THE LIVES OF INGOLF DAHL

Anthony Linick

authorHOUSE®

AuthorHouse™
1663 Liberty Drive, Suite 200
Bloomington, IN 47403
www.authorhouse.com
Phone: 1-800-839-8640

First published by AuthorHouse   9/12/2008

ISBN: 978-1-4389-1401-5 (hc)
ISBN: 978-1-4343-8003-6 (sc)

Library of Congress Control Number: 2008908616

*Printed in the United States of America
Bloomington, Indiana*

This book is printed on acid-free paper.

1. PRELUDIO

"You may start the life now." In an age that forever reminds us of our deficiencies and our mortality, this imperative has become a fundamental axiom. It was the motto of every member of my family and I proclaim it too, I, who look back ruefully on decades of my own attempts at getting the job launched properly at last.

It is precisely these many botched beginnings that come into focus now, now that I am to try once again to tell the story of my little family, and, in telling it honestly at last, clear the wreckage that inhibits a last new beginning.

My memory disappoints me. I long for an invigorating wind that might expose at last all of the dusty corners we once inhabited. Every year the task grows harder, and yet the urgency of the task remains central. In other ways, I am among the most fortunate of biographers.

When my parents died in 1970, I had the melancholy task of cataloguing their possessions and papers. My stepfather, the composer Ingolf Dahl, left some twenty large file folders containing professional and personal correspondence. In addition, I recovered his "daybooks," those annual pocket-sized diaries that I had always believed to be little more than appointment calendars. I was wrong. What I redeemed were forty-three years worth of intensely detailed and intimate daily excursions in autobiography.

My mother, Etta, also left a considerable written record: fiction, correspondence – especially letters to her often absent husband – and meticulously recorded observations on my own early childhood. Add the reminiscences of other family members, the recollections of dozens of bereaved friends, volumes of family photos, and I was uniquely situated to complete the history of a family whose secrets were yielded up only with the last breaths of their determined guardians.

They were not who I thought they were: my parents. And this meant that I too had been living a lie. We were not just naive innocents at war with the world, but a troubled family governed by imperatives whose history I would now have to master. I could see that I had a singular opportunity of understanding at last the very forces that had made me such an amateur at living.

Many of the facts I now unearthed proved to be immensely wounding, and it was many years before I was able to make my first attempts at telling our story with any frankness. This is but the most recent attempt.

What separates this account from the rest of its still-born predecessors is that this time I am determined to use my own youth as one focus of the family biography, to give the dwarf his place among the giants. I need to tell the tale as I experienced it, augmented of course by all those useful materials I have dragged along as sacred baggage for over a third of a century. I do not intend to obscure the true story by beginning it as I saw it on the spot – or heard about it from my parents, however incomplete and erroneous this telling turned out to be, but I will leave until the final chapters of this volume the true complexity of the tale as it was at last revealed to me – long after it was no longer possible to question the architects of its earlier, artful disfiguration.

Every autobiography should be an exercise in liberation, and that is why I too look forward to breathing the fresh air that such an inquiry summons. You may start the life now.

PART I

TO 1945

2. MAMMI'S BOY

I knew, in that intuitive fashion that young children seem to possess, that my stepfather was not like any other father I had ever seen. He spoke a very strange English, and when he and my mother wished to exclude me from their conversation they adopted a tongue that he was far more comfortable with, German. He wore clothes unlike his American contemporaries, as though he had dropped into our midst from an alien planet. He seemed to have no religion, no work schedule that could be compared with that of any of the other fathers, and he was sick all of the time. He didn't seem to have any other relatives, and this was strange, for even a small child like myself had a number of these. As I became older I learned that he had left his people behind in Europe, and I was naturally keen to discover as much as I could about them. Here is one version of their history, both as it was presented to me then, and as it can be augmented by my own researches now.

On his mother's side, the Dahls can be traced back to the early 19th Century. The family came from Fargelanda, a small village in southern Dalsland, seventy miles north of Gothenberg. Ingolf's maternal grandfather, Anders Julius Dahl, was a mechanic and maker of precision instruments. Among his achievements was the manufacture of equipment, including a spectroscope, used in the Polar explorations of Nansen. Anders Julius Dahl seems to have affronted society's conventions on a number of occasions. He faced jail in Sweden because he refused conscription, claiming that he would never be able to shoot another man. He was active in trade union activities in Norway and Sweden and in supporting the nascent Social Democratic Party. To escape the wrath of authority, Anders Julius Dahl sought work and asylum elsewhere, frequently moving his family across the map of northern Europe.

During my visit to Sweden in 1979, Ingolf's sister, Anna-Britta, informed me that her grandfather had married Albertina Edstrom, a servant girl, only *after* the first of their three daughters had been born. The birth of the second daughter, Ingolf's mother Hilda Maria, took place in Gothenberg in 1888, but most of Hilda Maria's education was completed in the Norwegian cities of Oslo and Bergen. All of Anders Julius Dahl's daughters accepted some form of menial employment during their teens.

For a while, around 1902, the family lived in Berlin, where Julius scrimped to provide his girls with a commercial education, courses in stenography and typing. Hilda Maria worked as a secretary in Hildesheim and then for a German bank in London.

Ingolf's great-grandfather on his father' side, Benjamin Marcus, was born in Germany in 1806. His son Siegfried, a head clerk, had three children, Elsa, Paul, and Walther. The middle child, Ingolf's father, was born in Hamburg in 1880. Paul Marcus compiled a family chronicle, and in it he describes his own childhood as both pleasant and suburban. He pictures himself as an ambitious and successful law student, one who studied in Munich, Kiel and Berlin. He was particularly interested in non-religious philosophies but, unlike Julius Dahl, he had no objection to military service. After he obtained his law degree from Kiel he served in 1902 and 1903 as a member of an infantry regiment stationed in Altona. In 1906 he became a junior partner in a Hamburg law firm which specialized in patent and trademark cases. A few years after beginning his practice he visited London, where his sister Else had just given birth to a son, also named Paul. At the youngster's crib he met Hilda Maria Dahl, a slender maiden whose hair was wound over her ears in snail-like braids. Paul Marcus found his future bride clever, musical, artistically talented, gifted in sewing and other handiwork, good with languages, and well-liked by others. Photos from the period show us an exceptionally pretty young woman, a bank secretary who favored peasant costumes. Julius Dahl was evidently not too thrilled about his daughter's infatuation with a member of the hated bourgeoisie.

Paul and Hilda Maria were married in 1911. They took up residence in Hamburg and here my future stepfather, Walther Ingolf Marcus, to use his full name at birth, was born in 1912 on Violastrasse. Three other children were born in the next six years: Gert in 1914, Holger in 1916, and Anna Britta in 1918. The Marcus family took up residence at Holunderweg 7 in the Gross Borstel district of the city, and here Pappi (pronounced as though it were spelled Poppy), knew happiness, success, and respect. Ingolf's father was active in the parents' council, not only of his own children's school, but also in that of the city of Hamburg. He also held political and legal positions within the city. In 1921 he became active in the Social Democratic Party and he joined the Masons. Paul Marcus was particularly active in the Monistenbund, a political-philosophical movement which preached unity and internationalism. He belonged to many clubs, societies, and charities, and frequently spoke at the union hall. Professor Walter A. Berendsohn, who delivered Pappi's eulogy in 1958, remembered Ingolf's father as a champion of intellectual liberty and human rights. But during the First World War Pappi had been attached to a unit of German counter-espionage, working chiefly as a censor. He was awarded the Iron Cross, a medal his children used as a toy. During the War he suffered from a lung complaint, which required a period of recovery in Davos.

Kurt Stone, a classmate of Ingolf at Hamburg's famous Lichtwarkschule, wrote to me in 1979 that his former schoolmate had the advantage of coming from "an exceptionally well-to-do and culturally active home." Here, according to Professor Berendsohn, generous hospitality was offered to a wide circle of "highly educated. spiritually active people." Pappi considered himself to be a patron of the arts. At his home friends gathered for the *Leseabend*, a communal book reading and discussion. All of the children had music lessons, and when the prodigiously talented Ingolf showed his early potential, Pappi bought the family a beautiful Steinway grand piano in walnut. This instrument spent World War II in Sweden, but it arrived in the United States in 1947, and I spent many hours playing under it or listening to my stepfather manipulate its keyboard from my privileged position beneath. (The last time I saw it, after it had recrossed the Atlantic, the piano was supporting a tray of kitty litter in the Stockholm flat of Ingolf's niece, Karin Marcus.)

Artists, academicians, and professionals frequented Holunderweg 7, but there was one figure who was not welcome – Pappi's father Siegfried, who seemed unable to get along with Hilda Maria or to recognize the genius in young Ingolf. Mammi (pronounced as though it were spelled Mommy) considered her father-in-law mean and vulgar. In 1920 Siegfried Marcus attempted suicide on the grave of his wife, having prepared a note which read, "If I can't think anymore, I don't want to live." He died of natural causes the following year.

That Mammi should have recoiled at the mean and the vulgar seems entirely consistent with a personality that hungered eternally for the innocent and the childlike. However great her intelligence, however sophisticated her manipulation of her husband, Ingolf's mother somehow retained a self-serving and infantile nature, elements of which she succeeded in transplanting to her eldest son. I have the impression that Mammi really longed to be one of the children. While servants cooked and cleaned, Mammi played – arranging parties, dressing up in costumes, taking leading roles in the circus shows and dramas staged by the children in the attic. Throughout her life she read, wrote, and illustrated children's stories, and her children were fed on a steady diet of Selma Lagerlöf. Mammi's was a world inhabited by princesses and trolls (that is the Dahls and the Marcuses) and, in great fear that Ingolf might really grow up, she persisted in sending him annual collections of the latest fairy stories every Christmas until he was in his mid-twenties. I still have many of these volumes.

Surely there was no happier time for Mammi than her early years as mother. The quest to recapture this magical period was intense. When her first grandson, Stefan Ingolf Bjornsson, was born, she wrote to my mother, "Etta, you cannot imagine how strange it is to have this little chap in the house. I have always the feeling he should be mine, and has been delivered to the wrong address." As Stebbi (as Stefan was nicknamed) grew older, Mammi lost the battle to have him called Ingolf, but she at least gained a new audience for her fairy story recitations – although, she reported, "I have made the story less cruel." I first met Mammi when I was nine, and I found her to be delightful, but then we were both children. She visited the United States in 1959 but even then she wished to perpetuate the childish patter, much to my mother's annoyance. I had to drag out my ancient stuffed elephant, Jumbo, so that he could have arguments with her teddy bear, Nalle Puh. It is not surprising that Mammi slipped into senility at an early age.

Gemutlichkeit and drollery, Mammi succeeded in making childhood into an idyll. All would have been perfect if Pappi had not frequently interrupted the fairy tale with a dose of reality. The Marcus parents did not believe in corporal punishment. If Mammi ordered Pappi to "punish these children," the request itself became the occasion for merriment among the guilty. After all, Mammi's wrinkled brow of displeasure was a sufficient warning that love might be withdrawn, even for a moment, and her idolatrous children would soon desist in their naughtiness. But

Pappi shouted, he had a fierce temper, he broke the calm which Mammi represented in all her benign wonderfulness. Anna-Britta, my source for so much of this family history, remembers an incident that reveals something of the role the others assigned to the father in this family. One evening the parents planned to go out. Ingolf staged a scene, refusing to be parted from his precious mother. When the screaming had proved unsuccessful and the parents had departed, he took a pair of scissors to a curtain. When the parents returned an enraged Pappi decreed that, as a punishment, he would not buy the family a radio. Everyone blamed *Pappi* for being unreasonable. Thus he became something of an outsider in his own family. He was dismissed as a social democrat who behaved like a burgher, a man of the people who was proud of his *own* accomplishments, a savage in this sanctum of saints and aesthetes. The family dined without him, and in this way the unimportance of the father was clearly established. Anna-Britta says that Ingolf began an emotional rejection of his father that, ironically, paralleled Pappi's rejection of Siegfried Marcus. When Ingolf returned from a visit to Lausanne, Pappi would want to know how much French he had learned, and Mammi would want to know how much chocolate he had eaten.

There was another impediment to perfect happiness, Ingolf's health. As a child he suffered from eczema and asthma, a disease that never left him. He was allergic to hay, straw, seaweed, and feathers. His asthma was so acute that several times he was sent to sanitaria and mountain convalescent homes. In 1924, when he was twelve, he spent three months in the Kindersanatorium in Konungsfeld in the Schwarzwald. A school report for 1923 describes him as asthmatic, often sick, and very protected by his home (for which we can read Mammi). When he was thirty, Mammi was still recalling "all the hours in the day and night I have nursed you, and bad hours were among them when you suffered heavily and I could not help you." In 1952, when Ingolf had knee surgery, Mammi wrote, "Don't carry on with the elbows or some other precious part of your beloved body, my son. There is not one part I have not especially nursed and dressed up when you had eczema, and I love the whole of you." The delightful mutual dependence established in this period of Ingolf's youth always excited Mammi's nostalgia.

When he was twenty-one, Mammi sent Ingolf a hand-illustrated book of her own poems, accompanied by the plaint, "I can no longer wash you or care for you. You are only little in my fantasy." "Well, my sweet son, you long-legged big boy, once sucking your finger nestling your curly head at my shoulders" – this is Mammi addressing my stepfather at age thirty-two!

Mammi's rectal thermometer was evidently omnipresent in the lives of all the children, but the special care lavished on Ingolf naturally caused its share of resentment and jealousy. Anna-Britta, who once failed to recognize her mother because she had been away for so long with a convalescent seven year-old Ingolf, played nursemaid to her dolls in imitation of Hilda Maria and her ailing older brother. At times the other children agreed that Ingolf was not sick at all, that his sudden bouts of illness were attention-getting devices. "Because of his gifts, he is more easily hurt than the other children," Mammi wrote in 1936, but this cannot have been an explanation that would have satisfied his siblings or his father.

It is worth noting, before too pathetic a portrait is painted, that Ingolf's illnesses were only episodic and that at other times he lived a normal, even athletic childhood. At the sanatorium he learned to ski. He enjoyed swimming, diving, and hiking. To correct posture faults he took up gymnastics. The family photo album shows a beautiful blue-eyed blonde-headed child with a sweet and wistful expression developing into a handsome and robust teenager, proud of an athletic build and eager to display his physical prowess.

Some of these physical activities, boating for instance, he shared with Gert, two years his junior. Gert also demonstrated considerable artistic talent, and in later life made a career for himself as a painter, mosaicist, and sculptor in Stockholm. Indeed on our 1990 trip to the Swedish capital we visited a tilted marble cube by Ingolf's brother that sat on an outdoor plinth at the top of Karlavagen and in 1995 we visited the Bagarmossen underground station, recently decorated in translucent color wheel panels by Ingolf's eighty year-old brother. The two brothers were not particularly close as adults, each evidently considering the other's work over-intellectual and lacking in emotion.

There was also an athletic affinity between Ingolf and his younger brother, Holger. Their mutual love of the mountains brought them together for a number of expeditions in later life, when the age difference was less pronounced. Holger became a civil engineer in Sweden, an inventor and a businessman, and he enjoyed a very successful career with AGA, one of the country's largest manufacturers of electronic and mechanical equipment.

Ingolf's closest personal ties, even in youth, were with his sister. Anna-Britta may have been six years younger, but with her he seems to have shared a spiritual kinship. In a letter written to Ingolf during World War II, she wrote, "It sounds as if I were your mother and not your little sister, but somehow I feel that neither I nor you can face grownupship as others do." Ingolf's "exaggerated, childlike, naive characteristics" may have offended Gert, but Britta was always more tolerant and empathetic. I could add that I have maintained a relationship with all of Ingolf's siblings, each of whom is still alive as I write this in 2008 – and with some of their children as well.

As youngsters the four Marcus children seem to have been a close-knit unit. Family albums are full of group photos, taken not only in Gross Borstel but also at Volksdorf, where Pappi maintained a small country property. Nude bathing parties alternated with elaborate costume affairs, in which Ingolf is pictured as a feathered Indian or a princess. For a number of years the children shared a very large bedroom in which Ingolf, Britta, and Holger would fall into slumber while spinning out their own endless Tolkien-like fairy tale, while Gert, claiming to be sleepy, called upon the others to shut up. Pappi implied that Ingolf's superior position in the group engendered jealousy and resentment, but Anna-Britta claims that Ingolf was essentially so good-natured a child that he never lacked for friends.

The family also had a dog, an aristocratic Airedale named Crimhilde von Angertal. "There are three divine creatures," Ingolf once said, "Greta Garbo, Marlene Dietrich, and Crimmi." The quotation is curious only because it omits a fourth divinity, Mammi, but this omission was made good at a later time. I was, of course, very distressed as a child to hear Crimmi stories, since I was forbidden to keep any pet myself.

In addition to his musical talents, Ingolf was also gifted, according to his father, in drawing and speech. At age eight he was writing verse dramas; by fifteen he had completed and illustrated his first novel. His sensitivity to the world of nature was also the subject of family self-congratulation: little Ingolf at the art museum exclaiming not over the beauty of the paintings but over the birch tree planted in the courtyard. A school report filed in 1923 comments on his intellectual and personal development: "Very clever...Knowledge unusual for age...Classmates find his ways to be calm and superior and they feel he tries to appear older than he is and they make fun of him because of [his] style of speech. Very gifted and intellectual...his perceptions and thoughts are often not his own but those of his enlightened and educated parents...Very stimulating for the class."

If children were sometimes uncomfortable in the presence of the prodigy, many adults were drawn to the gifted, good-tempered little boy. When he was eleven, a Professor Herkenrath, who had a room in the Gross Borstel house, sought the privilege of introducing Ingolf to the cultural landmarks of Europe, travelling with the child (who complained of homesickness) to Switzerland and Sweden.

Musical studies began at an early age. Pappi records that Ingolf's first music lessons were offered by Herr Lyon of the local elementary school. Then there were piano lessons from Frau Holle and, as his remarkable abilities developed, Ingolf was taken to Edith Weiss-Mann, a well-known pianist, who instructed him not only in keyboard technique but in music history and theory. Curiously, my stepfather chose to leave out of the list of his tutors, in subsequent biographical summaries, the name of Robert Muller-Hartmann, composer and lecturer on musical theory at Hamburg University. Appointments with Muller-Hartmann are listed on a regular basis in Ingolf's journals from 1928 to 1931.

When he was eighteen, Ingolf and Edith Weiss-Mann gave a recital, subsidized by Pappi, at the Hamburg Musikhalle. Ingolf included a suite for two pianos that he had written himself. It is hard to know when he began composing, but it was an early habit for him to write pieces for other members of the family since Gert played the violin and Holger the flute. A cantata for Mammi's fortieth birthday was completed when he was fifteen and a flute piece for Holger's thirteenth birthday soon thereafter. There are a number of juvenile compositions that survive in the Dahl archives of the School of Music at the University of Southern California, but I have the impression that he destroyed many other youthful works. What ever became of the "Workers Symphony," which the son of the social democrat intended as his first excursion in symphonic form?

A good deal of Ingolf's musical education was also undertaken at the Lichtwarkschule, which he attended form 1923 to 1931. Herman Schutt, the school's musical director, saw to it that my stepfather had many opportunities to exercise his talents as performer, conductor, and composer. "My first concert!" Ingolf noted enthusiastically on December 4, 1928, when he performed Schubert, Biber, Reger and Brahms in a chamber music concert at the school. Where other students presented papers as part of their examination, Ingolf was allowed to submit compositions.

The Lichtwarkshule, an unusual institution that encouraged freedom, creativity, and experiment among its pupils, was a well-known progressive high school. All of the Marcus children attended, as did Helmut Schmidt, the future chancellor of the Bundesrepublik, who was a contemporary of Britta's. The school sponsored many excursions for its pupils, and Ingolf, who was widely travelled as a teenager anyway, visited a number of sites in Germany as part of school outings, often succeeding in slowing down the entire museum party while he dawdled before some exciting canvas. An extended 1930 tour to Berlin, with a side visit to the Bauhaus in Dessau, may have been among these school excursions. At the Lichtwarkschule Ingolf studied German, English, Latin, History, Geography, Biology, Physics, Chemistry, Mathematics and Art, as well as Music. He seems to have had no weak subjects, and to have been particularly gifted in languages and the humanities. Since his university education was much more specialized in focus, it is fortunate that he obtained such a good general education from his Lichtwarkschule teachers, who enjoyed an outstanding reputation. The school itself was a victim of the Hitler era: already in the Twenties it was referred to as "the red shitfield on the Stadtpark;" it suffered a Nazi takeover in 1933 and closed its doors a few years later.

Two of Ingolf's classmates have provided portraits of Ingolf as a student at the Lichtwarkschule. Liesl Glogau (Dr. Elizabeth Glogau Estrin), for whom Ingolf wrote violin pieces in 1928 and 1929, remembered Ingolf's blonde, wavy hair, his blues eyes augmented by glasses, his sensuous lips, and his individualism. He was the only member of the class who wore the high-necked Russian blouse, rope belted. "He was pampered at home," she wrote, "so his adolescent rebellion was against rules that might hamper his self-expression: the school paper QUER KOPF, that he edited, had no capitals for nouns or proper names and no punctuation marks; his compositions bore no key or rhythm notation: the value and pitch of each note was separately indicated. His poems were 'free verse,' but there was an exuberance in all his creativity. He could rave about Baroque architecture and be fascinated by American popular songs."

Kurt Stone remembered my stepfather as an uncommonly bright and extraordinary student. His self-confidence "enabled him fearlessly to talk to the teachers and other more elevated creatures. If a teacher explained to the class what *Figaro* was all about Ingolf was likely to say that he had not only seen many performances at the Hamburg Staats-oper but in Venice and Zurich as well and that the Hamburg performances were deplorably inferior. . .When a teacher was sick, it was often Ingolf, rather than another teacher, who was asked to substitute...Naturally, he soon grew extremely proud of himself, and just as naturally, there were plenty of kids who not only envied him, but to be candid, hated his guts. Very few, if any, were neutral...Fortunately, his rather pronounced pride, if not arrogance, gradually diminished with increasing maturity, and by the time I began to work with him, editing and publishing his music in the early 60's, he was a remarkably appreciative, sensitive, even modest colleague and friend."

At an early age, Ingolf became an avid concert-goer. No wonder he always looked balefully at me when I disdained a free ticket to a chamber music recital in favor of some other teen-age amusement. The Hamburg Philharmonic, under the direction of Karl Muck, provided him with endless hours of instruction in the art of music making, undoubtedly whetting his appetite for a career in conducting. In Hamburg and other German cities, Ingolf had the opportunity of observing Furtwangler, Mengelberg, Knappertsbusch, Monteux, Böhm, and other great figures of the podium. Similarly, the youthful Ingolf witnessed performances by a series of distinguished soloists including Schnabel, Horowitz, Gieseking, Milstein, and Kreisler. Once my stepfather stopped the car in front of a house in Beverly Hills. "Rachmaninoff lived there," he confided. I had not known that my stepfather had twice seen the maestro perform in Hamburg concert halls in the Twenties.

Evidence for a description of the young Ingolf has come largely, to this point, from the recollections of his siblings, family records and letters, and from the reminiscences of contemporaries. When my stepfather was fifteen and a half he began to keep a daily journal, a habit he maintained from 1928 to 1970. These "daybooks" might really be described, in their early years, as overgrown appointment calendars, with the emphasis on lesson times, *Wantertag* itineraries, concert fare (and his reaction thereto: "Mahler's 4th!!!!"), and notations about the weather ("gloomy" or "heavenly morning"). They are useful in establishing chronology even in this larval stage; they confirm, for instance, that Ingolf completed three vacation trips to Sweden between 1928 and 1931, though it is clear that such trips were focused on Gothenberg and the little town of Lerberget in western Sweden, that is on visits to Mammi's youngest sister, Clara Lindblom,

The journals are very frustrating. They are addressed to the world and they are private at the same time, full of obscure references that will never make sense to anyone but their author. For me, there was the additional problem that for the first sixteen years of their existence, Ingolf wrote in German. Although I had studied this language at university, the texts were far beyond my capabilities as a translator, and therefore I reworked them with the assistance of my neighbor in East Lansing, Dr. Oscar Bock, a retired professor of German at Michigan State University. We were still unsuccessful on many occasions, and Dr. Bock was always at the mercy of my reading of the original text, from which, on many occasions, I failed to extract a meaningful German sentence. Ingolf's habit, from first to last, was to squeeze out, in a truly atrocious hand, thirty-five lines of script on a tiny cramped space where entries for three or four days shoulder one another for room on a three by five inch page. He also used a variety of unstable writing instruments, running inks, fading pencils. And, as if these obstacles were not enough, there are occasional dateless passages tucked in as addenda and some jottings in mirror-writing. Fortunately, many of these problems disappear with time; Ingolf gradually chose a somewhat more spacious format and a less fragmentary style. By 1931 the daybooks had become fully developed records of the day's activities and the diarist's thoughts and feelings. It would be stretching a point to argue that the journals are themselves of literary quality, but they have remained the single most useful source for me in my attempt to understand my stepfather and his secrets. Most notably, they provide a record of his complex emotional and erotic development.

It is not possible to date Ingolf's first sexual encounter from the journals, but Anna Britta has told me that Ingolf had his first love affair when he was sixteen. Young women found him attractive and he responded by involving himself in a number of affairs. An eighteen year-old Ingolf completed a novel fragment in 1931, *Der Maskentanz der Chaos*, which features a character named Eva. She addresses the following words to a character called Alf, a thinly disguised version of the author: "You think all others admire your genius, but you have been misled. I have formerly hated you myself because you were unbearable, blind, self-infatuated. Your parents pampered and coddled you, so did your teachers. They built a wall around you. I tell you this because I love you." I consider this character analysis to be a sign of self-insight, but Ingolf would have much more ground to cover in this area in the years that followed. The 1931 journals are full of the names of the latest untouchable love object. He was, however, still able to draw himself away from these infatuations in order to concentrate on his work.

In the spring of 1931 he enrolled at the Hochschule Fur Musik in Cologne. Here he remained until the summer of 1932, enjoying his first period of independence, his first experience with the world of professional music, and all the traumas of late adolescence. He tried to make some gestures in the direction of career, but his emotional life was always in an uproar. The daybooks reveal a tormented soul who can write that "Life is terrible, a dance above the abyss" at one moment and, after a successful rehearsal, that he is "bursting with happiness" and "filled with music."

In Cologne Ingolf studied music history, conducting, theory, and composition, participated in the choir, and took piano and clarinet lessons. His composition teacher was Philipp Jarnach, once Busoni's secretary and a friend of James Joyce in Zurich. It came as a surprise to me to discover how little training in composition my stepfather actually had – for he was never a formal student of the art again. He found his association with Jarnach to be extremely stimulating and he also profited from his association with Hermann Abendroth, the director of the conservatory. Ingolf also studied French and Italian in Cologne, languages he planned to use during extensive travels in 1931 and 1932.

In mid-July, 1931, he traveled to Munich and then continued on to Salzburg, Vienna, Trieste, Venice and many other cities in northern Italy. The journals are full of his enthusiastic appreciation of the artistic treasures that he encountered: Baroque castles, stained glass, monasteries, and palaces.

On August 7th, 1931 he and a hiking companion, Ferdi, were involved in a dangerous escapade while crossing an Austrian glacier. Rain began to descend in streams and fog clouded Ingolf's glasses. The elevated chatter of the hikers gave way to a silent desperation. Ferdi fell into a crevasse, but managed to extricate himself. As hail and thunder moved ever closer the young climbers threw away their ice axes, fearing that the metal might attract lightning, but the crampons on their boots continued to give them shocks. Ferdi again fell and Ingolf as well, but the glacier flattened out and they were able to catch a backpack as it rolled by. A path in the snow was at last discovered and a hut reached. "Oh God, we are still alive," Ingolf wrote, "that one can go through such a thing!" It was patently obvious to me, as a child, that a trip to Knott's Berry Farm was hardly likely to equal the adventures of the young Ingolf, and that as a traveller I might as well consign myself to a second class form of existence.

In May, 1932, Ingolf undertook a solitary expedition to Paris, eighteen days of sightseeing, socializing, museum and concert going, and angst. A whore accosted him between the Opera and the Madeleine, abandoning her prey only after he spoke to her in German. Curiously, there are also references to conversations in English during this trip. This was the language he used with Joaquin Nin-Culmell, to whom he had an introduction, a pianist and composer who was the brother of the famous Anais Nin. The musicians played their own compositions for one another and Ingolf attended a concert given by Nin. Our hero wandered about a great deal on his own, through Montmartre, along the Boul' Mich; he sat at the Dome and tried to drink in the ambience of wicked Paris. Inevitably there was an unsuccessful flirtation at his hotel. The Paris daybooks are full of judgments: "*Electra* is again religious art; Sacre Coeur is kitsch; the deepest contemplation is a kind of spiritual lust; all great art is surrealistic." For further inspiration he read Mann's *Magic Mountain* ("my Bible") and reflected on the achievements of Napoleon ("the greatest of all men, my God").

These divine analogies should perhaps lead us to a consideration of Ingolf's own religious views. This is because it is clear that he visited churches not only as a student of art history but as a prayerful supplicant. This son of an atheist family, a man who would steadfastly eschew all allegiance to organized religion, this life-long free-thinker, is always calling on God, a deity of some beneficence and purpose, albeit a deity unknown to the worshippers at Ingolf's side in the churches of Paris. Indeed, Ingolf's God is always being asked for that which everybody else's God forbids: erotic success in some illicit adventure.

On May 26th, 1932, during a visit to Chartres, Mary is invoked and Ingolf often seems to have favored churches built in the Virgin's honor, that is shrines in which the mother figure again offers blessings, comfort, and love. It is easy to see the association between the mother of God and the mother of Ingolf. Mammi, too, favored images of Mary, and had several on her walls in Gross Borstel. Throughout his life, in moments of desperation and pain, Ingolf invoked Mammi as his true goddess: if only she could come to him, if only she could be here now – such prayers for help were commonplace. It would be hard to quarrel with Ingolf's apt self-evaluation in a journal of the period: "The key to my nature: sentimentality and hysteria."

Two days after his visit to Chartres Ingolf returned to the "horrible cathedral towers" of Cologne – "so ends little Ingolf's outing in freedom." In fact, he was spending his last few weeks in Germany. Following a period of extensive travel here and in Switzerland he began, in August of 1932, a six and a half year sojourn in Zurich, a city toward which two other troubled souls were also hurtling – my parents, Etta and Leroy Linick.

3. THE TALONS

My mother was born in 1905, on or about October 28th. Her birthplace, Bialystock, a Polish city then located in a western province of the Czar, suffered a pogrom the following year, but Etta (or Anuta, as she was perhaps officially named) and her parents, Russian Jews, escaped unharmed. What had brought them to Bialystock in the first place is unknown. Etta's father, Isadore or Israel Stuk (there are many versions), had been born in Lidvinka, in Russia, in 1881; her mother, Fenya (Fanny) Rovinskiia (Rovinsky) in Elizabethgrad the same year.

From my mother I gained the impression that my grandfather was often on the run, and once even in jail, because of his participation in left-wing politics. In the year of Etta's birth there was, of course, an abortive Russian Revolution. When it soured, my grandfather decided to put some miles between himself and the Czar's police – just as Julius Dahl had sought to distance himself from authority. Soon after Etta's birth my grandfather migrated to America and, after obtaining a foothold in New York, sent for the rest of his family. Etta was approximately two years old when she and her mother undertook the long voyage, steerage class, from Odessa.

In the United States my grandfather changed his last name to Gordon. He was a tailor by profession, and on Cherry Street, in Brooklyn, he set up his own shop. In the rear of these premises a second daughter, Lillian, was born in 1910. A picture of Etta standing beside her handsome father survives from this time. He holds an iron. She looks pensive. She was, my Aunt Lillian reported, a sickly child with a greenish pallor.

Soon after Lillian's birth, the family undertook a second great journey, this time to Los Angeles. To have arrived in this infant metropolis in 1911 makes them almost pioneers and Etta could remember when Western Avenue was so named because it was on the western side of town. The Gordons lived on Woodlawn Avenue, near 51st and Main, in a section that today might be called Watts. The girls went to Main Street Elementary School and Jefferson High. Grampa Gordon, as he would eventually be known to his grandchildren, opened a tailor's shop on Normandy Avenue.

The is no doubt that my mother was an abused child, at least that is how we would refer to her today. There was physical abuse, but perhaps the emotional distress engendered by her unhappy and mismatched parents was even more substantial. The marriage of Isadore and Fanny was a disaster. It eventually sank under the weight of economic, personal, even ideological burdens. Grampa Gordon was an eccentric in all things. He was a food fetishist who would suddenly get it into his head that tomatoes or grapes could, alone, constitute a healthy diet. Steaks made of mashed peas were a staple of the Gordon dining room, with Fanny reduced to slipping hot dogs to the girls under the table.

Grampa Gordon also fancied himself an inventor. He enjoyed experimenting with gadgets and, later, costumes. He decided once that it would be possible to drive across the country using soapsuds instead of oil in the crankcase. He was also a womanizer. In the old country, Fanny had caught him in the act with her own sister. Now it was the hired girls in the Normandy Avenue shop who were the prey. Etta's parents were divorced around 1923, and thereafter had nothing more to do with one another.

My grandfather had a great passion for politics. He followed every moment of the Revolution of 1917 (and the establishment of the dictatorship of the proletariat in his homeland) with enthusiasm, and looked eagerly for the triumph of the communist system elsewhere. Like other Jews of his generation, those who chose Marx over Zion, he avoided and anathematized other Jews, and insisted that, instead of any religious training, his daughters attend meetings of the Young Socialists in Boyle Heights – where most of the other participants, including other migrating members of his own family, were, of course, Jews. It is reported that Grampa Gordon paid for the benches in the meeting hall out of his own pocket.

Since he had only an eighth grade education, political discussions with my grandfather were always conducted on an emotional rather than an intellectual plane. I overheard such discussions during those annual pilgrimages to his Inglewood home undertaken by his daughters and their families during and after World War II. I remember him telling my poor bewildered cousin Stevie that, "Geography has nothing to do with the laws of supply and demand!" On another occasion, my mischievous Uncle Morry argued that if Grampa Gordon loved communism so much, perhaps he should join the Communist Party of the United States. My grandfather's eyes narrowed to tiny slits behind his thick glasses as he passed a hand through his thick, wavy white hair. "They know where to find me, if they need me," he responded at last. Indeed, he seems to have joined nothing more sinister than the local Russian chorus.

In 1938 Etta described her father as "asocial in the extreme, also egocentric, iron both in purpose and energy; disdainful of most people." She certainly suffered herself from these traits. The prettier, younger sister was clearly favored over the plainer, older one. Etta's intelligence and her musical talent failed to win her a central place in her father's affections. My Aunt Lillian has described a scene in which Etta, having carefully copied some music needed for a performance, was interrupted at the piano by her father, who tore the score in half, shouting, "You call this music?" Etta learned well, according to her sister, how to hide the hurt of rejection, to approach the world with a stubborn self-sufficiency. This is surely a fair characterization of the Etta I knew as well.

I have always had the feeling that my mother came to forgive her father for many of the tragedies of a childhood suffered in his unhappy house. Grampa Gordon mellowed too, if this is possible, and even lived with Etta and my father Leroy for a short time in the year or so before I was born – still moody, but often generous and accommodating. In 1952 he wrote to my mother and stepfather, "If you feel like to ask for something dont be bashful after all I'll do my best." He also told my father, in a rare moment of insight, "I hope you'll be a better father than I was."

Two years after her mother's death, Etta described my maternal grandmother in the following terms: "Emotional: tendency to extremes, spoiled as a child & often felt persecuted, was vindictive; idolized me to unfortunate degree, was something of a man-hater. Well liked & very sociable: of child-like charm even in middle age." From this description is is not hard to deduce that the relationship between mother and daughter was only slightly less troubled than that between father and daughter. Etta could truly describe it as a love-hate relationship. Although proud of her daughter's accomplishments, Etta's mother acted in an obsessive, possessive manner toward the older sister, fearing any signs of independence, and pining after Etta when she at last broke free.

Fanny was remembered by Lillian as a short, pretty woman, much spoiled by an indulgent father. She possessed an outgoing nature, and often appeared to be jolly and fun-loving. She was also adventurous, among the first to wear her hair bobbed, an early defender of women's rights. In 1926 she and Etta rashly decided to hitchhike on their own all the way to Yosemite Park.

Behind the facade of the charming trailblazer, however, lay much bitterness, festering hatreds that erupted in episodes of hysterical screaming and melancholia. Etta was often the victim here too. Fanny was preoccupied with her daughter's sex life, accusing her of sleeping with every boy she met. Lillian recalls an ugly scene in which mother beat her sixteen year-old daughter in a closet with a coat hanger over just such a suspicion. This interference in the development of my mother's emotional life had its predictably unwelcome consequences. Lillian says that Etta recoiled from any strong attachments to men, habitually shunning all outward displays of emotion. Resentment of the mother and hostility toward the father lead her to seek the earliest possible escape from what she called the "talons" of the family.

Before her marriage in Russia, Fanny had worked as a governess. After her divorce. she became a practical nurse and performed menial tasks at the Kasper Cohn Hospital, a forerunner of Cedars of Lebanon, that medical colossus on Fountain Avenue that played such a large part in our lives. I was born there, Etta worked there during the War, and here the energetic Fanny, suffering from motor difficulties, loss of speech, and a toxic thyroid, died on May 6, 1936.

4. A TIDY LITTLE GODDESS

The schoolroom was one safe haven from the instability of life on Woodlawn Avenue and here Etta achieved standards which a peeved Lillian would have to live up to a few years later. My mother's talents were particularly strong in the verbal and artistic areas. She enjoyed singing, drawing, and sculpting, and would have spent more time with dancing, if this had not been Lillian's special enthusiasm.

I was certainly surprised to discover that my mother had also excelled in sports, for when the sports bug bit me, thirty years later, I found her to be an extremely reluctant participant. I do remember her boasting of her role as "jumping" center on the girls' basketball team; she *must* have been good at jumping, because her mature height was only a fraction above five feet. Boyfriends referred to her as "petite," and on her application form for U.S. citizenship in 1923, she listed her weight as eighty-five pounds. Etta referred to herself, with typical self-deprecation, as a "runt."

The hazel-eyed teenager had many friends of both sexes, and with them she enjoyed frequent outings to the beaches and the mountains. At Jefferson High and later at college (where they both belonged to the International Club) she enjoyed the friendship of Ralph Bunche. I remember how thrilled I was, after having heard his name mentioned in our home in almost reverential tones, when the U.N. diplomat called to speak to my mother one afternoon in the early Fifties. She was out, and I had to take the message from the winner of the 1950 Nobel Peace Prize. Evidence indicates that Etta possessed an outgoing nature that had won her many loyal friends. I can also remember how often I was informed, as a bored and isolate teenager, that – at my age – my mother had *never* suffered from friendlessness or ennui.

As her father withdrew from the family circle, it became necessary for the girls to make contributions to family finances. Lillian worked in a dime store and Etta, almost the "man of the house" by now, began to work as an accompanist at ballet schools and at dance recitals, where she often prepared her own arrangements. She persisted in this line of endeavor throughout much of the Twenties. Together, she and Lillian saw themselves as "Two Against The World," a world that had already provided a fair share of turmoil. The bond between them always remained an extremely close one and yet, given Etta's decision never to let the outside world share any of her inward distress, it fell to me to tell her sister, eight years after Etta had died, many of the secrets that are themselves the subject of this narrative.

In 1923 Etta graduated from high school and entered the University of California, Southern Branch. The campus referred to is the same one on Vermont Avenue later occupied by Los Angeles City College. Etta belonged to one of the last classes to graduate from the University at this location. It was soon to move to its new home in Westwood, and to change its name to the University of California at Los Angeles, U.C.L.A. Etta's undergraduate career, during which she majored in music education, does not appear to have been particularly brilliant; her transcript shows mostly B's and C's. Etta was never very good in science or math and, although she undertook a full program each year, we know that she was also working, and that she could never devote her full energies to study.

Constance Buchanan, a close friend and fellow music student, has left an interesting portrait of my mother in the era of the flapper. Etta, she wrote, was a "small neat presence, tiny but not fragile. Her ankles were sturdy, her walk purposeful. There was energy and strength in that compact body. I am reminded of those figurines from ancient Crete – those tidy little goddesses." Connie also added that Etta "wore her hair in braids pinned firmly across her crown, a style which became her, but was not fashionable in the 20's. The features of her face are lost in a blur of animation."

Connie confirms that Etta was serious about her degree, and not at all drawn to the Jazz Age lifestyles of her fellow students. On the other hand, Etta played real jazz piano, shocking some of her fellow student teachers, who believed that nothing less than the *1812 Overture* was permissible in a music appreciation class. Etta graduated in June, 1927, with a Bachelor of Education degree and a teaching credential. Thereafter she applied for work in the Los Angeles City School District, and she did succeed in finding work as a substitute pianist (at $100 a month) for a short period of time the next winter. Her assignment was at Hollywood High, where my father, Leroy, had graduated only a few years earlier.

The Linicks, to add just a few words about my father's family, were the desdendents of Aaron Linick, a rope-maker from Tykocin, near Bialystock. After a term in the Czar's army, Aaron Linick migrated to Frankfurt, where a generous Jewish community helped him establish a workshop. There were numerous children, including my grandfather – eventually called Adolph – who was born in 1869. In 1892 he migrated to Chicago, where he left behind the Orthodox culture of his father, who, however, joined his son in 1904. There was an early return to Germany for my grandfather, who came back to Chicago in 1898 with his bride, my grandmother, Augusta Faller of Wertheim. My aunt Elsie was born the next year and my father Leroy in 1907.

Adolph Linick made a great success of life in the Midwest, working as a pioneer in the entertainment industry, beginning with penny arcades and moving on to ownership of a chain of early motion picture houses in Chicago. He numbered many of the early entrepreneurs of this industry as his associates, including Adolph Zukor, Marcus Loew, William Fox, and Carl Laemmle. His son-in-law Sidney Weisman followed him into this business and there was soon a grandchild, Virginia. Not surprisingly, my grandfather was drawn to California, which he visited a number of times before making a permanent move in 1923, when he was 54. He had made a fortune in Chicago, and California would be for him a place of retirement. He bought a large house at 1343 North Laurel Avenue in West Hollywood and here husband, wife, the Weismans and a teenaged Leroy took up residence. Elsie and Sid had a second child, Richard, in 1926. (Members of my family were still in residence at Laurel Avenue almost eighty years later.)

My grandmother died during a return visit to Chicago in 1925; while the family was in attendance Louis B. Mayer, for whom Sid occasionally worked, entered the house on Laurel Avenue and had cousin Dora Faller, whom Adolph later took as his second wife, remove all of my grandmother's crochet work on the grounds that sight of it world be too upsetting for the grieving family.

My father, a shy *luftmensch* in a famiiy of entrepreneurs, graduated from Hollywood High in February, 1926, and his father took him on a melancholy European trip soon thereafter. Leroy returned to Los Angeles in July so that he could begin musical studies at U.C.L.A. My grandfather's second marriage was not as happy as his first had been – he and Dora were even separated for a time in 1931 – but they somehow found it comfortable to remain with one another in their old age. I remember them as a couple, when they were once again living at Laurel, in the cottage at the rear of the property.

Leroy had suffered from poor health at many times in his life and the pattern began in infancy. A childhood ear infection, in an era long before antibiotics, lingered for months and left him virtually deaf in one ear. In California his record of poor health persisted. In 1924, when he was a junior at Hollywood High, he was lucky to survive an attack of diphtheria. When he and my mother were married in April of 1928, he had just recovered from a severe mastoid infection that had required surgery, and he was still in bandages during the City Hall ceremony. Naturally the pair moved to Laurel Avenue, but Leroy was soon to break off his undergraduate studies so that he and Etta could work at the Konservatorium der Berlin.

The two met at U.C.L.A. and by the time Etta was looking for employment they were engaged. The event came as a complete surprise to my Aunt Elsie Weisman, who was such a keen chronicler of Linick family legends that she issued the first of a *three volume* family history in 1986: "One afternoon Leroy came home with a girl whom he introduced and announced that they were engaged! Her name was Etta Gordon, who was completing her course in music at U.C.L.A. and whom Leroy had met through a mutual friend. He had never even mentioned her before and we were dumbfounded. She didn't seem at all like the type of girl he'd been interested in. She was a year and a half older than he, not a bit pretty and her style and clothes did nothing to enhance her looks. But we soon found out that she was very intelligent, congenial, had a terrific sense of humor and was fun to be with."

When the stock market crashed in October, 1929, it wiped out the great bulk of my grandfather's estate. Chicago holdings were liquidated and stocks, in which he was heavily invested, became virtually worthless. He never recovered financially but he seems to have taken this reversal of fortune philosophically, and he had, after all, no great craving for extravagant living. His retirement was not pinched, in spite of his great losses, and his son-in-law Sid Weisman proved to be as successful as a real estate entrepreneur in his own day as my grandfather had been as a showman in his.

There remain only a few observations that I would wish to make before turning back to other characters. My parents' subsequent divorce and my mother's new affiliations had the effect of reducing my contacts with the Linick-Weisman family. Of course I saw them on an irregular basis on occasional visits to Laurel Avenue, but this homestead, and the comforts of the warm family life enjoyed there, were not mine to share. Much of the history of my paternal forebears came to me in a filtered form, an occasional hint from my mother or some half-digested gossip exchanged at a family gathering. Regrettably, I had to wait for many of the actors in my own life drama to pass away before I was able to close the gap that had separated me from this side of my family. That such a gap existed is obvious from the extreme poverty that *my* part of the family would endure in the early Forties. By this time we were far removed from the prosperity and generosity that had once been synonymous with my grandfather's name.

5. TO THE CITY OF G.

Ignorance rather than reticence prevents me from commenting in detail on the nature of the relationship enjoyed by my parents, newlyweds in 1928. For Leroy, who agreed to speak to me about these matters in the late Seventies, Etta, though not pretty, seemed to hail "from another world." He was referring to the obvious differences in social class, but also to the fact that her intelligence set her apart from the rest of the bubble-brained flappers. To quote Connie Buchanan again, "Etta was on good terms with herself...She had confidence in life already while the rest of us were still dithering and timid." Was Leroy also searching for someone who could provide the stability and warmth missing since the death of his mother? Of course Etta's self-assurance was only a pose, but my father had very little experience with women when they married. "She robbed me of my virginity," as he put it quaintly a half a century later.

Etta, by contrast, was no stranger to the love affair. In her marriage to Leroy she seemed to be searching not for sexual fulfillment but for the stability that would end the chaos of her own family life. The Linicks represented wealth and security – although if this was a primary consideration in Etta's mind it represented a horrible miscalculation: the stock market crashed a year and a half after the wedding. Leroy, to put it more positively, was a bright, good-looking, calm, gentle presence – qualities which were hard to duplicate in Etta's world. The two loved one another but there does not seem to have been any great passion in their relationship. According to his sister, "The relationship between them seemed quite platonic – they were never particularly lovey-dovey. We really enjoyed having Etta with us – she was such good company, pleasant and even-tempered."

In the summer of 1928, as we have noted, Leroy interrupted his musical studies at U.C.L.A. and he and his new bride sailed on the *Resolute* for Germany. A year was spent in touring, visiting, and study. Etta and Leroy lived at Flotowstrasse 11 in Berlin, and from here they undertook excursions to Cologne, Prague, and Switzerland. Much time was spent in visiting my father's relatives, Linicks, Kahns, and Fallers. Both of my parents studied music. Etta, for instance, was enrolled at the Stern'sche Konservatorium der Musik from October, 1928 until June, 1929. She took courses in singing, and had introductory instruction in harmony, counterpoint, and composition. Professor Alexander Von Fielitz commented at the end of the year on "her excellent musical talent and great zeal; Mrs. Linick possesses a very beautiful soprano voice."

Each of the newlyweds suffered an illness. Leroy dislocated a toe and tore a ligament and had to spend two weeks recuperating in Konstanz, where photos of the smiling invalid always remind me of the young Clark Gable. Etta had an appendectomy in Berlin, and always believed that a change in her metabolism could be dated from this point. No one would ever describe her as tiny again – a lifelong battle with calories had begun.

Etta used to enjoy telling the following tale, which, I suppose, had for her the value of containing an object lesson for a son not gifted in foreign tongues. One day, while she was lying in the hospital, she attempted to ask the sisters for the chamber pot. She was greeted by gales of laughter, for she had actually said, in her primitive German, "I have to make a lake."

The story illustrates Etta's philosophy of language learning, if not of life: the desire to plunge boldly ahead, making all the mistakes of the novice, but learning much in the process.

Etta possessed only a minimal knowledge of German when the trip began in 1928, but she had a great facility for languages. When the couple returned to California, via the Panama Canal, Etta resumed her accompanying work in dance studios, but she also took some German courses at U.C.L.A. This was just as Leroy was beginning his senior year, in 1930. The couple moved into the bungalow at the rear of Laurel Avenue and a small studio was fixed up for Leroy, who continued with his musical studies, hoping to qualify as a teacher in the subject. However, it was as a German major that he graduated from the Westwood campus (with high honors) in 1931.

That fall my parents returned to Europe, undoubtedly supported by Linick family resources (for which we can now also read Uncle Sidney), for a further five years. The consistently unlucky Leroy had decided that a career in music would not be possible for someone with his hearing problems, and that he now wished to do graduate studies in German literature instead. The departure of my parents meant that they missed the social event of the season, the New Year's Eve Party at the Weisman's in honor of "Hard Times." A bemused Fanny and Lillian *were* present. Invitations were penciled onto toilet paper and the party was supposed to take place at the Weisman cabin in Big Tujunga, but it rained so much that the guests, dressed as tramps, partied at Laurel Avenue instead.

Leroy's studies at the University of Berlin were interrupted a number of times in 1932 by student riots, the first tremors of the cataclysm that would soon engulf all of Germany. In October, having been made unwelcome at the University because of his Jewish background, he transferred to Cologne, arriving in the city just a few months after Ingolf had left it. Etta, however, remained behind in Berlin, where she was now studying theory, counterpoint and composition with Harald Genzmar, an assistant of Hindemith.

Connie Buchanan was present in Berlin at this time and was able to supply a portrait of the Linicks of this era. "They had a rare gift as a couple – together they exuded an aura of love which I describe inadequately as 'parenting.'" The Linicks introduced Connie to the works of Kafka and

Hindemith and took her to the concerts of Kipnis, Furtwängler and Walter. She and Etta embarked on a self-made art course, reading all the pertinent texts before entering the relevant room of the Pergamom Museum. Etta, as addicted to judgments as Ingolf, expressed satisfaction with Cranach, Klee, and Kollwitz, but – with her hardened mistrust of sentiment – dismissed "the masochistic saints and martyrs" of the medieval section. She provided picnic lunches when she and her friends had to wait in long theatre queues and carried smelling salts for the benumbed upper balcony martyrs at performances of *Parsifal.* Cards, ping-pong, weekend excursions in the Harz Mountains, Leroy's dirty jokes and much insincere clowning before the camera characterized these days as well.

Etta was taken up by the gaiety of decadent Berlin. In one nightspot she joined musicians in the band, took over the piano, and played a version of *Rhapsody in Blue.* Connie adds, "This was a single act of self-assertion but it might have been more...I think this might have been a form of personal reaction to threat." The threat was not merely from Nazi thugs. Her marriage was not an ideal one obviously, and at this point Leroy was studying in another city. My mother also had a crush on her music teacher. Then she developed a nervous tic and a chronic dyspepsia, which she treated with charcoal tablets. She lost animation. Soul-searching provided some insight and she regained her equilibrium. "She seemed moved to define herself as a person," Connie added. In any case, the events of 1933 required a new seriousness. It was no longer enough to laugh at the antics of the Hitler Youth. As the swastika was raised on German flagpoles, Etta and Leroy were reunited in Frankfurt on the first stage of a journey that would bring them to their new home, Zurich.

"We are writing to you with a deep sense of relief at being out of Germany," Leroy wrote to his family on April 5th, 1933. "As foreigners we were never molested and never in danger...but having eyes and sensitivity, we were in a continuous state of revolt against the existing dictatorship... For months we have been living in an atmosphere of unspeakable atrocities, physical and psychological, brutality, flight, horror, suicide, everything."

Etta was twenty-seven when she and Leroy took up residence in Switzerland. Ingolf, who had arrived in Zurich only eight months previously, was a very young twenty, but it would be some time before their paths crossed. Leroy began work on a doctoral dissertation, having to begin graduate work from scratch, at the University of Zurich. His chose as his thesis topic Subjectivism in the Work of Georg Kaiser, the expressionist dramatist. Etta also took classes at the University. By this time both of my parents were seeking other sexual partners, and both had begun psychoanalytic therapy.

In 1933 and 1934 the Linicks were treated separately by Dr. Leo Kaplan, a Freudian, and author of *Grundzuge Der Psychoanalyse*. Conveniently, Dr Kaplan lived downstairs from their flat on Gladbach Street. I asked Leroy in 1979 why he had sought psychoanalysis. He told me that he had been suffering from introversion and depression. Etta, he added, had no particular problem, but this was obviously a matter for Dr. Kaplan to sort out. Treatment lasted for about a year and was terminated by the analyst, Etta's a few months before Leroy's. Both of my parents claimed to have profited from the experience and Etta used the insights gained in these sessions to construct a semi-fictionalized account of her life, *The Talon*, which she completed in 1938, after bringing the account up to a period shortly before my birth. I found this document among the papers I recovered from our home in Hollywood in 1971; it has been extremely useful in recreating her moods and desires in this troubled decade.

In *The Talon* all of the major characters in her life drama receive thinly disguised *alter egos* and Zurich becomes the "City of G." Dr. Kaplan is thanked for helping Etta "to sort out the sense of my huge hatred for her who was my mother...It was taught to me how this had always diverted me from the ecstasy of a man's touch...I learned patience from him who first pointed out these things to me and he was as a father." Leroy, rechristened Galby, "was in these things as in all things understanding and in this peace of comprehension we lived together." Dr. Kaplan "taught us to read the deeper meaning of our flameless union." Galby learned "how his flame had in the many years spent itself in scattered spluttering. And he was able to gather and right it. Yet when it emerged at last it was nowhere near the bright flame of me. Too long our flames had not touched. Only our hands." It was this unavoidable realization that freed Etta to enter into a relationship with another love-starved searcher, Ingolf.

6. HEART OVERBOARD

"The streets of Zurich are clean; too spotless, indeed, to be really attractive. Zurich is almost alarmingly hygienic; the whole place has a tinge of vegetarian restaurants and expensive boarding schools." These are the observations of the novelist Klaus Mann, whose encounters with the city were contemporary with those of Ingolf Marcus. Zurich always seems to fare poorly when it is compared to the other inter-war capitals of Europe – Berlin, Vienna or Paris – cities that could be described variously as bohemian, jolly, or wicked. Compared to these sites, Zurich always managed to retain an aura of Protestant disinfectant but such a characterization misses a good deal of the picture. Banks and burghers were important, but the city also enjoyed a cosmopolitan ambience in the 1930's, an atmosphere clearly in conflict with outward appearances.

The cultural life of Zurich was a rich one, and the city had long been a haven for a number of artistic figures, including Wagner, Busoni, Joyce, Hesse, and, in the Thirties, Thomas Mann and his family. Zurich had also been the city of Lenin and Tristan Tzara – the surrealists had issued one of their first manifestos here during World War I. Switzerland's neutral status also had the effect of filling its cities with an international cast of students, artists, and distressed wanderers in flight from war and the threat of war. My parents would now be included in this company. And my future stepfather had already become one of Zurich's semi-exiles in August, 1932.

There is a regularity in the pattern of *his* activities that prepares us poorly for the turbulence of the emotional life he was experiencing at the same time. He undertook additional musical studies, he enrolled at the University term after term, his assignments at the Municipal Opera increased in importance and frequency, there were always creative projects on the horizon, and he enjoyed a wide circle of friends waiting to meet him in the cafés. Every free day provided the opportunity for skiing or mountaineering, and every summer was devoted to more distant expeditions. But chiefly Ingolf took his own temperature: the thermometer under the tongue provided evidence of physical disease on innumerable occasions; the fevered journal entries measured the well-being of the soul, and these too recorded the evidence of a profound malaise.

Ingolf suffered from ill-health throughout his years in Switzerland. Asthma was chronic, but it was only one of a number of problems affecting his chest: catarrh and bronchitis occurred with some frequency. Fever and colds plagued him and he reported sinus and throat problems also. "Not feeling well," is a phrase that appears with considerable regularity in the diaries. Then there were attacks of dizziness, feelings of weakness and fatigue. Ingolf made all of these problems worse by adopting an irregular sleep schedule. Either he would come home too late to sleep or he would sleep all day long. Sometimes he overslept and missed vital appointments. "I swallow a thousand pills," is a typical entry.

Matters were particularly bad in the first few months after his arrival in Zurich, a city whose muggy climate also disagreed with James Joyce. Ingolf spent the first week of September in bed with an attack of asthma. A doctor was summoned. Sprays and medicines helped only a little. For days the patient was too weak to climb the stairs. Two months later there was a more severe episode, and another week was spent in bed, with the patient, unable to swallow or talk, suffering from high temperatures and nausea. A worried Mammi called from Germany, memories of childhood illnesses oppressed him, and the tears came. For solace he read Schiller and the invalid's anthem, *The Magic Mountain*. At last oatmeal and zwieback, the foods of childhood, stayed down. But late in January,1933, a high fever and chills sent him back to bed for a further two weeks. A nurse was summoned. Days passed before he could make his first walk, "*Welt bist du schon*" on his lips at last.

It was Ingolf's siblings who first expressed doubts about the physical origin of their brother's many illnesses. Was he a *malade imaginaire*? Emotional crises *could* send him to bed, and asthma in particular seems to have been related to attacks of anxiety. Ingolf recognized this possibility himself, often commanding himself to *will* the problem away. It is also curious how quickly the physical crisis disappeared when a trip to the mountains presented itself. I remember that I often fabricated illnesses as a child in order to obtain the attention that my stepfather was receiving in the next room. *My* mother had no patience for such strategies, but Ingolf had been raised by quite a different figure. Nevertheless I would not be prepared to dismiss his behavior as mere play-acting. His physical sufferings were intense, whatever subterranean influences may have played a part in their origin.

To overcome the debilities of the flesh, he doggedly pursued a routine of strenuous exercise whenever possible. On Lake Zurich he found time for swimming, rowing, and sailing. He walked long distances in town and used a bicycle for longer journeys. He went to the gym often, and in later years he took up the *Waldlauf*, using a six-mile course to complete a run through the woods. It would be easier for him to conquer the body's weaknesses than the soul's maladies.

The Swiss mountains, dismissed by Joyce as "those great lumps of sugar," offered to Ingolf the most dramatic and most rewarding escape from the problems, physical and emotional, that plagued him in his Zurich years. Marko Rothmuller, an Opera colleague and later Professor of Music at the University of Indiana, remembers how Ingolf would complain on cold and cloudy Zurich days, "And to think that a few hundred meters above us the sun is shining!"

Over ninety mountain trips are recorded in the Swiss journals, everything from afternoon outings to nearby Utliberg to week-long expeditions in the highest Alps. All but three of the fifty-four named summits exceeded five thousand feet in elevation. Twenty-three of Ingolf's conquests topped the ten thousand foot mark, with Castor, south of Zermatt, at 13,864 feet, his highest summit. For skiing Ingolf favored an area immediately south of Lake Zurich and extending in a wide arc from the Furka Pass in the west to Klosters in the east. The Stoos, Etzel, Piz Sol, Titlis, Ibergeregg, and Davos slopes were chosen on innumerable skiing weekends. Many sites were visited summer and winter – Braunwald in the Linthal area was such a place, and here Ingolf welcomed Mammi and Pappi when they visited Switzerland on their twenty-fifth wedding anniversary in 1936.

Ingolf ascended many peaks on skis. And he combined other forms of exercise: hiking and bike trips or skiing and sunbathing. Snow remained on some slopes throughout the year and he enjoyed skiing in shorts or crossing glaciers in crampons and swimsuit. There were minor accidents and discomfitures: a twisted knee, a fall on the rocks, rain-soaked clothing or a sun-burned nose, but to Ingolf mountain triumphs almost required such honorable marks of the struggle. Much of this can be seen as an obsessive quest not to succumb to the body's weaknesses. And if his skiing should be sloppy or his breath short, self-recrimination was sure to follow. Joy was the one permissible emotion here, and the elation of the mountain experience was intense. "Ingolf is happy...The heart rejoices" – this is the language of the heights and it appears again and again in the diaries.

Mountains were also a place of escape. Here one could leave behind all of the unresolved conflicts, professional, creative, and romantic. Occasionally an image from this chaotic world would rise even to these heights, but on the whole Ingolf was successful in banishing the rest of the world from the mountains. The purity and clarity that eluded him on the streets of Zurich began at the horizon. A beautiful view, an evening of song in a Swiss Alpine Club hut and "the heart lives again." I have known several people for whom the beauty of nature represents a threat, its perfection made to stand as some intimidating reminder of the incompleteness and incapacity of the viewer. Ingolf was not such a person; if anything, he measured human environments, as we will see, against the standards which only mountains can achieve. Lakes like liquid silver, edelweiss in a meadow, larches etched against the pale blue heavens, red and blue shadows at sunset, the "spring-smelling moon," the odor of flowering trees, the sound of cowbells or birds – all these satisfied his thirst for perfection.

One other thought might be added about life and mountains. Life is a series of loose ends, of unfinished business, partial successes. An absent-minded procrastinator like my stepfather could never be wholly satisfied with the imperfect rewards of daily living. But a summit reached or a planned route completed represents a victory that is undiminished and undiluted. That is why Ingolf never liked to turn back without reaching his mountain goal, and why, if a summit eluded him, he would return a second or a third time to complete the conquest. In Southern California I remember our making several stubborn attempts to reach the tops of otherwise quite unrewarding mountains, like Condor Peak. Not to have done so would have been to forego that rare opportunity of saying, "I *finished* this." And this is why, as a proper child of Ingolf's household, I have surpassed mile 4,000 in my own quest to conquer the long-distance footpaths of Britain and why, more than a third of a century after his passing, Ingolf keeps me silent company on these journeys.

Ingolf treasured his mountain moments so dearly that he often had to run to catch the last train back to Zurich, changing his clothes in the train compartment, arriving breathlessly just in time for the evening's performance. And more than once, when the curtain had fallen, he was back on another train, heading for the heights again.

His address in Zurich was Russenweg 10, the home of his father's sister and her family. Living among cousins must have provided many challenges for someone who liked to keep as many secrets as my stepfather. On the other hand, there were many advantages, not the least being the presence of servants. I find it hard to imagine Ingolf, at any stage of his life, undertaking the business of maintaining his *own* living space. At Russenweg there was always succor in times of ill health and, of course, there was a piano.

Ingolf was a pupil at the Conservatory of Zurich in 1932 and 1933. He studied piano with Walter Frey and conducting with Volkmar Andrea. Frey was a distinguished Swiss pianist of international reputation, who specialized in the interpretation of modern piano music. Ingolf's audition took place on September 20th, 1932. "I play like a pig" is the literal translation of Ingolf's self-appraisal on this occasion, but the interview seems to have gone excellently on the whole, with wise comments from Frey and enthusiasm for his new teacher from the pupil. For Frey Ingolf mastered works by Prokofiev, Hindemith, Debussy, Brahms, Saint-Saëns, Mendelssohn, and Bach. Ingolf also enjoyed playing the piano in chamber music evenings with friends and in the cabaret style reviews that were popular among the students of the time. At one Stadttheater show in March, 1935, Ingolf and his colleague Willi Hausslein dazzled an audience with a two-piano version of Etta's favorite, the *Rhapsody in Blue*. This seems to have been well after formal instruction from Frey had ceased. Ingolf describes his teacher's comments after one his last lessons, on May 7th, 1933, as "much better than I deserve."

Volkmar Andrea was also a well-known Swiss musician, a frequent visitor to the podiums of European concert halls. He was the chief conductor of the Zurich "Tonhalle" concerts when he interviewed Ingolf on September 30th, 1932. Andrea was seen by his new pupil as straightforward and likable, but progress was slow. Ingolf describes his work during the lesson of December 1st as "disgustingly miserable." "Dear God," he added, "let me learn conducting!"

With some assistance from his family, Ingolf was soon able to provide for his own livelihood through participation in the many musical organizations of Zurich. His income was never better than marginal, and he attempted to supplement it by working as a nightclub performer in hotels and cafes. As early as 1932 we find him working on his popular song repertoire (*Schlager*), examining, with a certain distaste, sheet music for the latest jazz hits from America, rehearsing tangos, or checking out "Sonny Boy." An audition at the Bellevue on October 28, 1932 was described as a "success," but no engagement followed. The day was not a complete disaster, for that morning Ingolf had participated in his first rehearsal as a professional – a celesta part assigned him by Andrea in an orchestral work by Busoni. There were other occasions when he appeared in Tonhalle ensembles, but his most enduring professional association was with the Stadttheater, the Municipal Opera of Zurich.

His duties at the Opera were varied; each year he seemed to take on more responsibilities. His work permitted him to observe many masters of the musical arts at work, and I have no doubt that it was this internship that convinced him that music would be his own life's work. His own techniques and his knowledge of the repertoire developed markedly during this six year's apprenticeship at the Opera. The period gave him the solid foundation needed for a career in music, and the Opera came to dominate his professional life, quite surpassing his other studies in its demands on his time.

The Stadttheater, under the leadership of Karl Schmid-Bloss, enjoyed a reputation for excellence and innovation. In 1937 it presented the world premiere of Alban Berg's *Lulu*, and in 1938 the world premiere of Hindemith's *Mathis der Maler*. Ingolf was heavily involved in both of these productions. From the Zurich production of Shostakovich's *A Lady Macbeth of Mtsensk* he retained some set designs, which he returned directly to the composer in California twenty-five years later. The Stadttheater also presented the works of Swiss composers: Othmar Schoek and Arthur Honneger appear frequently in Ingolf's journals. But chiefly the Opera presented the classics, which Ingolf loved dearly, and operettas, which proved wearisome.

All of Wagner's operas were performed in the period 1932-1938; *Die Meistersinger*, which had been completed in Zurich, was mounted annually. Ten Verdi operas and six by Richard Strauss were offered in the same period. The Stadttheater prided itself on world premieres of operettas too; there are plenty of references in the journals to such titles as *Two Hearts in Three Quarter Time, Polish Wedding,* and *Heart Overboard.* Ingolf conducted many of these operetta performances, and, from the orchestra pit, he assisted in a number of ballet performances as well.

There seems to have been very little opportunity here for familiarity with that modern music in whose defense Ingolf would later battle so tirelessly. What modern fare did appear at the Opera, the Tonhalle, or in chamber music concerts excited him tremendously. In 1932 he pronounced Hindemith's new oratorio, *Das Unaufhorliche,* "the greatest music of our time," and in large letters he added in his journal, "ART IS STILL ALIVE." The following year, after many rehearsals of a Honneger opera, he wrote, "*Amphion* is in me," After a Stravinsky concert in November of 1936, Ingolf was seized with a violent emotion, describing the composer as "our greatest today." In 1937 it was Schoenberg's *Kammermusik* which caused delight. In fact, Ingolf possessed a capacity for enjoying music of all periods. Bach was a special favorite, but both Mozart and Mahler could bring him to tears. "Oh Beethoven!!!!!!" he wrote after a performance of *Fidelio* in 1933. Later the same year he argued that, "Notwithstanding everything, *Tristan* is the greatest opera that there is." Later, as we shall see, his tastes became less catholic, but in Zurich his patience only seemed to wear thin at operetta time. In 1937 he pronounced Jaromir Weinberger's *Schwanda, The Bagpiper* "a terrible piece," and Hans May's *The King of the Gypsies* "junk." Perhaps it was in memory of his own youthful enthusiasms, however, that he always defended my passions when I became a devotee of classical music in my late teens. At this time my listening habits did not extend much beyond the Romantic chestnuts, every one of which my mother denounced as sentimental drivel. But my choices were upheld by Ingolf, who no longer listened to such fare himself, as part of the necessary education of a music lover.

A youthful acceptance is also extended, in the daybooks, to most of the performers and conductors he encountered, if not to every one of the singers he was obliged to coach. "Schoeck has buried alive Bruckner's *Fourth,*" may be considered a rare example of a totally negative comment. Horowitz, Gieseking, and Menuhin all made Zurich appearances in the

Thirties and Ingolf had the opportunity of seeing Karl Böhm, Wilhelm Furtwängler, Bruno Walter, and Arturo Toscanini, as well as his conducting teacher Volkmar Andrea and Robert Denzler, the music director of the Opera. Concerts in 1934 in which Denzler conducted the *Eroica* and *Die Meistersinger* brought raves, "every measure full of life. Unbelievable beating of the heart." Similar enthusiasm was voiced for Furtwängler's *Tristan* in 1936. In August of 1938 Ingolf traveled twice to Luzern for concerts by Toscanini and Walter. He described the 29th as "one of the most beautiful days of my life," for on that day not only did he hear Walter conduct but he held in his own hands, at an exhibition, a signed copy of the score of *The Magic Flute* and Beethoven's own sketches for the *Ninth Symphony*.

Of all of these hero-worshipping episodes, however, none rivaled the excitement generated by the visits to the Opera of Richard Strauss. In November, 1932, the composer arrived to supervise a production of *Frau Ohne Schatten*; his presence had an electric effect on Ingolf, who pronounced the visitor "quite, quite great, a god!" In 1934 Strauss, in a light suit, arrived unexpectedly at a rehearsal of the same work, amused by the rowdy behavior of the orchestra. "Will I see him again?" Ingolf asked plaintively, but in June, 1936 Strauss returned to conduct his *Arabella* and to supervise the Stadttheater's first production of *Die Schweigsame Frau*. "We are floating in seventh heaven," Ingolf added, "I've never seen him conduct so beautifully." In one of the family albums there is a photograph in which Strauss, surrounded by the Opera staff, memorializes one of these visits at an outdoor banquet. Pictured at one corner is an admiring Ingolf, already balding. My guess is that the photo belongs to the 1938 visit, for only by then had he moved sufficiently forward in his professional life to stand this close to greatness – during the 1932 visit my stepfather seems to have served chiefly as a page turner.

It might be appropriate to add something here about Ingolf's own career at the Opera, an apprenticeship which proved both valuable and full of frustration. He was required to fill the role of performer on a number of occasions, playing keyboard and percussion instruments in the orchestra, and it was a complaint of his earliest months at the Stadttheater that he was given only celesta and xylophone parts. But he often played the piano as well – during dance recitals for instance – and his journals record that he played the organ during performances of *Die Meistersinger* in 1934, *Lohengrin* in 1937, and *La Forza del Destino* in 1938. In 1937 he assumed the role of the on-stage clown in *Lulu*, playing both bass drum and cymbals.

More typically, Ingolf was asked to assist in auditions or to play in rehearsals for the Opera's soloists. He then moved on to rehearsing and coaching both soloists and chorus and, on occasion, sections of the orchestra. He also acted as stage manager during a number of productions. Rehearsals often lasted all day long and Ingolf seems to have spent many an exhausting day running back and forth between them, scandalized by the weaknesses of some of the singers, shocked by displays of temperament on the part of the conductors. After a disastrous rehearsal in 1934 he wrote, "Denzler is becoming more and more of a problem."

My stepfather's titles at the Stadttheater were varied and oft-changing. He served as chorus master; he is listed as opera coach (*Korrepetitor*) in the program for *Lulu*. His name appears under the heading "Musical Assistance" in the *Mathis* program. Titles alone do not adequately describe his responsibilities. These were particularly diverse in the frantic weeks that preceded *Lulu's* first night. Preparations had to be made for a "fantastically good" lecture on the opera by Ernst Krenek, a composer whom Ingolf would meet again several years later in California. But our clown and *Korrepetitor* also had the task of supplying the Zurich journalists with press materials. His willingness to undertake any assignment eventually brought him the reward of a new title: Assistant Conductor.

His own podium assignments were almost exclusively in the world of light entertainment, operettas, Christmas programs, children's shows. Some of these conducting assignments began as early as 1933. Where other performers usually received encomiums in the journals, Ingolf rarely gave *himself* the highest form of self-evaluation. In December, 1933, he reports that he and the others, including a "disgusting" orchestra performed very badly in the Christmas show. "I am moderately satisfied," he wrote after a performance the following January, and a ballet evening in October, 1934 was described as a "great success for me." But a wrong cue in December's puppet dance lead to despondency. In the fall of 1936 he gave high marks to his first performance as conductor of Paul Burkhard's 3 *X Georges* – "it goes fantastically. Everything is flawless and full of bounce," but the next month he left the stage "terribly disappointed in myself." In January of

1937, with everyone else satisfied by his initial appearance as conductor of Ralph Benatsky's *Hearts In Snow*, the boss even calling him in to congratulate him, Ingolf was pleased only with the first act.

Some of his conducting assignments were in Winterthur and on the Swiss radio, but most of the time he was not the principal conductor of any of the productions, and the matinee performances, which he was frequently assigned, often had poor houses. Ingolf was repeatedly thwarted in his attempt to secure better conducting assignments and his frustrations, in which Opera politics and the fact the he was not a Swiss subject may have played a part, spoiled much of the pleasure he should have drawn from his years in Zurich. He experienced considerable jealousy over the preference accorded to his good friend and colleague, Willi Hausslein. "Hausslein takes my place," he wrote after a rehearsal in November, 1933, "Why?" Tears fell in June of 1935 when a conductor fell ill and someone else was picked as his replacement – "to lead that which I should have conducted." A bitter Ingolf attended a banquet following the premiere of Schoeck's *Massimilla Doni* on March 13, 1937: "I suffer from always being the second one. Willi gets all the press acknowledgement for himself and for all my work I get almost nothing." "I can not always be second," he wrote again a few weeks later. In the meantime we see him complaining about Willi one day and, on the next, accompanying his pal to the nearest bar. In the Sixties, these matters long forgotten, Ingolf used his influence to secure a visiting professor's appointment in the School of Music at U.S.C. for his one-time rival.

It is hard for me to picture the health-minded Ingolf I knew as the typical cigarette smoking, beer, wine and cognac swilling undergraduate, but in his student days, and these included virtually the entire Zurich period, he had not yet taken up the somewhat puritanical habits of later years. Drinks are often referred to as "injections that help," and he describes himself as being drunk or hung-over on many occasions, including one in which hashish was added to the mixture.

There were many opportunities for dissipation in this staid city on the Limmat – torch-carrying student festivals, dances, masked balls, Mardi Gras-like *Fasching* festivities, and *Sechselauten* hijinks in April, during which *Der Bogg*, an effigy of winter, was exploded amid bell-ringing and fireworks. "I walk through the streets of Zurich," Ingolf wrote during the 1935 festival, "seeing many faces from other planets." In *Steppenwolf* Hermann Hesse describes the masked ball of the Municipal Art Museum which he attended at the Baur au Lac Hotel on February 6, 1926. Ingolf attended and performed at just such gatherings at precisely the same time of year and in the same hotel just a few years later.

Some contrast can be made between the decadent flavor of the costume ball or the "amusing transvestites" at the Albis bar and other social activities less likely to produce a hammering in the head or fur on the tongue. For Ingolf these included chamber music evenings, parties at the home of his teachers, visits to the Scandinavian Club (where he often performed), official post-concert banquets, and revue or cabaret evenings, where Ingolf often participated in the entertainment. He also attended the salon of Herr and Frau Reiff, a Zurich cultural institution described by Thomas Mann in Chapter XXXIX of *Dr. Faustus*. There are plenty of references to ping-pong, rummy, word games and hot chocolate – enough to remind us that the increasingly chaotic nature of his emotional life never caused him to abandon his foothold in normal life, although, for Ingolf, the normal (as we will see in the concluding section of this biography) was always full of complexity.

"Oh what a complicated life," he wrote as he headed toward one of Zurich's many nightspots following an evening's concert. His daybook contains the names of some two dozen restaurants and bistros, some of them associated with theaters, hotels, or railway stations. Coffee houses, vegetarian restaurants, and Spanish wine bars also have to be added to the list, as do bakeries and the ubiquitous *konditorei*. The popularity of such meeting places waxed and waned in the six years Ingolf remained in Zurich, but some names appear again and again: the Rom, the Dome, the cafe Odeon (once frequented by Lenin and Joyce), the Albis, the Corso, the Gorgot, the Bettini, the Kronenhalle, and the Veltlinerkeller. In 1967, as my wife and I were completing our first grand tour, my misty-eyed mother escorted us on a tour of some of these places, for some of them were still going strong. We sat at a table in a crowded wine bar drinking red wine and eating nuts with a crowd of boisterous businessmen from Yugoslavia.

A year after Ingolf's arrival in Zurich, night life was enriched by the addition of Erika Mann's satirical literary cabaret, The Peppermill. The

Mann family was in the early stages of its flight from the Third Reich in the autumn of 1933, when they settled in Kusnacht, a few miles south of Zurich. They remained until September of 1938 and thus their stay was contemporaneous with that of my stepfather, who seems to have known at least four of Thomas Mann's children. Erika Mann is mentioned several times in 1933, and on August 25th Ingolf reports a "terribly nice" boat ride with her to Kilchberg. Some historians give the official date for the Swiss re-establishment of The Peppermill at the Cafe Zum Hirschen as January 1st, 1934, but Ingolf reports seeing an enrapturing performance given there by Erika and Therese Giehse on October 7th, 1933.

Ingolf met the novelist Klaus Mann for the first time on September 11th, 1933. They met again on several other occasions during the next few years. On April 1st, 1937 Klaus attended a performance of *Hearts In Snow*, which Ingolf conducted. Ingolf also records a nice chat, on March 7th, 1934, with "the smallest Mann," Elizabeth. Michael Mann, who studied violin at the Zurich Conservatory, is not mentioned until 1936, but his friendship with Ingolf lasted for decades and he was one of the two witnesses at the California wedding of Ingolf and Etta. Thomas Mann himself also appeared in Zurich to give readings from his latest works, and Ingolf appears to have attended such a gathering in November, 1933, and to have awarded the evening a record eleven exclamation points.

Some support for the thesis that my stepfather was leading a complex life must surely be evident when we consider that when he arrived in Zurich in 1932 it was *not* to pursue a professional life in music but to attend university. The *Tagebuch* for the fall of 1932 is full of references to classes he attended at the University of Zurich: psychology, Buddhism, Italian, Roman Art, Leonardo. His enrollment book suggests that he did not officially enter until the summer semester of 1933, but perhaps the distinction between regular student and auditor is unnecessary because the university system Ingolf knew was so different from the one he taught in, years later. The lecture was the chief method of instruction. Students would present their registration books for the instructor's signature at the beginning and the end of the term, but there were no course grades at Zurich and no tests, though students were required to prepare and deliver papers. Degree candidates would present themselves for examination at the end of their university studies, but their progress *toward* a degree would be difficult to measure. Ingolf took seventy-nine classes from May 1933 to July 1938, but there is no evidence that he ever offered himself for examination. I was surprised to discover that he was not "majoring" in music at all, but in art history. How faithful he was in attending all the classes for which he paid fees is not clear, but Michael Mann's wife, Gret, did remember seeing him in her art history classes. He did not bother to have instructors sign the *Testatbuch* at the end of the summer semesters in 1937 and 1938. The busy professional life he was now undertaking must frequently have interfered with the schedule of a part-time university student.

A bike ride, a run in the woods, the first good skiing weather, despondency and elation – these were among the things that must have taken precedence over a lecture on Holbein or Pompeian wall painting. Ingolf seems to have enjoyed the ambience of university life and to have suffered here as well – attitudes always related to the state of his love life. The student associations, the hostels, the eating halls and the cafes favored by his student friends provided the background for a chaotic social life, but from this background there emerged friendships that would alter his life forever, including, of course, those with my mother and father.

Ingolf signed up for one course in theater, four in philosophy, eighteen in music, and fifty-six in art. He studied every era of European art, especially the Renaissance and the modern period. A dozen of these classes focused quite specifically on matters of aesthetics, that is on matters of form and value in evaluating works of art. Ingolf's penchant for viewing life through aesthetic spectacles must have received official endorsement in such scholarly enterprises and since I, too, have inherited something of this family mania, I do not know whether to look with horror or gratitude on those University of Zurich professors who taught Ingolf the principles of aesthetic valuation in the 1930's.

In spite of the large numbers of courses, only twelve instructors were involved in Ingolf's university education, only two, for instance, in music: A.E. Cherbuliez offered courses in music history; Fritz Gysi taught courses in style, analysis, and criticism. Eight instructors lectured on artistic subjects; Ingolf enrolled in five classes taught by Heinrich Wölfflin, author of the influential *Principles of Art History* and one of the founders of modern art history. Ingolf took fourteen courses from Professor Escher and seventeen from Professor Stadler.

Not surprisingly, Ingolf used his travel time to study art as well – in Switzerland, northern Italy, at the Louvre and the National Gallery. His travels in the south were plotted to bring him into direct contact with the artistic wonders of the past – from the Greek theater in Syracuse to Verocchio's Equestrian Monument of Colleoni in Venice. The latter, which Ingolf viewed in June of 1934, left "a deep burning impression in the soul." In January, 1936, an opportunity to see Matthias Grunewald's Isenheim altar in Colmar left the student of art speechless, his soul affected as if by a heavy draught of intoxicating wine – "There is no sense in *writing* about it." In the fall of 1932 he attended a Picasso exhibition in Zurich on six separate occasions, studying the pictures until he knew them all by heart. It is no wonder that Ingolf could move easily from musical to artistic subjects in his own lectures in later years.

He did not neglect the other arts. He mentions a variety of authors whose work he read while in Zurich: Goethe, Rilke, Schnitzler, Hoffmanstahl, Kafka, Hesse, Rolland, and above all Thomas Mann. He attended the theater with some frequency, the Greek dramas, Pirandello and Ibsen are mentioned – with Aase in the latter's *Peer Gynt* reminding him of Mammi. The cinema also fascinated and delighted Ingolf who, in a rare departure from his usual exacting posture, seems to have enjoyed everything that flickered – the expressionist *Dr. Mabuse*, the surrealist *Blood Of A Poet* ("the greatest film in a long time"), films by Jean Renoir, Rene Clair, and Leni Riefenstahl, Chaplin farces, *Green Pastures* ("a splendid Negro-Bible film"), Hedy Lamarr in *Ecstasy*, Greta Garbo in *Queen Christina* ("tears"), Elisabeth Bergner in *As You Like It*, "wonderful" *Mickymaus* and "splendid" *Snow White*.

One difficulty in a life devoted to the pursuit of beauty is that if such standards are applied in the social sphere they magnify the aesthetic dimension in human relationships out of all proportion. Beauty becomes the sole standard by which to judge the potential partner; it dooms beauty's slave to a life of disappointment in a perpetual quest for the unattainable object. Appearance is above all the fixation of the adolescent and Ingolf would take a long time to leave this period of his life. As a consequence, the record of his Zurich love affairs and infatuations is a story of frustration and failure. "Sorry to have become twenty-one," he wrote on his birthday in 1933.

The journals indicate that Ingolf often went to the movies with young ladies and, indeed, he seems to have enjoyed a successful sexual liaison, at a hotel on the banks of the Limmat, with a girl called Traute on December 15th, 1932. My evidence for this conclusion comes from his habit of circling the date in his daybook and adding his partner's name in large capital letters whenever significant occasions presented themselves. Eva's name is circled on January 3rd, 1933, during a holiday visit to Hamburg. It is not always clear, it might be added, what last names his partners went by. Sometimes he uses only initials or speaks of the mysterious "her," and it is quite obvious that some of his friends shared the same first name – there were clearly two Evas, for instance.

Ingolf was clearly preoccupied with sifting the passing scene, finding just the right feature or face that might set his heart racing. The lakeshore beaches were thus a site for courting and assignations and a place for my stepfather to fall in love with beautiful, unreachable faces. "Why can't I die?" a lonely Ingolf complains, "Beauty of life. Why not for me?" Occasionally the crush would become disfunctional, with Ingolf's entire schedule distorted so that he could be in a position to catch yet another glimpse of the love object. Possessing the heart of the adolescent and the tenacity of the adult, my stepfather spent much of 1933 and 1934 locked in a debilitating unhappiness because of just such an infatuation. Depression, tears, and heartaches are reported again and again. Days without a sighting are like living in a "black box." When the beloved one is seen with other students at the University, the outsider responds, "I could tear my heart out." For many months Ingolf did not even have a name to accompany the face which so bewitched him. Then he found a way of searching through the beloved's coat pocket, looking for a clue, but chose the wrong coat! "Everything is finished," he lamented, "That one has to suffer so much because of another human being." Nothing happened when Ingolf slipped a note into the right coat pocket – "Everything is over, I should hang myself." The winter vacation brought on a period of despondency, for it meant that there would be no more opportunities to be in the right spot when the beautiful one happened to walk by. A visit from Mammi brought some consolation, but when she departed on January 17th, 1934, it was time for the fixation to return.

Interestingly enough, the obsession triumphed in importance over the possibilities of *real* relationships – which Ingolf enjoyed at the same time. At the theatre ball held at the Baur-au-Lac Hotel on February 10th, Ingolf danced with Maya Kubler, a ballet star whose work always enthralled him. "I will sleep with her yet," he boasted, "she is everything to me… I would like to possess her completely." In April, it was the star of a production of *Salome* who excited his passion: "*Die* Schulz is fantastic. Let me kiss your mouth."

Yet none of these preoccupations eclipsed the quest for the unattainable object. Ingolf was at last able to supply a name for the enthralling face, but this discovery was coupled with another bit of unhappy news: it was examination time for the beloved, who might therefore soon leave Zurich. A disconsolate Ingolf sent a bouquet, perhaps anonymously, on examination day. "Spring comes, everything is blooming and I sit in my cocoon and can not go out. There is no way out," he lamented. I do not know how seriously to take the many entries in which Ingolf speaks of hanging himself, opening the gas tap, or cutting a vein, but there is no doubt that his suffering was intense. As it turned out, the torture did *not* end with examination time, and Ingolf had to endure many more months of encountering the love object during concerts or in the bars or in the halls of the University, each one accompanied by a complete failure of nerve on the part of the smitten suitor. At best he would make some anonymous gesture, such as sending the loved one some concert tickets, but when the downbeat fell and the seat remained empty, depression would ensue. "The proper Ingolf mood" is summed up on June 23rd, 1934, as one that "stands in a melancholy fashion between things. Jazz music, a singing violin, the moon in an aromatic meadow, and a quiet, tired longing."

On July 6th Ingolf participated in a review at one of the lakeside entertainment palaces, perhaps aboard ship. The review succeeded "beyond expectations," but Ingolf saw something that caused hell to open up – the love object in the arms of another. The next day Ingolf left Zurich for seven weeks of holiday in Germany and Sweden, where the Marcus family would soon reside. He arrived in Stockholm on July 13th, ill and miserable. He was well enough in a few days to sail with Gert, to make music with Holger, and to tell his sister Britta all he could about life and death in Zurich, but there is no doubt that he was suffering from nervous exhaustion. He reports mysterious crying jags and other signs of emotional strain that only the warmth of Mammi could assuage.

"If Mammi did not exist...." The phrase belongs to April 28th, 1934 and to the despair that lovesickness had engendered. "There is only one person who is really interested in my life: Mammi," he added a few days later. Now that he was close once again to his source of eternal hope, Ingolf felt better about himself: "Mammi is a shaft of light in this melancholy... As long as Mammi is alive I live also...We are nothing compared to her. We are her subjects. The way to life is to work and forget...Only live, live somehow, and wait, so that one will be allowed to follow Mammi over the threshold."

It is true that the depths of despair experienced in the summer of 1934 never seem to have been sounded again. Much melancholy is in evidence and much anger. But anger often chooses an external object, while despair is a form of self-destruction. Ingolf returned to his old life, his professional commitments and a wide circle of caring friends, less obsessed with the unattainable object (though this is surely a matter of degree) and better able to undertake new adventures.

Friends from Hamburg arrived on the scene, dancers exercised a special fascination, and Ingolf undertook brief affairs with a number of these figures. But neither he nor his lovers could be described as stable personalities – the fights, the yearning, the sulking all contributed to a most complex social life. On November 18th, 1934 Ingolf was escorting a singer he was smitten with when they encountered a jealous dancer on the Quaibridge. "I live in a novel and am quite crazy," he concluded. The dancer soon returned Ingolf's pajamas in protest and Ingolf took the singer to the Hotel de la Balance in Baden, registering as Gert Sandstrom. A second tryst followed on February 3rd when the singer and Gert Sandstrom spent the night at the Hotel Schwarzerhof in Winterthur. Circling the date, Ingolf added, "It is beautiful." Four days later he went searching once again for the still unobtainable object.

The singer, having seen off the dancer, had a more difficult task in combating a phantom. Such was the strength of Ingolf's infatuation that he wrote to his current lover, "Give me up." He continued to see the woman; they attended balls and other social gatherings, they went to the movies, they went walking on the Zurichhorn and the Rigi, they dined at the Odeon, they went to the beach, Ingolf played his compositions for her, but he resisted all attempts to resume the half-begun romantic attachment. The spring of 1935 was once again dominated by sightings of the statue on the pedestal, but help was at hand at last from a most unlikely source – because on December 27th, 1934, Ingolf met Etta.

7. HEARTS IN SNOW

Every time I think about the union of Ingolf and Etta, the more improbable the success of such a liaison becomes. The two came from such dissimilar worlds; there cannot have been many like Ingolf in Etta's universe, and I do not remember encountering any references to Americans in any of Ingolf's journals prior to this point in his life. I don't suppose her German was as fluent as it eventually became, and Ingolf could not have had much practice in speaking English. Furthermore, Etta was, from the start, only a short-term visitor to Switzerland, and Ingolf had never considered a life outside of Europe. Although attractive to men, my mother was not one of those beautiful faces that so enthralled Ingolf. He was twenty-two when they met; she was twenty-nine, a far more sophisticated and mature figure than my future stepfather, and with much more experience of life and its realities. What they did share, initially, was a profound enthusiasm for cultural and aesthetic experience. Ingolf, who had been rejected by many a lover for being "too cultured," would find a soulmate in Etta. My mother was one of those women who nurtured creativity, one who was prepared to sacrifice her own ambitions to the sacred task of fanning the flames of genius. In Ingolf she found a challenge at last worthy of her energies.

They met, as I have stated earlier, on December 27th, 1934, probably during a rehearsal for a review in which she sang and danced. Ingolf makes the first mention of her by name on February 2nd, 1935. There was very little of the romantic in their early friendship and, indeed, Etta tells us in *The Talon* that her initial reaction to Thast, my stepfather's *alter ego* in this fiction, was full of ambiguity: "At first, when I came together with Thast I hated him...The sight of Thast's face was once hateful to me...It was a furious feeling...After I hated him, after this had gone I knew it was because else I would have loved him too much."

The journal for spring 1935 shows Ingolf and Etta setting out on walks together. The two have coffee, she comes to the theater with him, they go boating on the lake. During a "very beautiful" picnic on May 11th Etta read to Ingolf notes for a novel she was writing and he returned the compliment by telling her all about his infatuation with the beloved object. A few days later they were together when the loved one walked into the *Studheim* and Etta was able to see the source of Ingolf's obsession. He would phone Etta, and get her to agree to meet in some spot where a sighting might take place; Ingolf would be delighted when his new companion arrived ("Thank God, finally a human being"), but there would always be an eye directed toward another table. Ingolf first notices his affection for Etta on May 19th: "I'm afraid of her because I wish to possess her." Two days later he had extracted a promise from her, though its nature is not revealed in the journals.

It is fair to say that the Linicks had what would later be referred to as an open marriage, each having the freedom to engage in affairs outside the marriage bed. Therefore there was no embarrassment when Ingolf phoned Etta at home. They chatted about the loved one, they had drinks at the Gorgot, they worked on the next review, and Ingolf frequently joined the Linicks at mealtime in their flat and he was happy there. Leroy recalls finding Ingolf and Etta in the flat when he returned after having spent the evening with a girl from Budapest. Without saying anything, a mischievous Ingolf walked to the piano and began to play Brahms' *Hungarian Rhapsody*.

On July 4th the pianist took Etta to the movies; he was most upset when she told him, "Don't kiss me!" His response was the pretence that, after all, he didn't care anymore. But the next day found them looking at pornographic books and walking around the Zurichberg. And on July 9th the two registered at the Hotel Adler in Bremgarten, Ingolf signing the register as Gert Dahl, and Etta as Constance Lawrence of Southampton. My stepfather could not resist turning the tryst into an expedition – a bike ride there, a walk in the woods, and several plunges in the River Reuss. Etta, less of an enthusiast for such things, was plagued by horseflies, became exhausted, and sighed frequently. At night it was beautiful in bed – "I am very happy," Ingolf reported. The next morning he biked back to Zurich alone, while Etta took the train. That evening the two met again and Ingolf made a startling prediction in his journal: the next day was to be the unattainable object's "death day."

I have no doubt that it was Etta's influence that produced this declaration. It was not just a matter of having a replacement ready, should the loved one really "die." Etta must also have been passing on some of her analytic insights to her lover, helping him to understand some of the dynamics of his own personality. "Thast too was a cripple when he came to me," she wrote, "Thast with his face of warm marble and his strong square hands. Now I know why he came. It was because there was about him the mark of the talon and on him too it was deeply burned...A talon forgotten is a joy more fierce than any other joy." Clearly Etta had recognized that Ingolf's access to maturity was blocked by his dependence on his mother: "Thast was at times a man," she wrote, "Then there were these other times when he was again a youth. A youth among his small brothers and his small sister and his mother. For all of these he has a love which when it envelops him makes him once more a boy." Etta preferred to remember "those other times when we were as a man and a woman are. So magnificent that for two latelings like ourselves it was almost beyond believing. And Thast would slip boyward."

With much trepidation no doubt, but emboldened by a presence who was determined not to let him slip boyward anymore, Ingolf had determined to seek a meeting with the phantom at last. July 11th is referred to in the journals as "the great day!!!!" but no information is included to indicate how the fateful contact was finally made. Two days later, after a noontime meal, Ingolf refers to the once loved one as "so stupid," not a very complete description of a personality who had dominated his fantasy life for two years. The statue on the pedestal is not mentioned again for half a year when, shedding a final tear for the memory, and proclaiming that he is no longer haunted by this vision (which "no longer suits me erotically"), Ingolf seems to escape from his obsession at last. The kill-or-cure venture undertaken by the trembling idolater had, as Etta no doubt hoped, resulted in a cure.

The way was now clear for the next stage of Ingolf's relationship with Etta. Things did not always go smoothly. "I contrived from time to time," she wrote in *The Talon*, "to lift myself out of the full tide of unaccustomed and deep passivity which I knew in his embrace: by stinging him with harsh words or writings." Nevertheless, Thast was proving to be, unlike Galby, "the flame of my flame...At last at Thast's side I had become a woman in the whole meaning. I moved for the first time my flame from under the family talon and brought it to Thast and was grateful. The Thast thing was overwhelming to me in my fresh womanhood and I was a being which looks at its reflection exultant yet somehow terrified."

On July 14th, three days after the specter's "death day," Ingolf and Etta renewed their affair in Ingolf's room. "It goes amiss," Ingolf wrote, "but this only proves our love. And we are both tranquil and happy." Soon thereafter Etta helped Ingolf pack for his summer holidays, which began with a flight from Zurich to Frankfurt and a train ride to Hamburg. On July 21st he arrived in Stockholm for a two-week stay in some contrast to the emotional collapse of the year before. Etta was waiting for him at the train station when he returned to Zurich.

One rival may have been vanquished, but Ingolf still had other romantic entanglements that prevented him from concentrating wholly on my mother. The spurned singer returns at this point. "She wants "it" from me and is waiting for an answer," Ingolf reports. He went shopping with his former lover, still agitated by her proposal, but there next appears a saccharine piety in the daybook, "I want to be pure in order to get clarity from God." Surely he tried some other excuse on this importunate girlfriend, and her name does not reappear for six months; somehow, they managed to remain friends throughout his remaining years in Zurich.

On August 24th Ingolf said goodbye to Etta on a bench near the Theater and traveled to Bern for a meeting with yet another woman from his past. Barbara Kruger-Sachse, to use her married name, was a friend from Hamburg for whom Ingolf had also suffered an unrequited erotic yearning. "May God give me fulfillment," he prayed as the two took a second train in the direction of Schwarzenberg. "Barbara I love you, only you," Ingolf wrote, "you remain my highest hope." Her voice alone seems to have had the most overwhelming effect on him but that night he slept alone in his guest house bed and Barbara revealed that she belonged "body and soul" to another. A jealous Ingolf returned to Zurich alone on the 26th and Barbara resumed the status of friend and confidante. Now only Etta had the power to engage Ingolf's passion and for the next eight months she became the central figure in his private life.

He dragged her along on many walks and a climb up the misty Etzel. They went to see Chaplin's *Modern Times*. They played the gramophone at the home of a friend, went to concerts and art museums together, they drank vermouth at the Gorgot and the Veltlinerkeller, and they talked about books. Both enjoyed reading aloud; when Etta was ill Ingolf came to read Hesse. They also continued to share one another's bed.

"It is quite beautiful," Ingolf wrote after the night of September 26th. "Heavenly" was the word used to describe the visit of December 5th. "Things are going quite well right now," he wrote a few days later, "I am happy." On January 24th, 1936, Etta came to help Ingolf write some business letters. "We are stimulated by boots and glasses," he wrote. The phrase "I love Etta" begins to appear in the daybooks.

On March 7th the lovers were disturbed in Ingolf's room by his cousin Ernstli, who barged in knocking and singing. Furious at the interruption, the couple repaired to the Veltlin to regain their balance. Five days later Ingolf commented on another night of love – "It has never been like that before. There is no unpleasant aftertaste as with the others, but a beautiful conclusion." On the 14th he wrote, "Ingolf goes in odd ways: sometimes he believes that to have a wife and child is to possess something precious above all other things. A woman who waits for me at home and covers the evening with her warm body. It should come like that!" "How Etta means everything to me," he added on April 21st.

Unfortunately an icy wind was about to separate the unlucky lovers; on April 21st Etta had also learned that her mother was gravely ill and facing surgery in Los Angeles. The next day she called Ingolf to tell him that she would now have to depart for America. Leroy needed to complete his dissertation; he would remain in Zurich and join his wife in California a few months later. Fate had frozen in mid-breath the romance of the most unlikely of lovers.

"Like a black hole, the view into the future bursts upon me," Ingolf wrote. That evening he and Etta dined at the Kronenhalle, awash in the melancholy of parting. The next day, at the Corso bar, "farewell chokes our throats." Their last day together was April 26th. After breakfast at the Linicks, Ingolf and Etta took the train to Einsiedeln, site of the famous Benedictine monastery. The candles lit before the image of the "black Virgin" seemed to be burning down for the lovers. They took the boat back to Zurich, the sight of the beautiful peaks mocking their despair. A meal in the Veltlin followed and Ingolf played the piano for Etta while the two drank coffee in his flat. He then walked her home and the final embrace was exchanged. "She is gone," is the only entry recorded on the 29th. Etta evidently called Ingolf from Paris and, from her transatlantic ship, cabled him the news of Fanny's death, but the two must certainly have felt that final farewells had been said.

8. THE GREAT DEPRESSION

The emotional hardship endured by the parted lovers continued for months. Etta was not willing, at this point in her relationship with Ingolf, to sever all the ties to her old life. She had noted that, "Before I left Thast he had begun to find in himself a great resentment at my being partly bound to him and partly to Galby." But such sulking was a long way from the kind of commitment that Etta would need before abandoning her marriage. For good or ill, it was Etta and Leroy who tried to put the pieces back together again when my father returned to Los Angeles after completing his Ph.D. work in Zurich in 1936.

Leroy had a great deal of difficulty obtaining full time employment. His sights were clearly drawn on the German Department at U.C.L.A., but the bad luck that hounded the man was about to intervene again. Nothing better typifies the dramatic dichotomy in the fortunes of the Weismans and the Linicks than an incident involving one of Leroy's German professors, Dr. Diamond. Dr. Diamond had long been a champion of Leroy's interests and had succeeded in making sure that Leroy received his Phi Beta Kappa key, even though he had switched majors in his senior year. It was clear that Leroy could now look for some assistance from his old mentor in getting his own academic career launched. But some time before my father's return to America, Dr. Diamond was killed in an accident by a car driven by my cousin Virginia's future brother-in-law, the entrepreneur and art collector, Frederick Weisman. Baba and Sid Weisman (no relation) paid a call on the German Department and returned cheered by the promise that Leroy, in the interim, could finish out Dr. Diamond's schedule. But this was not to be.

Although Leroy was employed for a few months as a translator and secretary to Dr. Rolf Hoffman at U.C.L.A., this window of opportunity was closing. The popularity of German both at U.C.L.A. and on other American campuses was in decline, especially as war loomed closer. Leroy also believed, though this may sound a bit too much like a movie plot of the era, that U.C.L.A.'s German Department was full of Nazi sympathizers and that several professors were not happy at the prospects of adding a Jew to the faculty.

Sid once again intervened, using his association with Louis B. Mayer to get Leroy a job, in December 1936, at MGM in Culver City. My father worked for a salary of thirty-five dollars a week in the research department, translating German books as possible movie material. When Mayer left MGM this department was phased out, but Leroy eventually found a permanent position at the studio as a screen-story analyst, reading, summarizing, and recommending scripts and books that might make it to the silver screen.

For Etta, these months were times of continuing introspection and sadness. Medical records show that on June 22nd, 1936, a "depressed" Etta was treated by our cousin Julius Kahn. "I have always until this fancied that I lived well," Etta noted in *The Talon*, but "to live well is to hearken to the underside of the mind and not alone to the top...I spoke often to Galby in that time and I said that in our life there was no taste and no pulse. I spoke out to Galby and I said that our life had no color. He too saw this. But his eyes were riveted as were mine to the top of things. The tops of things are unrevealing. Beneath can be festering."

A new chapter and a new complication began: "Bewildered we made together a last cramped gesture to bind a tie which in all underneath honesty had long since begun to loosen. It is hideous yet we know that it is so. Thus the child."

During Etta's pregnancy, to further confuse matters, Leroy met an old high school sweetheart, Delphine Weiler, my future stepmother. "He is not a man swept easily from his feet but she gives him that which teaches him he is alive and that is the thing I do not give him nor does he give it to me...At last Galby spoke out and I told him he must go to her. And full of chiding in himself as well as in great joy he went."

There were many painful discussions about the future. "He says I have never seemed like his children's mother. This is a strange thing to say to a woman in whom there is a child. His child. And yet it is not so strange as it is late...When Galby and I speak out we are tortured but we are fearless and we are not bitter." Etta's pregnancy delayed, but did not restrain the inevitable divorce. This would require the assistance of the courts of law: "These are weird. There sits on a bench a man before whom one stands and one must say then that there has been a brutality. One cannot use the word mistake nor can one explain that all of these things had one day to come... Into the courts Galby and I will not go until the child has come into the world...Thus the clasp of Galby and me overlaps into the new era when we will each burn brightly elsewhere. And this is good. A good friend is good. He must not be called by any other name when he is a friend, but that he is a friend is good."

Across the Atlantic, another friend, Ingolf, was having a very difficult time adjusting to life without Etta. He writes much less about his private life in the post-Etta journals. Old names continue to appear, or reappear, new names are added, but there is very little to tell us about Ingolf's relationship to any of these figures. We can be certain that none of his new lovers produced in him the intensity of passion that he had felt for Etta. There are practically no daybook entries during Ingolf's last half year in Zurich.

In the summer of 1936, seeking balm for his wounded spirit, he spent his entire summer holiday in the mountains, four weeks of bikeriding and hiking in the Alps. Some of his experiences were memorable. On July 11th, for instance, he spent a day in Italy en route from one Swiss location, Soglio, to a second, Splugen. Bad weather returned all day and before much of a start could be made, Ingolf had taken refuge from a cloudburst in a hayloft. Formalities at the border occasioned a long delay and Ingolf coasted down to Chiavenna soaked to the skin. The town did not delight him and he had trouble changing money. He bought some fruit and pedaled north, but as the route rose the temperature dipped. A veteran of the Ethiopian campaign accompanied him as far as Piamezzo, where Ingolf took refuge from the wind and the rain and had a hot bowl of soup. Near Monte Spluga the rained turned to heavy snow, but at the border a kind Italian soldier sat the shivering cyclist down and gave him some coffee. Ingolf describes such a day as an "adventure," and though it lead to bronchitis and a severe cold, the achievement of attainment, which such an endeavor signaled, must certainly have been a treasured moment in a year of turmoil.

The adventure in question, and other mountain experiences in general, may also have provided creative stimulus for the fledgling composer, for the original manuscript of the *Pastorale Montano* is dated "Monte Spluga, 1936." Ingolf never wrote "program" music and the work in question, part of a subdivided and re-edited *Piano Suite*, cannot be considered a pictorial invocation of mountain scenes. If pictures are needed, it would be more fruitful to imagine the musical materials swirling around in the head of the composer – as the snow pelted down from above. Ingolf *did* associate musical motifs with specific individuals – several appear in his journals – and other projects had similar personal elements. In 1933 he completed *Three Songs to Poems by Albert Ehrismann*, a Swiss surrealist whom Ingolf encountered frequently in the Zurich cafes. *Variations on a French Folktune* was dedicated to his brother Holger and dates from the summer of 1935, when the two played flute and piano duets in Stockholm. A *Rondo* for piano four-hands was completed in 1938 and presented to Willi Hausslein. And, of course, there would now be many pieces invoking Etta's name.

As we shall see, Ingolf rarely found composing easy, and projects were often begun, dropped, and begun again. On May 3rd, 1934, there is a reference to the Piano Suite, which Ingolf claims he is beginning for the "167th time," but his prediction that "Now it must come" was overoptimistic. We find him still working on the first movement, "Preludio," in May of 1935. A second section, "Fuga Alla Burlesca," is dated the same year, but we have seen that "Pastorale Montano" was not completed until 1936, and a final section, "Finale," was not added until 1943. Eglisau, a small town on the north bank of the Rhine, seems to have provided brief sanctuary for the busy musician, and when a free day suddenly appeared he would jump on his bike and in a beautiful room in a cheap hotel he would find the necessary isolation to compose. Ingolf compares himself to Orestes in the Temple of Apollo, but in Eglisau the Furies were not allowed to enter. It could now be asked, in what form would Etta next return to Ingolf, muse or Fury?

In the wake of her deteriorating relationship with Leroy, Etta, not surprisingly, was spending more time brooding on her interrupted love affair with Ingolf: "I feel that if he is living, it is most surely the same in his heart for me as it ever was. I do not know. He walks about in the city of G. and sees the water we watched together and smells the red leaves and looks at the white peaks which always he pointed out to me with their names. And it is wretched with him." Etta had written to Ingolf with news of the pregnancy in late April, 1937, the same month that, reading *Steppenwolf* again, he was making a symbolic connection between Etta and Hermine: "Oh Hermine, how terrible it must go with me until you come. But if you did, would I be capable of loving you as you deserve to be? Yes I would if you came in Etta's form. If only you would bring to me some human nearness and warmth. I am so grateful for so little."

Ingolf reports receiving the letter with news of the pregnancy on May 19th. It sent him into a tailspin of despair, and he failed to respond for months. This explains the oft-repeated lament in *The Talon*, "From Thast I have not heard in long." He did write to Barbara Kruger about the devastating effects of what must have seemed a final farewell to happiness: "That it would be forever my mind told me, but not my feelings, which did not wish to believe it. Since everything only confirmed the fact that Etta was for me the 'real one,' the thought of having lost her was too depressing to be carried to its end." News of a child, he wrote, "was a bad blow for me;" it convinced the abandoned lover that his relationship with Etta must really come to an end. The journal entry for May 19th is even more bitter in tone, "It cuts my heart, I have loved her so much." To Barbara, he added, "It hit me so hard that until July I could not find the way to wish her well."

In *The Talon* Etta reports receiving Ingolf's response in August. "The letter from Thast. For me it is in his heart as it has always been. There is no joy in his life without my life. He is glad for the child. This he says because he believes that Galby and I are glad for the child. But the underneath of his words is seasoned bitter brown and poorly hid...I will write to Thast how it is in reality with all this...The letter to Thast grows huge. He will be a bewildered one...Thast will read this and in him there will be chaos." Before she could dispatch this letter a postcard arrived from Ingolf from Einsiedeln, where – fifteen months earlier – the two lovers had looked at the monastery candles on their last day together: "In it he speaks of the lighting of candles...Candles one lights for the dead...A candle for a dead thing." Would Ingolf see that their love was still alive? "He may not want me because my running from him might have drained him of desire... Would he still fold me to him as though the great time of hurt had not passed?"

And would it be possible to picture Ingolf as parent to the unborn child? "I have never thought of Thast as a father of children," Etta states at the beginning of her story, but this is then revised, "Thast loved little folk always and would speak to me often of this child or that and how it was in him for little children...I can now clearly remember how at the side of Thast in those overwhelming full woman times of me I wanted of Thast a child." "Thast could love this child," is the conclusion. Letter after letter went to Zurich, a compendium of Etta's hopes and fears: "To help me over the startling movement of the child in myself I have fancies of how it will be with Thast. I see him alight from a ship, from a train...By now he has surely heard my cry and goes about in the city of G. and goes about and about and about. Sets pen to paper and crumples it. And again the pen. And knows. And thinks. And feels." So Etta brings her story to its conclusion.

Ingolf does not tell us directly how he responded to Etta's letters. But on July 19th, 1937, the journal entry reads, "Screaming for Etta." In his letter to Barbara the following year he notes that the summer of 1937 was "a very difficult time for us all. It is overcome now and we don't think of it anymore." Early in January of 1938 he records with enthusiasm the birth of that problematic child who now completes his stepfather's biography – "Anthony Linick born!!!!" The birth, he wrote to Barbara, "did not change anything in our decision...all difficulties are only a stimulus to overcome them." The decision reached by the brave transatlantic correspondents was twofold: that Ingolf and Etta would become man and wife, and that Ingolf would make his home in Los Angeles, California.

Appropriately, he set out on a farewell visit to his family in the summer of 1938. He included stops in Paris, London, Cambridge and York before sailing from Newcastle to Gothenberg. He arrived in Stockholm on July 1st. It is not clear how much Ingolf told his parents about his relationship with Etta, though Anna-Britta, with whom he had spent several weeks of Alpine hiking the previous summer, would have known everything.

Brother and sister said goodbye on July 11th, but Ingolf and his parents traveled together for another two weeks, including some days spent alone with Mammi in Visby on the island of Gotland. Mammi is described as melancholy throughout this period, but at last the time to say farewell to her eldest and dearest son had to arrive. Ingolf took the steamer back to Germany from Trelleborg on July 24th – "Mammi sets down her case in order to wave to me."

Ingolf continued to work at the Opera, which had clearly turned into a dead end for him, throughout 1938, but he did this in order to have something to occupy his time and energy during those anxious moments while he awaited approval of his emigration visa at the American consulate. To assist him in obtaining this precious piece of paper he had been provided with affidavits, guaranteeing his support, from Leroy and from Morris Keller, my aunt Lillian's husband. He hoped to be able to depart as early as November, and to leave from Hamburg, where Pappi's bank account could be used to pay for his passage. Eventually he chose to depart from a French port, but his visa did not arrive until November 23rd and it was several weeks before all the unfinished business of life in Europe could be brought to a conclusion. Many farewells had to be said to relatives and friends, to Opera associates like Denzler and Willi, and to the Stadttheater's director, Karl Schmid-Bloss, who publicly thanked Ingolf for his high musical standards at a farewell party.

Margrit, his aunt's maid, helped Ingolf complete his packing and, at 3:29 on the afternoon of January 16th, 1939, he boarded the Basel train and began the long journey westward. "Farewell, Zurich!!!!" he wrote in his diary. Three of his friends accompanied him as far as the border and others met him in Paris, where he spent two nights. On January 17th he phoned Stockholm for the last time and the next morning he took the train to Le Havre and boarded the *SS Manhattan*. The social page of the *New York Times* tells us that Ingolf's shipmates included Otto Kruger and Edward Everett Horton, but a meeting is unlikely. There are no details concerning the crossing in the journals, but the weather is known to us from another source because on the same night that Ingolf boarded the *Manhattan*, two other men boarded the *Champlain* in Southampton and began a stormy transatlantic journey, arriving in New York on January 26th, 1939, to find a welcoming party made up of Erika and Klaus Mann. These two travelers were Christopher Isherwood and W.H. Auden. Ingolf arrived alone a few hours later, an impoverished, obscure twenty-six year old exile. He spent less than two weeks in New York, visiting, sight-seeing, and making some professional contacts, but it is clear that he was not willing to be deterred for long in completing his journey to California. His anticipation must have been intense. He left New York on February 7th, travelling west by bus, spending each night in another seedy hotel. His journals are full of astonishment at the unaccustomed sights of an America still gripped by dust bowl and depression: gingerbread houses, gas stations in the guise of windmills, neon crosses, papooses, cowboy hats, mesas, gold mines, cactus, even a Navajo wearing a version of the hated swastika!

Ingolf Dahl, for he had decided to use his mother's last name in America, would soon be part of an unusual *menage*. I had just passed my first birthday and my parents had just filed for divorce. These "friends" were still living together, enjoying what Leroy liked to call " a divorce without a separation." On January 17, 1939, Ingolf's last night in Europe, my father had written to the Weismans, "Etta and I intend to go on living under the same roof or in close proximity to one another as long as the fates permit, for we are very good friends, function excellently as co-translators, and have a darling son to bring up. On the other hand it would be dishonest and unethical of us to go on living together, pretending to be happily married husband and wife. We are not and scarcely ever have been." Without love, however, continuing the marriage would be "a hypocritical subterfuge." "The parents," he continued, "end up having done neither themselves nor their child a favor. Instead of such a patchwork solution we are going to give Anthony two friendly parents." Etta and Leroy earnestly pursued this ideal ever after. If I could not be the issue of a happy marriage I would at least be the product of a civilized divorce.

Leroy concluded his letter by proposing to move his family to an as yet unbuilt domicile on a lot he had purchased in the San Fernando Valley, northwest of Reseda. I do not know what became of this project, though this failure rescued me from a youth wasted among walnut trees, tract houses, billboards, and drive-in movies. Eventually Leroy sold his two acres, typically too soon, and some developer got to turn them into the next mall, twenty-five years later. We continued to live in Culver City until May, 1939, when we moved to nearby 3125 Bedford Street in Los Angeles

34, a spot very close to my future high school, Alexander Hamilton. Leroy had his own room, Etta had her room, I had my room, and there was, of course, a room for Ingolf.

He had arrived in Los Angeles at 6:45 pm on the night of February 15th. A few days later Leroy drove Ingolf and Etta to the mountains where, in a resort appropriately called Switzer-Land, the two lovers spent several days in solitude beside a rushing stream: "To be able to sit with you again at the fireside, and again to feel your hand, to talk of yesterday and plan for tomorrow and again to share joys and sorrows. What was begun is not at an end." Thus Ingolf summarizes in verse the reunion which brought to an end almost three years of tormented separation.

9. EPIPHANY

I was born on January 6th, 1938, on the seventh floor of the Cedars of Lebanon Hospital on Fountain Avenue, just west of Vermont, a section of Los Angeles I would call East Hollywood – if there were such a place. During my mother's confinement, a son was born on the same ward to Mr. and Mrs. Bing Crosby. I have never indulged in the fantasy that these babies were switched at birth, for never was a son more convinced, in the marrow of his flesh, that his father and mother were *exactly* who they said they were: Leroy and Etta Linick of 4037 Higuera Street, Culver City.

Even before leaving hospital, my mother had composed a poem to describe my first moments of waking life: "My father is a Ph.D. / My mother tries to hit high C. / What difference does it make to me? / I sleep and eat and pee." At six weeks, identifying a pattern that has never lost its intensity, she added, "He doesn't care what happens as long as he gets his food."

What a serious practitioner of the child-rearing art my mother proved to be! My father was holding weekly seminars in lay psychoanalysis, and, not to be outdone, my mother demonstrated her passion for the intricacies of infantile development by recording with religious zest every act and utterance of her son in a volume entitled *Your Child Year By Year*. This *Parents Magazine* publication put innumerable questions to the conscientious parent, and there was space to reply on a weekly basis for the first year, and a monthly one thereafter. Thus it is possible for me to speak with authority about my height, weight, health, personality, motor and language development, digestion and elimination at every stage of my early life – even though I have no memory of any of these details. My wife and I christened the volume the Baby Tony Book when it fell into our hands. Etta had found the space provided by the publishers insufficient. In 1940 she switched to a supplementary record called a *Deskaide*, so that nothing of any relevance to the science of childrearing or the wit and wisdom of Baby Tony would be lost.

I know that the devotees of this science are forever at war (Etta, for instance, belonged to a school of philosophy that favored the bottle over the breast), but a careful reading of these precious volumes convinces me that my mother adopted toward her late and only child a misplaced perfection compulsion – so many other things in her life, as we shall see, having turned out messily. Readers raised in a more permissive era can only smile in awe at some of her obsessions.

She reported frustration, when I had reached the ripe old age of twenty weeks, about my hands: "We tried to keep his hands out of his mouth by tying his nightgown sleeves over them, but now he puts *them* into his mouth." Time to clamp on the celluloid handcuffs and turn our attention to a little precocious toilet training.

"In order to save a diaper from being messed," she noted when I was four weeks old, "I placed a piece of Kleenex under him on the table and he moved his bowels on that. After this time I put him on the paper after every meal and grunted for him, which he imitated and very seldom from this time on messed his diapers." A few months later, no doubt regretting her over-optimism, my mother returned to the task with a doomed attempt to get me to move my bowels into a pottie; I was twelve weeks old. At fifteen weeks, she had convinced herself that I knew the difference between "wee-wee" and "grunt-wee-wee," and that I would often do either on request. During the twenty-third week she reported a little backsliding: "I believe he recognizes the sound if not the significance of a displeased "no-no" on my part. He looks earnest and puzzled and even sometimes gets obviously kittenish as if he'd like to divert me from the subject at hand (subject is: grunt-wee-wee in the diapers instead of in the pot)." It seems that I had been grumbling about sitting on this receptacle. "I don't blame him," she added, "It's too small for comfort. But he looks charming sitting on it."

Charming stinker! In spite of all these conscientious efforts to produce a *Wunderkind* of the water closet, Etta had to wait until I was a year and half before I *asked* to go "pobbie." "Since then he has been pretty consistent in asking during the day," she exulted, "general rejoicing!"

My father was working at the MGM studios, only a few blocks from our home in Culver City. Also close at hand were the Selznick Studios. When I was eight months old the pediatrician's nurse called to inform my mother that babies were being auditioned for a part in *Made For Each Other*, starring Carole Lombard and James Stewart. My mother crammed me into the stroller and we were off. When we arrived, we were driven to Stage Twelve, where the casting director sheepishly pointed to another infant, who had just been chosen. The lucky brat was abandoned as I was admired, handled, and exclaimed over. Everyone agreed that I would have been a *far* more suitable choice, "The next day we left some of his pictures at the casting office," my mother concluded. And *concluded* is the right verb. There were no callbacks and so ended Baby Tony's brief career in Show Biz.

I might never have recovered from the over-zealous attentions of toilet-trainer and stage mother had Etta not learned to relax a bit. In this process I suppose I can be grateful that there had now arrived in our lives a new and distracting figure, much in need of mothering himself – my future stepfather. Four months after my mother's short legs cost me a chance at cinema immortality, my parents filed for divorce – so that *each* could remarry. Baby Tony was about to experience more than the usual confusions of a broken home.

10. FOR THE SAKE OF LOVE

In spite of the joys of their mountain reunion, despair and estrangement were the overwhelming emotions during Ingolf's first months in California. Migration had brought him to Etta's side, but the price to be paid for this romantic gesture was very high indeed. Ingolf's early years in America were characterized by displacement, isolation, illness, unemployment, and emotional collapse. During his first weeks in Los Angeles he was taken to see the sights: Hollywood Boulevard, Grauman's Chinese, Bel Air, Beverly Hills, Westwood, the ocean at Santa Monica. Every relative, Weismans,

Linicks, Gordons, and Kellers, was trotted out to have a look at the new arrival. Our bicycle-riding European recoiled in horror at his first experience of a motorized suburban culture. On his first full day at Higuera Street, the journal tells a pathetic story – "*Heimweh!*" – homesickness. Two weeks later he was felled by a serious asthma attack, surely a form of culture shock. No wonder that the stricken emigré summarized his desperate position with the phrase, "Everything for the sake of love."

For the next few years he would attempt to make this unfamiliar world more tame by finding in it some parallel to the one he had left behind. Wasn't the view of the snow against the green hills on the Ridge Route almost like Zurich? The rain lashing the top of Mt. Wilson, couldn't this evoke that distant adventure in Splugen? A day in the U.C.L.A. library reminded him of similar moments on the campus at Zurich. San Francisco's Sutro Heights are compared to the Zurichberg, Laguna Beach to the Baltic, Palos Verdes to Italy, the San Simeon Highway to the Riviera. Ingolf read only one paper regularly during his early years in California, the *Neue Zurcher Zeitung*. He feasted on letters from across the Atlantic – though Etta had to to answer most of these. In many of his customs and habits, it was clear that emotionally he was still very much the European.

Ill-health had been an all too familiar feature of the life he had left behind. Unfortunately, he escaped none of these traumas through migration, and the war years were full of a patternless recurrence of all those health problems he had experienced in Zurich – asthma, bronchitis, weakness and dizziness, chest and throat complaints in infinite variety. Things were particularly bad in the first year, 1939, a year in which eczema returned and hemorrhoids required surgery. By September he had lost nine of his 149 pounds, and two months later he was undergoing weekly allergy treatments at the Good Hope Clinic, whose services he was permitted to use because of his extreme poverty. Asthma continued to bother him, however, and only in the period from the fall of 1943 to February 1944 was there any relief. His greatest difficulties were between 4:00 and 6:00am; additionally, the medicines he used for his asthma, ephedrine and tedral, kept him awake. In 1943 anemia was treated with liver and iron shots.

In 1944 he was asked by one of his many physicians (now including my cousin, Julius Kahn) to write out a health history. His specific complaint at the time was bronchitis, but he added some general symptoms: "no resistance or stamina, constant tiredness, need too much sleep, unable to do my work." My parents were both cultists of the basal metabolism test, and Ingolf appears to have undergone his first in May, 1945. He was much annoyed by the result – "my metabolism is normal and I feel like hell," and soon thereafter thyroid tablets were added to the arsenal of medicaments that held such a fascination for his intrigued stepson. Needless to say, the Armed Services pronounced Ingolf 4-F. He did not need an official confirmation of his situation.

The entry for January 5th, 1945, can be taken as a typical cry of despair. Ingolf had been working at the Warner Brothers lot in the Valley, recording music for the film *Of Human Bondage*. The lovely drive in the mornings," he wrote, "over Cahuenga and down Barham to the Valley, with the deserty hills in the background. And the drive home, after a day of work on the closed stage, with the deep purple clouds and the *air*! God, let me get healthy and well. Everything else will come by itself then." There is an irony in a man with weak lungs choosing to live in Smogville. But the deterioration in the quality of Los Angeles' air was a post-war phenomenon, a consequence of the lifting of restrictions on travel and the influx of the motorized millions to Southern California. Smog bothered Ingolf considerably in later years, but by then it was too late, and his roots had been re-grafted to California soil. The culture shock had passed and Ingolf had made his home here.

The health report filled out in 1944 also contained a section on physical exercise. "Always sports," Ingolf had written, "but mostly in spite of my health and not because of an abundance of it." It took him a year to get back on skis, and gasoline restrictions would soon eat into his opportunities to escape to the mountains, but it is possible to see the names of his favorite ski resorts – Mt. Waterman, Big Bear, Gorgonio, Baldy – as they begin to recur in the journals of this period. And the names of many summits in the San Gabriel Range, which Ingolf hiked for thirty years, make their appearance as well. Before long he had a small circle of hiking and skiing companions, most of whom had no connection with his professional life. His first hike took place on April 19th, 1939, in the company of Raymond Spottiswoode, the film scholar, who also introduced my stepfather to wildflower collecting soon thereafter. "It is finally again like life," Ingolf wrote after crashing through some underbrush in Tujunga Canyon. Thus

Los Angeles' physical setting helped win the allegiance of the semi-exile, whose first months in his new home were, in other respects, replete with disasters and wrong turnings.

Foremost among the practical difficulties were questions of livelihood. Ingolf arrived in Los Angeles with a lot of telephone numbers, but little else. Describing himself as "Conductor, Arranger, Composer, and Pianist," he set off in the spring of 1939 to find work, inhibited by the poor public transportation system, always conscious of his status as a foreigner and an outsider, slowed by ill-health.

His first efforts seem to have been directed toward the Los Angeles Philharmonic and its famous conductor, Otto Klemperer, to whom he had written while still in Switzerland. Nothing came of this at the time, and he turned next to the film studios. He seems to have offered his services to the composer Max Steiner at Warner Brothers, but his participation in the studio orchestras of the time was still off in the future. By the end of June, 1939, Ingolf was forced to fall back on one his old Zurich skills, coaching singers. This he did privately and sporadically for the next few years; the income must have been minuscule. His only happy professional moments came when he was socializing with other musicians – in many instances, a camaraderie among refugees.

"One of my most beautiful days," was Ingolf's summary of March 25th, 1939, a day spent in the company of Paul Hindemith. The composer of *Mathis* and his former musical assistant spent much time reminiscing on this day, but Hindemith did not make Los Angeles his home, as did many other European composers. One giant who was already well-established in Los Angeles was Arnold Schoenberg, who taught at U.C.L.A. from 1936 to 1944, reduced, so the pathetic rumor used to have it, to spending the war years teaching music appreciation to bored Bruin coeds. To make up for it, a new music building on the Westwood campus was later named Schoenberg Hall, and this is where my wife and I took *our* music appreciation classes some twenty years after Ingolf first encountered Schoenberg, his circle, and some of his pupils.

The latter included George Tremblay and Leonard Stein, later director of the Schoenberg Institute at U.S.C. Ingolf reports seeing the author of the twelve-tone system at Kerkhoff Hall on April 14th, 1939. A few days later he attended a class given by Schoenberg in the Education Building; the master played his own *First String Quartet* on the phonograph, and Ingolf spoke to him briefly afterwards. Evidently my stepfather was considering returning to the university in order to obtain a Ph.D., and it is interesting to speculate how his musical development might have been altered had he chosen to work with Schoenberg. Their relationship did not move in this direction, though in the following years they met socially several times, often at the home of bassoonist Adolphe Weiss, who had also studied with Schoenberg. Through Weiss, Ingolf also met two other composers, Edgar Varese and Joseph Achron. Their names pop up on the social calendar with some frequency in the early Forties.

Ingolf also had a number of professional contacts with Schoenberg. In 1942 my stepfather conducted a performance of the *First Chamber Symphony* and on December 18th, 1944, a performance of Schoenberg's *Pierrot Lunaire*. Ingolf and Carl Beier produced their own English language version of this work and won the composer's enthusiastic endorsement for their efforts: "The translation is wonderful and I can't think of anything better." Ingolf also joined with others in a seventieth birthday tribute to the composer in 1944, my stepfather sending along one of his own compositions. I cannot tell which one it is – Ingolf often dashed off birthday canons for his friends, but he must have been pleased by the master's response – "This is really a highly artistic work of musical craft," Schoenberg wrote, "It's admirable how you could manage to build your two phrases in such a manner that in retrograde the initial form appears again but in reversed order of the voices. Also the answer in the diminished fifth is explained by this. Congratulations are reciprocate – but in [my] case only for the achievement of having remained alive." The brown ink which flows toward the signature of the great man has not faded in sixty years. And the letter, one of two from Schoenberg which I still possess, lies framed just above my writing desk as I work on this chapter – all these years later.

On May 25th, 1939, Ingolf ascended a California podium for the first time, a premiere spoiled by the aforementioned hemorrhoids. The occasion was a brief run of Schiller's play, *William Tell*, for which Ernst Toch had written incidental music. Ingolf grew quite fond of the older composer as a consequence of this collaboration – "a dear man" whom he often visited in Santa Monica. *Tell* was performed at the El Capitan Theater and its run came to an end on June 3rd. "It goes well in every detail," Ingolf commented on the first performance, but there was no way for him to build on such a success, and the summer months were full of fruitless job-hunting.

As the four of us moved to Bedford Street in May, "cold-blooded" suggestions were made to Ingolf by other members of the family, Weismans and Kellers, about alternative (for which one can read non-musical) forms of employment. Ingolf was horrified by the idea, and he would not be moved from his quest for musical employment. "Never before have the tears been so close to falling," he wrote on July 2nd.

The next month, however, he secured work as a pianist with the Edith Lorand orchestra. Rehearsals began at the end of the month, and on September 14th Ingolf found himself beginning an eight-week stint at the Palace Hotel in San Francisco, playing the light classics at teatime and in the evening. Surely he could not have expected that his first lengthy work assignment in America would come 500 miles from Los Angeles and in so trivial a capacity. He tried to make the best of his time – he haunted the San Francisco Opera and he renewed a friendship with a Cologne colleague, Carl Fuerstner, later a member of the Opera faculty of the University of Indiana. Nevertheless he was often so bored that he was willing to spend hours chatting with Edith Lorand or the other band members.

When the orchestra disbanded, Ingolf stayed up north to accompany Miss Lorand in classical selections at the Burlingame Country Club and the Del Monte Lodge. A program for the latter appearance describes Edith Lorand as "The World's Greatest Hungarian Violinist-Conductor." Ingolf was also profiled in the hyperbole sweepstakes as the former "First Conductor of the National Symphony in Zurich."

He maintained his association with the Hungarian firecracker for about a year, doing occasional arrangements, rehearsing for concerts that never came off, showing up for rehearsals that were suddenly cancelled, putting up with Miss Lorand's efforts to improve his popular appeal – "See more movies; listen to more radio." Etta, writing to Dinah Spottiswoode in August, 1940, offers a portrait of Lorand etched in vitriol: "The woman is an enormously gifted violinist in her own field, that is the field of Hungarian gypsy airs and Viennese waltzes. That is the beginning, the middle, and the end. Unfortunately for her, there is not too great a demand for this type of music, which curtails her activities in the first place. In the second place, she has a vicious, obnoxiously egotistical personality which has 'queered' her with many an agent."

In the summer of 1940 Ingolf was named "assistant musical director" to Friedrich Fejer. Described by Etta as an "impossible impostor," Fejer and Edith Lorand were evidently attempting to make film shorts for distribution by, to use Etta's own words again, "moving picture slot-machines." All this sounds like an idea whose time had passed with some of my paternal grandfather's early efforts in Chicago. When some music was actually rehearsed Ingolf found that Fejer "has no idea of anything and is more stupid than had been presumed. I control myself but am as cold as ice and leave without saying goodbye."

In undertaking work with Edith Lorand, Ingolf was beginning a pattern that lasted for many years: although he had sacrificed a life and a career in Europe in order to be with Etta, the necessity of finding employment often forced him to abandon my mother as he took to the road in pursuit of demeaning musical jobs that enlisted only a fraction of his interest, talents or abilities. Undoubtedly, he *had* given up much for the sake of love.

11. A RECURRENT ENCHANTMENT

I wish I could say that generalizations about the love life of Ingolf and Etta come easily, but in fact their relationship was so complex that it has taken me years to fathom its depths, and I am still baffled. The evidence that does exist is often elliptical at best. Outsiders, who were often deliberately *misled*, do not help a great deal; nor do I intend to deal fully with the mysteries of their relationship until the concluding chapters of this volume.

My Aunt Lillian notes that from the first Ingolf and Etta refrained from demonstrative displays of affection, although at home their embrace was clearly able to drive Baby Tony into an Oedipal rage. Lillian argues that they were manifestly a couple, fiercely loyal and proud of one another, even a handsome pair, she with her heavy lipstick and dark upswept hair, he with his athletic build and charming foreign ways.

What each expected from married life is not easily divined, even when such expectations are alluded to in letters that have survived or from entries in Ingolf's daybook. The two enjoyed an occasional and middling sex life. "It is again beautiful with Etta," Ingolf wrote on April 16th, 1939, "and that was necessary after the last horrible time." The consistently pleasurable experiences that Ingolf describes, however, were more social than sexual – a walk in Griffith Park, a trip to Crystal Lake, a visit to the Santa Monica pier, endless movies. When Etta came to San Francisco during the Lorand engagement, Ingolf took her to Finocchio's, the transvestite palace, where they had a grand time. Tucked into a scrapbook of the era our sentimentalists preserved a small matchbook from the establishment. When I examined it in 1979, it still contained two matches, one of which, though forty years old, blazed instantly to light my wife's cigarette. Imperfect as their love may have been, whatever Ingolf shared with Etta was precious to them both.

On November 8th, 1939, Ingolf reports receiving an "indescribable" letter from Etta. "What could be more beautiful," he added, congratulating himself on winning such a woman as a wife. I have no way of knowing precisely which letter is referred to, as none of the ones he preserved bears a relevant date, but there is an undated letter from her, written in German, which points to some of Etta's feelings on the periodic nature of Ingolf's sexual attentions. Our love is big enough to accept such periods, she argues; we have to be able to accept the disenchanted periods and be prepared for the recurrent enchantment. It will come again, she assures her lover, adding, I only feel compassion for you because I love you above everything. Rather than have lovemaking out of guilt or habit, Etta implies, she would rather wait for the passion to return – if only other couples could be as honest. On November 17th, three days after his return to Los Angeles from San Francisco, Ingolf reports, "It is again infinitely beautiful."

In 1940 two weddings took place. On February 10th, Leroy married my stepmother, Delphine Weiler. Ingolf reports that at the conclusion of the ceremony Etta embraced her first husband in a simple, natural, and moving gesture. He also describes the weeks leading up to his own marriage as a time of emotional stress and difficulty. On March 15th he and Etta must have had a good fight – "catastrophe," "very severe breakdown," though the cause is unspecified. But a few days later the two sold a typewriter in order to buy the wedding rings that, half a century later, still lie in an envelope in my safe deposit box in Maida Vale. On March 21, 1940, accompanied by Michael Mann and Carl Fuerstner, Ingolf and Etta were married at the Los Angeles City Hall. This unlikely pair would survive thirty years of marriage!

Because of Ingolf's asthma, Julius Kahn advised against a high altitude honeymoon, so the newlyweds settled for a few days at the Weisman cabin in Tujunga. Then they and Baby Tony returned to our new residence at 3501 London Street, near Silverlake Boulevard.

The first years of married life were clearly difficult ones for Ingolf and Etta. When Ingolf heard Bruno Walter conduct Mahler's *First Symphony* on December 20th, 1940, memories of happier times flooded forth, punctuated by a suppressed cry for "Mammi!! "What is there that I haven't lost, a world thrown away," he added soon thereafter. "These are difficult days," he wrote during a period of illness in March, 1941, "and I am sick and so full of yearning...Nobody cares for me at all."

It is interesting to note how often, in his catalogue of miseries, he couples the economic with the erotic. "Terrible depression over financial, personal situation," he wrote in May of 1940; in July, he noted, "the material and erotic problems become worse and worse." Whatever the cause for what she clearly experienced as a rejection, my mother became despondent in turn. "Etta is becoming more problematic. What am I to do now...Etta is again difficult and I am so anxious, perplexed, wretched."

A talk between husband and wife, the first of dozens to come, led to some clarification, though it would be many years before the two could openly and honestly face all of their problems, and even then solutions were hard to come by. Etta tried to explain some things to Ingolf. Ingolf tried to coax Etta into being more reasonable. That summer the two began work on a children's opera, which they hoped to see produced in local junior high schools. I don't believe that much music was ever composed for *Sandy And The Singing Rocks*, but a libretto was completed and this collaboration between them seems to have been among the happy occasions, like walks in the hills, days on the beach or the occasional dinner at Melody Lane or the Gourmet, in an otherwise unstable relationship.

Time did not heal these wounds, and by 1941 the two were taking short vacations apart from one another. In April of 1942, Ingolf again reports that, "Etta is very down these days...Objective grounds – curfew and further restrictions. Subjective – my long illness and the erotic distance." On September 22nd, he adds, "Crisis the entire time, however it is not a crisis one gets over." There are many references to "my enduring incompleteness," "my many-layered wall." "Life is so difficult and severe," he concluded, "If only I could grasp it and hold it."

It is interesting to note that Etta had an explanation for the deficiencies she now detected in Ingolf's personality. Writing to Connie Buchanan in 1943, she argued, "Ingolf is an almost classic example of a person who has never stopped resenting his emergence into post-natal life...Everything he does is a contest between himself and life. It was probably not conscious on her part, but his mother bent over backwards filling his childhood with the prettiest, most amusing, most glossily sentimental and otherwise escapist things she could think of. She succeeded in fitting him with permanent rose-colored glasses...rooting out any will to struggle, be independent, in short to face life for what it is." Etta then added, "The fact that he was ill a great deal of his childhood did its part, too, toward fostering both his introversion and his narcissism...Like so many another creature with the need to compensate himself for having to live against his inmost wish, he turned very early to art. He tells me he wrote death dramas on the typewriter at eleven."

Did Ingolf try to hang himself in 1942? On September 15th, after leaving the daybook blank for two weeks, he tells us that he has a severe neck sprain. Neck problems recurred throughout his life, including cervical arthritis and disc troubles. Like other afflicted patients, Ingolf really *did* have to hang himself from an apparatus attached to the door.

Etta was willing to grant that Ingolf could be positive toward art, "otherwise he just swims along somehow, ignoring the problematic or even mildly annoying, at times pretending for all he is worth that such things cannot be and that if he just gives them enough rope and scope they'll go far away and hang themselves...It is agony for him to make even the smallest decision, because decision is an expression of will, and Ingolf doesn't really will anything." This ungenerous characterization would soften, I feel, in later years, when it was easier to see that Ingolf's decision to value life as it *should* be, in preference to life as it actually *was*, carried with it a certain courage, the bravery of the creative spirit. But Etta wrote her bitter analysis before Ingolf had taken many steps toward establishing his credentials as a composer, and it is no wonder that she should have been bitter over his many outrageous qualities and jealous of the emotional sublimation which robbed her of the loving response that should have been forthcoming in her mate.

It is clear from the daybooks that his relationship with Etta was worsening steadily. "Don't yell at Ingolf. It hurts my ears," Baby Tony protested on November 12th, 1942. Elsewhere, Ingolf comments on Etta's bad temper, her "difficult" behavior, her rejection of him, the onset of hysteria. A day together in the mountains, a rare instance of lovemaking, did nothing to alleviate the problems. "A heart-to-heart talk is due," Ingolf wrote on February 17th, 1943, "she doesn't want to be with me unless I talk and I simply can't make myself do it." A denouement is reported the next day, and Etta's letter to Connie gives us a pretty reliable summary of what they did talk about. Etta complained about the boredom and drudgery of housework and Ingolf advised more reading aloud, more films and more fun.

My stepfather clearly approved of the idea of Etta returning to work – "it is of great psychological importance that she should use her brain again as a human being instead of a shut-in slave of the houschold which she has been for too many years." But when Etta worked all day long at the medical library at Cedars and had most of the domestic chores as well, Ingolf was "too busy," she complained, to stop at the cleaners, though he had plenty of time to look at sunsets or go to the mountains. "What I call facing things, looking at them in all their ugly aspects," she wrote Connie, "he calls being negative…When this something happens to be a connubial problem (sex is also 'unimportant,' embarrassing when problematic, and at best, 'minor') you can see why I have gone rather pale around the stamina… Ingolf always admits freely that he is wrong or inadequate. That is a fine trait, but actually has no practical value, because his rate of changing himself is glacial."

Was Etta beginning to realize that change was, in fact, beyond her husband's capabilities? "Ingolf's preoccupation with himself is not selfishness," she wrote, "for he is in his own way as generous as he knows how to be -- he is simply egocentric to a degree that makes him practically useless in any set-up requiring cooperative living." Interestingly enough, Ingolf read and copied this letter to Connie – "like one of those hostages who were ordered to dig their own graves" – but it is unclear whether Etta showed it to him or he just discovered it around the house. Typically, he responded to each of Etta's charges with phrases like, "She is so right," and "I have compassion for her, for me." He has added to his copy of the letter, "The worst thing, in spite of all we love each other."

The two stumbled forward in tandem, sharing times of pleasure as well as those of turmoil. They frequently ate lunch together at Etta's workplace; they took moonlit walks in the hills. They read through *Porgy and Bess* (Etta enjoyed singing "Summertime"), and there were rare moments of reconciliation and sexual fulfillment, particularly when Baby Tony wasn't around to cramp their style; "It is again lovely," Ingolf wrote on October 23rd, 1943, "Finally the sex is beautiful. I love Etta." "I do love you so," Etta wrote the following March, "I hope you never forget it. After all, would I fight & fuss & complain so if I didn't feel at base that there is something worth fussing, fighting, and complaining for?" In their occasional euphoric moods, the idea of giving Baby Tony a younger sibling was discussed. On May 24th, 1943, Ingolf responds enthusiastically to the idea, when it is raised by Etta, and then immediately has his doubts. Nothing – or no *one* – resulted from these conversations. My mother used to suggest wistfully that she had always wanted redheaded twins, which I assumed meant in addition to, not instead of, me. In fact, Baby Tony was to have all the pleasures and deficiencies of life as an only child.

It is clear to see that in the war years the moments of unhappiness far outweighed these idyllic fantasies anyway. "Etta is gloomy and despondent and speaks of the end (which?)," Ingolf writes on June 27th, 1943. In her brooding misery the catalogue of her husband's faults grew ever larger. She complained of his vagueness, his absent-mindedness, his absorption in a thousand things other than his wife: "Music, Mountains, and Me," this seemed to be his priority list. There was also resentment over the nature of his work, the untidy "arrangerie" of his life as a commercial musician, who, when he finally got up, had to spread out his musical homework in the living room.

Then there was his habit of apologizing for his weaknesses, of agreeing with all of Etta's criticisms, and doing nothing about them! And chiefly there was the disaster of their sex life, the need for tangible expressions of his love: "I feel a sort of desperate need to encircle you in some way, to have some sort of contact with you, to touch you at some point, and as a result I hang around in that silly fashion wondering why I am so cross and why I am unable to tear myself away and *do* something," she wrote, "And I know I have a very irritating effect on you too because I make you self-conscious."

Much to Ingolf's embarrassment his wife would not stop talking about sex. She offered hints on technique. She talked about sexual cycles (Ingolf proposed his own as an excuse for infrequent performance), together they worried about medical causes and wondered if Ingolf should see a doctor. On October 30th, 1943, Etta, perhaps reacting to a passionless conjugal duty call, declared, "No more sex between us," a threat that was often repeated and always, eventually, withdrawn. A letter from Ingolf to Anna-Britta, dated only November 13th, may belong to this period; it certainly addresses the issue of his love for Etta, which, he admits, "sits deep in the pit of my stomach and it burns and it has kept alive through all the adversity." Admitting that "day after day I fail anew in giving this love a practical expression," Ingolf noted a quirk in his own personality: "Everything that I do not have at the moment has the strongest and most magnetic influence on me." When this love is present, however, he is overwhelmed by *other* "not now" desires.

Through her decision to remain Ingolf's wife, my mother accepted the phenomenon of his frequent sexual lethargy, balancing the inevitable bitterness with those special moments of erotic fulfillment she was still able to find in his arms. If "marriage" was not the right word to describe their relationship, Etta had determined that she would keep the man she loved – a decision that I would date from about 1944 – even if she would have to share him with every one of his many other obsessions and preoccupations. Thus, after four years of unhappiness in marriage, it is not surprising to note the recurrent diary entry for July 29th, 1944, "It is beautiful with Etta."

Curiously, the subject of their romance disappears as a central preoccupation in journal entries in the later Forties, pushed to the background of a life which was wholeheartedly devoted to music-making and career building. It is also obvious that Etta rejected, for some time, Ingolf's rare attempts at love making, finding the retreat from such affections to be more disturbing that the pleasures to be derived from their wayward onset. On January 17, 1946, he mentions "the fatal talk with E

– which this time really ends before the blank wall. I am dumbfounded and just can't accept it. She is right, but it just can't be."

12. HELL TO BE POOR

Our London Street home was small and dilapidated. Etta had no room of her own, there was no hot water, spongy floorboards sank beneath the feet, the sink was made of wood, none of the doors shut properly, and the moss-backed neighbors sniffed when Ingolf and Etta dined by candlelight on the back porch.

When he wanted to practice Ingolf had to go to the home of friends, like Connie Buchanan – his own upright was too rough-cut for such fine usage, and he could not afford anything better. He had no studio in which to put a decent instrument and no parlor in which to receive guests or students. My parents ran up a long list of social debts, which they felt themselves unable to repay at London Street. "And in this town," Etta lamented, "entertaining is a business investment." London Street *was* cheap, she admitted, but this was an absolute necessity in those days when jobs were so hard for Ingolf to come by.

Without any labor saving devices Etta spent tireless hours trying to create order and a dust-free environment in a household full of kiddy clutter and the personal and professional effects of an absent-minded husband. Ingolf was, of course, useless in the household, except on the most infrequent basis, regarding such endeavors as "stupid work."

A car was a requirement of life in Los Angeles, and Ingolf did earn his first driving permit within months of his arrival. His first car was named Black Peter – he insisted on naming all of his cars and, in later years, even some of mine, a droll practice that always made me cringe. Peter was a 1931 Model A Ford Roadster, a convertible whose top, if it still existed, was unserviceable. The vehicle was essentially a two-seater, but there was a rumble seat into which I would delightedly slip, even falling asleep on the way home from late outings, the lid closed over my head, lucky not to die from inhaling carbon monoxide. Maintenance of the "sweet buggy" did fall to Ingolf, and Peter was nursed through his own share of illnesses: flat tires, a sick speedometer, starter and battery troubles, and windshield wipers that wouldn't work. More than once Ingolf describes his progress through the teaming streets without benefit of wipers or top, though occasionally Etta, who did not drive, would hold an umbrella over him while he peered forward through his steamy glasses. Peter proved to be an additional strain on the precarious family finances; Ingolf reports his outrage, in 1939, at having to pay 54 cents for three gallons of gasoline!

I used to get a chuckle when my faculty colleagues would boast about their working class backgrounds, condescendingly implying that, in contrast, I had the benefits of a privileged upbringing. Needless to say I did not go without the essentials; and Aunt Elsie never stopped buying me toys and other infantile requisites. But such largesse did not affect the basic economy of life in London Street. I am reminded here of a story of Etta's. One night only a single can remained on the shelves of the London Street larder; it had lost its label so that it was with some trepidation that its lid was pried open when the dinner hour approached. It contained pumpkin!

Ingolf records a bitter scene on July 9th, 1940. "It's hell to be poor," Etta had snapped. "This cuts through me," Ingolf added. In fact, he appears to have applied for unemployment benefits on several occasions thereafter. This must have been an additional agony for him, for my parents hated the notion of receiving charity or being economically dependent on others. Other families can look back at the Depression of the Thirties as the low ebb in their financial fortunes. My family always looked back to London Street in 1940.

In almost everything I have written so far, the memories of my childhood are those of my parents, not my own. In *my* first memory I am very small; I am a helpless, inert blob who nevertheless feels the stirrings of a grand emotion. I have been left in the care of a neighbor. Surely this is a memory of London Street. It is a recollection of some silken Silverlake teenage baby sitter of the early Forties. The baby sitter has brought some of her friends to have a look at the infant with the big brown eyes and the blond curls. They form a semi-circle of smiling faces above me, a horizon of approval. The baby sitter is extolling my virtues in the coy voice used to address babies and dogs. She is besotted by my beauty. I look up and see the exquisite skin and deep red hair of her adorable head. I love her too, but I am only an inconsequential *thing*. To symbolize the pointlessness of this romance, the giant beautiful smiling head is withdrawn and my babysitter tweaks my bare belly button with her cool hand. I am electrified by this touch. Her sisters laugh in approval. I lie there in hopeless adoration. Nowadays, I cannot fall asleep if I am lying on my back.

I had troubled sleep at our next port of call as well. Higuera, Bedford and London Streets have left no memories that I can summon, beyond a shadowy sense of light and dark, grass and sky, and the image of my beloved baby sitter. My spatial world begins with our move to 1211 N. Westmorland on September 13th, 1940. I was two and a half.

Our stretch of Westmorland lay between Fountain Avenue, on the north, and Lexington, on the south. The street continued to the south for another block, reaching Santa Monica Boulevard. A block away, to the east, was Virgil and two blocks to the west was Vermont. This large six-block area was to be my world for almost five years. Westmorland, of course, was within walking distance of the Cedars of Lebanon Hospital, where Fanny's story had ended and mine had begun, and here, after several abortive starts with government offices, Etta secured steady employment in 1942 as secretary to the director of nurses, secretary to the medical staff, and medical librarian. The income was a necessity, given the precarious and impermanent nature of Ingolf's wages, but Etta's departure left my stepfather with the occasional unwanted domestic chore, and left me in the care of housekeepers, babysitters or home alone.

I don't think the neighborhood was ever elegant, although its surfaces were probably more polished than one can detect from the patina of decay that covers it today. Low stucco houses, three-storey apartments, and weathered frame bungalows rubbed shoulders in a rather haphazard manner with churches, hospitals, and one large sanitarium, which covered an entire block between Lexington and Santa Monica, a walled stronghold that leaked death, dark with protective trees and vines clinging to all its gates and fences, a place of especial dread to the children of the area because of its impenetrable silence. There was only one dividend in this wilderness; among the tendrils of the vines that encircled the sanatorium's perimeter a large tribe of back and orange caterpillars hid from the fingers that would transport them into the narcotic safety of our glass jars.

Palm trees accented the skyline and, below, desultory efforts were made to keep fruit trees alive. A neighbor had a rarity, a loquat tree, the fruit of which, when snatched unripened by bored children, always disappointed.

Just to the north of 1211 a hill reaches a gentle crest and the street then descends in a southerly direction, a gradient sufficiently exciting for a little boy in his red wagon to roll precipitately downward, coming to an abrupt halt as the wagon left the pavement and pitched its passenger into Lexington Avenue. A line of wooden bungalows accompanied the fall of the hill on its west side and across the street a stucco church, which was visited on Sunday by men in black suits, presented another alien and mysterious corner. Our house (it would take us many years to get back into one of these) was the highest of the bungalows, and between it and the next house there ran, parallel to Lexington, a dirt alley, another place of opportunity and menace.

The house to the north was owned by Mr. Zahn, our landlord, a figure of especial terror. He was always at war with his tenants and it didn't help matters that he carried a gun or that he kept unpredictable chickens in a pen along the alley. He didn't approve of our life style and would leave occasional illiterate notes of protest, when he wasn't borrowing our telephone. In particular he felt Ingolf should be doing a better job with the appearance of Black Peter, which collected dust under the pepper trees that lined the sidewalks on Westmorland. This is precisely the kind of domestic chore that Ingolf could be depended on *not* to do with any enthusiasm or consistency. It did rain a lot.

If one could make a safe passage past the chickens then the next attractions were the low roofs of two garages on the left. It was possible for even a small boy to climb to the top of these structures and to observe the passing scene or to bedevil, from above, those taking the dirt path between the garages down to the dwellings on a large lot that fronted Lexington. There was at least one house near the street, but back closer to the garages was the house of the Smith family.

The Smiths could have been Tom Joad's cousins, and it is worth remembering how recent the Dust Bowl exodus was when we moved to Westmorland. Indeed, the film version of *The Grapes of Wrath* was released the year we arrived, following by one year the publication of the novel. The Smiths were actually from Kansas, not Oklahoma, but they too had washed up on our shores in search of a better life. I don't remember a Mr. Smith, but I do remember a fat slattern of a mom and a tribe of progeny, including my best friend, Joanie, and her older sister, Anita, who sometimes served as my babysitter. A visit to the chaotic interior of the Smith house was always a venture into the unknown. They freely shared what food they had, but it tasted like nothing I was familiar with, and I usually found a way to decline the invitation. Every garment was passed on to the next child of the same sex, so that it was possible to see little Sissy wearing the giant holey bloomers of an older sibling whenever she spread her legs on the equally punctured sofa. Mr. Zahn also disapproved of the Smiths.

Life was a little more wholesome out of doors. In the front lawn of the property we played endless games of hide and seek and the other childhood games involving pursuit and victimization. On Sunday mornings we had a go, before their owner was up, at the funny papers in the chunk of newsprint that had been deposited on someone's front porch, I always wanted to know what peril was menacing Brenda Starr this week.

Our tiny backyard, in which a vain attempt to aid the war effort with our own victory garden would soon get underway, was always in the shadow of a menacing apartment building that also fronted on Lexington. Wash lines stretched across this tiny space also and here Etta, who had to wait many years for her own washer and dryer, hung out her blouses, my t-shirts, and Ingolf's nightshirts.

On Fountain, between Westmorland and Virgil, there was a small market, a shrine dedicated to my appetite for sweets. I was delighted to learn that I could redeem glass pop bottles for a new Dad's Old Fashioned Root Beer, and I often took my wagon through the neighborhood, searching the scrap piles for glass treasure, clanking up to the market with my windfall.

Another shrine was the public library on Santa Monica, near Vermont. I cannot remember when I learned to read, but I believe it was early rather than late and that I was always ahead of my contemporaries in my verbal abilities. At the library my mother would select books to read to me, but I was soon able to make my own choices. I was particularly fascinated by the adventures of the Nitwits, those silly stick figures who ran with a lollipop in their mouths, bathed in the water before testing its temperature or crossed the street without looking. The Nitwit books used only black, white and red so that a scalded Nitwit could present us a backside dramatically reddened by his inattention. I was fascinated by the body's dislocations following these acts of mental folly: the lollipop permanently lodged in the Nitwit's throat; the flattened Nitwit who stepped in front of the steam roller!

When you returned to 1211 N. Westmorland with your treasures, liquid or literary, you ascended a set of steep steps to a front porch, then passed into a front room in which a utilitarian piano sat, and on into a dining area that overlooked the alley. On your left, as you entered the house, was my bedroom, then a bathroom, and finally Ingolf and Etta's bedroom – into which the ill-matched lovers had crammed two large beds. A kitchen ran along the back of the house and there was a screened back porch as well. Flies buzzed through holes in the screen at all times of the year. There was also a mysterious dirt cellar underneath the house.

Westmorland was a place of refuge, as any home should be, and, as we shall see, I spent a great deal of time in it alone, but I did learn that even home can be a place of menace. One day I returned to find no one about, but there was an eerie sound issuing from my parents' bedroom. I cannot describe it accurately but it was chilling, a repetitious, shrill clamor, like a cuckoo clock gone mad. We had no cuckoo clock, and I was horrified at the possibility that some malign creature might have gotten into my house. Naturally there was no way I could investigate this peril, and I had to turn tail and rush into the safer streets, where I knew a number of hiding places.

Curiously, I did not tell my parents about this episode, somehow concluding that the incident must somehow be my fault, or that, at any rate, I could not provide the rational account they would have expected from an otherwise unfanciful child. And to this day I can not get any closer to an explanation – courting pigeons, one of Mr. Zahn's chickens, I will never know what this specter was doing in our house.

What I did know was that my world, even with its appearance of suburban domesticity, was not a benign space. If menace was not supplied by the much-feared Latino *Pachucos*, ranging the streets in their zoot suits, or the ring of local hospitals with their pain-filled wards, then terror was as close as an unexplained sound pulsing insistently in a usually quiet corner of my own home.

Westmorland also had its daily tensions, less dramatic than those outlined above, but far more enduring and upsetting. There must have been an emotional electricity pulsing though the rooms of this house, a current which a child would have found puzzling and threatening, for here it was that my parents conducted their struggles for economic and romantic survival. One of these topics, the love affair of Ingolf and Etta, has been examined at some length; we can now turn to the other great struggle, for it was from 1211 N. Westmorland that Ingolf set forth in search of his livelihood.

13. CROWD PLEASER

When Ingolf's work with Edith Lorand came to an end, he had to look for other forms of employment, assignments where his musical skills might actually put food on the table. One source of income was accompanying. His facility at the piano and his sight-reading abilities made him a useful participant in those endless auditions that Hollywood singers were always being summoned to at MGM, Columbia or Universal. Most of those he accompanied on studio calls have long ago disappeared into the mists of we'll-call-you obscurity, but I note that Patricia Morrison, whom he accompanied on the Republic lot in August, 1943, did enjoy some success in the B movies of the era.

Ingolf also played for a number of professional singers in recitals: the baritone Lee Gilmore, Miss Sherman Pall ("The Negro Lyric-Dramatic Soprano"), opera stars like Margit Bokor and Lauritz Melchior, and Fortunio Bonanova, the "Spanish operatic star of two continents, MGM star for South America, Mexico, and the United States." Violinists, like Miriam Soloviev and Bronislav Gimpel, also used Ingolf's assistance. Recitals often included a solo spot for the accompanist and, when called on at such moments, Ingolf would play short works by Bach, Chopin, Grieg, Liszt, Strauss, and Villa Lobos. Accompanying bass-baritone Edward Boyd at the Assistance League Playhouse on April 9, 1940, Ingolf earned one of his first local reviews. Richard Drake Saunders noted in the *Hollywood Citizen News* that, "Ingolf Dahl proved himself a highly meritorious soloist with an admirably enunciated Bach D-minor Toccata, followed by a Chopin Mazurka in response to warm applause." Ingolf's only comment on the occasion was the gripe that he been forced to use a "terrible" piano.

Indeed, he could never tell what kind of instrument might be provided by the Women's Club of Long Beach or the Pottinger Sanatorium or the Valley Hunt Club. That his best efforts were being offered up to an audience consisting of "dreadful, macabre women" was a perpetual complaint. Another unhappy dimension of this line of work was that it often entailed travel. In November, 1940, he followed Margit Bokor to Logan, Utah, and the following February he accompanied Miriam Soloviev in Tucson. He undertook tours with Bonanova, whose showbiz shamelessness always embarrassed him, to Sacramento and San Diego, and for his loyalty he got to accompany other members of the "Latin American Tunes & Rhythms" troupe, including Inesita, "incomparable Flamenco dancer."

In 1941 Ingolf saw an opportunity for securing steady work as an accompanist, at a somewhat higher level, when he heard that Yehudi Menuhin was looking for a pianist. Ingolf's admiration for the young violinist, whom he had first seen in Hamburg, had always been immense. He describes a concert given by the sixteen-year old prodigy in Zurich in October of 1932 as "an evening of the highest happiness." The naiveté and simplicity of the artist's soul had caused a twenty-year old Ingolf to cry, "Oh God, give us all a child's heart." In 1939 he had heard Menuhin play the Bach A-minor concerto in San Francisco – "a splendid, unique concert, quite perfectly played." Menuhin was living several hundred miles up the coast when he agreed to see Ingolf. On September 1st, in a great state of agitation, Ingolf took the overnight train to San Jose and the next morning completed a short journey to Los Gatos, where Menuhin picked him up in a truck. Ingolf played Brahms and Mozart. "It goes badly," he reports in an idiom for which I will not seek an English equivalent, "my heart falls into my pants. He seems to be unsatisfied but says nothing." A nice day with the Menuhin family followed, and Ingolf returned to Los Angeles, where Etta and I were waiting at the train station. Two days later a telegram arrived with the bitter news. Menuhin had "made other arrangements." "Failure of failures," Ingolf records in his journal. "What now. It is terrible."

(When I was making my first attempt to write about the life of my family, in 1979, Menuhin was living in London and celebrating his fiftieth anniversary as a performer. One day I was entertaining Ingolf's sister, Anna-Britta, and there the maestro was, sitting at the next table in our Hampstead pub, destined always to be on the periphery of our lives.)

Ingolf's disappointment in the Menuhin matter was colored by the dreary employment prospects that remained. On August 7, 1940, he reported excitement over a job offer from Lazar Samoiloff, an entrepreneur of the vocal business whose Bel Canto Studios and Opera Academy were located at 610 S. Van Ness Avenue. He and Etta discussed the offer at some length that evening. "A weekly salary of any kind will look good to us," Etta argued, and by early September, Ingolf was teaching repertoire, interpretation, sight-reading and solfeggio. Samoiloff took out an ad in the *Citizen News* announcing this addition to his faculty (and misspelling Ingolf's last name as Dhal), also issuing copy which read, "His personality is so charming and his teaching so inspirational I know that every singer, whether beginner or accomplished vocalist, will find a new appreciation of music under his guidance."

The Russian impresario mounted productions all over town, usually in high school auditoriums. He was Founder and General Director of the Burbank Grand Opera Company, and Ingolf participated in many of these concerts, as well as in productions under the auspices of Vladimir Rosing, who taught acting at Samoiloff's. By December of 1940 Ingolf and Samoiloff had quarreled over a production of *Aida* and the employer's refusal to let his employee have time off to do some studio work for Miklos Rosza. Meanwhile Ingolf's salary had been lowered by fifty dollars. My stepfather records nine exclamation points after the "Hurrah" that brought his work for Samoiloff to an end on March 19, 1942 – "Again a chapter comes to an end."

Needless to say, Ingolf had found ways of accepting other employment while working for Samoiloff. Two weeks after the Menuhin disaster he was asked to participate in another audition. This time he was successful and on September 27th, 1941, he boarded a plane at the Lockheed Terminal and set off on a two-week tour as a member of a company headed by the famous ventriloquist Edgar Bergen. Ingolf accompanied the musical numbers in the show, which made stops in Salt Lake City, Denver, Omaha, Des Moines, Chicago, Louisville, Evansville, and St. Louis.

The journals do not give many details about the shows themselves, but a number seem to have been played to empty houses in cavernous theaters. Ingolf never took to group travel, the crowded hotels, the spaghetti dinners, the enforced camaraderie. On the other hand he seems to have been genuinely fond of Bergen himself, and to have enjoyed his company on a number of occasions. Some of the shows, in which Charlie McCarthy and Mortimer Snerd made their appearance, were mounted specifically for children. Because of bad weather the troupe traveled from Des Moines to Chicago by train instead of plane. In a dreary Iowa train station, Ingolf watched Bergen entertain bored children with magic tricks: "He is quite charming." In later years, Ingolf never failed to switch on the radio when it was time for Bergen's radio show. Over the inanities of this and many another silly comedy show of the Forties, a high-pitched whinny of glee would issue from my stepfather's throat – "My husband's girlish cackle," Etta called it.

Ingolf was getting closer to radio work himself at this point. Earlier in the year he had become a soloist on KFAC's *Beautiful Music*. A few weeks after his return from the Bergen tour he became a regular panelist on a KMPC quiz show called *Are You Musical?* "This time," he wrote after the show of February 8th, 1942, "I distinguish myself."

Only a few days earlier, Ingolf had participated in another "apparently satisfactory" interview for an accompanying assignment. Rehearsals began in February, 1942 and by March 6th he had completed his first tour with a figure whom many believe to be the highest paid female entertainer of the era, the English superstar Gracie Fields. The tour took Ingolf to Fresno, Sacramento, San Francisco, Oakland, and Portland and in March there was a brief coda in Arizona, with stops in Phoenix, Tucson, and at an RAF camp in the desert.

The relationship between the immensely popular Lancashire mill girl and her pianist blossomed, and Gracie, over the next few years, began to employ Ingolf for all sorts of engagements, stage shows, radios programs and tours. Aboard battleships, at servicemen's canteens, at bond rallies and hospitals, Ingolf accompanied Dame Gracie, as she would become in her retirement, a true star whose earthy good humor and powerful voice had made her a British cultural institution

Gracie took Ingolf with her on a New York tour from May to July, 1942, and, as we shall see, on an extensive Eastern trip from February to May, 1944. There were also short trips in California and several weeks at the Cal-Neva Lodge, on Lake Tahoe, in the summer of 1946. Gracie also saw to it that Ingolf held a position in the orchestra of her many radio programs, and he supplied arrangements for many of the musical numbers. The first of these programs lasted from the end of November, 1942, to July, 1943. Another began that fall and lasted through January, 1944. There were two additional shows that year, one beginning in June, another in November. The work was not steady, as this schedule reveals, but Ingolf at last earned enough to drag our family out of the poverty cycle.

The first of the extensive tours with Gracie began on May 23rd, 1942. Ingolf traveled by train, reversing much of the route he had traveled by bus in 1939. In Dodge City he was awed by the sight of a father pushing forward with outstretched arms to embrace his soldier son. On the 27th he checked into the Hotel Bedford in New York, "expensive and not very nice," and soon thereafter he was conferring with Gracie and looking down from her apartment on the "human ant heap." Gracie appeared in the "Top Notchers" variety show on 44th Street in a bill that included the dancer Argentinita, "Think-A-Drink" Hoffman, and, in his Broadway debut, Zero Mostel. Opening night was May 29th: "Again the dress coat, again a premiere. Agitation, but everything goes splendidly. Gracie is very successful." Backstage Ingolf translated love letters for an Italian juggler. There were also some out-of-town bookings. Ingolf mentions a ball at the Westchester Country Club ("Ed Sullivan is here"), and, with sirens screaming, a ride in a U.S. Army car to West Point, where Gracie sang, he played Chopin and Casella, and both dined at the general's table. From June 30th to July 4th, Gracie appeared in another variety program ("Fun-For-All") with Jimmy Savo, at the Scarsdale Theater.

Ingolf scrambled around Manhattan on a sore left foot, perhaps an early instance of the gout that occasionally plagued him. He had time for a number of visits and, when Gracie had no bookings, for additional work. He looked up his old Hamburg piano teacher, Edith Weiss-Mann and Trude Rittman, a fellow student at Cologne, now beginning a long career as a Broadway arranger. He also had time to visit three old flames. One of the Evas was living in New York – "She is somewhat more distant," Ingolf wrote, "but this is no doubt because of the long separation." The Zurich singer who had dispatched the Zurich dancer was also in New York, and so were Barbara Kruger and her husband. After the latter visit, Ingolf reported, "I am still, as before, in love with her. She is still beautiful and enigmatic."

Ingolf's alternative employment opportunity certainly provided him with a fair share of unattainable faces, but "they don't see me," he complained. This new assignment was in the orchestra of the Ballet Russe de Monte Carlo, to which Ingolf reported on June 21st. The conductor of the ensemble, Franz Allers, was a successful Broadway conductor whom Ingolf remained on good terms with for years; indeed, I remember going with Ingolf to a Los Angeles performance of *Plain and Fancy* that Allers conducted many years later. Ingolf's work for the Ballet Russe continued after the Gracie tour ended, and when he returned to California he played with the ensemble when the troupe offered performances in San Diego and Los Angeles in July and August of 1942. Ingolf played for rehearsals as as well as performances and particularly relished playing the big solo part in Gershwin's "New Yorker," which was staged in the Hollywood Bowl. When he received his check for his work with the Ballet, he wrote, "What a shock: for the first time wealth after so many years of poverty." "I enjoyed my work with the ballet very much indeed," he concluded, "because it was the closest to the theater atmosphere I have been in in this country and memories of Zurich kept coming up all the time. The work was all the more stimulating and interesting because I knew I would have to do it only a short time...Besides there are some very great artists in this company whose work to witness was a memorable experience particularly Slavenska and Youskevitch and Nijinska and Agnes de Mille as choreographers."

In addition to the financial rewards that came to Ingolf as a result of his new association with Gracie Fields, it has to be added that my stepfather enjoyed the company of his new employer tremendously. He had a genuine respect for her abilities and valued her friendship greatly. At Christmas time, 1942, he presented her with a jar of Aunt Etta's Original Cranberry Sauce. Gracie kissed his hand in thanks, and, Ingolf, his heart beating, was overcome with affection. His comments on the shows they did together are also full of superlatives, He was a natural audience for her wisecracks and reminiscences, and seems never to have tired of her patter, however many times he may have heard it. When the Cleveland concert of April 14, 1944 was reviewed, the *Plain Dealer* reporter noted, "I am not certain whether Ingolf Dahl, her amazingly facile and accurate accompanist, or myself had a better time last night. Certainly her most appreciative audience was on both sides of the footlights."

Even when they were not working together, Ingolf was a frequent visitor at Gracie's beautiful home above the Pacific Ocean. I remember these visits too and I always had a good time. Ingolf also introduced Gracie to the snow in 1945. For years, in short, our family was dominated by her presence, our radio always tuned to her shows. As other children grow up on nursery tunes, I was weaned on "Walter, Walter, Take Me To The Altar," "The Biggest Aspidistra In The World," and "Don't be Angry With Me, Sergeant."

Gracie, too, seems to have been extremely fond of her pianist. At the end of the first radio sequence she gave him a watch. She kept up a cordial relationship with my parents for the rest of their lives, and several times tempted Ingolf to return briefly to the world of show business. In April, 1979, five months before her death at 81, she wrote to me that, "Ingolf just was one of the best accompanists I ever had, and he needed so little rehearsing, he automatically seemed to guess what I was going to do next." It is no wonder that, in October 2006, my wife and I therefore paid a visit to Gracie's mausoleum on Capri. It bore the legend "Cerio," which must be the local transliteration for "Cheerio!"

A number of interesting comments are recorded on the subject of his first radio work with Gracie: "This is a very easy and at the same time well paid job and the first one which has any resemblance to a 'steady job' which I have had so far (I consider four consecutive weeks as 'steady!'). It is really quite grotesque that the harder you work on something as a musician and the more you put yourself out the less it pays, and that for something like this, where I play just oom-pa-pa for a few hours every day I get very good money." He did not mention the extra wear on the psyche caused by the mindless dialogue, the scripted jokes, and the inflated patriotism. "An Australian sergeant I met told me this story and he swears it really happened," Gracie told her nationwide audience in November, 1943, "The British medical officer was giving the Expeditionary Force a little talk on tropical diseases – especially malaria. 'It has been my experience, men, that the best remedy for malaria is first of all quinine – and then whiskey, whiskey and more whiskey.' A big, red faced corporal raised his hand. 'Where can I get it, Sir?' 'What, whiskey?' 'No Sir – malaria.'" (Laughter and Applause). "In 1942, patriots in the occupied countries began to scrawl the letter V on the walls and on the sidewalks," Gracie informed her audience in February, 1943, "That year too, the letter V first appeared on the back of every package of Pall Mall cigarettes." Sponsors changed. "The Gracie Fields Show was brought to you by those two famous Bristol-

Myers products: Ipana toothpaste for your smile of beauty and Mum for your winning charm." On St. Patrick's Day, 1943, "for all the Irish boys who are helping to take the hit out of Hitler," Gracie sang "Danny Boy." In July Ingolf noted that, "This is the last week of our radio show and it will be a strange feeling to be without it after so many months. We were getting into an awful rut though, particularly Gracie. You can't do a daily show (and repeat the same numbers over and over again) and be good, or even interested."

Ingolf's work as Gracie's accompanist led to his participation in a number of new ventures. He played for her when she did guest appearances on other shows, such as *Duffy's Tavern*. He helped her record programs for the BBC. He appeared briefly at the piano in a film which she made in December, 1942, something Ingolf refers to as a "short," which was shot at Warner Brothers. Because Ingolf was supposed to be impersonating Gracie's English accompanist a back wig had to be fitted over his balding dome, and the one selected belonged to Charles Boyer! Ancient family gossip, if I recall correctly, also states that Ingolf appeared briefly on screen in some capacity in *Stage Door Canteen*. In June of 1943, Gracie sang in a big Russian benefit (those were the days) in the Hollywood Bowl. "I did some arrangements for her," Ingolf reports, "for huge orchestra. I was quite excited about it because it was a nice change. I put in 'harp vomit' and tried to make it sound as 'Hollywood' as possible and I think it did. The whole thing would have been all right if it hadn't been for the conductor (one of these innumerable movie Russians with the name of Yascha so and so) who paid not the faintest attention to what Gracie was singing and finished one number while she was still in the middle of it."

In the summer of 1943, emboldened by his success with popular audiences, Ingolf undertook a unique assignment, which began on June 9th, his thirty-first birthday, as soloist at the Bar of Music. His repertoire continued to be a classical one, though the works chosen had to fit a narrow range – "They have to be extremely brilliant (not *too* difficult though, because I don't want to practice too hard for this job), popular, *loud*, melodious etc...I haven't introduced Schoenberg to the barflies yet." Much of what he played he already had at his fingertips from solo spots on Gracie's tour shows: Chopin, Liszt, Albeniz, Strauss waltzes, Casella, Debussy and De Falla. "I was quite nervous," he reported on opening night, "but now have found myself and I find that the less I care *how* I play the better do I play. The 'what the heck' attitude actually seems to inspire my pianism." This is a statement, full of bravado, which is utterly inconsistent with the usual self-critical comments that salt his dairy. On August 23rd, a week from the end of this assignment, he noted, more characteristically, "Play poorly, but very successful evening."

With an eye to improving his employment prospects, Ingolf was also taking lessons in "swing." The decision was made after he had approached Gracie about the possibility of doing some solos on the radio show. She had told him that the bandleaders considered him a "good classical pianist," but inadequately trained for popular solos. A few days later he began to study "swing" with Lou Maury. "I hope I learn it," he added, persisting in his lessons for some months, often with no time to practice his homework. He seems to have hoped for some work with local jazz bands after his Bar of Music gig, but this project collapsed. Ingolf was, after all, not an enthusiast of jive, as it was then called, nor of the world in which it flourished. "The worst thing is that I very consciously and outspokenly *hate* it...The more I have been looking into the commercial field and into the monstrous exploitation of 'music' (radio, film) the more I come to regard swing as the arch enemy of everything we are, and I believe there is no compromise possible." This is a very strange statement from a person whose career in the world of entertainment for the masses still had a number of years to run, but we can better understand the depths of spiritual sacrifice Ingolf needed to make as he kept plugging on in an environment in which he was so uncomfortable as an artist.

On January 14, 1944, he reports a conversation concerning salary, "which I lose," with Gracie's husband, Monty Banks. Nevertheless Ingolf's contract gave him a hundred and fifty dollars a week, plus travel and lodging expenses during his stint as accompanist and, at a later stage of the 1944 tour, when he was also to act as "assisting artist," three hundred a week.

On February 10th, 1944, Etta accompanied Ingolf to Union Station in downtown Los Angeles as he prepared to undertake his second long tour with Gracie. "She is sad," he reported, "and I am absent." To while away the time on the tedious train journey he read *The Turning Point*, the autobiography of his friend, Klaus Mann: "Sex, senses, bohemia, our age," he sighed, "and where is our world?" Mystery stories, a favorite diversion, succeeded the Mann book. In Chicago he raced over to the Art Institute to view his old friend, Picasso's "Les Saltimbanques," and on February 14th he checked into a cramped room in Manhattan's Hotel Empire. Gracie opened two nights later at The Waldorf, "a triumphant success for her."

Gracie remained in New York for a month, doing her own show, making radio appearances, and playing benefits. Ingolf reports seeing Mrs. Roosevelt at a Red Cross benefit at Madison Square Garden on February 29th, and "The President!!" himself at a Washington gathering on March 4th. Fritz Kreisler performed on the latter occasion, producing in Ingolf the cynical comment, "Everybody stands for him, what a farce: the forces of the world pretending to bow to the forces of the spirit." On March 15th Gracie took her act to Boston's Copley Plaza. On April 9th, as "assisting artist," Ingolf began a long odyssey, mostly by train, that included stops in Providence, New York again, Baltimore, Cleveland, Detroit, Grand Rapids, Lansing, Detroit a second time, Dayton, Louisville, Indianapolis, Cincinnati, London (Ontario), Toronto, and Ottawa. In Toronto a brass band marched Gracie from the train station to the hotel. The tour ended in Canada, and Ingolf returned to Los Angeles, after stops in Boston and Chicago, on May 19th.

As I was reading though the journal for 1944 I was surprised to discover that Lansing had been on the itinerary. On April 21st (a grey, gloomy day), Ingolf and Gracie had arrived to play a college concert. The college is not specified, but the possibilities are limited; the two had obviously made an appearance on the Michigan State campus, where, in 1965, I took up a post in the Humanities Department. I decided to see if ancient copies of the *State News* were available on microfilm in the library. They were. I found myself doing research in my own campus daily, a publication which I had hitherto utilized chiefly to raise my blood pressure.

Gracie's visit had been extensively covered. Under the caption, "Amused Audience Hears Britain's Gracie Fields," the reviewer recorded that, "Gracie Fields took No. 1 on the laugh parade last night and an audience of approximately 4,000 kept her coming back with more songs in that untireable Fields manner." The reviewer continued, "With shades of 'over there' in her repertoire Gracie Fields showed an MSC audience why she is the world's biggest little morale builder. She burlesqued through 'My Hero,' ran as close a second as anyone ever will to Frankie Sinatra in "This

Is a Lovely Way To Spend an Evening;" and rolicked (sic) through "I Never Cried So Much In All Me Life" until she had even staid professors lapping from her hand." There was also a good description of the performer in action: "Gracie also did justice to the most critical eye with her beautiful gowns and her inevitable chiffon scarf which she tied around her head or neck or just waved. Always the essence of perpetual motion, Gracie punctuated her singing with shrieks, moans, and even a little touch of a hip swish."

The review also contained a paragraph about one staid professor's stepfather: "Ingolf Dahl, young American concert pianist, played the highbrow and semi-highbrow in as exciting a manner as Gracie put over her songs." In his diary, Ingolf noted that the concert had been very successful ("lots of college kids"), but the whole experience, one of so many one-night stands, had evaporated by the time he visited us in East Lansing many years later. He had forgotten all about the earlier visit and failed to recognize the auditorium into which his daughter-in-law would spend so much time trying to lure customers on behalf of the Greater Lansing Opera Company in 1979.

As the *State News* review indicated, Ingolf often played alone, while Gracie, who sang over forty songs a night, rested her voice or changed her costume. "Dahl's playing was an excellent background at all times," the *Cleveland Plain Dealer* reviewer wrote, "His solo work was particularly to the crowd's liking also – well selected and played with enough color and exhibition to strike the popular fancy." Typically, Ingolf used the solo spot to play "Night And Day," a medley of Strauss waltzes, "Malaguena," "Clair De Lune," and a version of *Rhapsody in Blue.*

In the summer of 1944 unemployment worries recurred, and the assignments were again sporadic. On July 19th he had an assignment at the Hollywood Canteen, and at the end of August he followed Gracie to San Francisco for a show at the Treasure Island Naval Base. Thereafter, for close to a year, he found his chief employment at film studios and on radio shows.

He had worked in studio orchestras as early as 1941, when he had performed the celesta part during the recording of the score for *Lady Hamilton*, starring Vivian Leigh and Laurence Olivier. (Poor Mammi went to see this film three times in Stockholm and failed to hear a single celesta note above the orchestral din.) Regular assignments at the studios did not begin until 1945, when Ingolf played in orchestras which recorded music for *Of Human Bondage, Flying Flivver, It Happened in Springfield, Plantation Melodies, Law of the Badlands, Nobody Lives Forever, Blood on the Sun, The Clock,* and *Wuthering Heights*. Ingolf also did some arranging and some orchestrating, perhaps even some composing, but much of what he did in these endeavors was *sub rosa*, a helping hand offered to other composers who got behind and needed quick and confidential assistance. Gail Kubik has acknowledged that Ingolf orchestrated 40-50 pages of *Thunderbolt* and it would appear, from fragmentary jottings in the journals of 1945, that Ingolf did work of this type for Gil Grau and Leigh Harline as well.

There were several other more unusual opportunities in the movies (not forgetting Charles Boyer's wig). On December 6th, 1943, Ingolf auditioned for the part of Frederic Chopin's hands in the film biography which starred Cornell Wilde as the rest of the composer. Ingolf didn't get the part. On July 31st, 1944, he spent the day at MGM as one of twelve pianists backing up Jose Iturbi. And on April 26th, 1945, the *Hollywood Reporter* announced that "Paul Dessau, conductor and composer, and Ingolf Dahl, composer and pianist, were signed yesterday by Hunt Stromberg for arrangement and direction of special musical sequences for *Young Widow*, starring vehicle for Jane Russell and Louis Hayward which William Dieterle is directing." The picture, not released for some months, presented the buxom Ms. Russell in her first major role. Ingolf recorded the piano music for this film and had the task of teaching the actress how to give the impression that she was manipulating the keyboard herself – eat you heart out, Cornell Wilde.

Gracie's last radio show for the winter took place on January 30th, 1945. By May Ingolf had a new assignment as an arranger for Tommy Dorsey's RCA radio program, a job that lasted through August. In this manner Ingolf at last broadened his arranging expertise beyond that needed for "There'll Always By An England" or "The Trek Song." Now, because of the many musical guests on the Dorsey show, the assignments were varied and hurried. Jeannette MacDonald had to be rehearsed in a new version of "Vilia;" Dorsey and the choir needed an arrangement of "Summertime," Melchior needed one for "Because;" Roy Rogers was going to sing "Don't

Fence Me In." Ingolf did much of this work in Lou Bring's NBC office. "Work finished (three numbers at 5 this morning. So sleep all day (get Tony breakfast)" is the entry for May 31st. On June 24th, suffering from bronchitis, he wrote, "Sick. How will I get over this week?" Ingolf evidently had to finish "Baia" and "Dream" and a piano solo for Diana Lynn, but he accomplished the task with incredibly long hours. Rehearsal for this show took place on June 30th, "and for a change I am satisfied."

The Dorsey show was the last of Ingolf's *full-time* assignments in the world of popular entertainment, although there were still many part-time jobs to come. The radio work had been so time-consuming that the journal entries for 1945 contain no commentary on the steps which lead to the next major chapter in his professional life. Nevertheless, we know that in the fall of that year, after six years of job insecurity, poverty, trivial assignments on the fringes of show business, travel separations, and the postponement of a career in classical music, Ingolf Dahl was appointed, at a salary of thirty-five hundred dollars a year, to the position of lecturer in opera repertory, film and radio music, and conductor of the University orchestra of the School of Music of the University of Southern California. There he remained for the rest of his complex and troubled life. "In 1945," a relieved Etta quipped, "college started working its way through my husband, and he became a man of letters, most of them unanswered."

14. ORPHEUS ASCENDING

Ingolf's eventual transition from a life in show business to one rooted in academia and artistic endeavor was not as abrupt as might be imagined. This is because, from the start, he had always tried to keep in touch with the world of music making at its highest level, a world he struggled to rejoin after his Zurich apprenticeship. His work as performer, organizer, musical craftsman and composer was undertaken not merely with an eye on future prospects. For Ingolf, this was a labor of love, however unrequited.

In 1939, while still very much the outsider, he seems to have made regular appearances on the piano at musical soirees sponsored by Madame de Zaruba and in 1940 he began playing with the McCarthy-Peet String Quartet. It took me a long time to discover musicians named McCarthy and Peet, but I learned from one of my mother's letters that the mysterious names in question belonged to the *sponsors* of the venture, heiresses ("matron patrons," "culture vultures," as Etta described them) who had chosen to fund the ensemble. In the fall of 1940 Ingolf also began to make appearances, this time as soloist, with the Brodestsky Ensemble, at the annual Bach Festival sponsored by the First Congregational Church. The musical director of the church, Arthur Leslie Jacobs, also began a Festival of Modern Music, held annually in May. Ingolf played regularly here too, beginning in 1941, and two of his own works were later premiered at the spring festival.

Having failed to make much progress with Otto Klemperer in 1939, Ingolf was intrigued to receive a call from the famous conductor the following year. Klemperer had decided to organize a new chorus, The Los Angeles Choir. Ingolf was to serve as *a capella* director, without remuneration. According to Etta, writing in August of 1940, "Klemperer has no idea how to organize a chorus but at the same time is so self-sufficient that he will not take suggestions from any one else. His manner is very brusque and arbitrary and no dares cross him because he is the great K." Auditions for the new ensemble were not properly publicized, and Ingolf ended up with "a flood of ladies and a dearth of gentlemen," who, when they bothered to show up at rehearsals, had to battle against the sounds of adjacent gymnasia on the campuses of local junior high schools.

Ingolf's task was to prepare this very amateur group to sing Bach chorales, Beethoven's *Missa Solemnis* and something eventually called *Trinity* by an obscure, newly-Americanized composer named Otto Klemperer. As Etta remembered it, the work included sections on America, Austria, France, and Christianity, and called for simultaneous singing of "America," "Drink To Me Only With Thine Eyes," and other melodies including the "Marseillaise." She pronounced the work "a scream." Ingolf's comments are unrecorded but his great admiration for the maestro was in eclipse. The Hindemith concert conducted by Klemperer on March 23rd, 1939, had been "a terrible disappointment." When Klemperer assumed direction of a Chorus rehearsal on July 10th, 1940, Ingolf regarded the conductor's performance as "again disappointing. Must one give up hope for his improvement?" But on September 4th, Klemperer congratulated his assistant on his work with the Choir – "Hurrah!" a gratified Ingolf wrote.

Only one member of our family seems to have been immune from the assumption that Klemperer must be treated like a god, and that was Baby Tony. Etta records a visit to Klemperer on May 12th, 1940. The "witty colossus," she informs us in her *Deskaide*, "was recovering from a brain tumor operation, but, as he claimed, all the medicines had made his blood bad and resulted in a boil on his leg." It was explained to me that I would have to behave myself and I evidently chafed under such restraint. Etta had to take me out into the garden several times, and suggested that I pluck a pink geranium and present it to the invalid. Klemperer, who was already "smitten," according to my less than impartial mother, then proceeded to entertain me in his "booming, heavily accented English. He kept shouting at the child, 'Iss there a liddle man in thiss radio? Where iss the liddle man?'" I was not especially amused. The next day, possessing already a role model closer to home, I lay down full length on the bed and said gravely, "I'm not feeling very well."

Klemperer and Ingolf remained on good terms for years. When his contract was suspended by the Los Angeles Philharmonic, the conductor wired Ingolf on November 24th, 1940, asking his young friend to advise all concerned that he planned to sue – "damage to me colossal morally financially." In 1943, after attending concerts in which two of Ingolf's works had been performed, Klemperer requested a private session in which he could examine the pieces more closely. "He was awfully nice," Ingolf wrote, "asked me to play everything over again, and genuinely participated. He seems to be very much better, though a bit quiet and depressed." In October, 1945, Klemperer conducted two Los Angeles performances of the *Fifth Brandenburg Concerto*, with Ingolf taking the harpsichord part. "A dream come true," Ingolf wrote proudly of this experience. The following year Klemperer delighted Mammi and Pappi, who had stopped backstage after a concert in Stockholm, with praise for their talented son.

When the late Peter Heyworth was working on the second part of his Klemperer biography in the 1980's, he paid me a visit in Maida Vale, so that he could examine any relevant materials still in my possession. One of these was the previously noted irate telegram, which I have since framed, along with correspondence from many of the other great figures Ingolf knew among his musical friends and associates.

94

Klemperer's chorus, as we have seen, proved to be a considerable trial for Ingolf. He did make some useful contacts however, and in the fall of 1940 took on some paying assignments with other local choruses. One of these was the Los Angeles Oratorio Society, the official chorus of the Philharmonic, which Ingolf directed as guest conductor on a number of occasions, beginning in 1941. Unfortunately one of Ingolf's first tasks was to conduct a work by Albert Hay Malotte, who was described by Ingolf as a "comical, naive crank." Malotte had written a famous musical rendition of "The Lord's Prayer," and had now graduated to a version of the "Pledge to the Flag," which Ingolf conducted at a Royce Hall concert in March of 1941.

Richard Lert, the Society's permanent director, was married to the writer Vicky Baum, author of the novel *Grand Hotel*, which had been turned into a famous film in 1932. A 1940 invitation to the Lerts gave Baby Tony another chance to show his stuff. The great attraction was the Lert's swimming pool, and I insisted on being taken into the water the minute I arrived. The novelist undressed me while Ingolf went to fetch my trunks and Wolfgang Lert adjusted my water wings. Once in the pool, I could not be dragged out – even refusing the bribe of cookies! "The climax came," according to Etta, "when he saw Ingolf dive from the board. He wanted to do likewise at once. So Ingolf stood on the board, held the naked infant in his arms, and dove...when they came up Tony discovered that he had 'eaten' a little more water than he cared for, and asked to be dressed. He then consumed innumerable cookies, made several wee-wees in different secluded parts of the garden, and romped a little with Murphy, the Irish setter puppy."

In addition to choral work, Ingolf also had the opportunity of conducting a number of local orchestras in the early Forties. This was the time when a Federal Orchestra, a division of the W.P.A., still existed, and on July 16, 1942, Ingolf conducted scenes from *Faust* and *Aida* in a concert given by the W.P.A. Symphony. Some of the ensembles of the period were manned by studio musicians, who got together in "study" orchestras to read through interesting scores, including new compositions. Ingolf was also asked to preside over such ensembles on several occasions. In 1940 he was elected to the Executive Committee of the Hollywood Theater Alliance's Music Council (with Victor Aller, Richard Lert, and Joseph

Achron) and at the inaugural concert, on December 15th, he conducted Darius Milhaud's *Three Little Symphonies*. According to Isabel Morse Jones, in the *Los Angeles Times*, the pieces were "charmingly played by a small orchestra and brilliantly conducted by Ingolf Dahl...Dahl will bear some larger conductorial responsibilities." It was only in 1942, incidentally, that Ingolf met Milhaud, who was living in the Bay Area and teaching at Mills College in Oakland.

Work with studio musicians inevitably drew Ingolf into friendships with a large circle of film composers and arrangers. These included Miklos Rosza, Hugo Friedhofer, Leigh Harline, Jerome Moross, Franz Waxman, Gil Grau, Arthur Morton, and Gail Kubik. The New Music Forum, which succeeded the H.T.A. in 1941, was also intended to provide a workshop atmosphere for the presentation of new music. Ingolf was Vice Chairman and David Raksin, still to write his famous score for the film *Laura*, was Chairman. The two began what was to be a lifetime friendship while planning workshops in the summer of 1941.

Ingolf's one-time employer, Lazar Samoiloff, was also president of the Crescendo Club, not a smart nightspot, as the name might suggest, but a unique private club for musicians (mostly composers), who attended bimonthly meetings in the president's private studio on Van Ness. The Club also sponsored monthly concerts that were open to the public. Ingolf mentions attending his first meeting in December, 1939; throughout the war years he played an active role in organizing and performing in these concerts, and through the Club, whose membership discussions were dominated by bickering and black balls, he met a number of well-established musicians and won the opportunity of demonstrating his skills as composer and interpreter of modern music.

Members of the club included Schoenberg and Aaron Copland, who appeared at meetings when he was in Los Angeles, George Antheil, Mario Castelnuovo-Tedesco, Miklos Rosza, Paul Pisk, Alexander Tansman, Ernst Toch, Adolphe Weiss, and George Tremblay. The club also played host to visiting firemen, including, in 1943, the pianist Jesus Maria Sanroma and the famous bandleader, Paul Whiteman. Ingolf often reported stimulating exchanges during such receptions, but that of April 7th, 1943, at which Whiteman was present, included an "unnecessary discussion of jazz *vs.* classics."

At Crescendo Club concerts Ingolf participated in music making with several new friends, including John Crown, the first of many future U.S.C. colleagues (including pianist Lillian Steuber, harpsichordist Alice Ehlers, and violinist Eudice Shapiro), whose friendship antedated Ingolf's position as a faculty member himself. Crown was a witty and clever Australian pianist and teacher who joined with Ingolf in a performance of the Dahl *Rondo* for piano four-hands at a Club concert on May 6th, 1940. Twice the two pianists gave local lecture-recitals on modern music for the piano, and Ingolf teamed up with George Tremblay for a similar presentation. Etta witnessed one of Ingolf's early speaking engagements, at U.C.L.A., in August of 1940. "Had he prepared the lecture on time, I would have helped him with it, but you know Ingolf!...Yet somehow he seems to live under a lucky star, and does just as well with his 'procrastination procedure' as I do with my Pedantic, Painful Planning...Ingolf's English was so full of quaint, juicy literal translations, made spontaneously from the German, that I have been warned never to correct him...Ingolf surprised me by showing all the marks of a very good lecturer, something I really didn't know was in him."

By January, 1944, the program committee for the Crescendo Club concerts consisted of Ingolf, John Crown, and another new friend, Sol Babitz. Babitz, a violinist and orchestra contractor, had a special interest in early instruments and jazz classics. His puckish sense of humor and the excellent hospitality that he and his artist wife May provided at their home on Cheremoya Avenue, made their house a frequent visiting place for our family. The house was always full of character and characters, eventually including my friend Eve, the eldest Babitz daughter, future L.A. confessional novelist and counter-culture journalist. Ingolf and Sol collaborated on many concerts, specializing in works of Stravinsky and Charles Ives. Together they prepared, with the cooperation of the composer, a modern edition of the Ives *Third Sonata* for violin and piano, which was published by New Music Editions in 1951.

In 1941 Ingolf made his first appearance under auspices that would be central to his music-making career for the rest of his life, "Evening On The Roof." The roof in question was part of a house at 1725 Micheltorena Street, upon which Peter Yates and his wife, the pianist Frances Mullen, had erected a studio. Here, just as Ingolf was arriving in America, they began a series of chamber music concerts offering the most modern fare in performances that represented the highest level of musicianship. Yates was responsible for establishing and stimulating many a career, and for reviving audience interest in hitherto neglected composers, like Ives. In spite of the assertion in the printed program that, "The concerts are for the pleasure of performers and will be played regardless of audience," the series attracted a loyal and sophisticated following, too large to squeeze into the Yates home. An odyssey among local auditoria followed, with a permanent home always the quest. The number of concerts attempted in the early years seems astonishing today. In 1942, for instance, Ingolf participated in seven Monday night concerts in the first half of the year alone. Thereafter his level of contribution was limited by other commitments, but throughout the war years he made regular appearances in chamber music ensembles and as a soloist, performing works by his contemporaries: Copland, Harold Shapero, Carlos Chavez, Gail Kubik, Virgil Thomson and many others.

Peter Yates was not a musician by training or profession. He was a civil servant, employed by the State of California, who wrote articles on music in his spare time for *California Arts and Architecture*. I remember him as a pipe-smoking, pedantic, but very decent man who turned an amateur's passion into a new life. His writings about new music, a chronicle of the modern movements he had helped to nurture, propelled him into the deanship of the School of Music at the University of Buffalo, where he spent his later years. In 1958 he and Sol Babitz began a new series of poetry readings by local authors. Peter himself wrote poetry and we cruelly referred to him as the Princeton Beatnik. Thus the roof was again used for public performances, alternating with Sol Babitz's living room. I was a regular visitor to these gatherings and, briefly, became a poetry impresario myself.

The original concert series still survives as the Monday Evening Concerts, with the institution at last finding its home at the newly-built County Museum of Art on Wilshire Boulevard. Yates gave up the directorship in 1953, and it was assumed for the next eighteen years by a most worthy successor, Lawrence Morton. Lawrence gave the series an international character, presenting dozens of West Coast and world premieres of modern compositions. It would be hard to name another American series that could rival the Modern Evening Concerts' record of devotion to contemporary music. Little wonder that the institution was itself the subject of Dorothy L. Crawford's estimable *Evenings On And Off The Roof*, published by the University of California Press in 1995.

In the early Forties, Lawrence Morton wrote music reviews in *Rob Wagner's Script*. His analysis of Ingolf's performances are typical of local press recognition, which found Ingolf a pianist equally at home in modern and Baroque environments: "His sympathy for new music is well known, and his performance of it...is marked at once by an intuitive grasp of the 'psychological states' from which the new music springs and by a scholarly understanding of the modern devices and techniques with which the modern composer makes his intention patent." Reviewing Ingolf's performance of the Bach *Toccata* at a Roof concert in November, 1942, Lawrence wrote, "His pianism can be taken for granted, for it has been proved time and time again. But everyone who heard him play the Bach pieces should have been grateful for the musical understanding that went into their performances. That kind of understanding precludes toying with the music, prettyfying it or even beautifying it."

Ingolf and Lawrence were soon to become collaborators on many a musical project in Los Angeles, and Lawrence became Ingolf's closest friend for a quarter of a century. A mutual respect for talent presided over the birth of this association, for Ingolf considered Lawrence to be the preeminent writer on musical subjects. In 1942, my stepfather wrote a few replacement columns for Lawrence, "When did you say was the deadline for my first '*Script*-tease'?," he queried, adding the complaint, "Do you want to discourage us word-poor musicians who are to follow in your footsteps?" Inspired by this stint as Lawrence's understudy, Ingolf published a few articles in *Modern Music* as well.

September 21st, 1940 must surely have been a memorable day for my stepfather. Hunting for Klemperer, with whom he wished to discuss the *Missa*, he caught up with one great conductor at the home of a second, Bruno Walter. Ingolf had met Walter before, in fact only a few weeks earlier he had received praise from Walter for his part in helping Miriam Soloviev prepare for a concert. Now, describing himself as a wide-eyed greenhorn, my stepfather was privileged to sit before these two great figures as they reminisced about Gustav Mahler!

That afternoon, Ingolf paid his first visit to the home of Thomas Mann. A number of the Manns had now made their way to Los Angeles.

Ingolf records a meeting with Klaus Mann on August 16th, 1939. Michael and Gret Mann were life-long friends of the Dahls, and when Thomas Mann took up residence in Pacific Palisades, it was natural that Ingolf should have come into contact with the great novelist during his visits to see Michael. The young men frequently played chamber music, while the senior Mann listened intently. My stepfather shared meals with the novelist on a number occasions. "Those eyes," Ingolf wrote after lunch on October 10th, 1942, "when they open wide they take in everything." After discussing *Carmen* and *Faust* with Mann, Ingolf reported himself to be floating on a cloud. Hugo Wolf's letters were the topic of conversation on July 28th, 1944. On August 26th, 1945, during a chamber music evening, Ingolf saw Mann "coming with red eyes out of his room...Werfel has died." On March 5th, 1947, Ingolf had lunch with Mann and played for him a brass quintet which he had written a few years earlier. "And he likes it," Ingolf exclaimed, "The fulfillment of *that* wish."

One day in May of 1988 I was surprised to discover, while reading a recent *New Yorker* on the way home from a hiking expedition, that a brash high school student, Susan Sontag, had also been a visitor to the Mann household, having succeeded in getting an interview with the living legend as he sat at his desk, politely fielding her questions. This memoir, in which Ms Sontag also mentions seeing Ingolf conduct at the Wilshire Ebell Theater, conjured up for me a series of memories. When the Southern California household of the Mann family was broken up, our family acquired several pieces of furniture, a chair, a lamp, and a desk – all of which we retained for years. In 1958 each of the pieces ended up in Ingolf's hillside studio in our new Hollywood home, the desk became his own and, after his death and its transportation to Michigan, mine. I used to indulge myself in the fantasy that Thomas Mann's pen, poised above the manuscript of *Dr. Faustus*, had once skipped its way across the surface of this humble piece of furniture, but Gret Mann, to whom I eventually put this question, supposed that the desk was more likely the one used by her mother-in-law whenever it was time to pay the family's bills! Well, maybe Thomas Mann leaned on it once or twice. It did not make the transition to England.

September 21st, 1940, was a memorable day for my stepfather, not solely because of Klemperer, Walter or Mann, but because the day began with his first meeting with Igor Stravinsky. "With Alexei Haieff, Ingolf Dahl was Stravinsky's closest professional associate from the early 1940's to 1948." So we read in Vera Stravinsky and Robert Craft's *Stravinsky in Pictures and Documents*, published in 1978. The nature of Ingolf's collaboration with Stravinsky and something of its origins can be traced through journal entries. The first meeting took place because he and Sol Babitz, who must have made the introduction, wished to audition their version of the *Violin Concerto* for the master before presenting it to concert audiences. Stravinsky offered his evaluation of Ingolf's interpretations prior to other performances as well. On February 16th, 1942 ("I alone with him"), Ingolf played the *Piano Rag Music*. Babitz and Dahl also played their version of the Ives *Third Violin Sonata* for Stravinsky the following April.

There were also many opportunities for Ingolf to watch Stravinsky conduct. One of these was on October 13th, 1940, when the Russian genius led a Hollywood study orchestra in Tchaikovsky's *Second Symphony*. "He conducts like a dancing demon," Ingolf wrote. In February, 1943, the younger man watched with enchantment as Stravinsky conducted *Petrushka*; a year earlier, Stravinsky had presided over the premiere of a "marvelous, stirring, exciting piece," the *Danses Concertantes*, which he had conducted "wonderfully."

Ingolf was himself involved in work on the *Danses Concertantes*, a piece which Stravinsky first mentioned to him in January of 1942. A two-piano arrangement was needed and the composer and his arranger conferred on the project on April 8th. Ingolf's work did not progress much until the end of the summer. There were additional conferences in late September and October and Ingolf finished his arrangement on November 4th, and the two met that night. The work was mailed to Associated Music Publishers on November 10th and Ingolf received a check for one hundred dollars, a big payday for him. "I consider myself exceptionally lucky to get into such close contact with Stravinsky," Ingolf wrote to his overseas family, "and to have been able to please him by my work. I don't need to say that I learned a great deal by doing this and I was more than fascinated to watch the work of one of our greatest masters at such close range."

Ingolf had the opportunity of seeing a number of Stravinsky works in manuscript, and the older composer often phoned his young friend when he wanted to share his latest creation with a sympathetic listener. Gail Kubik recalled that Ingolf was carving the Thanksgiving turkey when Stravinsky called him away one November afternoon so that he and Ingolf could read through the *Symphony in Three Movements* on the piano. Ingolf also seems to have had the responsibility of proofreading some of the maestro's work at publication time; several days of work were put in on *Norwegian Moods* in 1944. This was also the year in which another major collaboration took place.

In September of 1944, Ingolf spent several days recording, for the benefit of dancers, his own solo piano version of the *Scenes de Ballet*, which Stravinsky was composing for Billy Rose. There is now some evidence that Ingolf's role in the project was more extensive that that of arranger. In 1979, Leroy Southers, a student of Ingolf's at U.S.C. and later chairman of the music department at Loyola Marymount College in Los Angeles, wrote to me with more information about this matter. It seems that in 1968, over drinks after class at Julie's, a favorite U.S.C. watering hole, a somewhat tipsy Ingolf had told his students, in confidence, that he had assumed a major role in orchestrating the work as well, "He would go to Stravinsky's house every day or so, pick up the piano sketches, and take them home to orchestrate them." Billy Rose had wanted Robert Russell Bennett to undertake such a job, so there was an additional need for discretion in the affair. "In any case," Southers added, "Dahl's orchestration is perfectly in accord with Stravinsky's general aesthetic at the time, and in my view contributes a great deal to the period charm associated with the work." Ingolf's diaries do not clear up the matter completely. The entry for September 14th reads, "Afternoon and evening at Stravinski. Finished ballet. Afterwards corrections etc. It is so lovely. Dinner there. He likes me." In a draft of a letter to Leopold Stokowski written the following year, Ingolf does mention that "Stravinsky engaged me to help on orchestration of the *Scenes de Ballet*." This seems to be as close as he wished to approach the matter during Stravinsky's lifetime which, ironically, extended longer than his own. Ingolf had an awesome reverence for "the old man," and it would have been natural to claim nothing that might embarrass the master or assert his own importance in the matter.

Ingolf enjoyed the society and hospitality of the Stravinskys at their home above the Sunset Strip for a number of years. Etta, too, shared in this company on occasion, idolizing the small, witty, creative presence as much as Ingolf did. My parents were also extremely fond of Vera Stravinsky, a talented painter. Because of his work with the maestro, Ingolf often had meals with Stravinsky. Once they played Chinese checkers. Stravinsky gave his young protegé an antique map of Zurich, which hung on Ingolf's studio wall thereafter. There were also social evenings. On March 22nd, 1943, Ingolf reports a party at which Aaron Copland and George Antheil were present. "I am very happy," Ingolf enthused. Sometimes the Stavinskys, the Dahls, and the Babitzes went "bumming" together. On the night of September 16th, 1944, for instance, they went drinking, listened to Leadbelly, had dinner at Vesuvio, and went to a Russian film. Somehow the subject of Koussevitsky's interpretation of Stravinksy's music came up. Detecting a note of disapproval in the maestro, Etta said, "But he loves your music so much." "Alas," Stravinsky replied, "it's a measureless love."

In February of 1943 Ingolf published the first of several articles on Stravinsky, a review of *The Poetics of Music* in *Script*. Ingolf noted Stravinsky's preference for compositions that were "well organized, lucid, concise (if not always 'profound')," and the composer's interest in working with musical traditions of the past. Stravinsky had been arguing against the idea that music can *mean* anything, or that it can express emotional states. As a composer Ingolf was himself clearly moving away from the overtly romantic, lyrical, or expressionistic musical elements enshrined by Schoenberg and his circle. Thus my stepfather was ready to follow his new mentor into styles that are usually referred to as neo-classical.

Little has been said to this point about Ingolf's California compositions. In fact, for a number of years, local audiences heard only work completed in Switzerland. It was not until 1941 that Ingolf responded to a new composition project, a request by bassoonist Adolphe Weiss for a woodwind quintet. Ingolf appears to have "finished" the work twice, the first time in July, 1941, but he was still working on the piece aboard the train that took him eastward on his first Gracie tour in May, 1942, and he seems to have finished it a second time the next month. Additional revisions were added three years later. The title changed too, eventually becoming the *Allegro and Arioso*. He heard the first full run-through on March 10th, 1943, at Weiss' home, and he was tremendously excited by its premiere, which he conducted on May 22nd at the Festival of Modern Music.

Local reviews were favorable but the early history of the work was disappointing. It was rejected in February, 1943, when Ingolf submitted it to a contest sponsored by SPAM, the Society for the Publication of American Music. Late in August he was crushed to hear that it had placed only fourth in a members-only Crescendo Club contest -- "very depressed after that, I feel alone, lonely, forsaken, frustrated, terribly isolated." On October 16th he received a wire from Lavinia Black, Executive Secretary of the National Composers Clinic, announcing that the work had been selected for performance the following spring. "I am very happy," Ingolf crowed, "the first great recognition." But months later a second message arrived form the NCC; the first telegram had been dispatched after only *one* of the appraisers had been heard from; votes of the remaining judges had demoted the work to "honorable mention" status, and the performance offer was withdrawn. The piece seemed to be cursed, but its qualities were eventually recognized and the *Allegro and Arioso* became a minor standard of the wind quintet repertoire. It was published by McGinnis & Marx in 1962, and has been recorded by the New Art Wind Quintet and the New York Woodwind Quintet.

The wind piece was the last of the Dahl compositions that belonged to a period of dissonant chromaticism, a style influenced by the atonal expressionism of Schoenberg and some of his famous pupils. James Berdahl, who wrote the first of several dissertations on my stepfather's music, even detected use of the famous twelve-tone row in the opening flute section of the Arioso movement, and Lawrence Morton has noted that the piece shared some of its aesthetic with the works of Alban Berg. Those familiar with this style will recognize that it serves well to convey, in spite of its dissonance, the lush emotions of Viennese romanticism. One can understand why the youthful Ingolf should have been drawn to it. But just as he chose to record his passions in his journals only, and to hide them from the outside world, so he now began to reject the Schoenbergian ethos. Perhaps it is no coincidence that just as he was turning his back on these traditions he was entering into his long and fruitful association with Schoenberg's great rival for preeminence in compositional innovation, Igor Stravinsky.

The first journal entry that mentions Ingolf's next great project, the *Music For Brass Instruments*, comes on February 18th, 1944, but "more on fugue," suggests that he had been working on the piece before this. The work was completed in Toronto, during the second Gracie tour, on May 3rd. Ingolf was again working against a deadline, since the piece was scheduled for its premiere, only twenty-four days later, at the Festival of Modern Music, whose director, Arthur Leslie Jacobs, had commissioned it. "It goes well," the composer noted, "everybody likes my piece. Additional performances at U.C.L.A. and on the Roof followed quickly.

Ingolf constructed one of the themes of this work from the telephone number of Universal Studios and one from the dog tag number of Gail Kubik, to whom the work is dedicated. The *Music For Brass Instruments* may be seen as Ingolf's first composition in a tonal, neo-classical style. In *Script*, Lawrence Morton called the work "the most integrated and unified" of Dahl's compositions to this point, "the most personal, the most appealing in its human quality...The spontaneous expression of approval and appreciation by a sophisticated audience, after a joyful and very American second movement and again at the end of the performance, should indicate to the composer that he has found here what he has long been seeking – the matter and manner of his own music." Ingolf was once again disappointed in the annual SPAM competition, which he entered under the pseudonym of Thane Abbot, but the work soon won the approval of Alfred Frankenstein, writing in the *New York Herald Tribune,* and of composers as diverse as Aaron Copland, Wallingford Riegger, George Rochberg, and Francis Poulenc.

It had been Ingolf's belief, while writing the work, that "there are hardly any performance possibilities at all for a piece of this kind," and indeed the number of ensembles composed of two trumpets, French horn, two trombones (and optional tuba) must have been small, but the work itself is credited with a revival of interest in the brass quintet. Within a few years Julian Menken of the New York Brass Ensemble referred to it as "*the* most outstanding work in brass repertory." "When Ingolf Dahl wrote his *Music For Brass Instruments* 30 years ago," Robert Posten wrote in the mid-70's, "he signalled the beginning of the 20th century brass renaissance -- new music for a medium which had slept for over 200 years. Dahl had the foresight to treat the brass quintet with the seriousness which it later proved to deserve." The work was published by Witmark (now a division of Warner Brothers Music) in 1948, and it has been recorded several times.

The vigorous jazzy rhythms have also served as the theme music for at least two radio shows, *TWA's World Adventure in Music* and Martin Bookspan's WQXR record review show. The brass piece has remained one of the most popular of Ingolf's compositions; I was thrilled to hear a performance by brass players of the London Symphony Orchestra during a concert conducted by Michael Tilson Thomas at the Barbican in 1991.

I have noted before that Ingolf had had virtually no training in composition since his sessions with Jarnach in Cologne. Stravinsky was not his teacher, in the formal sense, but in 1945 Ingolf did enroll, however briefly, as a student of the craft. He did this by participating in the Sunday morning master classes offered by Nadia Boulanger. He first mentions attending a session taught by this passionate and proficient exponent of neo-classicism on April 8th, 1945. The list of American composers influenced by the French mentor has been a considerable one and would include Elliott Carter, Virgil Thomson, Roy Harris, Leonard Bernstein, and Aaron Copland. Ingolf seems to have profited from the classes a good deal and he mentions that his teacher liked a string orchestra piece of his very much. "Great class," he noted on May 13th, "She is like a glowing preacher." Frequently, however, the pupil had no time to work on composition projects (these were Dorsey radio days) and no homework to show his teacher.

He completed only one work during this period, *Variations on a Swedish Folktune* ("one of the toughest assignments I ever inflicted on myself"), a work for solo flute which he dedicated to his brother Holger. The first public performance, with Leonard Posella as the soloist, took place at a Roof concert on April 29, 1946. The work was published by New Music the same year and recorded by Doriot Anthony Dwyer in 1952, the same year she joined the Boston Symphony.

"I was mildly amazed that you were working with N.B.," Aaron Copland wrote to Ingolf, "It never occurred to me that you had anything to learn." Copland already enjoyed a reputation as the dean of American composers, and he was president of the American Composers Alliance, to which Ingolf belonged, when he spent some time in Hollywood working on film scores. He and Ingolf met in February of 1943 when the two conferred over Ingolf's interpretation of Copland's *Piano Sonata*, which received its Los Angeles premiere under Ingolf's fingers at a Roof concert on March 1st. Copland (and his "coterie," as the *Los Angeles Times* bitchily put it) were present to join an audience "eager and vociferous in applause." Peter Yates called it a great performance, "an event that will not soon be forgotten by those who heard it," and Lawrence Morton wrote, "I know of no Los Angeles pianist better qualified than Ingolf Dahl to have introduced a work of this importance."

A few weeks later, on April 5th, 1943, Ingolf returned to the Roof to play a revised version of his own *Piano Suite*. The next day he replayed the Suite and Copland's Sonata at a private party attended by Toch, Copland and Sanroma. "It is thoroughly my evening," he exulted, but, as he drove Copland home after the gathering, he learned that America's most famous composer liked only the newly completed movement, finding the earlier sections "dated and Middle-European." Thereafter, Ingolf preserved the new part of the Suite as a section of a work entitled *Hymn and Toccata*, and never played the four movements together again.

In January, 1944, Ingolf produced his own piano version of Copland's famous ballet, *Rodeo*, which he played at a Crescendo Club concert, and he twice played the piano part in performances of Copland's *Second Violin Sonata* the same year. I think it can be argued that Ingolf was soon to write, with the *Music For Brass Instruments* at the head of of the list, a good deal of music that was self-consciously within the American musical idiom, and surely Copland must have been a strong influence in such compositions.

Ingolf met Copland again in New York during the second Gracie tour in 1944. This time he was captivated by the city, its turmoil, confusion, challenges, excitement, frightening crowds, and its temptations. He spent considerable time with Copland and other composers, Henry Cowell, David Diamond, Harold Shapero, Alexei Haieff, Arthur Berger, and Lou Harrison. He wrote some of the brass piece, as a matter of fact, in Lou Harrison's apartment. After a Boosey & Hawkes concert on February 21st he reports his euphoria at the opportunity of walking down the street arm in arm with Copland, Diamond, and Shapero – "my head swims." A Koussevitsky concert featuring music by William Schuman and Samuel Barber at Carnegie Hall on March 11th caused him to note gleefully, "*Every*body there backstage." Ingolf was thrilled to be accepted into this company of American composers; only a little over a year earlier, on December 19th, 1942, he had complained at a League of Composers function in Los Angeles, "Again I feel not a "native" but an outsider. No place for me?"

Many of the contacts Ingolf made during his New York stay were on behalf of the Musicians' Congress Committee, a group of professional musicians chaired by Lawrence Morton and including such diverse members as Copland, Milhaud, Toch, Raksin, Rosza, Kubik, William Grant Still, Hans Eisler, Harold Arlen, Hugo Friedhofer, Jerome Kern, and Lena Horne. Ingolf was attempting to stimulate the creation of a New York chapter and, though often frustrated in meeting people (and handicapped by his own late rising hour), he wrote to Lawrence, "The longer I stay here the more I realize that *everything* happens in the East and that we in the West are just backward hick people – a great handicap for the Congress." I would hastily add that, although Ingolf always retained the Westerner's jealousy of the East Coast musical scene, his assessment of Los Angeles' contribution to the national picture soon underwent a dramatic reversal. Gail Kubik did challenge him to move to New York at this time and Ingolf's response was, "But I couldn't *ski.*"

More work for the Musicians' Congress (its leftist agenda caused some of its members a bit of bother in the McCarthy era) took place during the Boston portion of the tour. Ingolf approached Walter Piston and the critic Nicolas Slonimsky ("He likes my compositions!") about the possibilities of a Boston chapter. In general Ingolf was happier in the Big Apple than in Beantown: "Boston demonstrates to you the utter unattractiveness, boredom, and stagnation of virtue!" In fact neither city had what Ingolf was looking for in his unique life style. After his appointment at U.S.C., the fate of our family was determined for good; we would all be Angelinos.

15. A CHORUS OF APPROVAL

A few words about the musical development in other members of our family might be appropriate, just as a kind of coda to the activities of the emergent star whose ascendancy we have been following in the most recent sections.

Naturally, there was the keenest interest in the musical instincts of the youngest member of the family, Baby Tony. Ingolf records, in the *Deskaide* on April 21st, 1940, some of my spontaneous evening songs, epics which enshrined such lyrics as "scrambled, scrambled, scrambled," and "ja, ja, nein, nein." Ingolf notes that "the tunes are not at all distinct, just a succession of tones, sometimes almost oriental sounding. He cannot sing a single tune yet, not even familiar ones (like 'happy birthday'), for which he makes up his own 'melody.'" Surely one can already detect a whiff of disappointment in this anecdote, a lament that extended to this two-year old's performance at the piano: "He sometimes likes to sit 'by myself' on the piano chair and pound on the piano." This hardly seems a promising start, but couldn't Ingolf see here that imitation was undoubtedly a form of flattery? Indeed, on July 4th, 1940, Etta records asking Tony not to mess up Ingolf's music on the chair. My response was, "But I have to, mommy, I have to prakkels."

She also notes that I was often asked for my views on classical music. At four I described a piece by Copland as "nasty." On January 15th, 1944, just after my sixth birthday, I pronounced a work by Stravinsky "strange and nice."

Ingolf records that a two and a half year-old Tony was taken to his first concert, a recital by his stepfather (Scriabin, Schoenberg, Krenek, Honegger, Hindemith, Telemann and Dahl) at City College on October 21st, 1940. My reactions are not known, but when Ingolf later took me to see the Monte Carlo ballet perform *The Nutcracker*, I was evidently enchanted: "The experience of my life: Tony with his dreamfilled shining eyes on my lap. He understands the music." The extent of my musical understanding and appreciation still needs to be catalogued, but it was clear that, no pre-school Wolfgang having been discovered lurking in the shadows of the upright, no attempt would be made at this time to induce to me to accept any other role than worshipful listener at my stepfather's feet.

The question of my mother's musical development is much more perplexing. After all of her own years in musical studies she now yielded the role of music maker almost exclusively to my stepfather. She would occasionally sit down alone at the piano and sometimes she and Ingolf would read through a score side by side. But she took no further part in rehearsing or performing, confining her musical creativity exclusively, during the war years, to the composition of popular songs.

Etta had a wonderful voice; it would be hard to describe her singing style, but she would certainly have been closer to Mildred Bailey or her idol, Peggy Lee, than to Gracie Fields, who was evidently not smitten with an Etta song, which Ingolf played for her on January 31st, 1943.

Six or seven of Etta's efforts from the period have survived. Writing under the name of Toby Bowman, she registered them and made demonstration records, scratchy do-it-yourself 78's, that I can no longer play today. They are splendid examples of the popular forms of the times, rumbas, blues, upbeat numbers. Etta's lyrics cannot convey the true flavor of the compositions, but I can include some samples: The chorus of "I've Got Those I'm Getting Outa Here 'Cause I Won't Be Wanted Here Blues" is as follows:

> I've got those I'm getting outa here
> 'Cause I wont be wanted here blues
> Somebody else is on your string
> And I'm the last one to hear the news;
> It seems that some little bird tipped off
> A few feathered friends in his tree,
> They flew around
>
> And told the town
> And fin'lly found
> Time to tell me...
>
> You could have knocked me over
> With a puff of smoke;
> When will it mend and beat again;
> This tired heart you broke?
>
> If you should try to be sweet again
> I hope I've the courage to refuse,
> I've got those I'm gettin' outa here
> 'Cause I won't be wanted here blues

"I Want A Letter From My Honey" is a far more lively evocation of the times:

> Verse:
> Since a certain seventh of December,
> Girls are cookin' on long-distance ember,
> They get their glow
> By way of A.P.O.
> They're a million strong
> With their wistful song:

Chorus:
I want a letter from my honey,
Ain't seen my chickadee in an eternity,
I need a letter from my honey,
Sayin'": Hiya, Sweet, you all reet
And rootin' for me?"
Could use a letter from my honey,
A swig of fox-hole news for those duration blues
And that ever-loving P.S.with the 10 smackeroos.
Postman, don't you pass up my door once more,
Don't slip me ads when I need scads
Of soothing' from another shore!
Let's have the low down on honey,
Can't find my lost morale
Lest you assist me pal,
Hand me my ration of paper passion
From the good man to his gal!

I regret very much that my mother did not pursue her musical interests, not because I am vain enough to believe that the world was robbed of some imperishable contribution by her withdrawal, but because she should have been carving out an identity of her own. "I feel like a crumb catcher or an echo or an empty vessel," she wrote to Ingolf in March, 1944, "I don't feel *real* but rather ghostlike and this is very bad." We are in a better position today, after the women's movement has made its point, to recognize the psychological dangers which Etta courted in perpetually subordinating her own creative impulses to those of her more talented husband. "I never believed that I would set the world on fire in any field," she wrote to Connie Buchanan, "but it would have given me a great deal of satisfaction to have developed along some line to the point where I could have been good at it...Something must be acutely wrong with me at bottom to have prevented me from mastering one dismal corner to the point where I could hold it up for admiration, if not wild praise."

Ingolf was not unaware of these frustrations in his wife, but neither was he able to see a way forward. It is very hard to imagine Ingolf thriving in the narrow environment of the household with *more* than one object of glory present, himself. It was no great tragedy in his life that the rest of us remained on the sidelines as a chorus of perpetual approval.

16. ON THE HOME FRONT

I don't remember the seventh of December referred to in my mother's song, and, to be honest, I don't recall, with the exception of its concluding moments, *any* episodes in the great combat that was World War II. I have very strong memories of *other* events that were contemporary with the war, and I can certainly recall the ways in which the war transformed the home front, but that this was a daily struggle, full of military setbacks and triumphs, seems to have been at the periphery of my consciousness as a child. I don't remember allied landings in North Africa, Italy, or Normandy, and of the painful re-conquest of the Pacific I was blissfully unaware. Evidently I did return from nursery school in 1943 to announce, "I think we ought to shoot Hitler in the wee-wee," and I *do* recall the anguished tears of my mother at the news of F.D.R.'s death in April, 1945. Later, of course, the events of the conflict became a matter of great fascination for me, but my war was fought, trench by trench, in the movie houses of West Los Angeles five years after the last shot had been fired.

The obvious reason that I followed the war at such a distance is that none of my close relatives was involved in combat. Ingolf, we have seen, was declared 4-F the first time the army got a look at him. His involvement in the war was chiefly on the morale building side, accompanying Gracie on bond tours, playing in soldiers' canteens and veterans' hospitals, performing in benefit concerts with titles like "Iodine for Russia" or "Wings for Norway." Leroy Linick, too, was rejected by the army on medical grounds, though he delighted in showing us his draft registration card so that he could deny a detail of his physical description as recorded by some illiterate clerk – "slightly balled." I remember seeing only a few people I knew in uniform: Stephen Weisman, who married my first cousin Virginia on her eighteenth birthday in 1940, my Uncle Morry Keller, who served out his war in Little Rock, Arkansas, and the composer, Gail Kubik.

The Dahls first met Gail in the fall of 1943. He was assigned to a unit of the Air Force charged with producing documentary and training films. Two of the former, *Thunderbolt* and the original *Memphis Belle*, were directed by William Wyler and scored by Gail. His puckish sense of humor and Coffeyville, Kansas speech patterns delighted Ingolf and Etta, and they repaid his jibes by sneaking out to attach notes to appropriate places on his bicycle: "Handel Bars," "Beware of Pedal Points," "Light Motiv." He had a thousand nicknames for us (I remember Ingleberry, Ettabean, and Tonybun), and taught me such useful expressions as, "Blow it out your barracks bag!" Ingolf's journals are full of admiration for Gail, and not a little envy. On November 27th, 1943, the two went to Hollywood Boulevard after the evening's Bach Festival concert. They each had five martinis. It never took much to make Ingolf tiddly, but his reaction to his new friend was not based on drink alone. Gail, so Ingolf wrote, is an extraordinarily enriching and harmonious personality – his "heart is alive." After sitting drunkenly in a bowling alley and supping on ravioli and coffee on Vine Street, Ingolf did not return from this exercise in hero worship until 2:30 in morning.

I might add, before leaving the subject of uniforms, that Grampa Gordon spent much of the war tailoring them for officers. And I had two, myself – a sailor suit and a soldier suit, both quite authentic miniature versions of the garb one could see so often in the street. There is an extensive series of photographs taking in Fern Dell where, dressed in my navy wool sailor suit, I play with Miklos Rosza's boxer, Mowgli. And there is also a photo of me, in my soldier suit, saluting with Steve Weisman at the end of the war. In fact, I hated both of these uniforms, which I found both confining and itchy.

War actually began for Ingolf, a man with friends and family in Europe, in the first days of September, 1939, only half a year after his arrival in California. "*Krieg!*" in large underlined letters is the only entry for this period in his journal. For him, the Christmas festivities of that December were already spoiled by war. On Pearl Harbor Day he writes, "War with Japan. What else will overtake us now?" A blackout was called a few nights later and in February there was an air-raid alert. Ingolf convinced himself that he could hear cannon fire in the distance – "This is it!"

To add to our ordinary economic woes, we now endured rationing and curfew problems. Gasoline rationing was a particular problem for Ingolf, who often worked at night some distance from home. Etta had the task of monitoring our coupons and ration books and she conscientiously saved everything for the war effort, every form of tin and metal, even fat, which was drained from the evening's cookware and stored in large jars.

113

At a number of points in the war restrictions on the movements of aliens were threatened, and Ingolf took every rumor to heart. California's Japanese-Americans, it will be remembered, found themselves in camps in the desert. What might me be the fate of those who still carried German papers? Reading about proposed restrictions while on tour in March, 1942, Ingolf became desperately depressed, "Perhaps I must leave California. This news spoils the rest of the trip for me. Where are Etta and I to go?" A few days later he applied for a position in the music department of Baylor University. Nothing came of this. As I was once denied the opportunity of life in Reseda, so now Waco, Texas, was withheld from me as well.

War also brought an interruption in the flow of correspondence between Stockholm and Los Angeles. Delivery was often delayed, often uncertain, and letters were subject to examination by the censors. To keep track of the transatlantic mail, each letter in this family correspondence was given its own number, a system that was maintained out of habit until 1949, when Mammi had sent off Sweden's letter number 223. The Stockholm letters of this period, with their melancholy account of dislocation and privation, frequently caused anguish in the helpless Ingolf, though, of course, Sweden was spared the full horrors of war because of its neutral status. Then there were those letters that spoke of the death of childhood companions, those who had fallen in the ranks of the Third Reich. When she reported, on June 9th, 1944, the death of Ingolf's skiing companion, Seppl, Mammi added, "I do not think he believed in the cause for which he had to die."

Ingolf had decided, from his earliest moments in the United States, that he wanted to be an American. The journal entry for June 10th, 1939, reads, "First Papers assured. Hurrah!" The following February, after a visit to the Immigration and Naturalization Office, he wrote, "I will be an American by 1942!" This prediction was premature, though we find him applying for Second Papers in February, 1941, and, with the Weismans as witnesses, undergoing a citizenship examination in January of 1943. He was sworn in on September 10th, 1943, and a family party was held in the back yard at Westmorland that evening. Evidently I became so excited that I had to be walked around the block several times to cool down. Ingolf wrote his family that he was "unspeakably happy." In the musical senses referred to earlier, and now in the wider cultural and political context, Ingolf ever after proudly considered himself to be an American, and he earnestly endeavored to fulfill the requirements of conscientious citizenship. By 1944, to make the break with the past even more definitive, he was writing his journals exclusively in English.

War was not a time of unrelieved tragedy for the civilian population of Los Angeles. The notion that the ordinary citizen's efforts could make a difference in a struggle that was universally supported created a feeling of comradeship that was impossible for Americans to duplicate in later generations.

How joyous were those holiday dinners to which my parents, through the U.S.O., invited lonely strangers in uniform. How triumphant we all felt on VJ day when the war we had *all* fought came to an end with Japan's surrender. I remember the effigy-carrying crowds that I saw below me as I sat atop Ingolf's shoulders while we waded through the singing and shouting masses on the corner of Hollywood and Vine in August, 1945. And of course I will always remember the 7th of December, though not the one in 1941, however. I'll always remember December 7th, 1992, the day of infamy on which my car was stolen in St. John's Wood!

17. TELEMACHUS WAITS

I have the feeling that Ingolf did not know what to make of the infant he discovered in Etta's arms in February, 1939. It isn't until June that "Toni," as Ingolf often spelled my name, is even mentioned in the daybook. Baby Tony must also have been mightily confused, for the arrival of one father figure was accompanied the withdrawal of another. After his marriage to Del, we saw less and less of Leroy, and – Etta would add cynically – less and less of his child support money. There were, of course, sporadic weekend visitations, increasingly stilted occasions dominated by the disapproving Del, but it was not until 1945 that I began to see my father on a regular basis; even then, there seemed to be no way to get close to this enigmatic personality. I had failed to win a secure place in the affections of one father, and now I would have to try my luck with this stranger who had come to live with my mother.

More and more I came to command Ingolf's attention and affection. We were soon like father and son, and Ingolf's feelings of love and responsibility were manifest to everyone. Particularly while he was jobless,

Ingolf remained at home on many occasions to look after me and later, when I was ill, he would rearrange his schedule in order to be near my bedside, sometimes cramming the other musicians into our small living room on Westmorland so that a rehearsal could go forward while he kept an eye on me. After a period of illness in 1942, he wrote, "He is well, god be thanked." As my verbal and motor abilities matured, Ingolf found endless satisfaction in taking me on errands and excursions, both near and far.

One of our nearby favorites was Barnsdall Park, on the west side of Vermont between Fountain and Sunset. This hilly promontory was known locally as Olive Hill because of the silvery groves that descended its flanks. On the top there were public buildings, including a gallery erected by Frank Lloyd Wright. Wright had been going through a neo-Mayan phase when he designed the indented walls of this edifice and Ingolf would hoist me onto the top of the ramparts so I could run their length, like a knight pursuing his enemies along a battlement. An even greater treat was being allowed to roll from the top of the hill to the bottom, over the spiky crab grass that cushioned the descent of the young human juggernaut. Ingolf would pick me up as I recovered from my dizziness before we started the walk for home.

Black Peter was needed to get us to other favorites, most of which were situated within the confines of the Griffith estate in the hills to the north. I loved the Griffith Park Zoo, lush Fern Dell, and the dusty walk ("Toni climbs so sweetly") to the top of brush covered Mt. Hollywood, a walk that begins at the parking lot of the famous Observatory. This marvellous structure, with its molded parapets and mounted spy glasses, invited the kind of fantasy that movie makers have been exploiting for years as the setting for films as diverse as *Rebel Without A Cause* and *The Rocketeer*. Long before either film was made I was dashing about this magic place in my own epic wanderings.

Particularly when gasoline was available, we undertook more distant expeditions. I have mentioned the strand at Santa Monica, but we also visited the one at Manhattan Beach, where the Weisman's had a summerhouse. There were also trips to the desert and to many mountain sites, including Mt. Wilson, Lake Gregory, Crestline and Mt. Waterman, where on January 16th, 1944, Ingolf added a new variation to the piggyback on the diving board lark by putting me on his shoulders and skiing down icy run number three as I shrieked in terror at the menacing trees. "Unbelievable sunset," a happy parent recorded in his daybook, "Purple mountains. Happy home, early to bed."

From the start I had difficulty knowing what to call Ingolf. I could not pronounce his name and, at seventeen months, got by with Eegoo. This version of the name delighted Ingolf and Etta. She used it as an endearment ever after, spelling it Igu, and her use of it was picked up by some of his U.S.C. students, who also used it with affection, albeit behind his back. On August 3rd, 1941, Ingolf reports that while walking to Olive Hill I called him "Daddy," a name heretofore used only for Leroy. Etta discouraged this usage, however, feeling that it would hurt her first husband's feelings. Earlier in the year, so she records in the *Baby Tony Book*, one of our cleaning ladies had referred to Ingolf as "Your Daddy," and I had emphatically corrected her, "Leroy is my daddy. Ingolf is my father." Later I learned to use the word "stepfodder," but, so Etta reports, I resented using this word from the start, preferring "Ingolf" always.

My wave of goodbye at train stations remained in his memory when he set off on his tours, my voice over the transcontinental telephone affected him deeply, my running towards him with outstretched arms after a period of separation was thrilling to him. Diary references to Toni's sweetness continue throughout the war years, and Ingolf never failed to dispatch an endless series of post cards, often featuring animal scenes, when he was away. He also made great efforts to ensure that holiday times for his stepson would be as blissful as those enjoyed, under Mammi's aegis, by *lille* Ingolf. He would laboriously color tiger-striped Easter eggs or search out Christmas presents that would delight. I still have my copy of Anderson's *Fairy Tales*, bearing the inscription, "To My Beloved Tony, Christmas, 1943."

Needless to say, my mother – writing from the unhappy perspective of the frustrated wife – found a somewhat sour way, in July, 1943, of explaining the relationship of stepfather to stepson: "I once thought that Ingolf's love for Tony was an expression of his own desire for parenthood. I can, by the way, never be grateful enough for it, though I was mistaken in its source. But I realize now that it is rather Ingolf's way of paying homage to his own childhood, his nostalgic re-living of that golden time when "life" was so remote, and he was an innocent, and justifiably irresponsible as a young God. Every sign of Tony's maturity breaks Ingolf's heart." Ingolf's journals do not provide any evidence to confirm this assertion – and the attitude may not be as unnatural as Etta makes out. I *can* say that it was a delight to have as a parent someone who was as skilful in the ways of the child as my stepfather. The great tragedy of my childhood was that he was so frequently unavailable when I needed him.

Etta tells two stories in the *Deskaide* that underline the issue of the absent father. In one I am slightly over two, and have begun to silence everyone in the house with the refrain, "Igu is sleeping." I am saying this because my stepfather spent so much of the daylight hours in bed. In another incident, a few months later, my motto is, "Poor Igu can't have num-num." I had picked up this expression from Etta, who had begun many a meal with the explanation that Ingolf would have to eat later because of a rehearsal or some other nocturnal assignment. These situations were so common that I recited the litanies all the time, even when the object of my concern was wide awake, his fork poised! The stories are a reminder that Ingolf was often an absent parent, not so much in the sense that he was absent from the household altogether – although he obviously missed months of my youth while on tour – but because even when he was present he was often so preoccupied with his work or his emotional state or his myriad more interesting preoccupations that I found it very difficult to obtain his attention. "Ingolf! You got a bad habit of reading when you should be eating" – so Baby Tony cries out in protest. Ingolf was a parent on his own terms, not the reliable male figure that a child like myself needed for protection and guidance, needed as a model.

It was obvious that our household had only one leader and it was not this will 'o the wisp, who dabbed shaving cream on my chin one day and returned to his father-hungry stepson three days or three months later, with tears of regret in his eyes. There was no way of offering a rational explanation to the male-starved child for his absences, his prolonged vanishing acts, his local disappearances, his absent-mindedness when he was at home. Like many another household in wartime America, ours was, therefore, a matriarchy. It was Etta who bore all the responsibilities for overseeing my development, for nurturing me on a daily and consistent basis, and for *discipline* – a word that was entirely foreign to my absent stepfather's vocabulary.

18. A RIGHT CROSS FROM HELL

My mother approached the science of childrearing with the clear conscience of someone who had done her homework. Most of her responses, even in situations that otherwise might demand the tentative and the experimental, were conditioned by strategies that had been forged in the clear light of reason. Indeed, if my mother was ever made uneasy by childish behavior it was because the latter lacked rationality, a failure that could be remedied only by a dose of sane and salutary discipline.

Just home from the hospital, three week-old Baby Tony had suffered from a sore throat and a high temperature. My mother noted, "The only real after-effect was that Tony became somewhat spoiled through having so much sympathy and attention lavished on him and had to learn to rely on himself for company all over again." How else would an infant learn the entirely admirable trait of self-reliance than by having his mother ignore his whimpering cries for attention? When I was three months old, Etta was convinced that her strategy was working: "For some time now he has been able to make a single, reproachful protest noise when I leave the room. But he seldom if ever cries for attention because he learned from his third week that he would be paid attention to only at certain times." In a section of the *Baby Tony Book* on character and personality development my mother has sketched the following scenario: "Situation: Left in buggy to sleep; Child's Behavior: Objection – whimpering; Duration of Response: Usually short; Method of Handling: Ignoring him." After reading these entries I no longer wonder why, as a child, I developed such a fondness for talking to myself or holding imaginary conversations with stuffed elephants.

At eighteen months, with Ingolf on the scene at last, Etta recorded another instance of her favorite strategy: "Situation: Mother being kissed; Child's Response: Tony says a loud No!; Duration of Response: Until Mother is free to pay attention to him; Method of Handling: Ignored, since he gets plenty of attention at other times." If Baby Tony got into squabbles with other children over a desired toy, Etta sent him back to the fray to fight it out himself. If he crawled toward the hot stove, Etta watched calmly to make sure that Tony would understand not to do it again *after* he burned himself. Stupid brat, it took me to two passes at the stove before I put two and two together. At bedtime it was *all* lights out; who wants a ninny for a son?

Despite these carefully constructed tactics for obtaining compliance with the rules of rational conduct, Baby Tony sometimes made only the slowest of progress. Heading for the bathroom during meals and daydreaming at the table (as though I didn't have a splendid role model here) were particularly exasperating sins. "I discipline Tony quite severely at time," my mother noted, "For being 'sat upon' he retaliates occasionally by getting rid of me in his thoughts and even in spoken declaration...Tony made a long train of cars. He explained that it was a funeral. 'Oh,' I said, 'who is being buried?' 'You,' was the prompt reply."

But getting rid of my mother can only have been a temporary expedient, the revenge of the disappointed attention-grabbing suitor. At all other times I endowed my mother with the magical properties of the all-powerful beloved object: judge, avenger, savior in one. I must certainly have believed in my mother's omnipotence after my tonsillectomy. This surgery was performed inexpertly in a local one-storey clinic not too far from our Westmorland home. But my mother, who knew her way around hospitals, found the post-operative care totally inadequate. In order to reclaim her beloved child with the minimum of resistance from the resident medical staff, she hired a cab, snuck in the back door of my ward, wrapped me in a blanket when no one was looking, carried me out the back door and down half a flight of steps, and escaped with her precious bundle in the back seat of the waiting taxi. When a mother can change the course of history in this dramatic fashion any doubts as to her wonder-working powers must be dismissed. How horrible, therefore, to risk losing such a benevolent presence through misbehavior, how awful to feel the wrath of her displeasure.

Not surprisingly, I became a most obedient and deferential child, dull in my dependable compliance. When I erred it was usually through inadvertence, some especially irrational act that I had perpetrated more through ignorance than will. I remember getting spanked only once, however, and perhaps the rarity of this penalty among the arsenal of my mother's punishments is what makes the incident stand out. I have no idea what the crime was. I also think it is possible, if the veils of repression can be lifted momentarily, that my mother did like to sentence me to periods of closed confinement in closets. This would make sense; until I recovered my senses I could sit and think about the consequences of the nonsensical.

In 1991 my cousin Julie told me that when she had been a small child my mother had responded to an attack of infantile hysteria, that ultimate decent into the irrational, by shutting her up in a darkened cellar until she recovered *her* senses. I can't say whether this incident is truly remembered or not, but I can see how Etta might have needed such a strategy to restore order to a chaotic world. The only defense one can make is that Etta punished out of love. My late mother-in-law used to have a motto, "I never punish a child in anger." I think the *forms* of discipline which I have been describing to this point, however ill-conceived, would survive this test – failures in the calculus of deportment addressed by a measured, rational response intended to bring about wholesome change.

But I must say I felt much more resentment at a later stage in my life, when punishments were the byproduct of anger, usually occasioned by some smart-ass remark voiced by an incautious youth. When maddened by such mouthings, my mother, the least athletic of adults, could unleash a lightning-like assault with her open palm on my unprotected left cheek, a right cross from hell that hurt for days, or so it seemed at the time.

It seems that this is the appropriate time to take note of an additional character flaw in the small child who was once myself. Responding to more queries on personality and character development in the *Baby Tony Book*, my mother took on the question, "Is he demonstrative in affection?" Her answer was "Not very," and she continued, "He occasionally likes to cuddle, more often his woolly toys than humans. Next to that his mother." In this way we have early, if undated, evidence of my rebellion against a world that was so inconstant in its provision of love and love objects. I recoiled from the hugs of adults I scarcely knew, and even in the affectionate swoops of those I loved, my own aunts or Aunt Gracie Fields, and, even in the embrace of my parents, I squirmed uncomfortably. It was as if my body were saying, "Don't think you can fool me into believing that you will be here whenever I need or want you. Inevitably I have been disappointed by the disappearance or the rejection of those I loved. Better I learn to live without such fickle attentions." My shoulders would dip, my back would pivot, and my body, freed from the treacherous arms, would move safely

121

and speedily to some corner of the room where I could not be trapped again.

19. BEYOND BELIEF

Writing to a friend in 1956, Ingolf acknowledged that the Christmas festivities that we celebrated in our California home were, in fact, based on those of his own Gross Borstel youth. Without any clear perception of the model, my mother and I were obliged to act out Mammi's *julafton* fantasies. "I think the most overpowering memories of my childhood," Ingolf noted, "are those of Christmases into the preparation of which my mother threw herself with all the fervor and devotion of a true Swedish soul. Weeks before the great date we would paint, paste, bake, make presents, poems, learn pieces of music (or later: compose a piece) to be played on Christmas eve."

Many of these practices were transplanted to the new world. As I matured I grew to resent many of them, but I have to admit that as a child I experienced the greatest delight in the installation of the tree, the pile of inscrutable presents, the seasonal taste treats, and the wonderful mystique of the enigmatic Santa Claus himself. I even liked the music, itself a selection of tunes that had once been popular in Hamburg. "It was rather touching," Ingolf wrote, "how my parents reconciled their deep-rooted agnosticism and anti-religiousness with the equally deep-rooted traditionalism of the way in which Christmas *had* to be celebrated in an all-out fashion. They even went so far as to write *new* (non-religious) lyrics to the old Christmas songs, so we could sing all the songs around the candle-lit Christmas tree without having to sing about Christian personalities or symbols." I can add that Ingolf restored the *urtexts* of these carols when the rituals were repeated many years later in Los Angeles.

Friends, relatives and neighbors were always scandalized by the notion of wax candles burning on the branches of a dying tree, but this, not phony American electric lights, had been part of the Gross Borstel tradition, and Ingolf would taste only the original flavor. Naturally the tree was only lighted when the family were present in the room, and there was always a bucket of water handy – and naturally as well Etta was always ready with a lecture to doubters on the number of electrical fires that *faulty wiring* had caused elsewhere. I loved the candles, even recognizing that their usage constituted another example of my parents' weirdness.

Fortunately no one outside our narrow household witnessed an even stranger rite, based on the Swedish celebration of St. Lucia's day, just before Christmas. In this cult, Etta, filling in for Mammi, wore a crown of lighted candles atop her *hair*, as she awoke the sleeping Ingolf with a tray of goodies on the designated day. She did it for the first time on December 13th, 1939, Ingolf's first California Christmas. "In spite of all the strangeness it is very beautiful," he wrote. Etta kept it up for years, always more for Ingolf's sake than my own, a poignant reminder of the lost world he had forsaken.

Easter celebrations at our house were also extensive, but there were no religious echoes here at all, since these ceremonials involved the cult of the Easter Bunny exclusively. All sorts of secret preparations with colorful hard-boiled eggs were undertaken on the Bunny's behalf, and these were then followed by a manic search on my part to discover where the mischievous creature had secreted his treasures.

When I was five or six these celebrations were expanded to include my very young cousins, Stevie and Julie Keller. As soon as the children were allowed to go outside, I winkled out egg after egg from corners of the lawn and spots under the steps, accomplishing the task so rapidly that my parents realized there would soon be nothing left for Julie or Stevie to discover. When my mother sought to interfere in the natural process of greed and acquisition by discouraging my egg-finding efforts, I was struck by a revelation. "You hid these eggs yourself," I protested, "there isn't any Eastern Bunny." When I received no denial, I was struck by an even greater truth, "And there isn't any Santa Claus either!" Thus in one blow, my youthful belief system lay in tatters.

In tatters, but not destroyed in its entirety. For there still remained the broader question of God, a figure whose name I had been hearing a lot, someone who seemed to be worth cultivating, if only on the most superstitious level. Needless to say, my parents had included no religious instruction whatsoever in my list of childhood experiences, indeed they would have been hostile had the matter been raised. I do remember attending a session of Sunday school by accident. One weekend I spent a night at the Yates house. Peter and Frances had three sons, Bart, Cochran,

and Johnny – the latter about my age. On Sunday morning they sent me
along with their kids to the local Sunday school, which seemed an extremely
joyless and vaguely threatening place, dominated by an alien mythology I
had yet to encounter in a Nitwit or Oz book. This, nevertheless, was about
as close as I got to any religious instruction in my extreme youth.

I had, of course, my own view of God. I could picture her, sitting on the
telephone wire in our back yard, a large figure in the full skirts favored by
my elementary school principal. There she rocked gently, a keen observer
of all that she surveyed, sort of like a mother in the sky.

I did put to my own mother questions on the nature of the godhead
and man's place in the universe. She records such a conversation in the
Baby Tony Book in April, 1944, when I was six. From this dialogue you
can learn a lot about Etta's no-nonsense approach to childrearing, and
also a lot about a son's deference to his mother in a world which lacked
an adequate father figure. "Tony asked again who made the world," she
reported, "so once more I briefly gave him the Creator theory and the
Nebular Hypothesis. Finally he said, *"You* made it."'

20. HOME ALONE

Sometime in 1942, when I was four years old, I became a pupil for the
first time when I was enrolled in the Atkinson's Glenwood Nursery School
on Lucerne Boulevard. I have almost no memories of the place, but to this
day I am overcome with nostalgia when I get a whiff of school soup bubbling
through the corridors and thus recall my earliest nursery school lunches, in
which soup and jello played a big part. I can also remember the trauma of
wet pants, having been overtaken by urgent urinary requirements during
a period when it would have been impolite, not to mention attention-
getting, to rise from the mats to which we were expected to cling during
nap time.

Ingolf greeted my enrollment with some relief, noting in a letter that I
had few friends and that those I had were not particularly stimulating and
that I had "developed some bad social habits...His very active little brain
required organization and guidance which he could not get in the house."
Ingolf does not specify which social habits he was referring to, but he was
undoubtedly right that, as in the case of my mother when she was a child,

I needed stability, which only the schoolroom could provide – precisely because things at home were so inconstant.

I do remember the sensation of unease that I experienced on the first day of my enrollment at the Lockwood Avenue Elementary School in January, 1944, when, as a six-year old, I was accompanied by my mother to its portals among hordes of cheery, screeching children, all strangers, and deposited here for my formal education. What I don't remember are the lessons, beyond the painful attempts I made to learn block printing with an array of Crayolas not nearly as rich in variety as the set I had at home.

I was now taking my lunch to school in a small satchel, which contrasted poorly with the metal boxes sported by some of my classmates. Often we would trade the contents of these packed lunches, thereby subverting the attempts of our mothers to insure a balanced diet. Etta searched through my satchel every evening to see that I had eaten what she had provided, turning up the occasional neglected Brewer's Yeast tablet (with which, like cod liver oil, I was dosed daily) or the dime I should have used to buy milk at recess (but which I had intended to spend on something far less wholesome on the way home – but forgot).

After a while, I suppose when I finally learned how to tie my own shoes, I was sent off to school on my own. No one, in our neglectful and preoccupied household, collected me at the end of the day either, even though this meant crossing the busy corner of Santa Monica and Virgil by myself; there was a signal. I managed to stay out of trouble most of the time, but I *was* hauled in, along with some older miscreants, who happened to be having a battle with soft drink bottles on the very path I used to cross an empty lot on the way home. I would never have thrown an empty glass bottle myself, knowing that I could redeem such objects for full ones. Nevertheless, protesting my innocence to the last, I had to endure the principal's lecture on the danger to young eyes of flying glass – before being allowed to return to my undoubtedly empty home.

One of the happiest moments of life at Lockwood came during the occasional patriotic pageant, which school officials staged as part of their morale building efforts on the home front. Behind a large American flag the entire school paraded in step around the playground to the strains of a Sousa march over the loudspeaker. I cannot tell you how proud I felt to be a participant in this stirring, martial display. Of course Etta did deflate the experience somewhat by providing alternate lyrics for the Sousa, "Be kind to your web-footed friends, for a duck may be somebody's mother."

Lockwood Elementary was a progressive city school. They even had a speech class at work on the stutter and the Midwestern twang of my friend, Joan Smith. I liked the orderly hallways of the place, the rows of desks, the chairs fitted neatly around the table, I liked the rhythm of effort and reward. I must have liked it a lot, because fifty years later I was still going to school.

I do not believe that I encountered the phrase *separation anxiety* until the late Sixties. One of my friends used it while describing her continuing resentment against parents who had *dared* have an evening out – in spite of her protests that the sitter they were leaving behind was totally inadequate, no match for the rising hysteria of their abandoned daughter. Of course, every child has lived through such moments, and survived them without lifelong resentment or the need to take scissors to the household draperies, as a betrayed Baby Ingolf had once done. I have often speculated on my own position in this collective anxiety; do I have any reason to include myself in this catalogue of victims, am I a surviving saint of separation anxiety? I am.

Certainly by the time I was a first-grader, I was often expected to return to a completely empty house on Westmorland Avenue. Ingolf, if he were in residence, would have started his working day at last, and my mother would not yet have returned from her work at Cedars. I disliked a completely empty house and almost immediately I would be out the door again and off to visit the Smiths, or some other friends. When my mother returned from work she would come looking for me and I could enter those no longer empty rooms with some assurance.

I do not believe that I was excessively timid as a child but I suffered from the usual traumas of the darkened bedroom; Etta did not believe in such things as nightlights and so my bedroom was really black. She records my first nightmare when I was a year and a half old: "He cried out sharply at 11 pm that night and wept out loud for the first time since his birth. It was very startling and unusual in Anthony. We comforted him as best we could for five minutes and then he went back to sleep quickly."

I do recall one other vivid episode, one that also required my mother's intervention. I dreamed one night that I was being attacked by Mr. Zahn's chickens. Somehow they had escaped their wire pen next to the alley and they were menacing my bedroom with their busy beaks. My mother responded to my shrieks by throwing on the light, going to my dresser, extracting an orange and purple striped t-shirt and shooing the nocturnal beasts away. Satisfied with this evidence of their departure, I resumed my normal breathing and soon returned to sleep. Nevertheless the night held its special terrors, and it was therefore with some anxiety that one night, when I could not have been much more than six, my mother proposed to leave me home alone!

I cannot remember why she had to be out at night, except that I did not accept the excuse as legitimate, any more than I accepted Ingolf's unexplained departures as justifiable. Sometimes Etta had to attend doctors' meetings at Cedars, where she was needed to take notes. Whatever the explanation for her absence or for her providing no sitter, the bottom line was that I was now expected to be a brave little chap and stay by myself. I was permitted the luxury of an open door, so that a ray of light from the living room could fall across the foot of my bed. I could also see the lights from the street if I drew back the curtain, for my bedroom faced Westmorland itself – that is I was ideally situated to hear every menacing footfall on the sidewalk nearby. To endure my lonely vigil, for I had no intention of going to sleep, I piled every stuffed animal and doll I had into the bed with me. I even climbed under the covers with my clock, a wooden owl known for his ability to see in the dark.

Somehow I survived this ordeal and, by having done so, validated the experiment in my parents' eyes. I was at the end of my baby-sat years. Soon sitterless, I cannot remember a single gum-chewing teenage beauty mounting the steps of our next home, which we moved to when I had attained the ripe old age of seven.

Incidentally, one day when I was in the first grade, *I* disappeared for several hours from my mother's life. It has always seemed very strange to me that children were allowed to roam the city streets of wartime Los Angeles with a freedom that today seems wildly foolhardy. Or perhaps it was just *me*, for I certainly enjoyed such freedom from an early age.

My absent father, Leroy, should have carried some memory of the peril that engulfs young children, because he had been part of the social circle in which Bobby Franks had disappeared one day in Chicago twenty years earlier. "I knew Dicky Loeb," he once boasted, leaving us to wonder if chance only had spared *him* from becoming the victim of Leopold and Loeb's compulsion.

Now, as I made my way home across the empty lot that served as the local battlefield, a somewhat older friend insisted that I accompany him to his house. I complied, not wishing to challenge his edict and not expecting that my absence would be noted by anyone at my own home. I believe the chap lived somewhere behind the Vista Theater, that is somewhere northeast of the grand junction of Sunset, Hollywood and Virgil. This I can remember; I have completely forgotten the boy's name.

When we reached his house, also empty, he told me that he was going to tie me up. I did not like this, but he was much bigger than I was, and I was afraid. He experimented with a piece of rope and then he made me stand, trussed up, in his bathtub. All of this took some time and it was now getting dark. I knew my absence would certainly have to be noted when my mother returned from work, and that she would certainly have to worry. My worst fears were confirmed when my abductor and I heard her voice!

She had been frantically revisiting the homes of each of my friends, searching into all of my hideouts, and now she seemed to be outside the bathroom window, mournfully calling, "To-ny, To-ny!" Inside, we both froze. I did not know whom to fear most, a mother who would be angered by my absence or this big kid, who was mumbling threats about my keeping quiet. I had no wish to be discovered in such a shameful posture anyway, so I chose to say nothing. After a few minutes the beloved voice faded into silence and all hope of rescue perished. To this day I find it disquieting that, in my treacherous silence, I let that worried woman walk away, yet I can also see this as an act of revenge on my part, I who had been abandoned too often could at last pass on some of the anxiety.

My captor was clearly disturbed by this visitation, however. He began to untie me, for the time had come to let me go. Dire punishments were to follow, so he assured me, if I should give any hint of this afternoon's ritual. Swearing a craven obedience, I scurried from the scene, rushing toward the last golden glow in the deepening blue sky. As I dashed up our front steps, my mother was about to call the police.

Needless to say I kept my word. I had, so I explained, just been playing, and I had forgotten the time. My mother was inclined to forget the whole matter the instant her son safely reappeared in her world.

My father never knew that *I* had been the Linick family kidnap victim and my mother, whom I feared and loved, never understood what had happened to me on this turbulent afternoon. I have kept my word for over sixty years, but I keep it no longer.

21. FILM NOIR

I think I may have some clues as to the origins of my young friend's experiments with rope. This is because I, too, at an early and suggestive age, became addicted to a cinema that feasted on scenes of peril and restraint. I know that such a description seems far removed from that festival of slapstick cartoons, heroic Westerns, and Disney features that served as the movie diet of the very young in the mid-Forties, but the very young have a way of finding their own messages in the blandest of fare.

I was taken to the movies several times by my mother. Together we saw *Dumbo* and *Bambi,* classic children's films which were then almost new. I cried in misery on both occasions. In *Dumbo*, I wept when the baby elephant was separated from his mother, an atrocious possibility for a child whose only reliable adult possession was his own mother. In *Bambi* I cried when the fire threatened the beloved forest creatures. Perhaps my mother had had enough of cinema-going with a dimwit, for by the time I entered first grade I was merely *escorted* to the doors of the movie house on a Saturday afternoon and left to fend for myself in its darkened interior.

I went to the "show," as we called such excursions, with increasing enthusiasm. I patronized three local movie houses: the aforementioned Vista, the Los Feliz – on Vermont, north of Hollywood Boulevard – and my special favorite, The Campus, also located on Vermont, just south of Santa Monica and opposite Los Angeles City College. Each of these reserved a part of their weekend programming for youthful audiences, and I was a faithful worshipper at such shrines – and an altar boy at their refreshment counters, where I could try to stretch the few cents that had been granted me by my penny-pinching parents. To this day I can see the lobby of the Los Feliz every time I catch the peppermint whiff of a Necco

Wafer. I did not like Necco Wafers, but they were plentiful and cheap and one could make a roll of them last for a long time in the dark.

Our Saturday diet began with a few cartoons – which I enjoyed, while dismissing them as trivial and unreal. The show concluded with a cowboy film of some sort, Roy Rogers or Bob Steele. I liked these too, and I soon had my own holster, cap gun, and cowboy hat to signalize membership in this masculine fraternity. My greatest delight came from none of these, however, but from the *serials* that preceded the feature: tales of good and evil in which the triumph of the good would have to wait for *next* week's show, while a triumphant evil remained poised to undo the moral universe by doing in the hero or heroine.

Germans and Japs featured prominently as the evildoers in the adventures of Batman or The Phantom, and there was a lot of rope in evidence as the innocents in need of rescue were made to pay for their loyalty to the nation. How would our hero *ever* escape from the coffin dangling over the alligator pit? *What* could be used to stop the knives that were closing in on our hero as the walls of the elevator edged mercilessly closer to his costumed skin? The answers to these questions were usually a disappointment: the *question* was much more intriguing and, mulling it over, I would exit into the blinding light of the California afternoon, where my mother would pretend to listen with interest as I described each scene. That life could be *so* cruel; of this I had been utterly unaware before becoming a moviegoer.

One of the serials I watched was also a western. In it, Native Americans served as the evil oppressors of the righteous, and I was transfixed by their menacing appearance and savagery. In one haunting episode, cowboys and cowgirls were tied to the stake as the flames grew closer and the Indians shrieked with fury. I was overwhelmed with glorious dread. The forest creatures in *Bambi* had, at least, a chance to run from the awful flames. But these pinioned victims, from *where* would their salvation come? I would never know, for I missed the sequel, and so the question continued to burn as a masochistic fantasy fashioned casually and indifferently in the back lot of Republic Studios under the wholly wholesome aspiration of selling some popcorn to kids.

It was not long after this episode that *I* decided to experiment – not with rope, but with tape. In loving imitation of the terrifying Apaches,

I decided to don some of their war paint. I didn't know it was *paint*, but I thought I could replicate the look by using adhesive tape from the bathroom cabinet. I tried some crosses on my cheeks and forehead and then I got carried away and by the time my mother appeared on the scene I looked more like *The Mummy's Curse* than *Dances With Wolves*.

And my friend and abductor? I think of him as the true Apache, acting out his own version of some serial seen in another cinema. He was auditioning for the role of captor while I triumphed once again in my portrayal of victim. Pauline Kael, with whom I had a brief correspondence many years later, entitled a book of her reviews *I Lost It At The Movies*. I lost it at the movies too, but what I lost was the innocence of childhood.

I tried to regain it on the airwaves. I missed a good deal of instruction at Lockwood Elementary because of a very serious attack of the measles, one which kept me bedridden for almost six weeks. This illness presented my family with a considerable problem, since Etta had to work, and Ingolf frequently had commitments away from home. The solution, when I was at last in a convalescent stage, was to leave me to my own devices for much of the morning, with Etta coming back from the hospital at lunchtime to check on how I was doing. To give me something to do while I was bedridden, someone came up with the idea of putting the radio in my room. Brilliant idea! Before long I was addicted to the charms of the little brown box, listening for hours every morning and sometimes, when I managed to fight off feverish sleep, into the afternoon as well. And what could so command the attention of a child in his seventh year? Soap operas.

The soap opera was enjoying a golden age in the Forties, with advertisers on the national radio networks having discovered that the daytime drama was an ideal way of drawing the attention of a largely female audience to the excellence of their products. Many of the sponsors were, indeed, soap manufactures; it was, after all, Oxydol's Own Ma Perkins whose low key adventures in the lumber yard we were expected to take an interested in. Patent medicines and beauty preparations also figured frequently in these commercials and, as a consequence, this part of the broadcast meant nothing to me. I was only interested in the intriguing tales of deceit, treachery, mistaken identity, and above all, love, that unfolded each day, like Scheherazade's gabfest, without ever reaching a conclusion. *Would* it be possible for Helen Trent to find romance, even though she had now reached a senile thirty-five? *Was* it likely that Our Gal Sunday, a simple country girl from a mining town in Colorado, could find happiness as the wife of an aristocratic English lord? The travails of Young Doctor Malone and the Second Mrs Burton never ceased to engage my sympathetic attention. Childhood illnesses never seemed as discomfiting after I had discovered soap operas, for I knew that the sickroom would soon expand to include the remedial presence of all those conniving *femme fatales* and deceiving charlatans who peopled my soaps.

How wholesome a guide to real life did the seven year-old have here? At the outset of my listening mania I would not have had much experience in judging how the rest of the world, as opposed to my unique family, was supposed to behave. Ma Perkins did talk a little bit like Mrs. Smith, but most of the stories had an edge of vitality and importance that made our Westmorland world shrivel by comparison. Such confusions over the source of the real were compounded when one of the actresses read the national news at the beginning of the hour and then, saying goodbye to her co-workers in the booth, continued as a character in the soap that followed. Certainly I discovered the potential for many economic and emotional problems that did not seem to be a part of our world. I, like my stepfather before me, discovered that there was an East Coast that claimed to be the center of all things exciting. Chiefly I discovered the importance of romance.

No listener felt more keenly the distress of the soap heroine than one seven year-old bed-ridden boy in Los Angeles in the last year of the war. How I longed for a successful resolution of her many heart-rending dilemmas. How I hoped the nefarious plots of her feminine rivals would turn to ashes. How I urged her to remain steadfast in her quest, undeterred by the cads and interlopers who could never know her true value, as I, her worshipper, knew it in my heart. The voices of some of these heroines were so rich in splendor that to hear them speak the most mundane sentence was enough to rekindle all my adoration. The potent burbling of the organ, cranking out the theme song of these daily romances, was particularly riveting. After that, only a very paltry version of romance could go forward without the mawkish sweep of "Ah, sweet mystery of life, last night I found you."

Of course I knew of such a pallid union. Still years away from understanding the authentic elements of soap opera in the lives of my parents, I could only see their relationship as a weak echo of the promethean couplings I was privileged to monitor every weekday morning from my sickbed. And as much as I loved these people, I knew that my parents *were* weird.

22. A FOXTROT TOO FAR

For much of my life I have had trouble with water. I have managed, without struggle or discomfort, to keep myself reasonably clean; it is water in its other manifestations that has served as a malign force. Keeping the water *in* the radiator, keeping it *on* the roof, keeping it from turning my churning stomach into a fountain, and keeping myself afloat on its unwelcoming surfaces – each has been a struggle.

It wasn't always so. On August 6th, 1939, my mother reports that "Tony went stark naked into the ocean's edge and was so excited about it that he cried when forced to come away." The following April I insisted on going into an ocean choppy with high waves: "Tony couldn't get enough, and had not only no fear but was visibly fascinated in a way that astonished and almost frightened us, so violent was his urge." The same month I wanted to go into the water with a crocodile at the Griffith Park Zoo.

Perhaps my disenchantment began the day I ate too much water in Vicky Baum's pool. Certainly the following months already reveal an antipathy. On July 31st, 1940, my mother reported, somewhat disconsolately, that, "Our fearless, young Sicgfried is beginning to show fear for the first time in his life. Our water-baby suddenly is not only indifferent to going in, but fights *against* being taken." At the time my mother felt that I was just going through a ninny phase because I was also telling Ingolf not to drive so fast and setting up a terrific howl when she departed for the store without me. In this way she failed to note that my distrust of water was specific, profound and permanent. I escaped my parent's preoccupation with this subject by agreeing to enter a little wading pool sculpted from the sand on Santa Monica Beach, and thereafter I often enjoyed the sun and sand, particularly if accompanied by little Anne Morton, Arthur Morton's daughter and Lawrence's niece, but this did not mean I was ready for body surfing.

Eventually my parents decided that I needed systematic instruction in the natatory arts. Down on Vermont there was a large public swimming pool called the Bimini Baths. I can still recall Bimini's chlorinated air, seeping into every surface of the cavernous tiled edifice, and the taste of vinegary water running down my nose. With the same relish I would later muster for a trip to the dentist, I would accompany my purposeful mother on the bus as we crept south to this shrine of water torture. She would blow air into my black water wings until they held me as tightly as a blood pressure cuff. Then I would be floated on the water of the pool while my mother tried to cajole me into believing that this was fun. It wasn't fun because after a while the water wings would be withdrawn and I would be expected to flail about with my arms and legs and somehow remain afloat. Inevitably I sank like a stone. My mother persisted in these endeavors for quite a while, and Ingolf gave it a shot too, with no better luck. Finally they decided to wait until I was older, and to pass the instructional chores onto someone else.

When I try to recall my first act of rebellion against *authority*, an active, willful rebellion against authority's public face, against the commonweal, I usually return to an incident that marked the end of the summer of 1945. It too involved water.

In the summer of 1945 my parents (otherwise known in the outside world for their much-praised rationality and sensitivity) conceived the monstrous notion that it would be "good" for me to go away to summer camp. The little girl who lived next door to the Kellers, Sheryl Balinoff, had endured a similar trial the previous summer. Because a letter home was a requirement for admission to the dining hall, Sheryl had distinguished herself with the shortest letter in epistolary history – "Dear Moth," and my parents were sure that I could do even better if I put my mind to it. I had great reservations about this decision to repeat the summer camp experiment with a new guinea pig, and the term of *my* sentence – six weeks – seemed unduly harsh. Nevertheless, one sunny July day I found myself making a final plea for forgiveness just before that treacherous pair drove off in a cloud of fine California dust after abandoning me at Duffy's Camp, a hilly ranchero next to the Pala Indian reservation, a hundred miles or so from home.

I soon discovered that I was both the smallest and the youngest camper, and that my best chance of survival in such a hostile environment lay in remaining as *invisible* as possible. This wasn't easy to do on the morning after I had befouled my pajama pants, or the day I was sick before breakfast because I had experimented with swallowing someone's toothpaste. Invisibility was not easy to achieve because our every activity was supervised by a corps of keen counsellors, eager to assure us that each successive life-threatening experience would be *fun*. I did not wet myself when they took us to a ruin at midnight and terrorized us with ghost stories, but I did manage to bounce out of the saddle of a huge steed that chose to canter when I wanted it to walk. In all, I hated Duffy's Camp and begged, repeatedly, to come home. Such entreaties were particularly intense when Ingolf and Etta arrived for a mid-sentence visit. There was no parole.

Eventually, however, the final week of purgatory rolled around. I had almost survived my punishment when plans were announced for a poolside presentation to parents on Pick-Up day. As the particulars for this extravaganza were revealed, my horror grew. At last I had learned, during my stay at the camp, how to swim, so I could complete one length of the pool, and I had managed an approximation of the fox trot, which I was to use to get my partner back along the pool's rim to the starting point. I was not prepared to begin the process with a headfirst dive into the cruel waters – diving being an art form which those cheerful boy scouts responsible for out aquatic life had neglected to pass on. I had visions of my limp body lying on the pool's bottom as the waters closed over my innocent head – but rescue was at hand: my parents wrote to Mrs. Duffy, saying that they would be whisking me off to the San Diego Zoo on Pick-Up day and, alas, I would not be able to participate in the poolside pageant.

When I smugly passed this information on to the sun-dried gym teacher who had devised this torment, I discovered that there was no justice in this world, a notion that has often recurred. She lowered her megaphone for a moment and said, "Okay, but you still have to participate in today's rehearsal." Once again I faced the prospect of passing out of this world forever as I disappeared into the chlorinated waves.

It was a memorable day. Mrs. Duffy had just told us of another disappearance – much of the population of Hiroshima had just vanished under the authority of the atomic bomb and, without any understanding of the import of this announcement, I would now somehow have to save my own life.

Just before it was time to hurl myself into the unknown waters I asked if I could go to the bathroom. When my request had been granted, I dashed over to the ripe, fly-filled shack that served as the boys' outhouse (if only I had known how to reach it on the night of my sordid "accident"). I sat down on one of the polished wood holes. That's *all* I did – I sat. I sat in the warm, foul air of that place for forty-five minutes, sat until the last strains of the sickening fox trot down the hill had faded away and I knew the dress rehearsal was over. No one had noticed my absence. I had survived.

It is no wonder that I ended my stay at Duffy's Camp with the least demerits (and the least merits) of any other camper. In this incident I had perfected a survival pattern that transcended childhood: when the demands of authority are utterly unacceptable, try to oppose them without drawing too much attention to yourself. Sly deceiver, inspired fraud, perhaps today we would just say "lateral thinker."

I doubt that this is what my parents had expected me to learn when they insisted on this character-building ordeal. The summer of 1945 had been a period of great change, changes on the world stage, and many dramatic changes in our world. By September we were in a new home, I had entered a new school, and Ingolf had begun his new job.

Ingolf with parents, Paul ("Pappi") and Hilda Maria ("Mammi") in 1914.

Mammi with, from left, Holger, Anna-Britta, Ingolf and Gert, 1918.

A teenaged Etta with Fanny and Isadore Gordon, her parents.

Ingolf at 16, July, 1928; brother Holder is seated behind him.

A teenaged Ingolf at the piano.

Etta and Leroy in Zurich, ca. 1936.

Ingolf conducting in Zurich, ca. 1936.

The Zurich Opera entertains Richard Strauss on September 26, 1938.
Strauss is seated on the left. Ingolf is standing on the right.

PART II

1945-1958

23. CORNING STREET

When our family moved to 1955 1/2 Corning Street I was seven; we departed in 1952, when I was an adolescent fourteen. In these formative years I lived within a west Los Angeles community that still embraced a faith in illimitable possibilities. I grew up among neighbors who either expected, as we did, to own their own homes one day soon – or who knew, almost from the outset, that the red tiles on their white stucco imitation rancheros would soon be abandoned for something even *more* glorious in one of the burgeoning suburban settlements of Southern California.

Emphatically, the Dahls were still renters, the tenants of Mrs. Meyerowitz, who owned an eight unit court on the west side of Corning, midway between Sawyer Street and Guthrie Avenue. Our apartment was at the rear of the property, perched atop the garages of the occupants on our side of the court. In the front unit, on the other side, my father and stepmother made their home. And a few bungalows to the north, at 1931, Etta's sister Lillian and the rest of the Keller brood lived. I would not have to go far on Corning Street to find a close relative.

My world was bounded by four great boulevards: Venice, which still had its red streetcar on an embankment to the south, a more distant Pico to the north, Robertson a few blocks to the west, and nearby La Cienega to the east. My home territory stretched beyond these boundaries on occasion, but only just – and not very often. For most of the time I remained happily within the middle class streets of L.A. 34, coming to know each pavement, the inclines and descents, and the treasured sites of empty lots where dirt clods could happily fly when the grass was high after the winter rains.

North of the Kellers our block was quite recent in origin, the work of a developer named Steinkamp, who favored houses in a Mexican style that none of the Mexicans could afford. Our half of the block was humbler, a mixture of bungalows, apartment buildings, and – of course – our court. A few tall palms, including one in the front yard of the Quaglinos next door, brushed the skyline – but ours was the generation that had to plant most of the other trees on this street. I have revisited Corning several times in the past decades, and it has shrunk. The street seems so narrow, the houses pinched together, and – like so many other urban areas – it offers a dispiriting vista of neglect and blight, its former residents long gone to happier pastures and its spaces occupied by the dark faces that used to do only the odd jobs. It hardly seems to be the street on which I would climb joyously aboard the fragrant heaven of the Helm's Bakery van in search of a doughnut or pursue on my bike the ice cream man's seductive Good Humor jingle.

To reach our front door it was necessary to climb a flight of red cement steps. After a turn to the right you entered the front door and passed, on the left, the door of my mother's closet, and thereby penetrating a living room crowded with furniture, bookcases and a piano in the northeast corner. My mother, at some sacrifice to her own comfort, had managed to cram most of her possessions into the closet. It was so dense with her effects that it was only when company was due that she managed to get the door closed. On the west side of the living room a break in the wall admitted you to a small dining area at the northwest corner of the apartment. This space flowed into the kitchen where, after a few more years of growth, I still had to stand on a block of wood to complete my dishwashing chores. The proximity of kitchen to living room created many problems for Etta, including the dilemma of how to prepare meals without assailing the nostrils of rehearsing musicians. Even when there was only one musician in the adjoining room, there were problems: "Just as I am about to make eggs," my mother complained, "Igu says perhaps we can have quiet now."

At the south end of the kitchen you joined a hallway from the living room, passing, on your right, a bathroom with an ever widening gap in the plaster above the tub, and thereby immediately reaching the two bedrooms, mine at the southwest corner and my parents' at the southeast. Ingolf and Etta managed, once again, to stuff two double beds into their small sleeping space. There were just five rooms at Corning Street – no more than at Westmorland – though we did gain one of the garage spaces below.

These spaces were reached by a gravely alley that separated the backs of the houses on Corning Street from those on Holt, a block to the north. The alley was itself a place of wonder and opportunity for a young boy. Racing to the bottom of the steps you could turn left past the eugenia bush for a sprint to the garage, which soon became too crowded with junk to accommodate Black Peter – or you could waltz across to the marble ring that we had scratched into Mr. Quigley's dusty parking lot (when his wonderful brown 1930's gangster Packard was not present) – or you could turn right and stroll up the alley to a door cut in the Kellers' back fence.

This latter route was also important for Ingolf because, shortly after our arrival, my aunt and uncle decided to offer to him, as a studio, a storage room on the right side of their garage. It was soundproofed and his old upright found a new home. Many of the Dahl compositions of this era were forged at the desk of this small secret space hidden in the respectable folds of suburbia. Neither it nor the house at 1931 Corning survives, though our court was still standing when I last visited the area in 1992. After forty years the eugenia bush, whose red berries made such an agreeable stain when propelled with maximum force against the white t-shirt of an opponent, still flourished.

Etta was engaged in a perpetual struggle with objects in our Corning Street residence. There were two culprits in the crimes of our disorder and one of them is writing this book. Etta was not above using her famous right cross when pushed too far (I remember answering the call of a playmate below by emerging onto our porch, my eyes still filled with tears after such a blow, and explaining away the obvious evidence of my distress by blaming the smog). A more typical assault against confusion is revealed in the following list, dated February, 1950, enumerating both the misdemeanor and its effect on my allowance:

Addams & Evil slung on sofa 4 days (1 cent per day).	.04
Pillow case exposed	.01
Money scattered on table	.01
Light on in room, 1 hr Friday eve; ditto Saturday	.02
Unbreakable mirror in living room 2 days	.02
Left disorderly room & bed to go out & play Sunday	.01
Left sloppy soapy sink Sunday night	.01
Sailor hat all over house 3 days	.03
Dirty sock 2 days in room	.02
My pincushion & scissors in room	.01
Gum papers on living room floor Sunday to Sunday	.07
Ditto pencil	.07
Request to put laundry pile away unheeded 9 days	.09

This was how Etta handled one of her miscreants, but you couldn't dock the allowance of someone who was three times twelve, that perpetually preoccupied presence who was my stepfather.

Etta described Ingolf as a man for whom, "When his action on an object is finished, the object no longer exists." Burning lights, ski wax on the piano, books left on the floor, his fountain pen left open – these were Ingolf's crimes, faults which Etta could never decide whether to attribute to his unique psychology ("creative, introverted, egocentric") or merely to bad upbringing. You don't live with such a person, Etta concluded in some despair, you "live around him...Any other attitude is vain and catastrophic." The people he lives with, my mother continued, through no malice on his part whatsoever, "become his vassals." "I have learned," she wrote, "to trot after him, turn off his lights, pick up his books." It turns out that as bad as Ingolf may have been in this respect, he was better than he used to be:

> In the 13 years I have known him ...he has taken more and more cognizance of his real surroundings and become less diffuse, insulated and isolated. But I do not deceive myself that I have had any part in it. As a matter of fact I think he has developed better since, gradually, I have let him be.

Because clutter was endemic in our household, every square inch of flat surface was prized. Etta's "desk" was the top of an old fold-in Singer sewing machine, so "when I need to sew," she wrote:

> I shove aside the metronome, Mozart's Clarinet Concerto, a few topographical maps, a pile of ungraded music seminar papers, a leadless pencil, a musicological reference work, a list of available dehydrated foods or whatever else is in that corner of the nearby Steinway, and deposit my books there.

Next to Ingolf's difficulties with objects, Etta listed his "battle" with time, a battle that we all lost: "It is difficult for him to go to bed at night; it is difficult for him to get up in the morning." "Dear Dear Dear," a note to Ingolf began, "When do you want to arise?" In the box provided for response Ingolf has written, "Let me sleep." "When will you need the car?" "12:15," Ingolf has answered. If he actually observed this schedule it would have been a minor miracle in the life of a man who, according to his wife, saw "schedule as a shackle not a friend." On another occasion Etta woke my stepfather at 8:30 because he said he had to be in his office by 9:30. This action was repeated until 9:20, when he got up at last. Three *New*

Yorker articles later, at 11:30, he arose from the breakfast table. Sometimes Etta had to quit the house before Ingolf's *levee*. Even then she managed to continue the care and feeding of her husband from long-distance:

> Sir, your tardy rising I foresaugh,
> These proteinous ovals, thus are raugh
> Forgive this one involuntary flaugh
> In your repast. Sincerely Etta Waugh

It need hardly be added that waiting for the chronically over-booked Ingolf to arrive for dinner was like waiting for Godot and therefore, with rare exceptions, the long-suffering Etta had to serve the evening meal twice.

24. SENATOR DAHL ON THE FLYING RED HORSE

In the seven years between his appointment in 1945 and his first sabbatical in 1952, Ingolf's responsibilities at U.S.C. became ever more varied and time-consuming. He directed the university orchestra, acted as musical director for KUSC – the campus radio station, taught courses in music appreciation, opera repertory, music of the classical and early romantic periods, and film and radio music; he supervised individual students in orchestration, composition and conducting. He lectured to large classes, conducted seminars, and had many one-on-one sessions. Such private lessons were often the most emotionally and intellectually exhausting tasks in his crowded schedule but in the early Fifties he formed sustaining relationships with a number of pupils whose work he genuinely admired – including Donal Michalsky, Donald Aird, Paul Glass, and Tikey Zes.

As if he didn't have enough to do in his own classes, Ingolf was also increasingly in demand as a guest lecturer in both professional and amateur settings. In June of 1950 he spoke twice, once at a symposium during a contemporary music festival at Stanford ("Talk goes well – have a real feeling of contact, even jokes go over unexpectedly") and once at City College, where his topic was "Contemporary American Music."

In the early Fifties he established at U.S.C. a Collegium Musicum for the study and performance of Renaissance and Baroque music. Ingolf always attempted to make students (even non-performers) participate in the making of music itself. Hours had to be spent locating music that amateurs might play or sing with enjoyment and profit. It was a never-ending chore, as was the constant revision of old lectures and the writing of new ones.

There were also endless term papers, which Ingolf considered it his duty to correct himself – even if he was a semester behind in completing this task. Setting examination questions for advanced students was another onerous chore. And then there were those endless committee meetings and other academic rituals chaired by his bosses, Max Krone and then, for many years, Raymond Kendall. On January 10, 1947 Ingolf was elected a member of the U.S.C. Senate, an honor he greeted with the emphatic comment, "Damn it!"

Great energies were required to bring the student orchestra up to standard and it is typical of the man, who could have more easily achieved the national reputation he coveted by seeking assignments as a conductor of *professional* bodies, that he devoted so much time to a *university* orchestra, an undisciplined student ensemble whose members, for good reasons and bad, failed to show up for rehearsals of the most difficult repertoire. Ingolf believed that the university was a place for experiment and the introduction of works that might otherwise go unperformed in Los Angeles. Consequently he insisted on putting himself and his young charges to the test over and over again. But there were never enough string players and the brass players had to perform at Trojan football games and there were conflicts with opera and choral productions that destroyed the integrity of his rehearsals. "Terribly depressing turnout," Ingolf wrote after a Bruckner run-through in 1948, "I wish I could find another job. My nerves won't bear it any more!" On November 11, 1951 he noted that a performance "goes as well as possible – lots of little things, but the general idea comes," but the pressures lead to a serious asthma attack that drove him away from the post-concert celebration drinks at Carl's bar.

Although there were annual concerto programs in which talented soloists could present traditional concert fare, much of the rest of the programming was imaginative and innovative. Even when the composer was well known Ingolf often selected works never before performed on the West Coast; in his first four years with the orchestra works by Haydn,

Beethoven, Bruckner, Debussy, Ives, and Milhaud received such "premieres." At other times he had the orchestra stretched between the Baroque and the ultra-modern, particularly as a festival of modern music became a permanent part of the spring semester. Ingolf insisted that a good deal of modern *American* music be played at such concerts – George Gershwin, Aaron Copland, Ernst Toch, George Tremblay, and David Diamond – and he offered a number of works by U.S.C. composition department colleagues like Ernst Kanitz, Halsey Stevens and Robert Linn or by friends like Gil Grau, whose *Symphonic Variations in Two Movements* was dedicated to the conductor. A friend of the future was Lukas Foss. At a rehearsal of a Foss piece on April 8, 1952, Ingolf admitted, "goes lousy all around, this time for sure I have overreached myself," but by concert time on May 7 he was happy to find "everything above expectation!"

His belief that his students had not only achieved a satisfactory product but that they had *learned* something kept him at the podium year after year in programs that, according to John Garvey of the University of Illinois, were "almost unbelievable for a college orchestra." Reviewing a December 6, 1946 U.S.C Orchestra concert, Lawrence Morton wrote that Ingolf had brought "to his work as conductor the same conscientiousness and full-blown musicality that characterizes his work as a composer, pianist, and champion of new music in the community."

Every family with a child will know something of the rhythm of the academic year. Ingolf's appointment at U.S.C. fixed this rhythm even more deeply into the bloodstream of our rituals. Our annual psychological clock was set to the university calendar with its semesters, vacations, and summer schools. "End of School – hooray!!!" Ingolf exulted on June 18, 1946. On February 11, 1947 the entry reads, "First school day. I dread it, but it goes better than expected." So the pattern was fixed and, half a century later, I remained in its grip.

In spite of his new foothold in academia, however, Ingolf continued to flirt with the world of show business – where extra paydays provided a supplement to his meager university salary. In the summer of 1946, for instance, he spent several weeks as Gracie Field's accompanist at the Cal-Neva Lodge, Lake Tahoe. "Gracie is wonderful!!!" he reported after their first show on July 2, but the beautiful mountain setting had failed to dispel in the accompanist periods of dizziness, weakness and chest complaints.

Another two-week session occurred in April, 1947, when Gracie performed at Ciro's on Sunset Boulevard. That same year our family celebrated Christmas early so that Ingolf could work with Gracie for another two weeks in Las Vegas. I find it somewhat hard to picture my often puritanical and disapproving stepfather in this den of luxury and vice, but Las Vegas was still in its infancy then, and Ingolf could let down his hair (what there was left of it) when he was away from home. "I don't play two good hunches at roulette," he records on December 30. The next night he attended a New Year's Eve Party thrown at the Flamingo by Gracie's husband, Monty Banks, at which Jerry Lester and Eddie Cantor were also present. "Let me grow, let me be strong and humble and grateful" was his somewhat saccharine New Year's prayer. When he was not needed by Gracie he spent much of his time as far away from Las Vegas as possible, with much desert sight-seeing and a good deal of skiing on Mt. Charleston.

Some eight years later, when Ingolf was deeply entrenched in his academic routine, the telephone woke him from a nap on February 8, 1956. It was Gracie, attempting to coax him out of retirement for another engagement as her accompanist at the Statler Hotel. "What an upheaval," he wrote, but after securing permission from his bosses for this unusual form of moonlighting, he accepted, and two days later, "like a boy waiting for his first date," he met Gracie for their first rehearsal. There were even a few arrangements that needed attention and once again my stepfather found himself pouring over "One For All And All For One." Opening night was February 16 (one "good" show and one "lousy"). "I play like a pig," he wrote on the 23rd, but he was more positive about the star of the show – "Gracie," he wrote on March 5, "surpasses herself. *Very* wonderful and exciting." "I play well, good crowd, she is terrific," he noted four days later, after a show that Etta attended. Ingolf was obviously a bit embarrassed by this showbiz comeback – so remote from his usual professional image – and he tried to keep news of the engagement from most of his colleagues. Around the house we joked about Ingolf "prostituting himself." One night one of his own students, Vernon Read, showed up in the audience with a date and had to chase his reluctant mentor down a hallway before the blushing professor allowed himself to be caught. Vernon was sworn to secrecy.

Indeed, more than once Ingolf shifted all of his school appointments so that he could *clandestinely* answer studio calls. He often played piano and harpsichord parts on the Warner Brothers sound stage for Max Steiner, whose scores for *Pursued* and *Woman in White* were recorded in 1947 and 1948. In 1946 Ingolf and John Crown were both called on to play piano parts in the musical biography *Song of Scheherazade* because, as Etta would have it, the producers must have thought Rimsky and Korsakov were two separate composers.

Ingolf's last major association with the world of commercial radio took place in the fall of 1946, just as he was beginning his second year at U.S.C. This was work which he undertook for the Victor Borge radio program on NBC, a national show that was broadcast every Monday evening at 6:30. Ingolf served as arranger and conductor on this show and even had a hand in preparing "The Flying Red Horse Theme," which Mobilgas used as its signature tune. I suppose my stepfather was not particularly impressed by the opportunity of working with Lucille Ball, Edward G. Robinson or Lana Turner, but he was thrilled when Marlene Dietrich sang "Ich bin von Kopf bis Fuss"–"How that takes me back. Oh Lord, oh Lord." For the Danish pianist-comedian who hosted the show Ingolf arranged Chopin and Brahms medleys, often working against impossible deadlines again. "Arrange Chopin medley and cues till 6 in the morning," he wrote on September 7, a task he evidently completed only with Lawrence Morton's help. I remember being taken to see one of the Borge broadcasts, safely ensconced with my mother behind the glass of the recording booth; Etta was always a sucker for Borge's oral punctuation routine. The last of the West Coast shows took place on October 21, when the series departed for New York and Ingolf was left to resume his more usual activities.

25. A SOUTHLAND FIELD DAY

Escaping for a short period from the drudgery and frustrations of student orchestras, Ingolf did have a number of opportunities of leading professional ensembles during the post-war decade. On April 17, 1946 he lead a group of Music Guild performers in Bach's *Musical Offering* and later that summer he conducted the first of several concerts given by the Beverly Hills Philharmonic Society, a group of highly skilled studio musicians who gave "rehearsal concerts" of works seldom heard by Los Angeles concert-goers. Strongly conscious of his own association with the premiere of the work, Ingolf conducted Hindemith's *Mathis* on September 11, 1946; in January, 1947 he led this orchestra in readings of Walter Piston's *Second Symphony* and Copland's *Rodeo*.

On September 19, 1949 he lead a Roof ensemble in Schoenberg's *Pierrot Lunaire*. "It goes well," he noted in his diary, and soon thereafter Schoenberg called to complement him on the performance, which had been staged in honor of the composer's seventy-fifth birthday. On October 7, 1951 Ingolf again conducted *Pierrot*, in Santa Barbara, but this time the event took the form of a memorial concert, for Schoenberg had died in July.

In the fall of 1949 KFWB broadcast a "Music of Today" program featuring ensembles conducted on several occasions by my stepfather. Writing in the *New York Herald Tribune* Virgil Thomson praised Ingolf's conducting of the Thomson *Sonata da chiesa*. After two months of rehearsals Ingolf ascended the podium to conduct the West Coast premiere of Stravinsky's cantata *Les Noces*.

Ingolf's major podium assignment in 1951 and 1952 was as musical director of Gian-Carlo Menotti's *The Consul*. The West Coast premiere took place on December 5, 1951, with a production designed by Carl Ebert and presented in Bovard Auditorium. Ingolf conducted more than twenty performances, including some in March at the Philharmonic downtown and some in San Francisco in April. As I recall, Ingolf hated this work, though he greatly admired some of the singers.

As a keyboard performer Ingolf had many responsibilities in the first few years of his life as an academic musician. He gave many solo recitals, particularly on KUSC, where he continued to introduce, often with insufficient rehearsal time, complicated modern and well as more conventional fare. In October, 1945, the Music Guild presented a Bach festival in which all of the Brandenburg Concertos were conducted by Otto Klemperer. When Alice Ehlers, a U.S.C. colleague, sprained two fingers in an automobile accident, Ingolf replaced her as the harpsichordist in the ensemble and enjoyed a great success. Playing the solo part in the *Fifth Concerto* Ingolf was the sensation of the afternoon and, according to one reviewer, brought the house down with his brilliant performance – "Wild applause and calls of Bravo, Bravo followed the close of the selection."

Honegger, Copland, Kodaly and Stravinsky were among the Twentieth Century composers whose work Ingolf presented in solo concerts during these years. In late 1950 he and the cellist Kurt Reher travelled to Arizona to play two concerts which included Brahms, Telemann, Grieg, Beethoven and Ingolf's new *Cello Duo*. The first event took place in Tucson on November 26 and appears to have been the occasion for Ingolf's first meeting with the composer Elliott Carter, who was in attendance.

Ingolf also enjoyed collaborating with the pianist of the Los Angeles Philharmonic, Shibley Boyes, in concerts of Mozart, Schubert and more modern works. The two gave a number of four-hand concerts over KUSC and on KFAC's Sunday afternoon series, which was broadcast live from the County Museum in Exposition Park. Shibley was a great favorite in our household, a painter as well as a pianist – her intelligent and humorous presence shining through a broken-nosed face. Her memories of work with Ingolf focused on his "child-like joy" and his "profound seriousness." "His standards of performance," she recalled, "were challenging almost beyond accomplishing – but this made playing with him so wonderfully exciting."

Ingolf was also proud of one other piano partnership during this period – because he had been chosen to participate in it by Stravinsky himself. This was a performance on October 4, 1948 of the maestro's *Double Concerto*, in which the second soloist was the composer's son, Soulima.

In the early Fifties Ingolf continued to maintain his reputation as both a solo and an ensemble player – "one of the greatest pianists in the Southland," David Raksin described him to an interviewer in October, 1950. On March 6 of that year Ingolf played the piano part in the first West Coast performance of Alban Berg's *Chamber Concerto*, a Wilshire Ebell concert conducted by Izler Solomon. "I am getting nervous about it," he wrote after the rehearsal on February 12, but by concert time all of the butterflies had flown away.

In May, 1951 Ingolf made his first appearance at the Ojai Festival, an annual event with which he was to have a long association in the future. On this occasion he participated, with members of the American Art Quartet, in the West Coast premiere of Aaron Copland's *Piano Quartet*.

Inevitably my stepfather's most frequent concert appearances were under the auspices of Evenings on The Roof, an organization which was allied for some seasons with Alfred Leonard's Music Guild in the presentation of concerts at the Wilshire Ebell Theater. Ingolf served on the boards of both of these organizations and I remember a number of strategy sessions in our living room on Corning Street with Peter Yates, Lawrence Morton, and the Roof's secretary, Mary Jeannette Brown. Ingolf could rarely say no when asked to serve on some worthwhile committee, especially in these early years. On February 10, 1947, the same day he became a faculty senator, he received news that he had been placed on two other bodies, including the Music Committee of the Hollywood Bowl.

Ingolf appeared nine times on Roof or Music Guild programs in the 1945-1946 season. The pace of this activity seems staggering today, with another concert looming on the horizon every two or three weeks. Most frequently he was joined with others in chamber recitals of music that he had no doubt helped to choose: Beethoven, Bach, Brahms, Satie, Schubert, Bartok, Copland and Mozart. The concert of January 7, 1946, so typical of the many in which my stepfather performed for Roof audiences, was referred to as a "field day" for Ingolf by C. Sharpless Hickman in the *Christian Science Monitor*. Ingolf and Shibley used a single piano to perform Harold Shapero's *Sonata For Piano Duet* – a "miraculous feat," according to the *Citizen News* reviewer, one that was so enthusiastically received that the pianists had to respond to the applause by repeating the first movement. ("You are truly a composer's performer," Shapero wrote.) Ingolf then teamed with Sol Babitz in the *First Sonata* for violin and piano by Charles Ives, and the concert concluded as Ingolf accompanied soprano Sara Carter in Hindemith's *Das Marienleben*.

Teacher, conductor, performer, for many a musician this would have been a sufficiently lengthy list of duties. But for Ingolf such a list would have left out the most important task of all, composition.

In 1946 Ingolf began work on a new piece, one that had its premiere at a Roof concert on January 20, 1947. This was the *Duo* for cello and piano, a project that is first mentioned on August 23, 1946. The first movement was completed by September 22 and the second by October 13. Two more movements were finished in time for rehearsals with Kurt Reher. "Kurt plays magnificently," Ingolf noted on the night of the premiere.

The work was praised by Gail Kubik, recommended to the publisher B. Schott by Stravinsky, and it drew a rave review in the *Arizona Daily Star* when Ingolf and Reher toured with it in 1950 – "Dahl's music has the breadth and depth of universality, an all too rare quality among moderns, and it is obvious why he has such an outstanding reputation." Noting elements of expressionism, perhaps inevitable in music for the cello, Lawrence Morton also praised Ingolf's new composition in *Script* "as a work of impressive size, serious intent, and distinguished achievement... It is thus a product of the same climate that produced the first movement of Stravinsky's latest Symphony and the whole of Aaron Copland's *Piano Sonata*." But Lawrence also noted that the *Cello Duo*, in embracing the Central European Romantic Tradition, covered ground "that Stravinsky actively rejects and that Copland considers American music well rid of."

"Completed" and "finished" are two verb forms that one may never use with any confidence when writing about the music of my stepfather. By 1949 he was revising the *Duo* and thereafter he excised one movement and presented it as a separate composition, *Notturno*. As late as 1969 he was still making changes in the remaining movements.

For Etta Ingolf played the first bars of a new solo piano work called *Hymn* in November, 1947, and by December 3 the work was finished. Practice was furious for the next few days and on December 8 the work was performed at a Roof concert, paired with the last surviving movement of the old piano suite, *Toccata*. The two were performed together as *Hymn and Toccata* for a number of years but when, in the 1960's, the pianist Ronald Tarr asked to play *Hymn* alone, the composer agreed, regarding the more recent work as stronger than its companion and discouraging any further coupling of the pair.

Commenting on the Roof concert in *Overture* George Antheil (the self-styled "Bad Boy of Music") gave Ingolf one of those favorable reviews a composer would rather not have – "The best work on the program was Ingolf Dahl's *Hymn and Toccata* for piano. At least it was the best constructed and most effective. But how sad to write neo-classical music in 1947 when that Parisian rage went out of fashion as long ago as 1936." Several years after Ingolf's death Michael Tilson Thomas commissioned Lawrence Morton to score an orchestral version of *Hymn* for a concert with the Pittsburgh Philharmonic, a version which the conductor also recorded on an all-Dahl compact disc in 1994.

The *Hymn* was only one of several compositions on which Ingolf worked in the concluding months of 1947; he also completed a trio for clarinet, violin and cello – begun the previous year. There is some evidence that the work originally bore the title "Souvenir de Suisse." It was dedicated to Irene and Eduard Hartogs, Zurich friends, and the idea for the theme was suggested to Ingolf by Edu, a clarinetist and conductor, who had noticed that the legend on the side of every Swiss railway carriage – SBB/CFF (for *Schweizer Bundesbahn/Chemin de fer Fedérale*) could be transposed into musical notation. This was precisely the kind of starting hint that Ingolf always enjoyed and with a six note motif (E-flat, B-flat, B-flat, C,F,F) he raced off into a playful, jazzy, melodic, strictly organized series of transposed, expanded, contracted and inverted variations on these notes. He even included a faint echo of the fifths and fourths of Swiss folk music and, as always, brought his soloists through a rough series of challenges by which the particular qualities of their separate instruments might be sounded. To me, the music has always seemed an especially happy and outgoing exercise, not diminished by a more thoughtful central section.

Eventually Ingolf decided to call the work *Concertino A Tre* but a proofreading error during Arrow Music's publication of the work several years later reduced this to *Concerto A Tre* and this became the official title. It was later published by European American Music.

The work was the first since the brass piece to elicit national acclaim and attention. Henry Cowell wrote Ingolf that it was "a wonderful piece, the best small chamber work I have seen for some time." Halsey Stevens told Ingolf ("to his modestly acknowledged glee") that the *Concerto A Tre* was "one of the very few works of another composer that I could wish I had written." Aaron Copland accepted the piece for publication on behalf of the editorial board of Arrow Music and it had a long career as a favorite among chamber music ensembles, a success hastened by a brilliant recording of the work on Columbia Records' prestigious Modern American Music series. Ingolf was first notified of its inclusion on June 26, 1950 when he received a letter from Virgil Thomson, chairman of a board of selectors, which also included Copland, Cowell, Goddard Lieberson and William Schuman.

Ingolf never set easy tasks for his instrumentalists. Writing from the University of Illinois John Garvey wrote the composer, "I regret to say that none of the clarinetists in the orchestra could handle the part, mainly because of the brainwork involved rather than any lack of technical facility." No such problem faced the ensemble which recorded the work for Columbia on December 15, 1950: Mitchell Lurie, clarinet, and the husband and wife team of Victor Gottlieb, cello, and Eudice Shapiro, violin. A very talented violinist and pedagogue Eudice Shapiro also helped Ingolf with the editing of the *Concerto A Tre* at publication time and she and Victor had also been part of the ensemble that provided the first public performance, a benefit concert for the Idyllwild School of Music and Arts on April 24, 1948.

A few weeks earlier, on March 8, another new composition received its premiere at a Roof concert. This was the *Divertimento* for viola and piano, which Ingolf had written for his colleague Milton Thomas, whose knowledge of the instrument was relied upon in the composition process and in later editorial revisions. Thomas had suggested that Ingolf write such a work before our family undertook a trip to Sweden and that is why, in August 1947, we find Ingolf sketching ideas while roped to his brother Holger on a glacier and in his tent after bad weather had driven the brothers from their course. In the event, there was a mighty rush to complete the piece in time for the first performance. Thomas came to rehearse the just completed first movement on January 29th – "It is good!" On February 23, the second movement "just ready," he came for another run-through. On March 1, a week before the concert, the violist arrived to rehearse the last movement, but the final coda was only in sketches. Indeed, the last note was not written until five days before the premiere!

Ingolf used an Appalachian melody ("The Mermaid") as the basis for one of the movements and the work has a very American flavor throughout. At the same time it is one of those Dahl compositions which seeks to exploit the full range of sonorities available to the instrument. Stravinsky, who attended the premiere, called the next day, describing the work as "the best viola-piano sound I have ever heard...A very serious piece." The work also excited Michael Mann, who called it "the most *effectful* piece I know in the entire viola literature written in the last two decades." He and Yalta Menuhin toured Europe with the work in the next few years. In August, 1950 the *Divertimento* received the publication award of the Society for the Publication of American Music, whose editions were first issued by Schirmer and then by Theodore Presser. After Ingolf's death

Protone issued a recording featuring Milton Thomas and Georgia Akst in an album whose cover collage was designed by Eve Babitz.

I think it has become clear that Ingolf's first few years as a full-time academician also proved to be extremely fruitful ones in his life as a composer, a period of great creativity and invention. These efforts were soon capped by a new major work, his first for large ensemble, the beginning of a movement toward orchestral music that would season his creative activity in the next decade.

Sometime in the spring of 1948 the saxophone virtuoso Sigurd Rascher wrote to Ingolf to complain of the lack of suitable concerti for his instrument and to express his desire for a largescale work which he could use on his tours. Intrigued by the possibility of writing for the saxophone, Ingolf began the task in earnest the next winter, evidently undeterred by the raised eyebrows of Stravinsky who, when informed of the project, said, "I don't know, to me a saxophone always sounds like a pink slimy worm." As usual, Ingolf was working against a performance deadline. The last note was added on March 23, 1949 and a desperate attempt was made to prepare the parts for soloist and orchestra. "At school, correcting parts, till 6 in the morning – hell," Ingolf noted on March 31. The music was dispatched on April 10 and the premiere took place on May 17 in Urbana, with Rascher as soloist and Mark Hindsley conducting the University of Illinois Concert Band. Naturally, two revisions followed this first performance, as Ingolf reduced the size of the accompanying ensemble. The *Concerto For Alto Saxophone and Wind Orchestra* has been a favorite show piece for a number of outstanding saxophonists including Rascher, Fred Hemke of Northwestern University, and Harvey Pittel, Ingolf's own student at U.S.C. Pittel had played the work 42 times by 1979, when he edited Ingolf's piano reduction of the score for the publishers European American Music, who also handle rental of score and parts.

A work that explores the tonal range of the instrument in a manner that might please a jazz saxophonist, the *Concerto* is full of diverting melodies, good spirits, and driving energy. It is certainly one of my favorites and I was always perplexed that the work had never been recorded commercially. This lapse was remedied in Miami in January, 1994 when Michael Tilson Thomas recorded the piece for Argo-Decca, with John Harle as the soloist, accompanied by the New World Symphony.

Ingolf did not "hear" the work until September 1, 1949, when Sigurd Rasher brought recordings of his performance to Middlebury, where Ingolf was engaged in summer school activities. Writing in the third person, my mother noted, "That is an experience that shakes both Ingolf and Etta to the core."

26. THREE FRIENDSHIPS

One day in the late Forties, as I was playing with my cousins in their driveway at 1931 Corning Street, I was surprised to see a large sedan pull up at the curb. The driver, a friendly looking man with a middle-aged face and round horn-rimmed glasses, leaned out of the window. We clearly recognized one another, though I was not quite sure to whom I was speaking. "Do *you* like music?" he asked. I responded with a loyal monosyllabic "Yes," and he reached into the back seat of his huge car and produced two 78 albums featuring work by his own sextet. I was being addressed by the King of Swing, Benny Goodman.

Ingolf and Benny had met in September, 1946, when my stepfather was serving as the musical director on the Victor Borge show. Goodman was a regular on this series and because of his great interest in classical music he and Ingolf were soon playing chamber music together. Ingolf mentions a Brahms and Hindemith session on October 20, Milhaud and Debussy on December 31. The Gottliebs were added for Brahms and Beethoven on January 9, 1947, and, of course, it was Benny Goodman who joined them in the first public performance of the Dahl *Concerto A Tre* on April 24, 1948.

Benny paid Ingolf a fee of $20 a "sitting" for what amounted to private lessons in the classical repertoire, but, Ingolf noted on May 15, 1947, "There is a real friendship." Most of the early sessions took place at Goodman's home but, after the arrival of the Marcus family Steinway from Stockholm at the end of 1947, some of these meetings took place on Corning Street – which is how the famous clarinetist had known which boy to offer his albums to. Ingolf did several arrangements for Benny as well, including a cadenza for the Mozart *Clarinet Concerto*.

The Dahls and the Goodmans saw each other socially on a number of occasions and Etta fell in love with another infant, the Goodman's daughter

Rachel. Benny and his wife Alice came to hear Ingolf and Gracie at Ciro's in April, 1948 – "What wonderful people," Ingolf added. Benny had also been present at the Roof premiere of the viola *Divertimento* on March 8 of the same year. "Did you learn all the jazz in my house?" he asked the composer afterwards. Ingolf also met a former member of Goodman's jazz ensemble, the pianist Mel Powell. Powell was embarking on a new career as a composer of "serious" music and he and Ingolf became friends. Powell's wife, the actress Martha Scott, was a particular favorite of Etta's.

Benny Goodman was also the inspiration for Ingolf's only significant composition activity in the early Fifties, a period during which the furious pace of his creative life began to decline. Indeed, in the three year period from 1949 to 1952 Ingolf completed only one work, a two-minute *Invention* for solo piano dated January 20, 1950, but not performed. But he did labor on another major orchestral piece, one commissioned by Goodman on December 30, 1949. "Very excited, apprehensive," Ingolf wrote two days later, as he began sketches for the *Symphony Concertante* for two clarinets and orchestra – a work that Goodman hoped to play with the classical virtuoso Reginald Kell. Ingolf met Kell at Goodman's on April 8, 1950, a day on which he noted some progress on the concerto, "bit by bit, slow, oh so slow." On July 2 he reported, "Three wonderful days on *Symphony Concertante* – sketch ahead and am beginning to get really into it." A half-year passed before, on December 31, he could add, "finish 8 allegro bars, very happy to be rolling again." "It looks good," he noted three days later. There was evidently enough material now for a brief run-through on January 20, 1951 at Goodman's, Ingolf making an instant reduction as he sat at the piano and bringing Merritt Buxbaum with him to tackle the second clarinet solo. The composer reports getting close to the end of the first movement on February 8 but when he re-examined what he had written he declared himself "disgusted – nothing new – a mixture of vulgarity and pretentiousness." Progress was also slowed because Ingolf evidently burned a sketch by mistake. On February 19 he wrote, "First Movt. finished – (?)."

On March 22 he showed the work to his U.S.C. colleague Leon Kirchner, but their examination of the composition convinced Ingolf that a better ending was needed. James Berdahl, who completed a doctoral dissertation on Ingolf's work several years after the composer's death, gives the completion date for the first movement as September 3, 1951. In the meantime Ingolf seems to have begun work on a slow movement as well, laboring on it from the fall of 1951 to the summer of 1952. The first complete version of the piece was not finished until December, 1952, three years after the work had begun. And then, of course, this turned out to be not the end of the story at all. The project, as we will see, was doomed – not least because of the difficulty of getting Goodman and a second soloist together for a premiere. Goodman commissioned many concerti from leading modern composers but it was Ingolf's bad luck to get lumbered with the *double* concerto impediment.

At the premiere of the *Viola Divertimento* on March 8, 1948 Ingolf had been complimented, as we have seen, by Benny Goodman and Igor Stravinsky. There was a third great figure present as well, and his comment was, "I wish you had written it for violin." The speaker was Joseph Szigeti, the great Hungarian virtuoso. Ingolf had met him in the early Forties and had visited the violinist's beautiful home in the Palos Verdes Estates as early as 1944 to play Mozart and run through the Stravinsky *Duo Concertante* with the maestro. The following year he had returned, with Otto Klemperer also present, for readings of Berg and Busoni on "a treasured afternoon" during which the conductor talked about Mahler and Nikisch. Etta and I were guests at Palos Verdes at least once. I remember the hospitality of Wanda Szigeti and the sun shining on the hedges of the beautiful grounds.

As Ingolf and the Gottliebs had played music with Benny Goodman so they also appeared for music-making sessions at Szigeti's in 1947. "Szigeti plays like a wizard," Ingolf noted after hearing his friend play the Stravinsky *Divertimento* in January of that year. In 1950, when Szigeti played Bach solo sonatas, Ingolf described the event as "one of the summits of experience."

In the summer of 1947 he and the violinist began work on a major editing project, a reconstruction of the Bach *Violin Concerto in D Minor*. After getting through two movements Ingolf discovered some additional original materials and started over again. The two spent a good deal of time working together at the Szigeti home in June of 1949, Ingolf fatigued and Joska querulous – "He is such a problem child – Wanda is just heroic, how can she continue to bear it?" "How bad to be imprisoned in all this work," Ingolf complained, "and the beach right below there, the yellow sand." Szigeti recorded the new version of the Bach concerto twice and in 1950 Boosey & Hawkes agreed to handle the reconstructed version on a rental basis and, after Ingolf had provided a piano reduction, to publish the latter. Here Szigeti was credited with "editorial collaboration and editing of the violin part," but we can assume that the lion's share of the labors on this project were undertaken by my stepfather.

Ingolf's friendship with Igor Stravinsky was to undergo a subtle change in the period we have now reached. My stepfather continued to see his mentor both socially and as a collaborator on a number of projects. Visits to the Stravinsky home at 1260 Wetherly Drive were still treasured moments for the younger man. Often he saw the composer alone; at other times the house was full of interesting guests. (Ingolf reports seeing Aldous Huxley there on April 14, 1952.) Stravinsky was a captivating raconteur and his accounts of travel experiences, dreams, and the origin of musical ideas never failed to fascinate his protégé. On a number of occasions the Stravinskys and the Dahls dined out together; thus in March 1947 the older couple helped the younger one celebrate their seventh wedding anniversary at the Beachcomber restaurant. The previous August Ingolf and Etta had been Stravinsky's guests at the Players, following a day in which Woody Herman had driven Ingolf and the maestro to a rehearsal of the *Ebony Concerto*. Stravinsky often appeared at rehearsals of his own work; during a run-through of the *Symphony of Winds* on January 30, 1948, Ingolf wrote, "The music is overwhelming. What a genius, what perfection, what sounds. Can one do anything beyond it?" As we shall see, Ingolf's idolatry did have its limits. Stravinsky's *Mavra* "seems just terribly off," he wrote a few years later.

When they met alone Ingolf often had the opportunity of hearing Stravinsky discuss his latest music, of hearing recordings of these works, and of examining works still in manuscript. "What a moment!" Ingolf enthused after such a session in June, 1946. The ballet *Orpheus*, in 1947, and the opera *The Rake's Progress*, in 1948, were among works Ingolf saw in their earliest stages. He also continued to benefit from the composer's suggestions on the interpretation of earlier works that Ingolf would soon play publicly. Ingolf performed the Stravinsky *Tango* and the *Piano Rag Music* on the same October, 1948 concert that had featured the *Double*

Concerto, benefiting from the maestro's advice during a run-through on October 3.

Ingolf also pursued a number of publishing projects at Stravinsky's request, acting as a kind of semi-official interpreter of the master's current thinking on musical subjects. Stravinsky suggested that he write the notes for the New York Philharmonic program at the time the orchestra presented the premiere of the *Symphony in Three Movements* on January 26, 1946. "We all read your Stravinsky notes," Copland wrote, "in fact I don't ever remember 'notes' getting such wide publicity. Sometimes the 'notes' seemed even more fascinating than the notes of the score." Ingolf wrote liner notes for several record jackets at this time and published three articles on Stravinsky's work: "Stravinsky in 1946" in *Modern Music*, "Igor Stravinsky on Film Music" in *Musical Digest*, also in 1946, and "The New Orpheus" in *Dance Index* in 1947. The interview that elicited Stravinsky's views on film music was completed on May 3, 1946: "He is so sweet and plays me records of the symphony – the *greatest* music! I am again overwhelmed." Ingolf also reviewed new work by Stravinsky as well as other composers in *Notes*. Finally, another project completed in 1947 was the English translation of the *Poetics of Music*, the Charles Eliot Norton lectures which Stravinsky had given in 1942. These were now published in a new edition by Harvard University Press.

This assignment came at a time when Ingolf was still busy with the Borge radio program, in September 1946, and he decided to enlist the aid of a French scholar as his co-translator in the project, Arthur Knodel. Knodel was still working on his Ph.D. dissertation and was at the beginning of a long career in the French Department at U.S.C. A very tall, large-boned and good-humored man, Knodel became a close family friend at this time. He was a frequent guest at our home, particularly at holiday and party times – when his wit and linguistic abilities were enlisted in our family's endless word game rituals. Like Ingolf, he suffered from a lung complaint, tuberculosis in his case, and he was enduring a period of enforced leisure in 1946, giving him time to work with Ingolf on the Stravinsky project. "We would retire to my upstairs room," he wrote to me in 1979:

> And there we would go over what I had translated in a first rough draft. We were quite ruthless with each other's suggestions for translating various difficult details, and I immediately came to

have great respect for Ingolf's abilities, and also for his tactfulness, because he was frequently adamant, but never crude or bullying. I remember that when the job was finally completed he insisted that my name be put before his – 'so that it can help along your career.' I protested, but that's the way it came out.

On February 17, 1949 Ingolf completed another unusual assignment for Stravinsky. The composer, claiming damage to his professional reputation, had sued the Leeds Music Company for listing him as the author of "Summer Moon," a watered down juke box version of music from the *Firebird*. Ingolf was called to the stand as an expert witness, ("balding, bespectacled professor," the *Daily News* had it) and he was quoted as attacking popular music as an "abomination," though close examination of the remarks attributed to my stepfather reveals that it was *popular versions* of the classics and not popular music itself that exercised the b.b.p.

The intensity of Ingolf's friendship with Stravinsky, at any rate, was about to suffer an eclipse. This was due to the arrival on the scene of the talented young conductor, Robert Craft, who became a member of the Stravinsky household at about this time. "Meet Robt. Craft," Ingolf noted on August 6, 1948, "cute college student type." The two younger musicians became friends and collaborators on many projects (not excluding the skits they rehearsed for the Stravinksy's New Year's Eve party on December 31, 1950), but Ingolf continued to experience ambiguous feelings about Craft's presence, for it meant that Stravinsky had *another* always accessible confidante on musical matters. Similarly, Ingolf was vexed by Craft's influence over the maestro – feeling particularly perturbed by the problem of sorting out the origins of statements attributed to Stravinsky in the many Stravinsky-Craft conversation volumes that were soon to appear. I remember Ingolf and Lawrence grumbling repeatedly about ideas in these books that seemed to them to be more Craft than Stravinsky, and Ingolf was also distressed by the artistic directions that Stravinsky took under the influence of Craft, who had a keen interest in experimental styles and who encouraged the composer Stravinsky to follow new paths that, for Ingolf, amounted to whoring after false gods.

In view of later even more radical challenges to conventional composition techniques (music created by scissors, sythesizer, computer or the throw of the dice) it is hard to appreciate today the ferocity with which the Stravinsky vs. Schoenberg debates of the 1940's were conducted by Ingolf and his associates. Adherence to one school or another affected careers, it strained friendships, it lead to rewards and punishments in the highly politicized world known as art. In spite of making his own preferences known Ingolf did insist on keeping the whole matter within proper proportions; he was never a polemicist and he also admired much of Schoenberg's work – if not the angst-filled formula-ridden offerings of his disciples. When George Rochberg began to write twelve-tone music Ingolf twitted him gently, "I hear you've taken the veil." After the spring modern music symposium in April 1951, Ingolf reported, "Poll: the atonal school carried the day (depressed)."

Even I, who had no knowledge whatsoever of the terms of the debate, was particularly sensitive to the side-taking nature of my stepfather and his friends. When a piece of music went missing from Ingolf's piano in 1949 – when I was eleven – I got a good laugh from the musicians at Middlebury when I blurted out, "Maybe a spy from Schoenberg stole it." "Big argument about chromaticism," Ingolf repeated on December 28, 1951, a day on which music student Larry Moss had come to lunch. That night I again succeeded in amusing my stepfather by trying out my French accent, "I hear Larry's in z'ozer camp."

Now the suspicion that Robert Craft had succeeded in getting the beloved creator of neo-classicism, Ingolf's ancestral breeding ground, to experiment with Schoenbergian techniques in some of his newer compositions seemed to Ingolf a betrayal of much of what he had come to believe, a rejection of the stylistic influences that were so strong in Dahl compositions of the period.

Furthermore Ingolf had accepted the great composer as a father figure; that his access to the Old Man should now be limited by even so talented a sibling as Robert Craft was a bitter experience. In spite of his many recent successes my stepfather's sense of accomplishment was always precarious; the loss of his role as Stravinksy's confidante was, to him, just another bit of evidence that he was losing his foothold on the ladder of success.

Ingolf Dahl was certainly a figure talented enough to have chosen a career as conductor, or performer or composer. Precisely because he treasured each of these activities, and teaching as well, he never succeeded in abandoning any of these tasks to concentrate on one alone, although such a gesture might have helped him to achieve that national reputation for which he so desperately longed. It was all very well for one *Los Angeles Times* reviewer to refer to him as the "resident-musician-extraordinary," but this inability to focus his musical gifts may have cost him the celebrity he thought he deserved. I also believe that there were deep-seated psychological problems that likewise inhibited his creative endeavors, but more of this must come later in our narrative.

There are many journal entries that speak of Ingolf's sense of grievance over the progress of his career in the late Forties and early Fifties. He felt undervalued both on and off-campus, and the feeling that he was not receiving the respect he deserved seems to have been a part of his personality at every stage of his life. In particular he longed to extend his recognition beyond the confines of the West Coast which, though it had an active and vital musical life, never seemed to get its proper share of attention elsewhere. On December 26, 1948 the *New York Times* did announce Ingolf's election to the League of Composers, the American section of the International Society for Contemporary Music. But such public recognition was rare and month after month he read in the national musical magazines of the triumphs of others whose achievements did not seem to measure up to his own.

One consequence of these bitter feelings is that he often seemed to be envious of his own friends. As earlier he had been jealous of Gail Kubik's success so now he expressed similar feelings not only toward Robert Craft but also toward Halsey Stevens, who – for many years – served as chairman of the Composition Department at U.S.C. On September 18, 1949, Ingolf wrote, "Envious of Halsey's promoting push and drive." A few days later an article about Halsey appeared in the faculty newspaper – "Very disgusted and fed up," Ingolf complained, "Why no word about my publications, performance, etc. The problem of social relations, promotion, etc. is burning. I must find peace and adjustment some place." Seeking an explanation for his own slow progress Ingolf then added, "At the basis must be disgust with my own inadequacy in the world." This theme appears again on January 1, 1950. An issue of the journal *Pan Pipes* had just arrived to bedevil him – "depressing," he concluded, "the world again into which its seems *so* difficult to enter – I am outside, unknown, should I wish for the strength of character to be content in obscurity or for the strength of will to break through? Will probably just muddle along."

Although the picture improved somewhat in later years, Ingolf was never able to make the breakthrough he desired. His unappeased hunger on this point (and Etta's unkind reminders and invidious comparisons) spoiled much of the satisfaction he should have drawn from his tireless efforts in so many fields. Unfortunately, he could not say no to any musical opportunity. He found it almost impossible to turn anyone away when they wanted something from him, and since he had so many gifts the procession of requests never came to a halt. And when others were not asking him to take on new responsibilities he was squandering his own energies with new tasks entirely of is own devising. "Tired," he wrote in May, 1952, "overwhelmed by all the things that should be done."

27. AMERICAN GOTHIC TREMBLAY & LAWRENCE OF WEST HOLLYWOOD

In 1946 Lawrence Morton used one of his *Script* columns to capture the flavor of a visit which he and Ingolf had undertaken to the home of George and Verabel Tremblay. Ingolf was just completing his first year at U.S.C. His attempt to combine a life of academic responsibility with one of creative endeavor was becoming increasingly common among American composers, but George Tremblay had chosen an entirely different method of pursuing his art – while still earning a living.

He and Verabel, a painter, lived in Chatsworth, near the Santa Susanna Mountains, and here George worked as a caretaker on large ranch properties, including the Griffith Estate. Only after completing his day of labor among the smudge pots, would this man with a hoe, this American Gothic Tremblay (as I referred to him in my continuing role as smartass) retreat to his studio, a rough-cut Schoenbergian whose only compromise with the economic patterns of his fellow composers was the occasional private student who managed to make the pilgrimage to what was then an isolated northwestern corner of the San Fernando Valley.

The Tremblays often invited their friends to enjoy a day in the sun, with much musical chatter, good food, plenty of booze, a swim, and – if Ingolf were along – a hike. Sometimes other family members were included, but often it was "musicians only." Ingolf's friendship with George began within a few months of my stepfather's arrival from Switzerland, and for many years trips to the "real Chatsworth island" were treasured episodes. David Raksin reminded me of a visit that had taken place during the War. It was Ingolf's turn to provide refreshments and he, naturally, delegated this responsibility to Etta. She was impeded by butter rationing and decided on an ingenious substitute. When the lads finished their walk and fell upon their food they discovered that their liverwurst sandwiches had been contaminated by *peanut* butter! In addition to David and Lawrence, Gail Kubik and Gil Grau might be present when Ingolf went to Chatsworth, and visiting composers were often included as well. Ingolf reports taking Roger Sessions there in 1950 for "long animated talks."

In the *Script* piece crafted by Lawrence a visiting East Coast composer is identified as Leblanc. Over thirty years later I asked the author for a fuller explanation and he told me that he was probably referring to Alexei Haieff. In fact, all of the principal characters received new names in the retelling: George became Al Fresco, Verabel became Persephone, and Ingolf is recognizable as Vercingetorix. An excellent portrait of my stepfather as he must have appeared to others in 1946 emerges as Lawrence attempted to show his readers that his friend, a *real* composer, failed to resemble Hollywood's version of the great creator:

> Unlike the composer in "Hangover Square," he does twenty laps a day around the track at the Y.M.C.A., he is an inveterate mountain climber and knows more about skiing than Gregory Peck learned for his role in "Spellbound." He is something of a sensualist, but a critical and disciplined one. The smell of sage and wild thyme, the taste of currants eaten without lavation, the view of a valley from a hilltop, the sound of a bird in the night – these will induce mild ecstasies in the heart of Vercingetorix. Yet he has never written a piece about mountains, herbs, wild fruit, or birds. The ecstasy of these delights occasionally found its way into his youthful works; but his mature compositions are rather in the neo-classical mode. He has a wife, a son, a car, and a piano, of which the last two are much battered from age and hard usage. He is generally late to appointments and his manuscript is sloppy.

We then learn that, when it was time to pick up Lawrence and Leblanc, Vercingetorix arrived an hour late, that on the way to Chatsworth the three talked about Esther William's figure, Olivier's *Henry V*, the food in San Francisco, and the "almost nationwide inclination of conductors to play second- and third-rate American music." The travelers took off their shirts and drank beer, arriving quite late at the lunch that Persephone had prepared. Even then Vercingetorix insisted on a swim and Al Fresco, who had a student waiting, had to dine alone. On the hike Vercingetorix had a visual paroxysm over the view, a gustatory one when a berry bush was discovered, an olfactory one when he sniffed some meadow grass. "The rest of us," Lawrence observed, "had a cigarette." "After dinner we played records of our own music and complimented each other on our modulations, our harmonic structures, our marvelous sense of form." The visitors filled themselves with Dago red and Al Fresco and Persephone fell asleep.

During a testimonial broadcast three years after Ingolf's death, Gail Kubik also remembered a Chatsworth afternoon. He, Lawrence, George, and Ingolf paid a call on Lionel Barrymore, who was studying composition with George. The professional musicians (all in their cups, evidently) were appalled by the bad Hollywood sounds in the actor's compositions – Barrymore's versions of Delius and Ravel. Ingolf alone, putting the milk of human kindness to its severest test, took the actor's efforts seriously and left him with a feeling of encouragement.

Ingolf first mentions taking me to Chatsworth when I was ten and there were several occasions when Etta and I – and even some of my friends – went along on these rural outings. The kids took bikes and spent some time away from the grown-ups, pedaling among the orange groves, but my strongest memories are of the musicians giggling and arguing beneath the grapevine and holding debates on Scarlatti and Scriabin as they walked though the sandstone rocks which made such good locations for Hollywood westerns. I loved visiting Chatsworth, where the squeaky-voiced Verabel and the lantern-jawed George were always very kind to me. I was particularly fascinated by a persistent rumor that George had actually had an unacknowledged hand in the composition of "How High the Moon," a piece of music I actually liked.

Today I am sorry that I was not present on December 28, 1949. On this day Gail stole an orange from a forbidden tree, George improvised at the piano with his student, Georgia Akst, everyone wrote and sang *a capella* pieces and, after plenty of drinks no doubt, Ingolf and Lawrence performed a version of the Walton-Sitwell *Facade*. The following year the Dahls, the Tremblays, and Lawrence "bundled" under a piano to get the full effect of Henry Cowell's attempt to play on the strings of the instrument rather than its keys.

Ingolf and Lawrence Morton were collaborators on many projects during the Forties and in subsequent eras as well; and after Ingolf's death Lawrence was, for more than a decade, my chief advisor in matters dealing with the Dahl musical estate.

The two men enjoyed a friendship of postcards and telephone calls, shared enthusiasms and peevish quibbles. "Violent discussion with Lawrence," Ingolf wrote on September 5, 1945 – "Multiple Standards Vs. Truth." Earlier in the year, when George and Ingolf had attacked Lawrence for spending too much time on political matters in his *Script* columns – and not enough on art itself – the critic first *proved* them wrong and then waspishly concluded, "Nuts (but not mine) to both of yez." These disputes were quickly forgotten and Lawrence was a frequent figure at our home, and one of Etta's best friends.

A bachelor, Lawrence belonged to a Jewish family that had settled in Duluth, Minnesota. He moved several times in the period covered by this volume, exchanging an apartment on Holloway Drive for one on Doheny and a third on Sweetzer – I began referring to him as Lawrence of West Hollywood. He numbered many important musical and artistic figures among his friends but he always had time for the struggling beginner as well. As he became ever more involved in the affairs of Evenings on the Roof (later re-named the Monday Evening Concerts) he naturally acquired a power over musical life and creative destinies that not everyone appreciated. He could be wickedly blunt and his caustic comments, usually reserved for private correspondence or telephone calls, were especially barbed. As a child I always enjoyed hearing him talk, for he had a great facility with language. When his crew cut head and his horned-rimmed glasses were tilted above our dining table I knew that I was about to hear some delicious wickedness through which some over-inflated reputation would remain forever sullied. Lawrence added to my indebtedness by coming up with a long series of imaginative holiday presents, which I treasured. These included a surreal zoo, which he had drawn with melted red wax, and a bulletin board which he had made himself and which I dragged around until it disintegrated twenty-five years later.

In 1993 I carried with me – on a return trip to Los Angeles – a large number of letters that Ingolf had received from Lawrence during those periods when one or the other was away from home base, and thus unavailable for those hour-long midnight chat-fests on the telephone. I was attempting to assist the musicologist Dorothy L. Crawford, who was completing a history of the Monday Evening Concerts, and hunting for materials that would reveal something about the private Lawrence Morton, the hidden spirit behind the public face. I'm not sure that the dozens of letters I brought with me were of much use, for Lawrence, who was an avid gossip when it came to other people's lives, was the most private of personalities, a man who seemed to have no relationships other than professional ones – though this seems hardly possible. Certainly nothing of a private life was ever hinted at by any member of my family; it was as though Lawrence had energy only for the life of work. In his Minnesota youth, so it was rumored, he had dated the actress Ann Sothern. Now he seemed to be, at all times, companionless. With the brashness of callow youth I once asked him, as we were returning from a late concert at Royce Hall during my college days, why he had never married and whether he might still consider this a possibility now. He answered, in a typically self-deprecatory manner, "Who would want to get into bed with this scarred old body?"

28. JOHN MUIR'S GRANDSON

Ingolf had learned of his 1946 Borge radio assignment only two days after returning from a two-week Sierra Club climbing trip in Grand Teton National Park. There is no question that my stepfather preferred small scale mountain expeditions, ones that could be enjoyed with just a few friends, in preference to outings with large parties of strangers – where embarrassing scenes over who forgot to wash the pots might easily spoil the mood. But when the opportunity arose for him to see a part of the mountain world otherwise hard to visit on your own he sometimes accepted the discipline of the group. Now that wartime restrictions on gasoline were coming to an end it was increasingly easy for him to range further afield from his home base in the mountains of Southern California.

The Teton trip of 1946 offered the first serious alpine climbing opportunities since Ingolf had left Switzerland. He loved this portion of western Wyoming and three years later Etta and I were introduced to the area as well. In 1946 Vercingetorix nibbled on black currants, sniffed the yellow daisies in the wet forest, dipped into the icy lakes, and delighted in glimpses of black bear and elk. On August 21 he records another unusual sighting: Norman Clyde, the legendary mountaineer, "like an offspring of John Muir," carrying a tremendous pack and looking rather like a gnomish wood sprite as he brought just the right kind of huge log out of the forest for the campfire. Ingolf climbed the South, Middle, and Grand Teton peaks during this trip. His feet frigid as the cold seeped through his tennis shoes, he at last got to try out the rope climbing techniques he had been practicing. One of his companions was Bob Newhouse, a Los Angeles psychiatrist who became a frequent mountain companion in these years. On the way down from the South Teton Bob got into the wrong couloir because Ingolf, mesmerized by the view and intoxicated by the air, was not as watchful as he should have been. "Fulfillment," Ingolf wrote of this day, his last in the mountains.

His membership in the Sierra Club and his involvement in a number of its mountaineering activities dates from about this time. For twenty-five years he identified himself closely with the conservation efforts of this pioneer environmental lobby; his participation in many of its struggles formed, as we will see, just part of the wider political efforts he found time to support.

On August 8, 1950 Ingolf began a strenuous two-week expedition in the High Sierras, walking in a northerly direction from Kearsarge Pass along the John Muir Trail. His companion this time was a young music student named Lawrence Moss. Larry came from a family of cultural activists and musical benefactors. His parents, Oscar and Sadye Moss, were generous sponsors of many projects, most notably the Evenings on the Roof and its successor, the Monday Evening Concerts. Larry had studied in the East but was now returning to Los Angeles to continue graduate work at U.S.C. He was a keen mountaineer and I was deeply impressed that one of *his* Sierra Club trips had been described in the *National Geographic*.

He and Ingolf became good friends, in spite of a number of differences. Larry, for instance, enjoyed fishing, which Ingolf denounced as a tedious waste of time. But while Larry fished, the former Zurich art history student took out one of his sketchbooks and made charcoal and ink drawings of the high peaks and the jewel-like lakes. To some of these he later added watercolor. The two men made a new camp every other day as they moved up the trail. Ingolf seems to have been perpetually resentful of the large parties of fishermen who moved from lake to lake on horseback. As he and Larry passed a group of such layabouts one of the latter was overheard to say, "There are some backpackers, feel sorry for the poor devils" – a remark directed at a man who, at his camp the night before, had pronounced the experience "heaven on earth." The next night Larry "gets fishing fever," Ingolf reported. This resulted in a very late, very dark, and very meager dinner when Larry's lonely trout fell into the fire. The campers came close to a fight according to Larry but Ingolf's journal records only a "momentary disturbance."

Ingolf named one little tarn Lake Etta and in it he took an icy bath with a bar of soap. He and Larry climbed Mt. Sill and were so exhilarated by the experience that, as they faced their last campfire meal, they could still maintain, "To hell with steak and martinis" – a boast they quickly forgot as soon as they returned to civilization.

To watch Ingolf prepare for one his long expeditions was torture for me. The maps, the canteens, the dehydrated foods, and the canvas would be exploded all over our living room, but an invitation for me to join in the fun of what would be a very strenuous outing was not forthcoming. Still, writing to me many years later from Yale, where he had become a Professor of Music, Larry was able to let me know some of the things I had missed. The two men, for instance, undertook a second Sierra trip in 1951. On August 15 Ingolf took a nap on some pine needles and woke to find a doe with two young fawns grazing at his side. That night he became feverish and took to his sleeping bag, Larry caring for him. The next morning he felt fine again and was able to continue in a hailstorm to a hut above Lake Helen. A few days later there was a "run-in" with "some detestable fishermen on horses." Larry wrote:

> Ingolf could, as you, know, be suffused with a righteous indignation, and at those times he could be very compelling. I recall how we once came upon a party on horseback (for him the very epitome of what he detested in the mountains) and one of them, who was smoking, flicked his – still lit! – cigarette into the brush. Ingolf was literally livid. He lectured them for what seemed like a half-hour, and then, when one of them attempted to dismount and pick up the butt, said, with the greatest disdain, "I'll get it."

Larry's account of this 1951 trip gives a good sampling of the type of chatter one might encounter on the trail with my stepfather. As they walked along the two men played musical guessing games and discussed Renaissance composers. "It amazes me," Larry recalled, "when I think of the chutzpah with which I as a wet-behind-the ears Eastman M.M. discussed matters with him as an equal, and the democratic ease with which he answered." One of Larry's hardest tasks was informing his friend that he wished to study composition with Leon Kirchner, with whom he enjoyed a stylistic affinity that he did not share with my stepfather. But the older man cut the younger one off with some annoyance – it wasn't necessary to explain such a thing – "it was self-evident that I would study with whomever I thought would help me most artistically, and such matters were beyond discussion, and in any event could have no effect on our friendship." I didn't realize, Larry latter added, "how rare such objectivity and selflessness could be among artists, and indeed have never found such nobility repeated."

But Ingolf was not above correcting his young friend and part-time student. When Larry, at a little tarn above Bullfrog Lake, used the expression, "That is the exception that proves the rule," Ingolf scolded Larry into admitting that the statement was illogical on its face. "All right, I renounce its use hereafter," Larry is supposed to have replied – which is why, several years later, when I had at last matured enough for inclusion in Ingolf's Sierra plans, he led a group of us to a body of water he had named Lake Renunciation!

In addition to mountain climbing and simple hiking Ingolf was also now finding many skiing opportunities, both in Southern California and further afield. He traveled to Mammoth Lakes for skiing in April, 1946, and, in 1948, to Alta, Utah in February, Sequoia in March, and Onion

Valley in May. The first and the last of these trips were undertaken in the company of Edi and Mimi Schaar, two Austrian friends he had met at Mt. Waterman during the war. In the years that followed this trio completed many skiing expeditions together and Edi also accompanied Ingolf on a hike up a portion of the John Muir Trail in 1948.

Etta and I were excluded, as non-skiers, from most of these winter holidays, though Ingolf did buy Etta her own pair of skis in 1947. She did not take to this (or any other) form of exercise; surprisingly, Ingolf made no effort whatsoever to give me instruction in the sport. What he sought in his skiing holidays was the ecstasy of isolation and this would not have been available if the rest of the family had been in tow. "What a day. Beauty & life," he wrote as he trekked up Kearsarge Pass in April, 1946. "I am hysterical with snow delight," he added after a day above Tahoe City in January, 1950, "just want to shout wet-eyed."

29. AT WAR WITH THE HYDRA

Ingolf liked to make fun of his profession's general indifference to wider social questions by beginning lectures with a quotation from Emerson's *Journals*, "How partial, like mutilated men, the musical artists appear to me in society! Politics, bankruptcy, frost, famine, war – nothing concerns them but a scraping on a catgut or tooting on a bass french horn." I cannot argue that political questions were central to my family's existence or that Ingolf found time to engage in them with any regularity, but political, environmental, and civil liberties issues did matter a great deal nevertheless.

In an interview in a campus paper in 1947 he was quoted as saying, "Political ideas or strong convictions help art indirectly rather than directly. However an artist should never shut himself off from the world. The more he lives in the world which surrounds him the better his art will be." In the program notes for Stravinsky's *Symphony in Three Movements* Ingolf had earlier argued that "one day it will be universally recognized that the white house in the Hollywood Hills in which this Symphony was written and which was regarded by some as an ivory tower, was just as close to the core of a world at war as the place were Picasso painted 'Guernica.'" Ingolf would have been among the last to make art a servant of politics but he was insistent that artists have their social duties – like any other citizens.

My parents belonged to the non-Communist left. In Europe they would probably have belonged to one of the socialist parties but in America there were usually comfortable as Democrats. They were always worried about Fascism in any form and they were most uneasy when Reverend Fifield of the First Congregational Church, site of so many concerts in the Forties, became known for his right-wing views. Ingolf was disdainful of artists who had collaborated with the Nazi regime in Europe – even his old idol Richard Strauss did not escape unscathed. But my parents also protested against the internment of the Japanese-Americans during the war. When the Republicans won the presidential election of 1952 the Dahls began referring to America as Taft's Reich and Ingolf went around saying Heil Nixon! But my parents never joined any left wing groups – indeed, Ingolf never participated in any grouping more radical than the American Association of University Professors ("very good solidarity," he reported after attending a campus meeting in 1947). The closest the Dahls ever came to American Socialism was their vote for Henry Wallace in 1948, an action undertaken because they were so convinced that Truman would lose anyway that they wished to register a last progressive protest. Truman had, of course, failed to live up to their greatest political hero, Franklin D. Roosevelt. "Roosevelt wins!" Ingolf wrote enthusiastically on November 9, 1940. On April 12, 1945, the day my mother burst uncharacteristically into tears at the death of the president, Ingolf wrote, "Can't get over it. If I could write music up to the occasion!" Only one other figure captured their allegiance in so profound a manner and this was Adlai Stevenson, for whom they voted twice – once by absentee ballot during Ingolf's first sabbatical. Ingolf reports walking in stunned anguish in front of the Zurich train station the day the press confirmed Eisenhower's victory in 1952. Four years later he and I attended a Stevenson rally in Hollywood. This event was Ingolf's first political rally, "a great and inspiring experience" – he had never seen so many people in one place. But he was depressed that such a great man had little chance, "And the thought of Nixon in the presidential seat is not a pleasant one."

If one examines the list of causes championed by Ingolf and Etta the inescapable conclusion must be that my parents were unashamed liberals. They wore this label proudly and consciously attempted to live by liberal precepts. They were early champions of the civil rights movement, they took pride in the accomplishments of black students like the future conductor Henry Lewis, and they tried to bequeath to me attitudes of tolerance and respect. It may seem a bit patronizing now, but it was in all innocence that they insisted I play with the children of the cleaning lady. From a very early age I was taught that "nigger" was an unacceptable word. Once Etta rushed into the living room to still my fingers on the frets of my toy ukulele because I was strumming "Ol' Black Joe" while a cleaning lady was in the kitchen. Curiously Etta was never comfortable with the word "Black" – remembering its use as an epithet – and throughout her life she preferred the word "colored." In 1943 Ingolf joined a committee of the Crescendo Club which sought an apology from a member who had made a slighting reference to blacks. Two years later, when *This Week* magazine published a feature on "The Face of America," Ingolf wrote a protest letter criticizing the publication for showing so few faces belonging to Negroes or women!

Ingolf's adherence to the principles of the American Civil Liberties Union was profound and long-standing. When I left California he even took out a Michigan membership in my name so that I would not neglect the causes for which this organization stood. Interference in personal liberty or free expression angered him considerably. I recall that he was particularly upset when local police insisted that even the innocent must be able to prove their identity on demand. Once when we were parking the car behind our apartment building I suggested we rip an offending bumper sticker off another car. He lectured me quite sternly on the need to protect political expression and even offered the famous lines attributed to Voltaire, "I may disagree with what you have to say but I will fight to the death for your right to say it." Naturally the McCarthy era was full of bitterness for Ingolf. When the senator from Wisconsin died, he said to me, "Well, the Hydra has lost one of its heads." When U.S.C. was threatening not to renew the contract of a colleague because of membership in the Communist Party in the 1930's, Ingolf immediately led a successful petition drive in which eleven members of the School of Music placed their own jobs on the line in protest. "Ingolf was not merely a go-alonger," Raymond Kendall wrote in 1979, "he believed in principles, and that was that." Ingolf was also a foe of militarism and from materials he collected in his "Civil Liberties" envelope I surmise that he was a supporter of draft resistance during the Vietnamese War.

Before my departure from California in 1965 he regularly conferred with me on the eve of every election, including the primaries, trying to make up his mind on how to vote on even minor ballot propositions.

The flavor of the Dahls' attitude toward social questions can also be tested through an examination of their charitable contributions, where incomplete records still survive. Their donations were never large, but my parents did support a variety of causes and organizations. During and immediately after the war they sent money to a number of agencies charged with war relief and refugee aid including, in 1945, the American League for a Free [i.e., Jewish] Palestine and the Emergency Committee to Save the Jewish People of Europe. We sent a good number of C.A.R.E. packages also. Check stubs, from a later period, reveal contributions to the NAACP, the Congress of Racial Equality, and the Southern Christian Leadership Conference.

Throughout his life Ingolf was also very passionate about the need for protecting the wilderness and he participated in many of the struggles undertaken by the Sierra Club. A hike of July 5, 1968 was spoiled for him by the presence of "motorbikes all over, hell." Indeed he had many a run-in in with the mechanical desecrators of nature's quiet, with hunters who felt his footsteps would startle the game, with rangers who sided with the hunters, with motorcycle enthusiasts who liked to test their machines by destroying the trails, with speedboat operators who felt they couldn't enjoy the lake without the sound of the outboard motor. Every new road slashed into the mountainside broke Ingolf's heart. His fury was aroused by any form of wilderness enclosure – and between the army and the TV stations not a few summits were lost altogether to hikers in Ingolf's lifetime.

Naturally he ignored Keep Out signs and there were unpleasant scenes because of this. Once we had driven to the bottom of a canyon and parked to begin our hike. At the end of the day we discovered a chain across the road as we attempted to leave. While we were undoing it an enraged ranger came up to chew us out – hadn't we read the sign? Frankly I hadn't seen any sign at all and, clutching at straws, I asked, "Are you sure it was there this morning?" Well, the ranger admitted, it had been added *during* our hike, and thus we escaped prosecution.

Ingolf was an active letter writer. Preserving Dinosaur National Monument became an important cause in the Fifties and protecting the San Gorgonio Wild Area was a paramount issue in the Sixties. When the ski editor of the *Times* printed articles favoring "development" of the region, Ingolf wrote a letter that typifies his attitude toward the proper use of wilderness:

> You imply that San Gorgonio is now closed to skiers and speak of "opening it up for skiing." This is misleading. The area is wide open for all skiers who want to use their legs to get there and who will prepare themselves properly. I am not a "young mountaineer," but I have skied on San Gorgonio for the last 25 years and hope to continue to do so...San Gorgonio is the last remaining wilderness in Southern California and it offers wonderful skiing for those who are willing to make the effort. Surely a mountain as magnificent as this is worth some effort and need not be added to all the other mechanized spoon-feeding means of today's recreation.

There were many areas of life where I attempted to place some distance between myself and my troublesome parents, but I was able to accept the Dahls' political agenda with zest.

30. WHY CAN'T IT OBEY?

Although Ingolf could never be said to have enjoyed robust health I have the impression that he was spared, in the immediate post-war years, from a recurrence of some of the worst episodes of the past. Without some relief from chronic ill-health he could not have undertaken the mountain activity I have described. But asthma continued to plague him and there were attacks of bronchitis, treated with sulfa drugs, in January 1947 and July 1948. Hemorrhoids bothered him again, especially during the trip to the Tetons, when he was forced to stay in his tent one day because it was too painful to walk. "Oh the body," he complained, "why can't it obey? I overcame so much already. Lord, let me overcome this too!"

An exhausting work schedule helped to undermine Ingolf's health a number of times in the post-war decade and, no doubt, his health occasionally made work much more arduous than it should have been. "I have only one wish for the new year," he wrote on December 21, 1949, "may I be stronger and healthier – it would be terrible to go on like this, no resilience, no thrust..." The last meeting of his Collegium Musicum class in January of 1952 had to be improvised because the instructor, after a bad chest, could not speak. "Rest day," Ingolf had written on April 15, 1949, "just sleep and try to get hold of myself." But the next day he was off on a solo skiing expedition to Gorgonio – and this is a reminder that there were still ways of conquering the body when the will was strong enough.

On January 19, 1951, while working out at the "Y," Ingolf twisted his right knee. For a while he suspected gout, from which he did occasionally suffer. Benny Goodman loaned him a heat lamp, but no improvement followed. Dr. Robert Portis taped the leg on January 30, but again there seemed to be no improvement. Worry and pain lead to apathy and depression. "The knee is not so good," Ingolf reported after a brief walk on the beach on February 19. Easter vacation was looming and he would be forced to forego any physical activity, in spite of his "hunger for outdoors." On March 23 Dr. Portis decided on cartilage surgery. This took place on April 16th. Ingolf lay in a painful, drugged suspension for several days. On the evening of the 17th he noted, "The night nurse: in the uncertain light the lovely face that makes all pain go." With crutches under his arm, he left the hospital on the 23rd, "still fuzzy in the head." Stitches were removed two days later, but I remember a long curving scar. Physiotherapy followed and by June 8 Ingolf was able to take his first post-operative hike, a trip with my Scout troop to Chilao. "It goes quite well," he reported, and after several more practice hikes he was ready for his second Sierra outing with Larry Moss.

A year later, in 1952, it was the left knee that began to give him trouble after a ski trip. He managed to run six laps at the "Y" on April 4, but the knee refused to get better and he became despondent as future ambitious mountain plans evaporated. On April 15 Dr. Portis decided to operate again and a surgery took place six days later. With complete anesthetic this time Ingolf seems to have recovered more rapidly, but there were post-operative complications once he was on his crutches – a painful right ankle which had to be bathed in wax and later taped. Pain persisted for weeks. On May 24 Ingolf reports a sore left foot – "Can hardly stand on it. What is it? Also poison ivy remains. I am so down, incapable of doing anything, just want to forget, crawl into a hole. Don't get dressed all day ...I am so miserable, why does all this happen to me?" Ingolf was still limping around in pain when the summer began.

Etta, too, had her share of physical problems during this period. On August 4, 1949, as we were walking back to the car from a picnic at Taggart Lake, she strained a calf muscle in her left leg. It received a further wrench while she was dancing with Joyce and Gail Kubik in Peterborough on August 13; on the 26th she pulled the calf muscle a third time ("oh those damned infantile bovines") while dancing on the green at Middlebury College.

On January 26, 1950 the tips of Etta's rubber glove got caught in the wringer of Aunt Lillian's washing machine and the fingers, wrist and a good portion of the arm followed. She was rushed to the emergency hospital, where a fracture was suspected. "Awful to go away with her hand like this," Ingolf wrote, but one can guess that after blaming herself for being so careless, Etta no doubt urged him to complete his scheduled ski trip to Squaw Valley. He did. In fact bruises and swelling were the only results of this incident, to everyone's relief.

Etta and I both suffered severe attacks of the flu in the late Forties and early Fifties and Etta's high fever was dosed with penicillin in 1952. One of the army of medical men treating our family at this time was Dr. Maximillian Edel, one of Stravinsky's physicians, a healer to the stars. Even I made it to his august chambers once. "That's Farley Granger," Etta whispered to me, pointing to a handsome chap sitting opposite us – but I was too sick to care. Ingolf was under treatment for his thyroid deficiency and Etta had an amino acid problem and a long struggle with hepatitis. She had a great deal of confidence in Dr. Edel and a reverence for the medical profession in general. Once she pointed to one of Ingolf's students, who suffered from severe acne, and said, "Max could cure that." "And if he doesn't," I added, "You can always demote him to Maxathousand."

31. OH, SHENANDOAH

In September, 1945, I entered Shenandoah Street Grammar School. I was midway through the second year of my school career and already behind in one important skill – handwriting. At Lockwood Elementary we had learned the rudiments of printing, but these precocious Westsiders had already plunged into the cursive. I never caught up, bringing home D after D on report cards, my sole deficiency in an otherwise exemplary academic record. My mother used to sit me down to practice my penmanship after school and I could always manage to produce a readable script if I pursued the craft diligently, but I lacked the requisite patience. To this day my scribbled notes are a mystery to any other reader, and even when I have taken pains over such labors the result still requires some effort. It is precisely this effort that many of *my* students, over the decades, have declined to make when given a choice between reading my commentaries on their own endeavors – or forgetting the whole thing.

In my other studies I forged ahead efficiently. I was a good reader, an accomplished speller, and mathematics still offered no unsolvable puzzles. After several years at Shenandoah one of my teachers, Mrs. Kersh, proposed that three of us skip half a year. My delighted parents offered no objection and I was thus transported from a class that finished every grade in winter to one that completed its work in June. Today I see many consequences, both negative and positive, resulting from this promotion, but at the time I considered it a great honor and soon made many pals among a slightly older group of children. Indeed a number of these new classmates remain friends over half a century later and for this reason alone I have reason to be grateful for this change in my academic circumstances.

I did not seem to be behind in any category of work and my wit and intelligence earned me the respect of my fellow pupils and my new teachers, especially Mrs. Marin (B-6) and Mrs Frisby (A-6). The latter selected me as one of Shenandoah Street's finest when it was our turn to send a delegation of tots to be interviewed by Art Linkletter on the *House Party* radio program of April 7, 1949. I was the first to be interviewed by the famous host, and I chatted merrily about my family's recent trip to Sweden, addressing my interlocutor as "Art" and getting a number of chuckles from the studio audience.

My popularity almost earned me the presidency of the A-6, but I lost by one vote to Bob Abel, whose 7-up commercials many of us will have seen on TV many years later. In spite of this political loss I was better off than I had been a few months earlier when I had proposed that Gary Ford, the class ne'er-do-well, serve as president of the B-6. I had even clipped auto ads from a magazine and showed up at school with posters proclaiming "There's A Ford In Your Future." But Mrs. Marin frowned on this nomination, feeling that Gary was not ready for such responsibility, and I had to retreat in a sulk. To make matters worse, when we exchanged anonymous gifts at Christmas I ended up with a board game called "Kooties," something no child would want to be saddled with. Even this was better than the humiliation of being denounced as a degenerate because some sixth grade prude had chanced upon a photo of some naked African tribeswomen in a *National Geographic* I had brought to school.

I still remember some of our A-6 projects. We were studying South America and to impress Mrs Frisby Richard Binggeli and I made special covers for our anthology of reports on each country of the continent. We began with combed plywood, which we shellacked. Then, as a cover adornment, we drew a map of South America on a piece of tin, using a special tool to cut into the unyielding metal surface. Richard, I'm sure, did much of my work for me, since I was never good with my hands, but I enjoyed doing the research on the Humboldt Current and gathering statistics on guano deposits in Chile. I could, incidentally, paint, and as I labored over an impressionistic camellia on a mother's day card an enthusiastic Mrs. Frisby said, "I'm going to give you an A in Art."

Mrs Frisby was a large grey-haired woman who was related to someone at the *L.A. Times*. She taught all the subjects, with the exception of the occasional group music lesson, and even supervised our exercises on Shenandoah's large tar-covered playing fields. I remember her scolding me for striking out in a baseball game, but when I hit a home run (well, partly Richard Zuccarini muffed a ground ball to right field and was too lazy to chase it) I failed to receive the congratulations I thought I deserved. This was because, as I strolled back to class next to my teacher, she noticed that bees were encircling my head, attracted no doubt by the sweet lanolin-enriched patina of the Wildroot Hair Oil that I had been applying to my hair. "Get away from me," she protested. I slunk off, as I had to do again when I lost the final round of the class spelling bee after forgetting to spell Indian with a *capital* I.

I suppose that the Wildroot was an early attempt at making myself more attractive to the opposite sex, in whom I had begun to take a wistful, if unfocussed interest. I remember riding my bicycle past the driveway of the unobtainable Georgia Rawls and I did pay a visit to the tree house of Gay Wood, who lived only a few blocks away from our court. I had a "girlfriend" on Corning Street, the Keller's next-door neighbor Sheryl Balinoff, and I seemed to be reasonably popular among the girls of the sixth grade. But there was about to be a great gulf in the social development of the sexes, with the girls sprinting away toward womanhood and the guys gauchely clinging to youth. Here was one of the tragedies of my skipping a grade, for to add to the usual discrepancy, I was now half a year younger than most of the girls in my class, and here I could never catch up.

In spite of my fondness for the classroom I was just as eager to hear the 3:00 bell as the rest of my friends, for the afternoon – in those lucky years before homework loomed – were treasured spaces for play and pleasures. The latter seem simple enough by today's standards. There were two convenience stores near the school, at opposite corners of Shenandoah and Cadillac. Somehow the school grapevine was always able to supply inside information on what might have just arrived at these emporia to delight the palate of ten-year olds. Three taste sensations actually drew crowds of running children, eager not to be kept in short supply as wartime restrictions on sweets began to fade. In one store you could get viles of purple or green syrup encased in tubes of wax – with the wax proving to be much more interesting to chew than the liquid was to drink. If this was not in stock, and you didn't want to settle for inedible wax teeth, you could get jaw-breakers – impenetrable candy balls that could withstand any amount of pressure from wax-encrusted teeth. At the other shop there arrived one afternoon treasures so rare that the storekeeper actually doled them out one to a customer – the first comic strip-wrapped pink wedges of Fleer's Double Bubble Gum. By the time you got home the gum would have softened to a consistency that permitted the blowing of bubbles large enough to stick in the Wildroot.

I walked to and from school most of the time, but in my last few months at Shenandoah I learned how to use the full-sized red Schwinn two-wheeler that my father had given me for Christmas. In the morning I would get started by using a box to climb aboard the saddle. When I arrived breathlessly at Shenandoah, after some elevation rise, I would come to a stop by crashing into the school's cyclone fence and hanging on for dear life. Riding home, a soaring downhill affair, with my mouth full of sugar, was always a delight, assuming I didn't have a handwriting lesson lurking on the kitchen table.

At home, on those hazy Shenandoah afternoons, I would head almost immediately for the street to see who might be available for play. The patch of grass between the court's two front units and the white picket fence out front made an entirely delightful surface for a miniaturized version of football. There were no end zones but you could, for the winning score, crash headlong into the hedges at either end of the yard. Here I first puzzled out the intricacies of the game, approaching the task in a very literal fashion: the end stands at the end, the tackle makes the tackles and the guard. . . he guards the end. A larger playing field could be obtained by using the open grassy spaces in front of the apartment houses across the street. In the unit at the end lived a new friend from Louisiana named Potchie. Across from his apartment was the home of the Goldbergs: Mr. Goldberg forever clearing his throat, harried Mary Goldberg, her hair already turned a steely grey, and whiny young Martin, who was my age. One of the chaps in our court gave me two sets of boxing gloves and Martin and I tried these out. "Hey, you made my lip bleed," Martin protested, retiring to sulk after a first round TKO.

Another set of court neighbors had a possession even more prized than a pair of boxing gloves, the Collie puppy Robin. I was allowed to play with her after school and what a wonderful sensation it was to feel her soft fur and to respond to her frisky antics. Naturally there were constant supplications on my part for a pet of my own. Once I convinced myself, after hearing some squeaking from a closet, that my parents had decided to surprise me with a pair of chinchillas, but perhaps it had only been mice! The usual excuse that was offered when I became importunate was that a pet would be sure to exacerbate Ingolf's asthma (this was before I learned the truth about his beloved Krimme). Later the excuse was that the family traveled too much and a pet would be a troublesome burden. In the event,

185

I never managed so much as a goldfish or a stick insect. The Robins of the world were always welcome intruders in a petless prospect.

It was an ideal time for a middle class child to grow up: depression and war behind us and the Cold War yet to come to the boil. We continued to buy war bond stamps once a week and we learned to fear the vaccinations that were jabbed painfully into our arms when our turn at the front of the dreaded queue came up. We feared impetigo and lice and behind this we always dreaded the great menace of our childhood, polio – for which there was still no vaccine. But most of the traumas of my youth were associated with quite personal horrors and private chagrins. I remember the terror I felt when, a new arrival at Shenandoah, I accidentally touched in the sand box the fused fingers of a poor boy called Weber – but what I don't recall is whether this was his real name or a nickname derived from his infirmity. I also recall the look of dismay on the face of Craig Cunningham's mother when, having sent me to the dime store for some paper napkins during Craig's birthday party, I efficiently returned – having relied only on my own ingenuity as a shopper – with sanitary napkins!

Shenandoah Street School still exists, though perhaps its children lack the affluence of their predecessors. The two-storey building that we knew has disappeared – a casualty of a design that was not regarded as sufficiently earthquake-proof. Only the auditorium, in which I performed skits with my Cub Scout den, and my many memories of the place, still survive.

32. I'LL TAKE SWEDEN

One of the things that most delighted me about extended family travel was that on such occasions I could have unlimited and simultaneous access to both of my parents, that is we could resemble, if only briefly, a normal family – an illusion my very conventional soul always longed to embrace.

We set out on the first leg of a family expedition to Sweden on June 12, 1947, departing not from Union Station but from Alhambra so that, according to Etta, "everyone could really see us off on the train." She maintained a journal of this trip, later made available to those we had left behind, and thus I am able to reconstruct her version of our experiences.

Our train journey, which excited me no end, took us to Chicago. At the Art Institute Ingolf paused nostalgically before *Les Saltimbanques* and he and Etta had a chance to argue over an exhibition of Swedish peasant art, a kind of warm-up for the real thing, I suppose. "Ingolf and I differ on the question of whether biblical scenes should or can be portrayed in Swedish peasant costume," Etta explained, "I think it is silly, tho it was the custom of every nation at that time to do it that way. The prophets & disciples with tail suits & brass buttons is just too rich for my blood." I am not sure which audience Etta was addressing with these pedantic asides, but it gets worse. When we went to an exhibition at the Nordic Museum two months later my interest in the jewel-encrusted gear of the Swedish nobility required Etta to announce that these costumes "are not typically Swedish as these kings and queens had a taste shared by most of the European nobility of that time and had their apparel made in Paris and elsewhere."

The journey to New York was made by air. This was not my first plane journey, since Etta and I had returned from San Diego to Burbank by air at the end of the long afternoon on which I had been rescued from Duffy's Camp two years earlier. The earlier experience had not prepared me for the turbulence of this flight: "Tony was slightly queasy so we chewed gum very hard and sang the Bell Song from *Lakme*, taking turns at being the flute and Lily Pons." In New York I saw my first Broadway Show, *Alice in Wonderland*, and made my mother take me to see a film about Australian pioneers twice. We visited Barbara Kruger-Sachse, Ingolf's old flame, and Etta pronounced her "quite different from what I had imagined her to be."

We left New York on June 20 and spent ten days on the *SS. Drottningholm*, a Swedish-American Line vessel whose toilet facilities, bunk beds, and unvarying menu perturbed Etta. I loved it and all the boozing Scandinavians whom I got to know while Etta was smoking at the bar. We played many games, including cards and the Baltimore game ("Tony shone with some of his answers: in Värmland I'm going to vex Valery, and in Xanadu I'm going to xray xylophones on xmas), though this game evidently degenerated into name-calling ("You awful ape on the Atlantic"). *Dr. Dolittle* was read aloud and I fell down a gangway, twisted an ankle, and got a swollen purple ear. Ingolf tried to get on with an editing project but Etta sought to bring him down to earth by making him talk to a music school director after she had succeeded in getting the latter interested in her husband's compositions. There was a trio which played at meals: "Ingolf and I were very much reminded of Wechsberg's *Looking For A Bluebird*," she wrote. If it was lucky, life for the Dahls occasionally lived up to art.

The great day of reunion was June 30, 1947. Anticipating the welcome scene, I was quoted as saying, "I know what. While Ingolf & his mother are loving each other to death I'll trade stamps with cousin Gunnar." Even more waspish was a prediction from Etta to Lawrence Morton, "Ingolf, if he can get off his mother's lap long enough, may write you . . ." I don't recall the dockside rendezvous in Gothenberg or the first embrace between mother and son in nine years, but I do remember that Ingolf loused up the rest of the afternoon by failing to check through all the rooms of a restaurant in which the rest of the family awaited him and the mix-up made our arrival is Odsmal, where the Lindbloms had a summer property, a very late one. Ingolf reported that he was delighted with his first day in Sweden, "the linden trees in bloom, the little street cars, the bicyclists in summer clothes, the warm-light fragrant summer evening, Europe." I too was thrilled by our first swim in the fjord in the light of the midnight sun and, in the next few days – enchanted by the strange and beautiful sights – I learned to love many things about this northern land, to which I have frequently returned as an adult.

Pappi was overjoyed to have all of his children together again and Ingolf was delighted by a new nephew, Anna-Britta's son Stebbi, and an infant niece, Karin, the daughter of Holger and Aina Marcus. Stebbi (Stefan) was four, just the right age for me to corrupt with every English swearword I could teach him. He was enchanted to have a worthy opponent for cherry-pelting combats at harvest time or for blueberry and wild strawberry hunts in the woods, and together we explored the habitat of the local hedgehog. We were soon settled into Stjarnvägen 10, in the Stockholm suburb of Lidingö, where Mammi and Pappi lived with Anna-Britta, who had married an Icelandic engineer, Glummur Björnson. "Big lovely talk with the sweet girl," Ingolf wrote of his sister, "She is very, very marvelous." Most of us spent a week at the Lindangets Herrgardspensionat near Orsa and Ingolf and Holger went mountain climbing in the north of Sweden, where the weather was so bad that once they were forced to retreat into another country, Norway. There was also much sightseeing, swimming and nude sunbathing (of which, as a nine year-old blue stocking, I heartily disapproved).

"The linguistic mix-up," Ingolf wrote, "is indescribable. At the family dinner we speak mostly German because Pappi's English isn't very good, Etta can't understand Swedish and so German is often the language common to the majority of the family (however Tony can't understand it, neither can Aina, and Holger and Gert talk it only very brokenly." The language barrier may be why I have so little memory of Pappi, who was always quite kind to me, still the forgotten man in a household dominated by his charming wife, who was, of course, any child's delight. Etta reports that she attempted to draw Pappi out by getting him to talk about his legal career, but other than telling us that his most interesting case concerned a parrot and perjury she added no details. Ingolf played on the Steinway which Pappi had bought for him so many years before in Hamburg, and soon thereafter arrangements were made to have it shipped to our living room on Corning Street.

There was also a crayfish party near Uppsala: Ingolf and his brother Gert got drunk on aquavit and I sprained my ankle again. A few days later Etta reported that I was more than a little bored during the tour of the Stadhuset "so his limp got a little worse." Essentially I had a grand time and Ingolf's journals are full of references to this. On August 17 we went swimming in the Kottla lake and Ingolf notes, "Tony swims with belt far out and is so sweet and happy."

Ingolf's own mood was mixed. He too loved Sweden and he was most pleased to be reunited with his family. But there seemed to be so much unfinished business in America, and he caught a terrible cold – which improved just in time for his strenuous mountaineering adventure with Holger, on the last day of which the two walked 40 kilometers. Ingolf also made contact with some Swedish composers including Ingvar Lidholm and Hilding Rosenberg. As one might have expected from earlier accounts of their relationship, his rapport with Etta continued to be uncertain and problematic but on July 12, "a day of Halleluja" at Orsa, he reports a breakthrough: "Evening for a walk with E. It is all very desperate – silent resolutions on the brink of the depths. And then, on her bed in the hotel, the miracle. I am so terribly happy. The world is whole again." The next day he, Etta and Mammi went to Mora to see a ceramic church decoration executed by Gert: "Etta is so near, it is so wonderful."

Etta's own reactions to the summer are harder to discover since her journal entries were meant for others to read. I detect here a continuing contempt for the world of man, a bitter, cruel depiction of its vices and follies. On the boat, "the steward is tall and handsome in an ox-like way with bovine intelligence to go with the frame." At the Gashaga restaurant, where the service and the food were both found wanting, the waiter was denounced as a drunk – "a red-faced joy boy, but no queerer than all the other Swedish waiters," and the hostess was pictured as "a strange looking anemic woman with black middle-parted hair and a brazen manner."

Even more interesting are her comments on Mammi, for she now had a chance to observe the enemy at close range, to see what it was in Ingolf's mother that had produced a son so unambitious, so sentimental, so unwilling to take life at its face value. Etta had a long, last opportunity to cement her impressions on the day we began the return journey with a fourteen and a half hour travel extravaganza, cooked up by Ingolf, which got us back to Gothenberg via three trains, a cab, two railsbusses and a ferry over Vättern Lake. Mammi accompanied us and, several years later, Etta recorded her observations on this day and on this woman in a handwritten fragment.

First, Etta says, the visit to Sweden "engendered in me a grudging respect for mother-in-law stories." "The only thing my husband learned at his mother's knee was to bury his head in it." "She is a lovely woman with two feet firmly planted in the air, who assured me when we made a visit to Stockholm. . .that in 10 years her son (balding, etc.) hadn't changed a bit." On the last train trip two little boys were wrestling in the aisle. "Hilda Maria shook her head – my children never fought she said in her gentle delicate way." Here, Etta reports, Mammi's eyes actually filled with tears as she said, "Their childhood was a paradise, a paradise." "You're telling me?" Etta reports thinking to herself. Mammi gave a coquettish tilt of her bobbed blonde hair worthy of Mary Pickford and like a "screen ingénue Hilda gets what she wants at the end of each film." Then it was time to reflect on the after-effects of such a pampered childhood on her husband:

"Paradise Lost" sums up his whole life. He has from her – let us give her her due – a certain dignity, a keeping up of the chin, a never descending in manner to anything like coarseness, in short a behavior of charming stability in the face of anything. This is true in his own home or elsewhere. And it is reflex...They both always cultivate this keen appreciation of forms & fine gestures. You don't discuss things which are not nice because it is not nice to discuss them. Then you avoid bothering with their solution, but you have a quiet life. When it gets too noisy & thick & troublesome you can always retire & take a nap or smooth things over with a box of chocolates.

On August 23 we sailed from Gothenberg on the *SS. Gripsholm*, arriving back in New York on September 1. A week of business and socializing followed and on September 8 Ingolf took delivery on a 1946 Nash Ambassador sedan, a huge blue monster destined to be the successor of the famous Black Peter. This car was also named Peter, but because this was such a step-up in class, its full name was Mr. Peter Pemberton. That afternoon our family headed west, a progress slowed by flat tires, shock absorber problems and a failing water pump. Ingolf drove relentlessly and, when not slowed by car trouble, covered long distances, reaching Pittsburgh the first night, Monticello, Indiana, the second, Osceola, Iowa, the third, Kearney, Nebraska, the fourth, Estes Park, Colorado, the fifth, Nephi Utah, the sixth, and Los Angeles the seventh. Adventure was over and it was time for Ingolf to return to U.S.C. and for me to begin a third year at the Shenandoah Street School.

33. THE COLLECTOR

Collecting is a form of control and one of my responses to the disorder of a life in which my stepfather might disappear at any moment was to throw myself into the collection business with a frenzy that only an addict of order can sustain. My choice of collectible objects changed markedly over the years, but the goal was always the same, to bring system and completion to the chaos of the world.

I began with simple objects like playing cards and marbles. The other children enjoyed the thrill of the contest in the dust of Mr. Quigley's oil-stained parking lot, but my only interest in marbles was in picking up new specimens of the prized object. I was particularly fond of the translucent agates, which I could hold to the light of the sun in an effort to penetrate their deep secrets.

From marbles I moved on to milk bottle caps. At the north end of Corning the huge Adohr Dairy had its distribution center. By climbing under the fence it was possible to penetrate a marvelous stockade made up of piles of wooden milk crates. My friends enjoyed the cunning reconstructions that could be made in the configurations of the crates – thereby creating their own fort – but for me this dangerous foray had no other object than the retrieval of some rare bottle cap specimen, a gold double cream or a purple skimmed milk.

The paper caps could be pasted into a scrapbook, but my next collection was harder to display. Soft drink bottle caps, with their agreeable serrated edges and their metallic density, were the new objects of fascination. There were many varieties to be collected in an economy that still made room for the local bottler. At Lucky's Market on La Cienega there was a soft drink cooler. You reached into the murky cold waters, dragged out the bottle of Nehi Orange or Dad's Old-fashioned Root Beer, and twisted the cap off on a device suspended over a narrow metal box. No one had any objection to children squeezing their small hands into this box and retrieving the discarded caps. I never passed Lucky's without dipping into this treasure chest in order to see if there were any new specimens for my collection. I would occasionally purchase a flavor I disliked – if it meant I could add its cap to my horde.

Two collections that again required the scrapbook involved city names. For a while I had a collection of postmarks; each page in the scrapbook represented a state and I would clip the circular legend with the town of origin off of every letter or post card that came to our house and glue it into the appropriate page. I did the same thing, in a separate notebook, with the names of towns at the head of newspaper articles.

None of these obsessions with fixity and finality could rival, however, my great affection for stamp collecting. I began with stamps inserted in relevant sections of a stock book but my efforts took a giant leap forward when I purchased an edition of the *Scott International Junior Postage Stamp Album* from Bonnie Lloyd, whose brother Rodney had grown bored with the hobby and passed the volume in question on to his younger sister. The Lloyds were the next-door neighbors of the Kellers and a few eyebrows were raised when it was discovered that I had paid only $5 to the innocent Bonnie for the cherished publication, which included many stamps already collected by her older brother. In the event I was allowed to keep the book. Although not quite as complete as the "senior" version of the Scott International, this heavy blue-bound book did include every country and colony that had issued stamps before 1940 and spaces for almost all significant issues. In short it had spaces that needed to be filled by an obsessed collector like myself.

Soon everyone was on the lookout for stamps that I might soak. My father subscribed on my behalf to an approval service and I remember sitting in his flat at the front of our court when the new candidates had arrived, offerings that provided intriguing glimpses into an exotic new world: red and gold Argentinian oil wells, multicolored Swiss waterfalls, blue and green zebras from the Mozambique Company (well, Rodney pronounced this Mo-Zam-Bi-Queue). I always chose a modest total from the approval book, in part because I had discovered that many of the proffered issues were post-1940, and there was thus no place for them in my stamp book.

This problem was remedied, in part, by the production of a second, post-war volume brought out by Scott in about 1947. I purchased pages and binder from the Village Stamp Shop in Westwood and spent the better part of an hour trying to squeeze the former into the latter as I sat next to Benny Goodman's swimming pool while the musicians had a rehearsal inside the house. In the event I was frustrated; there had been so many new issues from so many new countries that the binder failed to accommodate them all, and for years the U.S. (which had pushed itself chauvinistically to the front) through Czechoslovakia had to be pinned together as a do-it-yourself prologue to the volume in question. It was precisely the kind of untidy solution that would rankle in the breast of an order freak. Still, it was a pleasure to move up to the full-sized international edition and for most of my life I have continued to indulge the passion..

Ingolf had many overseas correspondents, so he was a useful source of stamps for my collection, which, from the start, rashly included the *entire* world in its scope. Indeed, he pulled out his correspondence files and removed many stamps from letters he had received from family members and Swiss compatriots years earlier. Sweden and Switzerland were always well represented in my collection and their stamps provided me with some connection to the mysterious past of the man who was my stepfather.

34. STARS IN HIS EYES

My passion for sports baffled my parents completely. Etta would listen patiently while I recited the latest acts of heroism on diamond or gridiron, but she did so with a tolerant disinterest. There was no point whatsoever in speaking of these things to Ingolf for American sports did not interest him at all and he hadn't the slightest idea how they were played. Repeatedly I tried to instruct him in the rudiments of baseball. On June 1, 1952, during our annual trek to Inglewood to picnic with Grampa Gordon, I evidently tried again. "Tony comes over and gives me an excellent explanation of baseball. He is so charming and intelligent and handsome! This baseball business is really getting us together." A few nights later Ingolf, Etta, and I went to see Portland play my beloved Hollywood Stars, then managed by Fred Haney. Ingolf noted, "It is rather entertaining," but he seems to have enjoyed the crowd more than the game which, if I recall correctly, was one of those epic struggles won by the home team with a homerun in the bottom of the ninth. Ingolf never attended another game, though I did get him to a U.S.C.-U.C.L.A. track meet when I was a college freshman, an event dominated by the performance of my classmate Rafer Johnson.

The only time I can recall Ingolf *playing* baseball was in 1961, when I took him to the country during a visit to New York and we played softball with some of my friends. A lazy pop fly descended as he danced beneath it at shortstop, his arms raised in self-defense. *After* the white sphere had landed at his feet he at last reached for it with those pianist's hands that he would never risk by actually touching a ball in flight.

As for football, I never succeeded in getting him into the Coliseum. For many years his office backed up onto Exposition Boulevard and he was often perturbed by the sound of 100,000 screaming fans interrupting his Saturday afternoon's concentration, but in twenty-five years at U.S.C. Ingolf Dahl never saw a Trojan football game.

The Stars were a Pittsburgh Pirates farm club in the old Pacific Coast League, a Triple A transition point for ex-major leaguers who couldn't quite cut it any more and a nursery for rookie candidates for the big leagues.

Before major league baseball arrived on the West Coast in 1957 the youth of L. A. had to make a choice between the Los Angeles Angels, a Cubs farm club, and the Stars – as these two took on six other rivals: the San Diego Padres, the San Francisco Seals, the Oakland Oaks, the Sacramento Solons, the Portland Beavers, and the Seattle Rainiers.

It was only a short bus ride to Gilmore Field, part of a sports complex on Beverly Boulevard that later disappeared under the watchful CBS eye. Bleacher seats down the left field line could be had for a few cents and, with friends, I would often show up for a weekend double-header. We all wore our gloves in hopes of catching a foul ball but we never succeeded. I loved the atmosphere of this arena, the smart crack of the bat on the ball, the cries of the vendors' "Hey Beverly Ice Cream," the chance to see my heroes – Frankie Kelleher, George Schmees, Carlos Bernier, Johnny Lindell in the flesh. The death of right fielder Herb Gorman, who collapsed in the outfield one afternoon in San Diego, was one of the great tragedies of my youth.

When I was not in attendance I listened to the radio broadcasts of the Hollywood games. Mark Scott, the announcer, did live commentary of home games but away games were *recreated*: the action coming to the studio by ticker tape and the announcer using sound effects, crowd noises and the sound of hickory on horsehide, to supply the listener with the "sound" of a game in progress. Such was my loyalty that for several years I sent away annually for the official group photograph of the Stars.

My interest in football was slower to develop but I can remember when Los Angeles still had a team in the old All-America conference, the Dons, and when the L.A. Rams were dominated by the heroics of Bob Waterfield. My first attempt to listen to a college football broadcast came on New Year's Day, 1948, when U.S.C. hosted Michigan in the Rose Bowl. I had been looking forward to this event with keen anticipation but I was suffering from the flu and fell asleep after the opening kickoff, awakening only to discover that the local heroes had been swamped 49-0. It was not until 1950 that I saw my first college game, going as the guest of Betty Anderson, the U.S.C. band secretary. This was a wonderful introduction to the intensity of the struggle, for I remember many injured players being carried from the field as U.S.C. overcame Notre Dame 9-7.

I was a much better spectator than I was a player, although I participated in all the impromptu street games of my peers. I owned a pair of roller skates, which I much enjoyed, and I would often clatter down the sidewalks on these. Once I went to a roller rink somewhere near Culver City but my chief memory of this area as a sporting region again comes as a fan. Mike Livingstone, my classmate at Shenandoah, had a great passion for midget racing cars and once he insisted that I accompany him to a dirt track nearby. He made me root for the eventual second place finisher, a driver with the wonderful name of Yam Oka. Mike knew his racing and cheered for the inevitable winner, a chap named Troy Ruttman. A few years later Ruttman won the Indianapolis 500.

35. ON THE ROAD

Our family departed on what proved to be our last great outing as a trio on August 1, 1949. Haunted by the sounds of *Pierrot Lunaire*, which he had rehearsed the night before, Ingolf headed Peter Pemberton northwards along the eastern side of the Sierras and deposited us by nightfall in a cabin in Carson City. Etta was again the official chronicler of our Eastern tour, taking notes as we proceeded. Months after our return she began to assemble a scrapbook with souvenirs of the expedition, including all those travel decals I was *not* allowed to put on the windows of the Nash. She completed a text as well, but never got around to combining all the materials in a single volume. Ingolf naturally added notes to his private journal as well and from this source we learn that, having won twenty cents on a Nevada slot machine, "Tony has the gambling fever."

Ingolf's use of the name "Tony" was already out of date. Some months earlier I had come home from school to announce my intention to answer thereafter to "Anthony" only. I don't know what prompted me to reject my childhood name, though there was a *girl* in my class called Toni and this might have had something to do with it. Anthony is a mouthful of a name by which to address a child, and it was inevitably shortened to "Anth" by my friends and "Anthie" by my mother. I have never been Tony since, although I have wondered what it would be like to try it again. Tony is the name of a wholly different *persona* that I have yet to inhabit as an adult.

On the second day of the trip Etta surprised Ingolf by asking him if *she* could take the wheel for a while. *He* was astonished, but *I* was in on the gag. For months Etta had been taking clandestine driving lessons from my Uncle Morry. Sometimes I got to bounce up and down in the back seat as she practiced her gear-shifting. Our family knew how to keep secrets. She had survived her lessons and secured her license without the absent-minded and frequently missing Ingolf ever suspecting a thing. Her Winnemucca turn-off was a bit too fast and the car careened around the curve, but she soon settled down and spelled Ingolf on a number of occasions thereafter. Etta was always an overcautious driver but she stuck with it for a number of years and thereby enhanced the mobility of our family. "To the everlasting annoyance of my husband and son and a great many honk-happy motorists," she wrote sometime later, "I try to stay within the legal speed limits."

We stayed in motels and cabins most of the way across the country, with Twin Falls, Idaho, as our second rest spot. At night Ingolf and Etta took turns reading aloud, with a Dr. Dolittle book and Verne's *Mysterious Island* alternating as the preferred volumes. We spent nights three and four at Jenny Lake in the Tetons and Ingolf took us to Taggart Lake, where he had been with the Sierra Club three years earlier. Our swimming clothes got left behind during this jaunt and Ingolf had to drive back forty miles to recover them. I'm sure I gave several peevish sighs while this incident unfolded; my parents' inefficiency was an eternal cross I had to bear. Also, they were always getting behind schedule or proposing deviations from the approved route, thus spoiling the charts and graphs with which I hoped to maintain an *orderly* record of our progress.

After a night in Lusk, Wyoming, we reached the Black Hills and visited Wind Cave National Park. This succeeded in reminding Etta of a painting by Braque, but she too was in a complaining mood: "The tourists surrounding one are tourists, loud and uncouth – the same race the world over." No doubt their presence was used to explain why it was necessary, over my protests, to "haughtily skip Mt. Rushmore," but there were plenty of specimens of the breed in Wall, South Dakota, where we spent a steamy night in a two-bit hotel. The next morning, amid strains of a newly improvised song – "Oh We'll Have A Cup of Coffee in Kadoka" – Ingolf used some subterfuge to make an *unscheduled* turn-off into the

Badlands National Monument. After a night in Luverne, Minnesota, there was a rest day in La Crosse, Wisconsin. Ingolf had brought an inflatable raft and, like Jim and Huck, we floated a few feet down the Mississippi! On August 10 we had breakfast in Tomah, Wisconsin. Again I could tell that I was traveling with people who did not operate by the standards of normal parents. "We enter a little restaurant," Etta wrote, "but soon after we are seated Vaughn Monroe via the ubiquitous juke box succeeds in ghostriding us out of the joint." For reasons as frivolous as these I had to wait another ten minutes for my pancakes!

From Milwaukee we took the ferry to Michigan and spent a night in Muskegon. Then it was on to London, Ontario (where I suddenly developed a British accent), Niagara Falls, and Albany. In Bennington, Vermont I paid them back for Mt. Rushmore by refusing to tour a *museum*.

This trip, far from having sightseeing as its *raison d'etre*, was meant to provide Ingolf with an opportunity to make contacts and to be taken seriously by the musicians of the Eastern establishment. Appropriately our next stop was the MacDowell Colony in Peterborough, New Hampshire. Ingolf would himself spend some time here as a colonist in later years, but in 1949 it was the summer residence of Gail Kubik. I went swimming in Coswell's Pond, slipped off the raft, and swallowed a lot of water before Gail fished me out. I had to spend the next day in a hotel bed, convinced I was coming down with polio. Ingolf didn't fare much better that weekend, passing out from too many martinis at a cocktail party given in his honor. Chastened, we made our way to Round Pond, Maine, where we were the guests of Richard Donovan of the Yale Music Department. I had a grand time at my first clambake, and went hunting for bullfrogs, but my parents sniffed when it was suggested that they might enjoy hearing a troupe of *folk singers*.

On August 19, a day on which Ingolf was refused entrance to the Crawford House restaurant in New Hampshire because he did not have a jacket, we arrived at Vermont's Middlebury College. Here Ingolf was to be a member of the faculty of the fourth annual composer's conference, which began on the 20th and concluded September 3. Among other composers present that summer were George Rochberg, Esther Williamson and Otto Luening – who delighted Etta with his versions of Chinese opera, a radio intermission speaker at a Brahms symphony, a Walküre rehearsal, a lecture on "Behind the Beyond and Beyond the Behind," and his renditions of "Dinah, the Embraceable Minah."

I remember the setting as one which mixed much hard work with a great deal of fun. I issued my own tabloid, called "The Hillside News," full of gossipy innuendo about conference romances, I filled an empty gin bottle with water (which, predictably, resulted in some rather weak cocktails the next day), and I accepted George Finkel's invitation to conduct a string quartet. At one party Etta sang the blues. Ingolf lost his asthma atomizer and had to wake up several people as he searched the campus for it, wearing an overcoat over his nightclothes. He performed some of his own music at Middlebury and showed other works to campus visitors, including Harold Shapero. At Breadloaf he played the Copland *Sonata* by flickering candlelight, a thunderstorm having interrupted the usual power supply.

When it was time for us to return to California, Ingolf chose an adventurous detour through Canada, with stops in Ottawa and Sault Ste. Marie, then a swing across the northern plains via Duluth, Dickinson, North Dakota, and Gardner, Montana. On our Yellowstone junket he selected a scenic itinerary which elicited an "Over-my-dead-body-we've-got-to-make-time" look from the youngest passenger. Our way was barred by bears at one point and one of them ripped a red scarf, which I had hung out the window. Etta notes that on one of the long afternoons, "Anth and I snuggle under the wool blanket in the back. This proves to be silly as he is allergic." Such a rash, one of my sociologist friends once insisted, is the classic symptom of a momma's boy.

Our last two nights were a reprise of our first two, with stops in Twin Falls and Carson City. We were running out of opportunities for our ritual noontime root beer floats and I had only one more day, from the passenger seat, in which to chop off all objects with my imaginary scythe. It was with considerable interest that many years later I read the following passage in Jack Kerouac's *On The Road*:

> I told Dean that when I was a kid and rode in cars I used to imagine
> I held a big scythe in my hand and cut down all the trees and posts
> and even sliced every hill that zoomed past the window. "Yes! Yes!"
> yelled Dean, "I used to do it too only different scythe – tell you why,
> driving across the West with the long stretches my scythe had to be

immeasurably longer and it had to curve over distant mountains,
slicing off their tops...

This is precisely the fantasy that I had often embraced on any long
distance car trip, especially when the view consisted of nothing more
dramatic than telephone poles, water towers, and the occasional diner.
Curiously, much of *On the Road*'s cross-country traveling, the adventures of
Sal and Dean, of Kerouac and Neal Cassidy, took place in 1949, the same
year that my family was on the road too.

On the last evening we stayed in a place called Pepper's Patio. This
gave Etta a final opportunity to deplore miserable humanity – "I talk to
a screwball dame, presumably la Pepper, with a yappy little dog named
Blue Boy and a mass of dolls on a sofa in a weird office-living room; and
dentures she is having done by a Viennese dentist who is expensive but
my dear people come from all over the world to him." That night Ingolf
dreamt that he had taken posthumous tea with Richard Strauss, who had
died the previous day. Two days after our arrival he resumed his duties at
the University and I had a new beginning as a junior high school student.

36. BLUNDERKIND

Etta's ambitions for her son provide an interesting commentary on the
problems of child-rearing in a world dominated by the booboisie: "On the
one hand teach him to acquire as much culture as possible. On the other
teach him to hide it carefully like a specially built shoe for a club foot."
Part of the process of producing a child deserving of a place in this family
included the inevitable music lessons.

Etta first mentions these in a letter to Mammi on September 26, 1945,
shortly after our move to Corning Street. It had been decided that *waiting*
for Tony to show an interest in playing an instrument might not be the right
strategy after all. "Tony," she wrote her mother-in-law, "has had his third
piano lesson from Miss Gunderson. He is making the normal progress but
works only under protest, a phenomenon to which I pay no attention and
master Tony must count aloud to his great consternation every day after
school." Miss Gunderson was a large, soft, wrinkled, many-layered lady who
had a record of success with some of the other neighborhood children. She

had met her match in me. Ingolf, to offer the right note of encouragement, wrote a small piece for piano six-hands, *Frere Jacques and the Morning Bells*, which contained "Three Blind Mice" and "London Bridge" as well as the French song. It was performed by Etta, Ingolf, and the youngest student of the piano as we crowded onto a single piano bench at Christmas, 1945. It was dedicated "To our boy Anthony," but a childish hand has ominously supplied an additional inscription – "Some Crazy Junk I'm supposed to Learn," and, even worse, a sinister drawing is appended as well. This shows a child taking a torch to a bombed-out piano and the comment, "Wath (*sic*) a Shame."

After the Steinway arrived from Sweden Ingolf made a fateful attempt to succeed where poor Miss Gunderson had failed. He even did an arrangement of "Nature Boy," Nat King Cole's current hit, in an effort to win me to the pleasures of the keyboard. Again I rebelled. I was resolutely unprepared to surrender my own precarious identity, one that – in our household – had to battle so single-mindedly in order not to be swamped by his. To become a carbon copy of the *wunderkind*, to compete in a world in which the standards were already so high seemed to me to be entirely unfruitful.

One day Ingolf became furious with me. I had come home from school to be confronted with evidence of an awful crime. In the walnut veneer of his precious piano there lay the visible evidence of my actual signature! Who knows how long it had been there before he discovered it. Perhaps it was merely the result of some ill-conceived penmanship practice in which, without taking the proper precautions, I had employed only a thin piece of paper, pressing too heavily when I wrote my name, an accident. Perhaps there was an unconscious motive in the gesture, a desire to establish my own personality and reject his world at the same time. I recall the incident so well because it was the only time I ever remember my stepfather threatening me with physical punishment. But pleading my eternal innocence, I succeeded in eluding the ruler that lay poised above my wicked hand.

After being allowed to hang out at Middlebury with Bob Bloom, the New York Philharmonic oboist, I came back to California convinced that the oboe must be my instrument. It was then pointed out to me that no one *started* on the oboe and that I would have to master the clarinet first.

Ingolf engaged the L.A. Philharmonic's Merritt Buxbaum as my teacher and, on the whole, I made much better headway this time and actually enjoyed some of my afternoon lessons in Ingolf's studio behind the Keller's house. But there remained the old emotional impediment to my success as a music student and the pleasures of the experience were overwhelmed by its anxieties: when would Ingolf come to listen to my progress, the god of our family come to judge its youngest sinner? One day I developed a severe rash beneath my lip. This was diagnosed by an expensive Beverly Hills allergist as a sensitivity to the clarinet reed itself, a conclusion reached after I had worn for one diagnostic week a piece of the reed strapped to my arm.

This unexpected intervention was accepted as evidence that I was perhaps not made for the musical life after all, though I knew well enough not to manifest my glee too pointedly at home. No one ever suggested a third instrument and my after-school lessons and the relentlessly half-hearted practice sessions came to an end. Needless to say I regret the whole matter intensely now. Throughout my life I have had continuing cause to curse my inability to play an instrument – as my wise, finger-wagging parents had warned me I would. No doubt I would make even worse decisions in my pursuit of an independent life.

37. BELIEVE IT OR NOT

From an early age I was an avid reader. Some of my reading was undoubtedly useful in broadening my perception of the real world – though with the exception of sober articles in *The National Geographic* or *Boys' Life* I preferred a real world that was quixotic and heroic. I had, so it seems, memorized Ripley's *Believe It or Not* – "seen on a tombstone in Iowa: I. Etta Hamburger." Along with the rest of the sixth grade I enjoyed the prose of Richard Halliburton, particularly his account of the earliest Everest expeditions, and the death-defying heroics of Jim Corbett in *The Man-Eaters of Kumaon*. This book had such a fascination for us that Richard Binggeli, who may or may not have gotten an A in art, went on to paint a slightly cross-eyed tiger in its honor.

In fiction I preferred adventure over every other form of narrative. I loved Jules Verne and Jack London and the entire family was devoted to

Hugh Lofting. My favorite adventure author was Stephen Meader and at one time I had read almost all of his works. Surprisingly, at an age when such books would no longer have a fascination for my peers, I was also wedded to the Oz books, having inherited a collection of these turn-of-the-century epics from the Weisman children. I once read a psychological analysis of L. Frank Baum's oeuvre, in *Kulchur* magazine (Fall, 1961), entitled "The Oddness of Oz." The author, Osmond Beckwith, pointed out that all of Baum's male figures are weak, ineffectual, emasculated beings who must rely on the superior managerial skills of strong female characters for their survival. This thesis may explain some of my fascination for Oz – since it recapitulated some of the dynamics of our family structure: Dorothy, Ozma, Etta. How I wished to be translated to Oz and to have some beneficent spirit guide me though my own adventures. This wish eventually took the form of the childish desire to move to Kansas. But when I demanded to know why we couldn't move to the Jayhawk state my mother defended her refusal by citing the priorities of *her* man behind the curtain – "We can't move to Kansas because there are no mountains there."

The importance of radio in the national imagination is hard to recapture in the present era, which is so dominated by the television set. But this latter-day rival was only in its infancy when I was growing up in the Forties; for almost everyone radio still had one postwar decade of influence over the collective imagination, although it might be said that in our household its specter never dimmed.

In the late afternoon there were many fifteen-minute serials that fostered an addictive fascination in a principled day-dreamer like myself. I thrilled to the patriotic escapades of Jack Armstrong, the all-American boy, the Western adventures of Tom Mix, and the air-borne endeavors of Sky King. Weekend and evening crime fighters also held me in their spell: the Green Hornet; the Gangbusters; Casey, Crime Photographer; Sam Spade; The Whistler. The Fatman always received the same fortune when he stepped onto the scales – Danger! and The Shadow alone knew what evil lurked in the heart of man. My mother would often listen along with me in the evenings, explaining away the many adult mysteries that I failed to unravel myself, and we would occasionally be joined by Ingolf for weekend comedy shows like Jack Benny or Fred Allen. I particularly enjoyed the ritualized patterns of such shows: in every episode a bit of byplay with Rochester, a song from Dennis Day, Jack's banter with Mary Livingstone, or Fred's weekly trip down Allen's Alley to visit Senator Claghorn, Mr. Peabody or Mrs. Nussbaum. I was also devoted to Bob Hope (whom I always favored over the wet Bing Crosby), *Burns & Allen*, *Duffy's Tavern*, *Baby Snooks*, *Life With Luigi*, *People Are Funny*, and *Fibber McGee*. The latter's famous closet represented, indeed, every storage place in our own cramped apartment, but of course we were never permitted the chaos of collapse which Fibber instigated every program, in spite of Molly's sensible warnings.

Two special radio favorites offered a whimsical view of teenage life that succeeded in giving me a totally false view of the misery that lay ahead of me: *Henry Aldrich* and *Our Miss Brooks*. This type of radio was not, I'm afraid, deeply wedded to the notion of real life: when it was not patently ridiculous in its villainies it was cloyingly sentimental in its view of family life – in short it provided an easy escape route for a listener who was perpetually unsatisfied with his own family structure.

Some new categories of radio programming brought me entirely outside the orbit of the listening habits of my parents, who would condescend to turn on the switch only for Texaco's Metropolitan Opera broadcasts – unless we were in the car when there was a mighty tussle over the dial, usually won by Ingolf, who would listen enthralled to large symphonic compositions that seemed to come to an end a dozen times before actually doing so – probably my first taste of Mahler. I now began to listen to sports programs and, after I entered junior high school, to popular music shows. The Fifties do not strike me as a particularly outstanding era in popular music. But I was mesmerized at the time by the rebellious vibrato of Johnny Ray and charmed by the sweet ballads of Perry Como and Eddie Fisher. The heart-rending pleas of these crooners, with their open expressions of forbidden emotion and their relentless struggle against dashed hopes, embodied my own search for a totally sympathetic admirer, some gorgeous creature who wouldn't tell me to clean my room or practice my handwriting.

Radio persisted in misleading me on the subject of romance. This was due, in part, to my habitual interest in the soap opera, whose heroines continued to elicit my warmest sympathies as I lay recovering from some childhood illness, and in part to my great regard for their more sophisticated evening counterparts who were relentlessly pursued to the accompaniment of the sweeping chords that announced the arrival of *Lux Radio Theater*. I was forever in thrall to the essential wonderfulness of the beautiful woman, a creature who might profit from the true-hearted interventions of such a loyal listener as myself. But in this category of dreaming even the radio could not rival the parade of unobtainable fantasies on offer in another much favored medium of my boyhood years, the cinema.

Movies were a part of my heritage and my interest in them could be seen as carrying on a family tradition. Both of my grandfathers had been involved in the business, Adolph Linick as a picture house entrepreneur in Chicago and Isadore Gordon as a tailor on the RKO lot. Grampa Gordon now made Cary Grant's suits and worked on the flame-proof costume worn by James Arness as *The Thing*. Ingolf frequently played in studio orchestras and Leroy had just helped organize the screen story analysts into a separate union at M.G.M.

There were three movie houses within walking distance of Corning Street, all on Pico Boulevard, and I spent long Saturday afternoons at each. The Lido stood at the corner of Pico and La Cienega, the Picfair at Pico and Fairfax, and the Stadium on Pico a few blocks west of Robertson. It often cost more to buy popcorn and jujubes than it did to get in, particularly when special rates were offered for kids, and I would always get my money's worth by taking in a double feature. Often I had no idea what I would see before joining the queue. Sometimes I would go with others, particularly for some twenty cartoon extravaganza, but usually I went alone, allowing no one to intrude on the deep reverie of these weekly escape attempts.

Many of the films I saw were several years old, but this did not matter since they were new to me. I retook every Pacific island along with John Wayne and the Fighting Seabees. I had a great passion for these war films, never tiring of their formulas and never doubting my own courage in similar situations. I often wore my sailor hat to such films – as a way of enhancing the illusion of membership in the heroic elite.

I also loved swashbuckling adventure tales, being particularly fond of anything starring Douglas Fairbanks, Jr., and I would not say no to any comedy starring Abbot and Costello, Bing and Bob, Red Skelton, Danny Kaye or The Marx Brothers. I saw a lot of college campus capers and much *film noir*, where I was mostly interested in making sure that the murderers didn't get away with it unless they were pretty. My parents tried to raise the cultural ante a bit as I grew older, taking me to see *Henry V*, *The Bicycle Thief*, *The Red Pony*, and *Oliver Twist*. Etta took me to see *Johnny Belinda* at the Lido but I did not understand that Jane Wyman had been raped and Etta did not care to go into such matters with me.

The first great film biography to win my fervent admiration was *The Jolson Story*, which was revived in 1949 when the sequel, *Jolson Sings Again*, came out. My classmate Mike Livingstone had made the entertainer into a Jewish saint and specialized in miming to Jolson records, so I too was caught up in the cult and never failed to glance mournfully at Jolson's tomb, which was visible from the freeway as it sliced through the Baldwin Hills.

As before, I was infatuated by the screen goddesses and I had a long list of favorites headed by the red-headed Maureen O'Hara and closely followed by Ava Gardner in *One Touch Of Venus*. From the films of the era I refined my wholly inaccurate vision of the opposite sex, seeing these glamorous screen creatures as perfect in their wonderfulness and myself as the one true champion who could rescue them from the shallow cads who failed to appreciate their mythic grandeur. Walking home in the twilight after an afternoon of such romance, with the flowering hedges releasing their perfume and the crickets adding their charming rhythm, I would be swollen with feelings of omnipotence and superiority. At home I would take the top off the quart bottle of Royal Crown Cola and pour a small portion of the brown liquid into a little shot glass we kept for mixing drinks. Fortified by several shots of pretend whisky my mood of mastery could last at least until Etta asked me why I hadn't burned the trash in the incinerator.

On one of my sentimental walks through my old neighborhood I had a chance to walk past all of the old movie houses of my youth, seeing at first hand what thirty years can do to a dream palace. The Lido had completely disappeared as a structure, the Picfair was a burnt-out hulk, and the Stadium, whose tower still beckoned, was no longer a place for worshippers of the cinema; it was a synagogue instead.

As we lived in such a Jewish neighborhood it was not surprising that I would come home from school one day with a series of questions for my mother. The first of these was, "Am I Jewish?" "Yes." The litany continued.

"Are you Jewish?" "Yes" "Is Leroy Jewish?" "Yes" "Is Ingolf Jewish?" "No."
The answers to such questions were clearly important in West Los Angeles,
where the failure to be Jewish could mark you out as a member of the
minority. I could feel this great ethnic dichotomy because my high school
would be divided rather evenly between Jewish and gentile pupils while
my junior high school had been eighty percent Jewish. I knew this because
on Rosh Hashana or Yom Kippur my classroom would be emptied of
everybody but the teacher, five or six shame-faced gentiles, and me – the
mock-goy, the boy whose parents would never have condoned absence
from classes on the basis of anything so frivolous as religion.

Now it is 1951. I am thirteen years old. What happens to Jewish boys
when they are thirteen? Jewish friends like Allan Solomonow were having
their bar mitzvahs, but there was no chance that *I* would be allowed to
participate in a ceremony which would be denounced by my parents as
some sort of barbaric ritual. Allan recruited me to sell raffle tickets for his
synagogue, a process that was often embarrassing because I was frequently
quizzed on my own Jewishness by suspicious customers who had never
seen me at *shul*.

My parents' refusal to allow me to participate in the rites of passage for
which I yearned was based on their objection to religion, not to Judaism
specifically. Indeed they were equally opposed to my attending church, a
subject that frequently came up when the pious elders of Troop 50 (which
met in the Westminster Presbyterian Church on Robertson) suggested
that this might be a good idea for me. A few years later when most of my
fellow scouts had enrolled in the R.O.T.C. program at Hamilton High,
across the street from the church, our group did attend a service during a
weekend retreat at Fort MacArthur. When I noted that the minister had
praised our piety and interest, Ingolf and Etta snorted in derision and
succeeded in wiping out any traces of self-satisfaction on my part.

I suppose that I can sympathize more fully today with their desire to
keep their only son from sinking into the arms of alien idolatries, but at
the time their anti-religious obsession seemed to be only one more item
of evidence in the inventory of my parents' oddness. At least they let me
worship at the movies.

Meanwhile the conventional family structure for which I craved could
be reclaimed only a few houses to the north, at 1931 Corning Street. This

was the home of Etta's sister Lillian, her husband Morry, their two children Stephen and Julie, and their dog, Lady. I spent a great deal of my youth here, acutely aware of all the disparities between this family and my own.

Morry Keller had tried his hand at various pursuits after leaving the army. He and a partner had tried to invent and market a plastic-handled pickle fork, one of which remained in our kitchen drawer for years. When this enterprise foundered he returned to his old love, the law, and eventually became a hearing officer and finally a judge in the state workman's compensation courts. Once he took me downtown for lunch at a soda fountain and I was ushered into the hearing room where he presided. Morry had an excellent sense of humor and a keen wit. Stephen, several years my junior, had what we would today identify as learning difficulties and coordination problems, and his progress through the same schools I attended was difficult. He was an extremely sweet and good-spirited little boy and I am certain I made him and his pretty younger sister, Julie, quite miserable with my bossy ways, marching them in close order up and down their own driveway, putting them through batting practice, pasting Julie's name on her forehead with sticky letters (I spelled it "July"), managing their affairs in general. Nevertheless they were the nucleus of my gang.

At the Kellers one could expect a remedy for all those deficiencies that were so manifest at 1955 1/2. Dinner was served only once, at the same time each day, and you had your choice between sweet or salt butter. You could read *Life* magazine. The World Series was a fact of life, an NFL game would be on the radio on Sunday afternoons, and the mostly collie Lady would be curled up on your feet. And – most wonderful of all – there would be a television set in their living room.

As the Fifties advanced TV aerials popped up on the rooftop of every household on Corning Street but *not* on the roof of my house. Ingolf and Etta, to my considerable anguish, refused to have a set, considering the whole enterprise devoid of interest, demeaning, anti-intellectual, crassly commercial. Yes, they nipped over to the Linicks or the Kellers on rare occasions when something was "worth seeing," but in all their lives they never retreated from their original stand. I suppose that my publication, in the 1970's, of several articles on television programming must be seen as a last act of revenge against those puritanical saints who withheld from me *Crusader Rabbit*, *Space Patrol*, *I Love Lucy*, and *Highway Patrol*.

Morry hired me to mow and water his lawn, my first part-time job. Once a week I would fetch the lawn mower from the same garage that housed Ingolf's studio and I would zip over back and front yards, a task made more difficult when the Kellers purchased a magnolia tree which they planted in the middle of the front lawn. I did not need much encouragement to hang around, finding the uncomplex structure of the establishment and my Aunt Lillian's unmixed affection for me to be a heady remedy for the chaos I encountered at home. To this day I am much more likely to have dreams set in 1931 Corning Street – which was eventually expanded so that each child could have a bedroom – than I am to find myself again in 1955 1/2. But you can't go home away from home again either. After the Kellers bought a house in Woodland Hills in the early Sixties some developer bought the property and pulled down every stick of those spaces that had once been so significant in Ingolf's life and my own. About the only evidence of the presence of my family on this site was the tree with its dark leaves and fragrant white blossoms. This alone survived, and the new apartment complex that rose on the ashes of our dreams was called, believe it or not, The Magnolia.

38. WE SING THY PRAISE ALWAYS, PASTEUR

For the recent graduates of Shenandoah Street School the next stage in our academic careers began with our enrollment in September, 1949, at Louis Pasteur Junior High School – on 18th Street, a few blocks east of La Cienega. Here we remained for three years, completing the seventh, eighth, and ninth grades. Pasteur was again within walking distance of Corning Street and, abandoning my bicycle, I completed the short stroll morning and afternoon in all weathers, pausing always on the way home for an orange and vanilla push-me-up ice cream from the little van parked a block away from the school.

Pasteur was an admirable institution in many respects and it still exists as a magnet school in its current incarnation within the public school system of Los Angeles. In my day it opened its doors to all comers, profiting from an intake of bright, ambitious, well-behaved youngsters who took their lessons seriously and gave their teachers only the wittiest of lip. Asking the blue-haired cancer suffering Miss Draper, "How long were you *a broad?*"

was about as wicked as our lot got. Later the remark seemed particularly ill-timed, when a weeping Helen Jewett Rogers, our principal, came onto the intercom to announce the death of our teacher.

I continued to make a success of most of my classes and undertook new subjects. In my English class Mrs. Virginia Probert actually introduced us to the pleasures of literature, although I did not take immediately to *Lorna Doone*. In this same classroom I had my first experience of the cold war, a "Drop!" drill during which we were expected, on command, to huddle protectively beneath our desks in readiness for the disaster to come: a sure sign that the Russians had got the bomb too.

At Pasteur I had a semester of typing, which provided me with the meager keyboarding skills I have struggled with ever since, and I took a year of Latin, which I loved. As a seventh grader I was a member of the glee club, much fussed over by Mrs. Alta Dale because of the prominence of my stepfather in local musical life – that is until she discovered that I was turning in no reviews of the many concerts she supposed I would naturally be attending. I also had grave troubles finding the proper vocal range, as my voice was changing, for the required solo rendition of "All The Things You Are." At a later stage I also had a semester of drama, earning a part in a one-act comedy in which I played a character called Noodles. Miss Annis Thompson, much feared for her habit of throwing her keys at recalcitrant players, had a fearsome time trying to get me to smile as we rehearsed curtain calls – I had spent most of my life resisting such demands for insincere expressions of happiness, responding at best with a lopsided smirk.

The duplicity of the adult world had its exemplars in my own home, as I was to learn again and again, but from Miss Thompson I learned something of this betrayal in an easier to detect fashion. We all had to audition for a place in her class and she enthusiastically signed all of our forms but I noticed that the rejected Dick Dardarian had received only her initials while the successful candidates got her full signature. Years after my lone theatrical foray I was walking down a sidewalk in downtown Los Angeles when I heard Steve Franklin shouting at me from across the street, "Hey, Noodles!"

Steve was, as I recall, prone to exaggeration. I once lazily swatted at one his pitches as it floated over the plate and got a line drive single to center

– "You've got a lot of power," Steve enthused. Such athletic triumphs were hard to come by. Once our P.E. teacher sent us out to teach ourselves the rudiments of soccer. On Pasteur's giant tarmac, a bombing range for the local seagulls, there were no goal nets and so two piles of coats were placed at either end of the field. When someone actually passed the ball to me I attempted to unload it in panic as rapidly as possible to someone on my team, missed, and saw the ball run innocently over the end line. As we were coming in to shower, another kid, much to my astonishment, said, "Hey, Linick, you scored the only goal."

In fact my days as a junior high school athlete were not glorious ones. I had no arm strength and could not chin myself or climb the rope, tasks that the athletic Allan Solomonow could complete while contorted into an L-shape. I was usually the next-to-last person picked for any team, often the last in any race, and in the great contests of the year, when all boys were divided into Bears, Eagles, Panthers, and Bulldogs, I was of no use to the Bears. I was somewhat uncoordinated and even had to correct, with the help of a physician, a somewhat knock-kneed lope. I tripped over the desk runner at the back of the classroom as I was being escorted in to see a film and cut my chin so badly that Etta had to be sent for, and I managed to get knocked off my Scwhinn by a wealthy lady driver from Cheviot Hills as I was making my way along Robertson.

With this record of athleticism, gym class was a torment for me, except when I strained my Achilles tendon and had to sit on the bench, admiring the endeavors of the cool guys to whom I didn't matter. I hated the beer-bellied instructors, the stench of the locker room – where I could never get my combination to work when I was in a hurry – and the embarrassment of having to shower with older boys. To make matters worse I was assigned a position in the ballroom and, in a bit of inspired horseplay, flipped a basketball at the forehead of an unsuspecting Byron Ackerman and separated the right side of his glasses from the left. Finally, as if this catalogue of humiliations was not sufficient, while I was undergoing a routine examination prior to going off to Boy Scout camp one summer, cousin Julius Kahn recorded the fateful diagnosis on my medical record – "slightly obese." The sugary substances with which I had been comforting myself were prohibited, and I now had to munch on unappetizing diet bars as my afternoon snack.

About the only place that I could be sure to succeed in sports was back on Corning Street, where I was the oldest boy and where I had two much younger cousins to boss around. We had our own baseball team, the Corning Stars, and Etta bought us blue caps and sewed on a yellow C so that they looked very much like the University of California cap I wore as a fifty-year old. Finding a place to play was not easy. The tennis ball we used would soon disappear in the plumbago of the Keller's back yard or over the short left field fence into the Balinoff's or over the right field fence into the alley. I was continually changing the rules and so I declared home runs to be outs. Sometimes we went over to the authentic dirt diamond at Adohr but here the dimensions were so great that any ball through the infield would run forever. And when we tried to play on Jerry Magadman's front lawn I hit a drive down the left field foul line and succeeded in breaking the front window of the neighbor living across the street. I tried, very briefly, to blame this tragedy on Stevie's pitching, but by the end of the day I was dutifully ringing the doorbell of the violated householder and asking for my ball back.

The happiness I could still draw from playing with these younger kids seems to me, in retrospect, part of my unwillingness to face the challenges of adolescence. Although I was fascinated by the exchange of dirty jokes in the lunch line, Bob Sagedy's lascivious wail over Debra Paget's breasts, and the whizzing pornographic pages of somebody's Tijuana Bible, I was particularly uncomfortable in any social setting involving members of the opposite sex. When some older girls moved next door I was allowed to follow them up to the glorious new Foster's Freeze on La Cienega, north of Airdrome, where whipped vanilla Frosties were served with a variety of toppings to those who had forgotten they were on a diet – but on the way home the girls would make me trail behind while they joked about my sheep-like qualities.

On Friday nights I was enrolled in a dancing class given in a community center building at the corner of Preuss and Robertson. Here I learned the waltz, the box step, and had another go at the fox trot. I found the whole process to be excruciatingly embarrassing and I was so uncoordinated that I did no better on the dance floor than on the athletic field. Still, the lessons were of some use to me on the luckiest day of my junior high school career. Pasteur's version of a prom was a dance called the Mardi Gras. Since *all* were expected to participate, the complex business of pairing us up with members of the opposite sex was solved in a straightforward and practical manner. Each sex was lined up by height and we marched forward to meet our properly-sized partner in the opposite line. Mine turned out to be the prettiest girl in the ninth grade, Joan Gish, earning me the envy of every other male dancer. We did quite well together but when Joan invited me to a party at her house I was so ill at ease at the prospect that I invented an urgent camping trip. Fortunately, I did a little bit better than this when we played spin the bottle at Marlene Weisbart's birthday party.

I don't wish to paint too dark a picture of my Pasteur years. There were many moments of happiness, although most of these were away from school. I managed to keep pace with the rest of the teenagers in the clothing styles of the time, at least after the *wrong* leather jacket from the Linicks had been exchanged for the right one from the "Chubby" department at Sears. It accompanied my turquoise, pink, and lime green fluorescent socks and my pre-Elvis blue suede shoes.

But a full appraisal of life at Pasteur would not be complete without some attention to a final dark chapter. One area of the curriculum that has all but disappeared was still very important in the life of male students in the early Fifties. Following the mandates of a society that wished to prepare its youth for the world of work Pasteur offered a series of required courses in the manual arts. In short, it provided an introduction to those very skills that the parents of *our* students, in their flight from the ghetto, prayed that their lads might never have to use again.

We started off with Agriculture and actually succeeded in growing a few vegetables in a patch at the side of the school. This was followed by Drafting, or mechanical drawing, where my motor skills kept me laboring with t-square and compass over geometric shapes while the more advanced students were designing the next generation of automobiles. I managed to complete Electric Shop without frying myself and I completed a corner shelf in Wood Shop after smoothing my triangular inserts to such a degree of fineness that they ended up supporting nothing larger than a thimble when the Linicks bravely mounted the object in their bedroom. My real troubles began with Metal Shop. I labored for long hours over a coal scuttle but Mr. Dinwidee ordered me to bring him tin snips with which he chopped a chunk out of the finished product, declaring, "We don't let D work go out of the Metal Shop." I protested that I had wanted to present this very scuttle to my mother (in case she had any coal that needed shifting) and I think I managed to sneak the wounded object out anyway in the sleeve of my jacket. Learning from my mistakes I earned an A on my next project, a pancake spatula, although, of course, it was entirely the work of a more dexterous friend.

I thought I was doing okay as an apprentice printer in Print Shop but one afternoon, while I was setting type, I must have annoyed Mr. Silvera by exchanging some non-verbal communication with Leigh Peffer at the desk opposite. "What was that?" my teacher wanted to know. "I just made a face at Leigh," I responded innocently. "I think you should continue," he replied, "Make some more faces." Under this command I tried out a variety of grimaces, eventually sticking my tongue out at my friend. In spite of the fact that he had ordered this display, the sadistic shop teacher decided to take umbrage at this disclosure of tongue, and marched me over to a sink where I was required to lick a bar of soap. I refused to gag or swallow or drink water and my courage, and the obvious injustice in the incident, earned me the congratulations of the entire class as we made our way to social studies. Interestingly enough, I never told my parents about this affair, sure that a maddened Etta would have created quite a stir in the corridors of Louis Pasteur Junior High School if she had gotten wind of the matter, thereby *increasing* my mortification. Mr. Silvera won some award a few months later as Father Of The Year.

39. APACHES IN THE FOREST

For most of my years at Pasteur the garage below our apartment served as the clubhouse of the Apache patrol of Troop 50 of The Ocean Bay Council of the Boy Scouts of America. Our cars never made it into this space, which was used instead for the storage of camping equipment and for the piles of newspapers that the Scouts were presumably collecting for some future paper drive. In fact the bundles remained there for months at a time, serving as excellent resting places for young teenagers engaged in non-stop chatter. Occasionally we would liberate them from their string bindings and hurl them at one another in an impromptu and spirited paper fight.

I had begun my interest in scouting while still at Shenandoah and had worn the blue Cub Scout outfit proudly for a year or so before a Boy Scout Troop was organized at the Westminster Presbyterian Church. Here we were organized into patrols under the benevolent calm of Dick Stead, a milkman, and the pastoral eye of Reverend Radcliffe. For several years we learned woodsy skills, worked on merit badges, did a lot of marching in civic parades, went on camping trips, and horsed around. There were initially two patrols, the lame Flaming Arrows and the competitive Apaches. Five close friends were my partners in this khaki-clad league and some friendships were formed that have lasted a lifetime.

I have the impression that my family had been California residents far longer than those of my friends, many of whom had moved to the state as young children. Richard Binggeli, the patrol leader, was from Sioux Falls, South Dakota. Of Swiss descent on his father's side, Dick was a very serious boy with wavy blonde hair, a vulpine set of teeth, and acne. He was an excellent student, particularly in the sciences, and a keen outdoorsman. He had a wry sense of humor, but he was occasionally a bit stubborn and literal-minded. It was Dick who insisted we meet every Saturday in our garage, where I was appointed patrol scribe – a role I have never abandoned.

Dick lived on Reynier Avenue, a block west of Shenandoah, with his attractive mother and a father who worked the night shift as a tool and die maker at McDonnell Douglas. A block to the south John Daly lived on Bedford, one of the streets of my infancy. Born on the East Coast, he had an English mother and a charming Irish father. John was a tall fleshy chap with brown hair and an allergy to peas; he had a florid complexion and a subterranean temper that I was to feel the full force of on more than one occasion. Like Dick, John was an outstanding student, particularly in mathematics and science. He too had a droll sense of humor; he was an articulate and passionate debater – almost always taking Dick's side in the interminable squabbles of the Apache patrol.

Leigh Peffer had lived in several homes to the west of the rest of us, usually on the borders of Culver City. His parents were divorced and his mother Edna had married an All-State Insurance salesman, Don Simpson. With his punk hair styles, broken nose, and passion for motor cycles he presented a much more relentlessly working class image than the rest of us, a stereotype reinforced by his somewhat checkered academic career. I found his candor and his humor refreshing and we soon shared a great enthusiasm for Indians – as we were still allowed to call Native Americans at the time.

Dick Dardarian was Leigh's best friend but he actually lived nearer to me, on Cheriton, a couple of blocks closer to La Cienega than Corning Street. A dark skinned Armenian lad, with brown eyes and black hair, Dick was a mischievous cherub who was always keen to set off on any new adventure. He had a Doberman named Gretchen and at puppy time I was sure to be present to see the half blind pups search for a drink. His older brothers had traveled through our schools ahead of us and knew a lot of ancient gossip about our teachers. Not a great scholar either, Dick was far more knowledgeable in sexual matters than the rest of us (it was he who identified and delineated the uses of the tampon we had found hidden among our newspapers) and his commentaries were taken seriously by the rest of us.

Allan Solomonow lived three blocks to the north in a mock hacienda on Shenandoah itself. Originally from Omaha, Allan had brought with him a mother who was chronically indisposed, a father who had been missing a chunk of his shoulder since the battle of Leyte Gulf, and a little brother, Howard (Butchie). Allan was also an outstanding student and a superb athlete, in spite of his short stature. He was a well-muscled wrestler (who liked to practice his new holds on me) and a fast runner. He had an usual walk, however, and one of his nicknames was "Paddlefoot." Allan and I formed a partnership to patent inventions. We invented (but did not patent) a jet car and a rubber bumper which would cut down on the severity of the inevitable accidents. Allan also shared my passion for word play. We invented a new, secret vocabulary to describe every portion of the female anatomy; indeed, Allan was always coaxing my mother to show him her navel (which we cleverly called a "marine"). Another specialty was spelling every word backwards: "Hello, Nalla Enyaw Wonomolos, this is Ynohtna Kcinil." I occasionally spent a night in one of Allan's bunk beds, a sleep interrupted by flying objects in the dark. I admired the groaning board which was always set before us in the Solomonow kitchen and, of course, the television set on which, after we had separated Butchie from Hopalong Cassidy, we would watch all our favorite wrestling stars, Gorgeous George,

Mr. Moto, Baron Leone, Argentine Rocca. Ironically, a few doors away lived a champion in a real sport, the famous but retired heavyweight, Primo Carnera. I still remember vividly how, after an evening at Allen's, I would climb aboard my bike (which I once traded to Johnny Orvis for some stamps until my mom found out) and race through the darkened streets down Sawyer, up the incline of our alley, down its hill, and along the back fences until I reached the Apache's garage.

Allen accompanied me in 1950 on my second two-week outing at the YMCA summer camp, Round Meadow, near Lake Gregory. Obviously I had gotten over my feelings of discomfiture engendered by the six weeks I had spent at Duffy's Camp in 1945; indeed, I quite liked YMCA camp after recovering from the initial trauma of a lost pack. I got to wear a "rag" around my neck, I listened enthralled to the ghost stories and participated in the sing-alongs at the camp fire, I made a lanyard during craft hour, and once I found two painted peanuts during the treasure hunt, each redeemable for candy bars at the camp store. There was only a minor emphasis on religion at "chapel" services, and Allan was even allowed to give a discourse on Judaism. Our counselors, each a recent high school graduate, were objects of extreme fascination. They were full of sex chatter and they had brought with them a minor pornographic classic, *Everybody Loves Irene*, which they selfishly refused to share with the rest of us. I had been at Duffy's camp when news of the atomic bomb first entered our world and I was at "Y" camp the week the Korean War began. Our counselors all said they were going to enlist as soon as we got back to town and I often wonder if any of them did. The great trauma of my second summer at Round Meadow came when Ingolf and Etta arrived to visit us at the midway point. They let Allan and me off on one side of Lake Gregory so that we could walk around its shore and meet them later on the other side. After a while we discovered that our road was not leading us to the other side at all and, a panicky hour later, we had to hitch a ride in order to be reunited with my worried parents.

At one time or another every one of the Apaches served as my "best" friend, if only for a few weeks at a time – for the enthusiasms and allegiances shifted rapidly as each of us struggled to define our own personalities. I note that Ingolf began to invite me and my friends to the U.S.C. concerts that he conducted (Etta never missed any of these). Allan accompanied me on December 14, 1949 and on the same date two years later Dick Dardarian, Leigh Peffer and I saw Ingolf conduct *The Consul.*

The next year many of the Apaches shifted their allegiance to the Scout's camp, Emerald Bay, on the northern end of Catalina Island. We took a small launch from Long Beach to Avalon, during which I got thoroughly and miserably seasick (my motion sickness, which often made mountain expeditions into a torment as well, persists to this day). Then we had a long walk (dubbed "the Death March") in scorching weather past the Isthmus and on to our camp, a mostly waterless trek made all the more poignant by the tantalizing presence of all that beautiful salt water washing the shores just below us. Dick Binggeli and I, assisted by the camp doctor, earned our First Aid merit badges, I became a proficient swimmer at last, and somehow I survived some cook's attempt at humor, peanut butter and mayonnaise sandwiches.

Ingolf was only occasionally present as a chaperone on Boy Scout activities, at which times I always managed to behave more immaturely than usual. It was Tony Daly who shepherded us to Camp Josepho in the Pacific Palisades the day we tried and failed to earn our cooking merit badges. The wise man had brought his own food, which he ate in the car, while we were burning the Emu (well, chicken) in tinfoil buried in a fiery pit. My stepfather was more likely to appear on one of the many hikes that we now organized independently of the Scouts, creating our own special club for this purpose, The Forest Patrol.

The Forest Patrol had its own green and brown flag and a membership that embraced all of the Apaches, plus additional school chums who happened to be in favor at the time. All would be packed into Peter Pemberton and Ingolf would drive us to some spot along the Angeles Crest Highway where we would try to bag as many summits as possible. This was in imitation of our leader himself, who belonged to a subsection of the Sierra Club, The Hundred Peakers, which awarded a certificate of merit to anyone who had reached 100 Southern California summits over 5000 feet in elevation.

It is a marvel to me that Ingolf persisted in these activities on our behalf – because our very first outing was such a disaster. On December 21, 1948, on the eve of my eleventh birthday, he took six of us for a camping trip down to the floor of Devil's Canyon. He hadn't calculated on snow and we were totally unprepared for the cold and the wet. Also, still thinking of us a tiny children, he had put four of us into a single pup tent. One of my pals, charged with drying our boots by the fire, got bored with this chore and allowed a sole to burn off. Another chum dropped his spearmint into the soup. The next morning, after a cold, damp, cramped night, we all wanted to go home. Ingolf led our dispirited lot on a four-mile hike up the snowy trail, with intermittent sniveling over cold hands and feet. It was a miracle he could keep his sense of humor under such conditions, but when he was asked where John was, his famous reply was, "Daly is following weakly." To keep us amused he tried to tell us the story of the *Nibelungenlied* and when we got confused he switched to a fairy tale whose monster keeps commanding the maiden, "Virgin, take off your shirt!" "What's a virgin?" we wanted to know. I do not remember Ingolf's answer – except that it was not the right one.

Ingolf led us on Forest Patrol hikes every few months, accompanying us to the Vasquez Rocks or, closer to home, to the Bronson Caves, both movie locations where we could have weenie roasts, play Ambush, and toss around papier-maché boulders. He charmed every one of my friends. His cultured attitudes, humane outlooks, love of the mountains, and his musical gifts affected many of them deeply and several, to this day, argue that he served as an important influence on their lives. Who else would have indulged Leigh and me in our desire to return to Devil's Canyon in June of 1952 for a weekend *as* Indians? We had researched the matter for months and made our own costumes, including shields, bead work, and headdresses. "Two adorable braves come," Ingolf recorded in his journal as we appeared for the first time with our war paint on. He took so many pictures that we got disgruntled, cheering up only when, at the dinner campfire, he told us the story of his freighter excursion to Tripoli in 1933.

By 1952 there wasn't much of a future left for the Apaches. Allan had gotten disgruntled over our Saturday meeting times, which interfered with his celebration of the sabbath, and Troop 50 had made him patrol leader of a new group for young kids, the Bat Patrol. The two Dicks, Binggeli and Dardarian, had also quarrelled when the latter called the former a "son of a bitch" and Binggeli, taking umbrage on his mother's behalf, had squared off for a cursory scuffle. In fact, we had just about reached the end of our careers in scouting. We had achieved First Class standing and many of us were working on promotion to higher grades (I had added Pathfinding and Stamp Collecting to my list of merit badges) but no sponsor could be found to guide us toward the ranks of Eagle Scout. When we graduated from junior high we also graduated from scouting. For my family there were even more momentous changes in the offing.

40. CONCERTO A TRE

Every child has problem parents and I don't wish to exaggerate the difficulties of my situation – for I never felt unloved or unwanted. In spite of his many absences, Ingolf, for instance, always managed to keep the channels of respect and affection open between us. Thus, while I was at Duffy's Camp he sent "the first letter I have ever written to you that you can read yourself," beginning the first of three installments of the "Story of Plumbo the Elephant." Journal entries indicate that he and I continued to spend time together at the beach and in the mountains and Ingolf even accompanied me to a Cub Scout meeting at Shenandoah and to Dad's Night at Pasteur.

Some of our earliest mountain experiences were quite memorable. We had a favorite spot on a stream near Mt. Pacifico (renamed Tony Water) where we splashed in the waterfalls and bathed in the rock basins and where, on May 5, 1946, Peter Yates led us in the stoning of a rattlesnake. Ingolf also records a tenting expedition at Buckhorn Flats on February 15, 1947. Looking at the date I see now why my memory of this outing is one of ill-tempered whining over being cold. A walk in the Baldwin Hills during which Ingolf and I asked each other riddles seems to have been a happier occasion. "He is so sweet," Ingolf wrote.

With his child-like sense of wonder Ingolf was a delightful companion and I remained very jealous of the time he devoted to such intangible preoccupations as practicing or composing. But in 1948 I was able to secure the attention of both my parents when we undertook a trip in August to San Francisco. In the Golden Gate Park Ingolf and I played Robin Hood and I fed peanuts to the squirrels. We were staying in Mill Valley in a home lent to us by Michael and Gret Mann and in a nearby stream we had great fun trying to catch crayfish with salami. We also drove up to the Russian River for a wonderful swim.

But there is some evidence that all was not well between parents and son, even on this trip, and that a kind of pre-adolescent rebellion had set in. As Ingolf and Etta headed out for a day at Stinson Beach I refused to accompany them, a surly Charles Addams Pugsley intent on my own preoccupations, which on this day meant charting the make of automobiles as they drove by the Mann porch. (Statistics were almost as important an obsession for me as collecting.) "He is such a problem sometimes," Ingolf wrote, and he was right. As eagerly as I looked forward to hiking and camping outings I was very likely to get bored or tired and spoil Ingolf's fun. In the previous July he and Etta had taken three of us lads up to Gorgonio. "Moods are somewhat low," Ingolf had reported on the ascent to Dollar Lake. In the morning I wanted to go home – something about having gotten mustard all over my sleeping bag. When Etta became altitude sick the issue was decided.

Increasingly it became harder to command Ingolf's attention, and I became quite resentful. I note that on December 16, 1950 the journal entry reads "Hike – Forest patrol," but the handwriting is my own! I had neatly filed my request for Ingolf's company in the little red volume, which – had I but known – contained so much explosive private material. As Ingolf helped me prepare for my Boy Scout trip to Catalina I evidently became tearful over the separation. "I try to comfort him as well as possible, he is so sweet – so much a child yet." On March 14, 1951 he pictures "Anthony coming out of his boy's sleep and telling us his dreams – so open, lovely, a moment to treasure for life!" "I wish I could be more of a companion than I am," he concluded.

Access to my mother was, of course, much easier to control. I remember one lovely afternoon when we traveled to downtown Los Angeles together, each reading our own books in the children's section of the Los Angeles Public Library, sharing out a bag of peanuts until they were gone and the books were finished. But there were obviously moments when Etta would have enjoyed not having a child around. One instance is recorded when I had been delivered in 1945 to the Emily Johnson Duffy Ranch Camp:

> Large lovely waves of deep quiet envelop me, and I luxuriate in them. This 'loneliness,' which should be everyone's occasional inalienable right, is certainly not going to be hard to take. For this particular

kind of breath taking it seems I had to wait eight and a half long years, and I intend to enjoy every moment of it.

Since this right was only rarely exercised I had little to complain about, although I suppose there were signs of resentment when Etta failed to produce Ingolf when I wanted him. For the most part this highly intelligent and gifted woman contented herself with a life of household drudgery and childrearing, not the life style she needed for her own fulfillment. She was always starting on some new writing project but her only finished work was a children's play entitled "A Tangled Yarn," which I, Julie, Stevie, and some of the other kids on the block, performed in the Keller's garage before a neighborhood audience. I played a character named Admiral Eversearch:

> You've read how I battled with hunger and thirst
> To get to the top of the Rockies first;
> And now that the Rockies are open to man,
> I'll discover the Smoothies as soon as I can.
> The Catskills, of course, owe their fame to me.
> But the Dogskills are something you ought to see.

When the meager rewards of such efforts had exhausted themselves my mother announced, in the spring of 1951, that she intended to return to college and begin a long struggle toward the completion of a Ph.D. in the German Department of U.S.C. Clearly this decision was an attempt to create her own identity, one that could so easily have been entirely swamped by the insatiable demands of the men in her life for attention, nurse-maiding, care and feeding. But her almost daily absence from home and her preoccupation with assignments when she had returned had a disruptive effect on our usual routines. "Etta works on Hoffmanstahl paper," Ingolf noted in May, 1952, "she is so far away." I, too, took this secession on Etta's part as a form of personal rejection. Etta had a book entitled *An Outline of German Literature*. I used my pen to make this read "Ban The Outline of German Literature." Add my mother's defection to my often thwarted attempts to command Ingolf's undivided attention and we have the beginnings of a new and somewhat troubling chapter in the relationship between parents and son.

My attempt to re-win their attention, to remind them of my own dependence, took the form of a return to babyish follies, a regression to earlier, simpler times. I played tricks on them – I poked a whole in the bottom of the milk carton and disappeared, hoping that I might return to an unexplained flood on the dining room table. I refused to eat my Brussels sprouts and Etta left me sitting in the dark until I had consumed the detestable objects. I *re-read* all the Oz books. I became devoted to my stuffed elephant Jumbo, and invented for him a whole circle of subordinate playmates, each of whom took on the shape of one of our many household pillows. Pillowmania ruled.

Bozo, my own, and all the throw pillows – Beethoven, Ruth, Red, Junior, Subsequently, Hence, Klopstock, and Heine – each received a separate (usually naughty) personality which I projected in a squeaky falsetto to the amusement (and no doubt occasional alarm) of Ingolf and Etta. The pillows were allowed to think and say many things which an obedient son could not, and there was always a degree of hostility in their dialogue. Etta has recorded a typical snatch of pillowish conversation. Bringing one of the pillows into the kitchen I asked, "Is this Mrs. Goodie's nursery school?" Taking her cue, Etta responded, "Why yes it is." "This is Junior," I continued, "He won't be any trouble to you. Dead, you know." Later I came to rescue my toy, "Come on Junior. Time for your afternoon burial." Etta indulged me for many years in these childish inventions. There exists a document in which she applied for citizenship in the Pillow Republic of America (which had its own stamps, currency, and newspaper). The application even bears the signatures of witnesses: Larry Moss, Richard Exner, one of her fellow graduate students and later a professor at Santa Barbara, and even John Waterman, one of her instructors!

Ingolf was seduced by this on-going fairy tale and his interviews of the reactionary and self-important Jumbo, conducted at annual family gatherings, became a feature of the festivities even when I was myself in graduate school. While I was still in my teens we even had a war, Ingolf taking the side of the Pillow's Republic of China and I defending the honor of the American pillows. The decisive battle was fought on neutral soil, the sand in front of the Moss beach house on Lido Island, with cardboard cuts-outs representing the pillows and peashooters serving as the weaponry.

Even after Pillowmania waned I continued to cast my voice whenever I wished to pursue some bit of nonsensical banter with my preoccupied mother, but finally, many years after the inauguration of this madness, she said, "I don't talk to pillows anymore," and that was the end of it. I had always been aware that the cruel and charming chatter was an exercise in childishness, and I would have been mortified if any of my contemporaries had been aware of *my* participation in so infantile a cult.

Still, it was harder for me to recognize aberrant behavior in myself than in my parents, who by all the standards of my peers and the conventions of middle class America were indeed "weird." They failed utterly to measure up to that conformist image, Mr. and Mrs. Happy Couple, which my bourgeois heart longed for. Our household *was* different. We were still renters and our apartment, in which not even a hamster was allowed to rattle his cage or a television set shed its blue light, was crammed with the artifacts of our difference, one that started in the parental bedroom into which *two* double beds had been crammed. My parents, who professed no religious beliefs, treated sports and popular music as alien cults. They wouldn't subscribe to any of the popular magazines, finding enough sustenance in *The New Yorker*, nor would they admit any of the more lurid tabloids then on offer in Los Angeles, preferring to remain loyal first to the *Hollywood Citizen News* and then to the *Daily News*. With our crazy mealtimes and the demands for sudden quiet (now it was my *mother* who demanded silence so that she could do *her* homework) it was obvious that ours was a most unusual household. Other people's fathers were not so preoccupied, so vague, so hard to pin down to any schedule. They didn't litter their beds with ear flents or dart about the house in old-fashioned nightshirt and cap, as Ingolf did. They weren't always pumping at their atomizer to combat asthma. (I recall my embarrassment when, at the corner of Pico and Beverwil, another driver looked over at Ingolf, his spray in his mouth, and inquired, "Taste good?") In short I had the distinct misfortune of finding myself a burgher in bohemia.

It wasn't easy on my parents to have such a child. "Children at 12," Etta wrote:

> in their deepest determination to be grown-up often wear a stern, implacable air, sometimes even edged with scorn in the presence of their elders. The elders having made valiant and feeble attempts to

grow up, and being now pretty sure they are never going to make it, sometimes seem humble, apologetic, even contrite in this twelve year-old presence. Like a daub next to a classic. Thus Anthony and his stepfather, or Anthony and his mother.

I could add that another essential disparity between *my* parents and those of my friends was that *I* had so many of them. Every time there was a commencement, as for instance that graduation day in June, 1952, when I left Pasteur, there they were – all four of them: Leroy and Del on one side, Ingolf and Etta on the other and the embarrassed graduate, whose pals had the decency to bring only two parents each, would be smiling wanly in the middle. I also had the everyday trauma of living in a family whose last name was different from my own. For years I had to endure that end-of-term ritual in which Etta, in the space marked "Parent or Guardian," would sign my report card with the odd phrase: Etta Dahl (Mother). It is also true that, in spite of my self-conscious attempts to correct the situation, I was forever addressed my some of my parents' associates as Tony Dahl, twice a mistaken identity.

There were also those traumas associated with the possession of so ominous a figure as a *step*father. Freud would need to add another chapter to *The Psychopathology of Everyday Life* in order to explain the curious reaction which the mere mention of this word has elicited throughout my life. Because of my love for Ingolf there can be no assumption that *my* use of the word *stepfather* carried with it any invitation to share in a negative connotation. But such is our society's unconscious dread of the step-parent that I have utterly failed to communicate my relationship to Ingolf on many occasions. "You say you're writing a book about your father-in-law?" "Anthony's uncle is a composer." From father to brother-in-law to grandfather, I have been offered half a dozen different ways of eradicating the onerous relationship that stepfather and stepson is supposed to conjure up in our world.

More understandable but equally irksome was my attempt to communicate the man's real name, a difficulty he endured as well, no doubt. In conversation it was almost impossible to convey anything of the unaccustomed moniker. People just couldn't get their mouths around those simple six letters and when you gave them a chance to write it out the variations were infinite. Ingolph, Einglof, Ingold, Ing, Ingols, Ingvef,

Ingoli, Ingloph, Inglof, Infold, Ingoff, Ingoils, Sngolf, Infolf, Ingoll, Ingulf, Indolf – these are a sampling of the spellings my stepfather received in correspondence. The rarity of the name became a subject of humor for that wag, Sol Babitz. "Hello, this is Ingolf." A pause would follow and Sol would ask, "Ingolf who?"

On the whole, however, I was not amused, and my parents were about to offer me still another challenging variation to normal teenage life. Since the completion of the *Saxophone Concerto* in 1949 my stepfather had lost much of his creative momentum. Little wonder that he saw the opportunity of a sabbatical leave from the University as the opportunity to rekindle his creative energies. The notion of taking off a whole year, however, had become a reality only with the award of a $3000 grant from the John Simon Guggenheim Foundation. He had originally applied for this stipend in 1950, listing Igor Stravinsky, Henry Cowell, Otto Luening, Raymond Kendall, Benny Goodman, Gail Kubik, Robert Craft, Aaron Copland and Middlebury's Alan Carter as references. The award had been announced in April of 1951 but Ingolf had asked that the grant be postponed for a year. Now, on April 18, 1952, two months before my graduation from junior high, my parents confronted me with a choice. They had completed their research on a likely site for the year abroad, one that would be mountainous and inexpensive, and as they prepared to depart for European shores I was told I could either accompany them, or choose to remain behind in Los Angeles and spend the year with Leroy, Del, and a six year-old half brother, Timothy, living at a house the Linicks had recently moved to on Rosewood Avenue near Doheny. What if I wanted neither?

Ingolf and Etta had realized how dependent I had grown on my many adolescent friendships and they went so far as ask if Leigh Peffer could be allowed to accompany us to Europe as well. On this day they had learned that such an idea was not possible (Leigh's family having the good sense not to cause so wounding a dislocation) and so I was faced with the choice of continuing my education in some overseas school for American dependents or beginning my first year of high school with my pals at Hamilton High School on Robertson Boulevard. It was a very difficult choice for me to make but after four days my craving for stability outweighed my sense of adventure and I decided to remain behind in Los Angeles. All those travel experiences for which I envied my parents, the practical knowledge of another language I might have obtained, the breadth of experience that exposure to foreign cultures might have brought me – all of these I gave up so that I wouldn't fall behind in Latin or algebra.

This is the way I look at the decision now, but it is also possible to see other less obvious factors in my motivation – most notably my purposeful desire to forge a personality so sufficiently distinct from that of my wonderful and strong-willed parents that it might have a chance to survive in a world dominated by their genius.

41. A HOMECOMING

When Ingolf left Los Angeles on June 25, 1952, limping around on a sore left foot, he traveled alone because he was not heading directly for Europe but to Tanglewood and the Berkshire Music Center. In the fall of 1951 he had received a visit from Ralph Berkowitz, Dean of the Center, and an invitation to head the newly-formed Department Five, the Tanglewood Study Group, which would parallel other existing summer study units: orchestral and chamber music (Leonard Bernstein), choral (Hugh Ross), composition (Aaron Copland) and opera (Boris Goldovsky). Ingolf had flown to New York on December 16, 1951 to confer on summer plans with Berkowitz, Copland, Ross, and Thomas Perry, the Center's executive secretary. Copland had announced Ingolf's appointment in an article in the *New York Times* on February 24, 1952, "We have secured the services of a remarkable musician from California." Ingolf arrived in Lenox, Massachusetts on June 27, 1952, and threw himself into preparation for work which he would also undertake in 1953, 1955, and 1956.

The Tanglewood Study Group was created, according to Copland, as a place where the intelligent amateur, musical enthusiast, general music student, and music educator might "join forces for the exploration, discovery, and performing-for-the-joy-of-performing" of music from the 16th through the 18th Century, with some 20th Century work which could be played by amateur performers also included in the repertoire. The group was expected to show its progress by offering some public concerts. Ingolf was an obvious choice to head this division because its work very closely paralleled his beloved U.S.C. creation, the Collegium Musicum. In the organization and administration of the group he could rely on the

Anthony Linick

assistance of members of the Boston Symphony Orchestra, including Florence Dunn, the orchestra's secretary. Building up library materials and discovering and copying music that could be performed by his new students was as time-consuming a task here as it had been at U.S.C.

When Ingolf met his students for the first time, on June 30, he was shocked to discover that many of them could barely read music. His introductory remarks elicited blank stares and the first run through of a Purcell work was so ghastly that he left the rehearsal stage terribly depressed. Bach chorales weren't much better the next day. The first concert, given on July 12, "goes so-so," he reported, "but they seem to be having a good time." Elliott Carter was part of a small audience that attended a second concert on July 26. The fact that his students came to love the work and the repertoire provided a degree of consolation for Ingolf, but "for a professional," he wrote to Lawrence Morton, "it is not easy to live with amateurs (never a correct rhythm or an acceptable intonation)." On July 14 a new group of students, including some good players, arrived to cheer him up, but with so many interesting activities taking place at the same time, it was often difficult for Ingolf to get his pupils to show up for rehearsals. Apathy and disinterest characterized more than one meeting and some of the participants complained that there was "too much old music." Still, Ingolf's colleagues congratulated him on a job well done at a faculty meeting on August 11 and, cursing himself for having asked for too little, he agreed to return the following year. The Center's administrators were very happy with the TSG's financial success. Tod Perry wrote to Ingolf in September that, "I have heard nothing but praise for your work on all sides. Altogether you had enrolled in your department 106 students, which is more than a quarter of the school."

Ingolf did not have much to do with orchestral performance at Tanglewood and he was not always able to give the resident B.S.O., which was lead by a variety of conductors, the highest marks. He felt that Lorin Maazel's concert on July 18 was "lousy," and that a Rubinstein Brahms concerto concert on August 7 was "disappointing." He had serious reservations about Charles Munch, the permanent director of the Orchestra (I always got a laugh when I referred to the B.S.O. as Chuck Munch and the Bunch), but Pierre Monteux's presentation of the *Rite of Spring* on July 26th was described as "the experience of a lifetime." Ingolf himself helped

228

augment the chorus for a performance of the Berlioz *Requiem* on August 10, enjoying the experience tremendously.

There were other rewards waiting for Ingolf at Tanglewood. He was very stimulated by the presence of so many distinguished musicians and, to the extent that his diffident and self-effacing nature permitted, he sought their company and friendship. One figure whose company Ingolf seems to have enjoyed repeatedly this summer was the Mexican conductor, Jose Limantour. Most of the rest of the people he spent his non-teaching time with, however, were composers. Copland presided over this group which included, in 1952, Luigi Dallapiccola and Lukas Foss. On June 29 Copland gave a dinner in honor of Ingolf, Foss, and Dallapiccola and on July 7th he moderated a discussion in which the three debated "Tonality, Atonality, Twelve Tone – Where Does the Future Lie?" at the Lenox Library. Ingolf enjoyed Dallapiccola's company, though the two had to talk in French. and he seems to have spent a good deal of time in the Italian's company, even though Dallapiccola's penchant for prophetical utterance rubbed my stepfather the wrong way. On July 23 Ingolf reports taking a short walk with Dallapiccola and Luciano Berio, though this time he had to test his rusty knowledge of Italian. Ingolf made a permanent friend in Lukas Foss, who was full of questions about the Los Angeles musical scene which he would join the following winter as director of the U.C.L.A. orchestra, a position that somewhat paralleled Ingolf's post at U.S.C.

Lukas Foss was one of these recurring figures in the history of Ingolf's relationship to other composers, a charming figure whose friendship could be valued while envy boiled beneath the surface. In the mid-Forties Gail Kubik had filled this role. Now we read about friendly arguments with Lukas over Mozart cadenzas one day and chagrin over his handsome friend's popularity the next. "Piano teams," Ingolf wrote on July 18, "They don't show up. Am furious. Lukas would not be stood up like that." Naturally all these composers listened to one another's music. "What does he *really* think?" Ingolf asked after Dallapiccola had listened to some recordings of Dahl music. For his part, Ingolf was impressed by one of the Italian's compositions, but the latter's famous opera, *Il Prigioniero*, got only a mixed review when Ingolf listened to a recording in the Lenox Library. "Would rather have taken a sunbath," he wrote, "This I know: it is not for me. It is tortured, lush (Hollywood) chromatics – some attractive sounds, but no reality – one bar of *Rake* has more youth!" Ingolf expressed a grudging admiration for much of Lukas' music. "He really has 'the manner,'" he admitted after listening to *The Jumping Frog* on August 6. A few months later he wrote, "Lukas makes beautiful music out of material which I would not look at twice!" Foss valued Ingolf's criticisms and later in this sabbatical year sent his new friend a recently completed manuscript. "Your comments," he wrote, "will be the first and probably the most astute."

On August 9 Ingolf reported himself "*very* excited about Etta's coming." At noon her train arrived ("She is so lovely") and the two spent three nights together in Lenox before returning to New York. Ingolf devoted some time to research at the public library on Fifth Avenue ("very annoyed not to find my publications there") and the next day, August 13, the pair sailed for France on the *Liberté*. Ingolf did not care for the voyage, spending most of the time reading novels, including *Inspector Maigret* in the original. He described the "enforced inactivity and resulting dullness in mind and body" as "most loathsome. As if a healthy person were told to stay in bed for 6 days." On the 19th the Dahls arrived in Paris and on the 21st (described as "the day!") they returned to Zurich: Etta had been away for sixteen years, Ingolf over thirteen. The two were deeply affected by this return to Switzerland and even on the platform in Basel they held hands and walked through the station with moist eyes.

As Zurich was to prove to be within a day's journey of their sabbatical home they were able to revisit this city of their youth on a number of occasions. They spent a week here in August, with shorter stays in October, November, January, and April. On their first visit Ingolf and Etta actually stayed at Russenweg 10, the house where Ingolf had lived from 1932 to 1939. On August 23 he reports arriving at the Stadttheater "with palpitations." Plagued by hemorrhoids, he nevertheless insisted on revisiting with Etta all those spots sacred to the memory of their courtship. At the Veltlinerkeller on the 27th he reports, "the place is just the same – and here we are, the pinpoint of years, the experience of love, of our lives." Writing to Lawrence following his October visit he added:

> I cannot quite describe the effect of the second Zurich trip. The sameness of the surroundings seen through such a changed body and soul. What would you say if you came to a restaurant after 14 years and found both both it *and* the waitresses identical?...At the

Opera the hatcheck ladies were sitting unchanged at their places
– including the one who used to wish me good luck when I, a green
youngster, used to go down into the pit and conduct.

Ingolf even recognized some of the faces in the audience as he slipped
into a performance of *Figaro* on October 5. "Zurich still makes the heart
beat faster," he concluded.

He also used his time in Zurich to catch up on family matters and
to visit old friends like the Hartogs, his piano teacher Walter Frey, and
Stadttheater colleagues like Willi Hausslein. The latter, he complained,
was the only one to show any interest in his compositions. Ingolf played
the *Hymn and Toccata* on November 6 at the Kulturkreis Zollikon, where
he delivered a lecture on Music in the American University. He received
some encouragement from Opera officials who were interested in his ideas
for a ballet for his old friend Maya Kubler. Nothing came of this at the
time but Ingolf did soon start work on the story of the ballet that became
The Tower of St. Barbara. He accepted and then backed out of an offer to
conduct a radio concert of American music in the spring.

It was now time for the Dahls to think about some permanent
accommodation for the year. Switzerland would have been ideal but it was
too expensive for their restricted budget and so, following the advice of
Ingolf's skiing friends, the Schaars, the two travelled eastward into the
Austrian Vorarlberg where they took a branch railway line from Bludenz
up to the village of Schruns. They arrived on August 29, 1952, and here
they found their home away from home.

42. LIVING IN A CHRISTMAS CARD

The Dahls arrived in Schruns on August 29, 1952. They were instantly
charmed by the village, which was surrounded by the tall mountains Ingolf
relished. Country walks began at the end of every street but there remained
a degree of civilization as well. Hemingway had worked on *The Sun Also Rises*
in one of the Schruns' hotels, a clinic and a spa now offered to rehabilitate
Europe's elite, and a skilift built with Marshall Plan funds stood waiting
for the first snowflake. Beneath this slick surface a peasant culture survived,
offering its market days, and its festivals during which native costumes

were still worn; the sound of bells on farm animals was often heard in the streets. In 1952 this region of Austria was still occupied by the French Army, whose soldiers added another element to the population mix.

Ingolf set about searching for accommodation and even looked at a room in a farmhouse where a barefoot brood peeped shyly at the visitors from America. But the location proved to be too remote and on August 30 my parents agreed to pay thirty dollars a month for some rooms in Frau Netzer's house at Montjolastrasse 529. The mayor himself helped Ingolf locate a piano and by September 2 he was at work. Schruns remained the home of the Dahls until mid-June the following year.

"Go for a walk up Silbertal," Ingolf wrote on September 7, " – just heavenly – what views, what air, would it never end." A week later he was picking heather from the hillside. When rain turned to snow on October 12 he reported that "emotion runs in waves over me. Under the trees the snow falling down, the haystack in the foreground, the path, and the yellow leaves, a big moment." When he was at last able to ascend the wreath of white mountains he was overwhelmed – "unbelievable, chest expanding, Thanks." By April he was already mourning the signs of a premature spring – "over the places which I last saw under deep snow – cherry blossoms." With his background as an art student it is not surprising that Ingolf was an excellent outdoor photographer. He took many slides in Schruns and I never tired of looking at them, vicariously participating in an aesthetic experience I had sacrificed for the sake of high school football games, Latin Club banquets, and *Your Hit Parade*.

When the weather permitted Ingolf and Etta ate lunch on a balcony of the Netzer house, soaking up the sun and feeding the jackdaws who came to visit them. Quarters at Montjolastrasse were cramped; nevertheless the Dahls arrived with two trunks, "Emma" and "Ivan," discovering that in transit Etta's peroxide had done in Ingolf's black suit. A local tailor was employed to make a replacement. At least one meal a day was taken at one of the town hotels, The Taube, the Krone, or the Löwen. There was a cinema in the village and here visiting theatrical and opera troupes also appeared. Ingolf managed one extensive walk a day and often visited the local sauna. In the winter he had a rubdown with snow as part of this regimen.

On September 8 Ingolf recorded the daily schedule he proposed to maintain: 9-1 compose; 1-3 lunch and nap; 3-5 compose; 5-7 walk; 7-8 dinner; 8-10 correspondence and orchestration. This proved to be the typical pattern for the year, though Etta undertook most of the correspondence, a witty and voluminous exercise that delighted many a recipient. "What a wonderful letter," Lukas Foss wrote in reply to one of these, "If only my wife would do that kind of thing for me! You are a fortunate man, Ingolf, no wonder you write good music."

Ingolf and Etta seem to have survived the enforced proximity of life on Montjolastrasse surprisingly well. There were certainly many minor vexations. Etta failed to endorse every one of Ingolf's composition projects and this left some hurt feelings. Ingolf stayed out longer on the ski slopes than he said he would and this upset Etta. When Ingolf made some suggestions to Etta about improvements in her appearance the whole matter, predictably, blew up in his face. But there were many activities in which the two participated happily as a couple. One of these was a six-hour walk which they took on Etta's forty-seventh birthday, October 28, 1952. As Etta wrote Lawrence:

> I could never describe the scenery because it has everything, farms, woods, snowcapped peaks. We saw many cute farm animals. Ingolf has amazing conversations with goats, only this time two peasant women gave him inhibitions. I pointed to a tree and asked Ingolf if it were a birch. Yes, he said, and that little one next to it was a son-of-a-birch. We shuffled on purpose through dry leaves on the forest floor, making as much noise as possible. Ingolf did talk to a turkey ...a little farm boy sat nearby – taking in this dialogue between the bird and what gave every evidence of being a man. The turkey gave Ingolf hell.

Etta had not come to Schruns just to make coffee and sandwiches for her husband. She too had many projects, most of them connected with her interrupted doctoral studies. She read all the works that she would normally have encountered in classes at U.S.C. and undertook the study of two languages needed as part of her doctoral program, French and Swedish. Only someone as gifted in languages as my mother could have learned one foreign language in another, but that is how she learned French in evening classes at the local German-speaking school. When this proved to be an insufficient introduction to the spoken tongue she tried to find someone to chat with among the resident French occupiers. She and Ingolf went to a local beer joint frequented by the French army (and sent back their red wine because it was too cold) and Etta tried unsuccessfully to snag a khaki-clad beret wearer in conversation. The delicatessen man helped her construct a sign for the bulletin board at French headquarters; Etta would swap French conversation for English or German. An officer's wife volunteered and, over knitting, Etta proceeded painfully forward with no subjunctive – "without which a civilized conversation simply cannot be."

Etta began to teach herself to read Swedish in the new year when, felled by a bad attack of the flu, she lay bed-ridden for several weeks at the end of February and the beginning of March. "The grippe never bothers me," she wrote, "on the rare occasions when I have it...I just go on doing what I was doing, only I do it in bed, where I do a great deal of studying anyway. The disease and I tolerate each other by mutual agreement, and outside of taking the necessary medication, I ignore it. It usually departs out of pique."

On February 17 Ingolf fixed her lunch and went to see the "Fool's Run," part of the season's Fasching carnival. Etta left a record of the dialogue which ensued upon his return:

> "What you missed," he exclaimed..." "Did you know," I said, "that according to this book there are no less than14 ways of saying the English preposition *of* in Swedish?" "There was a man who came down looking as though he was skiing on his hands, only he fixed up his legs to look like hands, and his arms to look like feet. It was amazing." I flicked a bare crumb at him, but I had to hear about skiers dressed as railway porters, bears, the duo of a Spanish toreador and his bull..."I not only need a teacher," I said coldly, "I need a dictionary." "Oh, how are you, any more temperature?" he asked. "It goes up and down." "I forgot to tell you, there was a group of a father and two daughters..."

When the Swedish dictionary arrived from Brentanos Etta discovered to her chagrin that, though describing itself as "the latest and the best," the volume contained archaic Swedish spelling and a set of less than useful phrases for the contemporary traveler, including, "I like very much a piece of good meat and spinage," "Here are chickens coming, will you try them?"

"You shall make a great-coat, a dress coat, two pair of pantaloons and two waistcoats for me," and "I want a candle to seal up my letter." Even with this kind of help Etta was able to pass her Swedish reading proficiency exam upon her return to campus.

Ingolf also endured several illnesses during this year abroad. To the chronic knee, neck and foot problems, minor heel and thumb injuries were added. The usual colds, bronchial and asthmatic complaints, were augmented by difficulties with thyroid levels and complaints about enervation and exhaustion. In October only eight of the twenty-nine diary entries contain no reference to health. The most serious problem seems to have been with a knee, whose uncertain status threatened the skiing opportunities that had lead to the selection of Schruns as a sabbatical site in the first place. On October 9, after a consultation at the local clinic, Ingolf began a series of treatments involving injections and shortwave. He supplemented this with knee bends and other forms of exercise, occasionally overdoing it in his frenzy to recover in time for the first substantial snowfall. He was still worrying about the knee in April, but in fact he seems to have gotten in a great deal of time on the slopes and he finished the sabbatical in better shape than when he arrived. In addition to local runs he completed nine overnight skiing expeditions, most of them in the spring. As might be expected, he was always finding fault with his technique or his stamina; to improve the former he enrolled in a local ski school. Ill-fitting skis, painful boots and unsatisfactory snow conditions conspired to spoil several days but more often than not his efforts were rewarded. Skiing down to Zug on March 14 Ingolf experienced what he described as "the most exciting powder run of my life. Flags of snow streaming behind. Blue sky, speed, slopes. Get goose pimples and want to scream with pleasure." On several trips he returned to beloved Swiss locations. "Emotion becomes almost too strong," he noted after taking the Parsennbahn on March 3, "That this could be given to me again." "Oh to be able to come back again!" he exclaimed after a day at Piz Sol on March 8. Arthur Knodel was not far off when he wrote the Dahls, "You live in a Christmas card."

In fact Christmas 1952 was not spent in Schruns but in Stockholm. On December 20 the Dahls set off on the only substantial period of travel during the sabbatical, with Etta chronicling what turned out to be a rather uneventful expedition in a *thirteen* page letter to be circulated among friends and relatives in California. In this literary venture she had been encouraged by the wide and appreciative reception that earlier missives had received. "I can't remember," Lawrence Morton wrote on October 6, "that I have ever before known so many people rejoicing in someone else's good fortune."

On the first day of their trip the Dahls travelled as far as Zurich. Ingolf read *New Yorkers* and my mother had a Schweizer-Deutsch conversation with a little girl named Anneli who pointed to Etta's lipstick and said, "*Du bist rot!*" In Zurich the two enjoyed a glass of amontillado at one of their old haunts, Pedro Gorgot's wine bar. In Basel, they paid only one dollar for their hotel room, a serviceless aerie four floors up. The next day they packed their own lunch and went by train to Colmar, where they visited the Isenheim altar of Mathis Grunewald – almost twenty years after Ingolf had made an earlier pilgrimage. In the afternoon the Dahls took the train for Strasbourg, Etta ate snails, and the two climbed the tower of the cathedral while Ingolf gave Etta a lecture on the differences between Romanesque and Gothic architecture. In Basel again they ate fondue at the restaurant of the shoemaker's guild and sang Christmas carols with the other customers. Ingolf had forgotten his shaving cream so be used some of Etta's shampoo.

The next morning these unaffluent Americans squeezed into the third class section of an Italian train and proceeded to Copenhagen. Germany still showed traces of wartime bombing and it gave Etta a queer feeling to be back in this country again. An executive from General Motors gave them a pack of king-sized Chesterfields (they were still smokers, especially Etta, though their favorite brand was Pall Malls). At a nearby table in the dining car a group of drunken American soldiers caused her considerable embarrassment. In Copenhagen the train station announcer got good marks for enunciation from my mother, but the Danish language itself was marked down – "the R sounds as though it is unsuccessfully and forever trying to scrape the scum from the beladen vowels." Ingolf was thrilled by the Baltic air as the ferry took them across the water to Sweden. On the train to Stockholm the two worked on the verses which would accompany Christmas presents. Trying out a few Swedish phrases in the dining car, Etta refused the offer of potatoes by telling the porter, "None on me, thank you."

Holger, Gert and Mammi were present at the Stockholm train station, Pappi waiting at home. The next day, Christmas Eve, Mammi turned the tree decorating over to Etta and then insisted on doing it all by herself after all, and soon thereafter my mother started to complain of appetite loss. "It is very lovely and harmonious," a sentimental Ingolf wrote of the Christmas celebrations themselves. Drawing on her old skills as ballet accompanist Etta played while seven year-old Karin Marcus danced. On the 26th Mammi wheeled in coffee and cakes and served the Dahls breakfast in bed. "It isn't her fault," Etta grumbled, "that I don't particularly enjoy it, especially eating sweet things early." That afternoon there was a visit to an exhibit of Gert's work and the next day Etta, Ingolf, Mammi, and Pappi went to see Chaplin's *Limelight*. "The folks love it, so we said nothing, but privately wanted to give it back to the limes and turn out the light." At home Mammi dragged out volumes of memorabilia. "I even purported to see incipient genius in a pencil scribble of Ingolf, aged 4, which looked exactly like a pencil scribble," Etta added sourly. "Pappi is so happy," Ingolf noted, but Etta seems to have noted only her own discomfiture; on December 29, she tells us, "I was beginning to feel the strain of so many events and a kind of veil was over all. I tried to pierce it by being especially wide-wake, and probably seemed to have taken benzedrine." On December 30 Ingolf entertained the Swedish composer Ingvar Lidholm. "I served coffee and liqueur," Etta wrote, "and due to a previously given high-sign from me to Ingolf's parents, we slipped away to allow Ingolf [and Lidholm] to talk shop to their hearts' content." "Pappi bears up very well at leave taking," Etta noted on January 2, 1953, It was to be the last embrace between father and son.

That night Ingolf and Etta stayed with the Lindbloms in Gothenberg. "I am so befuzzled by now," Etta wrote, "That I just have to lie inert on one of Laka's sofas." Dragging one of their heavy wardrobe trunks everywhere, the Dahls began a long train journey south that afternoon, cans of sardines and anchovies adding to the weight. Boarding a ferry Etta fell in the snow. The two sat up all night, dozing and reading mystery stories. Hamburg was passed at six in the morning. "It does not speak to me," Ingolf noted in his journal – as a little boy named Siegfried threw up at their feet. In Zurich Ingolf went to the dentist and Etta mailed the just completed photostat of a revised version of the double clarinet concerto to Benny Goodman.

On the night of January 5 the Dahls returned to Schruns and Ingolf once again threw himself into the struggle of composer versus composition.

43. A NOISELESS PATIENT SPIDER

The critical comments on the music of other composers – which Ingolf had included in his notes about Tanglewood – were now becoming more and more common as he worked toward defining his own style, a struggle which necessarily involved the rejection of directions taken by other creators. We have seen that he admired Schoenberg's music tremendously and it can be added that he had considerable respect for the *European* students of the master, particularly Alban Berg. After hearing a performance of *Wozzek* in 1951 Ingolf wrote, "overwhelming experience! This is in the line of the real masters." More to the point, he had also added, "in spite of its oppressive convincingness we must go our different ways." This is paralleled by a comment about an Ernst Krenek piano concerto heard the same year, "Interesting but not valid for me." Only in the case of Anton Webern do we find a truly negative comment about a pre-war Schoenbergian – "I wish somebody would put Webern in his place," he wrote in 1953, "a peripheral aesthete, cultivating exquisitely a garden 2 X 2 inches in size." More annoying to him, because more threatening to his own position in the musical world, were the *American* disciples of Schoenberg, the army of twelve-tone chromaticists whose music Ingolf, with *his* European background in the Twenties and Thirties, found old-fashioned, facile, and over-emotional.

Ingolf was a great defender of American music and indeed constructed concert programs – in a characteristically generous gesture – that included much American music that he did not care for greatly; other than Copland and Shapero it is hard to find consistent praise for any of his American contemporaries. He expressed admiration for Roger Sessions *Second Symphony* in 1950 but he was disappointed by Walter Piston, disliked Samuel Barber, and loathed Douglas Moore. When it was proposed that one of the latter's operas be performed on a Musicians Congress program in 1944, Ingolf protested that Moore "represents a phase of neo-romanticism in American music that a progressive organization should not support."

Ingolf admired Stravinsky's work passionately, and Hindemith's too, but he had only mixed feelings about Bartok. "He has an enormous amount of true 'feeling' and 'fantasy,'" he wrote Lawrence in 1953, "but in spite of the really great moments Bartok is not an integrated composer (as Schoenberg, Stravinsky, or Hindemith are) and therefore not a really great composer. In spite of the world's opinion to the contrary I am convinced of this." None of the post-war European music he was to encounter on his sabbatical really excited Ingolf and some of it, the music of Werner Egk for instance, he pronounced "horrible." And if you wanted to make Ingolf spin like a furious top, a Rumplestilskin of the concert hall, all you had to do was whisper two words in his ear – Carl Orff.

As soon as Ingolf sat down at the piano on the evening of September 2, 1952 his own composition problems began. Throughout the year he worked in an atmosphere of unsettling pressure. He expected a great deal of himself – "You must come back with much music, you must break through to the open sea, time is running away!" Others expected a great deal also. Describing himself as "one of the people who really believe in you as a composer," Robert Craft urged Ingolf to work hard during the sabbatical. As this period came to an end Josef Szigeti, complaining that Ingolf had been a poor correspondent, added, "I hope this means that you will return here with a wonderful 'baggage' of several exciting works because you have to *justify* your silence in some special way." But faced for the first time with unlimited opportunities to compose, unrushed, undisturbed, Ingolf found himself paralyzed by soul-searching questions fundamental to his own position as a composer.

Unable to answer such questions he sought refuge in diversions, positive and negative; even annoyances, after all, serve to divert one from the necessary task. On the positive side we might list the call of the wild. "Start work at 9:30," he wrote on January 14, "the sunrise, first pink mountaintips, then bright white. Sunshine fills the whole valley, hoarfrost trees on other side. Find it impossible to work. Musical impulses are at a standstill." Other factors were allowed to impede his progress. Downstairs *another* piano was occasionally sounded, the noise driving Ingolf crazy and driving him to have a word with the evil-doer. "Everything is spoiled," he noted on November 16 when the piano was heard anew, "So just sit and stew." Etta was instructed not to use the typewriter and she obligingly continued her round-robin letters in pen. There is no doubt that Ingolf also felt the pressure of his beloved wife's presence, that critical and expectant audience who heard every note as it was first played on the keyboard. "A forbidding proximity, Strindbergian," Ingolf complains at this point; Etta's presence "keeps me from expanding, stifles all 'give,' feel hemmed in on all sides, become nervous therefore, tense, irritable – nothing that can be done." (One can't help wondering what the presence of a bored and noisy teenager might have added to this mix.) At the end of the year Ingolf admitted that one of the big mistakes of the sabbatical had been his failure to insist on a separate or isolated studio: "there is a *deep* down inhibition when someone is around." Even when Etta left the house Ingolf had to report, "For hours nothing. The mind boarded up – drought. Everything I can think of I don't like." On other occasions, when he at last found himself alone, he used his freedom not to compose but to play the piano. He also complained that Schruns was *too* isolated, too removed from musical life, that he needed the inspiration of live performance.

"What I am praying for," Ingolf wrote on January 12, "one time, one idea, which will make the music stream, which will set fire to all I feel is tinder in me. But how deeply is it buried, how many layers over it, is it there at all?" Ingolf rarely spoke of himself in the language of psychology, but such a quotation is an indication that he recognized the presence of mental impediments which thwarted his deeper artistic impulses. "Nothing can please" he added on February 21, "no melody flows, it is a quibble with sharps and flats...a note neurosis." A week later, in a despairing mood, he asked, "Must I, then, conclude that my inward potential, of which I am convinced, will *never* be realized? How can I accept such a cruel, killing fact?" Not everything was darkness. Just as his health improved in the spring, so did his confidence. On April 3 he lay beside a hillside chapel – "a kind of euphoric happiness steals over me – a good Friday spell? Birds, sheep grazing, patterns of bare twigs overhead...And the feeling (illusion) that I may still find some music, some ways and doors."

When he did move ahead with his composition projects it was frequently at the slowest pace possible. "This writer works very slowly," Ingolf had informed the Guggenheim Foundation in his 1950 application. "My work goes slowly and painfully," he now wrote Leroy, "and sometime I wish I had more of what one calls 'routine' and 'technique' and wish I did not have to start at the beginning each time." "To whom shall I pray," he wrote on February 13, "What shall I do that *once* only a work will be given to me *quickly*! Always the same: After the first few bars of anything, something in me says NO! or STOP. And then the agony of slowly picking out the next note starts all over again." In May he noted, "At last, last, last, there are good days. I work just as slowly as ever (*afraid* of *continuing* after something good, sidetracked constantly) but there *is something*, I feel it blossoming a little."

When Etta stopped typing and picked up her pen what she usually heard coming from her husband was not the sound of melodies dashing over the keyboard but the sound of the eraser. Evidently he was breaking one of Nadia Boulanger's strictures in so doing, but Ingolf was never satisfied with the initial version of anything. "For every bar which I let stand," he wrote to Arthur Knodel, "(Sometimes even with continued reservations) there are 20 which have been crossed out." Like the noiseless patient spider of the Whitman poem he would later set to music, Ingolf's art was a tireless spinning of filaments with could replace all those ill-made threads which his sense of musical architecture had rejected as flawed beyond repair.

The *Symphony Concertante* for two clarinets and orchestra, "the big work" which Ingolf longed to produce for Benny Goodman, had already been on his desk for many months. A first movement had been completed and, after only a few days in Schruns, a second one was finished as well. Ingolf also started tentative sketches for a final movement in September, but it wasn't until the end of October that he was sufficiently satisfied with the revision of the first two movements to press on. The journals are a record of this halting process. "It will not budge," he wrote after working on the end of a cadenza on September 3. "Where is the third movement coming from?" he asked a few days later. With no answer forthcoming he returned to orchestration of the first movement – "it is *such* slow and tedious work – am furious for not having written a better sketch...so much to be added and every note reconsidered." "At last the currents begin to flow again," he wrote on October 11, "I dabble with theme of III, and even Intro. to III, but what is lacking is *phantasy*, the arresting moment, the surprise, the difference." On October 31 he wrote, "At nap the same depression overcomes me: the music is not good – not 'tight,' not interesting, using other people's stale formulas, not *harmonically* moving, going from tone to tone instead of from phrase to phrase." Writing to Lawrence on November 18 Ingolf added, "I slave so over a few main lines and only here and there the main harmonies in order to get the architecture first, and then work on the complete details later. In this way I may speed up the process." By the end of the month progress was at last reported: "Evening play last movement up to Variation IV for Etta – it seems to grow nicely." Two days later, with "amazing speed," a presto section was added. The last note of the score was completed on the eve of the trip to Sweden, that is on December 17, 1952. It was part of the ritual of such moments that Etta was allowed to draw the final double bar on the page. Ingolf rushed out to buy a bottle of champagne, then used a chamber pot full of snow to cool it. Lawrence, amused by a report of this scene, imagined his own version of details which the Dahls had not reported in their letter – "the tear-filled eyes, the tender embrace, the Mahler-like background music. Etta hovering about as though SHE had composed the piece; and Ingolf probably still debating the practicality of an A double sharp."

Depressed by his inability to find some project that would truly engage his passions, Ingolf turned to some shorter assignments when he and Etta returned to Schruns in January of 1953. One of these was the *Quodlibet on American Folktunes* for two pianos, eight-hands. His research into appropriate material had actually begun during his first months in Los Angeles, almost a part of his own Americanization process. He had worked on the music for years but now he forced himself to bring the project to a conclusion. "It is my purgatory," he wrote Lawrence on January 13, "but got to be done (I think). And so difficult. Why did I ever start it?" The *Quodlibet* is subtitled "The Fancy Blue Devil's Breakdown," wording derived from some of the six traditional American melodies used – "Boston Fancy," "Deep Blue Sea," "The Devil's Dream," "Old Fiddler's Breakdown" (or "Arkansas Traveler"), "California Joe," and "Old Zip Coon" (or "Turkey In the Straw"). The following summer Lukas Foss and two other pianists helped Ingolf make a tape of the work which led to its acceptance for publication by Walter Hinrischsen of the famous publishing firm of C.F. Peters. A delighted Ingolf wrote, on April 28, 1954, "Since my earliest childhood PETERS EDITION has been practically synonymous with 'music.'" Later the same firm began to handle the orchestral version of the

Quodlibet, completed in 1965. The public premiere of the eight-hand piece took place on March 7, 1954 at a concert sponsored by U.S.C's chapter of Phi Mu Alpha.

Another January project was the revision of the 1946 *Cello Duo*. Here it was that Ingolf extracted one of the movements as a separate piece called *Notturno*. "Am really happy with it now," he informed Lawrence in April, "cello part simplified here and there, Capriccio almost new (on the same material though), many harmonies and details improved. Think it is a good piece." "There is only one good thing," he concluded, "all my agonizing changes are real improvements, I only wish I could think of some of these things in the first place." But he had no luck with the publisher Schott or the Fromm Foundation when he sought publication of this work or the *Saxophone Concerto*.

A letter of April 14 describes revision work on the latter composition as well. Ingolf worked on a piano reduction of the *Concerto* and revised the second movement: "I just can't be trusted in writing anything quickly and at the same time of such substance that I would be permanently happy with it." In addition to some recomposing, Ingolf was also engaged in re-orchestrating: the original large symphonic band was replaced by a smaller wind orchestra. The work was not finished when it was time to leave Schruns and Ingolf continued to labor on it throughout the summer. But he seems to have abandoned altogether several other orchestral projects started in Austria, including an "easy" suite which he had begun, against Etta's advice, in February.

That month he also began work in earnest on the last major project of the sabbatical, a solo piano piece eventually entitled *Sonata Seria*. A start had been made in November, but Ingolf had abandoned work in order to complete the *Symphony Concertante*. The closing group and second theme of the first movement, he noted on February 20, "are going to be my ruin. I am just stuck there, run around, and fuss around in circles, a note here, and one there. *Once* to get really afloat and sail!!!" "The weather is incomparable," he wrote on February 25, "not a cloud – blue-white brilliance and glory. *Difficult* to stay indoors. But today for the first time a trickle...God give me a *door* to go through. I am shut in a cave, going in circles, if one could go straight on! And thus I polish this little section or that." After returning from his skiing trip to Parsenn he reported, "Feel quite stimulated...go at the SS with renewed drive." On March 21, their thirteenth wedding anniversary, Ingolf was able to play the first movement for Etta. Uncertain if he was going in the right direction he pushed forward with a second movement in April, but by the 17th he had reached an impasse – "decide that what I have of SS II is not adequate. Very depressed. Can leave only the e minor episode – even there some notes will have to be changed." On April 27 he announced, "A good day's work. Get opening of SS II into shape. Nothing else, but I feel, for the first time again, that I am *composing!*" The slowest progress is described; on May 10 "sit at piano and *can't* think for the life of me how to work up a brilliant pattern for the 'cold' place in the coda." Twice the movement was pronounced "finished," and by the end of the month Ingolf was at work on the third section of the piece. Only a coda was needed when the time came for departure. "Dedicate it to Etta, who else should have it? It is done!" he wrote on May 31. On June 3 he played the work for her with some emotion and some little depression over details that had to be reworked. These sections were completed in Tanglewood in July. On June 11 his Schruns piano was returned to its owner – "all that piano has given me," he reported, "am much moved."

The *Sonata Seria* has been described as "tragic" in tone and Ingolf himself used such adjectives as "serious," "heavy," "concentrated," and "introverted." As played by Charles Fierro in a 1973 Orion recording the work lasts twenty-seven minutes, making it – with the cuts and deletions which reduced the duration of other works – the longest of Ingolf's compositions. The work was published by Theodore Presser in 1955. In accepting the piece George Rochberg wrote, "It far surpasses in power and invention most contemporary piano sonatas that I know."

Throughout the year Ingolf had wrestled with a variety of artistic questions, matters of style and intention which further complicated his daily efforts. At the Tanglewood seminar on July 7, 1952 he had taken the neo-classicist's position in the debate on Tonality, Atonality, and Twelve Tone music. He had joked that he was a reformed ex-atonalist who had renounced his chromatic past with the fervor of one who has chosen "the clean life of the triad, the key, in other words, tonality, which fills those of us who have left the promiscuous bed of the 12 tone rows behind them." Tonality, he felt, provided an overall architectural design for a composition, it spanned the wide arch between movements, between sections, between phrases. Ingolf had also affirmed a reverence for the individual tone, the individual interval – the importance of this C sharp, this and only this C sharp, whose entrance can have the character of a ray of light or a sudden dark shadow, if well prepared. His opponents, he charged, had promoted an *inflation* of sounds "in which the tonal currency is spent continuously, thereby *devaluating* the individual tone..."I find in myself a boredom, bordering on annoyance, with the stale ecstasy of constant tensions on a small scale, which provide nothing but harmonic greyness in the long run... I am bored with the whining half steps and the harmonic footlessness of the 12 tone style."

Ingolf admitted that his fondness for the symmetry and order of neo-classicism might be seen as irrelevant in an age of anxiety, one in which the unity of a work no longer seemed possible, but he rejected the reactionary label, especially because it was the neo-Schoenbergians who were producing so much music evocative of turn of the century Viennese romanticism. "How is it possible that all these *young*, healthy people, inhabitants of the blue-skied west, could write such old, tired, strained, over ripe music?"

This was how Ingolf spoke in July, 1952. Seated before his piano in Schruns the doubts began almost immediately. Is one deceiving oneself, he asked in November, "in trying to subordinate almost every note to a far reaching scheme of tonality and key?" On April 8 he records "tears at the thought that I am doing nothing but re-write Stravinsky." On May 22 he asks, "Will the listener really experience my key-relations – arrived at with so much pain?" The solution to this dilemma, reflected in the *Sonata Seria*, was the inauguration of what James Berdahl identified as a new period in Ingolf's style, one marked by a "gradual turn toward the use of serial techniques as a unifying device within the framework of tonal music." The *Sonata*, Berdahl could conclude, was serious but not serial:

> Although it is a tonal work, the harmonic vocabulary used is somewhat more chromatic and considerably more dissonant than in the works of the preceding period. The open textures and jaunty exuberance of earlier works are not present; there are passages of extreme density, and the overall mood of the sonata, as the title suggests, is one of gravity.

Several years later I had occasion to mention to Ingolf that, as much as I admired the music of Stravinsky, I missed the tragic element that I, as an adolescent listener, found so appealing in the work other composers. Ingolf bristled defensively when I said this and sent the dull-witted collegian packing. But now I find it curious that Ingolf himself had found it necessary to transcend the neo-classical vocabulary in search of the darker emotions. It would only be a matter of time before some of the methodology of the serial composer (if not the 12-note row) was accepted and integrated into his music. Stravinsky too, one may add, was also concluding a rapprochement with these same musical traditions which *he* had once shunned.

44. ROSEWOOD

I had last lived in the same home as my father when I was fourteen months old. When I was returned to his household I was fourteen years old. He and I had never gone for long without seeing one another, particularly when the Dahls moved to Corning Street, but I have to admit that my father was always an enigma and a stranger to me. With all of his gifts, his wit and his intelligence, he appeared to be content to live out a life of banal domesticity, the embittered existence of the victim. With his gout and his kidney stones he seemed to be endlessly preoccupied with just staying alive, and this did not mean that there was very much left over to share with his first-born son, especially when Leroy became a father again in 1946.

Contacts with me were apt to be strained; he was forever pursuing the model of good fatherhood without any sensitivity to the developmental needs of the object of these efforts. I had just entered junior high school when he called me solemnly into his study and suggested we talk about "my vocation." It took me several confused minutes to discover that he wasn't talking about another car trip. Once he thought it would be *good for me* to get a glimpse of Mexico and on the way back from Tijuana he suggested I try driving a bit, even though I couldn't really see over the steering wheel yet. He decided to show me how to shave before I had any beard. I suppose it was part of Etta's strategy that a year together with Leroy would soften the tensions in the father-son relationship and permit a more natural evolution of our feelings. If such was her hope we would all be in for a great disappointment. I had, on the whole, a miserable year, another consequence of my position in so quirky a family.

The great impediment to any happy outcome this time was, of course, my stepmother. If my father was disappointed in life my stepmother, Delphine, was outraged over its inequities. She never ceased reminding everyone that life had treated her unfairly and that justice demanded a recount. Leroy never made enough money to satisfy her material cravings and, of course, she would never consider doing any work herself – boasting, in fact, that she too lazy. This did not stop her from informing me that, at fourteen, *I* needed a summer job. I got on my bike and combed my new neighborhood, stopping at stores and shops on Santa Monica and asking if anyone needed my services. I even presented a letter from Sid Weisman to a cigar-chomping supermarket owner who owed him a favor. "Done any box boy work?" he asked. Actually I thought he said "box boiler" – but in any event I didn't even know what a box boy was. After fifteen or sixteen refusals Del allowed me to do chores around the house while I anxiously waited for school to resume. I did the gardening and stacked the firewood against the side of the house. Del made me iron my own ROTC uniform.

My stepmother loathed most of the world but she had some particular objects of hatred. She was perpetually resentful that Leroy's sister and brother-in-law had prospered while Adolph Linick's only son had fallen by the wayside. The house at Rosewood was by this time part of the Laurel Avenue real estate empire and Del could never get over the fact that she and Leroy had to pay rent. When she challenged Baba about this one day there was a very unpleasant contretemps in the dining room, which contained an upright piano and one of the theater organs that had survived the family's withdrawal from the cinema business. "Everybody in the family hates you," Baba snarled – and he was right.

Because she was an active participant in Jewish charitable organizations she was forever thrown in with women who came from a much more prosperous milieu, and I suppose this rankled. I remember being taken to swim in the Olympic-sized pool of one of her colleagues – and feeling very much the poor relation. Who knows what resentments Del carried back with her to the Rosewood bungalow after an afternoon in the foothills. She and Leroy were always debating whether the next car should be a Cadillac or a Lincoln; meanwhile they drove a Kaiser.

Del was not unintelligent, nor unattractive – with her black bobbed hair – though rather mannish. She also made an effort to provide Timothy, who was six when I arrived in 1952, with a supportive and well-structured regime. Every night he had to say his prayers in Hebrew and great fusses were made if he showed any signs of illness. Del made it her lifelong task to know more than any member of the medical profession about the ailments of her family – driving the men in white crazy in the process – but she was actually very knowledgeable in such matters. She had never gone to college, let alone to medical school, but once again we have a good example of a woman whose talents were wasted for want of the right motivation and the right opportunities.

Instead she delighted in finding the dark cloud in everyone else's silver lining, infecting my father with the same pessimism. Del informed me that I would never get into Stanford (not that I wanted to) because I was Jewish. When I cracked my shoulder against a wall Del wanted to know why I hadn't done the dishes. Leroy, learning of my enthusiasm for statistics, gave me a deflating volume entitled *How To Lie With Statistics*. He reminded me that my favorite minor leaguers probably wouldn't make it to the majors. Later, when I showed him my first efforts at writing, he was consumed with locating technical errors and uninterested in the content or the structure. Del too considered herself the guardian of grammar. On a family vacation to Sequoia, during which all four of us, to my chagrin, were outfitted in the same denims and red checked shirts, I swallowed the end of a word in the sentence "I bet we('ve) seen twenty deer today" and Del whacked my leg over the agreement error. For a while I invited my friends to visit me at Rosewood. Richard Binggeli and I even composed the first two bars of a song we were certain would make our fortune – "Pearl Of Far Samoa" – on the white piano. But after a while I could see that my pals were made uncomfortable by the censorious atmosphere of the place and I desisted.

Del doted on her mother, Minnie, and we spent a great deal of time at the Franklin household, where my only solace was a piece of Minnie's Black Jack chewing gum and a cuddle with Chubby, her Chow. Minnie was never a pleasant creature and her sour disposition was further deepened after a mastectomy – which Del was certain the surgeons had botched.

The Franklins were particularly omnipresent on Sundays, when Leroy was expected to take the entire family out to a restaurant dinner during which Del would monitor everything we were allowed to order. Carrying with me these memories of the embittered conversation and the relentless critique of every mouthful, I have never been comfortable in restaurants since. The Nick-o-Dell was a family favorite because Herbie Franklin, Del's stepfather, could order his sweetbreads here and I *did* like the red leather banquettes. Sometimes we dined at the Sportman's Lodge in the Valley and I was charmed once when a pink-faced Bob Hope walked by our table.

Herbie was a rotund hen-pecked cipher who was often on the road selling mattresses for Burton Dixie. This is why Daddy and Del (as they were always known in the Dahl household) never missed a radio broadcast by Paul Harvey, whose show was sponsored by the bedding firm. This was torment for the Linicks, who also endured the right-wing Walter Winchell, because they remained ardent New Dealers. How they hooted as we watched Nixon's famous Checkers speech in 1952. And with what anxiety did they fire off telegrams to the President begging, unsuccessfully, for clemency for the Rosenbergs.

My father seemed to have no hobbies or passions in life, beyond reading – which he did for a living. His position at MGM gave him access to the Academy Theatre near us and he and Del would frequently walk over to see the films nominated for the next Oscars. He also maintained an aquarium with tropical fish, but this was mostly for Tim's amusement. He wrote some fiction himself but at this stage in his life he had no luck with publication. He took no exercise, although he would toss the ball to me in long games of catch on the sidewalk. He never accompanied us on one of our walks but he did agree to drive some of the lads up to Chilao for one of our camping trips. Dick and I constructed a heavy wooden chest with handles so that we could portage our goods overland – some backpacks would have been much more practical – and we spent two nights fending off the raccoons and discussing such important teenage topics as whether or not women could have erections. Dick said they could.

There were a few things about Rosewood that I enjoyed. The Linicks had always been great cat lovers and they now added the giant black Bum, with a white triangle on his chest, to the red tiger-striped Rusty and the neurotic, half-Siamese, crooked-tailed Danny. None of the animals cared for one another and there were constant fights, hissings, and – if you intervened – scratch marks on your hands. Leroy would take me up to the Baldwin Hills where there were sandy patches that he could dig into for cat litter. Every few weeks he would stop off, on our way home from school and work, to pick up some horsemeat for the animals. This would be cut into fine chunks and doled out in saucers. Needless to say the Linick household always had a feline odor about it, but at least my craving for pets was temporarily satisfied.

I also enjoyed having a little sibling and Timmy doted on me – when he wasn't punching my arm. He was a bright little boy doomed to grow up in a family of losers. Every Saturday we would climb aboard the bus and I would take him to Gilmore Field to see how the Hollywood Stars were doing. Manager Bobby Bragan actually put his players into shorts during the hot summer days, but they lost every time I took Timmy to the park. Eight years my junior, Timmy was just too young to be a real pal and, in spite of our closeness during this sabbatical year, we soon resumed our separate existences. As he sank deeper into what seems to have been the family's hereditary introversion he became harder and harder for me to connect with.

I tried out a few new enthusiasms during my year at Rosewood. I grew a dwarf orange tree from a seed. I repainted my Schwinn with metallic silver paint. I carved grotesque heads from bars of ivory soap. I emptied the Weisman basement of every issue of the *National Geographic* since the Twenties and catalogued every article by country. I watched a lot of television, catching up at last on all that I had been missing on *Juke Box Jury*, *You Bet Your Life*, and *Victory At Sea*.

I missed Ingolf and Etta very much. Etta kept up a string of instruction-filled letters and I tried to keep up my end of the correspondence by providing a series of passionless reports on my life as a tenth grader and by mocking my deserting parents by drawing cruel cartoons of their life in Austria, utilizing my own version of *Mad Magazine* characters. To add insult to injury I insisted on giving them every detail of U.S.C.'s Rosebowl victory over Wisconsin, an event of absolutely no interest to any of us.

There is one brief portrait of my physical development in a letter that Lawrence, our near neighbor on Doheny, wrote to my parents on February

7, 1953. At Christmas I had visited him so that he could give me a present. "He looked just wonderful," Lawrence reported, "tall, un-fat, bright in the eyes, eager in the face, well set-up in physique." This may have been how I appeared to others but the turmoils of teenage life and the agonies of life at Rosewood made me miserable more than once. And nothing symbolized these traumas better than my last day in the Linick household.

It was the end of August, 1953. As usual Del had been berating my poor father about one of his many failures. I would always disappear into my room when such scenes took place; I couldn't witness yet again his continuing degradation. On this day there was an escalation of their usual anger, with the cry of "divorce" echoing down the hall. This was followed by the unmistakable punctuation of blows: they were cuffing each other about in their fury. I was terrorized and knew, instantly, that I had to make my escape. I unhooked the window screen of my room and dropped to the ground, crawling on my knees toward the garage so that I would not be seen by the contestants from the window of the bedroom in which they were still duking it out. Having gotten to the garage unnoticed I slipped inside and grabbed my bike, pushing it silently up the alley, away from our house. When I reached the next block I began a twisting, erratic journey toward Corning Street, fearful at any moment that I would be pursued by the combatants and made to resume my place in their breakfast nook. I stealthily approached the Keller's house, where Ingolf and Etta, newly returned from Europe, were in residence; I even snuck in the back way, using the door in the alley fence and gingerly opening the back door. Here my tale of terror was breathlessly related to Etta, who agreed immediately that I would not have to go back to Rosewood. I never did. A few days later we moved to 3481 Clarington and it was here, after a decent interval, that the defeated Leroy picked me up for another one of those horrible Sunday dinners. The beaten man made no mention of the fight or the strange circumstances of my leaving but he did have one request, "Be nice to Del."

45. THE ROAD TO PALMS

On June 5, as the last of his working hours in Schruns came to an end, Ingolf received a visit from a former U.S.C. student, Sam Spence, and the latter's future wife, Friedl. The Dahls were persuaded to accompany the young couple on a short trip in a Volkswagen beetle over the Arlberg and Reschen passes to Italy. The night of the 6th was spent in Verona and the following day in sightseeing in northern Italy. Ingolf completed one last Alpine outing and on June 13 the last farewells were said and my parents began their return trip to America with a stop in Soglio, a favorite Swiss site where Ingolf worked some more on the *Sonata Seria*, using the rickety piano in the hotel. On the 16th they crossed Lake Como and spent a night in Bellinzona. The next day they preceded north by train, amid a "rush of over-powering memories" to Einsiedeln and the famous monastery where they had spent their last day together seventeen years earlier – "Here we are again, Etta *and* I." Ingolf, the atheist, prayed, "Give me the achieved mark – and let me come back here. Thanks for giving me my heart."

The Dahls remained in Zurich until the 20th and Ingolf played through the *Quodlibet* with Walter Frey. There followed three nights in Paris and a reunion with Gail Kubik. At the St. Lazare station platform on June 24 Ingolf was overcome with tears, "The farewell from Europe overwhelms me." They sailed from Le Havre that night, arrived in New York on the 30th and on July 3 took the train to Lenox and Tanglewood – "the circle is closed," Ingolf wrote.

On July 5, the eve of the first meeting with his new students, Ingolf attended a faculty meeting – "a little embarrassed," he noted, "because I asked for it and now have nothing to say." After some Buxtehude the next afternoon he felt more confident about this year's group and its attitude. "Everybody seems to be pleased," he noted the next day. The group presented a concert on July 18 but Ingolf remained depressed about "all the mistakes and amateurishness. But audience and big brass seem to like it." Ingolf again gave several lectures and participated in public discussions, debating "The Consequences of Recorded Music" on July 13 and speaking on "Musical Form and The Interpreter" on the 20th ("I think it is lousy but it does not show"). A Purcell program by the Study Group followed on August 1, but Ingolf was devastated by a cutting remark overheard while he was swimming later that afternoon, upset precisely because he agreed with the critic – "more than ever want to get away from all this amateurishness, this constant nagging inadequacy." There followed one more concert on August 13 during which the group presented a contemporary work by Allen Sapp. "It goes quite well," Ingolf wrote, but "audience is awful."

There were again many opportunities for Ingolf to supplement the meager musical rewards of Department Five with the richer coinage of friendship and collaboration. Lukas Foss was again present and again Ingolf felt a touch of envy. After playing through his friend's piano concerto Ingolf remarked that "compared to it my music seems naive, crude." A new friend was the composer Irving Fine, though Ingolf was disturbed that some of Fine's work bore similarities to his own. Carlos Chavez was also at the Bernstein-dominated Tanglewood this summer and Ingolf was pleased when Chavez expressed a liking for some of his music. A dinner in honor of the Mexican composer was held on August 10, but Ingolf complained, "Lenny monopolizes everything." On July 28 Ingolf played versions of the *Symphony Concertante* and the *Sonata Seria* for Copland, Foss, and Fine. It was a "wonderful evening," he enthused, "particularly the latter impresses. Very happy about it." Ingolf dined with Elliott Carter on August 7. Carter had written to congratulate Ingolf on the Guggenheim award – "You certainly deserve it. So many people get it these days that don't." Ingolf also played the new piano sonata for Arthur Berger on August 3 and two days later welcomed Mel Powell for a brief visit. It was a summer without a sour note ("Barney Childs quite impossible" comes close) but there was at least one ominous chord.

On July 11 Ingolf and Etta took the train to Stamford, Connecticut for a day's visit with Benny Goodman. Benny went fishing in the morning but after lunch Ingolf accompanied him on the first run-through (minus the second soloist) of the completed *Symphony Concertante*. "A high point of experience – he is in the music, with me, the piece convinces me completely...this I have long waited for," Ingolf wrote. But Benny disappeared again before Ingolf could talk business with him, that is before some plans could be made for a world premiere. As the months passed and correspondence between Ingolf, Goodman, Reginald Kell, and conductors made its desultory way across the continent, Ingolf's own faith in the latest version of the piece wavered and another long process of revision began. In the process a work of thirty-five minutes was contracted to one about half that length and Ingolf never really completed a final revision. The failure of his plans for this piece was among the long-standing disappointments of his artistic career.

On August 10 Ingolf and Etta left Tanglewood for New York; in a few days they managed to squeeze in a trip to the Metropolitan ("a frustrating taste of heaven"), and visits to Trude Rittman, Arthur Berger, and Mel and Martha Powell. On the 17th they flew to Chicago and checked into a hotel in Kenosha, Wisconsin, where they took delivery on our family's first *new* car, a grey Nash Rambler convertible which they named Genevieve – or Jenny for short. Then they drove at a fairly leisurely pace westward, spending nights in Dubuque, South Sioux City, Wray, Moon Valley, Grand Junction, (with a stop in Aspen on the way), Gallup (with a side trip to Mesa Verde), and Blythe (after a detour through Oak Creek Canyon). At 3:00 P.M. on August 25 they pulled up in front of the Linick's house on Rosewood, where I sat anxiously waiting, the green felt Tyrolian hat they had sent me perched proudly on my head.

Etta climbed with some difficult from the Nash, ten or fifteen pounds heavier than I had last seen her. My mother-the-coed hugged me amid my usual embarrassment at overt signs of emotion and our family was reunited. The Dahls and I (after my flight from the embattled Linicks) stayed at the Kellers for a few days of apartment hunting, and on September 1, 1953, we spent the first night in our new home, an upstairs two bedroom unit in a large apartment complex just north of Culver City at 3481 Clarington Avenue. The site was actually in Palms, a sub-community of down-market bungalows and unattractive apartment complexes which had been chosen because it was not too far from U.S.C., within driving distance of the studio on Corning Street, and within the school district whose teenagers went to Hamilton High School. With its gas stations, its convenience stores, its railway overpasses and its smog it would be hard to discover an environment less similar to the Europe my parents had left behind. Nevertheless here we all struggled against life for five years.

46. CLARINGTON

To the extent that my desire to remain in a very specific corner of West Los Angeles influenced our choice of residence, I must share in the responsibility for imposing on my parents an environment that was so cheerless and banal. On the other hand Ingolf and Etta were very stubborn people and they never really did anything against their own will for long. Etta soon adapted herself to life in a large apartment complex and Ingolf, as we will eventually discover, managed to spend a great deal of his time elsewhere. When we left 3481 Clarington five years later it was without much regret on anybody's part.

Our new location was an upstairs flat at the back of a courtyard near Exposition and National. The view from the front window included only other entranceways, and a glimpse from the kitchen or dining room windows revealed nothing more inspiring than gossiping housewives ascending the back steps from a rear courtyard. The two bedrooms faced west and offered us vistas of the sun setting over the garage roofs that separated our complex from an adjacent one, where a communal swimming pool was located. It was all too new and too middle class to fit the pattern of tenement living, but the atmosphere of noise, crowding, cooking odors, laundry room and wash lines did indeed approximate some of the features of that kind of life.

Ingolf kept Genevieve in the garage beneath my bedroom window and to watch Etta manoeuvre the car into its restricted space was to observe the triumph of improvisation over skill. In fact the garages had no doors to them, rendering them useless as teenage clubhouses, but there was storage room at the rear and Ingolf spent much time here rearranging his camping equipment.

My parents made a regular habit of going off by themselves on long weekend holidays during our Clarington years, sometimes staying in motels but, more often than not, roughing it. They undertook an outing to Joshua Tree National Monument in celebration of their fourteenth wedding anniversary in March, 1954, and in September they spent several days driving up Highway 1. Ingolf would have initiated more of these expeditions had Etta been more physically active – thus we find him complaining as they drove by Point Lobos, "I always want *physical* contact with nature and places, feel the water, the sun, explore the scenery." A useful accommodation proved to be the many trips they undertook to Baja California, where they selected some deserted Mexican beach and camped by the car for long stretches at a time. The first of these expeditions took place in June of 1955, when they happily broiled themselves for five days at Boca Santo Tomas. In November 1956, with Jenny having been altered so that the front seats could be lowered and a car bed thus created, the two took a camping trip north of Ojai. In July 1957 they returned to Baja. From Ingolf's journals and one of Etta's letters it is possible to get a good view of the Dahls in one of their idyllic moods. After several abortive attempts at finding a camping place they ended up at Cape Colnett, watching the dolphins and the sea birds, digging for clams, dodging a rattlesnake. They took turns reading *Love's Labour Lost* and Mann's *Felix Krull*. They dozed and baked in the sun. Ingolf read a Swedish mystery story. Etta gave *Richard III* a bad review.

I kept *my* cars on Clarington itself. As I couldn't drive yet these vehicles often sat out there for weeks at a time, the juice draining from their batteries and their bodies relentlessly soaking up the pigeon shit and tree sap. My first car, inherited via the Kellers from Grandpa Gordon, was a 1936 Studebaker coupé called (but not by me) Cookie. On one of our repeated attempts to move her to a new parking place after days of battery-draining idleness on the curb, the door on the passenger's side swing open as I attempted to push Ingolf down the hill, sweeping me into the street just as the car was gathering momentum. I sustained a sprained wrist and a gash in my chin, the scar of which I still bear. Cookie died before I earned my first driving license, though the car was used by Holger and Aina Marcus, who came to visit us in 1954. The Studebaker was succeeded by a Chevrolet sedan of the same vintage, passed on to me when the Linicks, after much debate over a new car, settled for Minnie's second-hand Plymouth. Rufus, as Ingolf insisted on calling this apple green fossil, had a stick shift and a dodgy transmission. Nevertheless I persisted in my efforts to manage its complexities and Ingolf, Etta, and Leroy all had a go at being my driving instructor. Leroy had the bright idea of taking me up to the huge earthen parking lot that occupied the northeast corner of the U.C.L.A. campus in the mid-Fifties and here, on Sundays, there was a huge expanse of territory for the novice driver to cover without worrying about hitting anything. After failing once because I couldn't resist showing off by reversing too quickly into a parking space, I obtained the treasured license. My driving career began at seventeen and I actually drove to school the final semester of my senior year, a distinction that later earned sighs of envy from my London students, who didn't really start driving until their return to the States.

I wish I could claim that I used Rufus to cover territory as wide-ranging as the Dahls, but most of my ventures were much closer to home. I do remember driving us all to Knott's Berry Farm to celebrate some high school evening with the senior class; earlier we had borrowed the car from Leroy to head off to the Sierras, with Dick Dardarian at the wheel, and it was used once or twice on camping trips. It was always a miracle that it survived these expeditions but within two years it developed a fatal howl and had to be scrapped. I switched then to a succession of Buicks, each time stepping down a model and back a few years. My first, purchased in 1957, was a classic model with those famous portholes. Mostly I used my cars for some privacy, that is as a way to escape to some friend's house or to sit and hold long and earnest discussions with my pals in the dark. How we loved to argue, how seriously we took our own opinions, how we loved to take sides against the odd man out (in a way, we were *all* odd). Our post-car feuds could last for weeks, but these disputes seem to have been part of our search for adult identity.

Incidentally, I did not find any new friends in this uninviting neighborhood of Palms and home life was often a lonely proposition for me; I missed the opportunities of Corning Street, where I could walk out the front door and find someone to organize or at least a cousin to bedevil. Fortunately Leigh Peffer lived close at hand and I would often visit him. He introduced me to *Mad* comics, Vernor's ginger ale, men's magazines, and the music of *West Side Story*. Together we plotted a bicycle trip across the United States, another dream never to be realized, and we reported to the L.A. Public Library to take tests in book-shelf sorting. I remember my excitement in figuring out that a full time job in the library could earn me $50 a week. We both passed the test but only Leigh bothered to take the job. His grandmother had a house on Exposition Place and behind this he had created his own studio, where I also worked on my own projects, artistic and literary. Leigh was a very talented artist and would soon be on his way to art college. I smoked a pipe.

When there was no one else to visit, and when I had grown bored with my vain attempt to read every work of fiction in the Palms Library starting with authors whose last name began with A (this must be how I came to read Hervey Allen's *Anthony Adverse*), I went to the movies. There was a small cinema, also called The Palms, on Motor Avenue, just a few blocks walk to the west of us. On weeknights, when I had no homework – or didn't want to do it – I would ramble over here and lose myself in Hollywood fantasy for several hours. The Palms specialized in second run popular hits and I saw a lot of really dreadful movies here, films like *Not As A Stranger, I'll Cry Tomorrow,* and *The High And The Mighty.* The manager of The Palms always made a special effort to welcome me to his theater, selling me my ticket and my popcorn himself. I was, after all, his *best* customer, and – lest we see this descent into the darkness of the dream pool as a social activity – I have to state that on many nights I was his *only* customer as well.

The interior of our new apartment was crowded with the usual array of second hand and cast-off furniture, complimented in the living room by the arrival of an ugly new sofa in a detestable nubbly wool of yellow, green, and brown – with the magnificent Steinway in the corner. There were definite limits, incidentally, on the amount of time and the hours Ingolf could use his piano since Mrs Gurace, downstairs, was not a lover of modern music.

There was a dining area in the new apartment, the only addition to our space in all these moves, and here Ingolf also kept his music cabinets and a primitive phonograph. I used this machine much more frequently than he did, playing through our meager record collection which included Britten's *Serenade For Tenor, Horn, and Strings* and Mendelssohn's *A Midsummer Night's Dream.* These were still the days when you had to listen to symphonies on 78's but eventually I began to buy jazz hits that could be completed without turning the disc over – I was particularly fond of Woody Herman's "Bijou." This was the period of time during which I became deeply enchanted with those Sextet records Benny Goodman had given to me. When the first great multiple album compilation of Goodman's band music was offered I announced my intention to buy the set, but Etta, insisting I would grow bored with it, would not permit this. Needless to say all of my music listening had to be conducted clandestinely, since no alien notes were to be sounded whenever Ingolf was present. I had a little better luck in my own room, where – with the volume low, I could persist in my loyalty to the lofty ballads of KMPC's *Lucky Lager Dance Time*. I kept detailed charts of my popular music preferences which, by the time I reached college, included a brief flirtation with Dixieland and an enormous affection for the big band music of the previous decade – which was undergoing its first great nostalgic revival on the airways. By the time we left Clarington I was listening to classical music on KFAC and keeping my enthusiasm for the romantic period well under wraps, so as not to incur the sneers of the Dahls. Popular music was undergoing a revolution that could only have caused my parents the deepest puzzlement – the birth of rock and roll. I remember the excitement which permeated our teenage culture when, after a brief introduction from Bill Haley And the Comets and the Crewcuts surreal-sounding "Shboom," we began listening to L.A. stations that catered for black audiences and heard The Crows singing "Gee" or the Penguins doing "Earth Angel" in styles wholly subversive to the blandness of the Pat Boone era.

Ingolf and Etta's bedroom remained the most crowded of all our living spaces at Clarington and was once again choked with two double beds. My own sleeping quarters were soon littered by teenage paraphernalia and collections, and it was Etta's chronic complaint that I always left the evidence of my latest passions all over the rest of the house, that is that I showed evidence of becoming a second Ingolf. In the latter stages of our years here I decided to become compulsive about my own space, and my room underwent a series of drastic shifts in desk, bed, bulletin board, bookcase, and radio as I attempted to make order in the disordered world of a young collegian. This was something that Etta welcomed warmly since household chores, she announced, were no longer to interfere unduly in her career as a graduate student, a role she pursued throughout our entire stay at Clarington.

47. INSIDE THE WALLS OF TROY

Etta had completed most of her Ph.D. course work by 1955, when she passed written and oral qualifying examinations. Before this date she had passed her French language proficiency exam in May, 1954 and the Swedish equivalent the following February. She then began a long struggle to complete a doctoral dissertation on a famous picaresque novel of the 17th Century, Grimmelshausen's *Simplicissimus*. In her re-introduction to academic life my mother had taken most of the German Department's offerings in philology and literature and a few courses in French and Art. Like many other "adult" students, her second time at the university was far more successful than her first; it would have been hard to predict from her mediocre record as an undergraduate on Vermont Avenue that Etta would eventually earn 26 A's and 4 B's as a graduate student at Figueroa Tech, as we liked to call U.S.C.

I have the feeling that Etta must have been a trial to some of her professors and to a good number of her fellow graduate students, all of whom were puzzled by the seriousness, dedication, and proficiency of this middle-aged dilettante whose motives in earning an advanced degree were obscure at best. For some of the more marginal students Etta's dogged presence in seminar must have been maddening. Then there were times when she pretended to be instructed by a faculty whose knowledge of the subject matter was often inferior to her own. She gave vent to this frustration in a sarcastic dedication that never saw the light of day – "to my Ph.D. Committee, without whose guidance this doctoral dissertation would not only have been possible but better." I think it is fair to add that one can extend a certain degree of sympathy to a faculty which must have felt under some constraint not to offend the wife of a distinguished colleague in another department. *They* couldn't please her because they were measured against the standard only he could achieve. And they could hardly do her in when Ingolf sent roses and a scroll signed by all of her friends in the School of Music to the German Department office on the day of her written exams. With a less able student this would certainly have been a problem.

Etta obviously thrived in the graduate school environment and she soon enjoyed a new kind of social life at U.S.C. Lunchtime in the Commons

Cafeteria – a period that could stretch for hours, saw Etta and her many university friends engaged in perpetual chatter and gossip on literary and artistic matters. Added to this circle were many of Ingolf's students, Ramiro Cortes, Bob Taylor, and Paul Glass for instance, all attracted by Etta's wit and eager to get closer to the master through his wife. Etta served as a kind of cultural den mother and my future co-editor, Don Factor, remembers that she played a pivotal role in the noontime conversations, winning the respect of a large number of associates, many of whom were only slightly older than her son.

I too had the opportunity of observing this scene at close hand because in the summer of 1954, just as I was about to begin my last year in high school, my parents secured for me a job in the Gifts and Exchange Division of Doheny Library. While my mother went to summer school classes I opened much of the library's post. In fact I enjoyed my work and it was particularly useful for a stamp collector to be in charge of opening mail. In the slack periods, moreover, I could always climb into the storeroom and sort through the gift of a large number of *Esquire* magazines with Vargas drawings of near-naked girls. After lunch, with Jenny's top down in the broiling sun, Etta would drive us back to Clarington to the strains of "Hey There" and "Hernando's Hideaway" on the car radio. At dinner there would always be the latest news from the campus – classroom and commons – what Drs. Waterman, von Hofe, Marcuse, Mohme, or Townshend had got wrong today, what Don's new Thunderbird was like, how Paul and his girlfriend Norma were getting along. Through my mother's gossip I got to know many of these people, some of whom were to matter a great deal in *my* life, but long before I actually met them in person.

When my parents had died I discovered a great many written documents which enabled me to reconstruct a truer picture of our actual lives. Some of these, as I have indicated in my introduction, were profoundly disturbing to me, but I was not at all surprised to uncover a good deal of writing by my mother, who was always jotting down ideas. In the mid-fifties, it became clear, she was working on a detective novel in which she was to play the sleuth herself. In several spiral notebooks she recorded sketches, one-liners, plot situations and dialogue, all of which she hoped to put together in a finished form at some time in the future. That time never came, and we can't even be sure who the murder victim was going to be – although I suppose there were several candidates among her professors.

Etta had not even decided on a style. In some of the entries she has cast herself in the role of Ma Grafton, a hard-boiled quipster who parodies the diction of the mystery novels that Etta and Ingolf devoured. On her way to burn papers in the incinerator Ma says, "Got to destroy some evidence." About to boil a fish, Ma says, "Got to grill a suspect." Preparing a meal of leftovers, Ma reports, "I'll just go view the remains." "The apartment did not have that 'lived-in' look,'" Ma notes, "but the lady did."

In another section of her notebook Etta adopts a stream-of-consciousness style at some remove from Ma Grafton's butch diction. I include a lengthy excerpt because it is so specifically autobiographical that it serves well to recapture the flavor of our lives. I can not date it precisely, but it probably comes from 1955 or 1956:

> Six a.m. Alarm goes off nose thumb at it did I make a note to refer to Schiller-Goethe letter where Goethe says to Schiller The good German public is going to like what I'm writing now there's a moral lesson in it shows he was well aware of his public though never catered to it better get the coffee on Goethe's remark rather snide good for him I'm running out of sandwich bags put it on list you fool you'll never remember it can I get the wash in the machine before we go to school? Yes but there'll be no time to hang it time to wake son panic panic I'll never finish the dissertation by the deadline but he had peanut butter *yesterday* let's try chopped ham they can't have rehearsal here on Thurs. evening unless they can stop at 10 PM sharp musicians in apartments and upstairs is a drag time to wake husband none of your business how finally pull away to what I was going to do what what what I won't use Goethe-Schiller bit, it looks like mere showing off so prove Grimmelshausen's reader consciousness another way it should be easy should I wear no it isn't back from the cleaners what? the address book was on your desk it was there yesterday we have a balance of two eighty nine but Thursday is check day I'll wear the grey skirt & black top cuts me off in the middle oh well where is my rough sketch of introduction oh here I wrote to Stockholm last time *you* write to your mother my thesis style is ghastly but if my doctoral committee at least agree with what I have to say I can polish the style later an introduction should be written at the end anyhow I can wash tonight about nine-thirty after the dishes I like to hang it out by moonlight reminds me of Schoenberg's P.L. did I or did I not set the automatic oven

control for dinner I'd better not eat lunch in the Commons I get into too many discussions & don't work but it's fun these composition students of his poking their sketches under my nose my protesting I don't read well enough away from the piano to do them justice they don't care they poke poke son is growing out of those denims I'd better scrap any reference to modern psychology in analyzing the leading characters of the novel it will look pretentious no matter how I try besides such reconstructions though interesting & perhaps legitimate are hazardous we are never going to get to school on time I'm sure the library will not have located the missing volume I want perhaps U.C.L.A. has it I'll bet a nickel I didn't turn on the automatic oven control – I'll call son at 4 he will give me a lecture on inefficiency he used to say gross insufficiency now sometimes shortened to Mrs. Gross but we both know what he means Sunday I will make a meat loaf, sear a pot roast so all it has to do is simmer after that which should last until Monday T. & W. leftovers I am absolutely head over heels in love with Diderot a sort of 20th century mind habituated to our multiform approach to things & our ability *faute de mieux* to live in a forest of co-existent opinions with the decision lying nowhere but he did it in the 18th C when logical certainties were plopping like plums in every other lap how amazing the campus post office will probably be closed for lunch. Had enough? Don't feel sorry for me, I get along fine. And for you I'll put in punctuation.

In 1957 Etta began a long tenure as one of the lecturers in a School of Music course in phonetics and diction for students of voice. The language departments were evidently resentful that the instructors for this course were not hired by them, but in Etta's case it would be hard to imagine anyone with a better background in German *and* voice. One of her students was the unknown Marilyn Horne, who became a good friend of Etta's before beginning a resplendent operatic career. My mother loved her teaching, though it occupied only a few weeks every year, and she spent a great deal of time in preparation. From her university life she at last earned some recognition for her own intelligence and charm, a sense of identity which could so easily have been swamped my the demands of her self-centered and needy husband.

48. HAMI

The Apache Patrol infiltrated Alexander Hamilton High School in September, 1952 – as tenth graders – and we graduated, after three years at this institution on Robertson Boulevard, in June of 1955. During my first year here I was living on Rosewood and so my father would drop me off directly in front of the main building on his way to MGM, and pick me up at one of my friends' houses on his way home. By the end of the year this meant Leigh Peffer's house near Venice and La Cienega, which I would stroll down to on Cattaraugus, pausing routinely to buy a licorice stick and a Pepsi Cola (still only a nickel), before letting myself into the usually empty house for a little homework and TV.

During the first half of the year I spent most of my afternoons with Dick Binggeli at his house on Reynier. He had a great devotion to science by this time and he had built a little laboratory in his garden where we would torture caterpillars by testing various chemical compounds on them. Working in Dick's backyard was dangerous because his mother had a very sharp tongue and no tolerance for noise. Swept up in his enthusiasm I joined him for courses in science offered by staff members of the Los Angeles County Museum on Saturday mornings in 1953 and 1954. One of these courses was mineralogy and for a while we both collected rocks; there is a photo of us, holding the Forest Patrol flag atop some summit, in which it appears I have grown breasts, an illusion caused by my habit of stuffing new mineral samples into my shirt pockets.

Dick and I also shared a devotion to the Democratic Party and we spent a great deal of time in the autumn of 1952 stopping cars and asking drivers if they would like a Stevenson bumper sticker, piles of which we had picked up at party headquarters. We had more luck in supermarket parking lots because there wasn't a great deal of traffic on Reynier, which meant we spent a lot of time tossing the ball back and forth between political harangues.

Dick and I also formed the habit, after science lessons in the Museum, of walking through Exposition Park to the Coliseum, where we could attend the home football games of both U.S.C. and U.C.L.A. It cost only sixty-five cents to get into such games and we could often move over to empty seats in a better part of the stadium which (before its trim-down) seated over 100,000 fans. We saw U.C.L.A. beat Washington on November 14, 1953 when only 13,302 fans showed up on a rainy day during which the King and Queen of Greece were guests of honor. We saw U.C.L.A. thrash Stanford 72-0 on October 16, 1954. I suppose it was useful for us to be on the winning side of *some* local teams since the Hamilton Yankees, after winning the first game we attended in September, 1952, never won another one in our entire three years at the school and week after week we would sit disconsolately in the bleachers while Hami was being thrashed by Dorsey, Venice or L.A. High. We even traveled to away games for these ritual humiliations and thus got to see University High School pulverize our team 82-7 in 1954.

I made one new friend while at Hamilton. Mikel Taxer was a Jewish boy from Iowa. He was an extremely lively and outgoing young chap who had no difficulty projecting his amusingly innocent personality. He was easy to tease. We made him a late entrant to the Forest Patrol and hazed him mercilessly during a creekside initiation. Dick and I "hypnotized" him and implanted some post-hypnotic suggestions which he enacted so perfectly that we could never tell whether *we* had succeeded or *he* was having *us* on. Part of our difficulty was that Mikel was an actor (and a dancer), perpetually abandoning us for lessons. He was often seen in campus productions and he borrowed a tweed suit of Ingolf's in order to appear as the Stage Manager in *Our Town* in December, 1953. He aspired to a career in show business and he was part of a small group at our school that actually got a foothold on this ladder. In Mikel's case, in spite of surgery to correct protuberant ears and a flattened nose, this amounted to parts in local dramatic productions, though in real theaters, but two other class members went further: Carol Nugent had a brief career as an ingénue, and Mike's great friend Luana Anders (well, we knew her as Anderson) enjoyed a kind of minor cult status after a variety of movie rolls. I must say that the rest of us were always a bit envious of this celebrity and liked to characterize the whole Hollywood world as "phony," having picked up the word from Holden Caulfield. We gave Luana an unforgivably hard time when she visited us in the summer of 1956, when Mikel, John and I had a bachelor summer camping out at Clarington while my parents were in Tanglewood.

Hamilton had a number of other show biz connections; some of our meaner looking kids had bit parts as students in *Blackboard Jungle* and both of the Stockwell boys, Guy and Dean, John's neighbors on Bedford Street, had gone to our school slightly ahead of us. I remember Guy McElwaine, who eventually became an agent and studio president, beginning a baseball contest by concussing Dorsey's first batter with a high inside fastball.

In John's backyard, about the time of graduation, it was decided that we needed to form our own club, We wouldn't wear brightly colored jackets like the Dukes or the Barons or any of the other social clubs on campus, indeed we could not do so because our club was *secret*. Nevertheless Dick, John, Mikel and I solemnly convened the Knights of the Golden Sword as a symbol of our perpetual friendship and a few months later we spent an entire evening writing, for the historical record, personal histories and predictions about the future, of our world and our fellow Knights. Still fulfilling my role as scribe I retained these documents for an eventual reunion. In 1992, over a third of a century later, we read them aloud in Dick Binggeli's living room in Marina del Rey. Dick had become a professor of anatomy at U.S.C. and a practicing psychotherapist, Mikel, who had trained up from San Diego, was a minister of the Presbyterian Church, and John, who listened by phone from Washington, was working, as he had for most of his life, for the Agency For International Development. The following year Dick and I continued to reminisce at our annual Christmas get-togethers but when we shared some of these teenage fascinations with Dick's daughter Claire, the pretty young school teacher looked at us cannily as said, "Gee, you really were a bunch of nerds, weren't you?"

Well, let's examine the evidence, at least in my case. During my first year at Hamilton I did hold political office. I was the treasurer of the Latin Club and the editor of its newspaper, *Pax Terra*. I helped arrange club banquets at an Italian restaurant, during which I wore a borrowed U.S.C. Trojan Marching Band helmet and we all wore togas. I remember Miss Kay McGrath telling me not to feel embarrassed when the snapshots of this event revealed my newly hairy legs. On the glorious night itself Mikel Taxer and I sang "When the Red Red Robin Come Bob Bob Bobbing Along," and I delivered a parody of the Funeral Oration from *Julius Caesar*.

As an older student, inspired by Mrs. Marjorie Bruce, our challenging English instructor, I was a member of The Future Teachers of America club, but other than a brief stint on the Senior Privileges Committee I took no part in other activities or sports, never went to any of the school's on-campus social functions, belonged to no service organizations, took no interest in school politics.

After a final semester in P.E. I followed Dick, John and Allan into the high school R.O.T.C. where our paramilitary instincts, still alive after the dissolution of our scout troop, could play themselves out in endless close order drill, formation marching, and the disassembly of the M1 rifle. In my second semester at Hami I was awarded the Best Private medal and got to go a ceremony at the Ambassador Hotel with Captain Kanalis. Although I hated the wooly khaki uniform (and clandestinely wore pajama bottoms beneath my trousers) I rather liked R.O.T.C. President Eisenhower had promised to end the war in Korea so it wasn't as though we were preparing ourselves for any imminent risk to life or limb. We got to go to Fort MacArthur and sleep in a real barracks for a weekend and, as we grew older, we had the privilege of bossing all the younger kids around and getting saluted. Although I started a semester behind my pals I rose to the rank of captain before my graduation and shared with them a kind of office in one of the small add-on bungalows at the rear of the Hamilton campus. I remember dismissing one diminutive private who wandered into our sanctum with the pun, "Out, out, brief Campbell!"

I cite this witticism as evidence that we must have been making useful progress in English Literature at the same time. I enjoyed almost all of my classes at Hamilton, which had a very good teaching staff and an excellent academic record under principal Walker Brown, and I did especially well in English and Social Studies. Indeed Miss Mason, also clandestinely, paid me to grade the papers of the other students in my U.S. History class. In spite of the fact that he was rather politically conservative, I had a great affection for Joseph Weston, my Civics teacher, and I'm sure it was Mr. Weston who served as my teaching role model above all others. Under his sponsorship a number of us worked downtown till dawn helping lug bags of ballots around at election time. Mr. MacLean, who taught University Composition to seniors, gave me an excellent grounding in expository writing. I took two years of French but I did not climb to any challenging levels in math, after Algebra and Geometry, or in science, after Biology. There were some unusual parts of the curriculum: a course in job finding (I wrote my own letter of recommendation rather than bother anyone for a real one since I had no intention of applying for a job), a class in Senior Problems, and, of course, Driver's Education – although this was not accompanied by any behind-the-wheel experience. I did well academically, appearing frequently on the honor roll as a Nevian (Alexander H. had been born on the island of Nevis), and graduating as a Sealbearer of the California Scholastic Federation. In my last semester I had a perfect report card – all A's, all E's, no absences.

My social life, by contrast, was particularly dismal during the same period. I fell in love for the first time on April 7, 1953; the object of this infatuation was an eleventh grader (that is over a year older than I was) named Berkeley Meigs. Berkeley, whom I had met in Latin class, was a very bright and outgoing scholar, the daughter of another U.S.C. professor and related to the author Rachel Field. We spent a great deal of time on the phone and she once came to Rosewood for an awkward visit, but I cannot say that we ever dated and soon she was swept away by pre-college enthusiasms. She went to Stanford (the same school that Del had told me I wouldn't get into) and it was on the Palo Alto campus that I last saw her in 1955 during my freshman year at U.C.L.A. Next I had a crush on a young girl named Sandy who sat several desks away from me in study hall. I liked her sultry Sephardic looks and long black hair but she disappeared after Christmas of my junior year. Or did she? Weeks later I saw that she was still among us, albeit with a new nose! I had loved the old one.

In my senior year I met several girls I liked and I asked Rochelle Silver to go with me to the Military Ball, an all-school affair for R.O.T.C. students at the Ambassador, in December, 1954. I had to wear my uniform and she wore a formal decorated with the gardenia corsage I had bought for her. She seemed to be immensely attractive but I never called her for another date. In retrospect I realize now that this was because of an incident that occurred when I picked her up in Rufus. As I was introduced to her mother, the latter, who had just presented Shelly with a little brother, took a close look at her daughter's date and said, "*He's* not Jewish!" – to which I protested vehemently, but sheepishly. Today I see that this ambiguity of identity, something my parents had nurtured assiduously, placed me in a very difficult social position. Hamilton was half Jewish and half not. But I couldn't lie to Gentile girls and telling the truth to Jewish ones inevitably exposed my ignorance and brought up such questions as: which temple did I belong to and where was I *bar-mitzvahed* and did my mother belong to Hadassah? – the same questions that Neil Klugman has to face from Brenda's mother in *Goodbye, Columbus*. These questions mattered in West L.A. in the mid-Fifties and they helped to feed the affective paralysis from which I suffered anyway. The spring Military Ball rolled around and I did not have the stomach to undergo another humiliation. I sold everyone else *their* tickets, as part of my duties as an R.O.T.C. officer, and failed to buy one myself.

I did spend a lot of time in mixed-sex groups during my senior year when our class, following an Hawaiian motif, chose to call itself The Kanoans. We adopted charcoal and sky blue as our colors since charcoal and pink were *the* great fashion colors of the era – I had a charcoal suit, a pink shirt, and ties, socks and belts in both colors. As a class we undertook a series of social evenings culminating in grad night at some beach hotel in Santa Monica. The day after commencement several of us had the top of our heads flattened at the barbershop in attempt to look really cool. Yes, you *could* say I was a real nerd. And a forgetable one at that. It took forty years for me to receive an invitation to a class reunion. And, seeking to repair the irreparable, I went.

49. FANFARES

There are many references to career crises and creative paralysis in the period following Ingolf's year in Schruns. "Have I missed the boat?" he asked after reading about the successes of his composing friends in the *A.C.A. Bulletin* on October 2, 1953. A "lost lost lost day" is reported on March 13, 1954, "where is the grip on life, on the task. There is *too* much (course work, post composition cleanup, correspondence, future composition) – all this stifles me, strangles me – so I lie in bed and read *New Yorker*." Five days later it was announced that Ingolf Dahl had been awarded a thousand dollar grant from the National Institute of Arts and Letters "in recognition of the clarity, formal logic and brilliant instrumental coloring of his chamber and orchestral music," but the celebration was

269

clouded by self-doubts – "Am I worth it? What can I do?" Four weeks later he reported himself to be "dry, empty, tense, unhappy."

Part of this tension can be explained as pre-creative pressure: Ingolf was preparing to do battle with the muses again. On June 1, 1954 he drove to the Huntington Hartford Foundation retreat at 2000 Rustic Canyon Road in the Pacific Palisades, where we was to live as one of the fellows for two months. "What peace, what a wonderful spot for work," he wrote on the first day. The setting was one of those marvelous Southern California locales, a wild canyon not far from my old Boy Scout Camp, Josepho, but close to civilization as well. Ingolf walked every day, took sunbaths, jogged through the woods. The bees, the walnut trees, the blue jays and the quail, the aroma of leaves, the architectural accomplishments of Charlotte and Emily (his cabin's resident spiders) – Ingolf's journals are full of references to the delight he took in his new environment.

There are not many comments on other guests at the Foundation (for whom he occasionally played Mozart sonatas), but he does mention a trip to nearby Saddle Peak on July 5 with C. Wright Mills, who was working on *The Power Elite*. There were also trips to the outside, necessary appointments and commitments, and reunions with the family.

The Tower of Saint Barbara, "A Symphonic Legend in Four Parts," was Ingolf's sole composition project at the Hartford Foundation, a response to a thousand dollar commission from the Rockefeller-sponsored Louisville Orchestra, which had engaged many well-known composers during this period. Notification of the award first reached Ingolf at Tanglewood when Lukas Foss phoned him with the news of July 19, 1953. "Terribly excited, bewildered," was Ingolf's initial response; this was followed almost immediately by a request for a deadline extension – "I work rather slowly and need a fair amount of time for the crystalization of that kind of balance between expressive and constructive elements for which I am striving in my music." Now, he determined, would be the time to proceed with his plans to complete a ballet for Maya Kubler in Zurich. The storyline had been drafted in the first three months of the sabbatical but little music has been sketched before the summer of 1954. "I am afraid of Barbara," he wrote during his spring paralysis, "may Barbara be kind," he added on his first day at the Foundation, "may I get *into* the stream, really flowing, rushing, *inside*."

The saint whom Ingolf invokes was an early Christian martyr whose image, complete with the tower of her imprisonment at her feet, he had discovered in a church near Schruns. The ballet is based on the saint's refusal to accept a marriage initiated by her heathen father, the king, or to abandon her Christian faith for his pagan beliefs. After a period of imprisonment Barbara is tormented by the fury of the king's people and is slain by her own father. The legend made an appealing scenario for the dance, but Ingolf was a bit ashamed of this trafficking in medieval Catholicism. Pappi too was evidently upset by the overt religiosity of the theme and Ingolf had to admit, "I feel a *little* uneasy about it myself," excusing himself by suggesting that medieval legendary is, after all, only another kind of folklore and "it seemed most appealing to me to turn to a Saint and try to use the story in general human terms rather than in a specifically religious connotation." I think that Ingolf's affection for strong female characters – Mammi, Mary, and Etta – must also have played its role in the choice of subject matter.

The writing of the notes enmeshed the composer in his own martyrdom, for no part of the process was easy. Rival musical instincts were at war during this period in his creative life. "Ingolf," he chided himself, "you are on the verge of becoming academic, the correct voice leading, the right counterpart, the balanced structure – watch out – the framework must widen to include a richer, more phantastic imagination." But on June 19, he warned himself, "The working must be as tight as possible, the special notes must always be searched for." After the conclusion of the project he added:

> Some kind of symbolism had to be found for the two worlds (or two personalities) that are in conflict: Barbara's 'inward' world, and the 'outward' world of the king. The contrast is achieved in several ways. The king and his heathens have diatonic but dissonant music, set for wind instruments, Barbara has chromatic but consonant music, set for strings. Opposition of keys also plays a part (e phrygian for Barbara, Bb for the heathens). This must not be interpreted in too literal a sense, or too mechanically. If there were not many shifts, evasions, insertions, subtleties, reminiscences, references, this would not be a living organism of music.

One constant element was an adaptation of a plain chant used on the feast day of St. Barbara, a cantus firmus which runs throughout the piece, forming the basis of a number of themes. In the second movement Ingolf actually used the notes of a B-flat major scale in a serial manner, though he still shied away from referring to this as a "row." "Am scared of combining the modal and chromatic," he wrote on July 5, but the deed was done.

He was already at work on the second section on June 19, "but am disgusted all day with what I find. Too tritely percussive, too Stravinskian, too asthmatic, only 'gesture' and no musical *shape*." But the next day he recorded happiness with his progress and by early July he was at work on the third section. On July 16, "the big terrifying plunge," he began work on the last part. Orchestration was completed in August and on the 26th a champagne celebration with Etta and the Kellers marked the end of what must be seen, for Ingolf, as a relatively rapid progress.

Although the ballet has never been choreographed, *The Tower of Saint Barbara* did receive its first performance in Louisville on January 29, 1955, with Robert Whitney on the podium. Whitney found the work to be "powerful and exciting," but also a "stark piece of music." Gerhard Herz, Ingolf's old friend from the University of Zurich, was present at the premiere – "The few who understand something about contemporary music were all very impressed...it is a work of great substance, composed with meticulous detail which will reveal itself only after repeated listening." The Louisville Orchestra presented the work several times that winter, including a performance in New York on February 19, conducted by Leon Barzin in a concert honoring recipients of the National Institute of Arts and Letters awards and one on March 5 which Ingolf attended while giving a guest lecture on Stravinsky in Louisville. "A very rare high point," he wrote, "the first chord shatters me and it is all on a very high emotional intensity plane. Take two bows, warm applause, wipe tears as I go off stage." The work was evidently considered by the Pulitzer Committee and for once a number of publishers expressed an interest in representing it. Ingolf eventually placed it with Shawnee Press, which still handles the parts on a rental basis.

The Louisville Symphony recorded the ballet in 1956 and I wore out our copy playing it repeatedly. When it was first played for Etta on April 12, 1956, Ingolf sensed that my mother wasn't responding with the appropriate enthusiasm, but I'm not at all certain that this is true. A newer recording of the work, which was revised in 1960, was part of an all-Dahl compact disc issued on the Argo/Decca label and featuring the New World Symphony conducted by Michael Tilson Thomas, recorded in January, 1994. That June, Tilson Thomas also played the work at Ojai. I wrote the program notes for this performance.

Ingolf's unhappiness over his inability to see Barbara danced was complemented by the lingering disaster of the *Symphony Concertante For Two Clarinets*. Throughout these years a premiere always seemed to be around the corner. In the fall of 1954 he worked on the latest revision, finishing it on December 11. Benny Goodman and Mitchell Lurie read through parts of the new version on October 14, 1954 – "Most of it sounds very fine! What may be the fate of it?" Ingolf asked. Benny promised to show the work to Eugene Ormandy and Leonard Bernstein and Ingolf also wrote to the latter in January – "I feel quite sure that you will find it to be your kind of music" – but the letter was answered by a *secretary* who wrote to say that the maestro was out of the country and that the Tanglewood program was already set. A similar attempt to attract Bernstein's attention in 1958 also derailed. Ingolf proposed that the work be performed at the Ojai festival, writing to both Benny and to Lawrence Morton, who was serving as executive director, but again there was failure. Ingolf remained on good terms with Benny, who had lost his copy of the original score, and he even edited the Mozart *Clarinet Concerto* when the King of Swing recorded a portion of it for *The Benny Goodman Story*, but gradually it became obvious that there was little chance that Benny would push the project through to completion, and Ingolf, inevitably, began to have doubts about the latest revision. On Christmas Day 1957 we find him looking at a copy in his Corning Street studio: "*What* to do with it? How to rescue it?"

Ingolf's journals also enable us to follow his reactions to other completed compositions during this period. On December 28, 1956 he sat down to play the *Sonata Seria*. "Am deeply moved," he noted, "I don't care for success – but here I did something which I myself like to play for pleasure." Playing a tape of the work on July 12, 1958 he added, "makes an even bigger impression – it gets better all the time – will I *ever* approach anything like it? The cello *Duo* was found wanting in certain respects when Ingolf and his colleague Gabor Rejto played it through in 1957, but a performance of the *Allegro and Arioso* by the New York Woodwind

Quintet at the Coleman Concert in Pasadena on January 19, 1958 elicited the opposite reaction – "They play my quintet magnificently. It's a big success and I am just electrified." For a time Ingolf had to content himself with past glories, for it is certainly true that after the completion of *The Tower of Saint Barbara* a brief fallow period ensued: "What can I do – what is still in store for me – am I really written out?" The sketches of barely begun projects – a series of serenades, plans for an opera for which no suitable text was ever discovered – these stared at him accusingly whenever he entered his studio.

Early in 1956 he was able to begin another major project – a *Quartet* for piano, violin, viola and cello. The work is first mentioned on December 18, 1955, only a few days before the formation of the American Chamber Players – "the first stirrings of a piano quartet – and terribly frightened at the same time. A new departure? A consolidation? How? The ocean of possibilities: Is there a contribution I can make? Go toward complexity? What agonies of searching are ahead of me?" Work began on January 1, 1956:

> Etta drives me to studio – there take a deep breath and begin...to start the new year with a new piece...Nothing but DANGER and OBSTACLE and HALT signs all over. Am I so completely dried up? Oh no, it *cannot, must* not be – but all the decisions to be made: how much freedom, how much prearranged material.

"Frightened to death of the Piano Quartet," he wrote on January 4, "anything I read, hear, about another composer gets me in a state." Sketches for the first movement were completed at the end of the month and the first bars of a second begun on January 31 – "such responsibilities: to find the thematic germs that will work, to find something that is distinguished (it really isn't yet, just some simple pretty chords and a piano arabesque, but that's all that enters my head now.)"

Work seems to have stopped at this point altogether but on May 18 Ingolf received news of a commission from the Fromm Foundation to be performed at the 1957 University of Illinois's Music Festival and he determined to bring the piano quartet to completion as a response to this commission. "Evasion evasion" was the order of the day for many months. Four bars were completed at Tanglewood on July 23 and a few more were added in August. Work on the first movement was re-launched in September and continued until October 28, Etta's fifty-first birthday. The American Chamber Players provided Ingolf with a run-though of the movement on the 31st but this proved to be a disillusioning experience – "it is over-written, confused, lacks charm and 'expression' ...the piano part contradicts the strings and doesn't add up harmonically to the sound of the whole...what to do with it now?" "The trouble is," he added later that day, "I have no *style* which will permit me to write safely and efficiently and well." On November 5 it was back to the drawing board, with some progress reported – "it goes, it flows, there is some courage and spirit in me, oh mysterious well-spring – would you were to nourish me more strongly." It was not until December 14 that Ingolf "finished" the first movement again. Progress then began on the second, slow movement. "Get something done," Ingolf wrote on December 23; on January 6, 1957, my nineteenth birthday, he described this slow movement as "one of the best things I have ever done – I always have a harder time with fast movements – when I can be lyrical I seem to be more on my own." By the end of the month Ingolf was at work on the last movement as well, finishing the piece on February 7: "Hurrah! Go out and buy martinis, get drunk with Etta and have a great time!"

The music was quickly copied and sent to Urbana, where Ingolf followed it on March 1. There a faculty ensemble was led by Soulima Stravinsky, to whose father Ingolf dedicated the work. A U.S.C. faculty group including Lillian Steuber and Gabor Rejto gave the Quartet its Los Angeles premiere on December 23, 1957. After hearing a rehearsal on the 23rd Ingolf wrote, "This is really one of my best, every note, harmony, sonority feels right. Very happy, at last." Etta attended a dress rehearsal also: "She likes it!!" Ingolf enthused, "It is a good piece (only the very end needs more work)." I also heard the composition at its Los Angeles premiere and remember being very impressed by it.

The Piano Quartet, Ingolf's first chamber music work in eight years, was a difficult piece of music written for an atypical ensemble and perhaps it is not surprising to understand why the *Quartet* never found a publisher. (It is, however, available through European American Music.) It is a major irony, however, that many of Ingolf's less ambitious compositions were deemed more economically attractive propositions by the music publishing industry.

One of the reasons for the long delay in bringing this composition to a conclusion was that Ingolf was once again experimenting with new musical methods. In the first movement he had placed the strings in *opposition* to the piano, in the second in *alternation* with the piano and only in the last movement in *combination* with the piano. The first movement was composed with the use of a five-note row, though Ingolf was careful to point out in the concert program that the notes of the series were a result of the base line of the opening passage of the piano and not a response to some rigid serial formula. The new departure in the slow movement was "basically non-thematic writing, in which each bar evolves out of the preceding one without any real *motivic* connection." The third movement is also based on a five-note carillon ostinato figure which, though not used in a strict serial manner, *is* subject to the kinds of transposition favored by the 12-tone composers. Describing this section as "playful and extrovert," the composer drew some contrast with the more expressively dissonant earlier movements: "The very idea of using carillon motives in the last movement was prompted by the necessity of finding sonorities which would seem natural and convincing in a medium that is as unnatural as the combination of three strings with a modern concert grand."

Ingolf completed three other works in this period, though none of them required the prodigious efforts needed to bring the *Piano Quartet* to an end. When a recorder player, Lili Lampl, asked him to write a work she might play with harpsichordist John Hamilton at a recital in the spring of 1956, Ingolf decided to write a series of variations based on "Les Graces Naturelles," a theme from Francois Couperin's eleventh *Ordre* for harpsichord of 1717. This was a theme he had heard another backpacker playing on *his* recorder the previous summer. He began work in February of 1956, complaining that he had to write "expressive music for non-expressive instruments." The work was completed in June and he set to work on an alternative version for flute and piano. This was first performed at Tanglewood on August 9 by Doriot Anthony Dwyer, a U.S.C. graduate who was taking up a career as a flautist in the Boston Symphony Orchestra. Andrew Imbrie, who heard the music in its new version the following year, wrote to Ingolf that, "The work was full of that unerring elegance and charm that I have come to expect from your pen." Lukas Foss offered an idea, which Ingolf accepted, and a new first variation was added in order to provide a better transition between the Eighteenth Century theme and the Twentieth Century variations which followed. This revision was completed in the early fall of 1956. *Variations on an Air by Couperin* was published in 1973 by Joseph Boonin Inc., and is distributed today by European American Music.

On April 17, 1956, Ingolf was invited by Isadore Freed to contribute to a new series of contemporary educational piano pieces which he was putting together for Theodore Presser. The work was to be playable by young pianists but Ingolf's contribution was too lengthy for the usual format and therefore the movements of *Sonatina Alla Marcia* for solo piano were published separately by Presser as First, Second, and Third Marches ("Alla Marcia Moderato," "Alla Marcia Funebre," "Alla Marcia Allegro"). Most of the work on the five-minute piece was completed in Tanglewood in July of 1956, though final corrections were made on August 23rd on a picnic table at Scott Lake, Oregon during a summer mountain expedition. After Presser's 1957 publication of the music, "Alla Marcia Moderato" was selected as one of the year's best teaching pieces by the *Piano Quarterly Newsletter*.

In the summer of 1957 Joseph Prostakoff requested a short piano piece from Ingolf for a collection of contemporary piano works he was editing for the publishers Lawson-Gould. Dedicated to Lillian Steuber, who premiered it on December 13, 1959, *Fanfares* was eventually published in 1963 in a collection entitled *New Music For The Piano* and recorded in an RCA album of the same title by Robert Helps. Ingolf had begun work on the piece on December 30, 1957. "Slow miserable pace," he complained, "But that's my speed, dammit." Nevertheless the piece was completed on January 27, after only four weeks on the work table.

Given his great commitment to composition and the slow pace of his creative toils one might imagine that Ingolf would have given himself *more* time to concentrate on this activity. Nevertheless these same years see him taking on all sorts of *additional* non-compositional professional responsibilities. Some did have considerable significance but many merely wasted his energies on trivial tasks that brought him the most paltry of rewards. These distractions can be seen, today, as defenses against the demands of more urgent problems, creative ones such as those outlined in this chapter and personal ones which still have to be dealt with at a later time in this biography.

50. A MARTYR'S CROWN

I was surprised to discover, in examining the detailed diaries of my stepfather, that Ingolf, after an intense period as composer only, resumed a very active role as performer, conductor, lecturer, Tanglewood department head, symposium participant, contest judge and Stravinsky worshipper in the years following his first sabbatical. All such activity, much of which he undertook in *addition* to his contractual duties at the university, has to be viewed as an escape from the demands of the creative process.

He not only appeared at many Los Angeles venues but traveled to play or conduct out of town on many occasions as well. In 1954 and 1955 he performed at the Ojai Festival, joining Eudice Shapiro in May of 1954 as one of the soloists in the Berg *Chamber Concerto* conducted by Robert Craft. At the same festival he accompanied Nan Merriman in Hindemith's *Das Marienleben* and played four-hand music with Shibley Boyes. Ingolf performed in Eugene, Oregon in January of 1954 and in Tempe, Arizona in March of 1955.

On April 17, 1955 he played his own *Divertimento* with Milton Thomas at the County Museum, a work they had earlier performed at a Monday Evening Concert on January 10. Albert Goldberg reviewing the latter event in the *L.A. Times* wrote, "Mr. Dahl played the piano part in sparkling style, quite as if he were not the composer." This statement is surprisingly in tune with Ingolf's rediscovery of the 1948 work at a rehearsal on December 12, 1954: "It is still a fresh, airy, lovely piece!" In 1955 he participated in nine concerts during the first half of the year alone!

The Monday Evening Concerts, as the Roof events were soon to be called, were still of great significance in Ingolf's musical life. He was frequently a member of the board of the sponsoring agency, the Southern California Chamber Music Society, and a figure who could be counted on in any musical emergency. On Monday, November 29, 1954, for instance, Lawrence Morton called him at 2:30 in the afternoon to ask if he could substitute for Robert Craft as one of the conductors of that night's concert.

With one rehearsal, Ingolf conducted three songs of Stravinsky and Ravel's Mallarmé songs.

If one concert event dominated Ingolf's musical life in the mid-Fifties it must have been the presentation, on January 11, 1954, of an all-Dahl program in Bovard Auditorium sponsored by the School of Music and the Evenings on the Roof and featuring *The Music For Brass Instruments*, the *Sonata Seria*, the *Concerto A Tre*, and the newly revised *Concerto for Saxophone and Wind Orchestra*. Peter Yates had been working on the project for almost a year and it had been the source of troubled correspondence between Schruns and Tanglewood on one side and Los Angeles on the other. Ingolf was returning to the Roof stage after several seasons but his nose was out of joint, if one can read between the lines, because in the interim his role had been filled with considerable flair by Robert Craft. When Peter decided it was time for local audiences to hear the *Saxophone Concerto* for the first time he took the initiative in seeking out Raymond Kendall and winning the School of Music's agreement to provide hall and orchestra members. Ingolf then began a long exercise in temporizing, changing the program here and there and threatening to pull out of the whole project at several stages. Peter wrote a letter to Etta complaining of the intransigence of this "legendary musico-maniac" – "We have observed him reluctant; we have watched him moving slowly into action, always looking backwards; and then the rush of fury vanishes into the smoke of the enemy ceasing to exist. We do not believe in the reluctant Dahl; we consider him a mannerism." When it was Lawrence Morton's turn to do battle as the new head of the concert series Ingolf's earlier whining about wanting "a few crumbs from Craft's table" was held up as one reason for pushing ahead with the project.

Much of Ingolf's reluctance can be explained by the fact that the *Saxophone Concerto* was still to be rewritten. He worked on it throughout the fall of 1953. "My brain is dull," he wrote on October 2, "I find every excuse not to get to grips with it." "I must loosen up the 2nd movement," he added on October 19, "find the freedom, the interplay." On October 31 he complained, "Decide that page 47 which cost me so many hours and days will have to be done over!" A feeling of panic descended in mid-November: "I feel clutched around the throat – frantic – I will not be able to make it." "At this rate," he wrote on November 22, "it will not get finished, at a faster rate it will not be good. This paralyzes me." Of course the work was completed on the eve of the concert. "Goes fairly well," was his laconic comment on the night of the performance itself.

By this time he was at the exhaustion point anyway, having taken on the assignment of conducting the Brass Piece and the Concerto as well as the additional responsibility of performing the *Sonata Seria*, which John Crown had informed him he would not be able to play only three weeks before the concert. To add to all this, Ingolf was also deep into rehearsal of a number of works that he and other Los Angeles musicians would perform at the University of Oregon only six days after the all-Dahl event.

After all of these heroic efforts Albert Goldberg gave the Bovard concert a somewhat sour review, "Mr. Dahl's compositions all have an expert and professional format, though they are not uniformly based on ideas that immediately rivet the attention. At their best they are stylish in a moderately conservative contemporary manner." Presumably referring to the *Sonata Seria*, Goldberg continued, "Sometimes he overestimates the listener's power of concentration in the direction of length and overdevelopment and there were instances when the music lacked what might be called stage sense; it remained so confidential that it failed to project the author's meaning across the footlights." Though the reviewer noted that the "audience was large and extremely applausive throughout," he failed to make *any* mention of the *Saxophone Concerto* or its soloist, William Ulyate.

National musical publications mostly ignored the event as well. And even Peter Yates, who had originated the project, reviewed it waspishly in *Arts and Architecture*. He praised the *Saxophone Concerto* but panned the *Sonata Seria* as MacDowell brought up to date. What had been a success in Bovard Auditorium shrank to insignificance in the retelling and Ingolf had a right to feel a sense of disappointment. He heard a recording of the concert a few weeks later. "It is very good," he wrote, "Sax. Co. is just thrilling. This gives me enormous boost," but soon thereafter the question of cuts arose again and another revision had to be undertaken.

In December 1955 Ingolf and three other performers decided to form an ensemble of their own. The previously mentioned American Chamber Players (or Chamber Pots as Etta liked to call them) included Ingolf at the piano, William Van Den Berg on cello, and the husband and wife team of

Milton Thomas, viola, and Dorothy Wade, violin. Much excitement was generated at the inception of the enterprise. "We want to give an unusual type of program," Ingolf wrote, "in which the four of us would combine different types of ensemble (from Piano Quartet to String Duo) in one program." The Players set out to find a "new, different, exciting" repertoire – which meant, as far as Ingolf was concerned, avoiding "the awful 19th century." He and Willy played the Dahl *Notturno* on a number of programs and other 20th Century works were featured, along with quite a few pre-Romantic compositions. Ingolf also began a series of "redistributions" of Haydn piano trios for members of the group to play. His goal, so characteristic of a musician of his elevated standards, was for the group to perform "outstandingly *superb* concerts not just good ones."

The ensemble survived only a few years. They appeared at Ojai in 1956, at a Monday Evening Concert, at the Museum, at local colleges, at the Hollywood Los Feliz Jewish Community Center and even at the Purple Onion nightclub. But Willy, who played in the L.A. Philharmonic, had many schedule conflicts, there were displays of temperament, and Ingolf was certain the others weren't rehearsing enough. "We aren't really great," he added after a concert at Marymount in 1957, "probably will never be." The end of the American Chamber players was in sight. How Ingolf could have imagined a happier outcome, given his own conflicted schedule, is a mystery.

Ingolf's relationship with the U.S.C. Orchestra continued to follow the earlier pattern of triumph and fiasco. "It goes well and is much fun," he wrote after a run-through of a Handel concerto grosso with the always problematic string section on September 25, 1953. But attendance problems plagued many a rehearsal; opera productions under Walter Ducloux's baton and band performances lead by William Schaefer drained away portions of the orchestra. "Very upset," Ingolf wrote on the eve of the student concerto program in January, 1955, "Because of the absence of wind players who are in St. Louis." Naturally there were petty rivalries and inevitable frictions but Ingolf managed to survive such collisions with faculty colleagues without losing their friendship or respect.

Walter Ducloux dates his first meeting with Ingolf to September 1953. Many years later he described their relationship:

> I count him among my most cherished colleagues and among the
> men who have most influenced me during my later adult years...We
> complemented each other in many ways, to the benefit of our many
> students: Ingolf was the better musician, with fabulous ears, delicate
> sensibilities, attuned to the intricacies of 20th century experiments. I
> was more of the hard-bitten professional conductor, hell-for-leather,
> breaking plenty of eggs to make omelettes...with Ingolf one always
> had a feeling that breaking eggs was, to him, a kind of cruelty.

I attended almost all of Ingolf's great orchestral days in Bovard
Auditorium. It was always a thrill to see old favorites like Henry Lewis
(who, before taking up a conducting career and marrying Marilyn Horne,
played double bass) or the red-headed percussionist Forrest Clark as
they took up their places in the student orchestra. Ingolf's programming
at U.S.C. continued to move from the extremes of Baroque Christmas
concerts by the Collegium Musicum to first performances of esoteric
student compositions. Ingolf liked to provide local *premieres* of work
from the 18th century but inevitably his principal energies were engaged
in presentation of 20th Century work, particularly at the May festival
of contemporary music, where he served as director. On May 27, 1955,
to provide a sample program, Ingolf conducted the U.S.C. orchestra in
Rounds by David Diamond, *Tzigane* by Ravel, *Nobilissima Visione* by
Hindemith and *Men and Mountains* by Carl Ruggles. "You are amazing
in your activities and your concerts," Harold Shapero wrote a few months
later, finding no parallel to them in Boston, let alone New York. "We really
have nothing comparable here," Joseph Bloch wrote from New York, "even
at Julliard." "Your concert programs are very exciting," Paul Fromm wrote
from Chicago in 1958, "and more important than anything that we can
hear at Orchestra Hall during the entire season. Music is really alive on
your campus. And the credit for most of it must go to you."

Reticence was not to be observed, we have noted, when Ingolf was
evaluating his own performance as a conductor. His frustrations were
particularly evident when he was working on U.S.C.'s Diamond Jubilee
Concert in the fall of 1955. "Very depressed about my conducting," he
noted on September 25, and on January 3 he added, "it should be getting
freer, looser, more varied, and it is getting more pedantic and cut and dry."
Rehearsing for the Los Angeles premiere of Blomdahl's *Chamber Concerto*

in February, 1957 he wrote, "am dissatisfied with my lack of authoritative *push* and arrogance." But happiness was reported at the concerto program on October 6, 1957, the sensation of the evening being a performance of the Weber *Bassoon Concerto* by Vernon Read.

In November 1957 Ingolf and the U.S.C. Orchestra combined with the Monday Evening Concerts to present a concert honoring Stravinsky's seventy-fifth birthday; Ingolf lead the group in *Dumbarton Oaks* and the west coast premiere of *Persephone*, but absences, latecomers, and other technical problems plagued the rehearsals. At the warm up on November 25, he protested, "all are late, some don't show up – HELL." Listening to a tape of the concert some weeks later all of Ingolf's insecurities boiled over in a devastating self-criticism, "Listen to part of Persephone, am just terribly depressed. Everything seems wrong." After raking himself over the coals for errors in tempi, phrasing, inflection, attack, and balance, he asked: "And for that I work myself to a frazzle – for that I court ulcers, is it worth it? At least, if out of all this there would be some real outer growth (like Bob Craft's –). What have I to show for this fall's exertion? 2 'kids' concerts –. There is something so wrong someplace. Where?"

Most of his podium activity in these years was confined to the student orchestra, where just getting through the basics must have foreclosed all real opportunity for the kind of stylistic growth he yearned for. He did preside over a number of professional ensembles during the same period but these experiences were also full of frustration. Ingolf conducted a performance on November 13, 1953 of Bartok's *Two Piano Concerto* at an I.S.C.M. concert, an experience that lead him to the quickly forgotten declaration, "*never* conduct pianists!" Proof that he had forgotten this vow came when he conducted Lili Kraus in three Mozart concerti at the Ojai festival in May of 1957. Rehearsals were problematic. "Kraus is difficult," he wrote on May 17, "I can't get the sound I want, am unhappy, am not aggressive enough, get stepped over by her." The *Times* reviewer was generous in his assessment of the conductor's efforts, "Ingolf Dahl's straight-forward, neat and unadorned direction of the orchestral accompaniments were models of a clear stylistic concept." "By mastering all of my resources of tact, diplomacy and gentle stubbornness I got things pretty smooth," Ingolf later reported, and Kraus "was so happy at the end that now she wants me to conduct her all over and even play (and conduct) the Mozart 2-piano

Concerto with her." On December 29, 1957 he conducted a professional ensemble in a performance of Schoenberg's *Serenade*, Opus 24, a project beset by defections, schedule conflicts, and rehearsals during which some players were missing altogether. "This," Ingolf concluded, "is my martyr's crown."

Five days after the all-Dahl concert of January 11, 1954, he traveled with other local musicians to Eugene, Oregon, an ordeal of a weather-stricken journey that Ingolf endured with the help of a book of Dahl stories, that is the fiction of Roald Dahl, no relation. At the University of Oregon he lectured on "Trends in Contemporary European Music" and presided over a concert featuring the Los Angeles Woodwinds, during which he and Edgar Lustgarten played the Dahl *Cello Duo*. Ingolf also provided a lecture-performance on the *Sonata Seria*.

On November 14, 1956 the Composers Council of the U.C.L.A. Music Department presented Ingolf in an illustrated lecture entitled "Quality Judgments in Contemporary Music," a talk which he would offer in revised versions on a number of occasions. I remember the tremendous tension that gripped our house in the weeks leading up to this presentation in Schoenberg Hall, where I was now taking *my* music appreciation class. "The day," Ingolf wrote, "am beside myself with apprehension. Work very hard all day on lecture. Not enough time. Give a dress rehearsal to Etta in undershirt – it goes very badly." But that night he enjoyed a great triumph, a standing-room only crowd, "I speak well and am relaxed, have contact, and it is a real success." After the intermission a concert of modern music was presented. Ingolf and Lukas Foss performed Hindemith's *Sonata For Piano Four Hands* and Copland's *Danzon Cubano* for two pianos. "Also the playing is fine," Ingolf concluded. Robert U. Nelson, the chairman of U.C.L.A.'s Music Department thanked Ingolf for provocative, well-organized and effectively presented remarks: "The large and distinguished audience gave every evidence of enjoying what you had to say."

On March 12, 1957 Ingolf flew to Spokane, Washington for a Contemporary Music Workshop sponsored the local music teacher's association led by Sister Harriet Mary, of the Holy Names Academy, a nun whom Ingolf grew to admire tremendously. While in Spokane Ingolf lectured on "Intelligent Performance Through Understanding The Creative Process," "Musical Analysis From The Composer's Point of View," and

"Interpretation, Repertoire and the Teaching of Twentieth Century Music."
"Work on lecture material in plane (get alternatively panicky and cocky),"
he wrote, "*what* can I possibly give to the 'simple people' piano teachers?"
"Feel that I make a good impression," he recorded after the analysis class
on March 13, but the next day, "rather fall on my face." Sister Harriet Mary
called Ingolf's visit "the most positive and constructive master session we
have had so far...It has been a great pleasure working with you, a musician
of such great artistry and integrity."

Another time-consuming assignment was accepted in the fall of 1957,
when Ingolf, saying he wanted to earn an extra $175 for a skiing holiday,
agreed to give a lecture demonstration on the "Music of Expressionism"
at Pomona College. The Claremont Colleges were exhibiting a collection
of paintings by the masters of German Expressionism and Ingolf's talk,
which I attended after viewing a wonderful exhibit, sought to draw
parallels between this art and musical equivalents. "It goes very well,"
Ingolf recorded on November 3, "both talk and music, but afterwards I'm
just shot." Works by Berg, Webern, and Schoenberg were performed on
this occasion, with Ingolf once again conducting an ensemble in excerpts
from *Pierrot Lunaire*.

Ingolf was also in demand as a guest lecturer in other divisions of
his own university. In January, 1959 he introduced a lecture on "Art and
Artists Around Stravinsky" in an art class, and in February, 1960 he spoke
to medical students at the General Hospital on "Conflicting Trends in
Twentieth Century Music." In May he spoke on "Parallels between Musical
Form and Pictorial Expressionism" to an architecture class. On March 5,
1959, with one day's advance notice, he agreed to fill in for Lukas Foss in
a lecture on 20th Century Music at San Bernardino Valley College. "Play
illustrations," he noted," – "sophistication for farm boys...the talk is good,
but does music get home?"

As we have seen, Ingolf believed that his national reputation needed
to be enhanced through contact with the East Coast musical scene.
Appropriately, after a year off, he returned to his old post at Tanglewood
on July 1, 1955. A few days later he told his Study Group students:

> Our group exists for the sake of the music we are bringing to life, and
> the pleasure that can be had from this activity... Being surrounded
> by so many brightly polished professional talents on this campus

the feeling of stifling and oppressive competition may steal into the hearts of one or the other of you. Let us dispel that notion right now. Our repertoire, our attitudes are different.

Ingolf was assisted at Tanglewood by Karl Kohn and Flossie Dunn, who had also helped Lukas Foss the year before. In spite of his brave speech, Ingolf records depression after the "absolutely awful" TSG auditions on July 4, though by the 11th he was able to report quite smooth readings of Lasso and Buxtehude. With many rough spots a "so-so" concert was presented by the Group on July 23.

Continuing his role as public lecturer, Ingolf also participated in the Composers' Forums, spoke at the Lenox Library, and gave other talks, including one on Beethoven's *Eroica* on July 27. Two days earlier he had participated in a Lenox Forum colloquium with Roger Sessions and Leonard Bernstein, debating the topic, "What Do The Next Fifty Years Promise For American Music?" Ingolf began by attacking over-generalization: "Europe *is* this or that; the American scene *is* this or that...It seems hard to believe that so many loose, disembodied concepts should be floating around under this ceiling in an age in which both semanticism and philosophy have been trying to teach us about the limits of statement."

When it was his turn to offer predictions Ingolf warned against the decline of the performing musician and bewailed a dehumanized future in which computer-synthesized versions of Brahms 5th or Tchaikovsky's 9th or Grieg's Second Piano Concerto might dominate the musical scene. This acceptance of synthetic tone production, he concluded cheekily, might be complemented by consequent genetic adaptation – babies brought into the world equipped with strong and healthy calluses on their eardrums. On July 18 Ingolf also spoke on Stravinsky, a lecture attended by Sessions and 1955's other composer-in-residence, Boris Blacher. "It goes extremely well," the speaker noted, "Everybody most complimentary."

Again there was much time spent with other composers at Tanglewood, particularly with Sessions (whose *Black Maskers* Ingolf pronounced "a little naive, but very skillful") and Blacher, whose *Divertimento* he described as a "nice lightweight piece." On July 28 Ingolf played the *Sonata Seria* for Sessions (He likes it!"). There was also time to renew the old acquaintanceship with Elliott Carter and to form a new one with Gunther

Schuller. Ingolf also met the famous Carl Ruggles, then almost eighty, on July 31. A letter that Ruggles wrote the next day contains the cryptic message, "Dear Ingolf Dahl, You were right. The first version of the 2nd measure is the best. Hope you can arrange to come up to dinner soon. It was a great pleasure meeting you." Many years later, when I showed this letter to Michael Tilson Thomas, he understood instantly its import. "This is just what I wanted to know," he said, the document having provided him with the clue he needed for the interpretation he would give from the conductor's podium of the opening passage of Ruggles' *Men And Mountains*.

Ingolf was less successful in his pursuit of the elusive Leonard Bernstein – "all these days: the frustration of not being able to get Lennie to listen to my Symphony Concertante." Nothing better illustrated Ingolf's role as the perpetual outsider in this cauldron of high-powered music making than his allusion to Bernstein on August 6 – "Walk around him and his class like a hungry dog with long eyes and tongue hanging out."

On July 11 Ingolf reported elation at the news that Ralph Berkowitz had agreed to his conducting the Department I orchestra in *The Tower of Saint Barbara*. As usual there was not enough rehearsal time and on the evening of the concert, August 13, Ingolf was upset to hear from Sessions that Thomas Mann had died. "A wave of emotion" came over Ingolf at the news – "what has died with him, my whole youth, a world of experience, of beauty, so immeasurably much." Etta, who remained in Los Angeles, sent Ingolf a long list of people to invite to the Barbara performance, but the event proved to be a disaster. The orchestra played with devotion and everyone seemed to like what they heard but the fringes of a hurricane lashed across the music shed during the concert and many, who could not hear the music at all, left before *Barbara* was performed. No "important" people showed up and Leonard Bernstein was on his way to Hollywood to conduct a work by Lukas Foss!

The following year, on June 13, 1956, Ingolf left Los Angeles for New York (a yowling infant interrupting his reading of *Catcher In The Rye*) and the next day he took the train to Providence, Rhode Island, where he served as one of twelve composer participants in a Rockefeller-sponsored I.S.C.M -League of Composers symposium in which composers presented their points of view to managers, conductors, and trustees of American symphony orchestras. "Meet with *all* the composers," Ingolf wrote after his arrival, "Aaron comes, *so* good to see him, he looks wonderful." Breakfast with Norman dello Joio and lunch with George Rochberg came the next day and Ingolf reports successful talks by Copland, Foss, and William Schumann. In an afternoon session, "I speak, glibly, but say nothing, dammit, very dissatisfied." On the 16th he took a train to New Canaan, Connecticut, sharing a compartment with David Van Vactor and other conference delegates on their way back to New York – "the professional world," Ingolf wrote, "seems very bright, close, open." In New Canaan Ingolf spent two nights visiting with Mel Powell and his family amid "very fine talks and stimulating conversation."

In New York he worked during the day on the *Piano Quartet*, had meetings with publishers, and visited old Hamburg and Cologne friends Franz Allers, Kurt Stone, and Trude Rittman. He spoke to Barbara Kruger Sachse – "the warm sound of her voice throws me into an ocean of affection – it is like in the old days. All of a sudden I am the gymnasiast, overcome by waves of youthful emotion and love. It's a great life." On the 29th he took the train to Tanglewood, where, with Etta also present, he spent his fourth summer at the Berkshire Music Center.

"I am so sick and tired of amateurs," he wrote on July 3, "I can't do this much longer." On July 9 he gave an early version of his lecture on "Quality" and conducted a Ben Weber piece at a Fromm concert. On the 16th he again lectured on Stravinsky and there were two public concerts by the TSG. "Goes well, considering," he wrote of the second of these on August 9, by which he meant goes well considering the fact that much of the ensemble failed to show up for a last run-through "because of Munch's improvised rehearsals."

Ingolf was at work on the *Sonatina Alla Marcia* this summer and there seemed to be less time for Tanglewood socializing, but Aaron Copland was only one of the other composers with whom Ingolf spent some time during the 1956 summer. Lukas Foss was there, as were Irving Fine and the Italian Goffredo Petrassi (for whom Ingolf played the *Concerto A Tre* – "he is so complimentary"). Ingolf also had brief meetings with Benny Goodman and Elliott Carter.

It has to be noted that Ingolf's circle of composing friends was growing ever wider in this period. In addition to Lukas and Ingolf's own USC colleagues in Los Angeles there were many other composing friends in Southern California at this time including Aurelio de la Vega, a Cuban composer whom he had met in 1954, Karl Kohn, who taught at Pomona, and U.C.L.A.'s Leo Smit, whom he met at the Fosses in 1957. Some old friends moved through Los Angeles during this period as well, including Gail Kubik in 1956, and Alexei Haieff in 1958, and, also in Los Angeles, Ingolf met Vincent Persichetti in 1957 and the Swedish composer Karl-Birger Blomdahl in 1958. Ingolf reports himself extremely impressed by Pierre Boulez, whom he first met at the Stravinsky's on January 15, 1954.

When I picked up my parents at the Los Angeles International Airport on August 12, 1956 I was welcoming Ingolf back from his last Tanglewood assignment, The "problem child," as he referred to Department Five – had declined in enrollment and his passion for the project had waned. He asked for a leave of absence for 1957, citing the need for composing time, but when the Tanglewood administrators asked for a three year commitment thereafter, Ingolf reluctantly resigned, recommending Karl Kohn as his successor, and passing on to his Massachusetts employers Dean Kendall's remark that U.S.C. faculty members were expected to teach at campus summer sessions with "reasonable frequency." "I know precisely how you feel," Copland wrote when the leave application had first arrived, "and won't urge you to go against the dictates of your artistic conscience." After the letter of resignation had arrived, Copland added, "I console myself with the thought that if Tanglewood can't have you at least we can hope for more compositions from you."

But this hope, we have seen, was continually sabotaged by Ingolf's inability to say no to any demand on his professional time and we can augment this account of his professional activities in the mid-Fifties with perhaps the best illustration of his penchant for time-wasting trivialities, his willingness to serve as composition judge. In early 1954 he agreed to be one of three judges in a contest sponsored by the National Association of College Wind and Percussion Instructors. Alvin Etler and Burrill Phillips were his colleagues in this competition, eventually won by Halsey Stevens. For a twenty-five dollar fee Ingolf served as a judge in a choral work contest sponsored by Kansas Wesleyan University in the spring of 1955. One hundred and seventy works were submitted under such pseudonyms as This I. Believe, Boghead, Ock O. Pella, and Pseudo-Sapling. Ingolf, who had been described by the promoters of this contest as a man with "an almost uncanny ability to get to the heart of a new work," picked "Raul Torres," who turned out to be his own conducting student (and Halsey's composition pupil), Ramiro Cortes. From the journal entry of April 21, 1955 it would seem that he did this in all innocence, though the other contestants might not have been so amused by this accident. Undaunted, he joined Franz Waxman and Lukas Foss in 1957 as judges in a composer's contest sponsored by the Westside Jewish Community Center in which "A Chanukah Overture" and a "Maccabean Overture" were the winners. Such activities cannot be what Copland had in mind when he encouraged Ingolf to follow the dictates of his artistic conscience. He twice served as a judge in 1960, once in Fresno, and once for a composition contest held in conjunction with the Utah State Fair.

Ingolf came very close to accepting the seduction of the non-creative in one other endeavor, and this assignment involved Igor Stravinsky. Our household was constantly preoccupied with the health and welfare of the "Old Man," and Ingolf sought the admiration and approval of Stravinsky in the way in which a boy might seek the encouragement of his dad. At the same time Ingolf recognized his dependency on the master, emotionally if not stylistically, and occasionally agonized about this too. On November 19, 1953, Ingolf and Etta attended a Stravinsky concert given by the L.A. Philharmonic – "seeing him come brings tears (how many more times?)... that giant, my father, to whom I owe too much, the magician...Oh if I could break the egg – but here I am dissolved in emotions and admiration." "What Stravinsky gives is *confidence* in the creative possibility," he added on November 18, 1955. "He talks to me as colleague to colleague," he noted after a concert on February 24, 1957: "What a man! He was in fine fettle and full of ideas, vitality, quips, etc... Afterwards I felt as if I had been re-charged by the most powerful 'life-source' imaginable. He has that vitalizing effect – it seems to come out of his pores, and I feel tremendously lucky that I know him so well."

Naturally, Ingolf took advantage of every opportunity to see Stravinsky, often going to rehearsal or recording sessions where the maestro might be present. Such a meeting took place on September 13, 1954, when *In Memorium Dylan Thomas* was recorded. "I.S. is tired," Ingolf notes, "apathetic. Craft rules over him." There were also several concerts in which Ingolf collaborated in presenting Stravinsky music. One of these was a Monday Evening Concert on October 19, 1953, when Ingolf was one of the soloists in the "jazz" music of Stravinsky. In 1957 Ingolf also recorded a talk for a CBC series on 20th Century masterpieces, choosing the *Symphony in C* as his topic. We have also seen that the *Piano Quartet* was dedicated to Stravinsky and Ingolf delivered one of the first copies of the work to the maestro's porch on June 17, 1957. At a Boulez recording on February 7, 1958 Ingolf brought up the idea of recording *his* piece – "Igor is there, he gives me cold shoulder when I mention Piano Quartet recording – so that's that."

There were also many social occasions at which Ingolf and Stravinsky met, usually at the home of the latter. "After the wonderful New Year's Eve at Stravinksy's," Ingolf reported on January 1, 1955, "(with champagne and Petroushka stories and very much fun) sleep late." On December 16, 1957 his journal states, "7 Dinner with Bob Craft – i.e., with the Stravinsky's at Cock & Bull. Etta joins us there. We laugh a lot and have fun." After a reception following a Monday Evening Concert on October 3, 1955 (during which Stravinsky was quoted as saying, "Only silence makes music possible," Ingolf drove Aldous Huxley home.

Two projects related to Stravinsky were of particular importance to Ingolf during this period. The first of these was a new course in The Music of Stravinsky, perhaps the first in academia, which Ingolf inaugurated at U.S.C. in the Spring term, 1955. Beginning in February he made many visits to Stravinksy's house in search of materials for the course, which he offered frequently thereafter. The research he completed in connection with his teaching and his long friendship with the composer made my stepfather the logical choice for a major assignment – and here we approach the seduction of non-creative tasks mentioned earlier – one proposed to him by Oxford University Press in 1958: the completion of a full-scale biography of the famous musician. Ingolf was flattered and excited by this offer and spoke to Stravinsky about it on May 10 – "he is very nice and wants me to do it (question: how much is he *really* going to cooperate, how much to withhold?)" Ingolf wrote a letter of acceptance on May 14, though he failed to mail it for several days. When he received the actual contract the apprehension really began to grow. On June 5 he had lunch with Gail Kubik at the Huntington Hartford Foundation – "he completely corroborated my own feelings about the book: do you want to be a composer and [be] considered a composer?" With trepidation, Ingolf approached Stravinsky on the 16th – "He is in top form, tells about everything and just sparkles." Nevertheless, Ingolf had decided to decline the project:

> Backing out at this point is going to be a little embarrassing and painful, but it can't be helped. The point is that if I want to be a composer I must be one and stop fooling around with side-tracking activities, no matter how attractive, flattering, remunerative, ego-bolstering, 'advantageous' they may be. So I have made up my mind at last. Rather be an obscure composer than a famous Stravinsky biographer, if that is to be my fate.

By saying goodbye to this project Ingolf also escaped the problem of addressing the "attraction and opposition of the father image," which, he admitted, had always been a part of his relationship with Stravinsky.

On June 18 he wrote to the publisher and turned down the assignment. "I will have to stick to my business which is music, not words." Stravinsky responded, almost as Copland had done when Ingolf had declined the invitation to continue at Tanglewood, sending his younger friend a note in large letters, "MUSIK KOMMT ZUERST" – Music Comes First. Ingolf then tried to help the Oxford University Press find another author, "Robert Craft would in some ways be ideally situated for the book. The one question I have about Craft concerns his ability (and desire) to pursue truly objective approaches to the subject (the recent widely publicized "Questions and Answers" by Stravinsky-Craft tell us almost more about the questioner than the answerer."

In the end Ingolf recommended Lawrence Morton – "His literary style is of the first order, and his superior intelligence equips him to write about music both with searching analytical thoroughness and readability (as well as urbanity and wit)." Lawrence accepted this assignment – which turned out to be a labor of Hercules – conducting endless research all over the world, and never producing a final text. Ingolf had been right to shy away from the task.

Nevertheless the project and his eventual escape from it preoccupied my stepfather during June and July of 1958, when he returned to the Hartford Foundation for a second stint, finding it "just as heavenly as I remembered it from 4 years ago. I have the same cottage as before – isolated, surrounded by green wilderness and animal life." The latter included pet spiders and raccoons, whom Ingolf fed regularly. Now that the decision had been made to concentrate on composing, progress was very slow indeed. Another piano sonata, and a trio for cello, violin and piano were considered but he spent a great deal of time revising the *Piano Quartet*. In fact 1958 was a watershed year for our family in many other ways, and Ingolf had plenty of things on his mind as he wrestled with the creative mission he had chosen to make his own.

51. UNBREAKABLE GLASS

We have to note that there was one additional detour from Ingolf's newly resolved emphasis on creative work, and it was offered to him by his own pupil, Paul Glass. Now would be the time to say something about Paul and his impact on our lives. He would have been in his very early twenties when he and I first met in 1956, when he was studying composition with my stepfather. Paul was an extremely talented young musician whose ebullient spirits and good looks won him a wide circle of friends. I always felt that he could have had a career as an actor, for he certainly had the manner, the appearance, and the connections. His mother was an actress and his father, Gaston Glass, was a production manager at Fox. But Paul loved music and, to the puzzlement of his family, chose to fashion for himself a career as a composer.

He fascinated my parents with his winning ways and his show biz gossip and he was loyally attached to both of them. He wrote to them frequently over the next few years, when he had moved on to study composition as a graduate student in Italy and Poland, occasionally exasperating them with his perpetual bullshit, his repetitive inconsequential chatter, and his endless stillborn projects. I got fewer letters but many more phone calls, often stretching over an hour in length, at the end of which I would have to agree to come over to his house in nearby Beverlywood immediately, a journey that always held the prospect that some aspiring starlet might be fluttering through or that an all-night talk-fest might not send me back home in Rufus until dawn. Ingolf spent a good deal of time with Paul at Tanglewood in 1955, often referring to him in the journals as "Unbreakable."

I was absolutely mesmerized by Paul and his effortless conquests of the opposite sex, and the time I spent with him – at parties, on hikes, and at his home – always played a memorable part in the journal which *I* kept from January 1, 1956 to June, 1957. Paul encouraged me in my own literary efforts and accompanied me to the poetry readings which Peter Yates and Sol Babitz began to sponsor in their homes in December, 1956. Paul, of course, used these poetry readings, which even returned to the famous roof on Micheltorena, to romance Sol's daughter Eve.

One curious aspect of our friendship was that Paul and I bore a considerable physical resemblance at this time, and strangers often took us for brothers. I was thus able to use Paul's ID to get an illegal drink at Peacock Lane the night a post-poetry crowd went to hear Dizzy Gillespie, and on other occasions I accompanied Paul and his friends to bars and jazz joints. Such was my infatuation with the brash charmer that I even arranged to spend a summer in his flat in Rome, where he had gone off to study with Goffredo Petrassi, but reality soon intruded and I had to turn in my ticket. Paul did accompany us on many local hikes and he was a member of a party that included Ingolf and Larry Moss on our expedition to the upper reaches of Yosemite in 1957.

In the spring of that year Ingolf became involved in one of Paul's successful composition projects, the film score for *The Abductors,* starring Victor McGlaglen and Fay Spain. Ingolf agreed to conduct the recording of this score, which took place on the Fox lot. His visits to the film studios had been infrequent in recent years, though I note that he did play in the Warner Brothers orchestra assembled to record Franz Waxman's music for *The Silver Chalice* in November, 1954. In June of 1957 he would also appear briefly on camera for Walt Disney, who was making the TV introduction to his *Peter And the Wolf,* and wanted Ingolf, who bore *some* resemblance to the famous Russian composer, to help him recreate his meeting with Prokofiev. Ingolf agreed to this as long as he didn't have to speak any lines, so all we saw as we huddled around the Kellers' black and white TV set was a stiff Ingolf marching woodenly to the seat of Disney's piano in order to play a little preview of the cartoon's music.

The Abductors, which used to pop up on the late late show on occasion, was a quite undistinguished film about the pillaging of Lincoln's tomb. Paul had written a very esoteric and dark score of considerable complexity and had insisted that his mentor conduct it. Paul also wanted as many of his friends as possible to be present on the sound stage on April 18, 1957, and there was a huge crowd of hangers-on. Etta and I accompanied the conductor as he arrived at the Fox gate. A guard, who directed us to the wrong set, said, "*Ingolf* Dahl? Any relation to Arlene?" A small studio orchestra of about twenty awaited their new director but Ingolf knew almost all of the musicians already. Lou Maury, his old "swing" teacher was there as was Bill Ulyate, local soloist in the *Saxophone Concerto*. Once Felix Slatkin, the only violinist in the ensemble, tiptoed tardily across the sound stage in order to play two pizzicato notes on his violin. The tuba player came up to Paul at one point and said, "Oh thank you, thank you." "Why?" "I've been playing in this orchestra for thirteen years and this is the first time I've ever had a solo. I'm even going to *see* this picture."

Hours passed in a rhythm that alternated between frenzied activity and mysterious pauses. Ingolf led the group through a succession of cues, stopwatch and pocket metronome before him, click tracks exploding on the screen above. At one point there was a two-hour break while Max Steiner took over the orchestra to complete some cues for *China Gate*. Copyists, who lined one wall, rushed to produce parts for the music which Paul had completed only at 9:00 that morning. Poor Paul was drooping with fatigue, a huge coffee stain covered his shirt, and once he fell asleep in his chair. Ingolf had to hold the score of the newly copied music in his hand in order to read the repeats.

The recording stage was also swarming with members of the movie music establishment, come to watch this performance and to listen with incredulity to Paul's way-out score. Bernard Herrmann was there, so was Hugo Friedhofer. Alfred Newman supervised the scene and was only one of the Fox functionaries amazed at Ingolf's ability to proceed in this complicated task at such speed and with such success. The bassoonist Don Christlieb later recalled that Newman was "dumbfounded at the ease with which Ingolf handled the small scoring orchestra in what was perhaps his motion picture debut." Precisely on the dot of seven Ingolf finished his task, thereby saving a lot of money in overtime and earning for himself the heartfelt congratulations of all. As we drove back to Clarington Etta began to fret. Had she turned off the flame under the lentil pot? She had not. The apartment stank for days.

After Paul returned from his studies in Europe he continued to write film music for a while; one of his scores was for the Olivia De Havilland picture, *Lady in a Cage*. He also rejoined our hiking group, one whose personnel had changed a good deal since Forest Patrol days. One day, as we were driving back from the mountains, Paul became fascinated by the fact that one of my graduate school friends, Kay Nelson, was dating Marina Fistoulari, the daughter of the conductor Anatole Fistoulari and the sculptor Anna Mahler. "You mean you're dating Gustav Mahler's granddaughter?" Paul asked repeatedly, beside himself with excitement. "I have to meet her, I have to meet her!" he insisted. Indeed, before we were out of the mountains, Paul had already seen himself as the right man for the job of mining the Mahler archive. An introduction was made and, as a couple, Marina and Paul attended the wedding ceremony which ended my bachelor days in 1964. Shortly after that they were married as well, though the union did not last long. Still, they remained on good terms and Paul took me to a party at Marina's in London in 1973, which was the last time I saw this friend of my youth. He had already abandoned Hollywood for Europe, settled in Switzerland, and begun a long career as a composer and teacher. I have not seen him in over thirty years, but I have spoken to him on the telephone. He is still unbreakable.

52. MEN AND MOUNTAINS

Ingolf had not been slow to resume his own skiing and hiking activities after his return from Austria in 1953. There were many local skiing expeditions over the next few years, often to Holiday Hill or Gorgonio, often with old friends like the Schaars, occasionally with students like Larry Moss or Vernon Read. Edi Schaar was also Ingolf's companion on two Sierra ski trips, one in April 1954 in the Kearsarge Pass area, one in May 1955 to Mammoth Mountain. Ingolf also undertook two long skiing holidays on his own, one to Tahoe in January of 1954 and one to Alta in April the following year. The journal entries for these years are full of the joys of the ski slope, but, "What unpleasantness in the city is awaiting me?"

Ingolf asked after a last day at Squaw Valley on February 4, 1954. His knees seem to have survived these outings well and his technique, further sharpened by lessons at Alta, improved.

Ingolf also took hikes on his own in Southern California, though Larry Moss and Donal Michalsky were occasional companions in the mid-Fifties. If he went with others on such hikes it was usually with me and other former members of the Forest Patrol. My friends and I still liked to "bag peaks," and on some days we could get reach as many as four closely-connected summits.

The mountain trip which Ingolf undertook on his return from Tanglewood in the summer in 1955 began on August 23 above Whitney Portal. Dick Binggeli and I accompanied him but when I became altitude-sick Dick climbed the Whitney summit alone and Ingolf spent the day with me at Mirror Lake. He then went off to join up with a Sierra Club group. He climbed Mt. Irvine, discovering on the morning of the 27th that a squirrel had been in his medicine bag and scattered Epigranol over everything. After sleeping among the sagebrush on the desert floor his group attempted the conquest of Mt. Williamson. "Go right along," he noted, "following Bill Colvig who races on." Thus we have the first mention in the journals of a figure who would become of great importance in all our lives. Here we also have the origin of the Couperin tune used by Ingolf in his variations for harpsichord and recorder – for he had first encountered it when Bill Colvig played it on his own recorder while sitting on a boulder on August 28, 1955.

Bill Colvig was a San Francisco electrician and Sierra Club group leader. He was the most energetic and skillful mountaineer I ever met and he became a favorite of mine, of Etta's, and, indeed, of many of my friends. Once Allan Solomonow sublet Bill's apartment beneath Coit Tower while Bill was off on one of his monumental world travels, for he tended to live frugally, save up money from work on large construction sites, and then take off on long mountain trips to Mexico or South America. He had a wonderful wry sense of humor and with his black bushy beard, checked shirts, and mischievous eyes it is no wonder he resembled some latter-day Pan, playing at his pipes. By the time the Sierra Club group had climbed Mount Tyndall and Mt. Russell Ingolf knew that he had found a dependable friend with whom he could share his mountain climbing enthusiasms. They even discovered that they had the same politics and enjoyed reading many of the same authors. Bill was also very musical.

The two had their next meeting that November when Ingolf flew to Fresno where Bill picked him up for a drive to Yosemite. Ingolf visited the apartment at 1403 Montgomery Street on the return leg of this outing; he later returned to San Francisco in January, 1956, undertaking a number of professional visits and actually doing some composing at Bill's. Then in March he and Bill again took part in a Sierra Club trip, this time to the Havasu country of Arizona. They explored the beautiful sculpted canyons and Ingolf took a lot of slides which he shared with the rest of us. Naturally I was beginning to grow a bit jealous of the mountain time Ingolf spent with Bill.

For instance, on August 15, 1956, three days after returning from Tanglewood, Ingolf left for San Francisco and a *four-week* hiking tour of the Pacific Crest with Bill. They visited Mt. Lassen and Mt. Shasta in northern California, the Three Sisters and Mt. Hood in the Oregon Cascades, and Mt. Shuksan, and Mt. Rainier in Washington. One of these volcanic peaks actually ate a hole in the seat of Ingolf's trousers. The two crossed glaciers, retreated in disappointment from some difficult ascents, and battled fog. Ingolf reported drying his wet clothes by the fire while reading *Moby Dick* on Mt. Hood. As he had done earlier with the Forest Patrol, he entertained Bill on long descents with the legend of *Das Rheingold*. After a night in the Rainier hut on September 1 he and Bill ascended the famous peak the next morning, and descended amid "mobs of sightseers who ask questions!" On September 4 a pain in Ingolf's right side convinced the mountaineers that more summits were not a possibility and they drove down the Oregon and California coasts, getting Bill's car stuck near the Russian River, where Ingolf and I had gone swimming eight years earlier.

The next summer, in what seemed to the rest of us to be a kind of compulsive quest, Ingolf undertook a *two-month* mountain sojourn which began on July 12, 1957, three days after he and Etta returned from a Baja trip. He and Bill joined a Sierra Club trip which began at Lyell Creek; then, after a return to San Francisco, they drove to the Wind River Range in Wyoming on August 2 for a week's expedition. When this was over they drove north to Canada for two weeks of climbing in the Rockies. Ingolf's journal pages are always crowded when mountain scenes are being described, though the 1957 daybook itself fell into Dike Creek on July 20, turning several pages pink and baby blue.

In Wyoming Ingolf complained of Bill's habit of outpacing the mountain goats, describing himself as, "quite tired, my knees hurt, and worst, feet are full of pains of all sorts." Having finished Sullivan's *Limitations of Science*, a book which excited him tremendously, Ingolf turned to *Anna Karenina* after a day on the Gannet glacier while Bill read *Mad* and *The New Yorker*. A thunderstorm drove them into a cave on August 11, where they discovered some pictographs. They failed to get a ride back to their car in Dubois and had to spend a night on the windswept prairie. The next day they had better luck from a toothless truck driver and later from a cattleman.

After hunting for a laundromat in Butte and completing some shopping in Calgary they began the first of two assaults, from Banff, on Mt. Assiniboine, a prominent, steep, glaciated alp. On August 18, after a late start, they took a long time finding the route and Ingolf fell several times trying to get up the snow. They reached the base of the summit pyramid, after crossing a glacier and missing a narrow hidden crevasse, but they had no time to reach the top and had to retreat. "Turn back – am very unhappy because this seemed to be the *day* if mountain were for us at all." The next day, with an earlier start, the mountaineers made better progress, though in icier conditions, but clouds began to thicken in the west and a thunderstorm dumped heavy hail on them. Once again they had to retreat.

The disappointed climbers continued on to Lake Louise, and climbed three peaks: Mt. Whyte on August 22, Mt. Lefroy on the 23rd, and Mt. Victoria on the 24th. Descending from the latter they were swept up in a snowstorm so powerful that it had obliterated their own earlier footprints. On August 26 they went canoeing on Lake Louise before returning for an ascent of Mt. Castor on the 29th and an attempt at Mt. Sir Donald on the 31st:

> Trail climbs, see Sir Donald, wears a cloud hood. At stream Bill feels continuation of trail on other side, which proves a mistake. Go up and up it, pleasantly. At last we have to traverse back the whole way, lose an hour. Across roads, ravines, down to Vaux glacier and up moraine, first on rocks, then grass, with a fine traverse across wall, to

col. Here climb begins (it's late already) and it is really great, more than I've ever done. Difficult reaches, high pitches, always very steep and *real* climbing. Snow on north ledges complicates things. But it is wonderful, although Bill loses heart and is down again. Because of lateness finally turn back (there are still so *many* slow pitches ahead!)...Lunch in the lee, sun comes out a little. While eating, the look straight down, how did we ever get up, how to get down? Then descend very slowly, belaying pitch by pitch. Some rappels, which are fun. It clouds up, and a storm comes over, while still on ridge.

I have to marvel at my stepfather's endurance, for he was forty-five when he undertook this exhausting regimen and more strenuous, if less extended, challenges were still to come. These feats seem all the more remarkable if they are set against the continuing health problems that bedeviled him. His left knee continued to cause problems on a sporadic basis. Starting in 1955 he was required to pay more on his life insurance policy because of hypothyroidism. A pain in his left foot was diagnosed as Morton's Neuroma and on December 29 of the same year Ingolf again underwent surgery, an operation that had to be delayed because he had contracted an infection from a cactus needle during an unsuccessful attempt on Condor Peak on December 11. (Ingolf blamed vanity; if he hadn't been wearing shorts in order to improve his tan the accident might not have occurred.) A calcium deposit on a wrist tendon plagued him in October, 1956, and a gout attack exasperated him the following March. "Why does all this happen to me?" he had to ask again. Fortunately Benemid seemed to control his gout and episodes were rather widely spaced, but 1958 was not a good year – "in spite of taking 4 grains of thyroid," he reported on February 21, "my basal metabolism was about as low as the machine would register." In April he was felled by German measles; on the 19th he noted, "These things are terribly wrong: can't focus at all, dizzy, weak beyond description (feeble), lifeless." This is the plaint of a man who had spent two months of the previous summer in the most strenuous of mountain activity.

It was at the end of their 1957 expedition that I first spent some time with Bill Colvig on his native turf. John Daly and I had driven up to San Francisco for a few days holiday before beginning our junior years at U.C.L.A. I found Bill, who now served as our guide to a North Beach pulsing with Beat Generation energy, to be a delightful chap. The four of us went to the New Pisa for Italian food and had dinner at a Basque boarding house. While I was browsing at the City Lights Book Shop a clerk asked me why I wasn't at the trial. "What trial?" I wanted to know. In this way I learned that the store's proprietor, Lawrence Ferlinghetti, was having his day in court after having been accused of selling an "obscene" volume of poems called *Howl* by Allen Ginsberg. A few minutes later, sporting my first beard and *looking* very much the part, I found myself seated at the rear of a San Francisco courtroom listening to expert testimony from Walter van Tilburg Clark and Mark Schorer on the literary merits of the work in question. Several weeks later Bill sent me the newspaper accounts of Ferlinghetti's acquittal and additional editions of poetry volumes published by City Lights

Ingolf's next Sierra expedition with Bill was completed in the latter part of August and the beginning of September, 1958. Ingolf records days of beautiful vistas and strenuous mountaineering; he carried a pack weighing 54 pounds! On August 26 the two climbed the wrong mountain, mistaking Second Kaweah for Red Kaweah; they had better success on other summits but mosquitoes and cold nights plagued them.

Ingolf's new mountain buddy was proving to be an admirable addition to our circle of friends and before long I would be included in several Sierra adventures in his company; the first of these began on August 21,1959, when our party included Leigh Peffer, and Leigh's friend Bill Brun. The trip was a disaster almost from the outset. We drove at night to avoid the worst of the desert heat but as we headed up 395, north of Mojave, I noticed the temperature beginning to climb on the Nash's dashboard gauge. Ingolf, who belonged to the keep-on-truckin' school of radiator watchers, encouraged me to push on. Finally there was a damp splash on the windshield, steam and smoke boiled forth and the car came to a halt at the roadside. Ingolf and Willie (as we called Bill Brun to prevent confusion with Bill Colvig) hitchhiked to Little Lake and made phone calls. One of these was to Etta, who, when we had failed to keep our rendezvous further north, could expect to hear from a worried Colvig. The second was to a Lone Pine wrecker, who, after some delay, proceeded to tow us to Ellis Motors. We arrived at 3:00 A.M. and slept in our sleeping bags on what proved to be, when the sun rose a few hours later, the town's rodeo grounds. Bill, who had been *mis*directed by Etta to *Big* Pine, found us anyway and we all piled into his huge Nash Ambassador while Jenny, who had lost an expansion plug and suffered piston damage and a cracked head, was left behind to undergo major repairs. "What an incorrigible fool I am," was Ingolf's final reflection on this event.

Bill's car also overheated as we drove to the North Lake campground above Bishop, but we paused several times to put stream water into the radiator. On August 23 we began an ascent of the Sierra crest, each of us (with the exception of Bill) suffering some form of altitude sickness. Ingolf complained of dizziness and lassitude and suffered from asthma so severe he could hardly talk. After crossing Piute Pass a second higher challenge, Alpine Col, faced us. The scramble up this rocky chute was so exhausting that I could only inch myself forward and Bill retraced his steps in order to carry my pack. When we dropped to the other side, well behind schedule, there was little to do but bivouac at the first tarn, climbing supperless into the sleeping bags in our tents in order to endure a night of thunderstorms. The next morning, tired, hungry and wet, we descended to a lovely campsite high on a terrace overlooking Evolution Canyon.

Ingolf climbed several summits including Mt. Darwin, angry that no one was around to photograph him as he rappelled from the top. On the 28th we headed back, climbing Lamarck Col, where Bill used an eggbeater and some cocoa powder to make milk shakes with some left over snow. The next day we drove through Bishop, where Ingolf was overjoyed to report "*No* music" at the Golden State Cafe. In Lone Pine Leigh, Willie and I recovered Jenny and returned slowly to Los Angeles while Bill and Ingolf spent a few days in the Mt. Williamson area.

Bill made his first visit to Los Angeles at the end of 1959 and in May 1960 he returned so that he and Ingolf could climb Mt. San Jacinto from the desert floor, a vertical climb of over 8,000 feet! On July 29th of that year Ingolf flew to Calgary, where he again rendezvoused with Bill. Here he discovered that the San Francisco electrician was bent over double from a sprained back that threatened the success of the new mission before it had begun. Nevertheless the two drove to Canmore, and prepared to do battle once again with Mt. Assiniboine. Time was lost in arranging for a packer and Ingolf spent some of this in a rueful visit to a rural graveyard – "Italian, Czech, Russian, one Jewish, some old wood fenced in, the writing washed off the crosses, the stone split and almost illegible. No permanence of memory."

Rain caused another day's delay, but on August 2 the climbers were successful at last. It says something about Ingolf's persistent spirit that he would come so far to complete a conquest of this nature. In fact all of the summit victories on this trip came on second attempts.

Next on the list was Edith Cavell near Jasper, which the mountaineers first attempted on August 6. "Up at 3:30 to climb Cavell," Ingolf began his report:

> weather not encouraging, feel blue and under par – stomach bad, leave at 4:20 – just daybreak --over trail and moraine and snow to col, in two and a half hours; there very discouraged about weather (and I about my physical condition, will I make it, can I, how about technical climb, exposure, nothing to meet the problems with!... After four and a half hours decide to turn around. Fog closes in above, drizzles on and off."

Two days later the climbers decided to give it another try:

> Up 3:15, miserable cold morning, not feeling well, not enough sleep, just stumble around. Off at 4:30 still dark. Stomach so-so, on first moraine, blood in stool, but on anyhow. As sun comes up feel better – over familiar ground, "some interesting climbing – turns out to be simple. After it, no rope. Slow and steady to summit, which we traverse. Sunny and slight breeze...12:40 on top – stay till almost 3:00.

Four days later, during the long drive back to San Francisco, the two stopped in Oregon to climb Mt. Hood, whose summit they had failed to reach in 1956. Ingolf, as we shall see, hated quitters.

53. PROBLEM PARENTS

My friendship with Ingolf's students and my inclusion in the world in which these young men traveled had a great deal to do with my own attitude toward my stepfather and the image I held of him during our Clarington years. I was now old enough to go to his concerts not merely with Etta but with my own friends, with Paul Glass, for instance, and to sit among neutral observers who would join in the applause that greeted Ingolf's labors, to see his beaming face and his bald dome soaked in perspiration as he responded to the ovations in Bovard or Hancock Auditoriums. And just through the gossip of these U.S.C. students I was able to measure the degree of awe and respect in which he was held. On January 30, 1957 I met one of Paul's friends at a U.S.C. party. This was the young actor Jack Colvin (later familiar to TV viewers as the relentless pursuer of the Incredible Hulk). Jack spent a great deal of time telling me how much he admired Paul's teacher before learning that the man of whom he spoke was a rather close relative. Paul's brother Gaston and Leigh Peffer each asked me to obtain autographed pictures of the maestro. It is no wonder that I learned to regard Ingolf as someone special, a figure whose behavior was not to be measured by the standard of ordinary mortals.

One had, for instance, to forgive his chronic absent mindedness, those flights of inattention during which he could tune out the present in favor of some more pressing mental urgency. You could pass him in the U.S.C. Commons, his students reported, and receive no response to your greeting whatsoever from the preoccupied man. He was always forgetting things. One day, several hours after he and Etta had departed for a camping trip to Baja, I discovered on our front walk the beach umbrella and Coleman stove that Ingolf had neglected to put in the car. He often ran out of gas, he lost his fountain pen, his gloves, and his keys. During the war he was pulled over three times by the police because he had forgotten to fix Peter's amber taillight. Ingolf forgot his waistcoat when he first appeared with Gracie in Fresno in 1941 and two years later he forgot to change his socks so that a Boston audience saw him sit down at the piano in tuxedo and red, green and black argyles. He forgot appointments and inadvertently burned a sketch for a cadenza of the *Symphony Concertante*. He forgot a shovel on the Angeles Crest and our swimming clothes at the Jenny Lake Ranger Station. He forgot his sleeping bag on Mt. Whitney and he left his Swedish cup at Silver Pass. An army of analysts would have found steady employment unraveling the psychic intricacies of these gestures. His internal mental life – even that portion of it in which he consciously participated – was almost always more fascinating than the banality of daily life. Because he juggled so many balls he was forever preoccupied with something other than the task at hand. If he was chained to his chair at a meeting of the School of Music Executive Committee he was thinking about the latest problems in his composition, and as he was composing he was worrying about next season's repertoire, tomorrow's lessons, or next week's performance. One can even argue that Ingolf's success in the world and the many contributions he made to the lives of others represented a hard won victory over the constant seduction of a raging self-absorption. It would be hard to discern from his egomaniacal journals that here was a man whose generosity toward others, his fourteen-hour long teaching days, his immense efforts on behalf of audiences and colleagues would leave a lasting legacy of respect and gratitude in many of his contemporaries.

But there is no question that in some senses, along with my love for him, I also nurtured a sense of grievance against the man who chose to make so many other things more important in his life than me. This anger could only be expressed in an indirect fashion, for I was wellschooled by Etta in the necessity of exempting my stepfather from the familial requirements by which *other* fathers might be judged. *They* were not creative geniuses (and their children did not have to get in line behind the other disciples to get a piece of the master's time). I can think of only one instance of a direct assault, and even to so categorize it is to accept the notion that there is no such thing as an accident. On June 20, 1954, when I was sixteen, there was a family gathering on Father's Day at Palos Verdes. The Kellers were present and also Grampa Gordon. Only Ingolf went into the water and, bored and sulky, I walked up and down the pebbly beach. To test my arm I selected a small stone and threw it toward the Ingolf-inhabited ocean, not really aiming at anything but watching to see where the splash might register. The stone didn't splash because it hit Ingolf, wading fifty yards away, on the top of his bald head. He squawked. I apologized and the incident was so quickly forgotten that it doesn't even appear in his journal. In fact it was a far less serious episode, through semi-intentional, than a truly menacing one that I consider wholly accidental: a few years later – as a group of us were scrambling up a loose gully – I put my foot down on a boulder which, beginning to tumble downward, narrowly missed Ingolf's head.

It could be argued that I *was* guilty of another indirect form of injury. In 1956 I decided to write a novel about a 1954 Sierra trip during which Ingolf had taken a group, including Dick Binggeli, Leigh Peffer, John Daly, Dick Dardarian, and Mikel Taxer, to the Sierras. We drove both Jennie and Rufus to Onion Valley, crossed Kearsarge Pass, and stumbled in darkness into our first campsite at "Lake Renunciation." We all climbed Mt. Bago, an easy scramble, some of us made an unsuccessful assault on University Peak, and Ingolf and Leigh climbed Mt. Brewer during a "rest" day. It was our first experience with dehydrated foods – the powdered eggs, bean pot, Sierra Salad, and cabbage flakes of the Dri-Lite Company. The flavor of the beans was not improved when too much pepper fell into the dinner pot at East Lake. After a week the lads got desperately thirsty for malts, the sound of the radio, and magazines with pictures of half-naked girls in them. Consequently there was a rebellion when Ingolf wanted us to continue to the end of the trip, which was scheduled to include an assault on Mt. Whitney. "I hate quitters," he wrote of this mutiny. When, two years later, I was casting about for fictional names for the participants in this adventure I bestowed on Ingolf a most inappropriate substitute, his *real* name: Walter Marcus. But it was Etta who later drew me aside to tell me that Ingolf had been upset by this revival of an identity he somehow wished to suppress.

My chief complaint was not that Ingolf did not love me but that he found so little time in which to express this affection. There was never any question as to his feelings for me, and these were certainly confirmed in the journals. Indeed, in the 1953 volume I discovered a picture of me in my R.O.T.C. uniform! It was also evident that Ingolf took delight in my company. "Tony is wonderful," he wrote after a hike in October, 1953. "Anth is so adorable," appears as a description in February, 1954. Many comments refer to my mood. After a "nice" walk with mother and me in April, 1955, Ingolf wrote, "He is so chirping, a real high point." "Anth is so sweet and relaxed," he added in September, 1957, a sure indication that this was not always the case. It was not always so, in part, because of my failure to command, on a more regular basis, the full attention of this remarkable being whom we all loved.

If one culls the Clarington day books it is possible to come up with a substantial list of references to the times we spent together, on hikes, at movies, concerts and plays, just chattering around the house, walking in the rain. But the frequency of these happy occasions was so haphazard that Ingolf gave *each* its own review in his journals. On November 10, 1955, he notes Tony "has become a complete stranger," and on December 5 he adds. "Evening at home – no letters, just sit with E. & A. and shoot the breeze, very relaxed and warm and lovely – he is chirping again – how have I missed it, for how long have we been apart (and still are)." Ingolf comes close to recognizing that his own schedule served as the cause of this estrangement in a letter he wrote to Bill Colvig on September 15, 1956:

> Thursday night I did the copying of the Piano Quartet at home. It is so touching to see how Anthony brightens up and begins to sparkle when I spend one of those rare evenings at home (for the next 3 months I'll *have* to work on the quartet in my studio every free night). To see how my presence, banter, conversation effects the boy makes me feel very uncomfortable and guilty that I cannot give him more of the parental companionship which he so obviously needs, and so gratefully soaks up, and which is now mainly supplied by his mother. But I know that he realizes that the things for which he looks up to me are the result of all the hard work that keeps me in the studio at night.

On September 11, 1956, after Ingolf's session in Tanglewood and his long mountain sojourn, I wrote in my journal, "Ingolf left town on June 13, returned August 12, left August 15 and returned today. He's been home 3 days in almost 3 months & mother still calls this normal family life." This comment is a reminder that I was *not* able to accept every absence as a consequence of creative necessity and that the brunt of my dissatisfaction over the secession of my stepfather had to be borne by my mother. Indeed, it was almost as if I blamed her for taking part in a conspiracy to hide form me the true causes of Ingolf's wayward desertions. Many years later I learned that I was right. There was a conspiracy, an elaborate tissue of fabrication which I had been powerless to penetrate.

Etta had an answer, however devious, to my every objection about our abnormal family life. But we wrangled incessantly, in the early years of my college career, without ever addressing ourselves to the real problem. Etta's most reliable form of defense was a good offence – a summary of *my* faults: why didn't I ever make any new friends, why didn't I start a little theater group if I was bored, why did I want to spend my money on fleeting teenage passions when I should be saving up for something educationally beneficial? Etta was almost totally preoccupied with my intellectual development and determined to save me from the excesses of adolescent experimentation – as useful as these might have been in the development of my character. Ingolf, I might add, was far more generous than Etta in his tolerance of my infatuations and enthusiasms. One night the three of us drove home from a showing of *Umberto D*. On the car radio KFAC was offering the Grieg *Piano Concerto*. I wanted to hear it. The anti-Romantic Etta sneered and tried to turn it off but Ingolf countermanded her, "Let him enjoy it." Similarly Ingolf had a more positive attitude toward my attempts at poetry and fiction than my mother. "He wrote a poem himself today," Ingolf wrote to Bill in March, 1957, "not bad – but quite in the style of Ginsberg, without the 4 letter words, that is – it is a poem in defense of the intellectual – and I am glad he feels that way and expresses it." Etta usually had something to say about mistakes in form and my feelings were so easily bruised that I rarely showed any of my work to her. *I* would have no Mammi going gaga over any of my childish scribbles. Years later Etta was unrelenting, telling my wife Dorothy, "Anthony will never be a good writer. He can't spell."

On March 5, 1956, she wrote to Ingolf's brother Gert:

'Little' Anthony is now 18 years old and a young giant, taller than either his father or Ingolf. He is completing his first year at university and is intelligent enough but rather lazy intellectually. Quite a bit of his energy goes into pointing out to his parents how ridiculous they are, or in wishing he could just travel all over the world and write down his impressions. Both of these traits are common to his age and to be expected. Fortunately we can still remember ourselves at the same age, and a sense of humor is indispensable.

But no humor was in evidence on January 25, 1956, when Etta and I argued from dinner to midnight. Among the items covered was my assertion that Ingolf was rarely present and that – when he was – he often behaved like a "vegetable" who never heard what I said the first time. Etta's response was to challenge me to give an example of normal family life. When I named some candidates she countered that the happy couple I had nominated were "not very bright." "I really cut her into little pieces this time," I wrote after an argument on February 18, "mother was asking for it...She left the room telling me to go to the devil." Such debates were frequent and bitter and life at home was often bad for me, though eventually Etta and I found our way back to happier times, particularly as I developed new interests outside the home.

In retrospect, I know I should have gone away to university, or, at any rate, lived away from home while attending college in Los Angeles. But no one encouraged me to do either of these things and family finances would have made such choices almost impossible. With the money I did have for college and my excellent high school record there was only one logical choice: I would commute to the University of California at Los Angeles.

54. HAIL TO THE HILLS OF WESTWOOD

For the college applicant of the mid-Fifties the admissions process was a lot less complex than it became for my students in a later era. They had SATs and APs to complicate their lives but neither of these hurdles was in place when I was finishing high school. Entrance to the University of California was mostly a matter of good grades, though a separate English proficiency exam *was* administered. When I showed up on the Westwood campus to take this test I had the good fortune of discovering that one of the essay topics, on Conservation, had just been the subject of my term paper in my University Composition class at Hamilton.

Even though I passed this exam with a special commendation, thereby exempting me from Subject A, I decided to take another step up the ladder by attending a night course in English 1A at City College during the summer of 1955. Dick Binggeli was also enrolled in Mr. Otis Richardson's class. We would drive to the Vermont campus, where Etta had gone to college, have our class, which proved to be very useful to me, get the grades we had received on the previous night's paper (Mr. Richardson entered these in Japanese ideograms so we always had to go to Sue Quan, also U.C.L.A-bound, for a translation) and then, our evening labors complete, we would stop off at Curry's Mile High Cones on the way home.

My college education was paid for entirely by the Weismans. Aunt Elsie had told me some months earlier that instead of leaving me something in her will she would give me the equivalent of $100 a month for my university education. This sum was paid to me regularly for the next *five* years but, as part of the deal, I would occasionally have to put in some time at the offices of the Weisman real estate empire. These were located at Hollywood and Western in a building that had once belonged to Louis B. Mayer. My cousin Dick was also employed here and so, eventually was Maury Scharman, Virginia Weisman's second husband. Sid, sensing another *luftmensch* in the making, insisted that I work toward a license in real estate and sent me to Mr. Newman's school for apprentice realtors. Mr. Newman sat at the front of his classroom, drinking endless glasses of water, and listening to his own lecture on a tape recorder. I zoned out during the lesson on "metes and bounds," and dropped out soon thereafter – to go on the 1957 Yosemite trip.

Sid was by no means exclusively preoccupied with real estate. As far back as 1927 he had formed an alliance with a former rabbi, Herman Lissauer, in the presentation of a prestigious lecture series, The Los Angeles Modern Forum. This series specialized in bringing famous political, philosophical, diplomatic, and religious personalities to the attention of local audiences. Sid was a member of the Forum board for thirty years, succeeding Dr. Lissauer, on his death in 1957, as executive director. When he wasn't lecturing me in the coffee shop of the Hollywood and Western Building on another enthusiasm, Humanistic Judaism, he was off dining with Robert Maynard Hutchins or some other world-famous figure. Consequently my uncle had a lot of interesting stories to tell and he was a great raconteur, although even Elsie had to admit that he *could* go on a bit. Listening to Sid's endless stories was a small price to pay for the gift of a free college education.

As a matter of fact a *free* college education is precisely what the enlightened citizens of California provided for their sons and daughters in the mid-Fifties. How times have changed! When I entered U.C.L.A. (one fifth of the graduating class at Hamilton coming along with me) there was no tuition fee at all. You paid $50 a semester as an incidental (administrative) fee and your direct financial obligation to the university was complete. You did have to buy your own books, although used copies were often available, but $100 a month could go a long way. I used it to pay for clothes, movies, travel and whatever else I could sneak in without a lecture from my mother on "worthwhile" expenditure.

The Knights of the Golden Sword matriculated en masse to Westwood, John to study engineering, Dick pre-med, and Mikel theater arts. I didn't have a major for quite a while, overfaced by all the choices, but eventually I selected history and began to work simultaneously on a general secondary teaching credential. I was not a very successful student in my first two years at U.C.L.A. I found the giant campus awe-inspiring and intimidating and the large lecture classes off-putting and anonymous. Without the discipline of daily assignments I let things slide a bit. I remember an incident from my first year as a Western Civ student. Our teaching assistant, Sy Chapin, had been threatening us with a pop quiz for some time, but as he had never actually given one, no one took him seriously. Eventually the awful day arrived and the best I could offer on my paper was a limerick:

> There was a young man named Linick
> Who thought he was quite a cynic.
> With no tests in history to dread
> Voltaire, Montesquieu, and Rousseau stayed unread
> And now the young man's at the clinic.

There was a culture at U.C.L.A. I did not understand, a world of sororities and fraternities, of jocks and snobs. I met a lot of people, but made few new friends, clinging conservatively to my old pals, when I was not quarrelling with them. Dick Binggeli had a wonderful purring late 40's maroon Mercury and in the morning I would stand on my corner at Clarington waiting for a ride up to campus – where, if you didn't mind a ten minute walk – you could still find a free place to park. Sometimes I drove Rufus and on other occasions I took a bus up Westwood Boulevard. But I took no part in life at U.C.L.A. for quite a while, with the exception of my continued fervent loyalty to the Bruin football team. Dick and I attended all the home games in our white shirts and blue rooters caps, sitting in the card section and even manipulating flashlights for card stunts during U.C.L.A.'s night games. We also went to the Rose Bowl on January 1, 1955, midway through our freshman year, to see U.C.L.A. lose to Michigan State. Thirty-nine years later I returned to the scene of this crime but the same thing happened, this time at Wisconsin's hands.

My most memorable experiences during my early college years were always off-campus: poetry readings, outings with Paul Glass; the trip John and I took to the Bay Area to see our team play Stanford in the fall of 1955; a trip the next year when Mikel joined us for a "Three Go Wild in San Francisco" jaunt; the 1957 trip in which we met Bill Colvig. I also undertook that Sierra trip with Dick Binggeli in 1955 during which we spent some time in Yosemite after I had failed to reach the top of Mt. Whitney. The next year Leigh Peffer and I did succeed, reaching what was then the highest summit in the United States at 14,494 feet. (The admission of Alaska, and its Mt. McKinley, destroyed this distinction a few years later.)

In 1957 I decided, against everyone's advice, to undertake a long solo car trip through the Western United States. I had my Buick fitted with car beds and – fortified by a final bracer of Rachmaninoff's *Rhapsody On A Theme of Paganini,* which I listened to on John's stereo – I took off in the darkness. The trip lasted only two weeks. I broiled in the heat, got diarrhea in Oak Creek Canyon, had a blowout near Window Rock and took a stone through my radiator in Monument Valley – which had only dirt roads in 1957. By the time I had figured out the problem the engine of the car had fried. I spent three nights in a dollar-a-day hotel room in Cortez, Colorado before swapping the carcass of my car for a lesser cousin. It too developed water pump problems on the return journey, which I completed with a non-stop night-time drive, just like the Joads, across the Mojave Desert – César Franck's *Symphony in D* on the car radio mocking my attempts at adventure.

I entered U.C.L.A. as a freshman in the fall of 1955 and left the campus ten years later, having, in the interim, earned a B.A. in history, my teaching credential, a Ph.D., an Instructorship in the History Department, and a wife. This is not the time or the place to try to explain how this all came about, for in this volume I wish to concentrate on my unique family and *its* history, to unravel the complexity of relationships only partially understood by at least one of the participants in the struggle – me. U.C.L.A. was my world *apart* from my parents, and it is their tale, therefore, that must take precedence.

55. THE INVISIBLE WORM

Early in 1958, a year of very mixed outcomes in our lives, there occurred two quite specific family traumas. Both Ingolf and Etta lost their fathers. Pappi, who had been undergoing cobalt treatments for an "incipient" throat cancer, died rather suddenly on January 19, 1958. "Mine Lieber

Pappi is nun tot," a distraught Ingolf wrote. "This comes not unexpected," he added to Bill Colvig, "because he was quite ill and was old (77, which is a good ripe age). And yet it is only natural that one has a sense of loss, and of melancholy reflection on life and death in general. His old age, unfortunately, was overshadowed by loneliness."

On the same day that Ingolf learned of Pappi's death Grampa Gordon, after dosing himself with various quack cures, entered the hospital for a fatally delayed stomach cancer operation. On January 22 Ingolf reported, "Things are bad with him." After a visit to the Gardena Hospital on the 31st he added, "Grampa Gordon is at his lucid best – very tender, reconciled, farsighted. As it turns out, his last moment of grandeur." My grandfather died on February 2. His funeral, for which Ingolf purchased the grave, was in the Mt. Sinai block of Hillside Memorial Park on February 4, a day on which the mail brought Pappi's funeral program and copies of the eulogies. "They really made the tears come finally," Ingolf wrote.

Grampa Gordon's thirty-three bonds, once they had been recovered from the hole in which he had buried them, provided each of the sisters with several thousand dollars. There were some problems cashing them, as Etta explained to the family attorney, Toby Klinger:

> Not only did Dad keep his dough in dirt, he was orthographically quixotic, as witness naming me Etta Ingolf in the Equitable insurance papers. The Republicans downtown were not so concerned by my appearing as Dahl, Dall, and Dole (the latter makes me a British pensioner or a pineapple queen)...they were bewitched, bothered and bemildewed by father's calling himself now Isidore Gordon, now Isidore E. Gordon, now E. Isidore Gordon. He called himself as he saw himself, and was notoriously myopic.

The financial boost which this unexpected legacy provided our family permitted my parents to resurrect an old dream, that of owning their own home. Soon thereafter, much to my disgruntlement – for I was notoriously conservative when it came to change – they began looking at houses in the Hollywood Hills. On June 17, after several false starts, they saw a house in Beachwood Canyon at 2486 Cheremoya Avenue. "Looks lovely," Ingolf wrote, "can we have it?" "Thinking about that lovely little house all the time," he added the next day. On the 19th he recorded a triumphant "*We have the house. What a day. What a feeling!!*"

These feeling of euphoria did not last long. On June 22, three days later, Etta entered hospital for treatment of what doctors were fairly certain was a cyst. When Dr. Max Cutler began surgery on the 23rd cancer was detected and Etta underwent a radical mastectomy of the left breast. An anguished Ingolf who, with Lillian, had waited four hours to hear about the results of a procedure scheduled for one hour, went to see his wife after she returned to her room. "I love her so much, so deep down," he wrote, "she comes out and talks about checkbook (of all things!) – a few words, then she falls asleep." The next day the extent of the surgery was explained to Etta, with Ingolf at her bedside. "She is a woman of extraordinary spirit," he wrote to Bill, "(she would have to be, living with me –) and took it in stride. I am sure one will not find many women whose first words after the news is broken to them would be, I guess I'll have to go shopping for left sided falsies."

I was not in Los Angeles when this event took place. I had undertaken a long Greyhound Bus journey to New York, where Leigh Peffer and I hoped to spend the summer. It was to be my first effort at living away from home, but there was a brief period when I thought it might be best to return to Los Angeles at once. Ingolf's letter describing what had happened in my absence was waiting for me when I asked for my mail on my first morning in New York City. I was crushed by the news and walked aimlessly along the pavements in the cauldron of a Manhattan summer, Leigh by my side; somehow I couldn't get the lines of Blake's "O Rose thou ar't sick" poem out of my head. Ingolf rejected my suggestions about returning to Los Angeles. Etta was taken home from hospital on June 28th and made a good recovery. Thus I was able to overcome my despondency and to throw myself into New York life with zest. I began to make those new friends my mother had always encouraged me to find, and soon I made New York my summertime home, repeating the journey in 1960, 1961, 1962, and 1963.

While I was away that first summer Ingolf had a most difficult time juggling all of his responsibilities. He was, after all, living at the Hartford Foundation – and yet he never seems to have settled down there. He was always ducking out to keep an eye on Etta and to start the complicated work of packing for the move to Cheremoya. As if things weren't hectic enough he also had to report to the Santa Monica Hospital for regular treatments on another chronic ailment, a narrowed disc in his neck.

314

The move to Hollywood took place three days after his return from the Foundation, that is on July 31, 1958. Each of us had good reasons to turn our backs on the Clarington years and to look forward to better things from life in Beachwood Canyon.

Undated meeting of the Crescendo Club. George Tremblay is standing in the back row, second from the left and Ingolf is second from the right. In the front row Sol Babitz is standing at the left; Aaron Copland is seated third from the left.

Etta and Tony at Ferndell, ca. 1944.

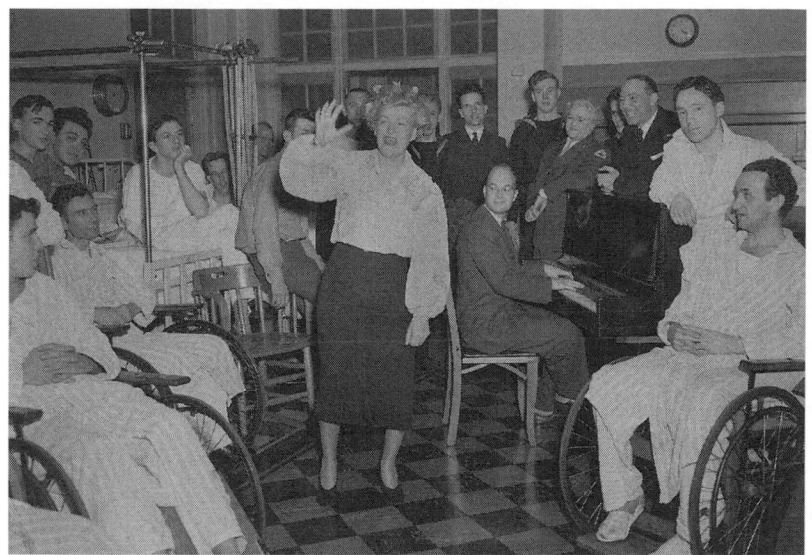

Ingolf accompanies Gracie Fields at the Chelsea Naval Hospital, 1944.

Jane Russell receives instruction from Ingolf on the set of *Young Widow*.

In Chatsworth, ca. 1950: back row – Lawrence Morton (l), Ingolf (r);
Front row – George Tremblay (l); Gil Grau (r).

The Dahls in Schruns, 1952 or 1953.

Ingolf attends his stepson's graduation from Hamilton High School in June, 1955.

Etta in 1955.

PART III

1958-1970

56. 2486

The Dahl's new residence, 2486 Cheremoya Avenue, occupied a most unusual location on the eastern flank of Beachwood Canyon, a mile or so north of Franklin. Many readers, without ever having visited this area, will still have an vivid visual image of this hilly region because of the famous Hollywood sign – perched on a bare patch at the upper end of the canyon. The sign, local historians will tell you, is made up of the surviving letters of the much longer "Hollywoodland," a property development of yesteryear. Having purchased their own bit of real estate much farther down the canyon's well-hosed slopes, my parents began to make a home that would, for them, never have a successor.

A bus made its way down Beachwood Avenue at less than frequent intervals, proceeded along Hollywood Boulevard, then down Fairfax. This precious public transportation link proved to be a lifeline for Etta, who gave up driving after her surgery. Isolation was the order of the day at Cheremoya. It was only five minutes from Hollywood and Vine, U.S.C. could be reached in half an hour, but the garageless house was inaccessible to motorcars. It was wedged onto a small plot of land eighty steps below Hollyridge and eighty-seven steps above Cheremoya itself. My parents could not have been thinking of their old age when they bought this house. The endless vertical trudging was an extremely tedious exercise, particularly if anything had to be carried, and the location was not exactly a favorite terminus for delivery boys. Etta gradually adopted the habit of picking out her groceries at a market on Franklin Avenue and having them delivered later in the day. For years Elmer, the Arden milkman, faithfully dropped down the hill with Ingolf's yogurt. Etta fell on the cement steps in 1959 and injured both of her knees.

There were occasions when it was possible to shut out the world at Cheremoya. Neighboring homes, except for some rooftops, were not included in the view from the living room window. When the smog was thin a marvelous twinkling panorama of L.A. lights appeared through the leafy arms of the Chinese elm. Ivy and succulents covered the exterior surfaces, a line of flowering oleanders served as a fence, cypresses and eucalyptus grew above, pots were full of Etta's rarely successful experiments in floriculture. A huge century plant welcomed puffing visitors to the property and next to the house itself stood a wonderfully gnarled dead fruit tree, identified – perhaps erroneously – as a cheremoya itself. Next to it a grapefruit tree produced a small but edible crop. A great deal of watering was necessary to keep all the other plants from suffering the fate of the cheremoya, but exactly how much moisture was required proved to be a subject of controversy between Ingolf and Etta; the former favored a watering regimen that was irregular to say the least.

The house itself had a unique design. Upstairs there was a large and long living-dining area, a bathroom, a kitchen, and two bedrooms. One of the latter was occupied by Etta and the other, a "den," served as my bedroom for several years. This was a comfortable room with combed plywood walls, a black flagstone floor, and a fireplace. Downstairs there was *another* living room, which Ingolf made into his studio, and, adjoining it, a tiny stand-up library, a second bathroom, and Ingolf's bedroom. The two double beds that my parents had spent seventeen years shoving into a single cramped bedchamber were separated at last.

The owner-builder of 2486 Cheremoya had never gotten around to uniting the two parts of the house. Ingolf had to descend his own porch, walk the length of the house on a cement path surrounded by ivy and lantana, ascend a set of crumbling stone steps, and reverse his direction on a flagged walkway in order to gain the front porch of the rest of his home. He had, at last, privacy within privacy. Communication between upstairs and downstairs was, for a number of years, difficult indeed. There was a telephone extension in the studio, though Ingolf frequently turned off its bell. If a call came for him Etta had to march outside, lean over the balustrade, and holler, hoping he would hear. When the call was urgent she would have to hike down there herself and rouse him from his nap. Eventually Ernst Toch and his wife took pity on my mother and, as a present, paid for a proper phone system to be installed, one which allowed Etta the luxury of *buzzing* her husband.

The Dahls undertook the decoration and upkeep of the property themselves – at least initially, but it was their first and last venture in do-it-yourself. Ingolf painted a good deal of the interior that first year, 1958. When William Schaefer asked him at an Executive Committee meeting what color he had used my stepfather replied by rolling up his sleeves, having cleaned his hands in time for the meeting but not the rest of his paint-speckled arms. Bill Schaefer was also puzzled by the tiles in the back hall, which seemed unusually spongy – learning to his horror that Ingolf had put these down on *top* of the old carpet. After their initial enthusiasm for decorating my parents gradually let the professionals take over and there was a good deal of modernization during the next few years. Etta became friends for life with all the workmen, for to tell the truth she was lonely much of the time in this Hollywood aerie and was glad to have their company. There were no friends or relatives living nearby and contacts with neighbors were usually the consequence of some dispute over a parking place or the collapse of a foundation wall onto someone else's property. An unsocial chap lived in a stilt house at the left side of the eighty-seven Cheremoya steps but after he had murdered his wife his company was shunned.

I'm sorry to say that in spite of all the improvements the house never lost its jerrybuilt appearance. Not even a cheery coat of yellow paint could hide the sag in the front porch, the constantly crumbling stairs, the windows and doors that never fit right, the omnipresent leak in the studio roof.

Many expeditions were undertaken in the fall of 1958 in search of new furnishings. Lack of cash is not a sufficient explanation for how it was that Ingolf and Etta returned from these forays into furnitureland with such a pedestrian assemblage. There were two terrazzo coffee tables, a sofa and chair in a bilious green Naugahyde, and some Danish modern chairs whose cushions constantly fell through the rubber webbing beneath. Much of the remaining furniture was late Walnutto.

The wall decorations were mostly reproductions or prints, since here too the Dahls chose not to invest any substantial portion of their income. Ingolf never acquired a work by Rico Lebrun, his favorite local artist, though the two were friends, and because of the commissioning costs he declined the opportunity of having his own bust executed by Anna Mahler.

The nicest room in the house was Ingolf's studio, where the Steinway found its last American home. Some of the windows were permanently sealed so that heat would not damage this instrument, and some efforts at soundproofing were also undertaken. The walls were covered with grass cloth and hung with framed sketches of music by other composers and by an antique map of Zurich, a gift from Stravinsky. Ingolf replaced our old 78 record player with a used long-play model capable of only the lowest fi. He also invested in a Wallensak tape recorder, which I used for many years thereafter. Upstairs and downstairs were both furnished with a full set of cleaning supplies in order to facilitate the work of the dour Gertrude Elliott, who came regularly to undertake chores which my mother, with her restricted arm movement, could no longer accomplish easily.

Beneath Cheremoya's long front porch, and again beneath the floor of the downstairs studio, two storerooms were located, and in these Ingolf found a final resting place for his topographical maps, his camping cookware, his tents and sleeping bags, his skis and all the other outdoor paraphernalia that used to be stuffed into our garages.

At Cheremoya the Dahls felt at home at last, and their love for this charming oddity only grew with the years as they proudly welcomed old friends and new acquaintances, at least those fit enough to make the hike, into surroundings which finally reflected something of the style and aspirations of the proud owners. The historian Francis Hackett visited them here, the poet Lawrence Ferlinghetti was a guest, so was the astronomer Fred Hoyle. Hackett, who had been a fellow resident at the Hartford Foundation in the summer of 1958, wrote, "Your home, with your boy there, and the sun on the rocks behind, with the goldfish under the greenery, and the two shelves of dwelling place, made us happy for what you've secured as your own – near enough to the University, and far enough from the crowd."

There were, in fact, two patios at Cheremoya, one below Ingolf's porch, a site for sunbathing and copying, and the one upstairs referred to by Hackett, a charming flagged courtyard surrounded by bougainvillea, in which a glass-topped wrought iron table provided the setting for many outdoor meals. To one side there was a small pond in which the Dahls attempted to grow water lilies and goldfish. They succeeded with the lilies but the local raccoon kept eating the fish and Etta got tired of suspending a wire screen over the pond at night. More welcome was "Butterbeak," the cheeky blue jay who would swoop down at outdoor meals to take peanuts directly from your hand.

We usually ate in the little kitchen, where a wooden breakfast nook had been built by the previous owner. And here you would find short Etta, standing at the sink on a little stool which enabled her to reach her counters and cupboards, while Ingolf, engrossed in some flight of fancy, sat with his arm curled lazily across the top of his head, his fingers absentmindedly picking scabs into the fringes of his shiny head.

There remained only one snake in this Hollywood paradise, an irksome impediment to Ingolf's contentment. "After lunch," he recorded disconsolately on July 3, 1960, "sunbath on lower porch, a breeze, blue sky – what a lovely place we have!!! But the ice cream man drives me batty."

Noise, unwanted, irritating, intrusive sound, was my stepfather's special torment. "This is the most grievous disappointment. From above, popular records – from next door the hi fi Beethoven – from down on Beachwood the teenager's rock and roll, from below the studio the piano playing" – so the catalogue ran. The distant sound of the traffic endlessly roaring up the Hollywood Freeway was another source of discontent.

Nothing caused more continuous grief, however, than the tunes of the Good Humor man, echoing in the narrow width of the canyon. Ingolf addressed the company itself: "I am writing this note to request that you ask your vendor to turn off his amplifier when he drives up the Beachwood area where I live because it is impossible for me to work when this disruption is going on." He also wrote to the City Attorney denouncing the amplified jingles as an invasion of privacy and as "aural billboards." Many times I heard him threaten to sue the ice cream company, but certainly he did no such thing. Though his own was imperiled, he did have to suffer in silence.

The plague of unwanted sound spread to other corners of his world. At Mt. Waterman they installed loudspeakers on the ski slopes. At Holiday Hill there was rock and roll on top, yodeling below. On February 1, 1960 Ingolf fired off another protest letter: "I have skied many times on Holiday Hill, even long before a lift was built, and I love the mountain and its fine slopes. But the 'music' which you amplify with loudspeakers all over the mountainside and which relentlessly and incessantly assaults the ear is enough to drive a person crazy."

Much later in his life Ingolf was slowly walking up one of his favorite ski slopes when the 'music' was interrupted by an announcement, clearly aimed at him, broadcast from a loudspeaker in a pine tree: "Nobody is allowed to walk up the mountain!" Sniffing a plot to extract a lift fee, my intrepid stepfather continued his uphill tramp. "If you don't stop," the pine tree said, "We're going to send the Ski Patrol!" Still, he kept walking, and the Ski Patrol failed to materialize. He once showed me a specially insulated cutting tool he had purchased to sabotage the wiring at one of these sound-blighted ski areas, but I never heard him say that he had actually carried out the act. I doubt it.

On July 13, 1953, at the Lenox Forum, Ingolf had begun his response to the question, "What Are The Consequences of Recorded Music?" by suggesting that one obvious outcome was that:

> Nowadays the most expensive luxury, the most exclusive possession, the most elusive delicacy is non-music, that is silence...The heavenly silence, given by nature, abundant as the air and equally omnipresent, has become extinct at all places of human habitation and has been replaced by the constant din of recorded and broadcast music.

Etta too craved quiet. After a noisy night out, her favorite expression, as she re-entered the Cheremoya cloister, was, "*Ah, le bon ordre du silence.*" For her the jukebox was the devil's invention just as, for her husband, a more modern, more sinister, more maddening spawn of the evil one was surely that disturbing presence known as Muzak.

Muzak drove Ingolf out of restaurants; it drove him crazy on airplanes. Michael Tilson Thomas remembers a period when all the Dahl students went around wearing "Muzzle Muzak" buttons. Ingolf refused to order textbooks at the campus bookstore because it was a subscriber to the hated system – which inflicted unwanted background sound on customers while simultaneously diminishing the efforts of the musicians who had recorded these same sounds in the first place. After his death I discovered that Ingolf had deposited in his Civil Liberties file an ad from the 3M company for its Cantata 700 Background Music System: "Educators are learning an important point from businessmen: properly programmed background music can relax or stimulate listeners as desired, can make them more receptive and attentive, can increase productivity and it can muffle distracting thought-interrupting noise." No better evidence for Ingolf's belief in the dehumanizing effects of this technological sub-species was needed. Yet when he protested at being bombarded by taped programs at the Salmon Lake Lodge in Sierra City the aggrieved proprietor responded that he was only offering to his customers a service similar to that provided by the Family Esterhazy or the Margrave of Brandenburg!

At the time I was rather amused by my parents discomfiture, regarding their protests as another sign of their eccentricity, their war with the world. But I could see that their suffering was genuine and as the years passed I found myself in many environments in which unwanted sound represented an intrusion which I grew to resent as bitterly as they had. I mocked no longer, but became at last a true son of these principled parents, firing off my own fair share of indignant letters and embracing my own share of disappointments in the process.

57. IN THE STEPS OF THE MASTER

Mountain expeditions in Southern California included an ever-shifting circle of part-time hiking companions, often including Ingolf's students, current and former. Just *which* students might be favored with an invitation to the hike remained a mystery whose pattern seems to have had no discernible rhythm. Students with whom my stepfather got along famously received no invitation; I'm sure I detected a note of regret in Michael Tilson Thomas' complaint that he had never made the list. On the other hand, some lesser fry turned up early on Saturday mornings for the ride though La Crescenta and La Canada and up the Angeles Crest highway. During the time I remained in Los Angeles one element in the trail mix may have been my own relationship with some of the other walkers. I was old enough to have friends among my stepfather's pupils and I would be insistent that a Paul Glass or a Donal Michalsky be phoned whenever an expedition was planned.

I do not remember walking with Frederick Lesemann, who became Ingolf's student in 1958, even though Rick must certainly be considered a Dahl protegé. Ingolf admired much of the music written by Rick, who assisted his mentor in many projects before joining the U.S.C. faculty himself. Douglas Talney, another student I knew only by name, also won Ingolf's admiration and, in 1960, during Lawrence Morton's leave of absence, Ingolf nominated Talney as interim administrator of the Monday Evening Concerts. My closest association with any of Ingolf's pupils, after Paul Glass' departure from the scene, was with Fred Myrow, who was actually my roommate and walking companion in 1960-1961, when I was living sans parents on Burnside Avenue during my second year in graduate school.

Another in a long line of Hollywood *wunderkinder*, Fred was a talented young composer who began to study with Ingolf at the age of seventeen, after spending some time under the tutelage of Darius Milhaud. Freddie was excellent company, full of boyish charm and wit, gifted in languages and other non-musical subjects. His grandfather was the famous music publisher Irving Mills, and his father was Joe Myrow, the song writer. The Myrows offered splendid hospitality in their Beverly Hills home and, when we had nagged him sufficiently, Fred's father would indulge our request for a rendition, on the living room piano, of his most famous hit, "You Make Me Feel So Young."

There was always a show biz aura surrounding Fred, who knew many people in the motion picture world – where he would soon be making his own way as a film composer. (At the Myrows I heard Fred's categorical assurance that Eddie Fisher would *never* leave Debbie Reynolds for Elizabeth Taylor.) Yvette Mimieux and Dennis Hopper, both in the infancy of their careers, were our guests during this bachelor pad period on Burnside and the studios were always trying to cook up a romance between Fred and Connie Francis ("Pop Meets Long Hair"). I note from one of Ingolf's diaries that Freddie was one of the guests invited to a "composers party" (along with other Dahl students like Ramiro Cortes, Mike Sahl, and Anthony Vazzana) which was held at Cheremoya on June 14, 1959; other guests included Halsey Stevens, William Bergsma, Leonard Rosenman, and Leo Smit. "Too many," the host concluded, "and I should have 'organized,' 'led' something, but fun anyway."

In the fall of 1959 a picture of Dmitri Shostakovich pouring over a score by Fred Myrow made the wire services. The occasion was a visit to Los Angeles in October by a group of Soviet composers, part of a good-will tour sponsored by the State Department. With only a week's notice, local musical organizations rushed to be ready, with Ingolf assuming a good deal of the responsibility for U.S.C.'s contribution and that of the Monday Evening Concerts, where he put together a special performance.

The visiting party included Fikret Amirov, Konstantin Dankevich, Tikhon Khrennikov, Boris Yarustovsky and two especially well known figures, Dmitri Kabalevsky and Dmitri Shostakovich. I recall standing outside Hancock Auditorium and having my hand pumped by both of the Dmitris who, I was informed, undoubtedly mistook me for one of the composition students they had met earlier.

The Russian composers heard the band rehearse a movement of the Dahl *Saxophone Concerto* and listened to a performance of the *Concerto A Tre*. Etta and Ingolf also accompanied the group to Disneyland. "They were wild for anything that whirled, raced, skimmed, floated, careened!" Etta recalled:

> But they also enjoyed the submarine ride (mermaids, sea monsters, sunken vessels, open buried treasure) and the "river" through the African jungle. When we passed dancing "natives" and the guide had to shoot a "dangerous crocodile," they clapped and yelled Bravo! While we waited for the little choo-choo to take us back to the main gate Dankewich made a heart-felt speech of thanks – you know: "better understanding..." "hope that..." "wonderful child-like spirit..." "charming wives" etc. etc.

During a panel discussion on the role of the composer it became clear, however, that there was a good deal of *mis*understanding. The standard by which the Soviet composers were obliged to judge a work of art – does it uplift and elevate the masses? – would clearly not be one in which Ingolf could find any comfort. Khrennikov argued that, "We regard it as absolutely inadmissible that a musician-composer would stand outside the movement toward humanitarian ideals and the uplifting of the masses," and Shostakovich described a piece of music he had heard at U.S.C. as "useful." "I think Shostakovich is paying inwardly for enforced simplicity," Etta observed astutely, "he is by nature quite otherwise."

At the end of the visit Ingolf gave a grateful Shostakovich a painting of the set done by the Stadttheatre's scenic designer for the 1936 production of *A Lady Macbeth of Mtsensk*. On the way to the airport Kabalevsky complained to John Crown that, "You seem to have either just hit tunes or music for musicians, nothing for the people." "Oh no," John replied mischievously, "We have lots of *conservative* music too."

Ingolf had the opportunity of seeing whether he was turning out conservative composers at a series of Student Symposia held annually by the West Coast music departments. These meetings often lead to despair – "Intellectually my sympathy lies with the Neutoner from the north," he wrote after the April, 1959 Symposium in Los Angeles, "but my ears or mind rejects their collectivism and chromaticism. And the people on my side of the fence bore me. Is there no way out?" On April 28, 1960 Ingolf joined a group of students in Rick Lesemann's car for the long drive to Provo, Utah, site of this year's Symposium. Such trips were always the occasion for fun; as the group returned to the car after viewing the Utah State Capitol someone shouted, "Last one in is a neo-classicist!"

Some of the group followed Ingolf to the ski slopes at Alta when the conference came to an end. There Ingolf cracked a rib. From comments made after the group had returned one could conclude, however, that the aesthetic injury had been more painful than the physical one. Writing to Lawrence Morton he summarized the B.Y.U. meeting by claiming that, "The John Cage latter day Dadaists have taken over. It was quite scandalous, in a depressing sort of way." In an undated fragment from this period the draft of a protest letter takes shape – "I realize there may be some schools which feel that the playground which they provide for the improvisation of their students should be extended to include the Symposium..." On April 27, 1961 Ingolf drove north with colleague Ellis Kohs for a Symposium at Berkeley. Here he met, twenty-nine years after their first encounter, his Paris friend Joaquin Nin-Culmell. At the concerts on April 29th Ingolf was particularly pleased by the contributions of his own students, Donald Aird, David Cohen, Harold Owen, and Roger Vaughan, but "Lesemann's *Trio* steals the show," he concluded. With many professional visits and one with Bill Colvig for good measure this had proven to be Ingolf's happiest Symposium outing.

On December 3, 1960 Ingolf took me and my two roommates, Brian Jenkins – a fellow U.C.L.A. history grad student – and, of course, Fred Myrow, on a hike to Monrovia Peak. The climb was an easy one, perhaps because this was Freddie's first encounter with outdoor adventure and, fearing a dose of over-protection, he had not even notified his protective parents of his participation in the expedition. We had reached the summit somewhat late in the day and Ingolf elected to take a more direct route back to the car, utilizing a fire road. The last part of our descent back to the canyon from which we had started was along a bare, trailless ridge which dropped rather rapidly. As we descended along the canyon wall we lost the sun behind the opposite ridge and had to inch our way down the steep slope in the darkness, Ingolf going ahead just a bit in order to find safe places for our feet. Fred, over-cautious and inexperienced, was negotiating much of this descent on his backside, losing the traction he might have enjoyed had he been leaning forward like the rest of us. He put a foot out to stand on what appeared to be a rock. It was not. In a second he had slipped past a horrified Ingolf. "Oh my God," the latter groaned. It was too dark to see anything but we did hear gasps and cries and the sound of falling rubble below. At last this stopped and we heard a moaning Fred trying to reassure us that he was still alive. He had tumbled some 300 feet, bouncing down the hillside at an extremely sharp angle, one which an anguished Ingolf duplicated in a few seconds of desperate scrambling as he tried to reach his fallen pupil.

By luck a ranger happened to be nearby and he helped Ingolf place some warm clothing over the stricken hiker. The ranger then ordered the remaining climbers to stay in our uncertain perches while he went to phone for medical assistance. Numb with worry Ingolf tried to keep a dazed Freddie in conversation, mistakenly calling him "John," and chatting away about Hoyle's theory of hydrogen atoms.

An ambulance took Fred away and (to admit to the most humiliating experience in my hiking career) the Sierra Madre Mountain Rescue Team, a bunch of volunteer amateurs, "rescued" Brian and me. They saw the whole outing as a chance to practice their roping techniques – which needed work; the rope they tied to my waist was too short and, while dangling in mid-air, I had to untie it in order to lower myself to the canyon floor. The exercise took about two and a half hours and we were now extremely cold, no doubt suffering from the shock of the accident and worried about our friend's injuries. We ascended a short dirt road in order to recover the car for the drive to the Sierra Madre hospital.

This we were unable to do because the car had been stolen! And with it, Fred's wallet and my own. The same sheriff who had filled out the accident report was flagged down so we could report the loss of our automobile. He let us get warm in his vehicle and drove us to the hospital himself. Initial x-rays indicated that Freddie might have a broken hip as well as other injuries. There was no restaurant in the town and the only food we could find was some cold chicken in a bar. Even Fred ate this, since the hospital had by this time closed its kitchen. I did not envy Ingolf the task of informing the Myrow parents about the incident, but they remained calm and cordial and a few hours later they arrived to give the rest of us a ride back to Los Angeles.

The next days were full of anxiety and discomfiture. Fred was transferred to Mt. Sinai for diagnosis. Carless, Ingolf had to depend on colleagues and students for rides. Then he borrowed a car from pianist Ronald Tarr, but its starter broke. And I had come back from the hike with a terrible case of poison oak.

Finally life began to improve. Freddie's doctors had discovered *no* broken bones and – with massive abrasions, a stiff neck, a twisted knee and, I believe, a draft deferment, my roommate emerged from hospital after a few days. Five days after the accident Jenny was discovered. Some kids had broken in just for a joy ride, coasted to the bottom of the mountains and abandoned her without stealing anything. On May 14, 1961, still limping slightly, Fred was back on the trail again (and again without informing his parents) for an ascent of Tahquitz Peak. He had survived Ingolf's most serious mountain disaster since that teenage expedition with Ferdi in the Alps, all those many years before.

58. IN ECLIPSE

In spite of the delight he experienced as the owner of a new Hollywood home, it is clear from the written records I later uncovered that – in all of the professional and artistic areas where he hoped to find satisfaction – Ingolf remained a disappointed man. At the university, on the concert stage, and especially at the worktable of his new studio, Ingolf's accomplishments often amounted to little more than a catalogue of frustrations. Or so he felt.

At U.S.C. he embraced a variety of responsibilities that brought him little reward and consumed far too much of his time. In the academic year 1960-1961 he filled in for Halsey Stevens as head of the Composition Department, accepting administrative burdens that he had usually managed to escape – though he often acted as head of Conducting as well.

In an era in which many of the most tortured passages in journals and correspondence express bitterness over career progress it is interesting to note that much of Ingolf's frustration was focused on his own university.

Here he found himself twisted in a knot of petty jealousies, complaining constantly not so much of the injustices of a fate which brought rewards to his colleagues (for he admired much of what they did) but of a destiny that robbed him of his own desserts. "Being beat, beat into the mud again," he complained in 1962, "try what I may, the things I do just don't *come off* right, and with Bob Linn they do."

The career of Halsey Stevens was still being held up whenever Ingolf wanted to lash out at his *own* "inadequacy." When Halsey told him, in November, 1958, of a proposed Boston performance of a Stevens composition, Ingolf recorded a bitter self-appraisal, "This is *arrival* – and I will never – ." In May, 1960 Halsey had to excuse himself from a meeting of the Theory Department because had a lunch date with George Szell – "that hurts," the green-eyed Ingolf admitted.

There are also a number of references to Ingolf's envy of Walter Ducloux, to whom he had at last yielded the University Orchestra. We find Ingolf at a party of the Friends of Music on November 23, 1958 where Ducloux is socializing with the "big brass" while my stepfather remains quietly in a corner, "hiding his light under a bushel," to use a phrase which Etta invoked whenever she felt it necessary to strike out at her husband's inability to propel his own career.

Ingolf, it is already fair to say, possessed a personality which was so laden with hidden and unresolved conflicts that it was never easy for him to switch on the politics of charm. Over and over it was his fate to watch more self-assured and socially confidant peers steel the limelight he craved. If a large crowd came to a Ducloux concert, if the orchestra played well without its old leader, Ingolf was envious. "I am again *consumed* with jealousy and envy," he wrote after watching his friend in action, "I had the *wrong* education, frittered away those years – did not have the repertoire, the conducting experience etc. I *should* have had – ." To add insult to injury, on March 1, 1959, Ingolf returned to conduct a contemporary concert at U.S.C., an arduous task considering the musical fare he had selected. When he arrived to face a very small crowd he discovered that the program listed Ducloux as the evening's conductor – "This hurts for a long time to come – ."

Ingolf's sense of grievance against his university reached a crescendo in 1960. On February 20 he was informed by Dean Raymond Kendall that he would *not* receive the sabbatical leave he had expected for the next academic year, having lost his place to two senior colleagues, one of whom was the dean himself. "I am really whopping mad about this cheapskate university of mine (the colleagues at U.C.L.A. don't get treated that way!)," an irate Ingolf wrote, a university "which would not even make the effort to dig up the money for a sabbatical for such a faithful teacher as myself, who needs it so badly."

To complicate matters, Ingolf was also invited at this time to be a visiting professor at Yale for the 1960-1961 academic year. He was tempted to use such an appointment as a way to establish a foothold in the world of East Coast music but – with his sabbatical now already two years behind schedule – he feared the consequences of losing his turn in line should he go to New Haven. On February 21, 1960 he wrote to Luther Noss, Dean of the Yale School of Music, to decline the invitation:

> The time has come when instead of courting success as a teacher (and a performer and conductor) I will have to court what may turn out to be failure as a composer. But rightly or wrongly, I have to take the more difficult, the less glamorous, the less profitable way (this sounds like a pose, but I don't think it is). It hurts to close doors – which have been so kindly opened to me and behind which such tempting prospects lie. But I have to open doors that lead inward and can only hope they they will not entirely refuse to budge.

Well, there is perhaps *some* posturing in this letter, but Ingolf's resentment over the shabby treatment he often experienced at his place of employment was genuine. And such frustration had its counterpart in his career as a performer too.

Ingolf's participation in the world of music making underwent something of an eclipse in the period 1958-1961. Some of this was certainly voluntary, for he knew, as he had written to Luther Noss, that he must limit such participation if her were to reserve more time for composition. But what he *did* do often brought him little joy, and to see others step into *his* limelight was also painful.

He made only five appearances in the 1958 concert season. He performed in a two-piano recital with John Crown at U.S.C. on October 5 and accompanied Eudice Shapiro in Pomona on November 2. Eudice was also one of his fellow players in a grueling recording session, spread over several days in late January, 1959, and devoted to music by Gail Kubik and William O. Smith. She then participated with Ingolf in a performance of the Dahl *Piano Quartet*, first at a Monday Evening Concert on February 2 and then at the San Francisco Composer's Forum on March 8, where the two also played the Stravinsky *Duo Concertante*. Ingolf's only other public appearance for the season was on the podium of an ill-fated March 1, 1959 contemporary music festival concert at U.S.C. Here Ingolf lead the school Orchestra is Milhaud's *Percussion Concerto*, Lukas Foss' *Ode*, and West Coast premieres of Berg's *Five Orchestral Songs* and a selection from Honegger's *Amphion*. (He had himself played in the percussion section during the *world* premiere of the latter work in Zurich, more than a quarter of a century earlier.) When he listened to a tape of the concert two months later he gave himself a pretty good review but added, "I *must* learn to get to the *depth* of a relaxed, filled tempo!!"

Ingolf made only four appearances on the local concert stage in the 1959-1960 season, and the last of these, a concert of the Collegium Musicum on July 15, 1960, was essentially an unreviewed private gathering. Because this was a period of time when Lawrence Morton was off in Europe doing his Stravinsky research the organization of the Monday Evening Concerts was divided among several program chairmen and Ingolf conducted two concerts during the season, including the inaugural offering on October 5, 1959, when he performed (from memory – because of a last-minute cancellation by Alice Ehlers) Bach's *Concerto in D Major* for harpsichord and strings, accompanied soprano Ella Lee in a Haydn cantata, and conducted Hindemith's *Concert Music* and the world premiere of Ernst Toch's *Music For Winds and Percussion*. A grateful Toch wrote to Ingolf:

> I feel the strong urge not only to thank you for all the effort and devotion you gave the performance of my piece but also to tell you my sincerest admiration for the outstanding rendition you achieved in the whole complicated concert...I want you to know how much I appreciate and enjoy the universality of your musicianship.

Albert Goldberg, the *L.A. Times* reviewer, gave the concert a rave notice, but Ingolf wrote to Lawrence, "I am so tired of half-rehearsed, half improvised concerts which under a great amount of tension have to be somehow 'pulled together' at the last moment. But I guess that's the only way it can be done." A performance of Lou Harrison's *Mass*, which Ingolf conducted on January 18, 1960, also failed to measure up – the choir didn't know the music, parts were illegible, and the instrumentalists "made some inexcusably wrong entrances."

On June 7, 1960 Ingolf participated in a performance of Stravinsky's *Les Noces* at Royce Hall. In this version (as in an earlier one in which Aaron Copland, Lukas Foss, Roger Sessions and Samuel Barber had been featured) four pianists substituted for the usual orchestral accompaniment. Stravinsky himself conducted, though Robert Craft had prepared the ensemble. Ingolf was joined in the piano section by Leonard Rosenman, Karl Kohn, and Leo Smit. As usual the event engendered in Ingolf that complex set of emotions which the presence of Stravinsky and Craft always invoked. On June 15, 1959 I had accompanied Ingolf to an earlier Stravinsky concert, also at Royce Hall. "The always breath-taking moment when he appears," Ingolf wrote, "smiling, bowing, great and small, intense." After the concert we went backstage, Ingolf hoping for a post-concert invitation to the home in which he had spent so many pleasurable hours during his apprenticeship. "And Bob at last asks us to come, so go and 'crash.' It is just great." I remember the evening well. This was perhaps not the first time I had met the maestro, but almost certainly the only time I had been a guest in Stravinsky's home. The old man kept refilling my Scotch glass and got me rather sloshed.

As for *Les Noces* Ingolf was more than upset to find himself in an auxiliary role. A number of times he had privately expressed his wish to conduct the work himself.

"He can be utterly charming, as you know," Etta had written of Bob Craft a few months before the concert, a sentence qualified by its first clause, "I'd like to shoot him myself." In her description of the Royce Hall concert she worked herself into a fine frenzy at Craft's expense, not neglecting to note, however, that Stravinsky's protége was feeling under the weather throughout the experience:

> The four pianists: Dahl, Rosenman, Kohn, and Smit were great but unhappy in rehearsal because the old man took everything too slowly and – alas! – doesn't really conduct anymore; he is physically strong enough, Thank God, for his age, but his movements are stiff and not sharply anticipating as they should be...In performance

the four pianists set the pace with Igor following and the chorus going along as best it could. I thought les quatres over did it, actually working a hardship on chorus and soloists...No one else seemed to feel this way...In rehearsal Bob was very insulting to the old man... When Igor came up to ask him something, Bob just let him stand there apologetically for four minutes while he (Bob) dressed down the percussion in dreadfully insulting language. Big mystery: granted that Igor has accepted Bob as son and guide, why does he also stand for being insulted, or doesn't he mind, and if not, is he masochistic in his old age?

My wife Dorothy remembered a Stravinsky concert at the County Museum of Art on Wilshire Boulevard during which calls of "Bravo!" following Craft's conducting sent a disgruntled Etta out into the courtyard in a minor fit of apoplexy. Ingolf never indulged in such outbursts, nor did he fail to record Bob Craft's virtues, but the tone of injury pervades many of his own comments. Recalling that he had read the third volume of the Craft-Stravinsky *Conversations* with such delight that he couldn't put it down, Ingolf added, "I dare say that there is much more of I.S. in Vol. 3 than there was in either of the other two."

Ingolf again made five concert appearances in the 1960-1961 season. One of these was also a Collegium concert, this time on May 24, 1961, and one, on the Berkeley campus, was as a last-minute substitute for conductor Gerhard Samuel in a December 29, 1960 concert featuring Marni Nixon in a program that included songs by Stravinsky and Ravel and Schoenberg's *Pierrot Lunaire*. "I am still too reserved," Ingolf reviewed his own performance, "although clean." Samuel, recovering from an automobile accident, attended the program and saw Ingolf's conducting as "meticulous, balanced, beautifully phrased – an intelligent overall view – a pure joy."

Ingolf also had the responsibility for the first of the season's Monday Evening Concerts, conducting Ramiro Cortes' *Chamber Concerto* and the Bach *Triple Concerto* (which he directed from the harpsichord) on October 17. Concert preparations were described to Lawrence as "a frantic last-minute patch job...in spite of all my efforts to get an early rehearsal start... But I feel such an old hand now at pulling things together." Four weeks after this concert Ingolf appeared on an NAACC program at U.S.C. in honor of Copland's sixtieth birthday. In a truly aleatoric gesture three pianists (Dahl, Lukas Foss, and Leo Smit) arrived on stage to throw a pair of dice by which Smit was eliminated as a performer, though he remained on stage to turn pages for Ingolf and Lukas in a performance of a four-hand arrangement of Copland's *Danzon Cubano*. On November 27 Ingolf made his last major local appearance before beginning his long-delayed second sabbatical. This was on an all-Dahl program at the Museum, also broadcast live by KFAC. With cellist George Neikrug, Ingolf played the *Duo*, Soprano Grace-Lynne Martin sang one of his earliest Zurich compositions, *Three Songs To Poems By Albert Ehrismann*, Ingolf and flutist Arthur Hoberman performed *Variations on an Air by Couperin* and an ensemble played the *Piano Quartet*. "What an effort," Ingolf wrote of this concert, adding the almost obligatory question, "for *what* returns?"

Only one other aspect of Ingolf's role as a performer in these years remains unexamined, though here the returns were immediate and spendable. After a number of years he took up again, on a fairly frequent basis, his role as studio musician. He knew many film composers and these friendships proved advantageous when it was time to hire keyboard players to record scores by David Raksin, Alex North, Jerome Moross, Jerry Goldsmith or Leonard Rosenman. Ingolf worked at Fox, Goldwyn Studios, Columbia, Universal, MGM, and the Todd A-O studios during this period. He rarely mentions the film he is working on in his journals, though North's *The Sound And the Fury* and Moross' *Huckleberry Finn* are listed. Ingolf did some recording for TV shows like *Twilight Zone* and spent many hours in the orchestra which provided the music for *Spartacus*. "I am sitting and writing this on the recording stage at Goldwyn Studios," he began a letter to Bill Colvig on June 13, 1960:

> The excellent pay seems to be in inverse proportion to the number of notes I have to play...Now I am sitting here counting rests...On the screen poor Spartacus and his friends are being crucified (I see that in the screen version they have given the picture a rather pre-Christian ending, although, as I read just yesterday in Anthony's Roman History book, Spartacus himself was killed on the battlefield...Had to stop here because I had to tinkle a few notes on the celeste (what a waste of the producer's money – because in the final dubbing it's going to be under dialogue and sound effects anyway, and besides – these notes are all doubled by the vibraphone, the harp, the

marimba, and god knows what else – speak of featherbedding – but of course I *can* use the money!)

Naturally, Ingolf was not able to give his own work in the studio orchestras full marks either. "It hits me stronger than ever," he noted after a session on May 19, 1959, "with everything I do there [is] just a little *something* wrong – nothing is every *completely* clean, realized, *controlled*." Such self-criticisms were mild, however, compared to the savage analysis he provided for his efforts as composer.

59. CONQUER MY OWN MOUNTAINS

When it was necessary for Ingolf to risk his fragile ego in any form of musical competition he always chose, with a certain persistent courage, to do so in the world of composition. In 1960 he challenged himself, on the ascent of Mt. Edith Cavell, with "serious questions about *why* I should, *can* go on with the mountains," adding that his foremost task was as a creator – "conquer my *own* mountains."

In the world of composition he pictured himself as a perpetual also-ran, even though not every bit of evidence sustains this image. An article on "Los Angeles: Culture Capital of the West" in a July, 1959 *San Francisco Examiner* rated Ingolf "one of America's top modern composers." John Edmunds, organizer of the New York Public Library's Composers Forum series, thanked Ingolf for suggesting West Coast composers by adding, "You would be delighted to hear the warm response from even disagreeable colleagues which the mention of your name always seems to evoke." In December, 1960 ASCAP announced its initial awards to "serious" musicians; Copland and Barber received the top award but Ingolf was among 39 other composers receiving $1250. In 1963's list he shared the top award of $2000 with a large number of other composers (including Rachmaninoff and Schoenberg, deceased). Even Ingolf could report an occasional triumph. At the University of Oregon summer festival in 1961 he crowed, "They tell me that I had a larger and considerably warmer audience than either Sessions or Foss, who were my predecessors."

Ingolf *could* savor a success in Eugene but Lukas Foss got invited to the Peppermint Lounge by Leonard Bernstein. There was an acute awareness on my stepfather's part that his efforts were at best peripheral. An article by Everett Helm on Los Angeles for a European music magazine failed to mention Ingolf at all in April, 1959 – "another bitter pill." Later that year Eric Salzman's *New York Times* review of the *Piano Quartet* carried the composer's name as Ingolf Dahn and informed the reader that the composer had "studied" a number of summers at Tanglewood. When no press showed up to review the Monday Evening Concert performance that he had arranged for the Soviet composers Ingolf wrote to Lawrence Morton, "My frustration: the *best* things I do are wasted, futile." Commenting on a U.C.L.A. Festival concert on June 3, 1961 Ingolf groaned – "all that's going on and I *so* on the outside."

Ingolf may have giggled over John Crown's characterization of Soviet music as "conservative," but he was also aware of an irony. What may have seemed like "music for musicians" in Russia *did* sound hopelessly conservative to those "composers" who twiddled the buttons in the sound factories of Darmstadt or Princeton.

His position within the musical world was again being undermined by new forces which he was quick to recognize as a threat to his own vision of style and his own definition of the role of the composer. He had made some accommodation with serial techniques, but with that wide range of compositional gestures which we associate with improvisation, chance, and electronic music Ingolf Dahl stood inflexibly and vocally opposed. When Lukas Foss began to write scores which required instrumentalists to improvise, Ingolf grew uncomfortable. A draft of a letter to Lukas begins:

> After having just listened to the Time Cycle for the fourth time I am just impelled to write a little note to you. Hastily, impulsively, and probably containing words which I might regret later on, but such is the nature of impulse. This music contains some of the most hauntingly beautiful pages that not only you have written but that anybody has written in our time. There are pages that are just pure unadulterated, unmistakable Foss – and here is a question: *Why* then did you find it necessary...to dilute what is strongest in you, and in which you are the strongest, with ideas that are undoubtedly fashionable, and even in their smart way attractive, but not much else?

Ingolf denounced "latter day Wagnerisms" in the work and told his friend that in listening to the composition he now skipped the improvised interludes altogether.

Anything which might remove the control of the composer in order to leave room for accident or realization by chance was, for Ingolf, not an act of liberation but one of dehumanization. He was not amused by John Cage or by electronic music, synthesized or taped. Though he knew it could produce some intriguing sounds, these techniques failed to inspire any lasting affection. It's easy to catch an echo of Ingolf's reactions to the many challenges now represented by the European avant-garde in the comments of one of his own students, Donal Michalsky, who went from the classroom at U.S.C. to study with Wolfgang Fortner in Freiburg in 1958:

> If you have been reading "Melos" you can do without my telling you that unless you are standing before an electronic music device you are not composing "live music of today" or if you haven't embraced the Webern-Boulez-Nono school you are a "dilettante" as Fortner referred to my partita after hearing it. He told me that it is very pretty music and nothing wrong with it except that he would not condone such work as fitting a student of his. He told me that I should experiment with 12 tone rows etc. – my music is not now. (I guess he means it is just simply music!)

On December 1, 1958 a concert of Karlheinz Stockhausen's music was given in Schoenberg Hall. On the previous day Ingolf had taken the composer and others on a long ride along the Angeles Crest Highway for a picnic at Cajon Pass. But Ingolf was certainly not a Stockhausen enthusiast or a devotee of "double-talk a la Darmstadt," and he found the German composer's report on this visit to Los Angeles in a 1960 *Melos* (in which Robert Craft was referred to as *the* conductor of the Monday Evening Concerts) "malicious and tactless."

As a composer it was easier for Ingolf to know which road to reject than which to follow. Writing to Bill Colvig in 1960 he summarized his position:

> The problem is that now a composer with each piece has to create even the syntax of a new work before everything else. To make

bricks long before one can even *begin* the actual architecture. There was a time (Concerto a Tre, or Brass Piece) when I was much more naive and surer and happier than I am now. – But I have to stick to it now and keep plugging along and try not to get discouraged after crossing out pages of sketches…If there is anything I *don't* have it is facility. I envy the solid 12-tone writers or neo-classicists their assurance. (In the way, probably, in which Catholics are envied by some for their *unquestioned,* solid reliance on their faith).

"What kind of music does the world want from me?" Ingolf asked on May 13, 1961, "that I can write?" "I don't feel well with the chromaticism of the 12 tone and the kind of pre-arranged approach," he added in September, "but the neo-classical harmony *bores* me." Increasingly Ingolf found himself isolated in his opposition to many of the trends which affected music in the 1960's. I remember there was considerable family annoyance when the Babitzes urged him to "get with it" in some musical matter but, curiously, the same phrase appears in Ingolf's journal in June, 1962. He had been listening to a concert of beloved vintage Stravinsky – "Horror, I am not with it – the incessant motor, the mannerisms – some of it stale and puny – What else *is* there for me?"

What he assumed to be a dependency on his mentor gnawed at his self-respect. He admired Rico Lebrun's painting because he felt the artist had overcome Picasso *"organically* from the *inside*! If I could only do that with I.S." Meanwhile the master was taking paths which Ingolf hesitated to follow:

> I have just received a score of Igor's latest (Cantata for Paul Sacher) and must confess I'm most distressed! It is just regulation-type Webern, and seems so without any of the spark and individuality that always characterized *all* his works! Such dreary factory-made sounds and rhythms (and *who* cares through how many notations he put his rows and rhythmic cells!…Only the third piece, dedicated to Father McLane, seems to have a little more *real* stuff to it. *What* is one to think and feel? I realize of course that this is the way Paul Rosenfeld felt about him in 1925, but at least then he wasn't imitating a bunch of Beatnik Post-Webernites.

Whenever the muse was hard to pin to the mat Ingolf found time to revise *earlier* compositions and in these years he found the opportunity to bring a number of partially finished projects to completion. The *Cello Duo* was revised in 1959. *Fanfares* was revised for a piano recital given by Lillian Steuber at U.S.C. on December 13, 1959. *Allegro and Arioso* was finally accepted for publication by McGinnis & Marx in 1960 and the piano reduction of the Dahl-Szigeti reconstruction of the Bach *D Minor Concerto* was published by Boosey & Hawkes in 1961. Ingolf revised the *Saxophone Concerto* in 1959 – "Due to cuts," he reported to Sigurd Rascher, "the proportions are much improved – originally I got carried away, understandably, by the delight in sonorities and the exploration of possibilities." *The Tower of St. Barbara* was revised for a concert by the U.S.C. Orchestra in 1960. "The piece will gain enormously be being not so discursive," Ingolf wrote Lawrence Morton. "There is something!" he reported happily in 1962, when he played the work through for Willie Hausslein.

The *Piano Quartet* was revised several times in advance of a Tanglewood performance in July, 1959. "*How* big an egg did it lay?" a worried composer asked as he awaited critical reactions. In fact Eric Salzman *was* rather negative in the *New York Times* but other evidence of the success of the piece continued to emerge. Copland wrote, "I myself was well impressed with the way the piece sounded. You were obviously working in an ambitious way and I think you carried it off with real flair." Karl Kohn called the piece a "superb and beautiful work," and, reviewing a performance in March, 1959, Alfred Frankenstein in the *San Francisco Chronicle* said, "Dahl's Piano Quartet...is a work of great eloquence, brilliant and inventive in its varied approaches to the medium." Ingolf completed another revision early in 1961 and it was performed at the University of Michigan's Contemporary Music Festival that spring. Wallace Berry, one of the performers, wrote Ingolf that:

> Your work was easily the best received of all that we played. I am especially pleased that members of the audience who expressed the deepest satisfaction with the Quartet ranged, in musical sophistication, from the most naive among our students and community concert-goers to the most sensitive and discriminating of our faculty...We who played the piece enjoyed it enormously (despite stubborn initial resistance from the cellist)...I have the greatest respect for your Quartet; it is moving, exhilarating, forceful. And difficult.

As gladdened as Ingolf must have been by such reactions nothing could compensate for his failure to bring new composition projects to fruition, nothing could ease the pain he experienced in wrestling with works that were never to see the light of day. In this stillborn category it is necessary to list a Chamber Symphony, which Ingolf worked at with little success from 1959 to 1961. "*Nothing* will come, I am absolutely desperate. I am *not* a composer, a faker, an imitator, a copyist – where to go, what to do?" – this plaint of March 18, 1960 typifies Ingolf's despair as he worked on the Chamber Symphony. "This situation is critical," he added on August 25, "and I try to fight it, but after five minutes of musical concentration, *bang*, the switch is turned off and I go off – ." "To refresh my vocabulary," he wrote to Lawrence the same day, "I am using a tonal row, and I feel like St. George fighting with the Dragon (with the work as the Virgin to be saved.)" To Bill Colvig he added, "I am telling myself that these things have happened before and that I've been able to overcome worse difficulties in the past, and that the thing to do is just keep slugging and try to keep going, inch by inch, each foothold and handhold at a time, just as in climbing a difficult mountain – but this is indeed a difficult time for composing music." In the end we have a rare instance of complete and total failure, the virgin perished, the peak unscaled.

Ingolf did complete three works during his first three years at Cheremoya. The first of these, a piano solo entitled *Sonata Pastorale*, was begun at the Hartford Foundation in July, 1958. We find him trying to return to the project the following March – "I must learn to concentrate, keep at it, not to digress constantly! That goddam wavering mind, no matter *what* I do –." "What nonsense did I do yesterday?" he asked on March 29, "After reading it through, get *so* depressed, there is just nothing in me now. Out of touch, out of invention, out of newness." Writing to Lawrence in November, 1959 he described the work as:

> Four short movements (the third is the reworking of a little thing I did years ago for Boulanger). It is simple, not difficult, and all in A major or related keys, so I should go into the routine apologies now about not writing "modern" music, but I will spare you these...But just to keep my franchise (or to keep my composing "visa" validated) there is hidden in the last movement, which is strictly D major, a real,

honest to goodness REIHE [row], which is consistently, discretely hidden, noticeable to nobody but myself...I am happy with it, I think it has a real "tone" and, whatever else one may say about it, it is *very* carefully written, but not academically so.

The four movements were intended to explore the musical ramifications of the term "pastorale" and in the last (a *fete champetre*) an outdoor festival is invoked in which characters from the Commedia Dell'Arte make an appearance. Ingolf described the sonata as "outgoing and direct" in nature, "a happier and lighter counterpart or companion piece to the *Sonata Seria*."

He agreed to give the premiere performance himself as part of his duties at Southern Illinois University's Contemporary Arts in America Festival in February, 1960. This he did with some embarrassment – since he had promised this honor to John Crown, to whom the work is dedicated; consequently this Illinois performance was not advertised in Southern California until after Crown's "first" performance.

Ingolf left for Carbondale on February 11. Over the next four days a number of events were held in his honor and a number of his pieces were performed. Ingolf conducted the Brass Piece ("I still like it") and played the *Sonata Seria* as well as the newer *Sonata Pastorale*. Of the former piece, Ingolf wrote, "It seemed to have made a deep impression, certainly on the musicians and the composers, but not only on them...I must confess that the older the piece gets the better it gets – it is *real* music in every note and sometimes I despair of ever being able to do something like it again." Ingolf gave a number of lectures at Southern Illinois and, in all, made such an impression that three graduate students in composition announced that they wanted to come to U.S.C.

John Crown presented the *Sonata Pastorale* to Los Angeles audiences at a Monday Evening Concert on April 17, 1961. "It's a big hit," Ingolf reported. Walter Arlen, in the *L.A. Times*, added, "Mr. Dahl's idiom is, of course, concise, compact, and entirely contemporary, but never harsh or self-consciously avant-garde. He solved the modern composer's problems brilliantly indeed by being fully himself and putting down only those notes he felt served his purpose rather than fashion." Peter Yates wrote to Ingolf, "I think one can count on one's fingers the number of successful piano sonatas written during the 20th century. Since Bartok's sonata in 1926 I doubt a half-dozen passable piano sonatas have appeared. Yours seems to me assuredly one of these...This is one of the few grand and unpretentiously grand piano sonatas of recent times." The *Sonata Pastorale* was published in 1971 by Southern Music Publishing Company and recorded by Charles Fierro in 1975.

The *Serenade For Four Flutes* was on the worktable as Ingolf prepared for his trip to Southern Illinois. "Morning *Start Working* on Flute Quartet," he wrote on February 1, 1960, "but it is like forcing mountains aside – every note is a problem, there is no flow, no continuity, no direction, no conviction – just force a few notes on paper – am so discouraged and disgusted with myself." The following month the picture had changed. Ingolf was happy with his work on the Serenade, and feeling guilty about such happiness. To Lawrence he noted:

> I am in a pretty low state right now. The work on the Chamber Symphony leads absolutely nowhere, obstacles are overwhelming, I am consumed by doubts, dissatisfactions, etc. – am also working on a little Flute Serenade for diversion – and it *does* divert me, but I hardly sit down to it but some urgent university or teaching chore has to be done (or gnaws on the inside and does not leave me in peace) and besides I'm doing it with a bad conscience, because the Chamber Symphony is the *big* thing, and that *has* to be done, but it won't budge.

A premiere of the *Serenade For Four Flutes* was offered at U.S.C. on May 2 and Ingolf began revision almost immediately. "Work on Serenade," the entry for July 2 begins, "Get stuck in another mystery story, finish. Oh, what a waste." The Serenade, dedicated to Doriot Anthony Dwyer, was described by the composer as a work in a "moderate, contemporary" idiom; it was clearly intended as "entertainment music." Ingolf's confidence in the work's commercial potential seems to have been sustained in the years that followed publication by Boosey & Hawkes in 1963. Hundreds of copies have been bought by flute students, it would appear, but it is one of a number of Dahl compositions that I have never heard performed myself.

Ingolf had worked briefly on a serenade for band in 1959 but progress on the composition later called *Sinfonietta* did not begin in earnest until January, 1961, after Ingolf had accepted an $800 commission (of which $682.39 went to the copyist) from the Western and Northwestern Regions of the College Band Directors' National Association. "I am not even able to keep a *fraction* of each day's assignment," he reported on January 8, 1961, "all the usual terribly awful depression follows." On the 14th he took advantage of a hot clear morning to abandon his work table and walk barefoot in the hills – "One can see the waves glittering... run all the way back – feel physically grand, shower, beer and late nap. Evening it goes better and get farther into the line-up of the first movement." Ingolf "finished" the work in April but revisions were inevitable, many prompted by his listening to a tape of the premiere performance by William Schaefer and the Trojan Symphonic Band on January 12, 1962.

Something of Ingolf's intentions in the *Sinfonietta* can be derived from extensive notes he prepared in 1964:

> I wanted it to be a piece that, without apologies for the medium, would take its place alongside symphonic works of any other kind. But in addition I hoped also to make it a "light" piece, something in the serenade style, serenade "tone," and perhaps also form,...You will remember that in many classical serenades the music begins and ends with movements which are idealized marches, as if the musicians were to come to the performance and then, at the end, walk off again...it was this tradition which motivated at least the details of the beginning and ending of the "Sinfonietta."

Ingolf's continuing affection for the sense of order he found in the classical period of music may also have affected another compositional gesture: "The form of the whole 'Sinfonietta' is that of a very large bridge or arch form. The sections of the first movement correspond in reverse order and even in some details to the sections of the last...the thematic material that closes the first movement opens, in varied form, the third. The middle movement, a pastorale nocturne, is also shaped like an arch." At the very center of the piece Ingolf included a gavotte-like section derived from excised portions of the *Saxophone Concerto*. Finally, he noted that in spite of its tonal-consonant nature, the first and third movements of the work were based on a six-note row. Thus we have in the *Sinfonietta* a combination of all of his stylistic interests, some more recent than others.

In its revised form the *Sinfonietta* proved to be a particularly successful work, one often selected by band directors looking for a showpiece. Reviews were good, if occasionally overblown ("His exploitation of the meaningful effects which lie waiting to be used in a big wind band were enough to make Berlioz himself envious"). The Eastman Wind Ensemble, under Donald Hunsberger, toured with the work in 1968, the year they recorded it for Decca and the *Sinfonietta* was published by Alexander Broude the following year.

60. TRIO

Etta was not at the airport on February 15, 1960, the day Ingolf, "dizzy with fatigue," stepped from the plane which brought him back from Southern Illinois University, a journey made sour by soupy muzak leaking from the loudspeakers over every seat. "Where's mother?" he asked, surprised to see me alone. "She has another cancer," I had to tell him, "and she has to have an operation tomorrow." There were tears in our eyes as we waited for Ingolf's baggage. As he pulled out a pack of cigarettes I asked him for one – and I didn't smoke. "Where?" he asked at last. I named the hospital. "No, where is the cancer?" he asked again. "The other breast," I replied, "the right one." Ingolf was stunned by the swiftness of this calamity; Etta had only learned the awful news four days before, but she had decided not to worry her husband just as he was about to undertake his Illinois trip. He now had to stumble through his teaching schedule that afternoon at the university and when the couple were reunited that evening in our kitchen there were more tears. "You tell me to trust in God," Etta said to him, "You, who are always telling us there is no God."

I recall that those hours I spent walking up and down the Cheremoya living room on the day of the operation, waiting to hear how the surgery had progressed, were among the worst I have ever experienced. "The operation was successful and the doctor is satisfied," Ingolf reported to Bill Colvig a month later, "They were able to remove everything (but what a frightening threat to hang above her future –)."

Etta's recuperation time was slower on this occasion for she had not been in the best of physical condition. She was tired. For six months she had suffered from unexplained fits of shivering, refusing to take the time to discover the cause of this malady (later diagnosed as anemia and cured with iron). Much of the spring was now spent in convalescence and fortunately I was able to provide some of the care which my absence in New York had precluded in 1958. By June Etta was reporting herself in splendid health. With amazing reserves of fortitude she pulled herself together and plunged back into life – though her arm movement, her ability to carry things, was even more severely limited. I remember her chipper patter as she hopped aboard the bus to Beverly Hills, where she had agreed to let Dr. Cutler photograph the "mangled old bag" for a textbook illustration of the double mastectomy. I also remember calling Ingolf aside in great solemnity in order to ask him *not* to take Etta to see *Psycho*, with its horrifying depiction of the knife wielded against Janet Leigh's chest. Once I heard my mother, in a less brave mood, say, "I want my breasts back."

For Etta, normal life meant continued progress on her doctoral dissertation, the culmination of the graduate studies upon which she had been engaged for a decade. Twice she had been forced to ask for extensions but neither hepatitis nor cancer had succeeded in undermining that dogged perseverance for which she was justly celebrated among her friends. Twice during holiday times Joan Schaefer helped her obtain quiet dormitory housing at U.S.C. so that she could concentrate on the thesis project without worrying about the care and feeding of the Cheremoya males. On September 1, 1960, while Ingolf was stewing in his studio over a revision of the *Piano Quartet*, Etta rushed in to announce, "It's done!" Revision and typing followed and the dissertation left her hands on February 14, 1961. Her final oral took place on May 22; I attended this ceremony myself, though not Etta's commencement on June 8, "crap and gown" day as she called it, an event spoiled for her because U.S.C. chose the same ceremony to award an honorary degree to Pat Nixon.

"Grimmelshausen's 'Simplicissimus': A Study of A Critical Deformation" provided Etta with another opportunity to illustrate the foolishness of man – represented in this case by the authors of 160 secondary sources, most of whom had been so anxious to characterize Grimmelshausen's work as a typical 17th century developmental novel that, according to Etta, they had failed to note that Simplicissimus (who, by chance had also undertaken a pilgrimage to Einsiedeln) fails to make much of an advance on the misanthropy, vanity, and deceitfulness that are *constant* elements in his character. Etta enjoyed a good polemic. She could exist for days in the afterglow of a quarrel with her professors over whether it was proper to use the adjective "edenic." It was; she did. *Now* there was a chance to show up the *Encyclopedia Britannica*, to attack "scholars of wide reputation but less than satisfactory scholarship" for their inconsistent, presumptuous, arbitrary, and incomprehensible interpretation of the text itself (when they had bothered to look at it all). The shortcomings of these chaps served as the intellectual fodder of our family mealtimes for years.

There is considerable evidence that Ingolf resented the time invested by his wife in this scholarly project. "How *can* she get finished?" he asked on December 19, 1959, "Wish it were over." The following March, as Etta was recovering from her second surgery, the two celebrated their twentieth wedding anniversary at a Chinese restaurant in Van Nuys. Haunted by his own lack of progress on the Chamber Symphony, Ingolf burst into tears, resisting Etta's attempts to discuss the nature of his emotional crisis. But the following December, as Etta was struggling through the final revision of *her* dissertation, a self-absorbed Ingolf noted "another E. crisis (which *now* I can't face) is in the works."

Ingolf's emotional state and his general physical condition continued to ascend the peaks and to drop into the valleys. His hiking and skiing were augmented by running, weight lifting and swimming in the campus pool. But there were also numerous chest complaints, asthma is mentioned several times, gout returned, his neck gave him trouble, strep throat and tonsillitis plagued him. I think Ingolf baffled his doctors to some extent; his recurrent episodes of fatigue, double vision, and dizziness could never be traced to a specific organic cause. "The news is very disturbing," he announced after a medical visit on September 15, 1959, "basal and other tests are all just *fine* – then what makes me feel so unfunctioning?" I note that Ingolf was rejected as a blood donor during this period because he failed to pass a hemoglobin test.

I wish I could propose a more comprehensive explanation for Ingolf's periods of general exhaustion, but I have to believe they were psychological in origin, and that they can be seen as a counterpoint to the creative paralysis that afflicted him at the same time. But it is not easy to find a specific trigger in the daily events that preceded such incidents, any more than we can say precisely what caused my stepfather to burst into tears at a performance of Bruckner's *Eighth* on March 23, 1961 – "deeply moved," he wrote, "as only music can do it (oh what have we lost)."

In spite of the trauma of these years my parents did continue much of their normal activity together, their trips to Joshua Tree and San Francisco in 1959, to Baja in 1960, their walks in Bronson Canyon, their dinners at the Nine Muses restaurant, their scrabble evenings, And they continued their love life. On Ingolf's forty-seventh birthday, June 9, 1959, he noted that his fifty-four year old wife "comes to wake me." "Etta wakes me and it is just lovely...as fresh as always," he added on October 9 of the same year. "Etta wakes me," he concluded three months after the second surgery, that is on May 27, 1960, "it takes a little time, but then just great."

Not so great, at least from Etta's perspective, was a visit from her mother-in-law, who arrived for a three-month stay in December, 1958. Mammi came to her son's lectures, to Collegium classes, to his concerts, he took her to the beach, the mountains, even to San Francisco. Mammi made a wonderful impression on everyone with her good English and Scandinavian charm, but Etta was not amused to see her husband drawn backward in time by this arch-fantasist. Even I earned a black mark from Ingolf for malingering at the time of the Yuletide festivities which he lovingly staged in honor of his mother's visit and his own youth. Much of the task of keeping Mammi amused (and out of Etta's hair) fell to me, since I continued to live with my parents until the fall of 1960.

Needless to say I should have found a way to establish a separate identity long before age twenty-two, when I moved away to join Freddie and Brian on Burnside for a year, but I found life at Cheremoya to be exceedingly comfortable and I continued to use the house as a home base. I graduated from U.C.L.A. in 1959 and spent a year working on a masters program in history while completing my student teaching at University High School and John Burroughs Junior High and earning my General Secondary teaching credential from the State of California. I switched to the doctoral program at U.C.L.A. in the fall of 1960. Early in 1959 Donald Factor and I (assisted by several friends including Leigh Peffer and John Daly) distributed the first issue of a little magazine that I would continue to edit for the next three years, *Nomad*. I participated actively in the Los Angeles poetry scene and developed a large number of new friends and contacts through my work (this also explains Lawrence Ferlinghetti's presence in our living room), spending most of my summers for a number of years among the avant-garde poets of New York.

In 1959, a rare Los Angeles summer for me, Ingolf wrote to Bill Colvig:

> I began to feel sorry for Anthony, who had been slaving away at dull school work all year, and now is doing more of the same in Summer School. I knew that if I wouldn't take him outdoors he would not go, so finally I suggested a Sierra trip to him and I am happy to say that he is getting very enthusiastic about it and I know it will do him good, so all that makes me feel like a good father.

Hiking, in fact, continued to be one of our most enjoyable forms of time together (not counting the Scrabble evenings in which I would invariably best my proud parents). Perhaps because I now had more of a life outside the house I was less resentful of the unusual schedule which made one member of our family so frequently late or absent. Ingolf had long ago given up any hope that I might develop any musical talents of my own and the only way that I could please him in anything remotely resembling this category of endeavor was my ability to identify, from a few bars, almost any piece of classical music that floated from the car radio. Of course KFAC had a rather limited repertoire but it never ceased to amaze Ingolf that I could outguess him on occasion. He also let me know, and not so subtly, that my academic interest, history at the time, was surely not as worthwhile as some study in the arts might have been. He never understood the essential fact that perhaps I had chosen a topic and developed my talents in alien fields of endeavor precisely because I wanted to be judged by standards that had not been set by my stepfather.

I spent a great deal of time with Etta at Cheremoya; I sensed her loneliness, her isolation in our hillside retreat. Ingolf wrote to Lawrence, soon after the second surgery, "Just wanted to mention that all through the last weeks Anthony has been just wonderful. A real man, with maturity, consideration, helpfulness. He was a great support to Etta during my absence, and a great help after our return." Even after moving to Burnside I returned frequently to 2486 for meals or social gatherings. "Evening talk with Anthony who is visiting," Ingolf noted on April 16, 1961, "and whose company is so pleasant." I make note of this pacific period in my relationship with Ingolf and Etta because there remained one additional bad patch – still to be endured by all of us shortly.

61. THE ROVERS RETURN

On April 12, 1960 Ingolf was awarded a second Guggenheim Fellowship. He had named Goffredo Petrassi, Carlos Chavez, Ernst Krenek, Ernst Toch, Roger Sessions, Lukas Foss, and two faculty members at U.C.L.A., Robert U. Nelson and John Vincent, as his sponsors. He then had to ask for a year's postponement so that the award could coincide with his second sabbatical, which was scheduled – two years late according to his calculations – for 1961.

A long period of travel began on June 24, first with a week in San Francisco and then with a two week assignment at the University of Oregon's Academy of Contemporary Arts, where he joined dancer Erick Hawkins and sculptor Theodore Roszak as guest artists. Ingolf gave eight lectures during the session, including many he had worked on before – "Quality Judgments," "Music and Pictorial Expressionism," "Art and Artists Around Stravinsky," and "Recent Trends in European Music." He lectured on Stravinsky's *Symphony in C* and gave a piano recital featuring works by Ruggles, Copland, and Shapero. On July 6 there was an all-Dahl concert which drained away considerable energy. Ingolf played *Hymn and Toccata* and, as we have seen, the *Sonata Pastorale*. He also conducted the *Music For Brass Instruments*; the *Serenade For Four Flutes* and the *Couperin Variations* were also performed. Ingolf seems to have enjoyed considerable success in Eugene, where access to mountain scenery would also have been an attraction.

On July 8 he flew to New York, spending several days in professional conferences. This was also a period in which he and I spent some time together in my summer home away from home. I took him with me to the country to visit some of my friends and also to some of my favorite Village haunts. On July 15 I helped him shop for meat – which he proposed to smuggle into Iceland for his sister and her family. Etta, now arrived from Los Angeles, secreted some of this carnivore's treasure in the lining and sleeves of his overcoat before I accompanied my parents as far as the Eastside coach terminal, where we parted for the year.

They discovered that they were *not* overweight, as they always feared, when they checked in at Icelandic Airlines – Ingolf in his heavy boots and meat-stuffed overcoat and Etta in her red three-piece wool suit, but there would be a *ten*-hour delay. Ingolf went upstairs to have a nap and a few hours later a puzzled clerk at Iberian Airways woke him with an inquiry, "Sorry sir, is this your salami?" Etta's sewing had come undone and one of the precious meat parcels had rolled over the edge of the balcony and plummeted like a bomb onto the desk of the Spanish airline. At last these gypsies were able to make their way onto the aircraft, Etta clutching her husband's ice axe.

The salami, the canned ham, and the sausages were received with enthusiasm the next afternoon in Reykjavik but the Dahls insisted on eating fish at the Björnsons', where they stayed two nights. Ingolf had his picture taken next to a statue of the first Ingolf, and the visitors went to see geysers and have a picnic on the lava. "Not a second alone with Py," Ingolf complained, though he did have a brief chance for a talk with his sister ("lovelier than ever") on July 18, the morning of the Dahl's departure for Gothenberg.

There Gunnar Lindblom took them to Odsmal so that Ingolf could visit his Aunt Clara and Uncle Henrik. "Sweden is the best," the Californian enthused – in spite of the rain that followed them most of the way to Stockholm the next day. A few crowded days of sightseeing and museum-going followed. Ingolf pronounced the Swedish capital "heavenly," though he did grumble that parts of the town were succumbing to modern anonymity. At home there was a difficult family crisis. "Mammi alone is quite a trial," he was forced to admit, "but Etta and Mammi together is impossible. Etta is at her worst around Mammi." Ingolf slept in the bed in which Pappi had died while Etta refused to get out of hers on July 20. On the 22nd mother and son went alone to Visby while Etta remained behind with Holger and Aina.

Ingolf and Mammi were reliving a portion of his farewell journey of 1938. They remained in the medieval city for four days, staying at a simple *pension*, and during the day there was swimming and touring. Ingolf was horrified at the traffic, the congestion and the noise. Bored Swedish teenagers used the narrow streets for drag races. Transistors blared everywhere, even on the buses. The band in the park played Ferde Grofé and Leonard Bernstein against a backdrop of town wall and sea. Back in

Stockholm Ingolf spent a day at the home of Karl-Birger Blomdahl; the composer of the space opera *Aniara* was described as "quite a guy."

On July 28, riding with Holger and Aina, the Dahls began a long journey south, traveling through Denmark and Germany. Ingolf visited the Mariakirche in Lubeck: "To see *this* again...much moved." Two nights were spent in Reinbeck, near Hamburg, and on July 30, "the exorcizing day," Ingolf and Etta took the train into the city of his birth. They visited an Ingres exhibition at the Kunsthalle, took a ferry on the Alster and a taxi to Gross Borstel where they walked along Violastrasse and Holunderweg. At night they went to the theater. "All this day," Ingolf concluded, "nothing cuts deep, touches closely – it is as if all this middle-European 'foreign scenery' had happened to someone else, of whom I've been told." In Hamburg, it seems, even the prince of nostalgia remained immune. By August 1 the Dahls had reached Strasbourg, parted from the Marcuses for a while and exchanged German impressions for French. Somewhere en route a distracted Etta lost her handbag,

"France-Strasbourg-miserable expensive hotel opposite station...all is so dirty and unpleasant and inefficient," Ingolf complained. The next day the Dahls revisited the cathedral, but Ingolf was too restless to enjoy it. In the afternoon they took the train to Paris. Ingolf had a miserable time in a phone booth trying to line up a hotel while Etta, keeping an eye on the luggage, stood disconsolately outside, still clutching the ice axe. On August 3 the couple took delivery on a new Peugeot 404, an anonymous grey vehicle whose color had been specifically selected by my parents because this was a shade least likely to reveal the layers of dust with which it would be encrusted in Beachwood Canyon. The car remained parked outside the Hotel Danube for the next few days while the Dahls, not daring to risk its fenders in Parisian traffic, walked all over the city, visiting museums. The Museum of Modern Art got a bad review – "both the selection and the exhibition methods were poor," Etta reported. After all the tramping about, her feet were beginning to give her trouble. The two bought a copy of *Le Malade Imaginaire* and read a part of it in the Luxembourg Gardens before going to a performance in the Tuilleries later that night. The next morning, August 6, feeling "childishly grand" in their own car, they began a tour of the cathedrals and castles of Burgundy, arriving in Zurich two days later, following another (unspecified) "crisis" with Etta.

After visits with the Swiss relatives the Dahls drove to their previous sabbatical home in Schruns and surprised Frau Netzer and her son Werner with a brief visit. "Very excited as drive up Montafon, back again, and the heart opens up," Ingolf reported. He had intended to undertake at least one mountaineering expedition while in Schruns but the weather was disappointing and after five days in Austria the Dahls returned to Switzerland. Here Etta remained in Lausanne while Ingolf, rejoined by Holger, took the train to Zermatt where, on Monday, August 21, 1961, in fulfillment of a lifetime's ambition, they climbed the Matterhorn.

The experience was traumatic. The brothers each had a guide, the brothers Eddy and Egon Petrig. Unfortunately, Ingolf later complained, Eddy proved to be one of the best in Zermatt, "an absolutely crackerjack guide, young, brilliant. He was bored with the Matterhorn, with me and my slow pace, and very quickly proceeded to fill me with the worst inferiority complexes, and subsequently brought out the worst in me." The marvelous experience of ascending the famous pyramid on a clear day was thus spoiled for Ingolf by his companion. "I have never climbed more miserably in my life and you know the vicious circle," he wrote to Bill Colvig, "the worse I climbed the angrier he got, and so he destroyed even more of the little self-confidence I had. He went very fast, which on the way up was undoubtedly necessary, but on the way down I was quite tired and toward the end I didn't do so well (even stumbled a couple of times over little pebbles." To make matters worse the Petrig bothers, who permitted their charges only one rest during the descent, talked about Ingolf and Holger in their own mountain dialect – "But since I've lived in Zurich for so long I understood every word, and boy was it uncomplimentary." At one point Eddy Petrig told Ingolf, "Dahl, you are a dangerous man," but, so Ingolf told Bill, "by that time I was already so demoralized and fatigued, and the former because of the latter, that I didn't give a damn." The incident nurtured in the forty-nine year-old Ingolf the gravest doubts about his endurance, his mountaineering techniques and his ability to handle high altitudes: "I have never pretended to be more than an amateur climber, at some time I knew a little *something* about it, but I do it so seldom that I forget from time to time what I once knew." These thoughts carried a particular urgency because he and Bill were planning an extensive Alpine expedition the following year.

After a 4:00 a.m. start the climbers were back at their starting point by 1:30 p.m. and able to make a leisurely return to Zermatt. The next day Ingolf recuperated with Holger, Willi Hausslein and two Fulbright-bound U.S.C. students, cellist Larry Lesser (future president of the New England Conservatory of Music) and pianist Ellen Mack. At an outdoor restaurant Ingolf even succeeded in getting them to turn off the muzak. At Raron he made a pilgrimage to the tomb of Rilke, walking over the paths in which the *Sonnets* were born. A peasant, standing with his dog, sharpened his scythe, sending a shiver of mortality down Ingolf's spine. Jets practiced overhead destroying the moment: "Under such conditions no poetry could now be written." At the grave Ingolf plucked an ivy leaf which, taped into the daybook, still retains its greenish cast all these years later. The party proceeded to Geneva, where the Dahls stayed with a cousin.

Ingolf had been on the road for two months and as yet no decision had been made on *where* this sabbatical year was to be spent. Anxiety on this score was certainly contributing to Etta's malaise but now the time had come to begin the search in earnest. The two spent a most unhappy period searching for accommodation – with Geneva and Grenoble each serving as a base of operation. Etta had her heart set on spending most of the year in a French-speaking country, hoping to improve her language skills. French-speaking Switzerland was considered too expensive so the couple headed south into France itself and visited some two dozen sites in the week beginning August 24. Ingolf wanted to be near mountains and skiing but some of the places he liked were too remote for Etta. Neither of the Dahls wanted to live in a city but they did hope to find a friendly village within striking distance of the usual metropolitan amenities. When my parents found a room *they* could live in, there was no room for a piano. When there was room for a piano, it was discovered the neighbors might object. Or Ingolf would complain that the room was too near to other noise, to the parade of motor scooters chugging by. Some delightful hamlets had no restaurants. Some had no hotels. In the meantime the Dahls found that France itself had problems. Smog choked the Isere valley and left them with sore throats and watery eyes. Bureaucracy and inefficiency plagued them whenever they visited an office and the Michelin Guide, *quel horreur!*, oversold the local museums.

Worst of all, the commitment to France was one-sided. Ingolf noted on August 24, day one of the search, "The conflict is coming out – I am so depressed – am *not* attracted to France yet have to adjust in everything to E's requirements – and my own? The reason for this year? A cold is coming on." One can imagine that this attitude soon manifested itself in Ingolf's reluctance to accept *any* of the proffered sites and that Etta grew increasingly resentful. On the 27th he describes himself as *"dead tired*, cross, antagonistic (toward E and vice versa)." A crisis day was reached on August 30. Ingolf placed a deposit on some rooms in Villard-de-Lans and the two sat down at lunch to discuss what to do for the ten days that remained before this accommodation became available. Tears flowed during this meal. Ingolf got Etta to concede that French studies were an embellishment, not the essential element in this year's sabbatical priorities. He then rushed back to his new landlady, extracted his deposit, and the decision was taken, amid "somewhat frayed nerves" (as Etta put it) to – and here we return to Ingolf's journal, "leave this goddam country *immediately*." That night the two began an exploration of the possibilities in the Rhone valley of Switzerland, first in Martigny and then in Sion.

A month after the French disaster, incidentally, Ingolf changed his mind! "Thought to stay at Mme. Masset's would have been just right – should have gone for 10 days to hotel and then *stayed* in V.-de-Lans. The trouble is too much impulsiveness." By this time the Dahls were already on the move again, academic refugees in search of a home,

August 31 had proved be full of the "agonies of frustration," though in a rare display of high spirits Etta had distinguished herself by throwing a bag of grapes to a fife and drum corps aboard a passing truck. On the next day the Dahls took two rooms in the basement of a house in a village recommended by Ellis Kohs, Montana-Vermala, east of Sion and high above the Rhone. This accommodation was available for four weeks only but my parents snapped it up in desperation and Ingolf even arranged for a piano to be delivered. The next morning, however, he phoned Frau Netzer in Schruns and begged to be taken back for a second year. "She is fluttery and vague," he reported, "will it work?" Three days later a letter arrived from Austria – "We can come!" Still depressed not to have found a new site, Ingolf accepted Frau Netzer's terms, but four weeks would have to pass before the Dahls could be settled down at last.

Ingolf seems to have had a great deal of difficulty in getting any work done in Montana. The tiny rooms of their flat proved to be cold and uncomfortable. "*Start* in my cell," he wrote on September 5, "start, start, start – how difficult, unused-to, the whole complex, overwhelming – what to write, what to do first? What next, what choices to make?" Frustration and depression followed him throughout the month and at its end there was self-recrimination over the waste of time. The only happy moments were spent away from the work table. Larry Lesser and Ellen Mack came for a visit on September 4 and the three played Bach, Beethoven, and Brahms in Ingolf's little studio. "The music playing," Ingolf added, "is like rain in the desert." Other pleasant occasions came during solitary walks in the nearby mountains. "I'm *living, living*," Ingolf reassured himself on the way to a summit, "here it is. I'm now." There were also some brief trips, one to Geneva, one to the Rilke Museum at Muzot. In Sion the Dahls bought a Hermes portable typewriter (it replaced a 1928 Remington) and had it refitted with every odd letter in the Swedish and German alphabets. Etta tried to amuse herself with French mystery novels and Scrabble squabbles. Since they had forgotten their English dictionary *I* was deputized to discover if Etta's use of the verb "to laze" was correct usage. Together my parents went to the local cinema to see *The Fugitive Kind*, so called, Etta insisted, "because the audience has an almost irresistible desire to flee." Ingolf noted that the fall climate reminded him of Zurich in 1932, but Etta complained that the high altitude of Montana made her sleepy and depressed. By the time she was acclimatized the four weeks were up and the Dahls could continue their pilgrimage.

On October 1 they crossed the Simplon Pass and began a brief Italian tour. Rain spoiled most of their sightseeing and they contented themselves with a visit to the Galleria Dell'Accademia Carrara in Bergamo, where they spent the night. The next day Lake Como remained hidden in grey mist as the Peugeot crossed the Splugen pass on the same route Ingolf had covered on bicycle in 1936. That evening they arrived again in Schruns, which remained their home until August, 1962. For three months they had been without a permanent address.

The Dahls occupied much of the top floor of Frau Netzer's three-storey house. There was a small back room but Ingolf despaired when he saw it – "How can I work there lightless, viewless. How can the fancy take flight there?" The problem was solved when the room was assigned to Etta. There was an unheated bedroom and a long living room in which Ingolf located his piano and worktable. The Dahls again had access to a long balcony upon which, when the weather was right, they could dine in the sun.

Ingolf found many changes in the village *and* many spots dear to memory. Ugly new roads were crowded with tourists, especially Germans, for whom Ingolf usually expressed his antipathy. The clinic continued to serve "American oil magnates, Egyptian potentates, and such luminaries as Von Karajan and Schwarzkopf," Etta wrote, "From our balcony it is possible to see a Cadillac driving slowly by the village blacksmith where some peasant has brought a young horse to be shod."

Etta prepared breakfast and a cold dinner and the two ate their noon meal at one of the town hotels. This midday period, which also included Ingolf's nap, was referred to as "Intermission" – it could stretch from 12:00 to 3:00. "Our reluctance to come back to this place," he wrote to Raymond Kendall at the end of his first month in Schruns, "where it was so perfect nine years ago proved to have been unnecessary. We see everything with fresh eyes and enjoy every moment of being here in these lovely surroundings." For Ingolf the life of the village continued to have many charms. The children's Christmas show, for instance, proved to be a "great experience. – In front row Erika Sahler, 6, in blue, an angelic touching lyrical face, a soulful beauty, the boys reciting poems, all mouthing at the same time, the fresh songs, the blonde boy in green sweater...the peasant faces – the beards, the lamb, the shepherd." Standing on his balcony with moonlight on the mountains Ingolf expressed an early but perhaps premature verdict on the scene – "What lucky people we are."

Part of the attraction of Schruns, as during the first sabbatical, was that it was not very far from Zurich, which continued to exercise its siren's call on its former son. Six visits were undertaken this year. On October 10 he drove into town to do some shopping and attend a concert – at which he saw one of his old music professors, Fritz Gysi. On the 11th he was walking down the street when he noticed a poster announcing that Stravinsky would be in town to conduct that very weekend. Having already made a dinner date with the Hartogs family he was in an agony of indecision – should he call the maestro at the Baur au Lac Hotel, itself the scene of so many memories? Finally he took the plunge. Stravinsky himself answered the phone. When Ingolf heard his mentor say, "Come and let me embrace you," he flew to the hotel. An account of the visit was shared with Lawrence Morton:

> He was alone and I had a very great time visiting, as you can imagine. I expected this to last for only a short time and had a dinner date with friends. As it turned out, he was in great spirits, time passed, I missed the right time to call my friends (who later gave me, deservedly, one of the worst dressing downs I have ever received), then Vera came and finally Bob and so we had dinner together. The maestro seems in excellent shape, and that is a real joy...Bob was in a very mellow mood, quite evidently enjoying himself on this trip.

Ingolf's grief over the discourtesy to his friends seems to have been considerable – "I have killed something because of wanting both again, and waiting irresponsibly until it was too late – acted like [an] impulsive child – will I never grow up?" Flowers and a letter of apology were dispatched. Three days later all was well again and Ingolf and Edu had agree on an Italian walking tour – "feel enormously released," a guilty Ingolf wrote.

The next visit to Zurich was on the way back from the Donnaueschingen music festival, a "trade fair" of the German avant-garde, also in October. He does not seem to have gotten much from the concerts there, but he did enjoy the company of friends including Karl Kohn, Ingvar Lidholm, and the composer-critic Everett Helm. On December 6 Ingolf took Etta to Zurich to look at an exhibition of Thomas Mann artifacts; they ate oysters and saw Jerry Lewis in *The Absent Minded Professor*, which Ingolf (anticipating all those French critics) pronounced "hilarious." The two went to plays by Dürrenmatt and Hofmansthal and a Frank Martin opera during their next visit at the end of March. Repacking his car near the theater, with a view of the mountains behind the lake including "all these beloved peaks," my stepfather spotted Robert Denzler, the musical director of the Stadttheatre in which Ingolf had put in so many hours of labor thirty years earlier. "Conflict of emotions," he recorded, "no, not talk to him, what's the use? Be little boy again: the only answer to *his* like is a good new piece."

Ingolf was often able to visit Willi Hausslein during these visits to Zurich; this he did on April 28, at the conclusion of a walking tour, and on June 27 when he and Etta arrived to see a production of Berg's *Lulu*, part of a cultural trip that also took them to Basel, Ulm, and Munich. In the latter city Etta chanced to see, at an opera performance, *her* old teacher from Berlin, Harald Genzmar. There then occurred an interesting sequel to the Denzler incident. Ingolf indicates that he would have liked an introduction to Genzmar, but Etta was unwilling to approach him and this lead to a peevish daybook entry, "*Her* shyness is OK?" Self-esteem may have been at a low ebb in both of the Dahls at this time. Life had not sent them back to the scene of their juvenile apprenticeships with the glory required by ambition, and each had found ways to avoid drawing attention to the shortcomings of fate.

The visit to Munich on July 1, 1962 was not Ingolf's first trip to the Bavarian capital. In another variation on composition-prevention strategy he had agreed to give a number of concerts in various German cities under the auspices of the United States Information Service. His performing partner was the cellist George Neikrug. They had played Bach, Beethoven, Boccherini, and the Dahl *Duo* at the Amerika Haus in Munich on November 23. While in Munich Ingolf was persuaded to participate in a recording session by his former student Sam Spence, who described the composition in question as "Warsaw Concertoish with a teen-age beat." Ingolf found himself a little out of his depth but "that soon passes," and he happily accepted double scale for his efforts. Ingolf was never happy for long in Germany. Writing to Bill Colvig about "Krautland," he noted, "Here we see the German illustrated magazines all the time and their content does *not* make one happy. The pretexts are negative of course, ('these were terrible people'), but under whatever pretext, they still manage to get pictures of the Nazis, of uniforms, of the war, etc. into almost *every* issue. They also feel terribly sorry," he could add with no irony, "for what happened *to* them..."

62. BE TRUE

Ingolf's travels, his mountaineering, his readiness to accept assignments that would take him away from his studio – all these diversions invite suspicion: why wasn't he composing? Well, he was writing *some* music, but he was unable to shake, even under the "ideal" circumstances provided by the sabbatical, any of the doubts and incapacities that had plagued him in

Los Angeles. "I feel *so* dried up," he wrote in Montana, "*so* inadequate (look at Henze's flow, his imagination, his flare, his diligence) you must write notes, notes, notes – where are they, where to start – feel so discouraged." There was little change in Schruns, where his autumn naps were haunted by dreams of inadequacy. "Start *slowly* to get wheels in motion," he noted on October 24, "turns out to be a *ghastly* day – no ideas, dried up...not even *stupid* notes – sit and stew." Three days later he announced "in the afternoon *set* myself task to write quickly within [a] week an organ piece, an *assignment* – but get stuck after 3 bars." "Worst afternoon," he recorded on November 7, "read some Maigret, can't *get* into it – and all the self doubts, *my* music is just between too naive and too difficult!" Things were no better the following April, "very depressed...*no* ideas, nothing – trash, cheap, naive, imitative – and get stuck the moment I start."

Ingolf's inhibitions were related, as usual, to profound questions of style. Too often he saw himself as nothing but a minor satellite of Stravinsky – "I know nothing, a foreflusher who has had luck in each of his half-mastered fields." Now, although he did not disagree, he was upset to see Stravinsky himself baldly state in an interview that he no longer saw the possibility of creating something new within the field of harmony. "Neo-classic harmony bores me – chromaticism, factory made, disgusts me – what else is there?" Ingolf asked on September 11. "All I do in the a.m.," he continued is futs around [a verb form he must have picked up from his stepson] with the rows (*why* rows??)...One has to stand for something – not be a reed in the wind, swayed into Allegro & Arioso dissonance one period, white music the next, back to expressionism the next."

Nevertheless Ingolf would now begin to write music, in the last period of his life as a composer, with some of the stylistic apparatus of the Schoenberg school, the serial row in particular. Ingolf adapted something of the method of "the other camp," but his goal would continue to remain at some remove from whining expressionism – and key-centered tonality was still a requisite in many of his later compositions. Ingolf's use of serial technique also remained free, avoiding mathematical or reductive approaches that would prevent him from achieving the sounds *he* wanted to hear. James Berdahl has suggested that, "He was able to achieve this synthesis by exploiting, rather than minimizing, the harmonic implications inherent in a twelve-tone row, and in fact, carefully constructing rows which would contain the greatest number of such implications." In adopting this technique Ingolf was sensitive to the "brutal" charge laid against the Copland *Sextet* by Lawrence Morton, who noted that it is possible to find 12-tone rows that permit one to write "the same kind of pretty music one used to write before." Ingolf's music could not be called pretty, but he was always aware that his lingering affection for key and harmony placed him in a rearguard position, a stubborn and isolated warrior doing battle against a sea of realizations, tone manipulations and electronic bleeps.

The only work he labored on with any success during this sabbatical was a trio for a combination of instruments which the latest Darmstadt reviewer had already pronounced "atavistic," piano, violin, and cello. Ingolf was working in response to a commission from the Koussevitsky Foundation in the Library of Congress, one he had accepted as early as September 12, 1957. Work was to have begun the following summer at the Hartford Foundation and Ingolf had made a number of important stylistic decisions at this time, but only a few notes were put down during that hectic July of 1958. Now, in a constant struggle against impotence and distractions, he would fight to bring the work to life. As usual, the process proved to be traumatic and protracted.

"Get at last the order and shape of Movt. I of Trio," Ingolf noted on September 20, "Makes me feel much better." As he worked on the second movement in October this happiness turned to frustration – "no idea will come – those few notes that do come are not worth keeping." Working on the third movement on October 31 he complained of "very small progress – it is either too chromatic or too primitive – what a thin line." By November 17 he was working on a fourth movement – "in the end there is always too much, and I want to stick *everything* into a single piece." Before this movement was completed or the final section begun, Ingolf had accepted, on December 4, an invitation from Ingvar Lidholm to have the piece premiered on Swedish radio on March 2. At the same time he had agreed to include, as part of his winter trip to Sweden, another concert with George Neikrug, this time in Berlin.

No sooner had he accepted these invitations than feelings of anxiety began anew. "Beginning to get panicky," he wrote on December 8, "which slows me down even more." "Getting terribly tense, nervous," he added five days later, "don't work well, *afraid* of notes, of not being up to the task, feel time creeping by and not getting enough done." Work on the last movement was interrupted in mid-January by a request for an article about the unfinished piece from the Swedish magazine *Nutida Musik.*

Complaining of a bad chest, the aftermath of the bronchitis that had also spoiled a ski trip, Ingolf left Schruns on January 17, with much music still to be written. After a brief stop in Munich he flew to Berlin later that day – on the first stages of a journey that would be remembered chiefly for its agonies and disappointments. It was a lonely odyssey, since Etta remained behind, partly because of the expense, partly because she could not face another visit with her mother-in-law, and partly because she, too, was suffering, physically and spiritually.

Ingolf's USIS concert in Berlin took place, after several rehearsals, on January 19. The musicians repeated the program they had offered in Munich and Nurmberg and received an enthusiastic response. Ingolf took two solo bows as the composer of the *Duo.* "I had almost forgotten," he wrote to Raymond Kendall, "what a pleasure it is to play in a hall that is really filled to the last seat with an interested audience."

He used the remainder of his time in Berlin to visit old friends, including Carlos Chavez and Boris Blacher and the singer Ella Lee. Twice he visited East Berlin, retreating to Checkpoint Charlie after an initial visit to the Pergamom Museum because he was hungry and had no DDR currency. A few hours were spent copying finished portions of the *Trio,* but Ingolf had no energy and his respiratory problems deepened. On January 22 he boarded a plane for Hamburg and a second one for Stockholm. He was taken to Mammi's flat on Norevagen in Lidingö, where he collapsed into a fever with a bronchitis which kept him bedridden for a week. A worried Etta called after receiving three dispiriting aerograms, but it was not until February 1 that he was able to get out of the house for the first time.

Ingolf never staged a true recovery in Stockholm and he described episodes of weakness and dizziness throughout the month that followed. "Am just not *here* and chest not right either," he reported on February 4. A doctor ordered three weeks of convalescence on the 6th. "I am so unhappy about my health," Ingolf noted six days later, "the chest is *not* right, feel weak, dizzy, hot flashes, no stamina at all and the sore spot in chest continues." A number of social events in his honor had to be cancelled and when he made it to a concert, on February 15, he noticed how pale and sick-looking he appeared in the foyer mirror. The climb up to Gert Marcus' atalier left him short of breath. Mammi, who fell ill herself, continued to care for him, her first-born son in need of a mother's ministrations after all these years. She dragged out the ancient photo albums one more time. "This visit is taking years off her," Ingolf wrote soon after his arrival; against his will he found himself "going back to where I don't want to go."

With only a month left before the first performance Ingolf returned at last to the unfinished composition. After completing (for the second time) a section of the fourth movement he wrote, "I am just incapable of doing anything right at the desk the first time." Working on the coda section of the final movement on February 6 he admitted that "the *outline* can stand, I think, but the notes are not all there." Laboring over another section of the same movement on the 10th he wrote, "Most of what the inner ear writes down and considered the outer ear rejects – so it has to be done over...Is the piece too far back in zozair camp? Dissonant and chromatic?" As Ingolf copied each section Holger had it run off and delivered to the other performers. At last, on February 12, Ingolf reported himself finished with the composing. Three days later he had copied the last of the score and delivered it to the cellist and the violinist. Furiously he tried to master the piano part and on February 20 he was ready to rehearse the *Trio* with the other musicians. More suffering was on the way.

Claude Genetay, cello, and Leon Spierer, violin, were first-rate performers but Ingolf soon discovered that working with them would be difficult. Spierer, the concert-master of the Stockholm Philharmonic, was preparing a program of his own and Ingolf felt that he was not giving the difficult new work sufficient time and that, furthermore, he "had very little chamber music experience and could not *listen* while he played." Now Spierer had to squeeze in a *Trio* rehearsal after a whole day of orchestral work and he, like the composer, was extremely fatigued. The first rehearsal was pronounced a "chaos...just plugging dully along – the simplest bar seems difficult." "This is going to be my professional finish – the little man who didn't make it, who didn't have what it takes," Ingolf complained after a "nightmare" rehearsal on the 24th. "The mood is vile," he reported two days later, "the piece doesn't work, doesn't jell – I just want to up and run in the opposite direction." "Hot words and shouting" erupted at the rehearsal on the 27th when Ingolf insisted on a four-hour session – "If it goes so badly *with* me, what would [a] performance *without* me be like?" "Another awful rehearsal" in another awful practice room took place on the 28th, "racing through [the] whole thing, no time to correct any faults, even the things that go, go without real rapport." At the dress rehearsal Ingvar Lidholm had to leave after the first movement – "he was right," a discouraged composer moaned, "rats leaving the sinking ship." In the evening Ingolf cried.

In addition to finishing the last movement of the *Trio*, copying all of it, and completing his rehearsal duties, Ingolf also had many other items on his agenda. He gave several interviews, including one in bed, and one press conference. He recorded (in Swedish) two radio talks and gave two lectures at the Music Academy. He also recorded the *Sonata Pastorale* for Swedish radio. One of the lectures was given to a class of Karl-Birger Blomdahl's composition students; Ingolf hoped to counteract some of the influence of Gyorgy Ligeti, who had recently addressed the same group on new sound combinations, but Ingolf's remarks on Stravinsky's *Symphony in C* found no response in the same class. Commenting on the many avant-garde works he was hearing in Sweden, and those of Bo Nilsson specifically, a resigned Ingolf argued, "They have no idea of what form really means, but they tickle the sensations most stimulatingly."

Musical fashion was clearly worshipping other gods in Sweden. Ingolf was vexed to see his little picture in *Nutida Musik* contrasted with a big spread about some "Japanese teenage post-Webernite." He was also annoyed at himself for letting Spierer walk all over him, and for letting the violinist do it just to keep a little piece. And on the night of the fateful concert Ingolf, in an "all time low," savaged himself as "a little appendage to I.S., no *real* ideas, everything pasted together with phantastic labor and trouble – the maker a mouse."

The *Nutida Musik* concert of March 2 was aimed primarily at radio listeners, but an invited audience was also in attendance at the Konserthuset premiere. This took place on the second half of an evening's program; during the first half Ingolf and his fellow performers continued to rehearse nearby. We have two eyewitness commentaries on the event itself, both by the composer, and they do not agree. The diary entry for March 2 indicates that Ingolf felt like crawling into a hole in order to have a good cry – "it seems so much like the *real* crush – the end of something. Playing too is no good, no rhythm, nothing really *there*, I am not a real professional either here or there." By the end of the month he was willing to put another evaluation on the evening. Writing to Lawrence Morton he agreed that, "The performance at least hung together and, I believe, the composition made its point, even though hundreds of details were messed up. On the whole I think it was a strong performance...Personal comment was very favorable (Blomdahl, Rosenberg, Wallner, even Ligeti!)"

On the morning of the premiere Ingolf felt the first twinges of gout in his right foot. That night he began to take colchicine, a purgative that is supposed to induce diarrhea and thus cleanse the system of the excess uric acid responsible for the attack. I, too, have used this largely outdated medicine and it has affected me the way it did Ingolf in Sweden. Here it caused not only diarrhea but also violent vomiting. When there was nothing left in Ingolf's stomach he vomited blood. He took once again to his bed, rising only on March 5 for his last interview with Swedish Radio. Unwilling to take any more of his medicine he limped around in agony until it was time for his flight to Zurich. On March 7, after seven weeks, he returned to Schruns and two days later, in spite of some pain, he was back on the ski slopes. On March 20, worried about his stomach, he underwent a thorough examination at the clinic in Schruns. "There is nothing wrong, what a relief!" he exclaimed. In fact the medical report diagnosed a slight gastro-duodenitis, but this health crisis, like the professional one, was soon overcome.

On March 16 *revision* on the *Trio* began. Two months were needed to complete the process. "It *must* flow now," Ingolf encouraged himself on March 23, but vows of this nature seldom produced immediate results. Ingolf concentrated his attention on movements four and five. James Berdahl has noted that the *Trio*'s sections reach a gradual intensification – "beginning in a light and playful serenade style and becoming more serious and complex." It was precisely with the more complex later sections that Ingolf had most difficulty, though after listening to a tape of the Stockholm concert he also found some problems in an earlier movement as well. On May 15 he "finished" the revision, but it took him many weeks to copy the new version and in the process portions of the work were recomposed. Ingolf found the first three movements to be "excellent" on May 22 and hoped at a later date to do some cutting in the last two. He admitted to Lawrence that the music was not so "radically different" in style, but good nevertheless, adding, "Do you know a style nowadays that is not dated?" To Harold Spivacke at the Library of Congress he described the work as a "grateful and effective one, if well performed." "It is impossible to look at [your] own writing *objectively* before starting it and while doing it. One has to work with blinkers," he later concluded, "If you look at it objectively (before and during) you'll never ever start." "I.D.," he warned himself while in Stockholm, "stay away from the fashionable techniques and gestures – they just lead astray, be true." But several months later he was still agonizing about his position in the musical world – "Where does one's responsibility lie? Toward humility, self-denial, conquering the self – or toward the puritanical virtues of ambition, self-advancement, recognition, public acceptance, the marketplace?" Ingolf's assessment of his own work in the *Trio* places him closer to the first of these two choices, but the costs had been great. "Oh how much time on *one* piece?" he concluded on June 25, "and what next?"

The sabbatical would end before such a question could be answered. In the fall he had succeeded in spending some time in revising earlier compositions such as the *Symphony Concertante* and the *Serenade For Four Flutes*. Working on a revision of the 1945 *Variations on a Swedish Folktune* he noted, "I *have* improved, know more since those days, thank heavens. But in re-doing it every note is as hard to come by (*pages* of attempts for one note) as it was then. I think I have a phrase on paper, in an hour it looks impossible again." Ingolf did spend some unfruitful hours searching for texts for proposed vocal works but he concluded the year with only the *Trio* to show for all his time abroad. "Get the Guggenheim installment," he reported on March 10, ("feel like a fraud)." All willpower and concentration were gone by the time summer returned, with its many mountaineering and travel distractions – "In afternoon *have* to finish Tey's *Daughter of Time*...feel guilty as hell about all this."

63. VALLEYS AND PEAKS

The tragedy of Ingolf's creative paralysis was only one of the problems affecting this crisis-beset sabbatical. Etta was suffering a decline in spirit as well, and the emotional outbursts which had characterized the months leading up to the return to Schruns only prefigured a more prolonged period of unhappiness.

It is not easy to say what caused this depression. I think it was, in part, a delayed reaction to the gravity of the cancer surgeries and their life-threatening portent, a reaction which Etta had succeed in disguising while the completion of the dissertation stood as an immediate goal. That mountain was now behind her. Although she had been encouraged by her professors to think of publication, and a revision of the thesis had been one of *her* goals for the sabbatical year, she soon seems to have lost interest in the project. "Regardless of how deathless the message is," she wrote to Fred Kahn on November 9, "there is no reason for anyone to devote 450 pages to it, and my message isn't deathless...There is absolutely no reason to suppose that it ever *will* be published." It also seems evident that Ingolf was not encouraging when he and Etta discussed the dissertation's future in the fall. Why he was so negative is unclear, but as the year abroad ended it is obvious that he blamed himself on this score, "E is farther away than ever, she seeks no contact, I find none (did I kill all that with the discouragement of thesis revision, in the hope of closer collaboration?? Was her *one* raison taken with it?)"

He also blamed himself for failing to make *her* back room headquarters in Schruns "a really nice place to be in." Such self-recrimination came too late, of course, as does my own. In the fall of 1961 I was going through a rather bad period myself. My letters from home were no doubt worrying to my parents, intentionally so, for I somehow located their role in the origins of my malaise. A Cheremoya retaining wall had collapsed in a rainstorm and I had to seek advice on how to get it repaired (I was living in Ingolf's studio this year, while Brian Jenkins and his bride Jean occupied the upstairs rooms). I had health and career problems too. When I proposed withdrawing from graduate school in order to complete military service Ingolf and Etta had a transatlantic tizzy.

Then there was Etta's chagrin at the failure of her French dream. Ingolf wrote to Lawrence that, though frustrated by their inability to find accommodation in France, Etta was being very sensible about it. But I don't suppose this disappointment was as easily overcome as Ingolf hoped – though it would have been hard for Etta to show the emotions needed in this situation. She succeeded better in registering her protest when Ingolf received a letter from Mammi, who wanted to visit Schruns – "Etta is again impossible, completely irrational, very depressing." The incident seems to have been one of those rare occasions when Etta granted herself the necessary anger.

She was, without any cessation in her love for her husband, mightily fed up with his chronic self-absorption, his ability to justify each act of self-indulgence, fed up with the myopia that blotted out her needs and desires. Dorothy recalled hearing from Etta about an incident in a Zurich bank during which Ingolf raised a critical eyebrow because *Etta* wanted to buy a blouse – with a scene ensuing immediately. It was not so easy to sacrifice so many aspirations to the egotistical demands of the artistic personality, especially when the creative dividends appeared to be so meager.

Finally we can add that Etta was again in bad health. Her chronic heartburn and other stomach problems became so severe that on December 15 she went to a nearby hospital for tests. "No operation for E," a relieved Ingolf wrote; nevertheless, digestion problems continued to sap her daily energy. She put an end to her formerly detailed correspondence duties, complaining that her round-robin letters simply encouraged her to indulge in "half-witticisms." Etta became increasingly withdrawn, to the growing consternation of her worried husband.

"Where *is* Etta, she's never seemed farther and I am depressed about it," he wrote on September 10. "If only Etta could come closer," he complained on October 23. When he did not hear from her while he was in Stockholm he noted "*how* dependent I am on her! Did I offend her at all!! Think of all kinds of things – so damn subjective. Very worried and just don't know what to do, what to think, so strange, when I'm away (this *subjectivity* again) I am pining for her – when we are together we have our problems." A letter from Schruns the next day allowed him to breathe again. On Valentine's Day, which the two always celebrated with ritualized sentimentality, he sent her flowers and phoned her. But he was perhaps never fully aware that his wife was suffering from what she later described to Dorothy as a "nervous breakdown."

I doubt that she used this phrase in 1962. The closest I have come to her own explanation of what happened was in a letter to my aunt Elsie, written on May 5, 1962 – "after I got here, my chin, which I had been keeping up for the last ten hard years...suddenly decided to do what comes naturally, and dropped. I permitted myself to collapse, and to date I'm unable to get excited about anything but living from day to day. No deadlines, no projects. This was long overdue."

The worst of the decline seems to have occurred while Ingolf was in Sweden: "I had collapsed into a kind of total apathy with heartburn. After about a week I was able to go to the doctor's." Frau Netzer, alarmed over her tenant's state, had intervened and insisted on getting Etta some medical help. This probably involved the stomach problem only. A severe gastritis was diagnosed and Etta was placed on a strict diet, told to avoid "airy" foods, and given some medicine, which she soon ceased to take because the phenobarbitol in it made her skin itch.

Ingolf's journals report the occasional happy moment with Etta – as the two played Scrabble and drank malaga or attended a local New Year's Eve Party. They took walks together and Etta read aloud Gerald Durrell's *My Family And Other Animals*. But there seems to have been no radical improvement in her mood during the remainder of the stay abroad, only rare rays of light. On March 14 Ingolf complains about Etta's belching, her remoteness, her lack of participation, her suggestion that he not try to write any more music for the rest of the stay. On their 22nd wedding anniversary, he notes, "in morning in bed E. begins to soften a little – I feel very ardent, in every way, wish we could stay in bed." Driving to Vaduz on April 11 he was able to report, "For the first time she opens up a little on way, more cheerful, singing, etc." "Try to get closer to E. in hall," he wrote on May 1, "but she evades again – so here is another crisis – she won't talk, I can't talk..." "It would be so lovely if E and I were closer," he sighed on May 9. Asked if she was getting excited about a forthcoming trip she answered, "As excited as I get about anything." "That's tragic," Ingolf reacted, "and *what* can I, must I do?" As he finished a revision of the *Trio* on May 16 he noted, "When I was in Stockholm I was only hoping to have my wife

374

close at the time I finished the piece – and here I am and still hoping the same."

Few friends found there way to Schruns during this sabbatical year and I can well imagine that feelings of isolation may have contributed to Etta's malaise. The Crowns came in late April, Willi Hausslein, Joan Schaefer, and Bill Colvig were there in July. In the previous half year only a visit by Fred Myrow, in late December, provided some direct contact with the world the Dahls had left behind them in Los Angeles.

On May 27 Ingolf and Etta did set out to pay a return visit to Fred, who was studying in Rome. This was the trip about which Etta could muster so little enthusiasm, even though Ingolf had chosen an Italian sightseeing itinerary that would ordinarily have engaged her imagination. "We are almost scared to go, with our jinx," Etta wrote Elsie, "The Tiber will probably overflow its banks, someone will aim at Pope John and hit us, or the diet I'm supposed to have will be unavailable (how do you say yoghurt in Italian?)"

Ingolf read Perry Mason mysteries in Italian as a way of preparing for the trip whose itinerary included stops in Venice and Sienna and much leisurely driving in Tuscany and Umbria. A number of sites were revisited twenty-five years after Ingolf's 1937 journey with his sister. The journals for this period are also very reminiscent of the Zurich daybooks – a catalogue of artistic and architectural wonders, each laden with a value judgment, i.e., "Rome as *city* nothing but ordinary town with fabulous monuments set in it." There were recurrent sources of discontent. Repeatedly Ingolf reports disappointment over locked doors at many sites his guidebook told him he could visit: the chapel in Padua, a church in Chioggia, galleries in Sienna and Perugia, the Capitoline Museum. One wonders how he found time to finish copying the revised *Trio*, a chore he completed in Porto Ercole on June 4. A second impediment proved to be the weather, which was often cold and rainy, obscuring views and driving these sun-worshippers indoors. Etta is mentioned only once during this trip, incidentally, which may be an indication that her mood in no way interfered with Ingolf's great pleasure. A photo from the trip shows her seated at a Sienna cafe, a raven eating out of her ice cream dish. "Play Mozart with Etta," Ingolf wrote on June 8, when the two were Fred Myrow's guests in Rome. Ingolf mailed the *Trio* to the Library of Congress from here and then took some time to renew acquaintanceship with Los Angeles musical figures, including Bill Smith. On June 9, in honor of Ingolf's fiftieth birthday, Fred arranged for some friends to perform the *Concerto A Tre*. The trip came to an end on June 19. For the fifth time Lake Como lay hidden in grey mist. At the Maloja Pass the Peugeot's radiator boiled over and the car spent several hours in the garage while Ingolf used the time to send off a wire congratulating Stravinsky on his *eightieth* birthday. Two months remained, mostly devoted to athletic rather than musical activity, before the Dahls were scheduled to begin their farewell journey from Schruns.

Outdoor endeavors provided for Ingolf a release from frustrations and an antidote to despondency that the more sedentary Etta could not take advantage of. When weather and health permitted (and sometimes when they did not), Ingolf used Schruns as a base for an extended series of mountain adventures. It was a poor snow year. Ingolf bought a new pair of skis on November 15 but on December 5 he was still dining on his sunny balcony. Rain washed away the new snowfalls and it was not until December 21 that he was able to get in his first skiing. Warm weather continued to destroy many opportunities throughout the year, though Ingolf did manage a good deal of local skiing in March and April. Several more distant ski journeys were undertaken, including three to the Piz Sol-Davos area of Switzerland and one to Corvara, in Italy, where Ingolf spent three days in January suffering from bronchitis. In June he undertook six days of ski mountaineering in the Otztaler Alps in the company of a local guide named Dajeng. As might be expected, Ingolf was displeased with his skiing technique. "Ski like a pig," he records on April 11; after his June outing Dajeng's criticism are listed – "on turn too much weight on inside ski – do turn *almost* on one ski, *always* on bent knees and always knees before body." In the spring Ingolf joined an outdoor exercise class in Schruns and he seems to have enjoyed this very much. Hiking, especially in a year of poor snow, was also one of his favorite activities. On November 16 he notes, "After nap, go for walk...a shepherd dog in middle of town, Fido, ask him if he wants to come and he does, *all* the way! Go up Kristberg and beyond, glimpses of Arlberg in evening light, *glorious*, then *run* down, long way. Fido catches up with me – a very touching goodbye at Montjola." In April Ingolf accompanied his briefly estranged friend, Eduard Hartogs, on a five day walking tour in Italy, north of Rapallo. In spite of wintry, miserable weather, Ingolf was able to report to Edi Schaar, "I am convinced that the most worthwhile, most enjoyable means of locomotion is *on foot*." From Schruns he climbed the Zimba and Seehorn peaks in July, a warm-up for a strenuous Alpine expedition along the Italian-Swiss border with Bill Colvig. Again lead by a guide, the two climbed a number of lofty summits between July 31 and August 9, including Disgrazia and Piz Roseg. Ingolf was aware that at his age he was probably facing his last opportunity to climb some of these peaks. This realization, he wrote Bill, "does not have as ominous a ring as it once had – partly because in my compositions I am finding even greater challenges to conquer than in mountains."

On August 14 Ingolf and Etta left Schruns behind. Their return to life in Los Angeles was beset by emotional difficulties. In Zurich they visited Gorgot's wine bar again, Ingolf complaining that in the meantime he had lost Etta. A warm embrace caused Etta to "go to pieces...She wants and wants not, but this is too rough on me, this tension and preoccupation – what can I do? Have we lost all communication?" Etta's reluctance to resume the role of lover is also revealed a week later. The Dahls had visited Reims, Amiens, Bruges ("rathaus lovely but this, too, has become a parking lot with [a] gorgeous background") and Gouda, and were spending a night in Bremen before shipping their car back to America. "In bed," Ingolf reported, "a tender moment which ends again in utter frustration, why does she make us suffer so, why these tortures?" The two took the train north, passing through Hamburg ('goodbye, towers of my youth') and Copenhagen before arriving in Stockholm on August 24. Ingolf, trapped in a round of family visits, avoided his musician friends, still embarrassed by the winter's debacle. On August 29 he and Etta flew to Reykjavik for a five day visit, during which Ingolf continued to complain of his inability to engage his sister in the kind of meaningful exchanges that had characterized their youth – "good talk, but just beginning to get some contact, don't talk about the important, just superficial."

On September 4 my parents ran for good seats aboard the inevitably delayed Icelandic Airlines flight to New York. I had a terrible moment, several hours later, when I called to inquire about their arrival time – only to be informed by some unthinking clerk, "We've lost contact with the plane." Nevertheless the Dahls reached Gander ("the new world greets us with loud Muzak and all-pervading lavatory smell") and a few hours later

I recovered them from the Eastside Airlines Terminal. They spent a few days with me in the apartment of Mitchell Goodman and Denise Levertov, which I had sublet for the summer. On September 8 we all boarded a plane at Newark and flew together to Los Angeles. Thus ended a year that each of us was happy to see come to an end.

Surprisingly, Ingolf was not anticipating the return to Hollywood with that joy that usually affects battle-scarred travelers: "Back to the smog, the stench, the superficiality, the hustle, the provinciality of LA, not to speak of the jingles of the ice cream man, which will surely drive me to insanity." Ingolf's love-hate relationship with his home city was now to take on a new note of despair – with many complaints about unsightly urban progress and inevitable comparisons with the European charms he has just left behind. "How uglified it is," he wrote of Barnsdall Park in November, 1962, "when one thinks how it was!" A year later a walk through downtown also lead to despondency, "Los Angeles, the flavor, the character is gone. Bunker Hill razed. Sad."

Almost five years passed before he was able to season his life in this smoggy city with another bite of European cuisine. In that time he took on ever greater responsibilities as teacher, composer, and performer. Through agonizing trials on many battlefields he pushed himself forward against the many internal and external forces that bedeviled his career. He achieved some notable successes. These utterly failed to bring him, or his estranged wife, the appropriate satisfaction or reward.

64. MEATY DAHL

Ingolf *did* have an early opportunity of exorcizing the demons of Stockholm. On January 18, 1963, in a haze of other people's cigarette smoke (the Dahls were struggling to give up their own bad habit), Ingolf flew east for the American premiere of the *Trio*. The expedition was an expensive indulgence but here Ingolf could put to rest the ghastly memory of that disastrous debut of the previous year.

As usual Ingolf found New York tremendously stimulating and he spent several busy days at the Museum of Modern Art and the Frick, at publishers' offices and in visits with other composers, including Aaron Copland, Vladimir Ussachevsky, Robert Gerle, Ralph Shapey, and Alexei

Haieff. At a publisher's party on the 23rd he records his only meeting with another journal-keeping composer, Ned Rorem.

On the night of the 24th Ingolf met the members of the Beaux Arts Trio, Daniel Guilet, violin, Menachem Pressler, piano, and Bernard Greenhouse, cello. With much relief he reported that they were friendly, though he failed to get them interested in touring with the *Trio* since, it was explained, they usually played Ravel as their "modern" work. They rehearsed the piece with the composer in attendance ("much is good but too pedestrian and no articulation"). Ingolf's own reaction to the music was increasingly positive: "Read through Trio in bed – remember this moment of real happiness – I can *see* it, I can touch it, it is a good piece."

On the 25th the composer flew to Washington where that night the American premiere was to take place in the Library of Congress. Ingolf was enormously excited by Washington, the capitol, Lincoln's Tomb. Harold Spivacke lead him on a tour of the Library's music division, where the manuscript of Schoenberg's *Pierrot Lunaire* proved to be a highlight. Then there was time to see the Emancipation Proclamation, letters of Lincoln and Jefferson and, outside the White House, Iranian students demonstrating against the Shah. "And here I am," Ingolf exulted as concert time drew near, "*my* work is to be played, in *this* place, *my* country."

In spite of some shortcomings, he was pleased with the evening's performance in the Coolidge Auditorium – "It goes well and is very well received. The audience is *with* it." Spivacke later wrote to Ingolf that, "I am sure you will admit that it was a difficult work and I feel it will be quite a few years before you can expect performances without some rough edges. That is the price you must pay for being truly creative and for writing something which is new and really different." A tape of the Washington performance, which he listened to on November 23 (the same day the musicians played the work for Madame Koussevitsky) convinced him that here was "a *great* piece."

After promising others and himself that he wished to concentrate on composing, it was perhaps inevitable that Ingolf (instead) had adopted an active role as a performer and conductor on his return from sabbatical in 1962. This included some studio work, including appearances, in February and April, 1963 – as he attempted to earn back the money needed to subsidize his Washington trip – on the sound stage that was recording

Alex North's score for *Cleopatra* ("good music, some of it very subtle and strong"). Typically, Ingolf felt frustrated by his studio call assignments – where his chief activity was "counting rests," and where he always found fault with his own performance. But the following December, working on a Jerry Goldsmith score at Fox, he was able to report, "This time real work, and I play well enough, so the ghost is exorcized."

Ingolf's first public performance after his return from Europe had come at a Monday Evening Concert on October 15, 1962. On this occasion Eudice Shapiro and Victor Gottlieb joined him in a performance of the *Haydn Piano Trio No. 8 in E-Flat*. This was one of a series of Haydn piano trios that Ingolf edited through a redistribution of the parts, following the example of the British musicologist Donald Tovey.

It was Ingolf's success as a Haydn arranger that lead to a second editing project this year, a request from cellist Gregor Piatigorsky for orchestration of a *Divertimento in D Major* – which Piatigorsky had earlier transcribed from a Haydn baryton trio. "I tried to make it simple, straightforward, thin," Ingolf wrote of his arrangement in August, 1963, "as much in Haydn's style as possible." The cellist replied, "I don't know how to thank you for your effort and time but I do consider it as a great honor and a sign of our friendship. Although for a master of your stature it was a 'kinderspiel' I know composers who are too great to do things one needs and at the time one needs it badly." The arrangement was to be utilized by Paitigorsky at a concert that he and Jascha Heifetz were about to give. Both of these virtuosi offered master classes under U.S.C.'s auspices in the 1960's and Ingolf was summoned to play chamber music with them on June 1, 1963 and at other times thereafter. His services were also required on July 24, 1966, but here Ingolf seems to have balked – "Heifetz and Piatigorsky want me to rehearse their concertos but not conduct it, nuts."

With Walter Ducloux on sabbatical Ingolf resumed his role as conductor of the U.S.C. Orchestra for the 1962-1963 season. The first concert was on October 28, Etta's fifty-fifth birthday. The orchestra performed Mozart, Webern, Beethoven and, in honor of the composer's seventy-fifth birthday, the *Fourth Symphony* of Ernst Toch. Ingolf was delighted with the result for once – "a grand evening – exorcising much of the past," and Toch described his enjoyment at the way Ingolf "brought everything, the smallest hidden items, to live and breathe." Walter Arlen in the *L.A. Times* called the concert memorable and praised the remarkably well-trained orchestra under the loving care and authoritative leadership of its conductor. In the Webern *Six Pieces*, Opus 6, a very young celesta player made his debut with the orchestra; his name was Mike Thomas, but, with the addition of a middle name, we will recognize him better as the future maestro Michael Tilson Thomas.

Other concerts featuring the orchestra followed, with Ingolf returning to his old complaint about poor attendance at rehearsals. In April Pierre Boulez arrived to conduct a Monday Evening Concert at U.S.C., with Ingolf, casting himself in the role of perpetual bridesmaid, preparing the musicians for the arrival of French star. Observing Boulez at work during a 1965 concert Ingolf noted, "He is terrific and I am learning a lot."

That other luminary of the European avant-garde, Karlheinz Stockhausen, also breezed into Southern California several times in this period. Ingolf was informed by post of one such visit in January, 1964 – "On the 18th or 19th he would love to go with you to The desert and see The Indians. He says that you are an expert in both and is hoping that you can liberate yourself on these days from all your earthly occupations." The drive to the desert seems to have taken place on January 19. Ingolf later wrote to Lawrence Morton, "Did I tell you what KH Stockhausen said to me when I told him what I[gor] S[travinsky] had been recently composing? He said, 'So he really thinks he is still actively helping to turn the wheel around? Oh, but he is deceiving himself very much there.'"

Speaking engagements in the summer of 1963 included some performance opportunities for Ingolf as well. In May he conducted the Dahl *Sinfonietta* at the University of Oregon and in July he played the *Sonata Seria* at Western Washington State College. The piano work may already have been at his fingertips because he had recently presented it on May 20 at an NAACC program at U.C.L.A, a concert which included compositions by three Dahl students, Fred Myrow, Paul Glass, and Rick Lesemann. This was an evening which produced a disgruntled review from Albert Goldberg in the *Times*, though Ingolf fared best under a subheading that has always amused me: "MEATY DAHL." "Just to be nice to the kids," Ingolf arranged and took part in a concert of work by the 1963 summer school composition students on July 26.

For Ingolf, the 1963-1964 season began with the Los Angeles premiere of the *Trio* at a Monday Evening Concert on October 21. A generous burst of applause and the warm response of the Washington press had now encouraged him to push ahead with the West Coast premiere, which took place on October 12. Ingolf joined Alexander Murray, violin, and cellist Larry Lesser in the performance. Rehearsals had been difficult. When the one scheduled for October 2 had to be cancelled, Ingolf wrote, "This is just like Stockholm – there is a jinx on the piece, cannot get it rehearsed once."

When it was all over Ingolf could point with satisfaction to reviews in Washington and Los Angeles. Paul Hume, in the *Washington Post*, described the *Trio* as "in the style that favors clarity in all things, that can be terse but that also shows a willingness to be amiable and zestful." "The most impressive thing about the program," Wendell Margrave wrote of the Washington concert, "was the first American performance of a trio written last year by Ingolf Dahl...The work is fearsomely difficult but was played in fine style by the trio. No composer could ask for a more dedicated and expert first performance. Mr. Dahl was in the audience and received, with the trio, an unusual quota of applause for a new piece." "The second Monday Evening Concert of the season," Robert Riley wrote in the *Christian Science Monitor*:

> was in homage to Ingolf Dahl, one of Los Angeles' most versatile, broadly gifted musical artists...This unassuming gentleman is equally expert as pianist, conductor, and teacher...Perhaps even more admirable than these aptitudes, though, is the unflagging zest for music of genuine worth, regardless of period or style, that he imparts to his students and associates...As a composer Mr. Dahl's output exhibits uncommon craftsmanship, indeed, his technical facility is inseparably fused with his atonal vocabulary."

The Los Angeles reviewers *were* intrigued by Ingolf's experiments in 12-tone technique. Albert Goldberg, noting that Ingolf's reputation had lead to a packed hall, remarked:

> He is too ingenious a composer...to resort to slavish adherence to serial principles. Rather, he has used the idiom freely and for his own purposes. The Serenata and Rondino have flashes of wit and

382

adroitness that are characteristic of much of Mr. Dahl's past work, and if the expressive intent of the other movements was not always as clear on first hearing they left no doubt of the technical skill in coping with involved problems.

Peter Yates, in *Arts and Architecture* argued in a laudatory review that:

The new piano Trio divides the progress of the dissonant harmony among the instruments so effectively that one seems to hear the violin and cello play piano, while the piano infiltrates the music of the strings. Instead of the dramatic conception of a conflict between the strict pitches of the piano and the inflected pitches of the strings, there is a complete mingling.

Ingolf could only have been gratified by the many personal comments he received from friends. "It is a *very* solid work," Aurelio de la Vega wrote, "a real addition to the literature." Don Michalsky called the piece a "delight of serious bouquets." Larry Moss reflected that, "It is so very elegantly worked out, the connections between ideas are so fluid, and the difficult balance problems in a Piano Trio so nicely solved." "Like any genuinely unique piece," Mel Powell wrote, "it is laden with wisdom and astonishing invention." The *Trio* "is more like the sensitive and musical Ingolf that I think I know," George Tremblay concluded, "than anything else of yours that I have heard."

Ingolf appeared only once on a concert stage in the many moths that followed – a performance of the *Sonata Pastorale* at the Santa Ana Public Library – because his energies were soon devoted to an event that crowned the musical season, for him and many others. This was the Ojai Festival, which Ingolf, a bridesmaid no longer, joined as Musical Director and principal conductor for three years, beginning with the May 1964 program.

Ojai is a small but prosperous community nestled cozily in a valley inland from Ventura. Its population has included a surprising number of wealthy and generous patrons of the arts; their sponsorship of the annual late-spring event helped create a musical enterprise of national significance in a site not easily accessible, even to music lovers from Los Angeles. The Festival "is managed," Dan Sullivan reported in the *New York Times*, "by upper class amateurs who, in a larger town, would probably be running the Junior League Worn-A-Bit Shop."

Ingolf had been preceded as Musical Director by a string of distinguished conductors including Thor Johnson, William Steinberg and Robert Craft, and his successors have included many luminaries as well, including Pierre Boulez and Michael Tilson Thomas – who honored his old mentor thirty years later by presenting a performance of the Dahl *Tower of St. Barbara* to 1994 audiences. "I feel somehow that you will not *dis*continue but *continue* my work," Lukas Foss wrote when Ingolf's appointment was announced in August, 1963.

Having successfully avoided the role of administrator for most of his life, Ingolf now found himself in a complicated and entangling web of bureaucratic responsibilities: programming, publicity, negotiations with artists and ensembles, conferences with the Board and, as the end of May grew closer, endless rehearsals. In many of these tasks he was assisted, throughout his Ojai years, by Rick Lesemann. Ingolf made several mistakes and endured a variety of crises. When one of the soloists asked for travel money *after* the festival had concluded, Ingolf, who had not budgeted this expense, offered to pay the sum out of his own pocket and to write the loss off as "'education expenses' – (my own education that is...)"

The 1964 Festival, which began on May 29, included concerts by the Berkeley Chamber Singers and the Los Angeles String Quartet, West Coast premieres of Schoenberg's *Piano Concerto* (with Lillian Steuber as soloist) and Mozart's unfinished opera *Zaide* (in a translation Etta helped to prepare), Ives' *Theatre Set* in a modern version edited by Ingolf, and the Dahl-Szigeti reconstruction of the Bach *Violin Concerto in D Minor*, played by Eudice Shapiro. So as not to slight the avant-garde there was even a concert of electronic music. The final afternoon featured Bruckner's *Mass in E Minor*, the Villa Lobos *Choros No. 3*, Hindemith's *Concert Music* and the Dahl *Saxophone Concerto*, with Fred Hemke as soloist.

I attended this program and remember something of the rapturous enthusiasm that greeted the efforts of the musicians. Albert Goldberg concluded, "Both as program planner and conductor Mr. Dahl decidedly won his spurs...In this first comprehensive view of his conducting abilities he proved himself remarkably versatile, conscientious and painstaking." A reviewer in a Ventura paper, Marvin Sosna, offered the following curious assessment of Meaty Dahl's performance on the podium:

> Dahl the conductor is a master, and there isn't much more to say, once that is said. He brings out strength from an orchestra in great rolling waves, yielding always to tenderness yet never to sentimentality. His approach to music is masculine, a surprising element in today's musical world; his music is highly personalized and hewn of solid sinew. To composers and audiences weary of the limpid and the nervous, Dahl comes a[s] a welcome reminder that beauty in not necessarily a feminine noun.

Etta, no impersonal observer, spoke in somewhat similar terms in a letter to Bill Colvig – "Ojai was a stupendous success…For Ingolf a vast personal triumph. All of his hours slaving over the scores paid off. I don't know another conductor who at one and the same time is so scholarly, powerful, well-disciplined, authoritative, yet romantic without being mawkish."

Frederick Fennel described Ingolf's selection of music as "a model of what 'festivals' can be and seldom are," and Lawrence congratulated his friend, "I hope you are comfortable and warm in the glory with which you swathed yourself this past weekend." Ingolf, however, was disappointed at the lack of press coverage. "I have the sense of futility, of waste, what for – " he complained on June 16. Attention paid by the press to the Cabrillo Festival up the coast was interpreted as "a slap in the face for me…, I just don't have what it takes to inflame, to carry along…" Listening to an unsatisfactory *Zaide* recording in December he added a characteristic plaint, "Makes me realize how good Ojai was, but it was good in a vacuum!! What for, all that work?"

65. THE DHARMA BUMS II

On August 22, 1963 Ingolf drove to San Francisco, where he rendezvoused with Bill Colvig. A year after their Alpine expedition the two were preparing for another mountain climbing trip, this time in the Oregon Cascades. Accompanied by Bill's brother, Dick, the two climbed Mt. Washington on the 25th and Mt. Jefferson on the 27th. After returning to the Bay Area Ingolf and Bill picked up *my* old school chum, Allan

Solomonow, for a drive over the Sierras, arriving in Bridgeport on the afternoon of September 2.

Here, on the courthouse lawn, they found another trio already arrived from Los Angeles, two of Ingolf's students (though separated almost by a generation), Don Michalsky and Jack McGuire, and me. This sextet camped near Twin Lakes and on September 3 began a week's backpacking trip, which, in spite of some bad weather, I have always regarded as my most successful Sierra outing.

Our goal was the California Matterhorn, the same summit whose ascent is described in Kerouac's *The Dharma Bums*. Lugging very heavy packs we struggled up the talus to a lovely wooded terrace the first day. Ingolf and Don went to explore the Dragontooth Glacier and encountered, by accident, an old mountaineering companion, the geophysicist Leon Knopoff. After dining on "Farina Chambree and Pudding Beure Ecossaise" we moved, the next day, to a lovely little lake beneath the peak and got thoroughly soaked when rain funneled through a grotto in which we had taken cover for the night. The next day we climbed over Horse Creek and Matterhorn Passes and on September 6 reached the summit in the late afternoon. "My first Sierra peak with Anth!" Ingolf recorded happily. He had forgotten Mt. Bago, nine years earlier; the sentence, in retrospect, would have read more accurately, "my *last* Sierra peak with Anth."

We were overtaken by rain and hail and had to make a hasty camp that night (Ingolf and I shared a tent) but the next morning the sun was shining as we crossed Burro Pass and stopped to have a cup of Orange Fizzy-flavored water. Another storm sent us bundling under ponchos at 10, 800 feet, but at last we descended to beautiful Crown Lake, where our last full day was blessed by more beautiful weather. I went fishing with a safety pin and Allan floated serenely on the lake's surface on his air mattress.

During the drive back Ingolf insisted we stop at some caves he had discovered in the gold mining country near Columbia. The advantage of this site was that one could swim in the dark waters and rely on the acoustics of the cave to improve our rendition of a canon by William Byrd – which Ingolf insisted on teaching us on the spot. The trip would have had a perfect ending here but, unfortunately, Ingolf drove the Peugeot into a curb in Modesto and burst a tire. It was the second accident of this year.

On March 31, after visiting Trude Rittman in Palm Springs, he had lost the car's sunroof in a gust of wind.

On June 20, the following year, I helped Ingolf celebrate a milestone in his career as a mountaineer. The occasion was the ascent of his hundredth Southern California peak, Sugarloaf Mountain near Big Bear, a conquest that earned him the 86th badge issued by the Hundred Peaks section of the Sierra Club. The day was not without its incidents. A large party of well-wishers accompanied Ingolf to the summit but the bottle of iced champagne which they expected to consume on top exploded at high altitude and its contents vaporized in an instant. Ingolf, as usual, had underestimated the time needed to complete the journey and this caused Paul Glass (and other guests in the walking party) to miss much of his brother's birthday party. "Feel nostalgic and rather sad that it's done," Ingolf reflected after his triumph. He kept on hiking, of course, and made a good start on his second hundred.

One can tell how much time Ojai took from his schedule by noting the number of summits "bagged" during these years: seven in 1962, after his return from Schruns, and thirteen in 1963, but only four in 1964, four in 1965, then fifteen again in 1966 – all but one *after* the Festival. A number of outings were devoted to "quantity rather than quality," as the hiking party climbed three or four easily accessible peaks in a day.

Ingolf had a troop of habitual hiking companions in these years; this included a number of students, present and former, such as Don Michalsky, Charles Fierro, and Paul Glass, friends of mine like Leigh Peffer and Kay Nelson, Don's colleague at Fullerton State, Paul Obler, and Etta's handyman helper Pete Thomas. Bill Colvig also walked in the Southern California mountains with Ingolf.

The hikes provided marvelous exercise for the body and the mind. I wish I could recapture some of the wit, and paranoia of trailside chatter. Ingolf and the musicians talked a great deal of shop and vented many a spleen at the expense of absent enemies. There were also many political discussions, where I would be expected to provide the historical perspective. We played guessing games, told jokes (though not, in Ingolf's presence, dirty ones) and there was inspired fantasy – should the Queen of Belgium *really* sponsor a competition prize for the world's best page turner?

I remember two pre-100th summits with particular clarity. On February 3, 1963 we climbed Mt. Harvard and Mt. Wilson from the Sierra Madre canyon deep below – accompanied by a stray black mutt addressed as Dog-Dog. We were so late that most of the descent on the Mt. Lowe road was accomplished in darkness but our reward was an unforgettable view through the clearest of air of the shimmering lights of the vast Los Angeles basin below. On the following April 26 we climbed Hines Peak, surprised to discover an icy summit and snowy trails. The winter scene inspired Paul and me to sing the *1812 Overture* as we plodded through the slush. Again in darkness on our return, Ingolf entertained us by beginning, one more time, the story of Wagner's *Ring*.

Charles Fierro was not only a hiking companion on whom Ingolf could rely for the most strenuous expeditions (including a brief Sierra trip to the Whitney area in September, 1966) but a favorite student and outstanding pianist. When Charles played the *Sonata Pastorale* on television at the end of December, 1964, Ingolf wrote to him, "I am not exactly spoiled when it comes to the performance of my music and therefore the experience of hearing the piece [played] with such command, flow, naturalness, projection and the kind of phrase inflection which an articulate performance requires, this was indeed something which made me very happy." Etta was unkind enough to suggest that Charles played the piece better than Ingolf himself, and, indeed, interpretation of Dahl piano music – on recording and in the concert hall – became one of Charles' special interests. I remember him as a gentle and soft-spoken hiking companion, striding along the trail in a blue pith helmet.

Donal Michalsky, who sported a red bandana tied around his forehead, possessed quite a different demeanor. A tall, beefy presence, Don had been an unmotivated linebacker for his high school football team. He and Ingolf shared many enthusiasms and pet peeves. Don maintained an even more rebellious distaste for civic authority and was constantly getting into minor scrapes with the police (even Ingolf got involved here when the two stopped to pee in an alley after a visit to a bar). Hikes with Don were flavored by the outraged yakkings of the two composers, keen to catalogue the latest assaults on nature, civil liberties or art perpetrated by the philistine "they." The flavor of this era, and something of Don's regard for his mentor, is related in a letter of September 25, 1964. Ingolf had praised a composition by Don, who replied, "I was and am aware of how "they" would regard the piece and what "they" would say about its place in relation to the new dogma but of course I did not compose it for "them" but for you and as a tribute to what you regard as musical and what I have learned from you." Earlier Don had driven away from the Ojai Festival "deeply pleased and honored to be your student-friend and colleague." Ingolf was an enthusiastic even envious admirer of his student's music. Writing about Michalsky's *Choral Symphony* to Lawrence Morton on January 17, 1967, Ingolf argued, "I have seldom been so moved or impressed by a new work – it is worth ten of Lutoslawski's 'Poemes"...There is not a single 'sound' in Don's piece."

Together Ingolf and Don completed a large number of outdoor expeditions including a a Sierra-Whitney trip in September, 1965, several overnight forays in pursuit of desert peaks and one bush-whacking struggle in fog and rain in the first week of June, 1964 – during which the two, in search of Mt. Ross, got lost and had to spend an unexpected mountain night in the damp. Anne-Marie Michalsky, worried about her missing husband, called the police but the Fullerton paper happily reported "Two Climbers Found Safe" when the wet hens at last emerged from the forest.

"I *need* exercise, yet will not take time for it," Ingolf complained on July 12, 1964. Nevertheless, as much as his arduous schedule permitted, he did try to keep in shape, not only as a hiker, but also as a swimmer, a skier, a runner, and a gymnast. There was practically no time for skiing in the winters of 1964 or 1965; when there was time there was no snow. In April, 1963 he had gone skiing with the Sierra Club at Whitney and Mammoth and he returned to the Sierras for skiing in June, 1966 with Edi Schaar.

On December 24, 1963 he plunged into the icy Pacific, just to say he had gone swimming on Christmas. Earlier in the year he had been exercising in the downstairs patio and had inadvertently brought his outdoor worktable down on his head. We can see from these adventures and misadventures that whenever possible he continued to find satisfaction in testing the body and any "vacation" would certainly have to include opportunities for physical activity.

66. CURTAIN CALL

Lawrence Morton's name appears with its usual frequency in Ingolf's journals of the mid-Sixties. The two were forever chatting on the midnight phone, sending each other notes, or socializing in one another's homes. "Long talks, but not enough," Ingolf wrote on September 3, 1963. There continued to be a great deal of professional collaboration between the old friends during this period as well. Ingolf was constantly counseling Lawrence on Monday Evening Concerts programming and Lawrence was Ingolf's faithful adviser on Ojai Festival matters. But it is obvious that the two were often at odds and that both enjoyed a good musical quarrel. Ingolf was upset by what he considered Lawrence's uncritical acceptance of the avant-garde; "an up to date but utterly useless concert" was Ingolf's review of the program offered by Lawrence on March 14, 1966. Michael Tilson Thomas feels that Ingolf was also jealous of Lawrence's advocacy of Pierre Boulez, "who was essentially, in terms of their mutual erudition and musicianship, the new Ingolf Dahl in town."

For his part, Lawrence had the responsibility for programming the latest in modern music, for this had always been the role of the Roof and the MEC, and he threw down the gauntlet as early as 1961 by declaring to Ingolf, "We are in a period, I think, when we must chose between two kinds of unsatisfactory composition, the avant-garde and the derriere garde." When Ingolf protested that this did not require the programming of charlatans and sensationalists, Lawrence responded in 1963 be saying, "On the lunatic fringe there are a few tassels that I find attractive." When Lawrence failed to compliment Ingolf on one of his 1966 concerts my stepfather grumbled, "Is he so completely wrapped up in the avant-garde?" That year the two also had a tiff over which voice (or what sex) to use in a performance of Pergolesi's *Orfeo*. "I treasure your last communiqué," Lawrence wrote (though surely with a short memory), "because it marks the first time in a quarter century that you have addressed me in a snit." Unfortunately Ingolf could not be so easily mollified. The *Orfeo* matter may have been insignificant but broader questions of programming impinged on his own sense of style and threatened his own position in the musical world.

There is an irony in much of this. Ingolf's advocacy of the music of his own generation had been manifest throughout the history of his own activity as a program designer. He remained to the end of his life an advocate for American composers and an active campaigner on their behalf among musical ensembles, foundations, and program planners, even with Lawrence, whom he accused of slighting Americans in 1964. The problem was that, in Ingolf's view, too many of his fellow countrymen, particularly the younger generation, no longer deserved a leg up, having gone whoring after foreign gods (or their synthesizers) and these striplings now occupied the places of composers of *music,* including those to whom Ingolf continued to offer instruction at U.S.C.

Writing to Gilbert Chase on July 27, 1963 Ingolf admitted "that sometimes I think back with nostalgia to those days of the forties where there was almost such a thing as a 'common practice' in the U.S. Aside from the question of how much of 'eternal value' was produced in that decade there was a common purpose by which I, for one, was quite swept away and I do not believe that I am imagining things when I note the absence of such a feeling today." Time had undermined Ingolf's position in the creative world. How could such a man – with such a long record as champion of the new – accept with any grace a role as troop leader of the derriere guard?

It is interesting to note that Ingolf did not abandon his search for quality in music; his oft-repeated lecture on quality judgments, first given in 1956, was frequently updated and expanded. His remarks show his dedication to objective criteria in evaluating works of art; he did not accept the assertion of Ezra Pound that "each work of art established its own criteria and may be judged *only* by these." Nor did he agree with Luigi Nono, whom he quotes as having stated, "A composer is following a worthy goal if he strives to completely baffle and confuse both the conductor and performers of his music." Similarly he was appalled when a young man approached him after an Ojai concert to ask, "If it wasn't true that the only new music worth considering consists of sounds that no one has heard before." "*Following* a technique, a style, a method, an idiom is not," Ingolf asserted, "a negative quality." Naturally he would not force all composers into the same idiom but he would judge them on the basis of the stylistic *unity* of their works of art, the ability they had demonstrated in pursuing the goals of their own style, and their ability to reject elements antithetical to their own intention. But "choices must be made on the basis of *something* beyond pure accident," and Ingolf felt that too much modern fare was being created by a process in which – by using chance, improvisation, computer, graph, scissors and tape – the composer had abandoned the personal responsibility for his own notes (or "sounds" in many cases) and thus broken the chain of human communication between artist and audience. Admitting that much avant-garde music was fun to listen to (once or twice) he argued that only tedium could result from works of art untouched by human hands, hearts, and brains. Life is governed by accident but art is governed by design. Now reviewers were calling works "highly organized and unified" that were mostly improvisatory!

Ingolf was fond of quoting Valery's dictum, "An artist is judged by the quality of his rejections." In musical terms this meant a search for *the* one note, the one harmony, the one rhythmic continuation, the active selection by the composer of possibilities, connections, elaborations and combinations. But such a method implies a vocabulary which many composers no longer found valid, and it is not surprising that Ingolf increasingly saw himself in impotent isolation, unable to proceed.

He began no new compositions in 1962 or 1963 and thereafter he often turned down commissions or suggestions from performers because he could not find enough enthusiasm for the project. (He even refused a commission to write a work based on the history of Western Washington State College!) "I wish I had written something during the vacation," he wrote on New Year's Eve 1963, "wish I had done a piece in memory of P[aul] H[indemith] (but time is going to go by, in dribbles, and I have no ideas, and that impulse will be gone)."

Only with the summer of 1964 was Ingolf able to find a project which could engage his creative energies. This was the *Aria Sinfonica*, the outcome of a $2000 commission from the Carolyn Alchin Foundation, which was awarded to Ingolf in the spring. He was the first composer to receive such an award, which was granted for the composition of a work intended for performance at the inauguration of the new Music Center in downtown Los Angeles. Raymond Kendall had gathered music and recordings of Ingolf's work for examination by the conductor of the Los Angeles Philharmonic, Zubin Mehta, whose assent was also needed before the commission could be awarded. Mehta evidently wanted a work for two antiphonal orchestras because he wished to exploit the possibilities of the new Center's huge stage, but Ingolf, overawed by the magnitude of the task that faced him, chose a more conventional ensemble.

A brief description of the *Aria Sinfonica* appeared in a Peter Yates review of the piece in *Arts and Architecture*:

> Aria Sinfonica is in four parts, related to the traditional operatic aria. A dramatic *Recitativo I* introduces the melody, which is then dispersed among the instrumentalists in a variety of brief combinations, followed by a quiet interlude and a *Cavatina* with three variations, for solo trombone, or oboe, clarinet, cello and violin, and for the strings. *Recitativo II* in a rapid tempo includes a duo for piano and harp; the orchestral part breaks and repeats itself in retrograde, the same notes in different orchestration. The concluding *Rondo* translates into orchestral *fiorituri* and a bravura *stretta,* the traditional display finale of the aria.

Ingolf's orchestral rendition of a scena, or extended operatic aria, was intended to supply parallels to the dramatic recitative in which the heroine depicts her plight; a melodic Cavatina in which she ponders the situation and proposes a solution; a second recitative in which she rejects her first idea and proposes a fresh solution; and a dazzling rondo in which the situation is resolved. Again a twelve-tone row was used but its harmonic application permitted the tonal coloration which Ingolf still preferred. The many passages for individual soloists represented Ingolf's homage to his friends in the Philharmonic, his respect for them and his challenge to them – for their tasks were not made easy. The work lasts approximately seventeen minutes and may be seen as the closest Ingolf ever came to writing a true symphony.

Early stages of the composition process were undertaken in Eugene, Oregon. Ingolf left Los Angeles by car on July 31, 1964. His first stop was Carmel Valley, where he gave a conducting lesson to a former student, Chris Nance. Then he drove to Weaverville on August 1 and checked into a motel: "Walk through the town, after. The spiral staircases, the mood of historical California – in an old big house an old lady, reading alone under lamp – thoughts of poor lonely Mammi – what if I were to knock and offer visit – as I pass, she smiles, lovely, about a passage in the book." On July

4 Ingolf noted that he *had* received a letter from Mammi "too depressing and guilt-evoking for words – she *needs* warm climate, she *needs* company. I could provide both and cannot." Letters in Mammi's shaky hand were soon to cease and in 1966 Anna-Britta reported that her mother communicated mostly with her teddy bear. Deep in senility she was moved to an old folks home on Vaxholm.

Ingolf's episodes in nostalgia remained pronounced. A week before his trip to Eugene my parents had paid off the rest of the mortgage on 2486 Cheremoya. "Not since Holunderweg," he reflected on becoming a home owner, "a feeling of pride, security, achievement...And the thought that just at the age at which I feel myself to be beginning Pappi was just about through." Pappi's "death day" was always circled in Ingolf's journals.

After three days hiking in the Trinity Alps Ingolf arrived in Eugene on August 4. Etta followed by plane and the two began house-sitting at the home of Robert Trotter of the University of Oregon's Music Department. Etta seems to have enjoyed Oregon, the aromatic air and "the lush green we don't have at home," though she was baffled by Claire Trotter's stove which had "some of those richly benumbered dials such as are found on the dashboards of planes and which I would gladly turn over to some co-pilot."

Ingolf took walks in the woods and worked out at the local gym. There were many visits with all the friends he had made after so many visits to Eugene. Complaining of "the weight of the world on my chest," of depression and doubt, of vertigo at the thought of having to conquer a work of such dimensions in a relatively short period of time, chastising himself as a talentless fake, Ingolf settled into a composition schedule. Feelings of futility are reported on August 7. "One needs two things," he noted on the 11th, "will power and blinders." "Sometimes I like some of the things I have been doing," he wrote Lawrence on August 20, "other times I get quite depressed." In an earlier letter he had acknowledged another problem, "I just can't shake the inhibitions which befall me when I can be heard while composing, even if it is by my own wife." On August 31 he began the long drive home and the next day the Dahls were back in Hollywood. Ingolf was now ready to begin a year of unprecedented labor, one which brought him, with the inevitable disappointments thrown in, to the summit of his career.

Even when he returned to the quiet of his own studio on September 2, the creative crisis continued – "an evening of utter depression – feel I *can't* go on – the piece *won't* be done or if it will it will be lousy – tears, frustrations, despair, don't know *wha*t to do." I was certainly not aware that my stepfather had reached such a low-point, for he hid these things well, nor was I cognizant of the fact that he was taking pills, Librium specifically, to counteract depression, though he does record that he borrowed a tranquilizer from my wife Dorothy on September 3. Later in the month and also in October there was a long struggle with asthma, so often a physical companion to emotional distress.

Ingolf, in fact, brought all of his physical afflictions into the Sixties, passing rapidly from periods of vigorous health to episodes of debilitating illness. He suffered from sore shoulders, knees, fingers, foot and neck and endured attacks of gout several times. He complained endlessly of fatigue, thyroid problems, the need for more sleep, of double vision. His teeth needed a good deal of work but this necessitated a succession of battles with receptionists over the office Muzak – which he dreaded more than the drilling. There were also stomach complaints in this period and numerous problems affecting the throat and chest: tonsillitis, laryngitis and bronchitis. On January 16, 1963 he endured a broncoscopy – "it felt," he wrote Bill Colvig, "as if they pushed the whole of Mt. Palomar telescope down my throat and into the bronchial tubes." None of his illnesses produced a permanent debility; on February 4, 1964 he notes how odd it was that after a strenuous hike he felt just great, "in top shape." Nevertheless illness proved to be, at the very least, an annoying inconvenience, particularly when it took him away from the worktable. Smog contributed to breathing problems in the fall of 1964 and on October 15 he took a cabin at Camp Angeles for some "glorious free air." Here he continued to wrestle with the length and shape of the *Aria Sinfonica*.

Harold Budd, a composition student, remembers Ingolf's delight over a passage of parallel 6th chords which he had given to the high strings in the new piece. "You know," the composer admitted, "no one cares; it's like pissing in the ocean." No one cares but the composer, whose preoccupation with details which no audience could divine continued to slow progress on the piece throughout the fall. November was a particularly fallow month. During the Christmas holiday Ingolf wrestled with his own self-imposed row – "why not just free chords??" – and the degree of dissonance and chromaticism he should permit. Copying of some sections of the work began on January 3, 1965. Driving to school two days later he admitted, "No matter how tense, worried, apprehensive, harassed a time this is – how happy to *work*, to *write*, to see forward to performance." The last tutti and coda were still missing on February 2; a week later he lay in bed hiding his panic with a pep talk – "You *can* do it – in two days you *will* do it." On February 14 it was done – "Lean on piano and have a good cry," he reported. Etta carefully drew the double bar on the manuscript and Ingolf rushed out to buy champagne. The next day his freeway drive to the university took him past the Music Center. He waved and shouted "Hi" – "I met the challenge."

Ingolf's anxiety returned in early April as performance time approached. He met Mehta for a conference on the work only two days before the April 15 premiere. "It is so hard to get *through* to him," Ingolf moaned. Sections of the orchestra were rehearsed that day ("piece is *good*, Ingolf enthused) but the Indian charm-bundle (or Zoobie Baby as was affectionately called) was much more preoccupied with Mahler's *Second Symphony*. On the 14th an anguished Ingolf complained, "He is *still* doing Mahler – at last 6:30 to A.S. – *first* time with winds – it is a mess – and gets only to end of 2nd movement. Tomorrow the performance, and not once through yet!" Seventy minutes of rehearsal time were allotted to this most complex of modern works on the morning of the premiere, April 15 – "still very shaky, tutti spots have been gone through just once, oh hell – ." A hug from Etta and a wave of emotion flavored the last minutes before the first downbeat. "Three curtain calls," Ingolf recorded, "standing and looking at the full hall, the moment of truth, so short, has arrived." This was the last time I saw him in a concert hall.

The program was repeated the next night. "To have heard you perform this music under Zubin Mehta's admirable direction," Ingolf wired the orchestra, "was indeed the high point of my many years of musical activity in Los Angeles" – but it was clear that the composer was none too pleased with the skimpy rehearsal time accorded his latest creation. When the Philharmonic played the work in Orange County on the 17th he described it as a "miserable experience," though a concert featuring the work in

Pasadena on the 21st was depicted as a "fairly good performance." Peter Yates' review of the premiere noted that:

> the several members of the orchestra who had solo parts showed their respect for the composer by coming well prepared and their playing separately and together in the public performance was consistently beautiful. The larger body, without solo parts, naturally took its lead from the conductor, and his lead was cautious. With the result that the performance was distinguishably on two levels; the music in its instrumental detail sounded very well, but the tuttis were undifferentiated.

The *Aria Sinfonica* received very encouraging reviews both from the critics and from the large number of friends who wrote to Ingolf to express their appreciation. "It was very much you and you at your very best, so clear and sparkling and such good, delightful music," Pauline Alderman wrote. Lillian Steuber added, "It seemed to me a complete unifying of ideas, imagination and knowledge unfettered or better, released in a really powerful work." Peter Yates said that the piece is "a true showpiece for orchestra, serious, but not solemn, a real test of musicianship and a joy for the listener." Alexander Fried in the *San Francisco Examiner* referred to a "decisive, concentrated score, shaping its ideas with impressive imagination and authority, and warming them with a temperate lyric feeling." Blair Hightower in the Pasadena *Independent* wrote that "Aria Sinfonica is a work whose neglect after its premiere would be shameful," and Albert Goldberg in the *L.A. Times* declared that the composer's "principal intention seems to have been to write a piece that would display the capacities of the orchestra as an opera aria displays the voice, and in that he was distinctly successful. The work does not yield all of its secrets on first hearing, but as an example of orchestral virtuosity it makes its points brilliantly."

But Ingolf was not convinced. Problems with the last section in particular began to haunt him and, until revision could be attempted, he wavered erratically in his own view of the composition. At one point he wrote that he considered the work "the most developed and mature piece I have written," but this did not save him from the same blackness that had overtaken him on a Stockholm street corner two years earlier. Where others saw originality Ingolf saw himself "writing like everybody else," the work "too fashionable...such small potatoes to come out of a year's hard work."

That none of these judgments represented a final word was illustrated by his repeated attempts to schedule the *Aria Sinfonica* for performance in later years and his search for a home for the work, eventually secured when rental of score and parts became available through the music publishing firm of Alexander Broude. Revisions had to take place first and in the busy spring on 1965 there wasn't time for this because on April 21st, after listening to the last of the L.A. Philharmonic concerts, Ingolf – with Ojai only a few weeks away – boarded a plane for Buffalo, where he would conduct the *Aria Sinfonica* himself.

67. DOWNBEAT

The pressures of Ojai and the *Aria Sinfonica* deadline prevented Ingolf from undertaking his normal share of performing and conducting assignments during the 1964-1965 season. His first public appearance had been on November 14, 1964, when he conducted the Glendale Symphony Orchestra in Brahms and his own *Tower of St. Barbara.* "The orchestra is an excellent one (all Hollywood studio players)," Ingolf noted, "They all loved 'St. B.' (including the hardboiled musicians, even some of old fogies did." The *Montrose Ledger*, perhaps following up on the Meaty Dahl theme, announced that Ingolf was a "conductor of great warmth and virility."

Four days later he began rehearsing the U.S.C. Symphonic Band in the newly revised *Sinfonietta.* "A good rehearsal," he wrote, "the piece is *fun*, it *works.*" Ingolf was preparing the band for a tour which began on December 17 when he and Bill Schaefer climbed aboard the band bus and headed for Tempe, Arizona and the thirteenth National Conference of the College Band Directors National Association. There was a warm-up concert at Brawley High School that night and the next day Ingolf conducted the ensemble at the conference – "They play their hearts out. Then standing ovation – am very touched – that this could happen to me." Just before the concert Ingolf spoke to the band directors about the *Sinfonietta* and gave his views on composing for the band in general; the next day he participated in a panel on the Educational and Cultural Responsibility of the College Band, noting that panelist Gunther Schuller "contradicts completely what I said the day before." Bill Schaefer recalled that Ingolf's appearance at the convention was a memorable and inspiring one. Keith Wilson, conductor of the Yale University band, wrote him, "When a composer of your stature displays an obviously serious interest in the band, not only by writing for the medium, but also by taking time to attend such a meeting and talking to band conductors, more progress is made in our field than [in] hundreds of clinics and demonstrations by our own colleagues, no matter how excellent they may be." A successful presentation of the *Sinfonietta* at U.S.C. on January 15, 1965 completed this happy chapter. Two week later, on February 1, Ingolf also conducted a Monday Evening Concert ensemble in the first Los Angeles performance of Ives' *Over The Pavements.*

On March 30 he had a most unusual assignment ("How amusing," he reflected, "*this* wrinkle of the musical career"). The occasion was the dedication ceremony for the new Los Angeles Country Museum of Art on Wilshire Boulevard's Miracle Mile. Here the Monday Evening Concerts would find a new home in the museum's auditorium and here Lawrence Morton would at last receive the office space needed to coordinate the famous series. To celebrate the inauguration of the enterprise a performance of Handel's *Fireworks Music* was staged, with real fireworks blasted from the roof and cued to the music, which Ingolf conducted below. While an invited audience sipped their drinks and milled about, the cameras of KHJ TV provided live coverage. I watched at home. Although the Handel went off like a rocket, Ingolf was annoyed at many other aspects of the evening. He did not like conducting music for a chattering mob – "*never* again the indignity of background music"– the musicians got to the champagne before the performance and some of them missed their entrances, and, after all of his labor – so I had to inform him – the TV people failed to identity Ingolf as the conductor of the orchestra! At least such irresponsibility was not repeated on April 12, when the local educational station, KCET, broadcast a performance by Ingolf and Larry Lesser of the Dahl *Cello Duo.*

Immediately after the troubled Los Angeles Philharmonic premiere of the *Aria Sinfonica* Ingolf boarded a plane for Buffalo. Buffalo had by now emerged as a new Mecca on the musical map and a number of Ingolf's friends from Los Angeles had followed the temptations of eastern promise. Peter Yates would soon accept an academic position here and Lukas Foss and Leo Smit had both left U.C.L.A. to take up positions in the city. Lukas was now conductor of the Buffalo Philharmonic and supervisor of a group of talented young soloists who gave concerts of mostly improvisatory music. Ingolf was not at all pleased with Buffalo's stampeding avant-gardism or with the decision of Fred Myrow to participate in Lukas' group. Other composers evidently regarded the experimental atmosphere with suspicion; Norman Dello Joio wrote to Ingolf, "I suspect your piece in Buffalo will strike a note of sanity in these confusing times." The ten-day trip, which began on April 21, was made under the auspices of the Rockefeller Foundation, which was sponsoring an American Music in the University conference in which Ingolf, Ralph Shapey and Harold Shapero appeared as featured performers.

Ingolf found much enjoyment in the company of old friends, including Foss, Smit, and Shapero. He was particularly grateful to Fred Myrow, whose apartment he used for practicing. "Thank heavens for his presence," the visitor concluded after an arduous period. It's clear that others had reasons to be grateful to Ingolf in return. Harold Shapero remembered that he had to conduct his own *Partita for Piano and Orchestra*: "I was a very inexperienced conductor and Ingolf devotedly went through my entire work with me, marking up the score, and showing me how to conduct every bar. It was a very touching display of friendship under hectic circumstances."

On April 28 Ingolf drove to Rochester where he heard the Eastman Wind Ensemble rehearse his *Sinfonietta*, "a thrill," he reported to Lawrence Morton, "hardly ever have I heard any of my music so well performed!" There was also time for a talk with students and faculty of the Eastman composition department. Ingolf's curious and unwanted association with the musical right wing is well authenticated in a comment of Robert V. Sutton, "Many of the more thoughtful students referred again and again to points you raised...In some cases the discussion took the form of baiting by the more conservative students acting as devil's advocates and enticing you into championing their position more eloquently than they could do themselves."

Ingolf played some of his own music at a concert in Buffalo on April 23, a day spent in an annoying and degrading search for a practice room and a piano to use it in. On the next day members of the music department at the State University College at Fredonia gave a Buffalo concert featuring several works by Ingolf, the *Viola Divertimento*, the *Serenade for Four Flutes* and the *Allegro and Arioso* – but Ingolf reported that nobody came, "it is just scandalous, the futility of it all." When the same concert was repeated at Fredonia on the 29th a happier result was achieved – "Performance better, large and very *warm* crowd of young people. Fun."

Rehearsals of the *Aria Sinfonica* began on the 23rd but Ingolf was unhappy with the orchestra and critical of his own shortcomings as a conductor – "not *the* pull, *the* magnetism, power, will, that great conductors have." The performance of May 1 was, in spite of some good local reviews, a disaster from Ingolf's point of view: "no balances, strings inaccurate, winds go berserk." Some instrumentalists played when they shouldn't have, others played "not one note right." "What became of my lovely piece?" he asked himself while mumbling all the right things at the post-concert festivities, "like my child run over by a truck." The next day he flew back to Los Angeles to begin the final stages of preparation for the 1965 Ojai Festival.

Ingolf had agreed to direct the 1965 festival as early as June 12, 1964: "They want me again – but reduced budget – elated and depressed." Ingolf offered to take a cut in salary in order to make more money available to his staff, but the Board thought a higher priority would be to attract musical stars to their festival. "They want me to get it for them wholesale," Ingolf grumbled. His task as director was, according to Etta, "twice the chore it should have been because of the limited budget. Many a good work had to be discarded because we cannot afford the number of oboes or brass it requires." The retired and wealthy business folk on the Board, among whom Ingolf and Etta made some good friends, also wearied their director with endless receptions and social gatherings at which he was rarely at ease. "Make speech about program," Ingolf noted during the Ojai Festival Ball on March 6, "dissatisfied with my clipped delivery."

"Am having Ojai nightmares," he wrote on February 16, "no soloist for final concert – no nothing – everything crumbling." Surely his preoccupation with the *Aria Sinfonica* in Los Angeles and Buffalo and his commitment to conduct Harvey Pittel in the *Saxophone Concerto* at U.S.C. on May 12 must have eaten into his preparation time considerably. There was much music to learn before the first orchestra rehearsal four days later. "Here we go again," he reported, "It goes quite well and I feel I've got it under control." There were a thousand minor crises. Soprano Grace-Lynne Martin found that she could not do a Mozart aria that Ingolf had programmed. "He had been in his own inimitable fashion," she wrote, "very patient with me, and when I suggested that I replace this aria with another Mozart concert aria, he immediately, without criticizing me, went to work to help me feel confident about the replacement of repertoire – all of this within a week or so of the concert!" After thirteen hours of conducting Ingolf drove to Ojai on the night of May 20, the eve of the first of six concerts in what Halsey Stevens called "a stimulating but beautifully balanced" exercise in Festival program planning.

Altogether Ingolf conducted three programs: these were supplemented by a harpsichord concert given by Alice Ehlers and Malcolm Hamilton, and a program of "American Pioneers of 20th Century Music" in which works by Ruth Crawford, Virgil Thomson, Adolphe Weiss, Wallingford Riegger and Charles Ives were set off by a brilliant pianistic display from Michael Tilson Thomas, who played music by Cage, Cowell, and Tremblay. Ingolf conducted Don Michalsky's *Fanfare After 17th Century Dances*, a Mozart Serenade and concertos by Ibert and McPhee on Friday night; Ramiro Cortes' *Violin Concerto* and Harold Shapero's *Serenade* on Saturday night; and Ruggles' *Men And Mountains* and Schumann's *Second Symphony* on Sunday afternoon.

His self-appraisals were, on the whole, quite generous, and the local papers were complimentary, but the inevitable depression was kicked off when a discouraging word was uttered by a reviewer on the Bay Area radio station KPFA. "This seems like the last straw," he wrote on June 8. Even after confirming plans for the 1966 festival with the Ojai Board on June 12 he reported himself, at the conclusion of this extraordinary year in his professional life, "confused, depressed, uncertain, tired."

68. THE WALL

Two weeks after the completion of Ingolf's first Ojai Festival he and Etta attended the wedding, on June 14, 1964, of Anthony Linick and Dorothy Goldstone. Many changes had occurred in my life in the two years since my parents had returned from sabbatical in 1962. For about a year I even returned to my old bedroom at Cheremoya, taking charge of many of the household tasks that my depressed and physically damaged mother could not do for herself. After two years of independence, first at Burnside and then in the studio downstairs, I found it quite difficult to return to the role of child again, and I suffered from the last stages of dependency and resentment for some months.

As I nurtured my own precarious sense of identity, I had attempted to keep my parents at some distance from my intellectual and social life. This task was now made doubly difficult by my return to the nest and, in spite of my yearnings for freedom, my parents remained the reference group to which all my efforts seem pointed. They were intensely preoccupied with my Ph.D. examinations and Etta coached me herself as I prepared for my German language proficiency test. During the last hectic week of May 1963, when I was scheduled to complete written and oral qualifying examinations for my Ph.D., Etta increased the pressure by regaling all her friends on the telephone as though I had already passed them. Even when the whole process was complete, Ingolf let me know that, given the obvious importance of the arts, he was slightly disappointed that I had chosen so dull and joyless a field as history. In this fashion he underlined why, in my effort to find a self that was separate from that of my parents, I had been drawn to such a choice in the first place.

Fortunately, Ingolf and Etta were both charmed by Dorothy and her sassy British ways. Etta was more than enthusiastic over her new daughter-in-law and when she saw our courtship reach its final stages she drew me aside and bequeathed to me, at engagement time, the diamond ring that Baba had once presented her – back in those glory days when his wealth lay undiminished. For over forty years Dorothy wore this symbol of the lost grandeur of the Linicks.

Ingolf was worried that my new liaison might keep me out of the mountains, but he soon realized that Dorothy was no more likely to prevent me from participating in a needed hike than Etta was apt to spike his own outdoor adventures. On the day of the ceremony at the Sheraton West Hotel he was full of parental emotion – "Go up to Tony's suite – help him into his collar – doing this the whole frame becomes visible – changing his diapers ("once!" – Etta), his first steps – the whole life together – and this is the last – he is so poised."

Dorothy and I lived at first in a small apartment on the last block of North Ivar. I had moved here in the fall of 1963 and here I wrote most of my doctoral dissertation on the history of the American literary avant-garde since 1945. We were within walking distance of Cheremoya and there were many visits. On November 15, 1964 I brought my new English relatives, including Dorothy's sister Naomi and her mother Anne, to a Cheremoya luncheon whose guest of honor was Gracie Fields.

I spent the academic year 1964-1965, a year of great triumph for Ingolf, as an instructor at U.C.L.A., but in the winter I agreed to take up a position as assistant professor in the Humanities Department at Michigan State University and we announced that we would be leaving Los Angeles in June, 1965. "Ingolf got all gooey over Anth's landing this," Etta reported, "launched at last."

I think that my decision to seek an academic post so far from Los Angeles must also have reflected my desire to cut the knot, to step away from the giant shadows that had impeded my movement toward the light for a quarter of a century. A resigned Etta declared herself "terribly pleased at his success but we will miss the children very much." Ingolf recorded, on March 25, 1965, only a few weeks before we all sat in the Music Center to hear the first bars of the *Aria Sinfonica*, "Anth calls canceling hike – very depressed about that – so cancel myself too. Need time, but need exercise too (And Anth –)." Even more despondency is registered on June 22, our departure day – "A handshake, that's all and watch the green VW drive down Beachwood, 'my son' at the wheel. Drive down the street after 26 years and out of my life – . Good luck, Anthony! May you find yourself."

My absence could only have heightened the sense of dislocation under which my isolated parents now lived. Etta had, after all, returned from the second sabbatical suffering from the same depression which had characterized the nervous breakdown in 1962-1963. An undated note in her hand, presumably written in 1963 or 1964, reads, "Dearest, I appreciate your wanting to take me on a trip but I have no 'Lebensgeiste' with which to undertake one and would have no fun." Drafts also exist, from the same period, in which Ingolf addresses himself to the problem of her withdrawal. There is no evidence that he sent any of these notes or that he verbalized his anguish:

> This is a sad situation. One of these days you will have to talk to me and tell me what's bothering you – or write me a letter again – as you used to do...what's wrong with us?...Don't I even deserve the

consideration of a letter?...Why can't you talk to me like a human being?...You have to talk to me, or write, if you want – how did we get to this point?...Have I pushed you into the shell in which you are now? Could I alone have built the wall that separates us now – surely you built as much of it yourself. Is there no way in which you can communicate any more?

The references to Etta's "wall" appear as late as August, 1964, when Ingolf is prepared to admit some responsibility for his part in her withdrawal – "Oh where is she – is it all my fault, I myself built the wall that is around E. And I want to love her and be close to her so much – what hell." Frankly, I have no memory of my mother behaving in a melancholic or introverted fashion on her return from Europe, and I was certainly in a position to observe her closely. It *is* certain that she knew how to hide her feelings, and, as I was to discover, to hide from me much of the reality of her life with my stepfather. But it is also likely that it was Ingolf especially who elicited the blank wall.

Etta did manage to press forward with a number of projects during these years. She did translations for Ojai, helped Arthur Knodel with proofs of a book, undertook business correspondence for her husband and taught diction to singers, not only at U.S.C., but privately as well. None of these activities, regrettably, really taxed her capacities or permitted sufficient exercise for her intellect.

In 1965 she began work on two pieces of fiction, one a wry sketch about an imaginary language, one an extended children's story. In "Strahenthian; Some Introductory Remarks," Etta demonstrated that she still retained a sense of humor – about adverbial forms at least – as she employed a stuffy academic jargon to illustrate how to say, in Strahenthian, "perpetually between heaven and earth," "now and then between heaven and earth," "scarcely ever between heaven and earth," "literally between heaven and earth," and "seemingly between heaven and earth." "Proof of Birchwarren's categorical contention," Etta continued, "that still another prepositional construction existed in the eighteenth century – 'characteristically between heaven and earth' – has been awaited with some interest in the field since he first published..."

Language is also the subject of "Eric Forth and Back," a story in which the hero visits a strange land whose vocabulary and sentence structure have been radically altered. "The Alligator," a poem, illustrates some of Etta's talent for verbal nonsense:

The cozy boats float hitherwither;
The alligator does not understand
the floating boating.
He slips away for wordage with his friend:

No paddling legs are on a boat; how does it float?
The alligator is at sea, at sea.

Just then a swiftylifty blows
And smacks the flopping rockaboats
Into a racy dashage on the blue!

Washed back, the alligator hugs the land;
Again, he cannot understand
Until his friend explains:

Atop a boat, as you will note,
A kind of canvas handkerchief sticks up
To make a puffy cheek or quiet wrinkle.
And this it has instead of paddly feet
For going when and where it whims.

The brainaged friend, who charges nothing
Deserves and gets a longly, lazy ride
Upon the alligator's back.

Now, seeing sailment on the sea,
No wonderage disturbs his pleasured eye,
Because he learned the boating how and why.

It was Ingolf's complaint that he saw too little of the Etta who indulged in such light-hearted moments. Either she stood above him as "the personification of the duty-drive," giving him a bad conscience if he wanted to take a day off, or she adopted a wholly negative attitude toward everything on the horizon and spoiled Ingolf's pleasure-seeking impulses. He grumbled that if they went together to an art gallery he would find the nice pictures to praise and she the awful ones to deplore. Even Lawrence Morton failed to escape her righteous disapproval, as a letter of April 6, 1966 demonstrates:

Dear Mr. Morton,

It has been brought to my attention that you, on hearing that I was unable to attend your party on April 4th last, exclaimed, on hearing the reason, "That's a lame excuse." I am writing today to congratulate you on your perspicacity. Due to the injury to my foot I was, indeed, lame; was any other type of excuse possible or even plausible? My excuse may have seemed tardy to you, and if it did, I can only compliment you once more; it was. It was tardy because since the bruising of my instep by a rough branch on the ground I had worn bedroom or other low shoes. It was only when I donned high heels (intending to grace your soiree) that I discovered how lame I had suddenly become. Since I was in some pain, I deemed it wise to go home and soak my foot. Might I suggest the same beneficial procedure for your head?
    Believe me to be, as ever,
        Your
           Ettadoll.

It was Ingolf's constant complaint that Etta was no longer available to him as a sexual companion. The anguished whining reminds us that there did persist a continuing physical attraction, a passion which, though periodic, always remained as one of the bases of their relationship. "A wonderful kiss from E. at midnight," Ingolf wrote on December 31, 1962, "but that's all it was going to be." "Just don't know what to do – wish I had a wife," he added the next day. "The same terrible scene" in Etta's room is described on their anniversary in 1963, "she is so unhappy and wants and doesn't and cries and I am *so* frustrated and unhappy." "E. is like a thundercloud – not a word," he added the next day, "goes and has coffee alone, locked in her room (should I go in?? Just for a repeat of the same scene?) Yet guilty to leave her like this, and yet I can't *penetrate* to her even if I stayed here." "E. comes to wake me," Ingolf was able to report on May 1, 1964, "her nearness." "When away from her," he reported while recovering from asthma at Camp Angeles in October, 1964, "the ties seem stronger... and then last week, when I was so bad she was so helpful, understanding."

Within a few weeks it was Etta's turn for sympathy and care. On January 3, 1965 she underwent surgery for bilateral ovarian carcinoma. Characteristically she did not even tell me of this illness, so as not to worry *me*, until I had returned from a job-hunting convention in Washington.

Her recovery was again remarkably rapid. "You are such a wondrous symbol for us all," Joan Schaefer wrote, but Etta's stern courage must certainly have been accomplished at the cost of a singular repression, for all of us chose not to dwell – because to do so would have been too painful – on the life prospects of a woman now on the mend from her third bout with cancer.

It was all very well for Ingolf to complain, a few months later, that "her spirits are not above her body," but it does not surprise me that this should be so. Nor that she should have retreated from an earlier act of courage, the decision not to smoke (Etta claimed she never inhaled anyway). "No thanks," she liked to say, "I've joined Ashtrays Anonymous," but there were moments when Etta lit up when that other latter-day abstainer, Ingolf, was not nearby to see. Once, by chance, he drove by her, smoking at a bus stop, and was overcome by a wave of "saddened sympathy."

My parents continued to spend much time (quality or not) with one another, in spite of Ingolf's busy professional and social schedule. They went to the movies, to the beach, the mountains, to concerts, they went to local eateries like the Self-Realization Fellowship Cafe and to fancier restaurants on special occasions and anniversaries. They read Gerald Durrell and John Cheever aloud. Arm in arm they strolled through the neighborhood. In February, 1964 they had celebrated the twenty-fifth anniversary of Ingolf's arrival in Los Angeles amid a "flood of reflections."

There were also some longer trips: in June, 1963, they spent five days in Baja, in August, 1963, and in June, 1965, there were overnight trips to Laguna Beach, and in June, 1966, they spent several days as the Tassajara Zen Mountain Center (where Ingolf disapproved of the "hoodlums, filthy-mouthed punks in hot springs, running around naked, mixed bathing, etc. no good – .") The following December they spent some time in Yosemite where Ingolf reported himself surprised at how well Etta did on the trail.

"After having said "no time" and "too busy" to social invitations for 2 years," Etta wrote Bill Colvig (neglecting to mention her own surgery earlier in the year) "we decided we'd better accept a few and also have some people over. So I was giving dinners in July, and also going to dinners elsewhere, fervently hoping the hostesses would have something I could chew with my beautiful new store teeth."

To recover from the strain of many active months Ingolf and Etta began their most extended vacation venture on July 31, 1965 – only a few weeks after Dorothy and I had left for Michigan, They spent one night in Carmel Valley, where Ingolf again gave a two hour conducting lesson to Chris Nance. The next day a long drive up the San Joaquin Valley and through Yosemite brought them to the east side of the Sierras via Tioga Pass. They checked into a Mammoth Lakes cabin at Wood's Lodge on Lake George. Here they remained for four weeks – "The dream come true!!" Ingolf enthused, "It's indescribably perfect and beautiful." Ten days later the spell had not worn off – "the drops on the branches, the clouds hanging over the mountains, the fragrant air – thoughts of Schruns and Switzerland. I love it – this is such a fulfillment." The Dahls enjoyed visits with the Schaars, the Kellers, and violinist Alex Murray while at Mammoth. Etta and Ingolf went on many walks, the two went rowing on Lake George with Edi and, alone, Ingolf spent several days ascending nearby peaks. There was also an enjoyable three-day excursion, back across the Sierras again, to the North Fork Ranch of their friends, the Wyles. Ingolf suffered some gout in his right hand, but this was nothing compared to his anguish over news of the Watts Riots back in Los Angeles. He had been even more strongly affected by the Kennedy assassination in 1963; Etta had declared herself "ashamed to be a member of the so-called human race."

Naturally there could be nothing as decadent as a complete rest at Wood's Lodge – Ingolf had come to Mammoth for a working vacation. There were two major projects, but the second – work on a long delayed *Elegy Concerto* for violin – could not go forward much because of the absence of a piano. Ingolf did spend the first ten days of his stay completing an orchestral version of his *Quodlibet on American Folk Tunes*. This project had been launched on July 17 back in Los Angeles and Ingolf had to work quickly to make it available for the August 22 "Bon Voyage" concert of the Idyllwild Youth Symphony at Bovard Auditorium. On the way to a meeting of the Monday Evenings Concert Board on July 19, Ingolf recorded, "Lawrence says I *must* get the Quodlibet done – that puts some temporary steam in me." "Progress is minute," he reported on the 24th but the pace quickened when he reached Lake George.

The composer was worried about the discrepancy between the simple material of the original melodies and the sophisticated treatment he was providing in his orchestration, but by the 11th of August he was able to mail off the completed score. By now he had lost his interest in folklorism and resented the time required to complete the project – and its inevitable revisions in 1966, when the work became available through C.F. Peters' Henmar imprint. Ralph Matesky, who conducted the Idyllwild Symphony on the Scandinavian tour which featured the work, reported that the "piece is a great favorite with the orchestra...wonderfully scored and most interesting to play – challenging enough to good school orchestras but not too difficult for capable young players."

Ingolf and Etta were still up north when the premiere took place; indeed the Dahls did not leave Wood's Lodge until August 27, when they made their way back to the Pacific for the Cabrillo Festival and visits with its conductor Gerhard Samuel and Ingolf's old friend Lou Harrison.

At home they fell into their perennial emotional patterns. Ingolf seems to have spent little time considering why a white-haired sixty year-old woman, seven years his senior, victim of a double mastectomy and a partial hysterectomy, should have lacked the psychological wherewithal for an active sex life. There were rare exceptions in her mood. "E comes so nicely to wake me," he reported on January 1, 1966, "memories of time past, she is so affectionate." Increasingly, however, even their intimate times together stopped short of the sexual and Ingolf records many a wistful protest. When Etta accompanied him to Pacoima Canyon on his fifty-third birthday in 1965 he noted that he had to face up to the facts – "I will never, never again be taken in by E., never feel her and be close to her." On September 14 the Dahls were introduced by the Schaars to their friends the Kohners (creators of the famous Gidget). "Etta shines," Ingolf noted, "and she is so lovely – wish she were my wife." "A long intense hug – if only," he wrote on July 19, 1966, "but a few sighs are all." On the morning of December 20, 1966 Etta crawled into Ingolf's bed in Yosemite, "My frustration is just terrible at these moments – does she feel nothing? Can she do nothing?"

In spite of this unhappy picture there can be no question that the love affair of Ingolf and Etta survived without diminution. "The necessity for E.," Ingolf wrote on January 25, 1966, "just the basis, that warmth, that belonging – may I have her always." "She is the best," he added a year later, "still the best – if I could only make her happy." And he did, in many ways. Michael Tilson Thomas reported that Ingolf (who discretely eliminated any sign of a second bedroom when it was lesson time in his studio) rushed forward to receive so rapturous an embrace from Etta after a 1965 Ojai concert, that, to Michael, this gesture seemed to be the very unrivalled epitome of love.

69. OFF THE MAP

Overwhelmed by the magnitude of details and decisions that had to be addressed in preparation for the 1966 Ojai Festival, Ingolf *did* limit his concert hall engagements in Los Angeles during the 1965-1966 season. On November 17, 1965 he conducted the U.C.L.A. Concert Band in a performance of his own *Sinfonietta*. On January 16, 1966 he lead the U.S.C. Orchestra in a performance of works by Halsey Stevens, Bartok, and Haydn, again chiding himself for his "limited conducting vocabulary – always the same gestures, no electricity and finally no authority," but citing, nevertheless, a performance "beyond expectations, a huge success." On April 1 he conducted a U.S.C. group at the Music Center ("goes fair") and two days later he presented a Collegium concert on campus.

There were also some out-of-town appearances. Ingolf had received an award from the Alice M. Ditson Fund of Columbia University in 1964, one that provided symphony performance subsidies for a work chosen by the composer and funds for the latter to attend rehearsals and concerts at performance time. One of Etta's letters indicates that Ingolf now proposed to use the funds in connection with a presentation of his latest orchestral work, the *Aria Sinfonica*, which he would conduct himself in Cincinnati.

He arrived in the city on the Ohio on December 7, 1965, and met the Cincinnati Symphony Orchestra on the 8th ("not satisfied with myself – not enough publicity pizzazz and vitality – too what the hell"). The 9th was described as a "Mt. Rainier day, very rough," though it ended with a "very nice relaxing evening in very congenial company" with Richard and Rosemary Waller, two orchestra members who were graduates of his own U.S.C. Symphony. The performance took place on the 10th. Ingolf described it as "cautious," "ruin my bows by letting trumpets stand – oh well." The next day he bought flowers from a "little colored girl sitting in the store – forlorn, wistful – want to say something nice, but what?" and made a visit to Max Rudolf, the orchestra's principal conductor. That night a second performance was also described as disappointing – "sloppy attack, sloppy rhythms – performance has no tension, and the little imprecision which just kills me – I am not so much above as I should be." With only three hours sleep he boarded a plane the next morning, had a brief altercation about the muzak, and stewed in his disappointment.

The following March the *Aria Sinfonica* was performed by the Oakland Symphony under Gerhard Samuel. Ingolf flew north for one rehearsal and again for performances on the 15th and 16th. His journal provides little information beyond mentioning that Colvigs and Manns were in the audience, but one can guess what his reaction was to a review in the *Oakland Tribune,* which dismissed his piece – a "rambling 12-tone rhapsody peppered with instrumental solos"– in favor of Morton Subotnick's *"Play (II)"* for tape and orchestra, which was described as an electronic venture "which bridges a necessary gap into a new era of expression which may ultimately be as significant as the introduction of the piano to the orchestra, back in Mozart's day."

Months of planning by Ingolf and Rick Lesemann were required to resolve the usual programming and technical problems associated with the 1966 Ojai Festival. I find it interesting that Ingolf had even considered a concert version of *Die Meistersinger*, but "no," he wrote on July 6, 1965, "[it] requires great singers – where are they? and the bombast and patriotism of the ending is just unstomachable for me." "Ojai is *not* shaping up," he moaned on October 30, "All morning sit in den and stew over OF programming." Groups he wanted to hire had schedule conflicts or were unavailable. There were again budgetary restraints. Closer to the event itself the usual rehearsal problems surfaced. "The mountain," Ingolf cried on April 30, "don't know where to attack it first. Panicky – don't know a *single* of the 11 pieces." Soloists and choruses were behind in their mastery of parts and this threw him into a fury. On May 14 (described as the "incredible day") Ingolf had rehearsals at 10:30, 2:30, 5:30, 7:00, and 9:00, each at a different location.

Not surprisingly he had selected a most unusual and stimulating repertoire. "We do intend to play a few more or less familiar works," he told Martin Bernheimer in the *L.A. Times*, "Things like the Beethoven *Septet* in its original instrumentation and Bach's *Second Suite for Flute and Strings*. But these are the exceptions. Basically I am convinced that we have no right to offer the same things one hears during subscription seasons and call our versions a festival." There was the usual Baroque concert, the world premiere of Copland's *Dance Panels*, the American premiere of *Il Cantico delle Creature* by the Danish composer Bernhard Lefkovitch, the West Coast premiere of Lukas Foss' *Echoi* and a special program called "500 Years of Experimental Music," which included Ingolf's new edition of Anton Reicha's 1803 *Two Fugues for Piano*, played by Michael Tilson Thomas. Doriot Anthony Dwyer was soloist in Nielsen's *Flute Concerto* and Leo Smit in Tchaikovsky's *Concert Fantasy* for piano and orchestra. Ingolf conducted works by Richard Strauss, Beethoven, and Stravinsky.

The festival, which began on May 21, broke box office records and was favorably reviewed in local and national newspapers. Shibley Boyes noted, "It does your friends so much good whenever you get the limelight – for we dote on you – and so many *in*ferior people and musicians get such undeserved acclaim and you are such a *su*perior people and musician." And Christie Lundquist, a young U.S.C. clarinet student, who was a special favorite of Ingolf's, added:

> You've just got to be one of the greatest things that ever happened to music...You possess that rare combination of unlimited talent and genuine humility that is so characteristic of really great people...I could tell by the reaction of the audiences at Ojai, both individually and collectively how much they appreciated you, not just for the masterly way in which you presented the concerts but for the charming way in which you presented yourself to everyone.

Ingolf was nevertheless unhappy. The festival had been a success but *he* had not, or so he felt. Daniel Cariaga had reviewed his conducting of Stravinsky's *Symphony in 3 Movements* glowingly – "Dahl's extraordinary gift for going directly to the heart of an extended work was never more in evidence" – but he had done so in the *Long Beach Press Telegram*. Papers as far away as New York and Washington had spoken well of the festival but largely ignored its impresario. "Here again a failure," Ingolf noted on June 1, "as a professional conductor I don't have the projection and power to register with the press."

Even before the 1966 festival Ingolf had made it clear that he would not be available in 1967. He resigned officially on June 15, writing to Theodore Lilliefelt, president of the Ojai Festival Board, "If these three years have been good years, as they have been to me, they were so first of all because they helped to serve the cause of the highest musical ideals, that is, both the ideals of the interpreter and of the living composer." Lawrence Morton took over the administrative tasks of the Festival and Pierre Boulez was chosen to ascend the Festival podium in 1967. Following this announcement, a board member was overheard saying, "I'm afraid that we are about to go on the map." Such are the fortunes of musical show business.

A disappointed Ingolf was already turning the pages of his atlas in search of another remote European venue, where he could tend to his hurt feelings in isolation, but in the year before his departure from L.A. he tried to remain busy with activities that offered considerably less glory than Ojai. On July 30, 1966 he flew to Bloomington, Indiana where, for one week, he served as director of a workshop for contemporary band music, sponsored by the Contemporary Music Project. "The whole thing is too foolish," he wrote on August 4, "*way* below me, nothing to get out of it." Nevertheless he pushed himself through a staggering number of symposia, readings of band pieces, and rehearsals before a final concert on August 5, where he conducted the "Dance variations" section of his own *Sinfonietta*. Two old friends from Europe, Zurich's Marko Rothmuller and Cologne's Carl Fuerstner, now both members of the University of Indiana faculty, offered him hospitality. Asthma plagued him during this stay, however, and he was too exhausted to enjoy a day of sightseeing and museum visiting in Chicago on his return journey.

He had begun a half a year's worth of post-Ojai concert appearances with a Museum program of June 20, when he conducted Ives' *Over The Pavements* for a small crowd so enthusiastic that he had to repeat the piece a second time. At the Monday Evening Concert of October 3 he was joined by Bonnie Douglas, violin, and Emmett Sargeant, cello, in another of the Haydn works that he had himself arranged, the *Piano Trio No. 3 in C Major.* "It goes fabulously well," he reported.

Four weeks later he returned to the MEC stage to participate in the world premiere of Stravinsky's *The Owl and the Pussycat*. He and soprano Peggy Bonini had played the work through for the composer the previous day, but Ingolf's opportunities for visits with the old man were by no means as frequent as they had once been. That Ingolf should have driven by the Stravinsky home on New Year's Eve, 1962, perhaps to see if some party were in swing to which he had not been invited ("but all is dark") tells us a lot about his feelings as an outsider. A dinner at the Luau *is* recorded on February 10, 1963. At Pierre Boulez's birthday party, given by Lawrence on March 25, 1965, Ingolf reports himself gratified to see the maestro, but "I am shy and the 'old' Ingolf, withdrawn and stupid feeling." Trying to compose a musical greeting card for Stravinsky on June 16, 1965 Ingolf complained that it was so *hard* to do, to overcome the repressed father love, the inferiority feeling." The two met again on October 25 at a Monday Evening Concert. Ingolf remarked that the Mozart had been good. The master responded, "Yes, but the Haydn, oh the Haydn is special." "Vera looks pale," Ingolf noted, "and complains of too much travelling and tiredness. Old man in flowing, outgoing, radiating." "Want to be close again," Ingolf sighed on July 4, 1966, "(father longing), but don't know how and besides – ." Ingolf remained on cordial terms with Robert Craft; a "nice long talk" is reported on January 25, 1965, but the undercurrent of hostility creeps out in his assessment of the concert of October 25 – "Schoenberg Serenade is delightful in spite of Craft."

In January, 1966, Ingolf received a thousand dollars as one of five recipients of an ASCAP award scheme established to honor Stravinsky's 80th birthday – with the recipients having been selected by the maestro himself. In the draft of his letter of thanks Ingolf responded to the honor by arguing that he considered the award an obligation to "keep faith with whatever creative work I am capable of," to "stay as much in tune with the presence of musical life as you are," and to "serve your music with all my capabilities." It should be added that Ingolf continued to draw large numbers of student to his course on Stravinsky's music at U.S.C.

After *The Owl And The Pussy Cat* there remained only a few more concert assignments before it was time to pack up again. In November Ingolf participated in an Alice Ehlers concert at Hancock Auditorium on the 6th, and performed in a program at San Fernando Valley State College on the 25th, standing in as a last minute replacement, with no preparation. On December 10 faculty, colleagues and students, lead by Christie Lundquist, presented an all-Dahl concert at Hancock. A scholarship benefit, the program included the *Piano Quartet* played by Eudice Shapiro, violin, Richard Ferrin, viola, Gabor Rejto, cello, and Lillian Steuber, piano, the *Music For Brass Instruments* conducted by Michael Tilson Thomas, who also played the *Hymn*, the *Concerto A Tre* played by Christie Lundquist, clarinet, Barry Socher, violin, and Johanna de Keyser, cello, and the world premiere of the *Duettino Concertante* for flute (played by Susan Cohn) and percussion, played by Barry Silverman. Ingolf supervised a number of the rehearsals, though he took no part as performer or conductor. A lost part created a last minute crisis as the hall filled to capacity. "Warm audience reaction," a nervous Ingolf reported, "at end of program when I get on stage the audience explodes – all get on their feet. What a moment!"

On January 11, 1967 Ingolf spent a day in San Diego where he offered lectures, took part in discussions, and again participated in a concert of his own music, including the Brass Piece. Finally, on January 30, after weeks of rehearsals, he accompanied Peggy Bonini in Hindemith's *Das Marienleben* on a Monday Evening Concert. On February 2 the two musicians recorded this performance. Ten years later it was issued at last as a part of Don Christlieb's GCS label Hindemith Anthology series.

The *Duettino Concertante*, which received its premiere on December 10, 1966, had been completed only one week earlier. James Berdahl suggests that Ingolf first began thinking about the piece during his holiday in Aspen earlier that year, but composition did not begin in earnest until July 19, when Ingolf asked himself, "How 'rowy,' how tonal, how organized?" "Nothing will come out," he complained the next day, "I am not even spending enough time at the desk to let something come out." "Agonizingly slow progress, distractions, sidetracks," were reported on August 22 and on many another day throughout the fall. Inspiration for the project came from the flutist Doriot Anthony Dwyer, who wished to record a piece with percussionist Everett Firth on an RCA disc featuring members of the Boston Symphony Chamber Players. The *Duettino Concertante* is an eleven-minute, four movement work, well-designed to reveal the full range of sound possibilities in this combination of instruments. Only the flute part was serially organized, though each of the movements is oriented toward a different key. Ingolf gave the percussionist some daunting tasks, including effects to be created by fingernails and elbow. For technical information he consulted Karen Ervin, a Los Angeles musician who participated in a second recording of the work, with flutist Louise DiTullio, for Crystal

Records. *Duettino Concertante* was published by Alexander Broude in 1968.

A few weeks after completing the piece Ingolf turned to another of those occasional exercises, a four-hand piano piece in honor of the fiftieth birthday of the composer Ulysses Kay, who was serving as a visiting professor at U.C.L.A. On January 1, 1967, Ingolf reported that he was happy to start the year composing, but eventually he found himself bogged down, out of vanity, in this time-consuming task out of all proportion with the objective – "but once I started it had to be good." A number of other composers contributed variations on a theme from the second movement of Kay's *Suite for Strings*. At a party at the Cortes home on January 7, Ingolf played the work with Ramiro as part of the evening's festivities. This trifle was to be the last bit of composing that Ingolf would undertake in Los Angeles for some time.

70. A PARAGRAPH IN HIS OWN LIFETIME

When I first tried to piece together this account of my stepfather's activities, one of my greatest surprises was the discovery of a long list of projects that seemed so peripheral to his central preoccupations and responsibilities. His gruelling schedule at the university left little time for creative work or professional development and yet he seems to have needed the distraction of additional labor. To be busy at *anything* prevented him from dwelling too profoundly on the many unfinished tasks that should have had a higher priority – or on the emotional dislocations that underlay his entire existence. Often his only moments of sustained introspection came in the narrower hours of the night: journal writing time.

Throughout the Sixties Ingolf continued to appear as guest speaker and judge and to offer his voluntary services in a number of capacities to young performers and composers; he even devoted a great deal of time and energy to the education of that frustrating and important lot – the music critics. None of these activities contributed much to his income or prestige yet he couldn't say no often enough.

A number of his speaking engagements *were* connected with performances of Dahl works in such sites as Eugene, Bellingham, Tempe, and San Diego. In 1965 he addressed a group of History of Civilization students at Occidental College on "Great Issues in Music." He presented his "Traditions and Synthesis" lecture at Santa Barbara in 1966. The Music at Noon series at U.S.C. also offered several speaking opportunities, and soon after his return from Europe he spoke here on "An American Composer's View From Abroad." Ingolf was often asked to speak to audiences about the music that was going to be played by the Los Angeles Philharmonic or some other musical ensemble. "I have the ladies' ear," he reported after talking about *Persephone* on January 11, 1963. The following April, hobbled with gout, he spoke in German at City College on Schoenberg's *Moses And Aron*, with the composer's widow (and that of Lion Feuchtwanger as well) in the hall. Every kind of audience seems to have listened to Ingolf at one time or another. He went from addressing a class of high school music students in December 1963 to participating the following May as a panelist at the Round Table on Creativity during the annual meeting of the Academy of Psychoanalysis. Ingolf, incidentally, took the question of artistic creativity with great seriousness and prepared diligently for his five minute statement. "It is a ghastly waste of effort and time," he concluded. Other panelists included Robert Lifton and Dorothy's U.C.L.A. English instructor, Jack Hirschman. The latter, Ingolf complained, "reads a tired old dirty beat 'poem.'"

Let us hope that Ingolf found more rewarding experiences as a judge. On May 3, 1963 he began a week-long northern trip, during which he served as a judge in the senior division of the 19th Greater Spokane Music and Allied Arts Festival. The trip did include a stop-over in San Francisco for visits with Bill Colvig and the Manns. Two other judicial tasks required no travel. In 1964 he again served as a judge in the Utah State Fair Competition and in 1965 he began several years of service as a judge in the composition contest held by Sigma Alpha Iota, "an international professional musical fraternity for women."

On May 22, 1963, only a few days after returning from Spokane, he flew to Eugene where he lectured on "European Music in the 1960's" and conducted the University of Oregon Symphony Band in a performance of his own *Sinfonietta*. On July 19 he lectured on "The Pictorial Arts and Artists around Stravinsky" at Western Washington State College in Bellingham and two days later he performed the *Sonata Seria* in a concert there.

That Ingolf should have spent so much energy arranging the *Quodlibet* for a youth symphony, as he did in the summer of 1965, is consistent with his commitment to young musicians – on whose behalf he was extremely active in this decade. Many of his own students, of course, were just in the infancy of their professional careers, but Ingolf also assumed many other responsibilities in connection with the Los Angeles Young Musicians Foundation and its Debut Orchestra. He was a member of the audition panel of the organization as early as 1963, then he served on its Music Advisory Council, and in 1965 he became Musical Director.

Auditions and board meetings were often tedious affairs, though suddenly there would be an experience that would make it all worthwhile – "the little blonde girl with pigtails playing Opus 11, No. 1 with intensity and understanding!!" Ingolf forgot altogether about a Royce Hall audition he was to have helped judge on June 13, 1964, but perhaps he recovered from his feelings of chagrin on the following October 22 when a young pianist didn't show up for the evening concert – "so I play *Scherzo a la Russe* from score, Mike conducts from memory." A number of young conductors earned their spurs at the head of the Debut Orchestra including Henry Lewis and Larry Foster. The Mike referred to in the previous quotation was Ingolf's latest and perhaps most successful protege, a young conductor with whom he worked on many campus and YMF projects, Michael Tilson Thomas.

Ingolf was able to assist fledgling musicians in additional capacities in the 1960's, chiefly through his membership on innumerable committees and as advisor to several national foundations. The Guggenheim Committee now wrote to him for *his* recommendations on candidates. He agreed to serve on the music panel of the California Arts Commission. He advised the Rockefeller Foundation on a number of projects through which orchestras might be subsidized in the performance of works by little known American composers. A Rockefeller proposal to place young composers in residence with American symphony orchestras induced Ingolf to warn against "money-spending gimmicks" and to insist that "many young composers whom I have had the pleasure to watch, observe, hear, teach, have had after their apprenticeship years only one need: public performance, publication, recording." As a consequence, Ingolf urged the Foundation to support "organizations, academic or not, that do struggle, under considerable sacrifice, to be constructive in their programming." This progressive impulse was also one that Ingolf tried to communicate to the many professional and musical organizations to which he belonged, a list which – after twenty-five years in America, must have approached several dozen – teachers' organizations, guilds for arrangers, conductors, instrumentalists, composers, scholars, sponsoring organizations, honorary organizations, trade unions – one could easily have become impoverished by the dues.

The Music Educators National Conference, to which Ingolf had belonged for several years, joined with the Ford Foundation in a Contemporary Music Project at this time, and in 1965 Ingolf became a member of the Project Policy Committee for Creativity in Music Education. One of the chief tasks of the organization was the selection of young composers for assignment, at Foundation expense, to school systems throughout the nation. Norman Dello Joio was chairman of the committee, whose director, Grant Beglarian, proved to be an arts administrator whom Ingolf grew to admire greatly, both as an executive and a friend. On October 6, 1965 Ingolf flew to New York for the first of a number of out-of-town meetings of the Project Policy Committee, an "inconclusive" affair which depressed him because of its embrace of educational jargon: "implement," "situation," and "meaningful" emerging as the three most overworked words. After attending a number of concerts and visiting his New York friends he flew back to Los Angeles on October 10, but on January 19, 1966 Ingolf made a return trip ("for once, *no* Muzak in plane!"), this time to Washington, for another meeting with Ford and MENC colleagues, "Plough through hundreds of scores," he wrote as the 78 candidates were examined before their assignment to school systems, "The talented ones write Avant Garde music without relation to reality – the dunces write illiterate junk, nothing in between." "Lunch with the guys" on the 19th included Virgil Thomson, Robert Ward, and Vincent Persichetti. Ingolf managed to get in some socializing and sightseeing before flying to New York on the 22nd. Here he saw a Dali exhibition ("what cheap sensationalism") and a "Spanish Civil War film," presumably *Funeral In Berlin* – "thoughts of my own precarious path through those years and here I am – must work, must produce more, that is the only demand of the future." Ingolf visited his old Lichtwarkschule friend Kurt Stone on the 23rd but on the next day he complained of being too tired "to get on the ball professionally, oh hell." Exercising at the "Y" he pulled a muscle in his left calf and had to limp off to Carnegie Hall, where he sniffed, "*How* much better my Webern!" In anguish, Ingolf applied hot compresses; his most recent accident had come on the eve of a scheduled skiing holiday in Aspen.

He arrived here on January 26 and soon recovered, attributing his strength the next day to the inspiration of the physical beauty around him. He skied every day until the end of the month, suffering the usual traumas of exhaustion, diarrhoea and Muzak on the slopes – "I am being smoked out of this world." The holiday was to have been a secret, that is Ingolf must have ducked out of some task back in L.A. because of "business conferences in the East," but on the 30th his walk through the Colorado town was interrupted by a "Mr Dahl, how are you?" from a U.S.C. student.

On February 1 he returned to Los Angeles – midway in a crowded professional year and ready to begin the final Ojai push. But with the festival behind him he returned to New York the following year for another round of CMP meetings. Much of his homework ("the reams of papers that were passed out") was completed on the plane east on January 17, 1967. "Not much material to choose from," he sighed the next day, when a final winnowing process produced this year's batch of lucky young composers. Ingolf was very disturbed by the impractical impulses of these novice artists on the one hand and by the "Ed. Psy." jargon of his colleagues on the other. Several drinking man's lunches left the judges bleary-eyed during the afternoon sessions – "a ship with a good crew but without a rudder." New York also offered Ingolf a party at Norman Dello Joio's on the 20th, talks with George Rochberg, and a reunion with the Kubiks. Gail was described as "so full of fun and understanding and charm and camaraderie." On the night of the 19th Ingolf witnessed a production of Stravinsky's *Agon* at the Lincoln Center – "the most shattering experience, sit 3 feet above seat, eyes and mouth open – tears of emotion over such artistic perfection, would it never end – at intermission see Ellis [Kohs], can't talk, am so shocked." The man who had devoted so much time to furthering the careers of young composers found himself still in thrall to a very old one indeed.

My stepfather never got around to telling the musical press, "You won't have Ingolf Dahl to kick around anymore," but his consternation at the performance of reviewers reminds us that his relationship with the press had always been full of problems and we can say that he regarded the education of these practitioners to be among his responsibilities as well. Writing to Bill Colvig on December 6, 1955 Ingolf noted how:

> Sometimes I have a talent for putting my foot in it: last Sunday, for example, there was a cocktail party for us after the concert. I was introduced to a gentleman with whom I had a lively and interesting conversation. When the talk came to the subject of music criticism I told him what I thought of it ("no good – useless – written by people who don't know much – there are only two readable ones: P.H. Lang in New York and Frankenstein in San Francisco, etc, etc.") and then the host came over saying pleasantly, "Oh I see that Mr. Dahl is hitting it off well with our San Diego music critic!"

There is no question that Ingolf was quite profoundly affected by reviews – whatever he thought of their authors – elated by good notices and distressed by bad ones. He routinely made a point of purchasing the papers on the day after concerts. "One bad review in *Times*," he wrote after participating in a Bach concert at the Roof in April, 1949, "disgusted and fed up." The power of the reviewer was always in his thoughts. When it was proposed that a major portion of a Monday Evening Concert be devoted to music composed during his first sabbatical, Ingolf responded in April, 1953, by saying, "I can hear the L.A. critics sharpening their axes already."

Ingolf did not like the language of much musical reviewing, with its endless attempts to use imagery from nature, psychology and other arts to describe the abstract and formal qualities of musical composition. He became accustomed to having Isabel Morse Jones describe the *Allegro and Arioso* as "capricious as the eerie north wind," and enduring the inanities of a reviewer of the Brass Piece who wrote, "Perhaps music as imperious and dissonant as Dahl's will be heard at the Day of Judgement. If so, sinners will repent in a hurry." He could be less tolerant toward reviewers who had the ability to analyze music, that is *notes*, but chose to fall back on "pseudo-descriptive" terms with little meaning – poignant, cheerful, strong, dignified. As an example of what *not* to write Ingolf proposed: "Its perpendicular planes set up an internal tension."

It was easy for reviewers, he felt, to score points in an era in which many musical features, removed from their true context, could have both positive and negative interpretations – "the dullness of these repeated notes" *vs.* "the rhythmic power and barbaric splendour of those repeated notes in the bass." If one were being negative "mannerism" could serve in the same sentence where a positive reviewer could insert "style;" "hodge-podge" could give way to "synthesis," "uncontrolled" to "imaginative." "chaotic" to "spontaneous" and "abstruse" to "thoughtful." "It is so much easier to write witty and well," Ingolf had noted as early as 1943, "in a negative way than in a positive." Ten years later he added, "Average humans without kindness are bad enough, but people who write and criticise without kindness and the 'larger view' are a real pest." Increasingly Ingolf came to hate the jargon employed in descriptions of avant garde music and evidently he wrote to the editor of *Perspectives of New Music* demanding an explanation of some of the more mysterious phrases.

An additional grievance which Ingolf carried against the critics was their habit of "influence-hunting." Attempts to place the work in a specific style often tempted critics to propose a specific derivation for the work in a composition by another creator. For many years he endured comparisons between his own works and those of Stravinsky, Hindemith and Copland. Not all of these comparisons were necessarily at Ingolf's expense and Peter Yates and Lawrence Morton were often able to suggest where Ingolf may have *improved* on the older composers. Ingolf never ceased warning himself against attempts to imitate Stravinsky; naturally he did not want reviewers to reforge the connection.

In all, he had a bad word to say at one time or another, about every critic, not excluding three Cologne reviewers who dissected a *performance* of the *Duo* which, in fact, had been cancelled from the stage due to a last minute illness! Even Alfred Frankenstein, mentioned earlier, was evidently placed on the defensive when he and Ingolf participated in a symposium at Stanford in June, 1950. Los Angeles reviewer Mildred Norton always exasperated him. With Albert Goldberg relations fluctuated. Ingolf felt undervalued on many occasions by the *L.A. Times* reviewer but when Goldberg gave a good notice to the *Aria Sinfonica* the composer actually wrote a letter of gratitude. "Dear Ingolf," Goldberg responded, "In this business we get so few flowers that I always feel the hell with ethics and cherish the compliments like a tenor."

It *was* rare for Ingolf to find something nice to say about *any* reviewer. A more characteristic tone emerges in a 1953 letter to Lawrence Morton (whose reviews Ingolf had treasured in the 40's). Douglas Watt had written some reviews in the *New Yorker* and Ingolf now wanted to know: "Don't you know anybody who can poison the food of Douglas Watt? He makes Mildred look like a real musician and is abysmally below the level of the rest of the magazine." Below the level of the rest of the magazine but not below the usual standard of music reviewing there, for in all his ravings about critics no figure ever received such abuse as the *New Yorker*'s veteran critic, Winthrop Sargeant. Ingolf loathed Sargeant and considered him to be an enemy of most of the progressive trends in contemporary music. Etta called him Winnie the Pew. When the NAACC bestowed a citation of merit on Sargeant, Ingolf resigned from the organization in 1960 – "To honor him thus (and for his objective attitude yet, which would be laughable if it were not so revolting) is a slap in the face of every serious-minded and forward looking member of the organization." In 1963, curiously, Ingolf expressed displeasure with the "epilogue blast at the critics" in Volume III of the Stravinsky-Craft *Conversations*: "It's unfortunate, silly, childish, out-of-place...It makes it almost impossible to attack Sargeant in a really *serious* way."

It is obvious that Ingolf did regard musical criticism in a most serious manner, so much so that he tried to write as little of it as possible. "Finish NOTES reviews," he reported on February 7, 1958, "(better not do it again, get too much riled up, spend disproportionate amount of time)." Instead he liked to lecture to critics and would-be critics on the necessities of their craft. This he did on December 17, 1954 at a symposium sponsored by the American Symphonic Orchestra League and at several mid-Sixties workshops which Raymond Kendall and the Rockefeller Foundation arranged for the training of music critics. "Uneven bunch," he mused on September 23, 1965 after meeting a group which contained one Hovhannes cultist and one aspiring reviewer who found Stockhausen "too harmonious." Ingolf's 1956 lecture on Quality Judgements was written with the critic in mind, and he kept it in a constant state of revision. In 1969 he and other musicians agreed to review Monday Evening Concerts so that concert-goers might read at least one informed, if self-published review.

Ingolf bore his greatest grudge against critics not for any negative comments they may have made about his compositions or performances but for their neglect to mention him at all. He was not the only one to notice a problem here. In 1966 Peter Yates, in *Arts and Architecture*, wrote, "Ingolf Dahl, whose authority as a composer is slowly coming to recognition, is not less gifted as an orchestral conductor. Among us, the career opportunist too often snatches the laurels, while the diligent workman stays inconspicuously at the job." But Ingolf wanted to be conspicuous. When Albert Goldberg reviewed the 1963 season for the *Sunday Times* on December 29, Ingolf described himself as "very depressed, everybody is mentioned...but it is as if I didn't exist in this town, what's the use?"

Reading through an article by Boris Kremenliev in *Melos* in 1965, Ingolf complained, "Berio gets 1/2 page, I'm not even mentioned...the ball continuously bounces away from what I do (it is not *that* little) – the dice *always* fall the other way –*I do not exist.*" Volumes on American conductors appeared listing his students, not himself. Reading under the heading "Sonata" in the German music dictionary *MGG* he noted, "Every American jerk is listed by W. Newman, but not I." In the Wright catalogue, which he examined in 1966, he found "all American piano sonatas are listed, except mine. What *is* this conspiracy??" The Ojai festival of 1966 was perhaps his last opportunity to secure the reputation he deserved as a conductor. But Irving Lowens' review of the event in the *Washington Star* contained no analysis of Ingolf as conductor at all. A 1940's letter to Margaret Harford had protested the absence of commentary on accompanists; now, after twenty years, Ingolf returned to the strategy of direct appeal by writing to Lowens, "Perfunctory conducting may deserve perfunctory criticism but it seems to me that conscientiously thought-out and realized performances deserve *some* kind of critical reaction, be it negative or positive..." His frustration at his inability to make a publicity success of his Ojai opportunities had been festering now for many months. In June of 1964 he had written Fred Hemke, the *Saxophone Concerto* soloist, that "to expect justice and responsibility and fairness from music critics is expecting too much." His bitterness impelled his friend Lawrence Morton to take up the matter with Albert Goldberg, to whom Lawrence wrote on May 26, 1966:

> You took no occasion to write a single praiseful sentence about Ingolf – not about his general planning of events, his conducting, his very fine interpretation of the Stravinsky and Copland pieces, his "composing" of the beautiful embellishments in the dances of the Bach suite, his scholarship and taste and interpretive imagination in the baroque program. Ingolf is, far and away, the best musician in the whole Southern California community – all of us lean on his knowledge and his abilities as a practical artist, and I think it is a pity that his extraordinary qualities go unnoticed and unappreciated in the press.

Such a testimonial from his friend came too late, unfortunately, to stave off the onset of a major depression over career prospects. I find it particularly poignant to discover that Ingolf criticized his own personality (which so many others loved) because it failed to measure up to the standards of charisma and back-slapping charm required by the times. He describes himself as out-of-tune at social occasions, wrongly dressed (he favored heavy European tweeds), ill-at-ease, self-conscious. In April, 1966, a friend with a movie projector showed an old film made on London Street. Ingolf was overwhelmed by a sense of failure, so little to show for twenty-five years of labor. The next day he drove by our old house and stood in front of it, "Does the grass not receive an imprint from the human life that happened on it?" Other bouts of nostalgic reverie had overcome him at the death of Hindemith in 1963 and Toch in 1964.

A month after standing on the London Street grass he received news that Leslie Bassett had won the Pulitzer Prize. When his own *Aria Sinfonica* was returned he noticed that the tape had not even been played by the Committee. "I am just not making it," he wrote on June 1, "I get close, but then the door closes – who can get up steam under such reflections of sobering, devastating truth?"

Reading about the triumphs of other composers in the musical press on July 17, 1966, produced another outburst, "I feel I'm not as bad and below them as all that, yet I'm getting nothing, nowhere – my music fizzles, conducting is unrecognized and when I *do* something good, no publisher, no discussion – all the other nincompoops get it, where am I failing that this nincompoop doesn't get it?" A certain courage was needed from a man who saw himself as nothing more that A Paragraph In His Own Lifetime yet could mount the Cheremoya steps that day and still choose as his motto, "*Durchhalten!*" – See It Through.

71. MENTOR

It is hard to say that Ingolf was ever at home on his own campus, with its "football president," as he grumbled in 1951. In March, 1965 his name headed a list of faculty in a petition pleading that any new music building might have windows that actually open, "so that our teaching hours would not have to be spent in the dungeonlike windowless atmosphere that is characteristic of so many other college music buildings." Indeed, for years the School of Music was promised much needed improvements in its facilities, though most changes took place after Ingolf's death. The journals are replete with other minor ravings about U.S.C. – would the *Daily Trojan* give enough publicity to the next concert? Would the bookstore ever turn off the muzak? Must he endure another Executive Committee meeting of "*surpassing dullness*"? Still, it is clear that Ingolf found life among his colleagues to be full of rewards and friendship and he prized the safety of this home base among the palm trees and red brick, especially after painful adventures away. His colleagues at a faculty meeting of September 18, 1962, his first since the disastrous second sabbatical, greeted his return with a welcoming round of applause – "how warming, cheering, reassuring," he wrote.

Just as Ingolf offered in his daybooks his own reviews of every concert in which he had taken part, so also did he leave a comment on many of the lectures and lessons he had given on campus. Here too the remarks are often self-critical. "Radio class good, even though rather unprepared," he wrote in 1947. "Cinema class," he noted in 1951, "it goes well – I'm relaxed and embellish the material considerably;" "Haydn lecture, it goes well and I'm fairly satisfied," he added in 1952 – these are the type of positive comments that become less and less frequent as the years pass. By 1954 he was preparing for his Music of the Classical Period class by calling himself a "dilettante, dabbling now in music history." "Better," he wrote of this same class five years later, "but will never be satisfied until it is *all* written out and reorganized. " "Need to do much work here," he chided himself in 1966, "feel so inadequate." To place these remarks in context we can add that he said much the same thing about classes in which he was the undoubted academic expert, his course on the Music of Stravinsky for instance. "Do not give good lecture," he wrote on October 29, 1962, "Must do *Noces* better next time." "Strav. I," he recorded on September 21, 1964, "59 in class – my lecture is too chatty, not meaty enough, superficial – needs tightening."

These remarks might surprise several generations of students, many of whom have described Ingolf's lectures as information-crammed exercises, full of musical illustrations played by the lecturer, presented in a lively language full of metaphor and imagery. Herbert Bielawa noted that Ingolf "was unusually articulate, in lectures as in person-to-person communication." I could add that Ingolf was certainly aware of student reaction to his presentations, though I do not believe he courted this overtly. He seems to have been genuinely surprised and deeply touched when a burst of applause brought a term's study to an end. "Last meeting," he reported in some contrast on May 24, 1954, "talk about rising romanticism, but students are not as appreciative...don't blame them, what lousy reports we had this semester!" His letter files are choked with unsolicited testimonials from long-forgotten students who wanted to express personally their appreciation for a course well-taught. (Such expressions were still possible in the era before instructor evaluation became a computerized industry.)

It has to be argued, however, that for many students Ingolf was a daunting and unapproachable presence. Without ever resorting to unkindness he managed to convey to his younger charges an insistence on perfection that must have left many of them backing away from the flame. Rick Lesemann reminded me that many would-be students never recovered from their first interview and Ingolf himself recognized that he was not at ease with beginners in any subject. "Not so sure of myself with these beginning orchestrators. How to proceed?" he asked in 1951. The same remark is echoed in the case of several composition students, where Ingolf admits, "I am not the right teacher." This was only one of the many reasons why Ingolf failed to succeed with some of his private students, for here matters of personality and musical style also affected the outcome of lessons. There is no doubt that he found some of his students to be a trial or that he was happy to have them miss their appointments or end their studies altogether. But to have to tell a student that he or she had failed or lacked the talent to continue was an impossible heart-rending task for Ingolf. "A horror of a day," is described in 1966, when Ingolf in the "role of executioner" had to tell a student that he had failed his exams. I also recall an ancient piece of gossip about a troublesome Asian woman whose opinion of herself as a composer failed to match Ingolf's view. To ease her rejection and help the lady save face Ingolf organized a campus concert of her music. A waspish Etta referred to this sad case as "Ingolf's Misfortune Cookie."

To thrive under Ingolf's tutelage a student had to accept criticism, to respond to it, and to avoid it by keeping on his toes. At a conducting lesson Ingolf would have students lead him in the prepared score, which he would sight-read at the piano, purposefully making mistakes – according to pianist Ralph Grierson – until the student detected the error and made the necessary correction. "Woe to the student who was not prepared," Leroy Southers added, "to write out a page, any page, of the score which he/she was assigned to conduct!" Rosemary Waller remembers that in her early days with the U.S.C. Orchestra Ingolf was conducting the rehearsal of an opera production:

> I succumbed to the temptation of watching the stage during a fairly long rest in the violin part. Predictably, I lost my place in the music and didn't make the next entrance. At the earliest opportunity during the rehearsal, Ingolf gave me one of the worst scoldings I've ever received from anyone. I have ever since been most grateful to him for that. Playing opera in a pit orchestra requires a special discipline and looking at the stage can be disastrous.

Southers, who also studied composition with Ingolf, noted that:

> When he was truly displeased with anything having to do with music, he could become awesome as he either sat in eloquent silence or expressed his displeasure in most certain terms...If he rubbed his temples, or raised his glasses, and rubbed the bridge of his nose, it was likely that he was extremely unhappy and that remonstrance would be forthcoming shortly. If pleased Dahl would become animated and though never effusive, would not hesitate to give praise.

That his conducting lessons were memorable may be measured by the fact that thirty-six years after his death Justin Davidson, in *The New Yorker*, could summarize some of Ingolf's teaching techniques: "a precise of stick technique: moving the hand up and down produces quick tempos and staccato articulation; moving it along a left-right axis will naturally slow the tempo and soften the accents; pushing out from the torso raises the volume; bringing the hands in toward the armpits will turn it down."

There does not seem to have been any one approach to the teaching of composition that Ingolf followed in all cases, though he does seems to have spent a good deal of time asking his pupils if what they had written truly reflected their intentions; could these be better realized in another way? He evidently gave students assignments that would require them to wrestle with their own weakest suits. "If a person was weak in rhythmical imagination," Donald Aird recalled, "he would suggest you write a piece for percussion only." Ingolf never fought to impose his own style on students, indeed he often felt reluctant to part with good ideas which he wished to save for one of his own compositions. "Should I have kept the idea myself?" he asked after a lesson with Paul Hedwall in December, 1965.

"I am getting worse as a teacher, just skimming the surface, more and more amateurish," he had written after a 1959 lesson, but few students could be found to agree. Many testify to his dazzling powers of analysis. "He could point to a chord in a Gabrielli sonata," according to Rick Lesemann, "and say '*that* is the dividing line between the Renaissance and the Baroque.'" His ability as a sight-reader was legendary and many people, including – according to Aird – Josef Szigeti, never encountered his equal. I remember that once, to indulge my passion for lush Romanticism, he sat down abruptly at the piano in his studio and, from a full score, played the first movement of the Rachmaninoff *Second Piano Concerto*, inventing his own orchestral reduction to accompany the soloist's part on the spot.

So profound was the respect for his teaching among his private University students that we can almost speak of a kind of cult of Ingolf Dahl, something he was aware of, even though he did not encourage it. Fred Myrow and other students sent Ingolf a *Father's Day* card! "When I began my work with Ingolf," Harold Budd wrote, "there was a clique of Dahl worshippers at U.S.C....the sort of folk who presume their worth in the world to be judged upon the accomplishments of others." Budd also added that when he had to leave the University in 1965 for financial reasons that "Ingolf spent many hours a week – gratis – seeing my work and giving advice. No one knows of the time given me; that, in my judgment, is a real teacher." A number of students reported that Ingolf had accommodated *their* busy schedules by giving them lessons at midnight and some recall that he found room for them by holding the lesson at Cheremoya, where they might be expected to join the master in eating kumquats, drinking beer or sampling Stravinsky's latest favorite, sweet vermouth and fernet branca. Most fortunate of all were those invited on hikes by their teacher.

"As a teacher," Don Aird wrote after his mentor's death, "Ingolf gave too much to his students. I can say that with a certain amount of guilt feelings now." It is true that Ingolf occasionally wondered if all of his university labors had been truly useful. "I feel so strongly," he wrote in 1958, "the waste, the waste of so many hours, years (the time on Film Music – the orchestra – not even the tape library shows many traces of the years of my work at S.C." But at least in the matter of his teaching there *was* some reward during his lifetime.

One such reward came with the success of his students in the wider world. Michael Tilson Thomas (or MTT for short) began studies at U.S.C. in the fall of 1962. He told me in 1978 that he was attracted to the School of Music because of Ingolf's reputation and that of the piano teacher, John Crown. He took some music history courses from Ingolf but most of the hours they spent together were in conducting class; with Ingolf these had a way of becoming private tutorials in music in general, for the teacher would use all of his powers of musical analysis to explain the score in question. Many of these sessions took place at Cheremoya and were proceeded by private lessons in German and lentil soup dinners offered by Etta. Michael was fond of referring to the Dahls as "my other parents," and there is no question that he too became a kind of surrogate son, particularly as I moved my life eastward. (This same sonship status could also have been claimed by Pete Thomas, no relation, a Santa Cruz student who did odd jobs for Etta.) Michael and I did not meet until my parents were no longer among the living but I do recall that he was often in their thoughts. Etta was fascinated by his family background in the Yiddish theater and I heard many stories at third hand about the famous Tomashevskys. There was a good deal of socializing with Michael's parents in North Hollywood and I often heard Etta boast of Michael's charm, talent, and success. Ingolf was greatly impressed by his pupil's gifts as a pianist and conductor. His Ojai appearance in 1965 was pronounced "*great*" by his proud mentor and on December 9, 1966 Ingolf records a "moment of truly great happiness: Michael Thomas plays *Hymn* so movingly that I am just melted." After finishing his work at U.S.C. – and before taking up a long series of conducting assignments with the major orchestras of the world – Michael went off to Europe for a session of Bayreuth and Boulez. "Boulez was very pleased with my work both conductorially and pianistically," Michael wrote on July 13, 1967, "for which dear mentor I thank you a thousand times."

In June of 1966 Ingolf received news that he had won a grant from the National Institute of Arts and Letters. With it he intended to spend a year composing, and recovering from the career disappointments that had followed his last year as Ojai's musical director. He had hoped that matching funds would be provided by his University, but these were not forthcoming. It was not yet sabbatical time but Ingolf was so determined to escape the scene of his disappointments that he determined to take off the spring term, 1967, without pay. An extra thousand dollars did come his way from the campus, but the source was an unexpected one. On April 26, 1967 Ingolf was named, on the basis of votes cast by graduating seniors, one of the winners of the U.S.C. Associates' Excellence in Teaching Award. He was not able to attend the banquet held the next day for he had by this time carried through with his plans and undertaken another period of extended travel. News of the award did not reach him until May 2. "That this too is granted me," he wrote, "extremely grateful and overwhelmed."

72. WINTER DAYDREAMS

Ingolf's 1967 leave of absence began when he arrived, unaccompanied, in New York on February 12. A suburban rendezvous with Gail Kubik followed. Ingolf played his *Aria Sinfonica* for his old friend: "Gail is just bubbling over, so much fun (what does he really think?)." A few days later, after responding quickly to a request for an opinion on some project, Ingolf received a thank you note from Gail, "You are without doubt the world's most organized man," Gail enthused mistakenly, "You should be coated in cellophane, reduced to 1/50th of your size, and worn as a necklace or watchfob by all civilized Americans."

In 1949 it was a visit to Gail that had brought our entire family into contact with the MacDowell Colony in Peterborough, New Hampshire. Early on the morning of February 14th Ingolf flew to Keene, New Hampshire, where a taxi took him to the artists' colony which would be his home for the next eight weeks. "Feel elated about this situation, " he recorded, "the studio, peace, worktime ahead." His first weeks in the wintry environment increased his feelings of well-being, though these were not to last forever (Ingolf was here to compose), but his affection for the setting never declined and his journals are full of joyful expressions of appreciation. The smell of newly sawn wood, the thrill of walking in the "palpable" cold, snow on the trees, everything delighted him. Trouble began only when civilization obtruded. On February 18 Ingolf wrote:

> Begins to snow lightly, *that's* too much, when will I see it *again*. So after 1/2 hour struggle to put on clothes and go for long walk. Straight NE over frozen snow – across country, down forest (too many roads all over!) along frozen river, across ice (if I *could* skate along the river!!) up on other side...then houses again, signs, dogs, hell.

The sight of skiers induced envy, and before long Ingolf was himself on rented skis at Temple Mountain, where "everything comes 'right' again." Soon he was on the slopes every few days, though he did grumble at Mt. Snow – "a commercialized, mechanized, overdeveloped resort – *not* my type." A roll in the snow in zero temperature followed a sauna on March 18. Ingolf also ran when he was not able to ski; he made the Colony into a gymnasium with his lung-shattering jogs along its drives. Much of the energy which he could not force into his creative work found its outlet in physical exercise.

Breakfast and dinner were taken with other guests but a basket lunch was delivered each day to the "lovely stone studio" where Copland, Foss, Bernstein and Kubik had worked before him. Without naming them, Ingolf noted that the other colonists included a moody taciturn sculptor, a black poetess, an elderly introverted gentleman novelist and lots of monosyllabic unintellectual painters. One of the novelists got into trouble ("Erosion!")

for saying, "I always write with the radio on." There were a number of other composers present, though one gets the impression that Ingolf felt most of their music was unplayable – "music to see, analyze, describe in the Yale Journal of Music Theory or the Perspectives."

A good friend and skiing partner was found in clarinetist-composer Nicolas Roussakis. Ingolf did squawk some when recording Roussakis' comment on his new chart music, "I don't always know what it sounds like, and often I do not like the sounds that come out, but I feel that my ears will just have to get used to my music." Before leaving the Colony Ingolf presented a seven bar *MacDowell Fanfare* to Roussakis, "a friendly parody," according to James Berdahl, of the younger composer's tone clusters. Together the new friends also arranged for clarinet and piano three solo piano pieces by Edward MacDowell himself; "Lover" and "From Dwarfland" were arranged by Ingolf, Roussakis worked on "By Smouldering Embers." The *Three Pieces* in the Dahl-Roussakis version were published some years later by Alexander Broude and were premiered at a March 25 Colony concert by the arrangers.

A great deal of time seems to have been wasted in rehearsing for performances at Peterborough, and Ingolf and Nick played through a great deal of piano-clarinet repertoire as Ingolf contemplated the problems of writing for this medium himself. A second concert was given on April 9 and a black-robed Ingolf also filled a gap in the choir for the Easter services at the Peterborough Episcopal church. All of this activity illustrates his difficulty in settling down to the task of composing itself.

"My work has been going slowly," Ingolf confided to Lawrence Morton on March 3, "and the problem of facing up so suddenly to the completely pressure-free, responsibility-less existence, the being plunked down in front of blank music paper – all this had at first a more paralyzing than liberating effect." Etta, responding to Ingolf's complaints about the slow start, tried to remove some of the pressure:

> Ask yourself what would happen if you did nothing but eat, sleep, read and take walks and socialize for a few weeks. Would that be so terrible?...If you can only bury your puritan conscience and do it in peace with yourself, I think there is nothing fatal in it, and it would probably do you a lot of good...I am deeply concerned about your attitude toward yourself and your work; there is a violent imbalance

there, increasingly frantic (from where I sit) and terribly dispiriting to watch, because of my love for you, in which you may or may not believe.

Ingolf worked on a number of projects at the MacDowell Colony simultaneously. These included a clarinet and piano sonatina, eventually entitled *Sonata da Camera*, a work for high school string ensemble called *Variations On a Theme by C.P.E. Bach*, and the long-promised work for violin and small orchestra entitled *Elegy Concerto*. None of these projects reached fruition in Peterborough and the only composition actually completed there was a solo piano work of forty-two seconds duration, *Reflections*, based on an eleven note row, and probably intended as the first movement of a longer work, never completed. Inspiration for this composition was a complaint registered by Frances Mullen Yates, to whom the work was dedicated. Frances had argued, after a concert in Binghamton, that the *Sonata Pastorale* provided such a challenge for small-handed pianists that she had built up callouses beyond the control of Revlon or Elizabeth Arden finger cream.

"Am still prone to pounce on distracting activities," Ingolf admitted to Lawrence. There were many other instances of the power of distraction – orchestration exams that still had to be corrected, the proofs of the *Quodlibet* needed attention, piles of correspondence waited for an answer. Three days were spent on liner notes for a recording of two Toch concerti. As panic set in on April 8 Ingolf recoiled from the efforts of sticking to a tightly confining work schedule. "I have to live like an animal," he confessed, "sleep when I'm sleepy, work when I'm bright. There are only 1-2 hours of the latter every day. Impossible to squeeze anything out 'on schedule,' when I'm tired and need sleep." Written so close to the end of the stay in New Hampshire, this comment may be taken as a reflection of Ingolf's disappointment over his general progress at the Colony.

Frustrations were also encountered during two side-trips to Boston. On March 9 Ingolf took the bus to the Massachusetts capital where he visited the Fogg Museum and attended a rehearsal by members of the Boston Symphony Chamber players of the *Duettino Concertante*. This turned out to be such a musical disaster, from Ingolf's point of view, that visions of the Stockholm nightmare circled above the composer's head and two weeks later he had a disturbing dream about the episode. A second trip was undertaken on April 2. Ingolf squeezed in many visits, including ones with Larry Moss and Harold Shapero. He was depressed by the faces in the bus terminal – "the ugliness of the people – the dinginess of the town." At night he attended a performance of *Rake's Progress* and visited backstage with Robert Craft. "I thought Bob did an excellent job," Ingolf reported to Lawrence, " but [Sarah] Caldwell should be shot, certainly before sunrise – Stravinsky should have a way of prohibiting such vandalism – couldn't Picasso protest if someone painted a moustache on his 'Seated Woman' at the Museum of Modern Art?"

After the last MacDowell concert on April 9 Ingolf prepared frantically for his departure from Peterborough. In the rush he lost his little music staff ruler, a prized possession. There was time to decorate the wall of the studio, which was soon to be reoccupied by Gail, with "suggested titles of works Kubik should compose here to speed up his acceptance by the Establishment and insure publication in 'Apogee.'" Among Ingolf's suggestions were works entitled "Triangulatory Synthetications," "Mobile Modules," "Intersecting Perspectives," "Prefabricated Assemblages," and one title that got in by mistake, "Sonata in A-flat."

Ingolf arrived in New York on April 11th and spent two days in talks with publishers, a night at the ballet, and a chat with Copland. There were baggage difficulties. Ingolf had to send some packages off to Europe because of overweight fears; he dropped his suitcase key on Second Avenue, but was lucky enough to find it again. On the 13th there were visits with Gail, Trude Rittman, Doriot Anthony Dwyer, and the Stones. Etta arrived by plane ("looks lovely, wonderful to have her again") and got lumbered with the ice-axe.

For two months Etta had shared 2486 with Rick Lesemann, who had occupied Ingolf's downstairs quarters while learning from Etta how to housesit the entire establishment after her departure. He did the gardening and she the cooking. She seems to have recovered something of her old spirit because Rick was astonished to see her in her bathrobe, the long gray braids of her wig swinging free from her head, a rose in her mouth, her feet skipping out a fandango. On the way to New York she stopped for a week in East Lansing to visit her son and daughter-in-law. Writing to Bill Colvig she offered her inevitable critique:

The kids and their friends spoiled me rotten with parties, dinners, etc., and I loved every minute of it. Also I have a new title. They have some academic friends who are Southerners, happily by birth only. As you know women down there are called Miss whatever-the-first-name is, even after they are married and live to be 99. So I am Miss Etta. I asked for and got permission to hear Anth lecture for the first time, so I sneaked in at the last second to an end seat in the last row. Unsurprisingly it was a very well organized and informative lecture (Socrates & Plato) but surprisingly very natural and not pompous. Maybe he shed the pomposity along with the extra poundage he had last summer. I wish he had kept his beard.

I too remember Etta's visit to Bessey Hall. After the class we went into the main office of the Humanities Department where I introduced her to my boss, Thomas H. Greer. The time came for the obligatory proud parent endorsement. "How did you like the lecture?" Tom asked. Dr. Dahl considered this thoughtfully and replied, "I thought it was *pretty* good, though I *do* have a few suggestions for improving it." These turned out to be only some additional illustrations. "When I made 2 tiny suggestions afterwards," she informed the Weismans, "he accepted them with good grace."

"Off to Yurp," Ingolf wrote on April 14, the day he and Etta arrived in Reykjavik at the beginning of another adventure-filled European odyssey. Two nights were spent in Iceland, with some sightseeing and Ingolf's chronic complaint about not being able to make any *real* contact with his sister, Py. The Bjornson family, however, was still in a state of shock from a recent tragedy: the previous summer Ingolf's nephew Gunnar had been killed by a bus while out on his bicycle.

After misplacing their camera at the airport, Ingolf and Etta flew on to Luxembourg on the 16th, a journey from winter to spring. They checked their baggage through to Zurich and spent a night in a Luxembourg Hotel – "these young people," a conservative Ingolf reported, "are all so orderly, sedate, tradition-and-moral rooted. What a world apart from the U.S.!" Etta ate hot dogs at a fun fair, "delicious as well as indigestible." On the 17th a train journey through "spring landscape and memories" brought the Dahls to Zurich at noon. By chance it was the day of the Sechselauten ceremony and a parade of flower-carrying guildsmen and brass bands marched through the streets. In the evening the death of winter was celebrated by processions of lantern-carrying bakers, vintners, and smiths. Ingolf and Etta crowded into Gorgot's wine bar where they drank malaga and ate hazelnuts and dried shrimps with some drunken students who toasted them and made them smoke hand-rolled cigarettes.

Five nights were spent in Zurich. Ingolf visited with friends and relatives, went to concerts and had several nostalgic rambles. On April 22, driving a Volkswagen belonging to Edi Schaar, the Dahls made their way to Schruns. "Here we are again – what a thrill," Ingolf reported that afternoon. Happy reunions with old friends followed and Ingolf, on Edi's skis, was on the slopes the next day.

During their visit to Yosemite on December 20 of the previous year, Ingolf had won Etta's assent to a third stay in this village in the Vorarlberg. "Big load off," he reported, remembering – no doubt – how unhappy his wife had been here during their previous stay. But on December 30 Edi had made a counter-suggestion, use of his family's summerhouse in Alt-Aussee in the Obersalzburg area of central Austria. This had been agreed and Schruns was therefore just to be a stopover point this time. On April 23, with weather conditions spoiling the opportunity for further mountaineering, the Dahls decided to push on, well ahead of schedule, to their new home away from home.

73. INTERVAL

The arrival of my parents in Alt-Aussee on April 25, 1967 was ill-timed. Winter had returned as they made their way eastwards and, under any circumstances, they were not expected by Edi Schaar's friend and neighbor, the widow Anna Gasperl, until May 1. Ingolf had also forgotten that water and electricity had to be turned on before their new home would be habitable. After dinner in Bad Aussee the travelers nevertheless drove up the road in the dark, the damp, and the cold. Etta had the key to Puchen 53 in her gloved fist, but how to find the residence in question was a puzzle. Puchen, it turned out, is a district, not a street, and the houses were numbered in the order in which they were built! This made it difficult to find Frau Gasperl at Puchen 182. Etta described what happened next:

At a corner there was a street light and 3 female figures of assorted ages, all wrapped shapeless against the cold, stood waiting for a bus... Unlike the fairy tales where the 3rd question gets results, here the *first* one did. The woman I asked said that we were in front of Frau Gasperl's house and "ours" was only 2 or 3 back. She thereupon tried to get Frau Gasperl's attention, but the house was dark. Our "helper" concluded that she was 2 houses off, across from "us," at a neighbor's. Down we trotted. Here there was a light but we couldn't rouse anyone until our helper scooped up a blob of snow and threw it at a window...Now began a comedy which we experienced in a kind of numb dream. Out popped Frau Gasperl and her sister Millie; they had been listening to a detective play on the radio. She did not understand at once why we had come so soon without letting her know. And so she scolded. But she is a warm person by nature...so in between scoldings she giggled....

Candles were lit and the Dahls entered their new residence. A neighbor (whose cow's milk Ingolf sometimes drank) turned on the utilities. The upstairs toilet was leaking through the ceiling onto the downstairs one. Also, none of the stoves were on and there was no heat. Millie mumbled politely that perhaps a hotel would be better for the first night but Ingolf lit one of the stoves and the rest of Alt-Aussee departed this miniature Siberia. Under feather comforters and blankets, in socks and sweaters, my parents tried to go to sleep. "It took almost too much courage to get out from under our wrappings the next day," Etta reported. To Bill Colvig she gave more details about this ramshackle ménage:

The house had to be seen to be believed. It is a kind of nucleus with accretions. For days yet another cubby room or closet or porch kept cropping up. The piano, bless Edi, was already standing upstairs in the room which became [the] studio. There are five tile stoves in as many rooms, and they take days really to get going, after which they can be cozy. The house is of stone, chilly and damp "by nature." The kitchen stove is a huge beast that also needs to be wood or coal fed. There is no refrigerator. The kitchen is the refrigerator. There is no running water...

It is a miracle that my parents escaped pneumonia in this setting, but they seem to have survived physically and there were no prolonged episodes of bad health similar to those that had ruined much of the previous sabbatical. The worst of Ingolf's asthma seems to have been left behind in

Peterborough, though he did endure several gout attacks in Alt-Aussee, including one in June affecting the right elbow, a particularly distressing incident since Ingolf was right handed and the colchicine did not seem to help. On June 21 he took a sauna in Ischl. The next day, perhaps because he had left its warmth too abruptly, he began to suffer in the chest. Aspirin helped his elbow but bronchitis set in and a day's skiing had to be cancelled – "hell and double hell." By June 29, however, he was well enough to begin a brief ski tour with a local guide – "He can't even set an alarm so it works," a disgruntled Ingolf wrote on July 1, the day he returned from an expedition to the Rauris valley.

Electricity failure and cold weather plagued Ingolf and Etta throughout their stay in Alt-Aussee, but gradually they became accustomed to the new environment. Etta loved the wildflowers, the strawberries and gooseberries, and a local salmon trout called *saibling*. Ingolf, who first described the village as "grey, unfriendly and uncomfortable," soon changed his tune. "Alt-Aussee is lovely," he wrote Bill on May 14:

> I have a nice work room in the house which we occupy – this is a blessing, to have so much room (contrary to the situation in Schruns) that we can both keep out of each other's way and I have a feeling of isolation and freedom in my work room. This looks out on meadows, the lake, towards Yosemite-like cliffs beyond...Weather had been magnificent for the last week (this European, alpine spring, with its flowers and scents, and meadows, and snow-capped peaks in the distance – just too much.)

The Dachstein dominated this setting and an unsuccessful attempt to conquer the peak was made on May 11. In a way Ingolf was using the occasion as a warm-up for a strenuous period of ski-mountaineering which he undertook with his 1962 guide, Dajeng, whom he met up with in Schruns on May 16.

During a driving break on the first day of this trip Ingolf plucked lilac from a farm house – "the smell and the 'here I go on the big one' feeling." A radio at lunchtime drove him out of a restaurant in Zams. Wishing to remain anonymous he checked into the Lowen Hotel when he arrived in Schruns, where something he had eaten gave him diarrhea. The guide took the wheel as they drove by Lake Como. That night they approached the Italian-Swiss border from the south along the Cervinia road but a fresh snowfall ruined their climbing hopes and Ingolf spent the day in Aosta. On the 19th an ascent of the Breithorn was attempted – "gorgeous air, thin light. Top slopes tough because of altitude. Almost no food (bad), try summit ridge *almost* to the top, but Dajeng in a shoulder deep snow gives up tracking." The next day the climbers slept in the Monte Rosa hut, Ingolf delighting in the sound of the yodeling Swiss youngsters and the sight of wild goats with enormous horns. "Almost unbearable" gout in the right foot menaced his chances on the next morning, when the ascent of the Monte Rosa began at 4:30:

> First slopes very rough, can hardly go and breathe, should have started much slower. At last get my wind…Glorious daybreak on the glacier world. Long plugging up the glacier step by step. Not easy. On spot by big crevasse have to take off skis to go around…Now the air gets thin. Have to stop every fifty steps and it takes *all* the will power to move up. Some big traverses, then see top and hut. With effort to ski depot, icy wind there. Dajeng impatient (but I *did* it in "normal" time – except the youngsters are all so much faster). Up on rope the last slope. Handshake. Sit in front of hut in the sun, the world below. Am overcome. Monte Rosa. Tears come and convulsive sobs. That this was still possible over so many obstacles (distance, time, money, health, age). Eat and drink a little and look. Down on rope…

In the hut that night Ingolf watched the celebration party of the other climbers ("I was ever an outsider in this world in language and everything else"), gazing into the faces of the young mountaineers "with the eyes of one who takes leave…Henceforth these mountains [are] left for them who come after." At 4638 meters (15,202 feet) Monte Rosa exceeded even the Matterhorn in elevation and Ingolf chose a worthy challenge for his farewell performance as an alpine climber. In fact he had intended to tackle other summits with Dajeng, but fatigue and bad weather caused repeated disappointment. Several days were spent driving around looking for suitable skiing spots but on the 24th Ingolf put his guide on a train in Zurich and began to think again of the more pastoral setting of Alt-Aussee.

Etta, who seems to have had no project more profound that the care and feeding of her husband, succeeded in making Puchen 53 livable. In 1967 she rebelled against her domestic destiny only once – and this by post

– during as interesting episode that began in Peterborough. Ingolf had experienced a nightmare in the early hours of February 28:

> Had murdered sister and someone else (forgot on waking) – walking along Hollywood Boulevard in despair, fright, must give self up to police – but before that confess and unload to the *one* possible person: mother – but feel guilty and nightmarish about this confession too – at last decide to – 'mother' looks exactly like E, so *is* E."

In the bathroom later that morning the dreamer dropped his glasses in the washbasin and cracked the right lens. Etta was called long-distance and given the chore of ransacking the chaotic storerooms beneath 2486 in search of a spare pair. After hours in this fruitless endeavor she received another call from the MacDowell Colony. Ingolf had remembered that he had already shipped the spare pair off to Zurich in a trunk. "I learned that you had pulled one of your M.B. Eddyisms again," Etta scolded:

> If leaving yourself unprotected against any kind of negative situation or emergency is being positive, you can have it. I just wish it didn't so often end up with me pulling the (your) chestnuts out of the fire. Better yet, I wish you were able to learn from such experiences, but you will go just as determinedly and blithely unprepared smack into the next one."

"And don't you make a genius-type signature," Etta instructed Ingolf when a check needed endorsing, "or they may refuse it (as they once did)."

Twenty-eight years of protecting her husband from the world continued. In Austria, Etta would not have to buy her husband's slacks at Silverwoods or lie to the office when he wanted a day of skiing, and there weren't any telephone calls to be screened before buzzing the maestro, but there was still a lot of correspondence to take off his hands – ("Poor girl, she's done nothing but write long letters since our arrival") – and with all the ashes that needed hauling from all those stoves Etta was soon claiming that she could put Cinderella to shame.

My mother spryly stepped along the village paths and over the fields at Ingolf's side many a day, a white-haired old lady. She became cross when Ingolf drove too quickly on the country roads. The two visited Salzburg and Linz and once a week they drove to Bad Ischl for shopping and pastry. At home they played Bach four-hand and attended the narcissus festival (Ingolf didn't win). There were a number of restaurants and hotels in the village and here Ingolf and Etta often took one of the day's meals. There was even a cinema. "From Moment to Moment," Ingolf mused on May 1, "the theme song has a fatal resemblance to both the *Symphony of Psalms* and Mac The Knife."

On June 29 Etta went to Schruns for a week's visit on her own. "Lovely to have her back," Ingolf wrote on her return. There seems to have been no recurrence of the introversion and despondency that had characterized her last stay in Austria. Ingolf had sent an apologetic letter on their wedding anniversary, "27 years ago tonight – so many of your apprehensions came true, but a few other things too, I hope to think." Etta replied waspishly, "One might imagine that I, perfect, gleaming on my pedestal, had spent the last 27 years mostly looking down where you – somewhere far below – were reiteratedly failing to come up to scratch. Surely it isn't all that one sided? Surely there were times when I disappointed you?" So the oddest of couples persevered.

In spite of its remote location Alt-Aussee attracted a number of visitors – whose arrival was charming and intrusive at the same time. The Michalskys were the first to arrive, on June 24. Don, who would remarry within three years, brought his first wife Ann-Marie and his daughter Katya. Ann-Marie was not in the best of moods, according to Etta, who reported that when she opened the door to her visitors Mrs. Michalsky's first comment was, "Don't you ever polish your shoes?" The situation was not too upsetting at first, for these friends departed three days later. But on July 8 little Katya appeared on the doorstep a second time to announce that her parents had *also* decided to look for a place in Alt-Aussee! This they did and thus, for another four weeks, Ingolf had one of his best friends living only a few houses away. Recalling Ingolf's behavior a few years later, Don wrote to Lawrence Morton that, "Even when we were neighbors, 300 feet apart, in Alt-Aussee Austria, I'd get mail from him and when I asked him 'why mail it?' he answered, 'Oh, I know what fun it is to receive mail from friends.'" In fact Ingolf was also trying to resist the temptation of spending too much time chatting and not enough time composing. "Waste much time visiting," he complained on July 8; on the 24th the entry reads, "Michalskys come to play scrabble (Katya with them) and it is really quite impossible." Still, Ingolf did enjoy his walks and talks with his former student. They went on several local hikes and one overnight mountain climbing outing. They also went out drinking more than once – Ingolf finally had an ally in his attempt to get the Muzak silenced. "Very nice yakking about music," Ingolf wrote on July 29, "(How one needs this mutual bolstering up – this time it's my turn to do it.)"

That same day Charles Fierro arrived for a brief visit and the three recreated one of their California hikes in an alpine setting. The day after Charles left another student, Winfred Blevins, also came for a short stay. Then there were family visits. On July 11 Holger and Aina, with their son Peter and Aina's sister Inge-Lisa came to stay, a visit that overlapped with the arrival of a number of Zurich cousins, who stayed in Alt-Aussee for a week. "All these invitations...and Don! as well," Ingolf wrote on July 13, "were a great mistake!"

Dorothy and I had no idea that we were the last in a long parade when we too arrived in Austria near the end of my parents' stay in Alt-Aussee and at the conclusion of our own eleven week epic tour of the Continent. By August 20, however, Ingolf had almost ceased his creative activities, and evidently looked forward to our arrival with considerable anticipation – "Excited that *the* day has come." Etta too was eager to see us. "You look like an expectant mother," Ingolf quipped. Our rendezvous took place in Salzburg. "Nice to see the kids," Ingolf wrote, "both looking fresh and cheerful. Have talkfest on way back." For several days we had the opportunity of observing for ourselves the unusual setting in which Ingolf and Etta had lived since April.

In fact we were astonished by the clutter, the makeshift nature of the whole enterprise. We were also discomfited, in the middle of the summer, by the cold, even under *our* comforters. In the morning I had to go outside to get warm. Etta had done a marvelous job under trying circumstances and had made friends with all the other little old ladies in the village. We were treated royally, dining out at a number of local restaurants and getting a tour by car of the beautiful countryside, where many of the fields had been newly harvested. On August 22 we went for a picnic on the nearby Grundlsee, with Ingolf objecting to the length of my rowing stroke in the boat we used to cross the lake, I sulked and it was decided that *I* was the

Grundl. My sore throat matched Ingolf's continuing chest complaint and Etta bought me a bag of Dr. Kepler's Bio-Menthol cough drops. Later in the day we went to Hallstatt and to Bad Ischl for pastry at Cafe Zauner. The next day, using some firewood as a net, I played ping-pong with Ingolf; Dorothy and I ran pass patterns in the grass behind Puchen 53, using a roll of toilet paper as a ball. Soon we would continue on our grand tour, with Etta as our guide.

In the meantime, Ingolf's struggles with the blank pages of sheet music on his desk continued to have a familiar ring during that half-year interval in which he managed to escape from the grips of his university career. What aesthetic stance to take? "Where am I, what must I do, where to stand?" he had asked himself on March 6, 1967 in Peterborough. On February 16, he had chastized himself for not being "*really* a professional composer." "There is no *flow* of music," he had complained on February 21, "no continuity of ideas – no being grabbed by *real* work." On March 29, by which time he was involved in a number of Peterborough projects, the self-flagellation had assumed a new form: "All this time the nagging thought that this time is being frittered away with little ditties, and that I should *now* concentrate on a big 'important' work..." However one defines "important," the half-year's leave did produced considerable rewards, for in it Ingolf completed two works for string orchestra, *Variations For String Orchestra on a Theme by C.P.E. Bach* and *Three Intervals*, the first full draft of *Sonata da Camera* for clarinet and piano, and substantial portions of *A Cycle of Sonnets* for baritone and piano and the *Elegy Concerto* for violin and small orchestra.

Ingolf first mentions work on the C.P.E. Bach variations on July 18, 1966, but after a false start nothing was added until Peterborough. On February 18, after four days work on the project, Ingolf decided to abandon it ("feel relieved"); two days later, after an emotional walk in the snow, the composing continued after all. "I am dabbling with a set of variations on a theme by C.P.E. Bach for string orchestra, for kids," Ingolf wrote Lawrence on March 3, "very easy, to play that is (very difficult to compose)...I can't find a away of amalgamating CPEB's harmonic style in the theme with what *I* want to do – and keep the whole thing *simple* and interesting." Because the work had to be written within the orbit of the theme's tonality the resulting eleven-minute work, Ingolf added, was "a distance removed from my other music now." He worked on Variation III during the April visit to Schruns, but the piece was completed in Alt-Aussee. "Something has to go," he wrote on April 29. Revision took a few more days (with more to come in 1968 and 1969) and on May 3 Ingolf celebrated completion of the composition with a glass of scotch at a local bar. Rick Lesemann, who supervised copying of the parts, called the work a "gem" – "How that *helps*," Ingolf responded on June 19. *Variations on a Theme by C.P.E. Bach* had been written for the American Federation of Musicians Congress of Strings, whose western section gave the piece its world premiere at Bovard Auditorium on July 12 under Walter Ducloux, who also conducted the eastern section in a Saratoga, New York performance later in the summer. The piece was published by Alexander Broude in 1974.

"In a *very* weak moment," Ingolf had also promised to supply a contribution to a volume of pieces for intermediate string ensemble edited by Ralph Matesky. The work was to deal in some way with a specific musical or technical problem but Ingolf failed to come up with a good idea until May 13 when, sitting on the balcony of Puchen 53, he had sketched the first notes of a work whose three movements were each based on a different interval. The first movement was completed two days later and he and Etta played it through in a four-hand piano arrangement which he had completed at the same time as the string version. "Nice," he wrote, "but awfully Strav-Bartok." A second movement was begun after he returned from a brief vacation on May 28 and the work was finished on June 2 and dispatched the next day. The intervals used by the composer were "Seconds," "Thirds," and "Fifths," but another movement, "Fourths," was added at the request of the publisher in 1969 and the work was re-titled *Four Intervals*. Dedicated to Aaron Copland, to whose *Piano Sonata* there is an allusion in the second movement, the work was published in 1973 in Volume II of Belwin-Mills' *Odyssey in Strings*.

The *Sonata da Camera* was also written in response to a specific request, in this case for a clarinet and piano work, by Thomas Ayres of the University of Iowa on behalf of a dozen or so other clarinet players. Ayres had written Ingolf about the project on February 7, 1966. Work seems to have started on March 1 in Peterborough but at the end of the month Ingolf broke off his efforts for two months or so, with only two of the four movements sketched out. With *Intervals* in the post he returned to his task and a third movement ("a little cloudscape") was finished on June 8 as Ingolf sat in his sunny back garden. "This is no *good* – has no style, the tonal sections stick out," he groaned after playing through what he had written on June 9, his fifty-fifth birthday. Revision began the next day. On the 15th a last movement was also begun, though Ingolf complained to Lawrence that the bright and jazzy patterns he sought were hard to write because he had no access to good jazz clarinet recordings. "At breakfast," on June 21, "Etta talks about sonority and vertical places – that triggers four good bars of 4th movement." A "finished" notice went up on June 25, but that night Ingolf discovered too many rough spots. "It looks better now," he added after a re-examination the next day, but, still dissatisfied, he withheld the manuscript until 1970, when he completed a revision. Ingolf had intended to dedicate the work to Nicolas Roussakis, with whom he had played so much of the clarinet and piano literature in Peterborough. *Sonata da Camera* was published in 1973 by Alexander Broude.

A fourth project of the period, begun in June, was also the result of a commission. As early as June 15, 1965, the baritone Maurice Allard had sounded Ingolf out about accepting a commission from the Helen Wilbur Foundation. Ingolf accepted this in November, 1966. For a time he planned to use as his text two pages from a Gertrude Stein novel and in June, 1966, he had obtained permission to use this material from Random House. But "Cantata From Ida" remained an idea only and there is no evidence that Ingolf wrote any music. Instead he decided to fulfill the commission by providing a musical setting for some sonnets by Petrarch, feeling that these would provide a more suitable vehicle for Allard. On June 5, 1967, while working on the *Sonata da Camera,* he noted, "Get set for *real* work on clarinet sonatina, instead the first 4 bars of Petrarch Sonnets want to be written. Do these also at night." A month later he noted, "Do only a few bars of Petrarch Sonnets today, but that's all, in that *intricate* stuff, that I can do." "Clean up yesterday's attempt," he wrote on July 5, "(is it getting too crowded?) But subjectively it seems better." The next day he finished the first movement. "Feel very ambivalent about it – sometimes think it is great – others that it is just no good (Vacillating in style, puny in content) and two weeks spent on *one* song, ridiculous – is that what I'm getting the grant for?" Months passed before he resumed work on *A Cycle of Sonnets,* which was not completed until the following year.

The *Elegy Concerto* for violin and small orchestra, which Ingolf worked on in Peterborough and Alt-Aussee, has a long but incomplete history. A work called "Elegy" was begun as early as 1944. When Victor Gottlieb died in 1963 Ingolf proposed writing a chamber concerto to be played by the cellist's widow, Eudice Shapiro. Ingolf reports sorting out old sketches on August 12, 1965, while at Wood's Lodge. "It is growing beyond proportions," he cried on August 18 and at the end of the month he abandoned work once again. "I had wanted to scrap the thing several times," Ingolf confided to Lawrence in July, 1967, "But in Peterborough I reached 'the point of no return.'" Transferring his sketches, Ingolf complained that some of the music was "too Bergian, too chromatic." "A fairly good day" is reported on March 1, but Ingolf was having difficulties with the Allegro section. "Fast music is always so much harder for me," he moaned on March 17, "the danger of tacking coda on coda." Two months passed before he looked at the music again on June 18, "what a mountain of work *that* is." On July 10 he began work anew – "I *must* go through with it, even if in the end it turns out a lousy piece. By August Ingolf was dosing himself with librium and reporting steady progress. "Work in garden on Allegro of Elegy and at last get into it," he reported on August 8, but on the 26th, the last day of his stay in Alt-Aussee, a number of important details were still incomplete.

As the comment about his garden illustrates, Ingolf liked to take his working materials out of doors, Many of the musical ideas incorporated in his compositions came to him while he was far away from his desk, inside or outside. He could "compose" in the oddest of locales, that is be taken by a useful musical construction almost anywhere. On August 1, 1964 he reports driving through Oakland, thrilled by a view of San Francisco glittering across the bay. Ideas about the last movement of the *Aria Sinfonica* suddenly emerged – "jot them down on the Freeway."

There are some examples of outdoor activity deliberately undertaken to stimulate the flow of ideas – "walk along beach in search of 2nd movement," he wrote on June 19, 1954, when he was working on *The Tower of Saint Barbara*. "Walk up the street to gather ideas for V," he noted on February 12, 1961, when he was writing the *Sinfonietta*. Mountains yielded the greatest amount of spontaneous musical material: ideas for the *Cello Duo* while walking on a trail in the Tetons in 1946, others to be used in *Hymn* while hiking in 1947, an idea for *Barbara* while skiing in the Sierras in 1954.

On April 30, 1967 Ingolf took a day off from composition in Alt-Aussee. When he arrived at the ski slopes he discovered he had forgotten his knapsack at home. He bought a bar of chocolate and hiked to the top. The snow was good but there was also time for a sunbath. Ideas for a coda in the C.P.E. Bach Variations made themselves known. He put on his skis, had a few nice runs and returned to incorporate this latest gift of nature in his work.

74. TRAVELS WITH ETTA

As the time for departure from Alt-Aussee drew nearer, Etta – who would now travel for the next two weeks with her son and daughter-in-law – padded about the village saying farewell to all the widows and waitresses. On the morning of August 24th we were taken to Bad Aussee, where Ingolf put us on a train, soon to depart for Attnang-Puchheim. No sooner had he said goodbye then he reappeared, five minutes later, with three mystery stories in English for Dorothy. Husband and wife said goodbye again, their next rendezvous scheduled for Iceland. While Ingolf was off on his own travels, including a visit to Sweden, we would be traveling with Etta on the continent and in England. Traveling with Etta was an interesting mixture of frustration and delight.

Even before we had stepped aboard the train Etta drew me aside to complain about the porter at the Bad Aussee station. Once this old chap had "forcibly" ripped the suitcase from her hand, cadging for tips no doubt, and she did not intend to be taken advantage of again. In fact, Etta was always on the lookout for the sharks who wished to make a mockery of her purse strings. Such crimes were, in any case, easier to deal with than emotional rip-offs, though we have seen many times before how her domestic unhappiness could boil over into a general condemnation of the vanity and foolishness of mankind. Dorothy and I had already endured a diatribe, while dining out one night, on the unctuousness of the head waiter at an Alt-Aussee hotel.

I would have to agree that Etta was well prepared to defend herself against the human flotsam which bedeviled her path. She had a calm and

449

dismissive air – in moments of vexation and crisis – that could withstand the attack of any foe. I cite by way of example an undated World War II letter to our cantankerous landlord, Mr. Zahn:

> We wish you would stop annoying us with notes, threats, and the like. You know just as well as we do that under the present O.P.A. regulations you cannot make us move and we do not intend to move...The present light arrangement is perfectly safe according to the Los Angeles City Department of Building and Safety, as you can find out for yourself by calling Michigan 5211, Extension 362...We do not intend to talk to you as you have proven yourself unable to do so in a civilized manner and your language is unfit for a child's ears.

Over twenty-five years later Ingolf described an incident at Mt. Wilson. He had parked his car at a viewpoint undoubtedly closed to the public by some agency, public or private – "A young man comes – berates us hysterically. Etta is magnificent, calmly parrying, not giving [the] slightest provocation but infuriating him more." Of course Ingolf was sometimes embarrassed by Etta's no nonsense approach to the world's misapprehensions. On April 20, 1966 the two of them attended a dinner party with Lillian Steuber and John Crown. Jascha Heifetz was another guest. Ingolf had already caused one scene when he refused to listen to a record by the Swingle Singers. Then Etta decided to challenge Heifetz over some misstatement and Ingolf had to silence his wife before she could ruffle the feathers of the violin virtuoso – "am once rude to E. who wants to correct J.H., but it passes." Etta may have missed a chance to correct Heifetz but she didn't lose too many opportunities elsewhere. She was one of those brave people who would turn around and stare fixedly at people who *talked* during the movie. For that matter, Ingolf too called for silence when the lights went down by hissing an angry "Psssssht!" And no one was ever better than my mother in getting rid of telephone salesmen. It took her only five seconds to detect the bullshit and then there would be a forceful but polite, "I sorry, we're not interested," accompanied by the sound of the crashing receiver.

Lawrence Morton, responding to a letter in which Etta had attacked half a dozen targets, begged for more of her "adorable bitchiness." But I am not certain that a life devoted to so much deploring, so many value judgments, so compulsive a search for phonies and charlatans (that means *you*, Tchaikovsky and Sibelius) truly represents the fulfillment of a personality which, at other times, could find so much to enjoy in life. "Superlative," Etta would say when she had been able to give something or someone a good notice; somehow even the pleasures in life came wrapped in a review. On our trip through Austria, Switzerland, Germany, Belgium and England I was lumbered with Etta's huge suitcase (and *we* didn't travel light in those days) and a hundred value judgments falling like felled timber from her pursed lips.

Etta tamed the world by rating it. We tamed Etta by ribbing her mercilessly. Banter was the easiest way I had to express my affection for this remarkable woman. With her laborsaving rituals and her arsenal of gadgets she was an excellent target, and she put up with all the jokes at her expense with good will. She did not complain when we put a rock in a pair of her socks for an impromptu ball game in the back garden at Alt-Aussee. She tolerated our insults when she ate her lunch too quickly on the Arlberg Express and ended up with heartburn. She accepted our joshing when we made remarks about her rapid streak through the Zurich station in search of a taxi, her short little legs skipping over the pavement in a pair of stockings that already had ladders.

We expected her to run out of steam quite rapidly, but for days she was always up ahead of us and always ready to begin the day's rating game. The creaking floorboards of the room above were cited as the cause of her early rising at the Hotel Augustinerhof on April 25. "If only you wouldn't sleep suspended from the ceiling," I began... Etta rushed out to buy a chopping board, of all things, and then we went on a guided bus tour of Zurich. Etta gave good marks to the French and English of the guide. At the Sonnenberg Gardens she jumped into the playground swings and pumped herself back and forth delightedly for several minutes. Dorothy suggested a sanatorium rest cure. When my wife bought her first mini-skirt that afternoon Etta pretended to be scandalized by its brevity. At the hairdressers the beautician got to hear the entire history of the young Linicks from a proud parent. The day concluded with a visit to Gorgot's wine bar. We were crowded into a table with three Yugoslavian businessmen. My mother, a faraway look in her eyes, was suspended thirty years in the past.

The next morning she counterattacked. She *talked* at breakfast, one of the blackest deeds in Dorothy's criminal code. Etta sulked because I hadn't left enough time to pay my bill (I had too!). She was keen to discover the slightest mispronunciation in my three words of spoken Deutsch. At Basle, where we went to see the Holbeins and the Klees, she complained that I never covered my mouth when I yawned. In Freiburg we dined high above the city; a long unscheduled walk in the woods led to recriminations from both of the ladies. On the way back to our hotel Etta excused herself to pee behind a tree. At breakfast the next morning she munched into a piece of moldy bread. "If you'd stop chattering for a moment," I suggested, "maybe you'd be able to see what you're eating."

We made our way north, Dorothy and Etta dissecting the costume and the social rank of every woman in waiting room and train compartment, and Etta adding analysis of their accents. In Cologne I called on her talents to do battle with a bitchy desk clerk who had overcharged us two D-Marks. My shoulder was sore from lugging her case on and off trains, Rhine ferries, up and down hotel staircases. By the afternoon of August 30, Brussels, Miss Etta *was* running out of steam. We had completed an afternoon's tramp through the city and she admitted that she couldn't do anything else like that again for some time. We spent our last full day on the continent in Ghent, visiting some people Dorothy and I had met in Spain. Etta charmed the socks off these folk and received many compliments on *her* French.

On August 31 we prepared for our journey to England. Etta bought another present for us, a bottle of cologne for Dorothy. Earlier it had been shoes in Zurich, a bottle of wine in Mainz. We took three trains from Brussels to Calais and the boat to Dover. The crossing was choppy and Etta, who had been placed in the liquor and cigarette line, collapsed on a sofa below decks. I stayed with her throughout the journey as a steward threw vomit sacks down on nearby tables. An Italian woman sat on my mother's feet, but she was too poorly to protest. On solid ground once again, she revived with a cup of British tea and, delighted by her first English sheep, sat quietly throughout the journey to Victoria. "I've never been to London," she was fond of explaining to people who knew her husband, "because there are no mountains there." But there was a shocking hill which we had to ascend after leaving the Sydenham Hill station. Trying to hoist Miss Etta's case on my shoulder I gave my neck such a crick that it ached for days. This didn't make me the best of sightseeing companions, though I did try to disguise my distress for my mother's sake; she seemed to be having a grand time. London was full of my Michigan State colleagues and their wives and Etta fell into an easy comradeship with all these people, trotting after us happily on many excursions to shops, museums, and the theater, At the National Gallery I did take the precaution of letting her proceed us by half a room, so as escape the afternoon's report card on the artists. On September 7, *our* return date, she saw us as far as Victoria, where I checked her case for her. Unexpressed at the end of this excursion was the melancholy thought that this might be the last opportunity for a mother and son ramble of this type.

The next morning she retrieved her case on the way to Heathrow, where she flew to Reykjavik and a reunion with her wandering husband. The next day Ingolf arrived from Stockholm, where he had visited *his* mother, now sitting out her senility in an old folks home on the island of Vaxholm. Dorothy and I had seen her there too, at the beginning of our grand tour. "I think I know you," she said to me. Later, Holger explained, she would tell all her friends that Dorothy and I were "her" children. Ingolf was sure that Mammi had recognized him "and is very happy. The gears jam sometimes, sometimes not, and sometimes wrong gears are engaged. But good health, hearing, sight, walking."

On the 12th my parents flew to New York and on to Los Angeles. Rick Lesemann and Michael Tilson Thomas were at the airport to greet the exiles returned.

75. THE QUALITY OF HIS REJECTIONS

The Dahls returned to Los Angeles on Tuesday, September 12. Only on Saturday the 16th did Ingolf find time to unpack his suitcase. He had planned his schedule so tightly that the day after leaving Reykjavik he was advising students at 9:00 in the morning. His first busy week back on campus was only a preview of the daunting academic schedule which stretched ahead for the twenty-nine months that separated this return to America from his next departure for Europe, in 1970. He taught summer school at U.S.C. in 1968 and in Hawaii in 1969, years in which his old Zurich friend, Willi Hausslein – through Ingolf's influence – also taught at U.S.C. in June and July.

"I'm really paying for my popularity now," Ingolf complained to Bill Colvig on February 9, 1968, "In my *graduate* music history course in 18th century music there are 70 students enrolled – sitting on the floor like at the Sorbonne." Teaching continued to be one of the most gratifying activities in a period otherwise full of professional agonies. "Collegium Middle Ages," he noted on October 11, 1967, "It is *fabulous*. They sing and play well and the music is just too thrilling – I'm very set up by it." The journals continue to provide a running self-appraisal of Ingolf's classroom performance, but I shall quote only that of November 17, 1969 – "All day work on 'Russian Music' lecture, and then leave my notes at home – . They applaud me after. And it *was* something of a virtuoso performance."

Ingolf cites fewer off-campus lecture appearances during this period, though he did succumb to an invitation to speak to the San Fernando Valley music teachers on "Problems of Repertoire" on January 6, 1969. On January 16, 1970 he provided another Philharmonic preview lecture, one which William Hartshorn pronounced the best in the twenty-five year history of such talks.

Ingolf had a great deal of respect for his new boss, Grant Beglarian. "He's going to come, hurrah!" Ingolf exulted on February 8, 1968. At a Contemporary Music Project meeting the following September Beglarian told him that is was "mostly because of you that I'm coming to Los Angeles." Beglarian bought a huge house from Dmitri Tiomkin and on September 13, 1969 he threw a party for the music, cinema and drama faculties. Here Ingolf stood chatting at the pool with Rick Lesemann. "I bet you haven't got nerve enough to jump in with your clothes on," Rick said. Etta, who was inside the house at the time, heard shrieks and applause outside – "Ingolf must be in the pool," she surmised, and she was right. Responding to Rick's challenge with an "Oh, wouldn't I?" her husband had fallen backwards into the water in his blue striped drip-dry suit. Another instructor jumped into the pool to retrieve Ingolf's glasses while Rick attempted to toss the Dean in for good measure. Surely such hi-jinks provided some counterpoint to all those hours spent in tedious academic meetings.

Ingolf continued to hold a position as Musical Director of the Young Musicians Foundation until May, 1968, when he resigned. "I know how difficult it must have been for you to cut that particular tie," Ellis Kohs wrote, "well, you will remain a sort of godfather anyway." In fact Ingolf kept a position on the board for another year. "Hear Stockhausen rehearsal," he wrote on May 19, 1968, "such a waste – but Michael is fabulous." The following January a disapproving mentor added, "M's avant-garde directions toward repertoire are disturbing."

One gets something of this same conservatism in Ingolf's record as a composition judge, a task he undertook for the YMF, Sigma Alpha Iota, and the Music Society of Santa Barbara. Examining the YMF submissions on October 6, 1969 he wrote, "Pretty sad – these dissonant, ugly, unheard offshoots of Sessions-Wolpe, what disasters." He was not much more pleased by the young composers he encountered on December 24, 1968 in the Santa Barbara contest. One work was "typical movie cue music – asthmatic phrases with continuous harping on a sickening 'theme song.'" A trio, "primitively improvisational and totally incoherent" was also rejected. A piece of "blatant kitsch," which he reviewed for the same contest a year later, was "like the melodious outpourings of an 80 year-old little lady from Pasadena." On the other hand Ingolf approved of a work that showed "invention, melodic curve, expressive depth, and multiplicity of levels." When the contestants were decoded it turned out that the composer in question was Paul Hedwall, a former student!

Contests required the expenditure of emotional energy but Ingolf also found more comprehensive ways of exhausting himself physically in mad dashes across the country for symposia and foundation committee meetings. In the year and a half from January, 1968 to June, 1969 he made no fewer than eight long-distance journeys eastward!

The Policy Committee of the Contemporary Music Project met in Washington on January 17-19, 1968. Ingolf mentions meetings dominated by "nonsensical abstractions." "I suggest a few practical things...The problem of present day youngsters...and the functional projects they *should* work for."

At the end of March he flew to New York to serve on a committee charged by the National Council of the Arts with selecting a winner of the Kodaly Fellowship. "On earphones for classical entertainment," Ingolf grumbled as he took his seat on the plane on March 29, "Mahler's 8th Symphony – for people to sleep by, as my neighbors do." Publishers conferences and a stop to visit Donald Hunsberger in Rochester brought this trip to an end on April 1.

On July 25 he made his way to Emporia, Kansas for a composer's workshop. "Their pieces are played and I comment – am not in top form," he wrote on the 26th, "and the light touch escapes me." Nelson Keyes, a former student, was Ingolf's host during this three-day trip but Ingolf stayed in a dormitory at the teacher's college – "can't sleep because of elevator, then TV, then loudspeakers in wall – the poor students!" The *Allegro and Arioso* was played during this visit – "I still like it" – and Ingolf performed the *Sonata Pastorale* – "If I could once concentrate and concertize, I could be good." Only fifteen people turned up to hear this performance – "*Never again!*" Ingolf roared, "can't cheapen myself that much."

"Dull meeting, superficial junk being thrown around," Ingolf complained during the next CMP meeting in New York on September 27. One month later, on November 1, Ingolf was back in New York for another CMP session – "I make a couple constructive suggestions. The contributions of each around the table say little about the subject matter, but much about the sayer. Lunch with the gang." Ingolf resigned his position on the Policy Committee soon thereafter but this did not seem to make much of a dent in his travel plans or diminish his participation in other Ford-CMP projects.

On November 15 he flew to Austin, Texas to give his "Tradition and Synthesis" lecture. Here he also conducted the *Sinfonietta* and the *Saxophone Concerto*, with Fred Hemke as soloist. On the return trip he managed to lose his paycheck, but he did enjoy a visit in Dallas with an old Hamburg girlfriend – "Spatz" (Margaret Hirsch) and her husband Walter.

A personal visit was also added at the beginning of the next trip east. On his way to Washington for a CMP meeting – and not daunted by foggy weather which required a four hour *train* journey from Chicago, Ingolf visited Dorothy and me in East Lansing on January 29, 1969. "9:30 in pouring rain in Lansing," he wrote, "Anth, under umbrella. He is so happy to see me, hugs me puppylike, I am too. Very nice drink and dinner and long yak. It is good to be with them." The next day he was given a tour of the "monstrous campus-city" that was Michigan State University, giving no sign of recognition as we passed the auditorium where he had accompanied Gracie Fields 25 years earlier. He attended a class in which I was showing Renaissance art slides – "a little too colloquial, funny paternal feeling, sitting in his class."

On June 9, his fifty-seventh birthday, Ingolf arrived in Rochester for a Ford-sponsored workshop at the Eastman School of Music. Don Michalsky had joined the CMP too and he frequently accompanied Ingolf on these long-distance junkets. Ingolf mentions drinking three Negronis with Don on June 13. The next day he completed the last of his eastern trips and flew back to Los Angeles before beginning a long summer session at the University of Hawaii. He should perhaps have attended a board meeting on December 30 of the National Opera Institute but by that time he was too preoccupied by his forthcoming sabbatical (and too ill) to undertake another long journey.

While he was in Austin, Ingolf was asked to change jobs. "The U. of Texas," he wrote Bill Colvig, "made me a fantastic offer to become the No. 1 composition professor, at an unbelievable salary for 9 months of teaching." Of course he turned this proposition down, and it does not seem likely that he ever considered seriously any of the job offers made to him by other universities. Occasionally he dangled such invitations in front of U.S.C. administrators, just to see if this would help his cause within the School of Music, but he never actively sought another job himself and even turned down invitations to be a visiting professor, as at Cornell and Yale in 1960 and Michigan State in 1963. He said no to offers of a permanent transfer which he received from the Peabody Conservatory in 1945 or 1946 and one from Julliard in 1954, and he responded negatively to "feelers" extended to him by Indiana in 1956 and 1967, Iowa in 1957, Hawaii in 1965, Utah in 1966, and Buffalo in 1969. He was also asked if he wished to be a candidate for dean or music department director by selection committees and administrators at Brooklyn College in 1953, Oberlin in 1961, Oregon (where evidently a formal offer was made in 1962), and Washington in 1963. Other institutions could offer more prestige and more money but few could offer the active musical life which Los Angeles provided and Ingolf needed, or that city's cultural and outdoor activities.

Much time *was* spent on the Oregon campus, as we have seen, and in the case of another of these institutions, Ingolf agreed to a summer school appearance in 1969. On June 15 he flew to Honolulu where, for six weeks, he lectured at the University of Hawaii and served as a guest-performer, with the Julliard Ensemble, during the East-West Music Festival. He seems to have enjoyed many things about Hawaii, though he was initially depressed by his apartment, located only a few steps from heavenly water, yet blessed with a view of "the assholes of apartments and luxury hotels." Rock and roll hit him from two directions and he was driven out of his patio by Beethoven's *Eighth*. The only cheering note in this environment was the presence of his own mango tree, though he ate so much of this fruit that he came down with a rash three weeks later.

At the University he lectured on the classics of 20th century music and presided over an elementary composition class. In both endeavors he encountered frustration. In the middle of his Expressionism lecture on the 23rd Ingolf asked himself, "What am I doing here...it doesn't connect, I'm way off, and as a result feel verbally inadequate to the subject." Schoenberg's Opus 11 went better the next day – "Sweep them along," but it seems clear that Ingolf's students were educationally unprepared to appreciate his sophisticated approach. "Am I being arrogant and snobbish?" he asked on June 27, "Yet, if I were to address in a similar fashion a group of bright, analytically experienced youngsters they would not want to be talked to about music of this kind and style." As it turned out, the keenest students had selected term paper topics on the works of Varese, Penderecki, Stockhausen – "all that dull stuff."

As for the student composers, Ingolf was horrified – "They are not producing and are totally untutored...only two of them have any background – the others don't know how to put 2 notes together." He began with primitive exercises. "Discuss variation form and what one can do," he recorded on June 27, "and I talk so well and clear-concise...they don't even take notes." Some progress was observed; one of the students "says I'm making him work harder than anyone has before – and I thought I wasn't getting through." Scrambling over Diamond Head on July 10, Ingolf forgot to attend a young composers concert – "am disgusted and embarrassed," but he was very touched when the class presented him with a bottle of Scotch on the last day of the term.

There were a number of Julliard Ensemble concerts in which Ingolf had some role. On June 30 he played the *Sonata Seria* ("I play much of it well...I have the audience at the end!)" He was also pleased with an Orvis Auditorium performance of the *Duettino Concertante* on July 7 – "They really come though and it is *very* successful." The *Trio*, in which Ingolf took the piano part on July 14, also went well, but he was annoyed by the lack of press coverage and the irrelevant reviews of all these concerts. Indeed one reviewer had spent more time talking about "the clown in the first row who took pictures...until his camera mercifully jammed" than about the *Sonata Seria* itself.

On July 25 the exercise came to an end. Ingolf, who had been slowed in his athletic activity by an injury to three toes sustained while running barefoot on asphalt, looked down into the crater rim at Diamond Head and exulted, "I am through, I done it, it is all over, I am free, the first free moment since September!" Five days earlier there had been another moment of exhilaration as men walked for the first time on the moon – "Overwhelmed. The astronaut jumps about in big strides, and we see it happening!!" Later he walked along a beach and saw a sinking half moon reflected in the ocean over Waikiki – "There they are asleep. The human grandeur once poured into gothic cathedrals now achieved this!"

On July 26 he flew to the island of Kauai for a week's vacation. "Paradise found," he wrote on August 1. Here he went walking in the nude in the rain forest and scratched himself while swimming on a reef. On August 2 he returned to Los Angeles for one final semester – before beginning his last sabbatical abroad.

76. EVERYTHING ON THAT CARD

In the two musical seasons that followed his return from Alt-Aussee Ingolf once again embraced an extremely active concert career. In the 1967-1968 season there were eight concert performances, though the first – on December 13, and the last – on July 21 – were fairly informal presentations by the Collegium Musicum. "Sounds good," he wrote of the latter concert, "but the crowd is disappointing. Why am I doing all this? Sense of duty to students..."

Ingolf appeared on two MEC programs, one on December 18, the second on January 8. On the first he conducted his own edition of a Telemann concerto and the Bach D-minor *Harpsichord Concerto*. The soloist was the elderly Alice Ehlers, making her final public appearance. Lawrence Morton recalls that just before curtain time Madame Ehlers looked up and said, "Did we rehearse this concerto?" "Ingolf and I were appalled," Lawrence added, "but she played marvelously – out of habit I suppose." Ingolf, too, noted in his journal, "Bach goes extremely well and all are pleased." An all-Haydn concert a few weeks later was also a success. Ingolf conducted two *Notturnos* and accompanied Dorothy Ledger in the cantata *Arianna a Naxos*. Because he had memorized his part some of his students convinced themselves that he must have been improvising at the keyboard. Then he joined Bonnie Douglas and Emmett Sargeant in his own edition of the *Piano Trio No. 4*. "Late start," Ingolf reported, "big crowd – all goes very well. Trio is *the* hit!"

On March 3 Ingolf was the featured composer in the Encounters series at the Pasadena Art Museum. He had been invited to participate a year earlier by Leonard Stein and a great deal of correspondence had flown across the Atlantic as Ingolf, in Alt-Aussee, chose the music he wished to program and the performers he wished to play it. The program was presented twice on concert night and Ingolf spoke about the pieces. He then accompanied Larry Lesser in the 1946 *Cello Duo*. "It might seem somewhat of a novelty," the composer wrote in reference to all the avant-gardists who had preceded him in the series, "to have a piece that ends in C major." The two musicians were joined by Eudice Shapiro for a performance of the 1962 *Trio*. "Happy time," Ingolf had written during a rehearsal of this "once-jinxed piece" – "the music is beautiful and the performers are *with* it." Highlight of the evening, however, was the first performance of the recently completed *A Cycle of Sonnets*, with baritone Maurice Allard, accompanied by Charles Fierro. "Beautiful music," Ingolf noted in his review of the evening, "grand performance."

A week later the Pasadena performers offered the *Trio* at California State, Fullerton, where Ingolf also gave his "Tradition and Synthesis" lecture. On April 22 they presented the work a third time at the Schiff Memorial concert at U.S.C., adding one of the Dahl-edited Haydn trios to the evening's fare. Ingolf's final concert appearance of the season was as guest conductor of the U.S.C. Orchestra in the world premiere of the work of one of his own students, *Venite* by Phillip Westin.

In spite of precarious health Ingolf pushed himself through a grueling number of engagements in the 1968-1969 season, including a string of fifteen April performances as conductor of Humperdinck's opera *Hansel and Gretel*. In addition to this special assignment, there were thirteen other concerts in an eight-month period between October and May! It would be hard to find any year in his musical past richer in accomplishment.

Eight of the concerts were offered by the U.S.C. Orchestra, whose podium Ingolf ascended again in the year following Walter Ducloux's departure from the campus. The season began on October 28, Etta's sixty-third birthday. Ingolf presented the world premiere of Ramiro Cortes' *The Eternal Return* and conducted Mahler's *Fourth*. "Wish you could have heard this," he wrote to Bill Colvig, "I had worked awfully hard for it and did the Mahler from memory (60 minutes of music – .) The hall was filled to overflowing and when I took my bow at the end the audience just exploded – I'd never experienced anything like it, and never will again – they just got to their feet and cheered and wouldn't stop." Walter Arlen felt compelled to mention in his *Times* review that the orchestra was "mostly girls this season," but added that, "the standards of the group have never been higher." Nothing was mentioned about the audience reaction, but the critic did comment on Ingolf's conducting of the Mahler – "It was lovingly detailed, deliberate in the right places, controlled, relaxed and genuinely warm."

On November 13 Ingolf presented the work of another student, *Analogies From Rothko* by Harold Budd, during a Music at Noon concert. "The tension is almost unbearable," he wrote on January 11, eve of the next U.S.C. concert, "the few rehearsals, the Ravel going badly, memorizing Webern and studying scores, the choral problems, and all of it weighs on me." Among other works, Ingolf was presenting the world premiere of Robert Linn's *The Pied Piper of Hameline*. "Big success, but small audience," the conductor wrote of this concert. Karen Monson in the *Times* said, "Rarely – very rarely – is a concert program as imaginatively and successfully structured...Much of the credit for the programming and for the consistent superiority of the performers goes to Ingolf Dahl..."

On February 19 Ingolf conducted orchestra and soloists in a concerto program on the Music at Noon series, to which the orchestra returned for an additional program on March 5. When John Granet played the Bach *Piano Concerto in F minor* at a Town and Gown recital on March 23 Ingolf reported, "We play well, but the reception is dismal – feel so out of place – quick back to the ivory tower where a few people love musical art – not this huge rich indifferent crowd." Ingolf's last appearance with the orchestra he had loved and nurtured for almost a quarter of a century took place on May 11. "It is getting better," he noted during a rehearsal on the 8th, "but all the attendance problems – ." "My memorization helps put tension and attention into the orchestra," he added on the day of the concert. A Mendelssohn overture was followed by the Brahms *Violin Concerto* (with Eudice Shapiro as soloist), Stravinsky's *Ode* and Hindemith's *Nobilissima Visione*. Ellis Kohs wrote to his colleague that the evening:

> was one of the memorable events of many years...Students in the audience and in the orchestra too must have sensed more deeply that ever that Music as a calling, as a profession, involved much more than showmanship, than technical proficiency or innovation. Rather that at the highest level it is concerned with the essential dignity and profundity of human life.

"So," Ingolf wrote, "the last is on a G major chord of Hindemith...The audience stands up and cheers and won't let me go."

Ingolf had also conducted the Young Musicians Foundation Debut Orchestra at the Music Center on April 19. "Enjoyable," he wrote on March 30, "If all rehearsals could slowly evolve a performance like this!" But shortly before the concert he reported himself "crazy with apprehension." Part of the problem was an ambitious program that included the *Aria Sinfonica*. On the 17th he reports tears of happiness at the orchestra's reaction to the work. Two days later he assembled his charges for a warm-up at 6:30 – "They hate to do it, yet it is necessary and results show it." From the first chord, he reported happily, "we are in it, crisp, vital, controlled. The A.S. is a great success, many calls. What a moment."

There were also four chamber music appearances in the 1968-1969 season. On December 1 Ingolf joined Eudice Shapiro and Mitchell Lurie at a Coleman Concert in Pasadena. The trio played an arrangement of Stravinsky's *L'Histoire du Soldat* and Bartok's *Contrasts*. The latter work was repeated at a Monday Evening Concert on March 10, at which Ingolf conducted Copland's *Nonet* and joined Eudice Shapiro in Stravinksy's *Duo Concertante*.

Two concerts were given in Fullerton. The first took place on February 13 and the second (in which Ingolf and Larry Lesser played the *Duo*) occurred on the same day that he conducted his last U.S.C. Orchestra concert, May 11 – "one of the toughest days I've ever been through."

It is hard to know why Ingolf should have accepted such an assignment on such a day, coming at the end of a busy U.S.C. season, only a few weeks after the YMF concert and all those performances of *Hansel and Gretel*. Carl Ebert was again in charge of this opera production, which had its premiere on April 8 and he and Ingolf spent many hours in auditions and rehearsals for the Guild Opera Company. Co-sponsor of the event was the Los Angeles City School System and all but one of the performances, that of April 26, were for school children – 72,000 of them in total! Ingolf had many memories of Zurich while completing this assignment ("the feelings of standing in the light green gangway under the pit, waiting for the house lights to go down"). He was unhappy with the acoustics of the Shrine Auditorium where he couldn't hear the last stand strings, trumpets or trombones – "they could just as well have played Yankee Doodle and I wouldn't have known the difference in the tutti passages...Also of course the players can't hear each other, the singers, when upstage, can't hear the orchestra." Shibley Boyes came to critique a performance. She thought Ingolf's conducting "wonderfully musical," but suggested he was trying for too many subtleties that would be lost or drowned out by 5,000 squirming kids.

Another chapter in the long history of Ingolf's service to young audiences had also been added earlier in the year when he had completed a rare assignment in a commercial recording studio. (The only other studio job of the period seems to have come on March 25, 1968 when he worked on Miklos Rosza's score for *The Green Berets* – a "horrible brutalization movie.") On February 12, 1969, however, the assignment was something quite different, for on that day it was Ingolf who, in playing the *Pathetique Sonata* of Beethoven, provided the notes which millions of children heard coming from Schroeder's piano in the film *A Boy Named Charlie Brown* .

It will not come as a surprise to learn that none of Ingolf's professional activities lead to any reversal in those dark career appraisals we have encountered before; he continued to stand aside in jealous envy while others achieved the recognition he thought he deserved. After the 1967 Ojai Festival Peter Yates wrote to inform him, needlessly, that it was generally conceded that he lacked the glamour possessed by Pierre Boulez. "MTT comes and visits," Ingolf noted on December 22, 1969, "to hear him talk (the Ruggles recording etc. etc., and all the things which I pioneered, and for which I was never at the right place at the right time, with the right people.)" After receiving only lukewarm reviews for the U.S.C. concert of May 11, 1969, a bitter Ingolf hissed, "That proves that I cannot move the scribblers to enthusiasm the way my inferiors can." "Feel bad about being so unrecognized," he wrote on March 5, 1967, after perusing the *New York Times*. After reading *NOTES* on December 29, 1968 he added, "What can I still do? Why? Who wants it? Why this struggle for professional recognition which in the really big sense I can never have anyhow?" "Is it my job," he asked on December 28, 1969, "to see that *some* of what I did survives in consciousness. How, how, how to be recognized?"

"Today's concert is a very special one," the program of the Fullerton Friends of Music read on May 11, 1969, "for Ingolf Dahl is departing from the concert stage to devote his creative energies to composing." The decision to choose, at last, to give up the life of the performer was an agonizing one for my stepfather, who believed that "the deepest pleasure of music can come only with physical contact and effort." Nevertheless he had made this "hellish" decision sometime in the fall of 1968. "Will I have the strength and willpower?" he asked on October 18, "It is going to be like cutting off an arm." "It means so much to me," he moaned to his sister on December 8, "and I am so good at it (and getting better all the time) that it will really hurt to give it up. But if, in my remaining years, I am still to create some good music I *must* give up other distractions." By the end of October he had announced his decision not to accept the baton of the U.S.C. Orchestra after May, 1969. "The flair and dynamism of Dahl cannot be replaced and he will be missed," *The Daily Trojan* editorialized on May 9. Four days after the final concert the orchestra gave its conductor a leather brief case – "I fail to find words for a speech which I should have made." In the previous month, as a symbol of the seriousness with which he regarded his decision, he had turned down a conducting assignment he would once have coveted, the opportunity to lead the Los Angeles Philharmonic in several concerts.

It is true that he was committed to some performing tasks in Hawaii and that twice Lawrence Morton (who was one of the many figures begging him to change his mind) succeeded in getting him to participate in Museum concerts that fall, but the commitment had been made and Ingolf would do the rest of his living and his dying as a composer above all.

His decision to give up the concert stage seems all the more heroic, if not foolhardy, when one considers that he was now practicing his compositional art in a musical world in which he felt out of place and uncomfortable. The work of his contemporaries exasperated him increasingly, and rampaging avant-gardism brought him to the fury point. Some of this loathing succeeded in putting a strain on his friendship with Lawrence Morton. On October 2, 1967, exercising an ancient concert tradition, Ingolf booed a piece by Sikorski at a Monday Evening Concert, then congratulated Lawrence on his "public success." He booed other MECs as well. He wasn't much more happy with an Ojai Festival performance of a work by Lutoslawski on May 25, 1968 – "too 'soundy' for the medium," he griped, especially when Etta said she liked it.

"Anonymous soundwaves" from Poland were not among his favorite listening experiences. "I misbehave in morning," Ingolf wrote of a CMP meeting in Washington on January 31, 1969, "when an involuntary 'Ugh" escapes me apropos Penderecki." Ligeti was probably the avant-garde composer he had the greatest regard for, but the army of dada sound manipulators now invoked a rage more desperate than any ever directed at Carl Orff.

A "godawful" happening by Ichiyama drew an S.R.O. crowd to a Honolulu concert on July 3, 1969 – "all those barefoot mindless ones taking in anti-intellectual 'waves' of bedlam." Even composers whom he had admired in the past failed in the final measure. On April 20, 1969 he attended a U.S.C. performance of an opera by Henze, a composer whose "flair" and "flow" he was always comparing with his own – "the lousiest – and *all* these many students wasting all that much time on *this*. – It is shapeless, noisy, grey, continuous tutti (and the thin places – Intermezzo – trite Weillish without his flair.) Force myself and E. to stay to end." In 1967 he chanced on an article in the *New York Times* that spoke of the musical equivalent of Tom Wolfe's *painted word*: "Boulez, quoted by Feldman in NYT, 'I am not interested in how it sounds, I am only interested in how it was made.' That should be *exactly* reversed! Who the hell cares how it was made? Except the 'non-musicians.'"

Needless to say Ingolf was passionately interested in how his own music was made, and questions of style never ceased their vexing insistence. "Was there any *choice* involved," he wondered in 1967, "that I took the Stravinskian way of writing only 'single pieces,' neither the style nor the musical method of which could be repeated, so that the writing of 'just another one' like the Concerto a Tre...became impossible, just as did any *bulk* of pieces?" "To write in a style that one feels secure, comfortable, cheerful in," remained a goal to the end, but Ingolf found that in 1969 this would involve the use of styles either imitative or old-fashioned – hence his despair. "While running on track the first moon sliver," was observed by the composer on October 4, 1967. Ingolf made a wish – "the big work again" – then he added, "Who am I kidding? "Why don't I just give up and not continue the fraud of 'composing'?" he asked the following November 26. Etta, observing the suffering of her husband, made this same suggestion repeatedly.

Nevertheless Ingolf persevered. "Am I a good enough composer now," he asked after the fateful decision about performing had been made, "to put everything on that card?" His record as a composer in this period between Alt-Aussee and the return to Europe in 1970, one in which so many professional and emotional crises blocked any progress, certainly called into question any vision of a prolific future.

Only two works were begun *and* finished in the period, and one of them, *Variations on a Theme by Halsey Stevens*, was a ninety second contribution to a seven-part 60th birthday tribute, scored for clarinet, cello and piano, which Ingolf completed on December 3, 1968. The other, *I.M.C. Fanfare*, was a one-minute work, published in 1973 by Joseph Boonin, for three trumpets and three trombones, which Ingolf completed in response to a commission from the International Music Council and UNESCO, tendered by Norman Dello Joio in May, 1968. "A *real* composer," Ingolf argued, "would write such a fanfare in an hour or so." In fact he began work on June 7 when he put down some sketches while looking from a hotel window at the deep valley and clearing clouds of Yosemite. In mid-July he began again, "at last seem to be getting *into* the art and joy of composing again," but he did not complete the piece until August 22.

Three works underwent revision. A final version of the *Cello Duo* was finished in January, 1969 and dedicated to Laurence Lesser, who played it in spring recitals in New York and Los Angeles with Michael Tilson Thomas. The final revision incorporated some suggestions made by Gregor Piatigorsky.

On June 30, 1968 Ingolf began revision of the *Variations on a Theme of C.P.E. Bach* – "going to be all right (with big cuts) if I can write a new second variation quickly." The dilemma was not solved until the following January. "The end is in sight," he wrote on the 9th, but the revised version was not completed until February 22. Six days earlier Ingolf reported himself finished with a revision of the *Aria Sinfonica*.

On October 18, 1969 he received a request from Matthew B. Ehrlich, an amateur flutist from Philadelphia, who wanted to know if the composer would be willing to provide an arrangement for flute and alto flute of the 1945 *Variations on a Swedish Folktune*. Intrigued by this challenge, Ingolf notes that on the afternoon after receiving this request "in one draft do most of it in the sun on lower patio." Finishing the job became a project for the next sabbatical as did completion of the *Elegy Concerto*, which Ingolf glanced at on December 29, 1969. He found reassurance in what he saw – "there seems to be some soulful music there." Another project postponed for a later time was a request by post on February 27, 1967 for a second brass quintet made by Arnold Fromme of the American Brass Quintet. Ingolf never seems to have made any headway here and besides, he asked, "How do we know that son of Lassie will be as good as Lassie herself?"

I don't know of any Dahl composition, no matter how critically treated by its creator, that did not arouse his affections ultimately. Even the *Flute Serenade*, which he had earlier panned, was described as a "wow" after a successful performance at a U.S.C. Composers Concert on April 21, 1969. He did despair, even after the RCA recording, of ever hearing a fully realized performance of the *Duettino Concertante*, but this did not diminish his affection for the piece. A Milton Thomas rendition of the *Viola Divertimento* on May 7, 1969 brought tears and, thirty-five years after they were written, he could pronounce the Ehrismann songs "very successful" when performed by his student Victoria Bond on January 6, 1968. On March 28, 1969 there was another chance to hear Donald Hunsberger conduct the Eastman Wind Ensemble in the *Sinfonietta*, which Ingolf pronounced "fabulous." After a scolding from Kurt Stone Ingolf returned the final proofs of this work to Alexander Broude the following June.

There were also three 1967 works, begun in Peterborough or Alt-Aussee, which needed completion. On January 25, 1970, with John Crown, Ingolf recorded the piano four-hand version of *Four Intervals*, now including the section entitled "Fourths," which he had worked on from August 8 to October 20 – "rather nice, but don't think it makes much impression on E., or the others."

On January 4, 1970 Ingolf also put the final touches on a revision of the *Sonata da Camera*, a process he had initiated in the last week of the previous November. "It is done, hurrah," he gloried, "under such obstacles." These two tasks of completion were not as substantial as that needed on a third, *A Cycle of Sonnets*, for here Ingolf had made progress in Alt-Aussee only on the first of three proposed settings of the Petrarch poems. Appropriately, he made completion of the work his first creative priority upon his return in September, 1967.

Even the first song was "not quite right" when he looked at it again on September 26, and it wasn't until November 7 that he completed the section anew. On October 17 the second song was started; it was completed only on Christmas Day. "Work on metric scheme of Intro and the notes," he wrote of the third section on New Year's Day, "(and in afternoon, it works!)" With a performance scheduled for March 3, feelings of panic had set in by February 1. "How lovely," Ingolf reported on the 9th, as he sat working on the composition while sitting in the nude (because of poison oak) as the rain fell outside, "Start with what I have of Sonnet III, *like it!*" The composition was completed on February 16. In this "vocal sonata" the keyboard part was intended to be the equal of the voice. James Berdahl described *A Cycle of Sonnets* as "one of the most complex and strictly controlled serial works" of the composer, "Although basically polyphonic, it is dense, dissonant, and highly chromatic. The piece is centered around the key of C minor, and the asymmetrical row contains that scale within its first seven notes." As we have seen, Charles Fierro played the piano part to the baritone of Maurice Allard in the premiere; later he accompanied Robert Hasty in the work at a Monday Evening Concert on November 24, 1969. To Charles, Ingolf wrote that the work is:

> excruciatingly difficult, in every way...but in addition to finding it ghastly difficult I found it also very, well – beautiful. Excuse my saying it – but after fighting through the notes myself, and thinking

– 'oh my, what have I done, this is so awfully overwritten and thick and over complex and thorny and unrewarding' I finally found the whole thing opening up just as I had originally planned it.

77. FOOLS ON THE HILL

Etta missed Alice Ehler's farewell concert on December 18, 1967 because she was not feeling well. The next day Ingolf took her to the doctor. "E is OK as I thought," he wrote. On January 4, however, he had to alter his diagnosis – "E. has to have a tumor operation, but it is safe!" (Ingolf's ability to ostracize the painful is well catalogued. He seems to have convinced himself that the 1964 surgery was "safe" too, yet the present crisis seems to have originated in the ovarian cancer of that year.) Etta had been experiencing sharp abdominal pains and now it was necessary for Dr. Sherwood Feinberg to remove part of the colon and the uterus. My mother entered the hospital on January 9. "It is much more severe than thought," Ingolf wrote the next day, "A blow. But no colostomy." He sat by her bed while she slept, "lovely, spirited," he reflected, "what a soul." Every night he went to the hospital to be near her. "How handsome you are," she said, looking at him with love and tenderness before dropping off again. "I'm so tired and weak," she complained on the 13th. By the 16th Ingolf was able to report a "fantastic improvement in Etta. Like a week between yesterday and today...Very happy about her progress." At her bedside he read aloud a story by John O'Hara. She was still in the hospital when he returned from a five-day Eastern junket on January 21. "Etta looks grand – am so happy to be with her, my love." My mother had again risen to dominate the physical with her wise-cracking spirit. "She is the sensation of the hospital," Ingolf enthused before taking her home on the 23rd, "I love her so much, am so dependent on her, and treat her so badly – ."

"She is doing very well and states that she feels better than she has in two and a half years," Dr. Feinberg wrote on April 1. "She is such a delightful patient," he added on June 20. Ingolf wrote a letter of thanks to the surgeon: "The other day, when I mentioned to my wife the occasion when, right after the surgery you came to talk to me about everything that had happened and what you were able to do under the circumstances she said, 'I bet if you were a dog you would have licked his hands!' That, so humorously and nicely expressed by her, is the gist of this letter." Etta certainly seemed to be in good spirits when Dorothy and I arrived for a visit in March of 1968.

It was the last opportunity I had to observe my parents in their native habitat. To me Ingolf and Etta were just the same dear dotty cranks, a couple whose relationship had never seemed more pacific and mutually supportive. But how hopelessly ignorant I was of their life beneath this surface.

Etta had her own circle of friends in her final years, visitors whom she could entertain at Cheremoya or spend time with on campus. Nancee Cortes and Leda Campo were two of her favorites. Often Ingolf would come up from his studio to find Etta gossiping with Christie Lundquist or MTT. Michael continued to write to her after leaving Los Angeles. "Dear Dear (5,280 times) Etta," he wrote on November 12, 1969, "I have also been conjuring you up whenever I feel an attack of the 'too much success too soon vapors' coming on. Usually just one good E.D. '*Humph*'... is enough to dispel them immediately." Etta never tired of chattering with the workmen and fix-it specialists – who always seemed to be underfoot, but she also spent a great deal of time alone, and Dorothy and I would wear ourselves out trying to suggest ways of reducing the loneliness of life on that hillside.

Of course she remained adamant on the subject of television (though she always had a lovely deplorathon in front of *our* set, where she would sit happily for hours during her visits to East Lansing). We urged her to get a dog, not only for company but for security. Every rational argument failed – who would walk it, who would feed it, who would take care of it during sabbaticals? Stubbornly she sat soaking her cracking feet in a pail of Epsom salts and when these were dry, she would read mystery stories or the *New Yorker* or make simple projects into complex ones.

How we used to rib her about her gadgets and *tchotchkes*, her special little gas cartridges for making fizzy water (lest she have to *pay* for club soda like everyone else), her penchant for multiple purchases of the same product, her *dozens* of vacuum cleaner bags, the lipstick shades she was so certain would be discontinued by the manufacturer that half her hoarded stock turned rancid before she could use it.

Many of her most convoluted solutions to the problems of everyday life came in the kitchen. Her sister Lillian characterized Etta as a cook who was "experimental and courageous, but lacking in intuitive flair." Etta's culinary triumphs came when she could boast that by combining three different kinds of Campbell's soup a delicious hybrid could be produced. I had few complaints at the time, though I can recall the scorched pigs-in-the-blanket, the rock-hard pizza dough, the watery lentil soup, the shriveled Swedish meatballs, the much fussed-over Rock Cornish game hens that yielded two mouthfuls after one had successfully completed major surgery. Her specialty was a "cheese pie," which she made from Philadelphia Cream Cheese, a drop of almond extract, and a crust derived from crushed graham crackers.

Although she could not understand a dress pattern, Etta did like to sew. She and Lillian would go shopping at the Broadway. Etta would insist that they take their own lunches and eat them in the dressing room of the department store (because, heaven forbid, why should you pay to be waited on?). Maybe Etta would be on one of her slimming regimens – no bread but a pint carton of boiled tongue consumed in one sitting. If Etta bought a garment a ritual exorcism would be performed over the object because no one in the rag trade had an eye for the correct relationship between button color and cloth. Throughout her life Etta had to rectify such aesthetic failures. Off would come the old buttons, on would go Etta's own selection.

My mother conquered the more manageable aspects of a daily existence fraught with emotional uncertainty by making charts and inventories. She made order out of Ingolf's business correspondence by maintaining the files herself. She made her own calendars. And she composed endless reminders, guideposts to progress, in a long catalogue of schedules and lists. A few have survived and they give only a small clue to the number and thoroughness of those that have been lost: "Fred 4:30, Mayfair, steak, bagels. Thrifty, make-up, sheer hair-nets, white adhesive. Instructions to Gertrude." I could not resist tampering with these lists and often enjoyed adding impossible items to the weekly shopping. Ingolf too participated in this game. To "cooking onions, ground round, wide scotch tape and *real* chicken," he added a footnote:

"According to Plato, 'real' is only something that is perceivable in relation to the manifestations of the 'ideal,' whereas on the other hand Schopenhauer maintains that only that can be real that is neither subject to the distortions of the will nor entirely determined by perception, however Nietzsche says that it is not..."

To Steak Tatar, he has added another proviso, "If this term refers to an Asiatic tribe which overran Europe in the 15th century there is one R missing – if, on the other hand, this term refers to the word of endearment uttered by departing friends there is one R too many."

These asides illustrate why Ingolf was such delightful company, when he was around. He enjoyed making humorous lists of his own, for instance he maintained a list of cat composers – Clawed Depussy, Darius Meow, Vincent Pussykitty. His journals rarely give us much evidence of this love of good humor, the buoyancy of his cackling giggle. In company he was not a melancholy figure at all, and he often demonstrated a ready enough wit and a deadpan delivery. Etta recalled visiting a series of weather-beaten statues in Sutro Park in 1943. As they approached a replica of the Venus De Milo, Ingolf stared seriously at the work and said, "There one can see what comes of too much thumb-sucking."

I continued to be amused by Ingolf's running feud with modern life, though I was not supposed to be. In his anti-ice-cream-man letter to the City Attorney he had insisted, "I am not an obstreperous crank," but of course he was – and a pity there aren't more like him – with his justifiable stream of indignant letters to the mayor's office, the police, Western Union, the telephone company, newspaper and TV stations. On December 31, 1964, the day Charles Fierro played the *Sonata Pastorale* on John Crown's KNXT program, Ingolf put pen to paper and wrote a *fake* fan letter in yahoo style – "The USC professor presented it so good and the playing was just delightful." When *he* got a got a protest letter from an angry physician, who inserted a prescription slip under the windshield wiper to complain about the presence of Ingolf's car across the street from his garage, the wily crank counter-attacked masterfully, "Dear Sir: It would indeed be appreciated if you would ask the police to come and paint red exactly that portion of the curb which you require for access to your garage, so that your neighbors would not unknowingly trespass on your convenience."

Nor should we forget, while trying to evaluate Ingolf's credentials as a crank, his long list of famous predictions – his assertion in 1956 that "electronic music" is just a freak," his claim in 1958 that rock and roll was nothing but a fad, or his wholesale denunciation in 1953 of *recorded* music. "Life is too short to listen to records," he told a Lenox Forum audience:

> How can one preserve the excitement, the sting of great experience, the "shock of recognition," when it can be duplicated on a reduced scale at any time at home...Easy access to music leads to dulled listening, only half an ear, half a soul...A third rate concert, a barely adequate attempt to sing and play some simple music by a community choir or an amateur orchestra is more valuable than 100 records by the Heifetzes, Horowitzes, and Furtwanglers combined.

Ingolf also protested the commercialization of many aspects of modern life accepted without demur by the rest of us. "Lucky the person," he mocked, "who owns a set of all nine symphonies by the great Toscanini." Rick Lesemann told me that when Ingolf was still an avid smoker, he sent his students out to the store to buy three packs of cigarettes. "Choose three kinds at random," Ingolf advised, "so we can say that we're not victims of advertising." He remained, therefore, in so many ways, out of step with most of his contemporaries. Even his clothes had a foreign flavor. When his Schruns suit wore out another was ordered from the same tailor. "Ingolf's clothes," Eve Babitz remembers, "always looked as though he'd had them forever already and would always have them," that "his ageless tweed-type suits and thick sweaters made everyone else's clothes look deplorable and skimpy."

Ingolf continued an active athletic life, even though good sense might have suggested that it was time to take it easy, and thereby combined obsession and idiosyncrasy. It was his boast that he could do 30 pushups on his 56th birthday. He continued to lift weights, and to run on the track and out of doors. A barefoot jog on Mt. Hollywood remained one of his favorite activities. He went swimming frequently, always recording the number of lengths he had completed.

He was disappointed that there was not more skiing in these years. "I belong here," he wrote at Snow Summit on March 12, 1969, "this is my deepest life – why should I suppress it? the blood sings and all fibers vibrate." With the Schaars he twice completed Mammoth ski vacations, once in April, 1968, and once in May, 1969. "Feel great and peppy, the real 'after-the-mountain feeling,'" he wrote on May 29. With the Sierra Club he also undertook a week's exploration of the Kanab region of Utah, also in April, 1968; in October he spent a weekend on a Colorado River canoe trip. His one mountain climbing expedition to the Sierras during this period came in late August, 1968, one celebrating the thirteenth anniversary of his friendship with Bill Colvig – with Don Michalsky making a third member of the party. Ingolf's last Sierra summit, the North Palisade, was conquered with Bill on September 2, a second, perhaps foolhardy attempt that seemed doomed to failure when the climbers, who had no rope with them, were unable to find a way forward. "Very dark thoughts about this, the last mountain gone, the last fling fizzles." Bill continued to explore an "impossible ledge" and stiff and tired Ingolf followed him up – "Some very hairy places, particularly one with smooth sides over snow tongue, almost no holds." At 3:00 they reached the summit, Ingolf in tears of exhausted gratitude.

In the Southern California mountains Ingolf succeeded in pushing his total from the 100 peaks conquered in 1964 to 140 five years later. A number of hikes were now made to desert mountains. On the ascent of San Ysidro on February 3, 1968 Ingolf reports that he fell into a cactus and a visiting Holger fell into a hole. Don Michalsky, Charles Fierro and Dan Lewis were among his mountain companions at this time; so was the psychologist Alan Glasser, whom he had met on the Kanab trip. On one of Ingolf's last Southern California hikes, October 19, 1969, there was an unnerving incident. "Toward the end," Alan wrote, "I could see that he was tired and offered to take the pack. Ten minutes later a huge rock was dislodged and smashed me to the ground. It hit square in the center of the pack and such was the force the frame was bent 90 degrees. Had I not had the pack, either my back would have been broken or I would have been killed outright."

As the time for the next sabbatical grew closer both of my parents experienced severe health crises. "E. is very depressed," Ingolf wrote on October 3, 1969, "found some blood in stool. So it is going to go on like this? With every irregularity a rush to doctors and panic? Difficult, difficult to come to terms with this, and how is that going to be in Europe?" By

October 20 the decision had been made to send Etta to hospital for exploratory surgery. This took place on November 5. Ingolf's entry for the date tells the awful news – "Had a terrible night, so little sleep, tension, uneasiness, wake at 7 – 'now they are starting surgery.' To hospital, Lillian there, wait and wait. At 10:30 Doctor Feinberg comes – how to evaluate his news? An ovarian type tumor, unremovable (!) that may ("most likely") respond to chemical treatment." In fact the disease had recurred in the area of the sigmoid colon and the small bowel.

Etta was aware at every stage of this prognosis and on November 22 she wrote us a long letter describing her stay in hospital. (Ingolf lost this letter, along with two sack lunches, but someone mailed the former anyway.) "Here goes the first writing I have attempted since several (2) weeks ago," Etta began, "when once again, and hopefully for the last time, they were sawing the lady in half." At the radiology lab, a week after surgery, a nice young doctor had told her, "Mrs. Dahl, we have seen these doctors driving around in their Rolls-Royces and often wondered how they got that way. After looking at your record, we now understand why." Etta reports that the radiologists "looked at my scar-covered carcass, now known as the freeway map with a new off-ramp," and decided that cobalt radiation would not be a useful approach. On the 7th she told Ingolf, "I have cancer and will always have it, but it is of the type that can be contained." He visited her every day until the 16th, when she returned home – "and always the question, 'how long??'"

Her reaction to Leukeran chemotherapy was good. She made repeated visits for blood tests to the office of Dr. David Rosenbaum. But Etta was very worried about the approaching sabbatical, the European cold, and the rigors of traveling with Ingolf. After talking her to the doctors on November 28 he reported, "E. is so happy with the results and the doctor's helpfulness, the big trip now seems within reach." "She is doing remarkably well," Dr. Feinberg reported to Fred Kahn on January 6, 1960 – my thirty-second birthday, "I cannot feel any abdominal masses. She feels well on an intensive chemotherapeutic regimen, and has no complaints other than hair loss."

As to the latter problem, so Etta informed us on January 24, "I had one of two choices: (1) Go to the conservationists and tell them they need no longer worry about the extermination of the American Bald Eagle, for

475

here I am. (2) Buy a wig...I got a beautiful white dynel stretch-wig which looks smashing...I am said to look younger in it, which doesn't hurt."

It seems mad that my parents were considering another European adventure under such circumstances but a Swiss doctor was found to continue Etta's treatment and preparations for the last sabbatical continued. Ironically, it was not Etta's health that dominated my parent's attention in the last weeks of their life in California, but Ingolf's, which suffered a serious decline that autumn as well.

Ingolf had suffered from gout in the hand in 1968 and in March, 1969, he sprained a knee. But the only illness requiring hospitalization was another neuroma in the foot, diagnosed in February, 1968, but not operated on until May. Well ahead of schedule he left the hospital after surgery, protesting, "I have to go to Ojai." On May 28 he went to have his stitches out. "Can you turn *off* the Muzak? he asked Dr. Portis' receptionist. "The Muzak cannot be turned off," she replied. "Then I'll wait in the hall." Which is just what this stubborn man on crutches did. Five days later he was tramping about Yosemite. "Very unorthodox treatment," his doctor concluded.

"Chest is not good," he had reported after several bronchial attacks in 1967 and 1968, "the devil *always* sitting in the tracheal tracts, and from time to time he acts." He suffered from severe tonsillitis quite a few times as well, and managed to return from Kauai with a bad chest infection, treated with antibiotics. On August 18, 1969 he reports terrible pains in the neck; by the 22nd he was experiencing dizziness, exhaustion and double vision and the traditional end of summer Sierra expedition was cancelled. On September 8 he was "dismissed" by his doctor but told that his problems would recur. Three days later an attack of asthma ensued and he spent a weekend in Tassajara with Bill Colvig and Lou Harrison, at the end of which he announced, "Can breathe again." Exhausted by two lengths of the U.S.C. pool on the 20th Ingolf mentions "emphysema" for the first time. Etta also wrote to us that Ingolf was suffering from this disease, but later tests lead to another diagnosis.

Asthma returned in early October. On the 19th Ingolf reported breathing so congested it seemed like not getting enough air through a straw tube. The problem was particularly acute when he tried to sleep. On the 21st he used an adrenalin injection. On November 7 Dr. Harris revealed a new complication – "a partially paralyzed diaphragm because of paralysis of one of the phrenic nerves." Ingolf learned of this dramatic deterioration in his physical condition on the same day that Etta spoke to him about always having cancer!

A series of doctors had a hand in testing Ingolf and suggesting remedies. Meanwhile the patient pushed himself through his usual round of exercises, hoping for signs of improvement, some of which he was certain he could feel. On the 28th of November he had to report, "My diaphragm is no good at all, getting worse, am terribly depressed." There was little progress in the neck disorder either. On December 15 Dr. Harris had to report that the paralysis was no better, that lung capacity was not improved and that Ingolf should probably not go above 6000 feet. "*Sometime*," Etta explained to us by post, "diaphragms can 'borrow' nerves from elsewhere and re-vitalize themselves in 6 months, but the doctors cannot guarantee it and don't know how to help the diaphragm to do this."

A pre-trip typhoid shot added to Ingolf's miseries on January 8. "Sleep with tedral every night, don't dare without it. What a wreck I feel like," he added on the 10th. A test on January 12 showed an improvement in lung capacity, though no improvement in the diaphragm itself. Bronchial spasms continued and some of the specialists appropriately questioned whether it was wise for Ingolf to undertake a trip to Europe at all. To shove this prospect from his mind Ingolf did twenty push-ups on January 22.

On January 25 the Dahls visited the Kellers for the last time. Ingolf left a strong box with my Uncle Morry, containing some important papers, including, as it turned out, a will. The next day he entered the hospital for a spinal tap. On the 28th he discharged himself, nonplussing the nurses, and drove himself home. Bent over from a sore back he made his goodbyes at the university on January 29. He wandered around dazed with painkillers for several days. He said farewell to Lawrence Morton on February 1. "Can hardly stand it any more," he wrote on the 2nd, "bottom of pain, weakness, depression, walk with last strength." Facing the prospect of a long flight and a longer drive at the European end of his journey, panic set in – "*What am I to do, to leave under such conditions?*" A last L.A. day was spent in pain so great that Ingolf could not stand upright. Etta too had been saying her goodbyes as departure day approached and many of her friends have told me that in her eyes the truth was made clear – you will not see me here again.

78. IN FRUTIGEN

Only Ingolf could have embarked on a year's sabbatical under the conditions that prevailed on February 4, 1970. He was undoubtedly too ill to travel, and his companion enjoyed only a precarious health. To save money he had booked two one-way tickets on a charter flight to Frankfurt – miles away from where he wanted to be. After leaving Cheremoya at 5:30 in the morning the Dahls were greeted by a series of delays that left them waiting at LAX for the entire day – though Etta did have time to witness the arrival of Spiro Agnew, come to bury some Congressman – "Turnabouts fair play," she suggested waspishly. Ingolf, bent over from his recent spinal tap, was in great pain. Their plane left at 6:15 that evening; after fourteen hours they landed in Germany, Ingolf having foolishly checked both tedral and atomizer in his suitcase. The night of the 5th was spent in Frankfurt's Hotel Adler but the next morning, feeling a little stronger, he sent his heavy suitcases on to Bern, put Etta on the same train, and headed for Paris alone. The two had arrived forty pounds overweight, having escaped extra charges due to the assistance of a porter who had taken pity on them. My stepfather had sent his skis on to Switzerland with another flight companion, U.S.C. musicologist Pierre Tagmann.

Ingolf arrived in Paris late in the afternoon of the 6th, complaining of a blistered bottom caused by the train's heating system. He took a room in the Hotel Lorraine and had a "totally lousy" ice-cold steak. The next morning he took the Metro to Issy, where he accepted delivery on the last 1969 Peugeot in stock, a dark green sedan. "The young mechanic who explained the car to me and saw the ecstatic gleam in my eye," Ingolf reported to Lawrence Morton, "said, '*Every* new car is beautiful.'" Poor Ingolf spent the next hour searching for a toilet, got misdirected by a policeman, and finally found a paperless café w.c.

That afternoon he began driving. He reached Troyes and slept for fourteen hours, rising to do his gymnastic exercises in the hotel room. The main road to Switzerland was "unspeakable," he snarled, "one thinks one is in Mexico." Bad weather spoiled the views – "all the 'history' weighing on these hills is not visible." As he drove, the idea of working on a piano concerto consisting of many short movements came to him. He stopped to relieve his bladder on a side road. "You write modern music? Like Honegger?" the border guard asked. "Back in Switzerland," the composer wrote, "But too tired and sick to feel the impact as so many times before." He spent the night in a Basle hotel and at noon on the 9th he arrived at the suburban home, near Bern, of his landlords for the year, Drs Hans and Hanni Stoller.

Etta had been here for some time, "systematically spoiled" by these kind and hospitable people, who now served lunch to Ingolf while Etta examined the new car. She liked the exterior but not the "bolster lumps" as she called the headrests (which she was too short to need anyway) or the upholstery color, "a cross between ochre clay and either kiddy or chicken shit." After a nap Ingolf and Etta followed their hosts on an hour's drive south into the Bernese Oberland and on to the village of Frutigen, their last home.

They occupied an entire floor of an eleven-room house which the Stollers had once used as both home and office for their general practice. Both of the doctors now specialized in anesthesiology at the Bern hospital and used the Frutigen residence only on holidays and at weekends. Pierre Tagmann, who was also on leave this term, had been instrumental in introducing the Dahls to surely the most pleasant and roomiest of their many overseas environments. The fact that their landlords were medical specialists must also have been comforting for my parents. On February 13 Etta made her first visit to Dr. Kurt Brunner, who would be responsible for continuing her chemotherapy at the Zieglerspital in Bern. The night before this first appointment the Dahls had heard Yehudi Menuhin, after all these years, in a performance of the Elgar *Violin Concerto*.

Etta found a well-equipped kitchen and a living room larger than the one at Cheremoya. A piano waited in Ingolf's studio. "The house turns out to be perfect," he enthused, "roomy, light, warm, all the conveniences, not too expensive, well situated, we are so lucky, this is the best yet."

Like Schruns, Frutigen combined the rustic and the modern. Perched on a steep hillside and surrounded by towering, tempting peaks, the village was also full of shops and restaurants. "I market nearly every day and wear my nylon tights under my slacks, plus socks, then boots," Etta reported to

Lillian, "The distances between shops are small and just about the time when the toes and thumbs start to make slightly painful objections, you pop into another shop and are saved, or there looms our 11-room 'cottage.'" The latter even had a garage for the new car; two blocks away was the railway line to Bern. Behind the house a stream, the Leimbach, was held in icy suspension between banks of concrete.

Relations between Ingolf and Etta followed their well-established course of attraction and retreat. "Etta is so very warm and outgoing and kind and nice all the time," Ingolf reported on February 25 – "it is very lovely." He "spoiled" her by keeping her in fresh flowers and he was obviously engaged in nostalgic contemplation of the strange set of circumstances that had brought Etta into his life. On April 27, driving alone to Zurich, he took a detour to Bremgarten and spent a long time looking at the unchanged Hotel Adler, where they had first shared a bed so many years before.

But when he was not acknowledging his debt to her, he was expressing his resentment, his feeling of being "reined in, pulled back, watched over, inhibited." On March 2, when her patience over his inevitable composing traumas was wearing thin, he entered a long diatribe:

> The continuous tension...Her automatic pushing-away reaction, no matter what is said and done. Always fighting, always rejecting – god how hard it is to live with that and never be able to unbutton, relax, be unguarded, undammed up. And even the words about my work are now being received with shrugged-shoulder silence ("why don't you give it up?"). This must steal me, still more, as it often has – ...."

Either Etta got blamed for indifference to his work or, when he tried to escape it with some outdoor endeavor, she was there to earn his resentment by reminding him that he had work to do, or that such exercise was contrary to the doctor's orders.

Etta had brought some of her literary projects with her but she spent hours writing letters. A long series went to her sister, full of pedantic instructions on European travel (which the Kellers were about to undertake and "half-witticisms," i.e., "Make yourself (copy out of book) the basic floor plan of a cathedral, never mind the variations. Don't be stupid like your sister who still doesn't know an apse from and apse-hole." A good deal of time was spent in wrestling with her wig – "No matter how I do my own hair," she complained on February 22, "there are spaces between me and the wig. Ingolf pats me on the head and says, 'Hollow, hollow, hollow.' And I say, 'You've always suspected, now you know.'" By March 14 she had filled the gap with a pair of white lacy stretch socks. Her health remained stable, in spite of a cold and a brief period of pain in May. Her doctors continued to experiment with the Leukeran dosage, monitoring its effect every few weeks in Bern. But the dominant factor in this last sabbatical was not her health, but that of her unhappy husband.

"The ambience could not be better," Ingolf wrote on February 12, "looking out of window in front of desk, a grey snowy mountain landscape with lovely open fields above – all so totally unreachable." In his deplorable state of health almost everything he had looked forward to in this alpine milieu was in some way spoiled.

His little daybooks, which had become ever more crammed as the years advanced, proved too small to encompass the full range of medical details which he wished to record – symptoms, dosages, the time of the latest attack or the elusive moment of imagined relief – and he maintained such medical addenda on separate sheets throughout the Frutigen stay. There is an abundance of disheartening information in this chronicle of desperation.

Almost immediately he began to complain of sleeplessness – "it was a bad night," he noted on February 10, "awake for hours, then took librium and benedryl and had to sleep it off." "Drunk with sleep," he spent the next day in "utter exhaustion." "Breathing is very difficult," he added in the afternoon, "couldn't do a *thing* now on skis...totally depressed and tired." "Depression is complete," he continued on the 12th, "the conditions are all perfect and (why??) I am in the lowest physical state. I cannot breathe, even level walking bad." On the 14th Hans Stoller concluded a *kaffeklatsch* by examining Ingolf with a stethoscope while the composer sat at his desk. An x-ray was ordered and Ingolf's landlord himself accompanied his tenant to the hospital.

On the 17th Ingolf journeyed to Bern for his initial visit with Dr. Rolf Hoigné. Suffering from a runny nose he stopped first for a meal in the Bahnhof buffet – "good fish lunch. Sit at window – outside the snow is falling heavily. The civilization of this restaurant – no muzak, very good food, very pleasantly served." Optimism presided over his meeting with Dr. Hoigné. "He thinks I am healthy except for diaphragm," Ingolf reported, but it has to be added that Ingolf's version of these medical visits and the advice given him by his physicians can not be wholly trusted, nor can we have confidence in his own prediction of a quick recovery ("chest is *better*!!" he wrote the next day). When I arrived in Switzerland a few months later, to put this optimism in perspective, I was told that at least one of the local doctors had said, following an initial examination, "I would not be surprised if this man dropped dead one day."

As Ingolf had failed, on many occasions, to understand the depths of his wife's despair, so Etta was now inclined to discount the intensity of the agony suffered by her husband. "Ingolf is rather demoralized," she wrote to Lillian on February 20:

> Partly I sympathize with him, partly I see the bad results of his early "upbringing," where non-think and physiological pleasures (non-sensual) were greatly encouraged. Here he is at a time of life when he should be in top creative form, or at last eager for at least some kind of life of the mind, and, although he does some reading, he mostly pouts because he can't fly around on skis. I hope he isn't going to become a bitter old man, but this is a possibility we may have to face.

Tests taken in connection with his first Bern medical visit were discussed on February 23. There is definite asthma, Ingolf noted, and the diaphragm is working at only 1/4 of its capacity. Thereafter Bern became a frequently visited site. On the 20th the Dahls had joined Pierre Tagmann for an evening of cabaret; on the 25th they returned for a concert by Ingolf's Zurich piano teacher, Walter Frey: "Etta helps me to take the adult attitude and not go back stage." A huge portion of vermicelli was followed by a near collapse on the homeward bound train – "the chest is awful. Another nadir."

On February 26 Ingolf felt well enough, or desperate enough, to attempt a day of skiing – "I'm functioning again, albeit reduced." The Stollers also took him skiing on March 1, a successful outing that left him "very tired and short-breathed." Ingolf rented an inhalation machine which ran on electricity and required the patient to add two chemicals. At the end of a day in Bern on March 4 he suffered asthma so bad that he could barely talk: "Take 5:21 train home. *Rush* to inhalation." His dependency on this machine increased thereafter, but on March 5 he was back on skis again. "Breath, in spite of Tedral, a problem again," he reported after this excursion. It was thus always a race to see which would wake him up more rapidly, his asthma or the medicine he took to fend it off.

"The nights are terrible," he wrote on March 6, "never sleep more than 4-5 hours." On March 8 Ingolf offered a summary of his position:

> What a ghastly, ghastly health mess I'm in – and no way out in sight. It is as if since last fall an axe has fallen. Now looking out of window at snow falling and thoughts of MacDowell, 3 years ago. Then I was able to do a run every morning, to swim, to have a hike up Monadnock – and now I cannot even move inside the house –. What causes it, what can be done, am I going to be a cripple from now on? Yet I cannot give up hope that somehow, as always before in my life, the asthma will clear up and I'll be strong again.

Etta drew his attention to a new moon as they stood in the parking lot of an Interlaken restaurant the next day. Ingolf bowed three times and wished for "health, health, health."

Skiing on March 10 was accomplished without asthma. "Is today a turning point?" he wondered. The next day Dr. Hoigné disabused him of this hope. A skiing trip to Verbier with the Schaars would have to be cancelled. Distressed that the asthma was no better, Ingolf's doctor ordered his patient indoors and proposed putting him in hospital but Hoigné did change his mind – no doubt Ingolf protested loudly at the prospect of confinement – and the patient returned to Frutigen with a new array of prescriptions, including a suppository for asthma. Ingolf was taking cortisone and Alupent and who knows what else, for in the middle of the night, when the attack was bad, he tried a little bit of everything. Each sign of improvement proved illusory, at best the result of enforced quietude, progress that was soon lost when he attempted any prolonged physical movement.

On the 22nd of March Ingolf discovered a new problem, a sore spot in the lower throat that haunted him with memories of Pappi's fatal illness. The esophagus was x-rayed a few days later – "they find nothing in throat (so it isn't Pappi's disease) but pain persists." The diaphragm seemed to move a little better on March 23 and no spray was needed for asthma that day. On the 25th Dr. Hoigné found only a little improvement in breathing capacity and some evidence of a bronchial infection. Again there was a warning against physical exertion – "If I had followed *that* advice all my life..." Ingolf grumbled, "why all of a sudden is my whole physical existence cut off with a knife, changed so totally?" "Am terribly depressed, despondent, what am I to do?...if I have to go to hospital, when will I be out in nature again, or on skis?"

On the 29th there was another false dawn – "*is this the turning point?*" The asthma seems so much better." To convince himself of this possibility he did fifteen pushups, with no immediate ill effect – and the next day he went skiing again, waiting in a long line amid "pushing, shoving, chiseling ruffians" and struggling with breathing spasms. These became so bad in the Bern train on April 2 that Ingolf reported himself "ready to give up." Nevertheless he finished four lengths at a sauna swimming pool that afternoon – "which *absolutely* knocks the stuffing out of me." He had difficulty making his way up the stairs at home – "it seems that Dr. H and I are just kidding ourselves about the effect of all these medicines." "I am not really living," he complained the next day. On April 6 he reached the sensible conclusion that by forcing himself up the ski slopes he was perhaps putting too great a strain on the heart, but he lacked the will to be a proper invalid, a "dead shell." On April 10 he went to see his doctor again. Patience was advised, but Ingolf was not patient by nature.

On April 22 he went to Bern to have most of his prescriptions renewed. The next day Etta reported to me that Ingolf "is sort of 'coming apart at the seams' and requires an enormous amount of rest...I think he had been over-extending himself, mostly his nerves, for many years and that he is now suffering the results."

Ingolf's impatience with the slow progress of his recovery impelled him to seek the advice of another physician, Dr. Albert Wernli-Haessig. Three days were spent in Zurich in consultation and tests, beginning April 28. "He thinks," Ingolf reported on April 29, "'contrary' motion of diaphragm is irritating the asthma." Supporting Etta's thesis that Ingolf's condition was related to nervous strain, the new doctor told his patient, "No conducting, no working for a deadline," and this put an end to plans that Ingolf had made to conduct a concert of American music on the Bern radio. He was nevertheless encouraged by his visit and tried to convince himself that the ban on physical activity would soon be lifted. The patient came for an additional interview on the 30th. He brought with him a long list of questions to put to the doctor, wrote the answers down on a shopping list, and then lost the list. Dr. Wernli gave Ingolf a new set of prescriptions and recommended a specialist in breathing exercises in Bern. Etta reports his protest at this point – "But I'm not the Yoga type!" "Well, he may have to become it," she added on May 3, "He hasn't gone yet, so we shall see."

On May 5 Ingolf convinced himself that "it does seem that now a new dawn is near, thanks to Wernli!!!!" In Bern the next day for x-rays, he offered a truer picture – "I *can't*, can't, can't any more – can't face more hospital, more weakness, more debility." Embarrassed that he had taken on a second doctor he went to Dr. Hoigné's office to "disengage" by reporting he felt "so much better." The next day a level walk proved so difficult that he returned home, counting the seconds that separated him from his spray. "It's really been downhill all the way," he admitted on the 8th, "in Troyes I could still do my exercises, now I can't."

On May 11 Ingolf reported for his first gymnastic breathing session – "does me a world of good," he declared. How rare it is to encounter a positive assertion in the tortured journals of this year. It would be far more accurate to accept Etta's verdict that – in despair over his physical well-being – Ingolf was becoming a bitter old man. The sense of persecution crackles beneath the surface of many of his reflections on life in these months of trial. On April 10 there had been a minor road scrape – "on freeway a crazy idiot wants to pass while I'm doing 80 – don't see him because I'm passing cars myself – what a fool!" In the evening he calmed down at an exhibition of work by Paul Klee, whose son he recognized in the audience at a concert a few nights later.

Ingolf was also perturbed because the trunk he had dispatched on January 6 did not arrive until April 27. He sulked because permission to stay in Switzerland for the year was not granted by the proper bureaucracy until March 23. Embittered by such frustrations and slowed by their many health problems Ingolf and Etta looked to escape the hellish situation that was life in Frutigen on a number of occasions that spring; at least four times they ventured forth on overnight expeditions.

79. FINAL JOURNEYS

On March 20 Ingolf and Etta travelled by train on a thirtieth wedding anniversary expedition to Zurich. They had a "grand time," Ingolf reported to Lawrence Morton, "even though I felt lousy." Etta went shopping for plastic rain boots with zippers, the two dined on oysters and attended a Stravinsky ballet evening ("the poor composer!"). At the Kronenhalle restaurant ("and still the same waitress, unchanged!!") Ingolf ordered a bottle of Veuve Cliquot as the clock advanced to March 21 itself. The next day he gave Etta a scrabble game ("which she almost bought for me") and the two snuggled together on their way to a surprise lunch which Ingolf had arranged at their old haunt of 1936, the Veltliner restaurant. "I nearly fell over," Etta reported, "we had a gorgeous meal finishing with cherries jubilee." They visited the Wesendonck villa, the art museum, and walked along the lakefront. In the afternoon the nostalgia tour ended with a visit to the Cafe Odeon. Where Klemperer and Stefan Zweig had once sat in marble grandeur, hippies now lounged beneath the crystal chandeliers. In the evening the Dahls attended a performance of Krenek's 1938 opera *Charles V*, a work so crammed with historical detail that Ingolf proposed giving members of the audience an exam as they left their seats.

On April 16 Ingolf and Etta put the Peugeot on a flat car at Kandersteg and had themselves pulled through two tunnels into Italy. The occasion was a performance of the *Music For Brass Instruments* by the American Brass Quintet in Como. Ingolf had accepted an invitation from Arnold Fromme and had decided to add several more days to a brief Italian tour. The first night was spent in Pallanza on Lake Maggiore, one of those sites that Professor Herkenrath had taken the ten-year old asthma suffering Ingolf to almost half a century earlier. The next day the Dahls moved on to Como itself, Ingolf complaining of the "horror of all the Lombardy smog drifting up into the lake country – can't see other side of lakes, no point to go to islands, even, no views, no snow mountains." Before the concert Ingolf and Etta stood in front of a TV store and watched anxiously as astronauts made a splashdown.

Ingolf felt that his presence made the performers nervous – "the audience seems bewildered." Performers, wives, and the Dahls had a post-concert restaurant party – which Etta pronounced "a grand, zany time."

On the 18th my parents drove to Milan and saw a performance of *A Midsummer Night's Dream* in Rumanian! Then they returned here on the 19th, bought tickets from a scalper and saw a performance of *Don Carlo* at La Scala. To their surprise this production featured a former Young Musicians Foundation scholarship winner, Shirley Verrett. "She brought the house down," Etta reported, "They scream Verr-ett! Verr-ett! Verr-ett! til we thought the elegant chandeliers would fall." The night of the 20th was spent in Cremona, but Ingolf reported breathing difficulties again – "asthma comes up each time I fall asleep – tension – I'm a wreck." They had taken the inhalation machine along, but the current was too weak to run it. "Getting up from the car can *hardly* manage the steps in the house," Ingolf wrote on their return, April 21.

On May 14 the Dahls left Frutigen for a brief northern tour. First stop was Freiburg, where two former U.S.C. students were singing in a production of Strauss' *Ariadne*. Ingolf was unnerved by mountain views – "It is just too agonizing to see it, to be in it, to be shut out of heaven, it just takes too much to fight that depression all the time." A journey through the Black Forest and Winterthur brought them back through Zurich on the 15th. Happy visits with cousins followed and both Ingolf and Etta reported delight at a cabaret evening that night and at a circus on the 16th. Gret Mann dined with them at the Kronenhalle and accompanied them to the cabaret and she later recalled how much my parents enjoyed themselves: "They laughed incessantly and talked a great deal. I kept wondering at their indefatigable vitality. It must have been one of their last good outings."

On May 17 Michael Tilson Thomas arrived in Frutigen for an extended visit. Ingolf was happily enjoying a few days of good health – "In morning," he reported on the 18th, "hike up the mountain with MTT – everything goes so easy, I can walk uphill without trouble, the difference is extraordinary, almost as it used to be." After breakfast that day the three began to discuss vacation plans. "Let's go to Greece," Etta chirped, not forgetting to add to Ingolf, "provided your doctor says you may go." For the next few days the trio consulted their travel books. Ingolf received permission to take the trip on the 21st, but while he was in Zurich he took a walk to the Witikon church. This had been one of the sites he had first visited after recovering from illness in 1932. Now he was too thinly dressed

487

for the weather and caught a cold. MTT, who later provided me with a great deal of information about this period, reported that several days were spent sightseeing in Switzerland and in trip preparation. Ingolf gathered daisies on a walk and gave them not to Etta but to some cows, whom he addressed as "Girls." Etta picked out her own trout in a restaurant fish tank with a small speech, "Aren't we nice and fat and full of life. But we can't live forever and I'm going to eat you." At the apothecary the Dahls ordered anti-diarrhea and anti-constipation medicine, only to be stopped at they left the store by a distraught druggist who had remembered at the last moment that he had reversed the labels. At noon on the 23rd the three flew from Zurich to "the shores of Hellas."

In Athens they checked into the Galaxy Hotel and walked up the Acropolis. Again Ingolf failed to bring a sweater and his cold got worse in the cool breeze. "After dinner," he reported, "I feel like a total wreck, all around. Asthma, dizzyness, weakness, headache, stopped up and painful left ear." The next day the three spent four hours at the National Museum – "the thunderbolt," Ingolf observed, "the greatest art there is. Walk on clouds." On the 24th they went to the Plaka, where a "grooving" Etta wanted to dance to the bazouki music. Ingolf had trouble with the Greek music because, MTT remembers, "he hated the augmented second." Etta went out alone the next day, entered a record store, and sang a tune which Michael had liked as a way of demonstrating to the proprietor what she wanted to purchase. More walking on clouds at the Acropolis followed. All of them cried in front of favorite statues.

On the 26th they rented a car, Ingolf's cold settling in as bronchitis, and drove to Eleusis, Daphni, and Thebes. Ingolf wrote some music on a piece of paper, his mountain top habit, and pressed it into a wall near the temple of Apollo at Delphi. Fearing pneumonia, his chest like sandpaper and "depressed beyond words," he had to spend an entire day in his bed at the Hotel Vouzos – "Take *all* medicines within reach." Michael attempted to climb Parnassus but his progress was halted by an outburst of rain. Ingolf told him he had to make an offering to the gods and the next day, before the precinct was open to the public, Michael climbed over a fence and poured out a bottle of wine half way between the temple of Apollo and the theater of Dionysus. "Leave it to Ingolf to get sick," Etta had joked, but on the 28th, feeling himself to be a terrible burden to the others,

Ingolf arose to a "California spring day," still suffering from chest pains, terrible phlegm, weakness and dizziness, and discovered that Etta was ill. A sacroiliac complaint, first manifested in 1968, had recurred. This is just an episode, she told the others on the 29th; it will pass and you must press on. She took medication for the pain, got in the back of the car, and passed out. Michael drove his invalids to the ferry at Itea and they set sail for Aeghion. "I am so far off," Ingolf noted. That night he collapsed in fever at the Hotel Xenia in Olympia.

"The nadir," Ingolf reported on the 30th, "never felt worse." The day was spent in bed again. A doctor came and prescribed two medicines. "In p.m. get a crying jag," Ingolf wrote, "my nerves are shot and help seems *so* far away, and the future *so* uncertain." On the afternoon of the 31st he was able to crawl to the Museum – "How perfect," he pronounced it. Etta had recovered – as she had predicted. She and Michael visited the same restaurant so many times that the proprietors took him for a gigolo, a conception so amusing that he and Etta played the game to the hilt.

An asthma attack was overdosed with Alupent when Ingolf feared he would choke in the early hours of June 1. That day the party returned to Athens and checked into the Grande Bretagne. Ingolf could not lie down without a "racking, painful, chest-destroying cough." On the morning of the 2nd a long distance phone call was made to Dr. Wernli in Zurich. An appointment was made for the following day and the Dahls booked a return flight. "Breakfast with MTT," Ingolf reported, "(I feel so goddamned *guilty* about the whole debacle and the burden on him) and *so* terribly *insufficient* because my conversation is dull and listless and unmusical and uninspired." Michael remained in Athens and that afternoon the Dahls arrived in Zurich and checked into a hotel – "feel lousiest, just have no *air* to breathe, can hardly talk." "E. is an angel," he added, "does everything... she is so gentle and loving in direct proportion to my helplessness, sickness, feeling old and slow."

After an awful night, Ingolf, accompanied by Etta, arrived at Dr. Wernli's office at 8:30 in the morning on June 3 – "the goal since last Saturday...Like the grail to the crusaders is this waiting room." After the administration of medicines Ingolf returned to his hotel room for another bad night. The smokers in the dining room increased his difficulties. He visited Dr. Wernli again on the 4th: "At lunch time bringing up mucus is such effort. I almost lose all the breath I have, exhausted...On the afternoon an attack of despondency and just want to cry and cry, but pull myself together. And E., Penelope, sitting all the time in her bed reading mystery story." After a third doctor's visit on the morning of the 5th Ingolf and Etta returned to Frutigen, "at station awful attack, can hardly get air after coughing...and now if I could be alone with piano and with my tears –." A day of recovery followed on the 6th but the next afternoon a new crisis intervened.

On June 7 Etta went to lie down after lunch, not feeling well. Ingolf went alone to see the Jodlerfest parade – "tears come so easily now (my nerves) – this tradition, security, ties, rationality, individuality in our ocean of a modern age." Etta vomited when he returned to the house. No medicine eased her abdominal pain and at 10:00 Ingolf decided to drive her to the Zieglerspital in Bern, where Dr. Stoller had arranged for her to be admitted. The drive was hell. Etta cried out in agony and throughout the hour it took to reach the hospital cloudbursts and thunderstorms lashed the highway. With Hans Stoller himself serving as anesthetist, a surgery was performed immediately. This lasted from 1:00 to 4:30 in the morning. A new carcinoma of the colon was uncovered, though the doctors were not certain if this had, indeed, been the source of the acute pain. Ingolf returned to Frutigen for a few hours and wrote special delivery letters describing the incident to Lillian and to me.

Back at the hospital he could report, "E.'s recovery is astonishing...she can even joke with the Stollers. Sitting there for 2 hours as the golden sun sinks behind the green gardens, the birds signing." "Poor Etta," he wrote on June 9, "one would not think that her frail body, so maltreated, could stand another such ordeal, but her spirit is such that it rises above everything." It was his fifty-eighth birthday. At the hospital Etta gave him a letter clip souvenir she had purchased in Athens. When he left she smiled a sweet wan "toodleoo." In Frutigen a pile of letters had to be opened; a portion of the house at Cheremoya was slipping down the hillside.

At about noon on June 10 the abdominal pain returned and Etta was placed under heavy sedation. Ingolf was summoned to the hospital. At her bedside he witnessed "that will, vitality, power, struggling to come through once more – the sudden wide-open blue eyes, trying to tell me something. The end." Etta died at 9:30 that evening. "The clock ran out,"

Ingolf wrote in his journal. To her many friends he addressed a handwritten mimeographed letter the next day, "Up to the last Etta was her strong, courageous spirited self."

That night Ingolf called me in East Lansing. We had just received the optimistic letter he had written after the surgery and the news was numbing, though not unexpected. He could now hardly talk. I offered to fly to him in Switzerland, but he declined. We called the Kellers. Using the addresses which Etta had carefully copied out of the family address book at home, Ingolf sent off a large number of death announcements in the next few days. He was assisted in this task by Pierre Tagmann, and his gratitude to Pierre, the Stollers, and the hospital staff was great. Later he wrote to Dr. Hoigné, contrasting the quietness and peace of the Zieglerspital with the factory bustle and incessant TV of the large California hospitals that he and Etta had been so familiar with.

Five days passed before the cremation ceremony, which Etta had requested. On the 11th he went to the hospital to fill out some forms. When he was asked "Date of marriage?" he began to cry. A walk along the river later that afternoon also brought on the tears – "The red sun sinking, how she would have – ." On the 12th he stepped inside the house in Frutigen for the first time since the tragedy, then returned to the Stollers home in Kirchlindach. He again tried to be in his own house on the 14th – "Now comes the hardest. Kiss Etta's turquoise little slippers, which I put last on her feet when I washed them a week ago, a world ago...If only my health were better so I could stand *up* to it all. In afternoon, E's grey nice winter coat, holding it to my heart, in front of bedroom mirror."

At his own request, Ingolf was the sole mourner at the Bern Crematorium on June 15. Etta's coffin was covered in flowers sent by well-wishers and Ingolf received permission to play the simple country organ in works by Mozart and Telemann that he and Etta had played together many times. He repeated the Telemann three times. He lifted a corner of the coffin. Then he sat on a chair in the cemetery, surrounded by birds, while the white puff of smoke rose from the chimney. "And at the end," he added, "just before leaving, a bird flies directly before my feet, rust brown and grey, and stays and looks and then flies off."

Ingolf was besieged by invitations to visit friends and relatives. To me he wrote, "For a while, at least, I'll stay here, where I can still feel

Etta's presence and besides I must be true to the two obligations I have toward Etta: to care for my health (which is bad again) and to work on my compositions." He sent me a rose from one of the funeral bouquets – "Your mother, dear Anthony, and my wife – the circle is closed: in Switzerland I first met her, and in Switzerland she was to end her days."

80. UNREELING THE FILAMENTS

"A cloudless beautiful morning," Ingolf observed on June 16, the day after the ceremony at the Bern Crematorium, "warm, lovely beyond words. A lilac twig, dark violet – how different its meaning today." Later that afternoon he mailed a laurel leaf, which he had plucked at the cemetery, to MTT, whose letter of condolence was full of the fondest memories of his departed other parent, "the carriage of the head, the tone of the voice – 'you've got to get on the ball and do it, man.'" On each day Ingolf discovered another reminder of his loss. On June 25 Etta returned in an afternoon dream – "She sits next to me, so very close and warm." On the 29th he sat at her desk and examined the pile of incomplete literary materials she had left behind – "a wave of emotion – the creativity of hers, the plans for stories, notes for own work, the unfinishedness..." There was time to emend one last shopping list: "Mon. cereal, salami, apple juice, radishes, etc." with a melancholy comment – "There was to be no Monday." On June 30 Ingolf went to the jewelers in Zurich and had her wedding ring enlarged so that he could wear it next to his own. More letters of condolence came pouring through the mail slot. "Dear friends," Ingolf wrote in a mimeographed letter of thanks, dated June 28, "the many messages of sympathy and compassion that reached me reflect in a hundred facets the light that shone out of Etta, a light that will continue to live in our memories." On July 10 he picked up some copies of a photograph of his dead wife and cried as he taped one of them into the back of his journal. "Can't do a thing," he wrote on July 16, "the loss of both 'anchor' and 'chain' is beginning to really hit me." Loneliness overwhelmed him in that big house in Frutigen. "I understand E.'s occasional outbursts of communication-urge about herself, her illness, her feelings," he wrote on July 30, "(how little of that we provided for each other)."

In his letter of thanks to those who had offered their sympathy, Ingolf had added a brief paragraph – "I must now spend the limited time that is available to me to do what Etta most wanted me to do: work on my music." This statement, with its convenient camouflage of all those moments when Etta had said just the opposite, was written on June 28, the day that he completed a composition dedicated to his wife, *A Noiseless Patient Spider*.

It came as some surprise to me that, given its trials and tragedies, Ingolf was able to complete *any* creative work on this sabbatical. Health was the omnipresent deterrent – "can't rise above the debilities," he had written on March 8, "to do big work." "A lost, lost, lost despondent day," he had added on March 31, "nothing is right, no ideas, no will, no drive, no appetites, no strength."

Creative work also had to be completed against the background of despair that marked his relations with music publishers. "No mail from any of the publishers," he had complained on March 22. A fuller list of grievances on the latter subject appeared some time later under the heading, "The things that are *not*.":

> (a) I finish the commissioned work for SAI, send it off, send two letters – it is one of my best pieces, certainly the most substantial of all the SAI series – not a word of acknowledgement – nothing. (b) the Sax. Conc. supposed to be in print long ago, nothing – not even an answer to my letter of inquiry. (c) Sonata Pastorale has been completely proofread *long* ago – where is the publication? (d) the Trio string parts are supposed to be autographed – no answer to my letter if they ever *found* the parts! (e) Boosey and my Reicha arrangement. (f) shouldn't CPEB Var. be here by now?

Given the limited energies granted to him in these months and the very few hours of the working day available for composition, it must be agreed that the time needed to engage publishers in fruitless correspondence might have been better spent.

To be fair, I can imagine composers with whom it would have been easier to work. Ingolf balked at supplying publishers with clean copies of his own music – especially large works where copying costs were prohibitive. "I cannot afford to compose anything I cannot copy myself," he had announced in 1948, but of course he had to retract this threat many times. His record of returning proofs on time was also rather blemished.

Dealing with an absent-minded grouchy and procrastinating composer may have been a burden assumed by publishers when they signed him on, but one needn't ignore the needless problems many of them inflicted on him in return. In 1966 Josef Marx had reminded Ingolf, no doubt correctly, that, "Publisher-composer relations are always beset with embarrassment: the composer attaches to his music a large slice of certainly necessary ego and the publisher has commerce in mind and nought else." No doubt Marx did not mean to excuse, however, the suffering that Ingolf endured at the hands of other publishers. Long and unexplained delays occurred in bringing works to print. Compositions suddenly went out of print. Publishers carelessly omitted Dahl titles from their own publicity catalogues. They lost contracts, failed to return signed copies of same, misplaced manuscripts, ignored the terms of agreements and delayed royalty payments shamelessly. Letters went unanswered. The staff changed so rapidly at many of these firms that the composer often knew more about the progress of a work though the publication process than the publishers themselves.

It was always Ingolf's hope that many of these problems could be overcome if *one* substantial firm would agree to publish *all* of his works, past and future, and great was his envy of composers who had such agreements with some of the better publishing houses. There was a time when he hoped that Alexander Broude might fill this role for him, but even before his death this hope seems to have evaporated. Ingolf's exasperation was especially evident when compositions were performed over and over again by outstanding soloists (as in the case of the *Cello Duo*) and yet failed to find any publisher: "It's been like this all my life – nobody wants to take just one piece, the big ones take lousy composers...and yet I am played. This is a hellish situation."

Style questions still provided major difficulties – to the end. "How to be 'relevant,' 'personal,' and 'important'?" he added on May 5. This problem was confounded by the musical offerings presented by Swiss Radio – "There are practically no sounds left that really attract me, excite me, with which I can identify," he wrote on March 3. "*Why* this foolish championing of new music?" he asked on March 19, after listening to an avant-garde concert, "When it isn't really worth anything?" "Very impressive," he described Ligeti's *Requiem* on March 27, "but what a world to live in, totally without melodic content – without line, that is, without song." How ironic, though hardly unique in the history of art, to observe this once fierce champion of new music issuing a final appeal to Lawrence Morton, in a letter of July 20:

> To be frank: the one thing for which I am starved more than anything else (next to normal breathing, that is) is a good piece of new music! Maybe they've always been as scarce, although I doubt it, and it's just that we are older, more blasé and harder to satisfy, but I've heard quite a few new things on the radio...and I tell you I'm just starved for something good, or interesting, or both.

In the meantime Ingolf never recovered from the bitterness he felt at losing what he believed to be his own just position in the musical world. On May 8 he expressed this baldly – "I'm out, out, out – so outside, and don't have the energy to fight for anything, make any moves."

The limited time he had for composing was often drained away in correspondence and editorial tasks. "All day on the Dutton Dictionary Bio & Article," he wrote on April 25, "I *hate* it, it is just like pulling teeth." The next day he continued work on a contribution to the *College Music Symposium's* feature on "The Composer in Academia." Responding to a Stravinsky statement that had warned composers against a life in the university, Ingolf courageously rejected the father figure (whose own ill health was a constant preoccupation) in his retort. "Economic facts are inescapable," Ingolf wrote, "and the Craft-Stravinsky quote, with its polemic overtones, is about equally far removed from the realities of a young American composer's circumstances as many of the young composers are themselves now removed from the realities of music making."

Indeed, Ingolf could not resist taking a swipe at the well-endowed trendy avant-gardists whose academic postings spared them the necessity of observing musical realities and encouraged "cloistered isolation; separation from music as activity; doctrinairism; abstract analysis – and eye-motivated note spinning; underdevelopment or deterioration of the mind-ear balance; growing disdain for the listener; over-involvement with the minutiae of craft..." "Who among the contributors to this issue," he asked, "would not prefer to have been invited to compose a piece of music instead of composing paragraphs of words?" So, inevitably, Ingolf's chief creative efforts *did* go into his own music to the very last, and the accomplishments of his last months are surprisingly varied and complete, even though he never succeeded in writing that piano concerto of many short movements he had first conceived while driving by Chaumont on his way to Basle on February 8.

There were two pre-publication proofreading chores and two revisions to complete. He worked on the proofs for the *Trio* in February and March – "dammit, it *is* such a good piece, every note 'right.'" Proofreading of the *Intervals* on June 24 ("working with music, hallelujah") was the first musical activity he turned to after Etta's death. In March he had also at last made a clean copy of the revised *Sonata da Camera*, inevitably making improvements as he worked. The project was completed on March 14, just as, to the composer's surprise, his own Brass Piece was announced on the local radio – "Quite shattering – and that lovely music." In mid-March he also resumed work on the flute and alto flute version of the *Variations on a Swedish Folktune*, completing this on May 2. More importantly, Ingolf also finished four new compositions while in Frutigen and made progress on a fifth.

The *Little Canonic Suite* for violin and viola had its origins in a brief canon which Ingolf had written in November, 1969, for one of his students, the violist Paul Polivnick, on the occasion of the latter's engagement to the violinist Kathy Lenski. On February 21 Ingolf expressed the belief that this work might be made part of a four movement canonic suite, and this he set out to realize in the next few days. "Rather nice," he wrote of the third canon on February 22, "but not formally balanced." The composition was completed in early March and copying concluded March 15. Because the canons were written in retrograde inversion, Ingolf hoped to provide a bit of fun at performance time by having the score placed on a flat surface so that the players, facing one another, could play from either end simultaneously. For practical reasons this method was not adopted in the published edition of this four-minute work when it was issued by Joseph Boonin in 1975.

The *Fanfare on A and C* was Ingolf's contribution to a volume of letters and tributes which Clare Reis put together for Aaron Copland's 70th birthday, November 14, 1970. Work was started here in March also, but the piece was not completed until the summer. On the 13th of July Ingolf summarized his activity for Lawrence, "finished a fanfare for 6 brasses for Aaron's 70th birthday album. It consists entirely of the notes A and C, but because of the different tunings of the 6 brasses I have broader pitch variety and I think it makes a *nice sound!* (Even got a little quote from 'Dance Panels' into a middle voice.)" *Fanfare on A and C* was published by Joseph Boonin in 1973.

A Noiseless Patient Spider is a work for women's chorus and piano obbligato, commission by Sigma Alpha Iota for its Modern Music Series. Etta had discovered the text in an illustrated Swiss magazine, a Walt Whitman poem taken from the collection entitled *Whispers of Heavenly Death*.

> A noiseless patient spider,
> I mark'd where on a little promontory it stood isolated,
> Mark'd how to explore the vacant vast surrounding,
> It launch'd forth filament, filament, filament, out of itself,
> Ever unreeling them, ever tirelessly speeding them.
>
> And you O my soul where you stand,
> Surrounded, detached, in measureless oceans of space,
> Ceaselessly musing, venturing, throwing, seeking the spheres to
>   connect them,
> Till the bridge you will need be form'd, the ductile anchor hold,
> Till the gossamer thread you fling catch somewhere, O my soul.

"Since my first impulses are primarily musical, and musical-formal, "Ingolf wrote to Lawrence on April 7 (about ten days after beginning work on the piece), "there are all these places in which in order to round out or to vary and repeat a phrase I need more syllables than the poem gives me, and one cannot always rely on the repetition of words." "Looking at first part of Spider," he noted on May 5, "who really cares if the equations are complete and correct? If the ear wants B-flat, why not write a B-flat, even if it does not 'fit'?" Ingolf was working on *Spider* when Etta had to be taken to the Zieglerspital on June 7 and he wrote some sketches in her hospital room. The appropriateness of dedicating the work to her was obvious and it was to complete this composition that Ingolf first turned his attention when he returned to new work at the end of the month. "The end moves me so," he wrote on the 28th as he finished the piece, "and the thought if only Etta could hear it – ." In the sketch book he added, "Sunday – and two weeks ago that terrible Sunday of leave-taking." Copying was completed on July 13; thinking about the amount of time involved in the project, he wrote, "People write symphonies and operas in that time!" *A Noiseless Patient Spider* was published by Carl Fischer in 1972.

Ingolf's last completed composition was the *Five Duets for Clarinets*. One movement had its origin in a birthday presentation which Ingolf completed for Donal Michalsky in 1964. Composition began again on March 13, with the first of what turned out to be a series of duets for B-flat clarinet reaching completion on March 27 (the same day that *Spider* was begun). Ingolf decided to dedicate this movement (Sonatina) to Don and to write each of the remaining sections with other clarinetist friends in mind. Don's original birthday present, in a somewhat rewritten version (as Invention on Two Intervals), was finished two days later and dedicated to Christie Lundquist. Work on additional movements took place in April and May, but Ingolf lacked the energy, physical and psychological, to press on with the task until early July. Part III (Cadenza Pastorale) was completed on his balcony on the afternoon of the 2nd and dedicated to Nicolas Roussakis. At one point Ingolf anticipated adding only one more movement but on July 7 he records, "decided Duets need a *short quiet* interlude before finale." Four days later he changed his mind, "decide to chuck the Invention on a Rhythm and leave it at 4," but on the 22nd he was again at work on this penultimate section. It was completed, against a backdrop of ever-worsening health and black despondency, on the 25th and dedicated to Robert Wojciak. The last movement, Canonic Rondo, was completed on July 31 and dedicated to Mitchell Lurie. Ingolf spent two days copying a work which Roussakis pronounced "delightful and enjoyable...a welcome enrichment of the clarinet literature." The work was published in 1974 by Joseph Boonin.

Ingolf began work anew on the *Elegy Concerto* for violin and small orchestra on July 17 – "I think I am at last getting *into* it again!" he added two days later. "I *must* finish," he wrote on July 20. He had written to Lawrence that the work had been 9/10ths completed by the end of 1967. Now, on August 6, and with plans no doubt to revise as he went forward, he ruled the bar lines of the first page of the score in order, at last, to produce an orchestrated clean copy of this expressive work. "The first step has been taken!" he wrote to me in some excitement. But no more music came from his inventive pen, and we must now turn our attention to an account of the death of Ingolf Dahl.

81. MARCHE FUNÈBRE

Three theories have been proposed to account for the passing of Etta's husband. The first is that he took his own life. When I visited U.S.C., a few weeks after the event, Grant Beglarian, who was not a believer in the theory himself, questioned me closely on this possibility, for it had evidently been mooted in the musical world. That ambiguous phrase in the letter to "Dear Friends" of June 28 ("I must now spend the limited time that is available to me") may have contributed to the belief that Ingolf did not expect or *plan* to live much longer himself. As late as 1993 Dr. Fred Kahn, my cousin and one of Ingolf's many physicians, accepted the suicide theory – "I think Ingolf killed himself." My initial reply to any questions put to me about the meaning of the "Dear Friends" letter was that Ingolf simply intended to indicate that only half a year of sabbatical time remained before his return to other duties. I am less certain of this interpretation today, but I remained unconvinced that suicide was ever directly attempted by my suffering stepfather.

A second theory, though clearly related to the first, argues that Ingolf lost the will to live, that he died of grief. Michael Tilson Thomas put forward this romantic thesis, and it does have the virtue of being harder to disprove, for it is extremely difficult to measure the depth of psychological factors in cases like this. Surely Etta's loss was an immense blow. Had she been present she would also have been in a position to insist on the hospitalization that her husband's condition increasingly demanded, a banishment to an institutional setting which this stubborn man continued to avoid at all costs. Alone in Frutigen, he concealed from others the full extent of his debility. Indeed health reasons alone can be used to account for his dying. Now we can examine the evidence as we observe Ingolf in the last two months of his life.

On June 18 he had another appointment with Dr. Wernli in Zurich. "It is better," he wrote in triumph, "the *diaphragm* is improved." Then he had lunch with Willi Hausslein in the Kronenhalle and drove home, suffering from asthma. This and the bronchial infection persisted. The

21st was described as "one of the worst days." On it Ingolf began traction again for his neck. It took a pill every three hours for him to sleep. On June 22 he reported, "Breathing is a little better, as least not the total panic of yesterday." Nevertheless Ingolf was embarked on what he called "sanatorium days" – filled with health business. The night of June 25 was a "fairly good night;" the next day I called from England where I was serving as chief-of-party to a group of 80 Michigan State summer school students, and Ingolf spoke optimistically to me about his progress. Dr. Stoller also arrived to give Ingolf a vitamin injection. This was the period when the last sections of *Spider* were reaching fruition. On the eve of completion Ingolf walked to a local church for a concert – "But alas, when I get home after concert, there is so much asthma again – it is to despair."

Admitting on the 29th, "I'm worse than before I got to Wernli," Ingolf drove to Zurich to see his physician. The latter was able to report "objective" improvement on x-rays and tests. At home a "*nice* walk, with another *glimmer* of hope," was completed on July 1. The next day he made an even more distant circuit on foot and needed no Alupent after dinner – "this is the best yet." On the 5th he tried a much more substantial distance, taking the train to Kandersteg and walking back for almost four hours – "2/3 of way terrible fight with breath, continuously. Can't breathe *out*. Stay and 'pray' – Lord let me breathe, breathe, breathe, breathe again. Rest on bench, finally take Alupent, from there on it is much better." On July 9 Ingolf had another consultation with Dr. Wernli, who was leaving for his vacation. The walk back to the house from the Frutigen train station was "surely the worst of all – just *barely* make it – people ask 'are you ill? – never so much out of breath, barely make it. A *wildly* uncomfortable evening – I swallow every medication in sight and inhale it." In this condition he went to his worktable to finish the Copland Fanfare.

"Each cough brings with it a state of collapse," he wrote the next day, "And just walking two steps is taxing beyond words. Am so depressed – how is this going to *go*?? What is going to happen?" "Feel rather lousy," he complained the next night, but on the 13th he deliberately avoided a meeting with the Stollers, perhaps fearing their reaction to his physical state. For several days he tried to spend the night without sleeping pills, but he was soon forced to give up on this experiment. On July 14 he described himself to me as "full of anti-biotics, cortisone, and more other medications than I can name, each on their own daily little schedules, plus inhalations and what have you. I'm not stirring from the house and am slowly improving (but then, there have been so many 'improvements' since we first got here). Anyhow, there's nothing to do but to follow 'doctor's orders,' much as I am fed up with them." His journal entry for the same day includes the command, "I think the breathing is slowly getting better, now *stick* it out, *stay* quiet!" Two days later he took an uphill walk after lunch at one of the town's restaurants. Out of breath, he barely made it back to the house and the "lifeline" sprays. In the evening he reported deep despondency at Etta's loss ("the anchor and the chain"). His stomach was now upset from too many fruits and berries. On the 18th he went walking again, a day followed by asthma that awakened him every two hours throughout the night.

July 19 was a glorious, cloudless day. On it Ingolf began work on the *Elegy Concerto* again, feeling so alienated from the unreachable world outside that he was forced to say, "Go away sun, go away nature, go away beauty, don't tease me, torture me." On the 20th, after completing three letters of recommendation, he noted, "I feel *strange*, very out of sorts, the breathing is all up and hottish, as if I were ill." Lawrence had written to ask the always logical question in asthma cases – could psychological factors be involved? Now an evasive Ingolf responded that he had done some digging in this area without result: "Not that there aren't likely to be many further layers farther down, just as in Troy. But my question is: after you have all this knowledge about your mental twists and turns, what then?" Ingolf preferred to believe that body chemistry alone, *metabolism*, might explain his present difficulties. When Dr. Wernli returned on August 10 (for Ingolf perhaps foolishly delayed seeing any *other* doctor in the interim) he would try to convince his Zurich physician that here the problem might be solved. But he could not have been doing himself any good in his own efforts to find the right chemical balance through this haphazard and desperate mixture of remedies. "Fill myself with tedral, " he noted on July 22, "just *anything* to get relief – I don't care anymore."

On July 23 he re-read his 1970 journal with horror – "the conclusion, awful, is that, since February I've got continuously worse, in spite of all doctors and medicines. What to do now? Where to go from here?...I would not even have the strength to practice the piano now." On this same day someone told him about a sanatorium near Thun, but he filed the idea away without taking any action. At the end of the month he twice went to Interlaken for visits with old friends, the Lilliefelts from Ojai on July 27 and the Duclouxs on July 29. A "truly exhausted nap" after returning from the latter visit lead him to complain, "*That* isn't functioning right. The trouble lies not in asthma but elsewhere!" "Spatz" and Walter Hirsch came to Frutigen for a brief visit on July 30 – "In evening I'm just so lousy again – can hardly make it from [restaurant] to home, the sprays continuously, and after, just sit at desk, taking medicines, waiting for it to pass."

On July 31, the day he completed the last of the clarinet duets, he turned down a local social invitation because of "recluse-ness." "Watch out, Ingolf," he wrote, "don't remove yourself, that's too easy!" He went for a long walk in the evening and had a glass of Scotch with no ill effect. But at 4:00 a.m. he was awakened with a bad asthma attack, cutting through the sleeping pills. In the afternoon the next day he was able to drive to Bern for a party at the Stollers. On August 2, however, he noted a "strong urge to get out, feel lousy, ill, weak, exhausted, insufficient, and *just don't know what to do.*" His walks, it seems to me, were, in spite of their consequences, a desperate attempt to prove to himself that he was still able to function physically. He took a long one now, ascending the banks of the Leimbach stream to a point higher than the one he had reached with MTT in May. "I could have gone further but it's too late," he boasted. But the next day he suffered a debilitating reverse, a day of exhaustion and asthma. He had agreed to accept the help of Frau Kallen, who came to clean at regular intervals, but he insisted on doing his own shopping – "can hardly get up the house steps with the groceries," he recorded on August 3. There was also a recurrence of stomach problems, gas trouble, loose bowels. In the evening he turned on the radio – "that awful R. Strauss – but my nerves are totally shot, I can't control my tear ducts at all."

On Tuesday, August 4, he went walking again. "This is again a *bad* day," he declared, "I must face the facts – I have not improved one inch since February-March." Asthma interrupted his afternoon nap and he had recourse to his medicines throughout the following evening, during which he tried to copy the clarinet duets. "Sprays won't work at all," he reported at 5:15 a.m. The medication induced diarrhea and knocked him out for most of the next day, Wednesday the 5th, which he described as "just a survival day...Try to get by with the minimum of motions of any kind." The night was awful again – "in spite of medications need sprays, am so asthmatic in horizontal position that I cannot sleep. A hell of a night...Still slight soreness in coughing, mucus sightly yellowish! But how can that have such a devastating effect?" The clarinet duets were finished, packaged and mailed on August 6, a Thursday.

"Feel just awful because of lack of sleep," Ingolf recorded in the early afternoon on one of his medical addendum sheets. "Too weak to do anything, and can't *move*," he added in the journal, "then at last start to rule the first score page of Elegy Concerto." His nap was interrupted – "the problem of horizontal position, if I could sleep upright!" Because he could not sleep at all he got up and wrote me a letter: perhaps he *would* visit the asthma specialist in Thun.

"What an awful day!" he protested in his daybook, "and outside hot, sunny, ideal August day!!" At 11:15 that night he again made an entry in his medical addenda – "what am I going to do. The Alupent inhalation *irritates* the asthma rather than soothes it...If I only I had enough adrenalin hypos...This is surely one of the worst nights." In his journal he added the phrase, "afraid of going to bed."

Some ancient recollection, perhaps of a youthful precedent for this moment, flitted into his ever-active memory: "40 years ago – " But these were the last words he ever wrote, for sometime in the early hours of Friday, August 7 Ingolf Dahl, fifty-eight, was overcome by a bronchial spasm; his heart pumped its last blood through his drowning lungs, and, collapsing alone on the floor of his Frutigen studio, he died.

Ingolf at his desk in Tanglewood, mid-Fifties.

Ingolf working with Paul Glass on the recording set for *The Abductors*, April 18, 1957.

Ingolf working with Igor Stravinsky, ca. 1959.

The Dahls celebrate 25 years of marriage, 1965.

Michael Tilson Thomas and his German teacher, Etta, 1966.

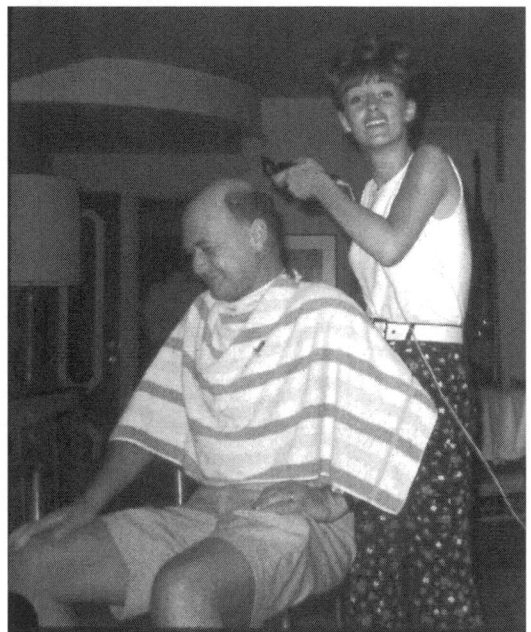

Dorothy cuts her father-in-law's hair, 1966.

Ingolf in 1967.

Ingolf (l), Don Michalsky (c) and Bill Colvig on a Sierra Palisades trip, 1968.

PART IV

THE ANSWERS ARE AT THE
END OF THE BOOK

82. THE ANSWERS ARE AT THE END OF THE BOOK

In the introduction to this biography I suggested that I would begin by offering the story of my family as I had lived it and knew it – concentrating on those aspects of the tale that represented the public face of the Dahl legend.

When my parents died, within a few weeks of one another in the summer of 1970, I experienced a series of shocks, each of which weakened my confidence in the notion that I knew them at all. The lies they had chosen to live by, I came to realize, had not only disfigured their own existence but had undoubtedly undermined my own sense of identity and assurance. To repair this damage was one of the reasons I decided to go behind that public facade – and to do so in the concluding section of this volume.

To begin this process I need to say something about my own whereabouts that fateful summer Sunday when it all began to unravel. On the afternoon of August 9, 1970, I was making an attempt to find a parking place near the entrance to our unit of Park West, a stolid collection of high-rise flats north of London's Marble Arch. My progress was impeded, ironically, by a hearse. Its driver approached me apologetically. "They'll be bringing the body down in ten minutes," he said. I backed out of Park West Place and left Dorothy with our bags, while I searched elsewhere. This mild discomfiture, it seemed at the time, was only the last in a series of disasters that had plagued my summer. At the profoundest level I still mourned for Etta. On an everyday basis there was all the turmoil and tension of supervising those 82 sophomores, who were taking part in Michigan State University's overseas study program in the Humanities. One could never foretell what crisis might have descended during my weekend stint as surly holiday chauffeur in distant Devon and Cornwall. As "chief-of-party" I had already survived disappearances, defections, dope smoking on the tours, and one pregnancy problem that mysteriously went away by itself. I was not in the best of tempers. Deep in my gut there was an undiagnosed kidney stone that would necessitate three hospitalizations in the next few months and I had already missed a week of classes because of this illness. Little things, which might have amused me, now made me peevish. For instance, while reversing my car I noticed that our weekend passengers, the

Platts, had left something behind: little Dixie Leigh's chocolate bar had melted all over the vinyl of my new back seat.

I was also troubled by a grave problem of cultural logistics. In a few weeks I was scheduled to drive my wife, her sister, and her mother to Frutigen, where we would visit my distraught and ailing stepfather. It was not easy to see how such a visit could succeed. My sister-in-law, twenty-three year-old Naomi, had already announced her distaste for mountains; she could, however, be expected to adopt a passive role, curled up in a corner with a book. My mother-in-law, Anne Goldstone, would certainly be more assertive. With her cleaning and straightening she was bound to upset any routine that Ingolf had managed to carve out for himself. I was also afraid that she might chide my stepfather for failing to provide any semblance of Jewish funeral ceremony for Etta, a suggestion so outside the scope of my parents aloof atheism as to seem ludicrous. He might say so. My stepfather was, after all, living out the first few weeks of solitude after thirty years of what many would describe as a close and ideal marriage. He would not need to be nagged regularly. I could picture the austere line of reproof in his brow, a Viking in the ghetto.

I found a place to park behind Park West. It was warm and muggy in London and I had a headache from driving on the wrong side of the road. I was not looking forward to a large family party that had been scheduled to start shortly before our return. But when we reached our door, Dorothy and I both noticed the silence, no sound at all where there should have been a din. Anne let us in; she had been crying. The flat was dark and empty and there would no longer be any need to worry about bringing my in-laws to Frutigen. "Ingolf has died in Switzerland," she said.

A few days later Dorothy and I flew to Zurich and on to Bern's airport at Belp, where we were met by Pierre Tagmann and taken first to the home of the Stollers, the Dahls' landlords, and then on to the very silent house in Frutigen. We were introduced to another elderly Stoller, a town official, who provided innumerable services to us over the next few days. But when everyone had gone there was a vast emptiness in that house. The Leimbach stream roared in its concrete banks outside – it was like living in a hurricane – and the wooden structure was dark and too musty for a man who had died of a lung disease. My guts were still not right and I lay down on one of the huge beds and wept.

The house was full of the artifacts of my departed parents. Ingolf had himself started to collect memorabilia in an envelope entitled "Dear Etta" – it contained a ribbon from the Frutigen Jodlerfest, a number of souvenirs from their short trip to Greece, a leaf of laurel that Ingolf had plucked while attending his wife's solitary funeral at the Bern crematorium. All of Etta's clothes were still in the house, Ingolf's battered brief case was there, indeed memories of my long life in their home waited in every drawer and under every pile. In Ingolf's study a dark patch on the carpet revealed the spot where the blood from the composer's destroyed lungs had leaked from his dying mouth.

On Thursday, August 13, Ingolf's funeral took place in Bern. It too was not a religious ceremony. An organist played Bach, a cousin delivered the eulogy in German. The Katzenstein's, Zurich friends and relatives of my father, or so I believed, were well represented, and there was a Scandinavian contingent as well. Ingolf's brother Holger and his wife Aina had driven down from Stockholm; his sister Anna-Britta Björnson had flown from Reykjavik. The hall at the Bern crematorium was full of flowers, many sent by colleagues from the School of Music, and back in Frutigen messages were arriving from the four corners of the musical world. People who had just survived the shock of my mother's passing were unable to comprehend that Ingolf had followed so quickly. I remember picking up the phone to hear Gail Kubik ask to speak to his old friend, and the haunting wail of Gail's tearful breakdown as I gave him the news. For other friends, Holger insisted on formal death announcements; we used the same address list that Ingolf had compiled in writing about the death of his wife.

Even more eerie, for many of his friends, was the arrival in the mail on August 31st of copies of *The Five Duets For Clarinets*, which the composer had asked Cameo Music Reproduction in Hollywood to send to the clarinetists. Don Michalsky received such a copy; on the 17th he had received a letter from Ingolf in Guanajuato, having learned of his mentor's death only the day before. Michael Tilson Thomas was called from the rehearsal stage at Tanglewood to hear the awful news.

After the funeral there was a stop in a nearby restaurant for coffee and cake. Some of the funeral party returned to Zurich and later that afternoon Holger, Aina, Britta, Dorothy and I found ourselves trying to maintain an air of business as usual over trout and wine in a little cafe on the road to

513

Kandersteg. While Dorothy and I were getting reacquainted with Ingolf's Swedish relatives something unforeseen began to pepper their conversation – Ingolf's siblings, at least in the sense I had always understood it, were not Swedes at all! And neither, I was astonished to learn, was my Swedish stepfather. The curtain had started its slow ascent.

83. ANOTHER AHASUERUS

At the funeral party that Thursday afternoon, held at our little inn on the road to Kandersteg, the conversation turned to the history of the Marcus family, and more specifically to the fate of Pappi, Paul Marcus, and to his stubborn refusal to abandon – until it was almost too late – the Germany of the Thirties. "And why should he have had to leave?" I asked innocently. "Because we were Jews, of course," Holger answered.

In this fashion I learned that the phrase Ingolf had supplied to all those music dictionaries – "Born in Hamburg of Swedish parents" – was not the whole truth, and that echoes of childhood conversations, when I had pressed Etta for more information about Ingolf's family – "What religion is he? "He doesn't have a religion." "What religion were his parents?" "Oh, Lutheran, I suppose" – contained only convenient untruths. I realized at last that the obviously Jewish Katzensteins, who had just departed for Zurich, were not *my* cousins, as I had foolishly assumed all these years, but those of my "Swedish" stepfather, a man who was, on his father's side, like so many other emigré artists of his era, a German Jew.

It took some time for me to arrive at any satisfactory explanation for this elaborate subterfuge, a falsification of identity that was offered by Ingolf and the colluding Etta to everyone, including their own son, as a workable substitute for the truth. One might ask why the matter was of any importance to me, but the answer to that requires a little explanation of my own sense of identity.

I could say that the mid-Michigan made me a Jew. In Los Angeles, with its large Jewish population, at JewCLA with its many Jewish scholars, to be Jewish was as unexceptional as being a Democrat or a carnivore. Having had no religious training at all, being Jewish, for me, was entirely a matter of cultural ancestry, and that it might in any way be seen as a debilitating impediment had not occurred to me until I signed on as an Assistant

Professor of Humanities at Michigan State University – five years before the death of my parents. Almost immediately Dorothy and I realized that we were very much out of step in our new surroundings. Other Jewish members of the faculty wanted to know whether we intended to make our Jewishness public, implying in this question that some of them had decided to camouflage such a regrettable lapse. Whereas the academic fights of the Nineties would feature battles to include cultural materials produced by authors other than dead white European males, in the Sixties some of my colleagues and I had a struggle to insert into the curriculum of our basic course in Western Civilization *any* mention of a Jewish contribution at all. There was one unit entitled "Judaism as a background to Christianity," but this slighting reference and the inclusion of excepts from *Mein Kampf* in a widely used textbook, *Classics of Western Thought*, were pertinent reminders that here was a culture whose sensitivities to Jewish matters was not finely attuned. Nevertheless I persisted. For several years I offered a course on the Jewish-American novel, enlisting the aid of a bemused Etta in preparing a Yiddish glossary for my students. After our department decided to deal with the non-Western cultures by offering separate courses in their cultural traditions, I put forward plans for a course on Jewish culture. I am told that members of the department's curriculum committee were uncertain that such materials could be made into a ten week-long course. "I might as well offer a course in Scottish cultural traditions," one of these doubters scoffed. "What would you teach on the second day?" was the bemused reply.

The new course, along with others on Jewish themes, survived to become part of a thematic program at the university, and for a number of years I was actively involved in questions of Jewish history, identity, and culture. These were the same years when I had to wrestle with a Jewish identity problem very close to home: why had my stepfather been at such pains to hide his own ancestry? As I turned my attention to a review of the Dahl journals and began my interviews with members of his family in 1979, the Jewish question was one of the matters that interested me most. Here is what I learned about my stepfather's true origins.

Mammi could certainly claim Swedish progenitors, but even she was educated in Norway and, from her teens, raised in Germany. During Ingolf's childhood, his teenage years, and for much of his Zurich apprenticeship, the Marcus family lived in Hamburg, *visiting* Sweden only on holidays.

Ingolf learned a good deal of Swedish from his mother and her family, but he never spoke the language like a native. He spoke, wrote, and dreamed in German for the better part of his first thirty years. He was, in short, a German, and he carried a German passport. He may have had good reasons for obscuring such a fact, but this is the truth.

In 1957 Pappi sent to his son a Marcus family tree, with an accompanying text. He noted that from the marriage of Benjamin Marcus, a manufacturer, to Fredericke Cohn, that six children were born, including his own father Siegfried, a managing clerk (*Prokurist*). Siegfried in turn had three children, Else, Paul, and Walther. One notes, even in the first names of the Marcuses, how speedily the process of assimilation was progressing among the German Jewish community. But Paul's siblings married Jews. His sister became Else Katzenstein and it was in her home at Russenweg 10 that Ingolf found accommodation during his Zurich years. Many of Pappi's relatives maintained overt Jewish connections but Paul was hardly a solitary figure in choosing a gentile as a wife. "On the eve of the First World War," according to Walter Laqueur, "there was one mixed marriage for every two among Jewish partners in Berlin and Hamburg."

At university in Munich, Paul tells us, he worked in vain for equal rights for Jewish students, even though he himself had already departed from Jewish society and turned to a study of non-religious philosophies. In 1906 he became a junior partner in the law firm of Drs. Otto Schmeisser and Julius Levy, but his tendencies were assimilationist and eclectic. He served his country loyally in the First World War and his city benefited from his cultural activism. His relations with his father, who may have viewed some of these activities ruefully, were not good. Siegfried failed to get along with his daughter-in-law and Mammi was appalled, for her part, when her father-in-law failed to show the appropriate reverence for the *wunderkind* Ingolf. Dismissed as mean and vulgar, Siegfried Marcus was asked not to visit Holunderweg 7. The process of rejecting the Jewish connection had thus begun well before Ingolf embraced its urgencies.

As a child my stepfather grew up in a household that had severed its connections to every aspect of religious ritual, Jewish or Christian; he was not circumcised or baptized, and his parents listed "no religious preference" in the appropriate spot on his birth certificate. Instead, Mammi found in her Scandinavian youth a rich store of satisfying annual rites and tribal customs and we were still living out her Christmas fantasies in California decades later. No room remained within the Marcus' lofty materialism or their pan-European vision of cultural tradition for a Jewish contribution. Jews were other people.

They were "other people" until Hitler knocked. Although there is not much evidence that Ingolf followed political events with any special concern, he did read the Zurich newspapers and listened often to the radio. Under any circumstances it would have been difficult to silence the clamor of events in Germany for they brought with them such devastation for the Marcuses of Hamburg. As Hitler reached for the mantle of German leadership some of Pappi's Gross Borstel neighbors suddenly remembered they had a Jewish family living in their midst. No one was more astonished by this rediscovery than Pappi himself. His children, who had survived for many years without any reference to their Jewish identity, now found themselves the objects of persecution. The blonde Ingolf managed to escape the worst of this; in appearance he was hard to distinguish from his Aryan schoolmates, and he left Germany in 1932 anyway. But the others, including his darker siblings, were not so fortunate. Shouts of *Judenschwein* followed them in the streets. Holger remembers a day in which even the fair-haired Gert was pursued by a posse of Hitler Youth.

It was Mammi's decision that the family must migrate. Gert and Holger were sent to Sweden within a few weeks of Hitler's accession. Mammi and Anna-Britta joined them in Stockholm in the spring of 1934. This left only Pappi, stubborn, naive Pappi, the social democrat who wouldn't believe that it could happen here, that it could happen to such a distinguished citizen, a holder of the Iron Cross. Life became more and more difficult for him. His name disappeared from the office door, he was legally forbidden to follow his profession, the empty house on Holunderweg was cut up into flats, its once proud owner hidden away in a maid's room in the attic. Although he undertook a number of visits to Stockholm during this period, Paul Marcus refused to be parted from his property and his hopes until it was almost too late. It was only with considerable effort that Mammi at last secured the necessary entry permit for her husband. Bereft of profession and possessions, he migrated to Sweden in January of 1939, the same month that his eldest son crossed the Atlantic.

Fate had determined that the Jewish Question would have to be re-answered by the Marcus family. Pappi's indifference to Jewish matters evaporated; and the man who had once fought for a generalized international brotherhood would now add concern for the state of Israel to his list of good causes. Anna-Britta joined a Zionist youth organization in the 1930's; even Mammi visited a kibbutz late in her life.

Anti-semitism can make Jews, but what about Ingolf? His responses were quite different: a complex, even irrational evasion of the burdens of identity.

Not surprisingly, Ingolf's references to Jews in his early journals are written in the voice of the gentile outsider. On the whole he seems to have liked the Jews he encountered. In 1931 he records meeting a Jewish family in Mannheim; they have two "nice" children, "He intelligent, she humorous and full of jokes." A few months earlier he had been taken in by a group of young Jews in Paris. They asked him to play his own music; he was surprised and gratified by their compliments. There are many references in his journals to Jewish women, including, of course, my mother. Such women seemed to have held a special attraction for him, particularly if they were of the "modern" type, self-assured, direct, and culturally sophisticated. This is the way Eva, the heroine of his youthful novel *Maskentanz*, is described. "Mean and vulgar" Jews were less acceptable and those who proclaimed their Jewishness were an anachronistic embarrassment. What is one to make of an entry in Ingolf's daybook for 1940, some two weeks after his marriage to my mother, "Etta gets on my nerves with her loud and obtrusive Jewish manner of speech"? (So ashamed was he by this observation that he actually went to the trouble of recording it in mirror-script in his journal.) But is it any wonder that Ingolf had internalized that same catalogue of Jewish deficiencies enunciated by the anti-semites of his era? This was the air they all breathed in those days. Of course he was deeply offended by overtly anti-Semitic behavior, but was he not perpetuating the work of the anti-semites by eradicating all evidence of a background that so many others had branded as shameful?

It was easy to do. Far from having roots in Jewish culture Ingolf could view Jews as a people standing somewhat apart from the Christian culture and the European artistic movements in which he took such delight as an art student and music maker.

That he might be ripped from this inheritance through the misfortune of having a Jewish father must have seemed the height of injustice. But one of his German friends broke off relations with him after 1933, advising Ingolf to "seek new friends, new human beings. Think what happened to Bruno Walter, to Klemperer and act accordingly. There will come some time in the future when nationalism will acknowledge the international validity of art. But at present there is only the fight for the existence of a nation." Under such circumstances it is not too surprising that Ingolf chose not to accept the burdens of Jewish identity. Unable to gauge the strength of American toleration and fearful that any overt adoption of a Jewish persona might serve as an impediment to survival and success in his new country, Ingolf chose to disembark in the guise of the ur-goy.

I would like to speculate on one other element in Ingolf's complex psychology. His rejection of the Jewish element in his background parallels other developments in his psyche. Ingolf's own sense of suffering and martyrdom, which we have encountered in earlier sections of this biography, has a Christian referent, with Mammi cast in the role of the blessed Virgin and her son taking the role of the remarkable baby Jesus. But rejected in this familial ideology is the Jew, Joseph, not the real father, not the spiritual force represented only by mother and son. Ingolf was thus able to combine traditional oedipal hatreds with dismissal of that haunting Jewish presence which so frequently spoiled happiness in youth and now, through its genes, threatened survival and preference in the present.

Ingolf was determined, all conjecture aside, to disguise the Jewish element in his past. The decision had been made before he arrived in the United States, and however his vision of America may have been altered by experience he never sought to alter the myth of gentile parentage; however many Jews he numbered among his closest friends and colleagues, he maintained the lie until the day he died. Anna-Britta believes that, in spite of their closeness, that brother never invited sister to visit California because her "Jewish" features might have given away the game.

I have dwelt on one aspect of Ingolf's cosmetic surgery on the past. Another process of rejection was also under way in the Thirties: Ingolf was about to expunge his German identity as well. The process began with the first moments of the Third Reich, and was accelerated by the exodus of the Marcuses from Hamburg. On his own visits to the city during the next few years, stopovers between Zurich and Stockholm, he found himself increasingly ill at ease and rootless. Many of his best friends abandoned Europe and migrated to America well before he did, and upon his arrival in New York he was able to visit Barbara Krueger, Liesl Glogau, his old piano teacher Edith Weiss-Mann and many other people he had known in Germany. During his last visit to Hamburg, in July, 1938, he spent a terrible week "among remembrances of distant youth." In correspondence in 1944 he and Mammi agreed they never wished to set foot in the city again.

Meanwhile Germany was an ache that could not be forgotten, even in Zurich. German conductors shouted "Heil Hitler" at the beginning of concerts; pro-Nazi hecklers interrupted performances of "The Peppermill"; *Triumph of The Will* played in Swiss cinemas; "Germany – what a country," Ingolf wrote after viewing this film in 1936. The fall of neighboring Austria, on March 11, 1938, was a particularly bitter moment for Ingolf, who reports a day spent in deep despair. After all, he carried German papers, and there were anxious moments at border crossings on a number of occasions.

The most complete surviving expression of Ingolf's attitude toward the German Question comes in a fragment which he completed as a journal addendum while visiting Saas-Fee on April 10, 1937. In the Britannia hut he had encountered some Nazis from Berlin. An "elementary senseless hatred" seized Ingolf, "I who couldn't hurt a fly." "German assholes," he wrote, "these Hitler lackeys – none of them is innocent; when I look into their maws or hear them speak the rage boils within me, blindly, from the depths." "How odd," he added, "I am German myself, so very much, for I myself speak this hated language, I long to be able to get *out* of my language, for everyone must take me to be one of those hateful people." How odd as well, Ingolf continued, "that I myself have been such an admirer of the German culture...and Mammi is much more German than Swedish." But so successful was the attempt of the Dahls to obfuscate Ingolf's German background that Etta could write to Lawrence Morton, while reviewing the linguistic weaknesses in a speech that Ingolf delivered on Music in the American University in Zurich in November, 1952, "He spoke in German, and alas, this language has slipped from him. He used it actively, of course, from 1931 to 1939." And what language are we supposed to think he used actively in the streets of Hamburg, at the Lichtwarkshule, or in Cologne before 1931? Or, for that matter, in his journals up to about 1944? Similarly, I have my doubts that Gert and Holger spoke German "only brokenly," as she advised in a letter for public consumption written during our visit to Sweden in 1947.

This deception on Etta's part illustrates, incidentally, how great a complicity she shared in her husband's elaborate counterfeits. When my strong-willed mother-in-law determined that Dorothy and I would have a Jewish wedding on June 14, 1964, the Dahls were offended. "Will all the men have to wear those stupid beanies?" Etta asked. Yes, but a yarmulke-clad Lawrence Morton, much to my surprise, came forward when Rabbi Morris Kaplan needed a Jewish witness for part of the pre-wedding ceremonial. Ingolf and Etta meanwhile sat at the head table like vegetarians in an abattoir.

In spite of his admission in the Britannia hut, Ingolf made a concerted effort, once established in America, to eradicate the German as well as the Jewish nature of his own background. When neighbors made anti-German remarks he feared that these were directed at him. When someone introduced him at a concert by saying, "He came from Germany," he cringed. And whenever he heard his own voice on tape he was agonized by "that awful Kraut accent!"

Fortunately, he was able to select another national identity and fob it off as his own. And this is but another reminder that we too often see the immigration process as one in which the oppressed gain new opportunities to celebrate their own national or cultural identity in peace and dignity when, for many, America was wonderful because it allowed one to forsake these very things.

For a time, Ingolf toyed with the idea of being Swiss. In a 1946 interview he is quoted in the Gatsby-like evasion, "I grew up in Switzerland," but then he added, speaking of his Zurich days, "This was a very happy time of my life," so we have obfuscation at every turn. The same year the *Daily Trojan* described the new member of the School of Music faculty as a "native of Switzerland" and a year later the *Trojan Owl* characterized him as one who was born in Sweden, raised in Switzerland.

Eventually, Ingolf chose to be Swedish. This claim bubbles up at the same time that the Swiss candidature is being shoved onto a back burner. A 1946 reviewer described the composer's *Variations on a Swedish Folktune* as "built upon the beautiful melodies of Dahl's native land." Most of his American associates came to believe in this Swedish mythology. I did. Only after his death did I discover the truth. I learned that the "Born in Hamburg of Swedish parents" line was essentially a fabrication. It was not a complete lie because *eventually* all of the Marcuses did secure Swedish papers. But it has to be admitted that citizenship did not suddenly make Pappi into a "Swedish parent," though Ingolf preferred to confuse the issue with a phrase that was unfeeling at best.

In fact it was a struggle for all of the Marcuses (including Mammi) to obtain Swedish naturalization, and in the process much red tape and discrimination had to be overcome. Sweden's reputation as a haven for refugees had not yet been earned in the late Thirties, when Pappi arrived at last. Mammi's work as a translator and secretary kept the family afloat while Pappi struggled to learn the language of his "native land." As an alien his movements were restricted and his suffering was great. Of course he was not allowed to practice law, and he had practically no income. The proud breadwinner spent his old age enduring a scolding from his employable wife every time he failed to get the family dinner started on time. Anna-Britta had to enter into a paper marriage in order to become Swedish enough to receive a graduation certificate from her Stockholm high school. And the Swedish Ingolf, who claims to have studied piano in Stockholm (which, if true, must have been for the briefest of periods during holidays) never mastered a fluent Swedish, though he could read the language without great difficulty. Mammi, of course, had tried to maintain a Swedish presence in her Hamburg household and all of the children had received Scandinavian names, "Ingolf" being the name of the Ninth Century Norseman who first colonized Iceland. In an effort to make Ingolf bilingual, Mammi had even spoken to him in Swedish during his infancy, but the custom had to be abandoned during the First World War, ironically, because the Germans took her Swedish chatter as the mutterings of a spy. With such tenuous ties to Swedish life and culture Ingolf nevertheless chose to represent himself as a Swede, not a German.

To cover his tracks more fully he indulged in another small subterfuge. Holger believes, as I do too, that (again in the musical dictionaries) Ingolf altered his arrival date in the United States from 1939 (the true date) to 1938 (a false one) in order to seem less like a war refugee, German or Jewish. For a while he was aided in this fiction by another erroneous emigration date, 1935, which appeared in some musical reference books, probably in error. But even those musical encyclopedias he himself supplied with information late in his life received the same, shifty story – arrival 1938. In his own hand, in the last few years of his life, he altered an existing biographical statement to read "left Europe in 1938 and settled in Los Angeles, California early in 1939." Even here, when it didn't matter to anyone anymore, he was playing with the truth – for the entire emigration process, from Le Havre to Los Angeles, was completed in 1939. Perhaps he could have persevered in neutral Switzerland indefinitely, but Ingolf was, in fact, a war refugee, whether he wished to admit it or not.

Only one additional gesture was needed to make the identity transformation complete. Walther Ingolf Marcus (or "Ingmarc," as he signed some of his youthful compositions) had to become Ingolf Dahl. The decision to adopt his mother's very Scandinavian maiden name must have been made before he left Europe. He is listed as Ingolf Marcus in Zurich concert programs but he was known by his new name in his earliest professional appearances in Los Angeles. Anna-Britta testifies that he told his parents that employment prospects in America would be better if he freed himself from such an obviously Jewish name as Marcus. The statement is puzzling for a number of reasons. Ingolf settled in one of the few parts of the world where having a Jewish name might have been an asset; moreover, Marcus does not seem to be so obviously a Jewish name as he might have supposed. We do have to remember that Ingolf did not know for sure that he would spend all his life in Southern California; had he pursued an academic career elsewhere then perhaps he would have encountered that same cold shoulder that some of my older colleagues had experienced at Michigan State. There were plenty of reasons why people, in terror, sought to escape from the stigma of Jewish identity in those days. When his sister questioned him more directly on the name change, many years later, he evaded her accusations of hypocrisy by staring sheepishly in another direction and beginning an unfinished sentence, "Well, you must understand…"

Curiously, Ingolf did not complete the legal formalities needed to make the name change official until almost four years after his arrival in America. He reports seeing a lawyer on the day after Pearl Harbor, that is just as the U.S. began its entry into World War II. On February 3rd, 1943, after a day in court, he noted in his journal, "I am Dahl!" Then he added, "Forgive me, Pappi."

Throughout his life in Los Angeles he and Etta maintained a discrete veil over his Jewish ancestry, not even confiding the secret to closest friends like Lawrence Morton. After Ingolf's death it took nineteen years before the association was made in print, in this case a casual reference by Robert Craft in an article in the *New York Review of Books* entitled "Jews and Geniuses" in 1989.

During his own lifetime Ingolf never seems to have admitted into his mental calculations the psychological costs of hiding his true self from the outside world. "By making a desperate effort to reject himself and to camouflage his Jewishness," Albert Memmi writes, "the Jew often ends up by not seeing himself except as an embarrassment to himself, a hindrance to his life as a man." How must Ingolf have felt when he discovered what a truly wonderful circle of friends and colleagues he had in the Jews of Los Angeles specifically and in the musical world in general? How agonizing to perpetuate his lies in the face of such an open and accommodating world? And what about the lies to me – was Jewishness so disgraceful that the presence of a Jewish father must be kept from your own Jewish son? This was the betrayal that haunted me as we finished our lunch on the road to Kandersteg.

"There is no absolute rupture between the first harmless verbal camouflage, as in name-changing, and for example, the furious fight against the self, or even suicide. They are," Memmi continues, "gradations of the same impulse, easily recognizable in the diverse and multiple aggressions which the oppressed inflicts upon himself."

And did he succeed in expunging the truth about his own ancestry from the wellsprings of the unconscious? Did he truly lose *all* sense of himself a a Jew? I will conclude with only two more incidents and then leave this matter for others to ponder. On the night of August 27, 1955, while camping with some Sierra Club friends near Mt.. Williamson, Ingolf had a dream. In it he is taken prisoner, in this case by the enemy of the moment, the Russians. "Why?" he begs to know from his captors. They reply, "Because J[ewish]." "No," the captive responds in terror, "Only half!" In June, 1942, there is also a revealing entry as Ingolf wanders desperately through the lonely streets of Manhattan, at home nowhere in the world. And how does he refer to himself in this moment of exile? He pictures himself, appropriately at last, as "again the eternal Jew, Ahasuerus."

Repression was the essence of Ingolf's psychological destiny and the many conflicts he endured in his creative and professional life have to be seen in part as an outcome of this constant effort to hide his true self. But ancestry and national identity form only a part of this catalogue of the repressed. I had only a few days left before a second great shock overwhelmed my image of the man who called himself Ingolf Dahl.

84. THAT TOPIC

A watershed summer, the summer of 1970. I had lost both Etta and Ingolf within a few weeks of one another, and my own sense of self was beginning to crumble at the edges. In London there were many letters of condolence awaiting response; more arrived every day and one, written on August 16, was about to change forever my perception of the family structure in which I had struggled and survived for over three decades.

The letter was from Bill Colvig, our old mountain climbing buddy, Ingolf's most loyal trailside comrade, a man I had known for many years, not only from the Sierras but through our trips to San Francisco and his return visits to Cheremoya. Bill had much to say on a number of topics before getting around to a unique subject matter. I cannot tell, re-reading the letter all these years later, whether he imagined he was carrying me over familiar ground or preparing me for a subject that would be entirely new – something, therefore, that needed the assistance of a sympathetic outsider, someone who could help me prepare for another ordeal in the aftermath of my stepfather's death. In the event I was in for a profound shock.

"And now That Topic," Bill wrote, "homosexuality." In this way I learned for the first time something that my mother and that many of the friends, lovers, and even casual acquaintances of the man had always known – Ingolf Dahl was gay.

I endured chaotic waves of emotion. I felt betrayed and enlightened at the same time. The answers to recent mysteries stood revealed: why Holger, for instance, had – only a few weeks before – recovered some gay magazines from a bookshelf in Frutigen, only to toss them into the wastebasket with the remark, "Well, these could not possibly be Ingolf's." And greater mysteries opened up like an abyss: how could I not have known, why was I not told, what dizzying truths remain to be discovered?

I carried Ingolf's music manuscripts and papers in his own battered brown briefcase when I flew alone to Los Angeles at the end of the summer. As I passed through customs an inspector fingered his way through the contents of the many envelopes in this case and unerringly pulled out only one, the one in which Ingolf had collected gay tidbits "For Bill." At least I wasn't surprised anymore.

At Cheremoya I retrieved Ingolf's diaries dating back to 1928; when these were combined with the incomplete 1970 volume, which Holger had retained for a few months, the total numbered forty-three; forty-three years of autobiographical memoirs, intimate and revealing in character. In the summer of 1971, when Dorothy and I lived for the last time at Cheremoya, we packed up all of this explosive material, Etta's writings, the family photo albums and slides, and many personal artifacts and took them with us back to Michigan. I threw away Ingolf's gay party costumes and more gay magazines.

What I retained I did not choose to examine or share. The materials just sat in a closet in my study in East Lansing, a menacing message from the past which I chose not to decode. Respect and cowardice – it's hard to determine which of these had a greater share in my reticence. Anna-Britta twice urged me to destroy all personal materials – "If I were you I would throw away all private correspondence you find, except perhaps from 'famous people.'" I was not prepared to do this. I had been trained as an historian and we do not destroy documents. I kept them, but I did not want to submit to them.

The issue was made more complicated in the fall of 1973. James Berdahl, completing doctoral work in the Department of Music at the University of Miami in Florida, chose to write a dissertation on *Ingolf Dahl: His Life and Works*. His request for family and personal papers was understandable, but I was not in a position to grant it. I completed a lengthy catalogue of Ingolf's professional correspondence and I was happy to help Jim with any other documents he needed, but, as I explained during his visit to East Lansing in January, 1974, I was unprepared to delve into the personal materials myself, let alone share these with a stranger. Holger, writing to Berdahl, also insisted on limiting access to information:

> I would like to get an assurance from you that you are prepared to keep confidential information for yourself, to be used only as a background for your understanding, not to be mentioned in any way in your dissertation or otherwise. Only three years have passed since Ingolf died and many people who knew him are still alive and therefore we must try to tell the story like Ingolf did.

But Bill Colvig, to whom I wrote on the subject, chided me for believing that a life could be fully understood with the types of limitations that Holger had imposed:

> It is difficult for me to comprehend how a man's life can be portrayed with any honesty at all by leaving out important details of his "private" life or "personal life" because these very details are what gives the man his individuality, his very special character...I can't think for a minute that Ingolf would have wanted "that" side of his life kept quiet.

To all the other anxieties under which I labored at the time, I now had the added dimension of guilt.

Berdahl's dissertation on the public life and compositional styles of Ingolf Dahl was completed in 1975; my confusion was not. At least two more years passed before I was able to begin that long postponed journey into the past, a sifting of the evidence, the necessary examination of the discrepancy between the public image maintained by these admired figures, Ingolf and Etta, and the reality that lay beneath. Curiosity overcame caution and the natural instincts of the detective, for historians love puzzles too, reasserted itself. Some seven years after the death of my parents I began my first attempt to unravel their mysteries, an attempt that reaches its fruition in these pages now. It has been a voyage of self-discovery as well. We have told the story as Ingolf and Etta did, but now, as I have done in the case of his family background and nationality, it is time to insert all those missing pieces from their private life.

85. SOMETHING HAS HAPPENED TO ME

Having taken a second look at Ingolf's childhood – and having added the missing dimension of his German and Jewish background – it is now time to consider his homoerotic past. Our journey into this clandestine world is one that will inevitably take us through many familiar landmarks in the tale, but our footsteps will be far more assured on this second voyage round my stepfather.

His first sexual encounter, according to his sister, occurred when he was sixteen; it can now be added that this encounter was with a man. "Something has happened to me," he reported to Anna-Britta, "I have been out. What a life! I'm so sinful." Ingolf's first lover was, according to his sister, the painter Eduard Bargheer. Edat, as he was called, was in his late twenties at the time. He had been employed by Pappi to paint murals on the house at Holunderweg and he had also completed portraits of the Marcus children. He and Ingolf remained friends for many years and kept up a correspondence when life brought Ingolf to America and Bargheer to Italy. Ingolf retained a series of lithographs by his former lover, and these hang on my walls in London all these years later.

Following a rendezvous at Edat's on March 18, 1930, the diarist has written, "O Ingolf!" – which we can interpret as a token of wickedness, delight, love, or all three, though it seems clear that by this time Ingolf had ceased to regard the homoerotic impulse as something sinful. His struggles with "normality" caused him to embrace feelings of guilt, self-hatred and incompleteness, but these traumas were not accompanied, at least at the conscious level, by any acceptance of *society's* rejection of the homosexual act. Nor do we find him exploring the fruitless and irrelevant question, "What causes homosexuality, especially my own?" "The great spirit of love has a thousand faces," would become a kind of motto for Ingolf.

In 1978 I took an afternoon's walk with Bill Colvig in a beautiful forested canyon above the Aptos home that he shared with Lou Harrison, and we discussed Ingolf's sexual nature. "Ingolf did not consider himself to be a homosexual exclusively," Bill told me, "He always insisted that he was bisexual." From the evidence extracted from his journals, this would certainly have been true in his teens and twenties, but there must be an added proviso: his preference and partiality – from the earliest days

– remained with men. It is no wonder that he has difficulty telling the Eva of his 1931 "novel," *Der Maskentanz der Chaos*, that she expects too much from him, and that his kisses for her are manufactured, an artificial ardor.

The pages of the 1931 journal are crowded with the names of those young men for whom Ingolf felt the thrill of passion. Two of these – Kurt, perhaps a student at the Bauhaus, and Erich – are also portrayed in the novel. Both affairs end in tragedy. But Ingolf also seems to have been attracted to women who were not reticent in their analysis of his character – I include my mother in this category. The Eva of the *Maskentanz* not only lambastes the Ingolf character, Alf, but warns him that Erich is nothing but a male whore..."You are wasting yourself on a man who is deeply beneath you."

Rejected in real life by Erich, Ingolf next turned to a figure identified in the journals only as Walter. "God, Walter, do you know what you give to me...I desire you and your dark eyes, your mouth." A few months later Ingolf is "wild with longing" for someone named Hans; at least four major affairs are recorded in 1931 alone.

Others soon followed. By the summer of 1932, when Ingolf was twenty, it was Wolf who "is the center of my consciousness"– this uttered only a few weeks before Hans-Dieter, another contender, breaks the journal keeper's heart once more. "I am in a deep valley...This is a mountain over which I must come...I can't get rid of him, out of the deepest grief I scream."

And when Ingolf had no specific dream object in his heart there remained a generalized longing for new liaisons – "The boy with the beautiful eyes. Will this become an adventure?"Traveling in Venice, in July 1931, Ingolf sees a sailor with an Italian boy at the Doge's palace, and the yearning begins again. In May of 1932, during his trip to Paris, he became infatuated with a medical student who was staying at his hotel. The young man had "unbelievable eyes" and these paralyzed Ingolf in the hotel's gardens – as they stared down from an upstairs window at the adoring visitor below. Two days after the infatuation began Ingolf writes, "He is more beautiful that I first suspected. He lives in me."The next day the entry reads, "I must have him. I love him. His eyes burn into me. I lust for his lips." Ingolf evidently haunted the hotel, hoping to encounter the young man. On the hotel piano the love-struck musician played the *Well-Tempered Klavier*, hoping it would produce some sign of recognition

– "When will he take me into his strong arms?" The following day it was Liszt and ping-pong at the hotel, more waiting, and the reward of seeing the love object return to the hotel with a blonde on his arm. On his bed Ingolf cried, a diet of bread and water adding to his misery as the centimes ran out. On his last day in Paris Ingolf tried one last time to attract the attention of the young Frenchman by playing loudly on the hotel piano. The young man appeared at his window – and slammed it shut.

In Paris Ingolf had received a number of love letters from his friend Wolf. The two had a stormy relationship. In the summer of that same year they walked, hiked, hitchhiked and argued through the Black Forest on their way to Switzerland, which they reached on August 12, 1932. On the 14th they passed through Thun, only a short distance below the town of Frutigen where, thirty-eight years later, Ingolf's story came to an end. Ingolf was on his way to take up residence in Zurich and Wolf to return to Germany. The two parted in Lausanne, where Ingolf concluded, somewhat prematurely, "Wolf is not for me. We are adversaries." His journal twice records in large letters a telling self-evaluation: "THE KEY TO MY NATURE: SENTIMENTALITY AND HYSTERIA."

It is hard to escape the fact that Ingolf's earliest sexual life was full of experiment, if not promiscuity. One of the worlds in which he traveled does resemble Isherwood's Germany, gay and grotty. "Frightful hangover following yesterday evening," becomes a minor refrain in the daybooks of the early Thirties. At the same time, a puritanical streak asserted itself when study or work demanded his fullest attention. When he had to record an "unprofitable" or "wasted" morning he did so with a sigh of regret. What we have here is a personality precariously balanced between the dissolute and the respectable: one night out with boyfriends and the next at some *Musikabend*, where he would be expected to play chamber music at the home of some burgher, to the delight of his hosts and the pride of his parents. It is not surprising that the phrase "*der doppelte Ingolf*" – the twofold or two-sided Ingolf, begins to appear in the journals.

I have no doubt that Ingolf attempted to disguise the more socially unacceptable side of his behavior from most of the members of his family, Anna-Britta being the sole exception. This did not stop his brothers, she recalled in 1995, from speculating on the origins of their youngest sibling's homosexuality. They were convinced that he had been seduced by a male member of staff at one his childhood sanatoria. I also discovered a 1935 letter from Gert in which the younger brother attempts to help the older one get over his infatuation with males and his inability to find happiness in the arms of a woman, problems which Gert related to Ingolf's immaturity or inexperience – rather than to any homosexual inclination. What Pappi was willing to put into writing on the subject also indicates that Ingolf's friendship with males was seen largely as an adolescent phase, one which would soon pass away. Writing about the Ingolf of 1931, Pappi added this sentence to the family history – "He often experienced heartfelt affections for young people of both sexes." But Anna-Britta remembers that Pappi was disturbed by effeminate mannerisms in Ingolf; the way he brushed his lips against the back of his hand irritated Pappi into shouting "Stop that!" more than once. The parents, worried about Ingolf's sexuality, sent a sample of his handwriting to a graphologist, who concluded that the author was a homosexual. There is no evidence that Mammi ever considered any aspect of the personality of her beloved eldest son deficient in any way, though Ingolf, particularly after the arrival of Etta, allowed her to believe that he had straightened himself out. But it is likely that Pappi's preoccupation with the issue lead to a deepening fissure between father and son. Neither of Ingolf's rather conservative brothers ever raised the gay issue with me, even though they knew I was writing about Ingolf. It as if Holger's advice to James Berdahl, "you must tell the story like he did," remained an official Marcus family position. But I *am* now telling the story as Ingolf did – at least in his treasured, cherished, and much-thumbed little red journals.

86. BUT NOT FOR ME

In Zurich Ingolf continued to find many women who were charming, fascinating or beautiful, and he did undertake a number of liaisons with them, as earlier references to his flirtations may have indicated. Some women were the subjects of a romanticized if distant passion, others assumed the position of confidante, like Etta. In his earliest years in Zurich Ingolf repeatedly ascribes this role to a girl named Alice – "I slowly walked through the old town of Zurich in a deep depression to Alice (opium)."

But affairs with women did not command his essential attention, and it is not surprising that social gatherings dominated by heterosexual couples left him unhappy and unsatisfied. Women did find him attractive and this bothered him – "Fraulein Tolenz is charming but there rises for me again the torturing problem of my partiality." During the winter trip to Germany, which he took as part of his first holiday in December of 1932, a time when he and Eva "slept together," it is not surprising to see Kurt's name circled as well. The latter seems to have been the art student who also appears as a character in the *Maskentanz*. Love letters from Kurt speak of Ingolf's beautiful lips and small teeth – "I have to hear you speak, to feel your brown locks and embrace your beautiful body." Ingolf carried such letters close to his heart, but the two never enjoyed a permanent relationship, they lived countries apart, and the political situation in Germany was soon to contribute to a final separation. Lacking the prospects for any permanent male relationship in Zurich, Ingolf, as in Cologne and Hamburg, fell back on the custom of idolizing the faces of strangers.

"The boy with the accordion" or the "peasant who played the brown clarinet" – male faces affected him especially. Sometimes the fact that "there are only pretty boys on the street" seemed "terrible" to the lonely Ingolf. Riding on a tram he is mesmerized by the face of a fair-haired youth with sunken cheeks and rough hands. A teenager with a wise face eats an ice cream cone. Does the beautiful boy with the horn-rimmed glasses represent anything real? In the mountain hut there is a young man with beautiful teeth whose tousled head Ingolf would like to take into his own hands – "I am, after all, perverse." And when that first winter vacation was over a sea of empty faces greeted him on his return to Professor Stadler's class and, scanning them, Ingolf asks, "Where is that which is real?"

It has to be noted that Ingolf was often infatuated with males who were not gay. Anna-Britta recalls an incident during which Ingolf, seated at his Zurich piano, eagerly tried to impress his latest love object who, behind the back of her brother, tried to steal a kiss from his sister. The failure of male friends to respond in a fashion which Ingolf craved may have been, as it was with the Parisian medical student, a factor in several disappointing encounters in 1933, when the "real" eluded Ingolf over and over again.

There was Werner, with whom my future stepfather enjoyed an evening's walk in March and a bitterly disappointing conversation a week later. "A kiss on his rough boy's hand" was all that Ingolf seems to have managed.

Hardi is first mentioned in May of 1933 – "If only he hadn't come into the dressing room with lilacs and his white peasant shirt everything would have been quite, quite different." For several months Ingolf and this boy seem to have pursued a troubled relationship. A mountain trip to Braunwald turned into disaster in early June: "I have cried into my pillow but he doesn't know it." It was all over by July – "Hardi comes with very bitter words. It doesn't matter to me. I know that trap already." To complicate matters, Ingolf also seems to have had an attachment to Hanna, a girl who often appeared at Hardi's side. In October, 1933, Ingolf developed a crush on a man called Tom, a member of the ensemble which performed *Two Hearts In Three Quarters Time*. Smiles were exchanged but not words and, to Ingolf's consternation, a wedding ring was detected on Tom's left hand. A few days later Tom was gone altogether and Ingolf was complaining, "What sense has the evening now?"

This pattern of sentimentality and hysteria prepares us for the depths of depression that followed the most prolonged of these infatuations, one which occurred in 1933 and 1934. His behavior on this occasion, the nervous breakdown which his disappointment engendered, has been described in a much earlier section, but by now the reader will understand that the love object was, of course, a man.

"Now I'm sitting at the University," Ingolf reported on October 18, 1933, "and he just came in." A musical notation is added, and, at some later time, the postscript, "That was the beginning of the end." "This daybook is quite totally pathological," Ingolf added on the 26th, a day in which he went to the campus just for a chance of seeing "him." "I have seen him and immediately longed for him" is the entry for the next day, but by the end of the month and after many tears Ingolf had already taken to his bed, faithful Alice in attendance, "sick because of *him*." "I am not able to live because I despise myself," he added, but the first November entry indicates a short period of recovery, "Saw *him!* He looks at me. He comes toward me. I am mad for happiness. I must speak to him." Ingolf lacked this courage. He dreamed that "his hand was lying on mine," but at the University, "he doesn't take any notice of me...My life belongs to him so much."

When Ingolf finally located the coat of the beloved and slipped into it a note with an unspecified "famous four lines," nothing happened. "His eyes follow me," the frustrated Ingolf wrote two days later, "I must not see him...Everything is over. I should hang myself." The winter vacation ended all chances of sighting the love object in his usual university haunts but Mammi's arrival offered some solace. When she departed on January 17, 1934 ("alone," her abandoned son wrote), hell began again, though, surprisingly, Ingolf could balance his unrequited passion with a pragmatic sifting of new candidates in both sexes. It was on February 10, 1934 that he recorded his lust for Maya Kubler – "the first woman I could fall in love with without conditions. She is unbelievable." The next day, as if to illustrate the essential problem, he caught sight of a fair-haired student whizzing down the ski slopes. Abandoning a companion, he decided to pursue the vision. When he finally neared his goal he discovered that the blonde head belonged to a girl! "It's not tolerable," Ingolf complained, "I would have driven the flies away from a sleeping boy, she drives me away."

In 1957 Ingolf wrote a letter to Bill Colvig in which something of the complex emotional atmosphere of early 1934 is recaptured: the letter also introduces a new male figure and a new relationship. The day described was February 17, 1934:

> During the carnival season I was taken to a fancy costume ball (an artists' ball) by my friend Ernst, to whom I was more or less a kept boy...Although he was a decent enough person he was really quite unattractive and much older than I and physically meant less than nothing to me. But I had just been through such a fantastically unhappy and unsuccessful crush that I was emotionally much too worn out and apathetic to resist when he made a big play for me. We went together for a couple of years, and once he took me to Venice. Anyway, there was a costume ball (always that eager anticipation: "maybe tonight -?", almost always disappointment afterwards) and I had made *quite* a costume for myself. Suffice it to say that it was in the style of abstract art, including metal ribbons, and it revealed quite a bit of skin. After the end of the ball I found myself in my room with several people whom I had asked to come up for coffee...Ernst had brought with him a young man who was costumed as a sailor and was very attractive. He was probably square, but yet intrigued by the other side. Ernst was teasing us in a rather cruel way (at one point he was saying: Come on, Hans, give Ingolf a kiss) but before any damage was done I had to leave with my skis. However, I did make a date with this costumed sailor boy to meet him next night after my performance [of the *Rhapsody in Blue*]...of course, he never showed up, and there was another blow.

In the diaries of 1933 and 1934 Ernst appears as a companion and, presumably, lover. The two take walks together in the rain, they have dinner, Ingolf makes coffee for his friend, they make plans for the summer holidays. But Ernst is described as "half-loved" only. "He is no problem at the moment and I am true to him," Ingolf wrote in June of 1934, but it is clear that such fidelity resulted only from the lack of more exciting opportunities.

Ingolf's relationships with other men in 1934 also proved to be unsatisfactory; none could rival the wholly loved but unattainable object. René, André, Jonny – the pursuit of these young men in the spring was undermined by that debilitating fixation on "him," a fixation that caused all other passions to pale. Thus in February we find Ingolf returning to his quest, at least to the point of discovering at last the name of the loved one. "Shock upon shock! " he records on February 26, "His name in Peter… Peter!!! This name I would like to shout out with all my strength." Peter's presence continually served to haunt his ardent admirer. Suddenly "he" is at a performance of *Arabella* – "the world turns round." At three o'clock Peter comes running down the steps. He is "radiantly beautiful, tanned, arrogant." Peter, it is discovered, eats his lunch at the student dormitory so, Ingolf explains, "I'll have to got there at noon."

On July 6th Ingolf saw something that caused hell to open up again – Peter at a lakeside review with a girl, a silly woman in a blue dress whose side "he" did not leave all night long – "I remain under the trees and see his hair directly in front of me and his hand grasp that of the girl. In the morning everything comes to an end. His eyes are darker than ever. I see him for the last time on the ship. Goodbye, Peter. My head floats away in the *Bahnhof* restaurant." The farewell on this occasion was Ingolf's own, for he was about to depart "on a journey to Sweden because of love-sickness."

The turbulent pattern of his erotic life continued after his recovery from nervous exhaustion at Mammi's side. Wolf made another appearance in Ingolf's life and then there was an affair with a Slavic dancer, who spent "the entire night with me, he can't resist me." This was the dancer whose jealousy was aroused when he discovered Ingolf walking with one of the Stadttheater's female singers on the Quaibridge on November 18, 1934. The next day it was the volatile singer's turn to cry on Ingolf's neck. She attended the December 19th afternoon performance of the Theater's Christmas presentation, a day which may have marked Ingolf's conducting debut, but the jealous Slav came up shouting at the interval, addressing his former lover with the impersonal *Sie*, causing the world to go quite dark. "He has such beautiful hands, such shimmering eyes... He is quite diabolically beautiful." So how could Ingolf give himself to the singer when the dancer remained so constant a preoccupation? On January 12th, 1935 flowers were dispatched to the man as Ingolf headed to the train station for a tryst with the woman. A "crazy" night in Baden followed, full of tension, disappointment, many tears from his partner, and at the end, Ingolf reported, "Everything is still in suspension." On January 17th the frustrated singer actually confronted her Slavic rival, returning to Ingolf with agonizing news. "He has been playing with me. He despises me because I am too feminine," Ingolf now admitted. References to the dancer all but disappear from the journals and those that remain indicate that Ingolf quickly recovered from this passion and that (one hopeful sign of maturity) he was even able to maintain a subsequent friendship with his former lover. But in spite of a second and more successful outing with the singer, Ingolf's life was still incomplete. Four days after this assignation he went looking for Peter in the *Studheim*.

Threatened by female passion, Ingolf now insisted that, "Peter is the god to whom I pray. I am raging with longing for him." The threatened singer seems to have known everything about Ingolf's long-term infatuation with the statue on the pedestal and she was now prepared to take action against this phantom – as earlier she had dispatched the Slavic dancer. As she and Ingolf walked down the street on February 14th she announced a campaign to "desanctify Peter." "That must not be," Ingolf protested, and a week later it was the lady who found herself banished from Ingolf's romantic life. "I can't. It's in the stars," Ingolf complained, "I can't have a wife." This must be seen, in retrospect, as an ironic utterance, for on December 27th Ingolf had met a new sympathetic listener, a rare spirit who could listen to these homoerotic yearnings and still love the teller of the tale, a woman who would succeed in desanctifying Peter when others had failed, the woman who would be Ingolf's wife for thirty years – my mother.

87. THE PLAN OF THE KNIFE AND THE BLOOD

My discovery of the written evidence left behind by my parents had a twofold effect. The missing parts of my stepfather's story made complete, at last, this enigmatic character who had played such a central role in my own life. But the more I learned about my mother, the more mystified I became. To this day *her* story remains the more baffling of the two.

Why, for instance, did she chose to love a man whose preoccupation with men must have menaced the very possibility of any permanent union? Could she have considered his infatuation with Peter, into which she was soon drawn as witness and coach, merely the last echoes of an adolescent homoeroticism? Did she really believe that the love of a good woman could bring about the desired cure?

It was not possible for me to ask either of the principal figures in this unlikely romance such pointed questions, but my father, whom I visited in Palm Springs in the late 70's, was willing to talk to me about a number of intimate matters, including, for instance, the psychotherapy that the Linicks had undergone in Zurich. Leroy was not comfortable with my questions, but he answered honestly. He also told me something of the open marriage philosophy which he and my mother had embraced from the very start of their married life, quoting Etta as saying to him in 1928, "I don't care what you do as long as you come back to me." But aboard the *Resolute*, on their first transatlantic crossing that summer, the honeymooner who slipped off for a night with one of the sailors was Etta herself. Leroy told me that he was slow to adopt the pragmatic approach to the demands of Eros which the liberated Etta so openly encouraged through her own behavior, but that during their Zurich days they were both seeing other people. Playing around did not suit his nature any more than it did that of the more mature Etta. The *Resolute* episode left him with a profound respect for monogamy and, he added mischievously, a profound distaste for travel by sea. He also confirmed that there was no doubt in the Linick household that Ingolf was gay.

So no one can explain why Etta allowed herself to embrace a fascination, both enriching and fatal, with the idolater of Peter. How could she give herself heart and soul to a man who was so keenly infatuated with this young man, one whom they had *both* come to observe, two tables away, at the student restaurant? Surely she must have sensed his "barrier," as Ingolf called it, though she would have been cheered by the resolution he seems to have taken at the end of their first weekend sojourn together. "Tomorrow evening," Ingolf wrote on July 11th, "is Peter's death day." A meeting had at last been arranged on the 12th, and on July 13 it was Ingolf who sat at Peter's *Studheim* table at noontime. It would have been poetic justice if Etta had been able to observe, from her own table, the great demystification taking place because there is no doubt that she had predicted the outcome. Finding the beloved one to be "so stupid," Ingolf was able to conclude, "Peter no longer suits me erotically."

Ingolf and Etta, in the early months of their own affair, had much to overcome in pursuit of their love for one another. There were rival affections, particularly on Ingolf's part, that threatened their happiness: some of these have been mentioned in an earlier chapter, some were to come after Etta had left, a long relationship with a chap named Heini, for instance. But even while the two were together there were monumental impediments. Etta was another man's wife, an American visitor, and the prospects for continuing the relationship on a permanent basis must have seemed dim. Then fate, in the form of her mother's fatal illness, intervened to snatch Etta away, just as the love affair was achieving its apotheosis, and Ingolf had to endure both separation and, months later, the news that Etta was expecting Leroy's child. No opera librettist could have fashioned a more bittersweet plot. But the greatest impediment of all, Ingolf's continuing affection for men, would not be mentioned as part of this family saga in years to come. Yet examining his journals it is possible to see just how large a part in his life this affection was, even *before* Etta departed Zurich.

Shortly after his return to to the city at the end of his 1935 holiday in Stockholm, Ingolf spent a night with a student from Basle named Hans. Unfortunately they had failed to lock the door and were discovered. There was a minor scandal and Hans disappeared without a word, leaving a pining Ingolf to complain, "He seems to be a coldly forgetful person." Months later Ingolf saw Hans while visiting a Basle Museum. Hans criticized his former lover for "being too cultured." "My old fate again," Ingolf added, knowing that this was the one charge that Etta, who was also sharing his bed, would never bring against him. Then on January 25th, 1936, Ingolf set out for a rendezvous in Colmar with Wolf.

Who knows what Etta would have concluded about Ingolf's sexual direction had she remained in Zurich? Her abrupt departure on April 29th left this question and the question of their entire future together in suspension. As we have seen in an earlier chapter there followed a long period in which Ingolf feared for the worst, especially when Etta and her husband made one last attempt to save their marriage after Leroy's return to Los Angeles.

Her pregnancy came from this attempt and it too, I discovered, was the subject of comment in "The Talon: A Novel Fragment by Etta Linick," the autobiographical sketch bearing the inscription "Copyright Screen Writers Guild, September 12, 1938." I have quoted extensively from this document already, but there is perhaps one remaining section that needs to be added now, another example of the surprises that awaited the son-biographer when I began my examination of the manuscripts left behind by my parents.

The pregnancy had just asserted itself when Leroy announced that he was in love with Delphine Weiler. Etta willingly agreed to a divorce, though it would take some time and, in those days, someone was required to take the blame in the courts in order to receive a bill of divorcement. Etta now refers in *The Talon* to the unborn child "as the epitome of our miserable union." She implies that there was a period when suicide held its appeal, but that such an ending was at last discarded. "I am too fond of Galby its father to people the rest of his life with two ghosts." Another remedy was proposed:

> It is the plan of the knife and the blood. The child knows nothing. It leaps and lies on this side of me or that. It will be born and reared but if it were now hushed by the plan of the knife and the blood there would no longer be the gravity of its existence...We believe that in this plan there is present pain yet future mercy for us all. It is a hideous plan only in name; in deed it is an honest plan and a good one.

The illegal operation was evidently scheduled. "In a part of me," Etta wrote, "there was resolution and thankfulness at the vision of starting my new life without the child who was conceived in error. But my flesh crept and I was confused in another part of me." In the event, no abortion was performed. At the last moment, Etta confirms, it was determined that "the child was already too long in me for the knife." I asked my father to confirm this account of my arrival on the scene. He distanced himself from the abortion idea, but agreed that Etta *had* made plans for such an operation. Thus I was born.

My mother always insisted that I was a wanted child, and I have no evidence, testamentary or emotional, to doubt that my presence on the scene was welcomed enthusiastically by all concerned. But when Etta refers to her *new* life she is talking about her new life with Ingolf who, cutting all ties with his European past, national, ethnic, familial, and erotic, had agreed to make his life at her side in the new world.

Thus I was soon to start living the life of a lie. Ingolf Dahl, Swedish native, come to be the lover of Etta and the father of the new infant, arrived in our house on February 15, 1939, when I was not yet fourteen months old. His name wasn't Ingolf Dahl (yet), he was not a Swede but a German, his people were not "Lutherans," but atheists and Jews, he was totally unprepared for the role of father (though he made much progress here) and as for his relationship with Etta – this we have already seen was bedeviled from the outset by his homoerotic disposition. We are certainly in a better position now to understand the complex and desperate nature of the early years of their married life.

88. MY DEAR CAPTAIN

When, twelve months after his arrival in America, Ingolf writes, "For a year I have not touched a boy," we have a cry of despair, not a triumph of reformation. His decision to marry Etta could not, given his very nature, carry with it the ability to expunge the homoerotic nexus of his sexual orientation. Etta may have deluded herself that this was a part of the past, but we can now see that Ingolf's "partiality" explains, at last, the great difficulties that this couple endured in the early years of their marriage: Etta's longing for physical contact, Ingolf's inability to summon the requisite passion.

Walking along Santa Monica Beach in July, 1939, Ingolf spots a figure who stirs a hurricane of emotions. Returning to the same spot a week later he finds the desired object in the company of others, outside his reach, and the quest continues. (In the same year and on the same beach, so Christopher Isherwood tells us, *he* carried out this search too.) A masculine figure at the La Cienega pool causes agitation for Ingolf a few weeks later. At Del Mar, the following March, a long-legged, tanned youth in faded red trunks makes the musician fall into "the bottomless depths...Will I ever possess such a one again?" Ingolf's wistful ogling had gotten him into some bother a month earlier. He had been dazedly staring at a candidate, encountered at a viewpoint in Elysian Park, when the recipient of the gaze snapped, "What are you looking at, Bud?" Embarrassed, Ingolf scurried away, his blood turned to ice – "This must not happen again."

During the Lorand tour in San Francisco in the fall of 1939 we find him searching in vain for a male companion and, failing in his attempt, brooding obsessively over the last of his Swiss lovers, Heini. A vision of the naked Heini "which throws me almost to the ground" overcomes him as he waits his turn in the allergy clinic. On March 16, 1941, Ingolf and Etta went to see *Kitty Foyle*, starring Ginger Rogers. Then a shattering occurrence: "Dennis Morgan seems incredibly similar to *Heini*." This experience took place months after that lonely San Francisco autumn in 1939, when Ingolf had filled a large box in the middle of the October 27th entry with the legend, "Screaming Despair for Heini." What makes this entry more pathetic is that it shares space with a comment about my mother, who was on a four- day visit to San Francisco – "I love her and we have it beautifully with one another and yet I am always so limitlessly gloomy and desperate." While Etta was able, in the early stages of their marriage, to gloss over Ingolf's deficiencies, to settle for a "recurrent enchantment," and to claim that, "We are not so much pathological as extraordinary," there would certainly be limits to her patience.

Ingolf continued to mourn the loss of male companionship, to moon over lost opportunities with cute male hitchhikers, to marvel at Apollos on the beach. A boy at a choir audition has a heavenly face, a sailor has brown velvety eyes and long lashes. Rehearsing for the all-Toch concert at City College in December, 1940, Ingolf sees a half-bare boy racing by on a bicycle, an angel, a slim blonde youth with golden hair on his chest. "Whether I'm awake or asleep," he writes, "I dream like an old spinster." Could the fact that "Etta is again difficult," which Ingolf recorded on July

17, 1940, be related in any way to Ingolf's obvious agitation at the presence of a baritone, who had stopped by the house for coffee?

That summer the Dahls were working on a children's opera. When I read what Etta had produced for *Sandy And The Singing Rocks* I was struck by her description of the character known as Valentine Cactus, a character who is:

> as prickly a cactus as you would ever want to meet. This unfortunate exterior hides a soft and even very romantic interior. This is Valentine's trouble. What use is his amorous disposition, if no young lady is brave enough to penetrate behind the needles...if only one would come along and not mind the danger of being stuck...something which up until now every lovely girl *has* minded *very* much.

It is interesting to contrast this unintentional parody of her relationship with Ingolf with her husband's plaint, written during his tour with Gracie Fields in 1942, "I should fall in love again. I would be happier in unhappiness. I would at least burn." Instead he was gazing at the beautiful, athletic male dancers of the Ballet Russe ("They don't see me") and fruitlessly cruising the streets of Greenwich Village in search of an adventure. "That's me in the mirror? At the expensive luncheon in the garden of the Museum of Modern Art? Where does life drift me? Why alone??? Oh could I show all this to Mammi...Am I so hideous? So negligible?"

The journal entries of this period resemble in their desperation the blackest moods of his Zurich days. It is at this stage that one is entitled to consider whether Ingolf really tried to hang himself. After leaving the daybook blank for two weeks he tells us, on September 15, 1942, of the dark urge (*der dunkel Drang*) and that he has sprained his neck severely.

It is with increasing desperation that he catches glimpses of unreachable happiness all about him. At the Bimini baths, for instance, while I am trying not to drown during my swimming lesson, Ingolf is ogling the other swimmers. Outside the NBC studios, where he went daily to play for Gracie's radio show, the eyes of a sailor dazzle him. On February 11, 1943, he stops to give two boys a ride. One of them, sitting close to the driver, puts his arm behind Ingolf's shoulders, prompting the query, "Why is life so difficult?"

Etta tried many times to get Ingolf to discuss their marital problems openly; each time she was met with rationalizations, evasions, and subterfuges. At one point Ingolf seized on the theory of sexual cycles to explain why he always seemed to be on the *wrong* cycle when Etta was in the right one.

In her attempt to fashion some semblance of an erotic life, Etta then tried an even more desperate tactic. On March 12, 1943, Ingolf played for Gracie at the British United Services Club. Glasses were lifted to "Gentlemen, the King!" At home he observed that Etta was writing a letter, wondering ominously in his journal, "To whom?" The next day he received two phone calls. One was from Igor Stravinsky. The other was from Etta. The letter in question was for Ingolf, and her call told him where he could find it. It survives, and I reprint it now. Of all the materials I uncovered among Ingolf's files in 1971, none, I have to say, brought me more trauma than this document. Not having read the journals yet I failed to understand its context and it presented me with a stranger for a mother, cheapening and dishonoring her image in my eyes. These feelings have long since passed. I know so much more about the origins of so unique a love letter:

> My dear captain:
> I have after much thought and deliberation made the none-too-happy decision that I am too young and lusty and sea-worthy a ship to stand idle in the harbor for the better part of my existence.
> I have decided that although you are and always will be the captain of my home port I cannot stand almost perpetually still with the weather beating on me until I warp when I should be out on the bounding water, whipped by the brine and full of cargo.
> If you have not seen the signs of my warping, then it is because – I do not condemn you – you have had eyes and ears only for your navigation charts, your beautiful marine drawings, your studies in latitude and longitude – all those things which for you are really gratifying if not even more gratifying than sailing your ship. And now you are coming to be recognized as the great navigator that you are and ever more charts and maps and writings on your art are being asked of you. You are well absorbed. As you sit and work you can look out over the sea, but rarely do you wish to sail out, for you can sail with no hazard whatever and with rare delight in the vast waters of your mind.

And down below I have always waited restless for those rare times when it pleased you to sail. And I do not wish to convey that these voyages have not afforded us pleasure and yet they have been too few.

Other captains have walked by where I was moored and wondered.

But though I have wanted to lift a flag in signal it has always been a half-hearted, semi-invitation with my eye always turned up toward your study window. Nor is it easy to go on a voyage with a strange captain (I recall with vivid abhorrence my days as a tramp steamer). There are so few captains with whom I would sail. They must be only of the finest. And when they are fine they are certain to be shy, as I too am shy for all my aching to sail. I seem only to care for captains who need courage, and I myself need courage so much. Then, too, the only captains I could care for are (since they must be of the finest) the type of captain who would prefer to have an unborrowed ship; one for his very own for always. Just as I myself would infinitely prefer at base to be the ship of one captain. So if and when I manage to convey to a captain that I will sail with him or he with me, we will both have to swallow our distaste for impermanence and sail out of mutual need.

On the voyages I know that there will be dangerous rocks. I have thought of these rocks and I have stood with my keel in the mud of low-tide and I know that there are many and scarcely avoidable. And I have shuddered and glanced up to where you live in your lighthouse and watched you lavish your inmost being on your marine art. And you have completed a fine bit of it and been spent, just as spent as if you had been sailing on a hard, stormy sea voyage. And it is in these times that I have come to the painful belief that it is more in my ship's-nature to sail at all cost and risk crash than to mark time in sterile waiting in port.

It has taken the better part of a year for me to make this choice which I now make with no little trepidation and with no great evidence of spirit. I have, if you recall, made mention of the germ of this choice as far back as early last fall. As always when I have spoken thus and pulled openly at my anchor you have momentarily become acutely aware that sailing is a fine sport, dropped your compasses and gone on several quick voyages to lovely ports. And on your return you were immediately engaged in converse with other navigators who heaped you with toil, some gainful and honor-bringing and much just honor-bringing, but all not only justifiable but necessary to your happiness and well being. And I know again that there would be a long voyage-less time with you steeped in your sedentary sailing.

I promise faithfully if and when I sail with another captain to sail only in the blackest night and in places where I cannot possibly be seen. And I promise to keep my decks spotless and to take great care to keep my hold free of strange cargoes of fruit. Since the taste I have for strange captains will only rarely be satisfied – by reason of their being only the finest – I will no doubt not be compelled to voyage away very often. But that I will one day glide temporarily off is certain.

You will see no change in my affection for you. On the other hand, a certain tenseness of my daily life with you will be absent. And this will be most welcome. I know of no captain at the moment who would want to take me out to sea. Nor can I imagine myself boldly flagging one. It is all very difficult. But it cannot be worse than the intense dissatisfaction of my contra-natural existence of the past many months, when I have stood and scuttled myself many times over in my imagination.

You know me well enough to realize that this is no mere clever ship's bulletin calculated to make you more voyage-minded. Whom would that in all honesty benefit? You have your natural inclinations and must abide by them. I too have mine and have reached the point where they are no longer adaptable to yours. May the sea-gods blow us both luck.

The tears fell as Ingolf read this letter. "She is so right," he noted in his dairy, "I have compassion for her, for me." Nowhere does he comment on the actual text, the elaborate and labored metaphor which Etta uses to make her point. This device is so typical of these strange people. Ingolf was often accused of substituting art for life. Literature, Etta complained to her confidante Constance Buchanan, was not for Ingolf something to enrich life; it is "the *real* thing." But Etta also found that life was easier if approached with the language and referents of the arts.

Did Etta persevere in her decision to seek out other lovers? She did, but only sporadically and on the whole unsuccessfully. On April 26th Ingolf noted, "Etta has doctor's meeting. I go to bed at 3, she's still not at home, comes about 4-5. Next morning don't see her. During lunch again read Dear captain, Oh God, has it come so far? I am horribly agitated, knowing that I am to blame." The following year, in an attempt to assure Ingolf of his own abilities as a lover, she wrote, "I prefer your love-making to anybody's and as you know I recently availed myself of the opportunity to make a comparison with a man who must have had two dozen affairs."

Etta had a number of motives in writing the Dear Captain letter, though – except for hints in the last paragraph – a frank discussion of Ingolf's "natural inclinations" was not one of them. She obviously hoped to awaken Ingolf's awareness of her need for a more frequent and fulfilling monogamous love life, and on April 20, 1944, we find her far off base in proposing to him, "It would be useful also, in trying to discover the true nature & extent of your sexual apathy to know how & if other women arouse you at all & to what extent" – this to a man who is overcome in the dentist's office with longing for Heini – "your hands, your stomach, your soft flesh."

On November 27th, 1943, Ingolf made his first appearance at the downtown branch of the YMCA, where the sight of so many naked boys in the shower room (including a black lad who received eight exclamation marks) proved to be very stimulating indeed. In his dreams of this period he is pursued by male lovers to whom he must surrender, but in real life he seems to have gotten no closer to a real affair than a date in December with a boy named Dale, who turned out to be a "boring, lifeless amoeba." There were moments when Etta directly interfered with his fantasy life. Once he brought home a skiing companion with whom he was smitten, but Etta deflated this love object by referring to him dismissively as "a nice kid." When my parents took a vacation to San Francisco in 1943 they were approached, as they walked along the street, by a sailor and two attractive boys in a car. This trio asked the Dahls if they wanted a lift. Without consulting her panting husband, Etta snapped out a quick, "No thank you." "I want to scream, to tear up something and to rage," a disappointed Ingolf added after this incident.

With this new evidence it has been possible to reconstruct the sources of the marital discontent that disturbed the Dahl household in the initial years of their marriage. In another partnership the word divorce would have been uttered, but there is no evidence that this oddest of couples considered this choice to be one of their options, for, as Ingolf noted, "The worse thing, in spite of all we love each other. My love to her!!! She is the only *woman* I could ever love."

89. THE HEART IS ALIVE

In February, 1944, Ingolf, as Gracie Fields' accompanist, returned to New York as part of a second, extensive tour. He visited old friends and made a visit to the YMCA on February 18th. On the 23rd someone smiled at him there. "We make a date for tomorrow night at my hotel. I have to swim forth and back to cool off." Later that night he called Etta, "her voice – so calm and clear. Etta –, my wife." The day of the assignation came: "I am feverish – frantic – hysterical. My head spins." When the door was opened disappointment walked in – "instead of Stevie, it's Bill. He stays with me, he is an angel." The next day (headed "At last!!!") Stevie kept his date. For the first time in over five years Ingolf had slept with a man. A few days later we find him trying his luck at the Boston Y – "I will accept the inconvenience of hs. [homosexuality] but I will *not* tolerate suffering and torture again. Is that possible? Isn't that a completely unrealistic construction?" Ingolf was about to test the matter, for on April 17th he met Douglas at the Boston Y.

Douglas was a gay collegian (with literary ambitions) whose studies had been interrupted by wartime service in one of the naval branches of the armed forces. Ingolf made a date with the sailor and in great excitement got through the evening's show, playing *Rhapsody in Blue* in the solo spot and thinking of the time, ten years earlier, when he had played the same piece as he looked forward to a meeting with the costume ball sailor in Zurich. The waiting had been in vain then, but this time Douglas appeared. "I am so happy," Ingolf wrote. "The answer to so many prayers is here. The solution. Don't sleep a wink all night but don't mind it." Ingolf was once again in love.

The next day was spent "on clouds," as Ingolf waited for another evening rendezvous, his thoughts full of the hair, the deep eyes, the lips, the hands of his lover. Douglas arrived in uniform. "I am the luckiest," Ingolf exulted. On April 9th, however, Gracie's Boston schedule came to an end, and Ingolf had to depart, terribly upset at leaving his new lover behind. As the tour progressed into the Midwest, thoughts of Douglas forced out all other considerations. "D. is in my head and heart and thoughts and blood incessantly." He then wrote to Douglas, proposing a second Boston rendezvous at the end of Gracie's tour and warning himself, "Ingolf you have to be prepared for a no answer from D. It *must* not throw you if it happens."The reply from Douglas remained his sole preoccupation for days. In Lansing on April 21st (no wonder he couldn't remember the M.S.U. auditorium) Ingolf wrote, "He *will* say no. He cannot constitutionally say yes. And against my better judgment I hope." On April 24th, after two weeks of suspense, Ingolf opened the long-awaited reply in his Louisville hotel room – "Come to me the minute your tour is over."

A complete hysterical breakdown followed, Ingolf unable to stop crying. "Something broke," he wrote, and I think we can generalize at this point by saying that, whatever the outcome of his affair in Boston, this experience had confirmed his absolute need for male companionship, helping him to overcome some of the barriers that had kept him from sexual fulfillment for so long. Life would be different from this point on.

When Gracie's show got to Cincinnati on April 29th Ingolf went slumming with two servicemen and ended up in a kind of sleepless octopus sandwich between the Army and the Navy. This all took place at the Netherland Hotel where his innocent stepson would deliver a paper at the Popular Culture Association convention a third of a century later.

From Toronto, where the tour ended on May 9th, Ingolf made his way in great anticipation to Boston. (I do not know what explanation he offered to Etta for this delay in his return.) Douglas, "more beautiful than I ever thought him to be," was at the train station. The sailor "borrowed" a rowboat on the Charles but an oar broke. Ingolf later remembered his partner's words – "First break it, then abandon it" – as prophetic; his own heart was about to suffer the same fate.

During the five days that followed Ingolf copied out parts for his new brass piece at the Copley Plaza during the day and at night waited for some sign of renewed interest in lovemaking. The night of May 12th is described as "utter catastrophe." When Douglas cancelled their meeting the next day, Ingolf wrote, "Hell has caught up with me...Go to Charles River Park and there, behind bush, cry my eyes out." In this deepest despair the first thoughts of a composition entitled "Elegy" came to Ingolf. He was still at work on a piece with this title twenty-five years later and one wonders if any of its musical materials can actually be traced back to this moment.

Ingolf left Boston, after more tears, on May 15th. "It was all fate," he later wrote to Douglas, "I don't blame you personally at all. You have no control over your feelings and it just happened that I didn't interest you sexually any more." In fact the two kept up a correspondence for a number of years, with Ingolf at first signing his letters "Ingrid" to confound the naval censors. Ingolf visited Douglas several times during visits to New York and when his young friend wrote of a disappointment in romance Ingolf offered advice which may be seen as a summary of his final thoughts on this episode in his own life, "Douglas, suffer! And sigh for joy that your heart is alive, that you are able to be intoxicated by the pain of its beat, by the size of its agony. You know what it means 'the heart is alive.' It happens so seldom in life. To most people never. It happened to you – suffer and sing, even if tears choke your voice."

Ingolf returned to Los Angeles, after three months, on May 19th, 1944. "Etta is there (long walk through the station to her, accelerando). Embrace, tears." Two days later he wrote, "Here I am in my 'butch existence' and a week ago – I can't believe it." Employment worries, suicidal thoughts, dreams of boys, tears, mad searches of the mail for the next letter from Boston, this was the fabric of his life for the next few weeks. "I have a choice of fraud or gay misery," he wrote on May 24th, "there is no other way." No other way for most husbands, but Ingolf was married to an exceptional woman. On July 19th Ingolf finished his work at the Hollywood Canteen, visions of Douglas disturbing him, and returned to the house. Etta was crying. She had discovered Douglas' letters. "At last I got her to see it," Ingolf reports, "The greatest of all triumphs!!! Thank you, Lord. It is beautiful with her." The following night another long and deep talk took place under the pepper tree – "She is so marvelous." With the evidence before her, Etta had at last agreed to accept as her husband the real Ingolf and not the fraudulent one. Three days later Ingolf noted, "Afternoon try to sleep first. Then Etta comes & it is lovely!!" In the Dear Captain letter she had notified him that he must share her, so now she had agreed to share him. The emotional costs of this sacrifice on all parties are not easy to calculate and everybody paid over and over again for this kind of detente.

"It was unfortunate," Douglas wrote in August, "that she should learn of your 'paramour' in Boston through an unkind turn of Fate. Her sense of values, her understanding, or, perhaps, her stoicism are not often paralleled.

Yet I wonder if such detachment is not gained at a constant expense of tears." This was putting the issue well. All that needs to be added at this point is that Etta, by her decision to remain as Ingolf's wife, agreed to accept as well his frequent sexual absences, balancing against the inevitable bitterness those special moments of erotic fulfillment she was still able to find in his arms. "It is beautiful with Etta," Ingolf wrote on July 29th and on April 1, 1945 he added, after another successful encounter with his wife, "I *am* bisexual."

Etta, in fact, remained his most frequent partner for some time – even though Ingolf was living in a new era in which he enjoyed her tacit blessing in his search for male companionship. Such a search continued to be full of disappointments. Another sailor approached him briefly with a pointed suggestion in the shower of the Y, but Ingolf never saw the chap again. A date was made with a young man who followed him as he walked along Sunset after visiting Stravinsky, but the next day the fellow failed to show up. In San Francisco, where he was accompanying Gracie at Treasure Island, Ingolf met some guys at the Y. who entered his hotel room and stole several objects, including a watch that had been a present from Heini.

With this sorry record and the constant tension over employment prospects it is little wonder that Ingolf suffered from depression for many months. "I am just a shell, with nothing inside, no thoughts, no feeling, no sex," he wrote on October 1, 1944. "I am so unhappy because I am not alive," he added early in 1945. In June of that year, however, there was a brief episode, the first that Ingolf felt comfortable enough to consummate in Los Angeles after six years here. While eating dinner at the Gourmet – during a break from some radio work – he met a young man named Byron. Drinks followed, as did sex in an office at the radio station. "He is very lovely," Ingolf wrote, "But those terrible qualms of conscience" (by which Ingolf meant, Do I tell him that I'm married?), "If I tell him, I would lose him and I need him." The problem did not last for long. Ingolf reports that the next day he was still "on clouds...I am loved again. The heart is alive," but five days later Byron had shown his deficiencies. He "doesn't show up well in society – quite cringing," and he lacked a brain. So, "it won't work out. Another failure (God, how much can one take?)." On March 31, 1945, after an all too brief encounter with a sailor in the Y shower, Ingolf returned home to color tiger-striped Easter eggs for Tony. "This is 'family,'" he wrote, "and order and the regularity for which I make my choice..."

90. TWO GUYS AND A GAL

Many things changed for our family in 1945. We moved to Corning Street and Ingolf, employment worries behind him at last, took up his post at U.S.C. From the evidence provided by the journals I would say that romantic or erotic matters, with one exception, were pushed very much into the background of a life devoted so wholeheartedly to career building and music making. Ingolf's relationship with Etta is rarely mentioned in the journals of this period, but when it does appear it is obvious that there has been little change. Visiting a Rubens and Van Dyke exhibition at the Museum on January 1, 1947, Ingolf reports, "Etta looks so nice and is so attractive, where is the solution to the half-problem?" "Etta is close and last night stirred me up. I'm so much attracted," he added on May 7. But these were rare instances of a spontaneous feeling which Etta, for her own reasons, seems to have been in the process of squelching just at this time. On January 17, 1946, he mentions "the fatal talk with E – which this time really ends before the blank wall. I am dumbfounded and just can't accept it. She is right, but it just can't be."

What was discussed is not clear, but there exists a letter dated only July 9, perhaps sent to Ingolf while he was touring with Gracie in the summer of 1946. Here Etta is quite specific about the direction of their marriage, how it is they have managed to survive to this point, and what she proposes to do (or not to do) about it. With the exception of the penultimate paragraph, which dealt with another topic, I now include this July 9 letter in its entirety. The insights that this document provide bring us as close as we can get to an understanding of that remarkably complex being who was my mother:

Igu dear,

I believe that you have been suffering quite needlessly in that part of you where all of us suffer deepest and most, namely in your ego, and I hope by the time you finish reading this your ego will have been somewhat mended. I am writing you this instead of telling you, tho you have heard some of it before, because I believe, with your tendency to ignore what you don't want to acknowledge (a surprisingly good and successful tactic in many instances) that in the past you have been inclined to treat everything I have said in the spirit of "this too will pass." Even as I write, I have no assurance that you will take what I have to say earnestly, and I probably will never know, since I have quite given up expecting you to express yourself. I'm not even angry about it. All I can do is express myself.

I realize full well that this kind of life I have selected for myself, like entering a nunnery, is off balance. But, like a nunnery, it offers certain advantages, among them an overt pattern of emotional equilibrium, no matter what goes on within the person. I can only hope that with time I won't acquire any "peculiar" characteristics, as a result of living thus unnaturally. But when I had reflected over a long period of time over the alternative, presented by a life of occasional intimacy with you, I chose it deliberately, having become increasingly cowardly about emotional upheaval and having had more than my fill of it. But it is very important to me that no one catch wind of my inner conflict from my outward demeanor, especially my raison d'etre (per forza), Tony, and to this end I have been working harder on my manner than the Bankhead ever slaved over the nuances of her best roles. I doubt that even my sister is aware of anything, and I never confided in her, in spite of our intimacy, by so much as the lift of an eyebrow.

Before I go further, I must anticipate two things. One, when I have finished you will come up with your leit-motif "you always look on the dark side of things," which I am perfectly willing to acknowledge by at least two-thirds, and two, no matter how objective I claim to be in an analysis of your character, you will believe that there is covert contempt in it, and that I am not being merely realistic, as I claim, but also antagonistic. Neither of these is true, but I cannot prevent your thinking them. I might suggest, at the risk of being way off, that you are possibly suffering from a certain amount of self-contempt, or self-antagonism, and that you have carried it over into me. But I have none of it.

My analysis of your character is, like anyone else's sincere analysis of anything, only a setting down or "this is how I see it," and makes no claim to authenticity in the absolute (if indeed there can be an appraisal of character in the absolute). Someone else, writing on the same subject, would size you up very differently no doubt. It is a little like two painters putting the same subject on canvas. I believe that emotionally you are and always will be an adolescent, although mentally, intellectually, socially, and professionally (with an exception I will touch on later) you are mature, and increasingly mature all the time. There is this very definite cleavage in you, and it is the basis for a great deal of your despair, as it haunts you enough without any reminder on my part. What I mean by delightfulness is this: adolescence is the time when adventure, experiment, novelty, love of hazard, contra-moral experience, enthusiasm, great spiritual energy, etc. are rampant. Most people become increasingly sedate, get over wanting to try new things, shy away from hazard, become crystallized. This has not and never will happen to you, to which for the most part I say thank God. You have something very precious which most people can only look back upon with nostalgia. In sex, adolescence is a jumble of quick, not deep, but very exciting experiences, an amazing succession of allegiances. Since it is a time of being "in love with love" it is not the object but the ever-new experience which is paramount. The sting is the thing, and since the initial sting goes out of an attraction to be replaced by boredom (in immaturity) a quick turnover of objects becomes a necessity. It is a time when we discover what wonderful instruments we are for producing sensations. Being a fine instrument yourself, and a narcissist to boot, it is natural that that early phase of your life should have tempted you not to relinquish it [after] all these years. (Already you are probably reading a negative evaluation into the above on my part which is not there; I even envy you at times for having escaped the trials of maturity so successfully.) Any text book will tell you of the logical association of self-admiration with admiration of the same sex. To the fact that you did not remain 100 per cent in that phase, and you are periodically able to go beyond it, I can certainly furnish proof. But for the most part, the obstacles, real and imagined, with which your entree into normal sex life is blocked, and your recurrent dips into self-love and same-sex love show you to be still quite bound to that earlier time.

It would be foolish of me to say that you can *never* change, tho I am inclined to doubt it; all I know is that I cannot be instrumental in effecting the change. Actually you are doing very well for the most part without changing at all, so that there is no urgent necessity for your doing anything about it at all.

I am genuinely sorry, for your sake, that I caught you inadvertently in an elaborate fib as to where you were and with whom on a certain date, since it is literally and figuratively none of my business. Naturally with your make-up, it is more zestful for you to carry on whatever you carry on in secrecy. It isn't exactly that it surprised me, and I have gotten over being hurt by it ages ago. I have not "retired from the field" to "punish" you for any "misdeeds." To punish you for anything would be ridiculous. You have to do, always, what you have to do, and no matter where it leads.

But one place it does not lead to, and that is marriage. In reply to your statement that I knew exactly how you were when I married you, I would say (aside from the fact that people about to marry are not prophets, but only hopeful and often erring humans) certainly I knew how you were when I married you, but I misjudged completely my own reaction to it, and my own ability to live a semi-islandic life. It is I who, in a sense, have failed, a fact which I can face squarely, no matter how dire the implications. It would be entirely presumptuous for me to presume that the woman doesn't exist to whom you could be successfully married (when I said that your make-up doesn't lead to marriage, I mean marriage to me, and marriage in general), all I know is that I'm not equipped to make a go of it. I can by all that's reasonable not hold you responsible for my failings or lack of power to adjust, or whatever you call it. There are probably many women who could fit into your scheme, quite unafraid of the risk of being taken for granted, and willing to be seldom sipped, shelved, and await the next time when you should be thirsty, without changing in the least bit. I'm a rotten sublimator, I feel ceremonious and leisurely about sex, and my desires are fairly constant and never marginal but always full front page. You don't mix the clay I'm made of, you are of quite different clay, and for either of us to feel responsibility about it is preposterous.

While as your wife I found it extremely trying, too trying, to adapt myself to relegating my feelings to the end of a long procession of rehearsals, articles, lecture preparations, fatigue periods, and occasional new-sting affairs (provided even then that you were in one of your pro normal sex periods) – as your housekeeper-secretary this can no longer be a source of trial to me, and it certainly relieves you of a lot of unnecessary guilt pangs which you never need have had in the first place. It may be that the present set up irks you, though as I see it, it has a great many advantages for you. If it irks you too much, or if you have found someone who is thankfully without my hyper-sensitivity, bless you, you have only to tell me about it.

I don't intend to "sell" you this present set-up if you find one better suited to your needs, but I will explain why I think it is advantageous. In the first place, I am accustomed to your professional schedule with all its vagaries and am willing to accept it; secondly, in your profession, while it is not essential, a bourgeois front is a good thing to have (do I imagine this?); thirdly, with the ever-present if not likely hazards that your affairs present, in a pinch or a show-down your having what to all appearances is a wife might stand you in good stead; fourthly you have a real need for some kind of family life, when you have time to indulge in it, and I know you cherish Tony (my gratitude for this knows no bounds). Possibly, even though you see some sense in what I have put forth, you would still rather be entirely free. You have only to say so.

At the outset I said that I thought you were suffering quite needlessly in your ego, and that I hoped to correct this. For I believe it is basically your ego, your self-esteem, and not your libido which has been disturbed of late when I have not responded to your timid manifestations of affection. I might have imagined it, and if so I beg your pardon, but it has seemed to me as though you have wanted to be affectionate the past few weeks before you left. It will and should therefore give your ego the boost it deserves to know that it has cost me plenty *not* to respond. You are indeed a man, no matter how many knots you are tied in, and I find you every bit as attractive now as I ever did. (That I am fond of you must be self-evident by now, and that no one is more ambitious for you or proud of you or more willing to help in your work must also be pretty obvious. If I bore you any malice whatever or blamed you for anything, I certainly could not find it in me to take that attitude toward your achievements or not want to participate in them.) That I desist from responding physically to your affection in anything but a superficial way, and desist also from making any advances of my own, is certainly not attributable to any lack of magnetism on your part. Rather, as I have explained, it is an index of my own lack of stamina and my acute memory of the galling frustrations of the past. I simply would be afraid and most reluctant to resume, which is no doubt cowardly, but there it is.....

Well, dear, I'm talked out, and have said everything I wanted to say, none of it very new. The main reason for my writing was that I just didn't want you to be in any doubt as to your male proclivities, and I couldn't see any sense in having dark thoughts about it when it's so easy to tell you that you are, as you have been, attractive to practically everybody, and to myself. To put it poetically, your beef is Grade A; but I have chosen, all things considered, to be a vegetarian. Meanwhile I look forward to your homecoming.

In earlier sections we have seen how Etta always relented in her decision to exclude Ingolf from her bed. Here we simply have additional evidence, provided by this remarkable letter, that Etta had once again determined to sublimate her happiness to that of the man she loved. And Ingolf, without ever freeing himself from the guilt feelings she engendered in such missives, was now in an increasingly better position to seek male companionship and even to fall in love again.

Before the advent of an unashamedly gay sub-culture, the Y.M.C.A. was one of the best places where homosexuals might make casual contacts. Ingolf frequently came here on prospecting expeditions in the late Forties, generally favoring the downtown branch because it was closest to the U.S.C. campus. On April 30, 1946, he was so attracted to a man named Stan that it was necessary for him to hide his embarrassment by jumping into the pool. The two met outside and went to Stan's place, where Ingolf used the telephone to cancel dinner at home. "Then lots of fun and games and great relief (even though he is oldish...Fortunately (*and* unfortunately) there is no love or complications. Just sex." When Ingolf returned home, Etta was still up – "how I know that I love her, from deep down," he wrote, "I don't think she notices anything." The evening's activities revived his nostalgia for Douglas – "I love Douglas," he added, though it was now two years after the fiasco of his second Boston adventure. The next day there was an evening meeting at the home of his boss – "Strange to straddle the worlds like that."

Another figure encountered at the "Y" was a future friend of many years, a man I shall call Fitz. The two met on March 6, 1947 and went to Fitz's home – "it is perfectly lovely. No love again, but strong and beautiful physical attraction." Fitz, if I have reconstructed the pieces correctly, was a court officer and pseudonymous author of articles in gay magazines like *One*. His home provided a kind of erotic safety-valve for Ingolf, who enjoyed for the first time at Fitz's social gatherings and costume parties, a purely gay society.

Finding a place for a quick sexual liaison was a problem for Ingolf. He even brought dates to his studio in the Keller's garage, where he had a couch, but, "It isn't quite right," he reported in March of 1947. Julie Keller, who was a pre-schooler at this time, told me that she remembers looking into the window of this studio from her own back yard and seeing a most perturbing scene – but not perturbing enough to raise an alarm.

Ingolf was often naive in his romantic entanglements, and Etta had to warn him repeatedly to be discrete. He never had an affair with any professional colleague nor did he mix his erotic life with his musical one – even though there were many famous gays in the latter – and he knew enough to refrain from involvements with other School of Music personnel or students (though there was one brief flirtation with a piano major in the spring of 1947), but *other* figures on campus were not excluded in Ingolf's early years at U.S.C. – and thus Guy entered his life.

Guy, also not a real name, was an art student when Ingolf met him at the campus pool on April 24, 1947. They headed for Malibu in Guy's car, Ingolf wearing his new friend's raincoat: "I am feverish and pray. So much overwhelming beauty next to me." "You want to feel if I have a heart?" Ingolf asked. Guy put his hand on Ingolf's chest – "guess you have a heart." After the first kiss Ingolf remained on clouds for days. The next night the two met in a cafe but the day after that Ingolf saw Guy with someone else in the "Y" pool. "After that I have to sit down and bury my head and can't think, it is all so crushing and strong." A draft of a letter to "Dear friend" was preserved in Ingolf's files; it must have been written on April 27, 1947:

> ...You probably know also how I feel about you, how terribly I have lost myself to you and the surging of the ocean waves the other night accompanied the lighting of a fire that is now burning without check. Don't think that I am unrealistic. I wish I were, but I'm not. I realize that the involvements of life exist and have existed for you as well as for me. They have to be accepted and you will find me reasonable and obedient to all the exigencies of the outer world, just as long as I can still see you...Your overwhelming eyes are before me wherever I go and your voice is in my ears. I beg of you, don't think that these are easy and cheap sentimentalities, thrown away at random. I feel, I really feel, and I haven't felt in such unthinkably long time...Let me see you again. Even for a few minutes, to look at your wonderful face and feel alive again...I enclose a little snapshot, taken recently, to remember me by and hope you will return in kind.

After seeing a "breathtaking" Guy on campus on the 29th, Ingolf called to make a date for the next night. Guy promised to spend a weekend with Ingolf. "My knees almost give way," the smitten composer reported, and there followed ten days of feverish anticipation as the weekend approached. "Does Etta notice anything?" he speculates on May 2. On May 4 he dispatched a volume of Keats to his young friend and on the 9th the day at last arrived – "and with it the *greatest*. My world changes these days. All that was lost is refound, solution to everything. And all is clean and pure."

On campus Ingolf played Handel, Schubert and Chopin for Guy, who said, "I didn't realize you were so good." Then Ingolf ran out of gas on 36th Street. After re-fuelling he drove to Corning Street and, with Tony's laughter ringing upstairs, tiptoed to the bottom of the stairs to leave a note for Etta in the mailbox. Guy rested his head on Ingolf's shoulder ("Oh Lord, how have I ever deserved such happiness") as the two headed out of town. They had coffee in Pomona and took a room in a motel in Redlands. "Fulfillment," Ingolf wrote, "Sleep little. *That* face next to me all night." The next day the two took a cabin at Camp Angelus and spent the day hiking and picnicking: "He is so wonderfully relaxed, simple and pure and the heart is alive...that life had *that* still in store for me. The wounds are healed." On Sunday the two made love again among the ants – "It is so overwhelmingly perfect that I have to cry." On their return the two stopped off for brandy in Colton and chicken in Pomona. Ingolf arrived back on Corning Street in some trepidation, "But E. is helpful (only pale and anguished I feel) and passes over it."

It is not clear how much Guy knew about Ingolf's other life because on May 14, as they sat sipping cognac in the studio, Ingolf records that, "I tell him about myself and he says, 'I'm not going to see you again.'" Ingolf cajoled his lover out of this resolution and the two continued their affair over many a public dinner and many a drink in the next few weeks, Guy protesting that he was keeping Ingolf from work and Ingolf "drowning in the ocean of his eyes." They managed another weekend at Camp Angelus in early June. Anxiety gripped Ingolf as Guy announced, "In a relationship such as ours three things are necessary: sympathy, understanding, casualness." Jealousy had already intruded when it became obvious that Guy had made a beach date with someone else. When Ingolf arrived home from his second weekend in the mountains he found Etta sweet and affectionate toward him and a sudden wave of love for her overwhelmed him. On June 5 he and Guy had lunch together: "And everything is clear & peaceful, there are no doubts, no fear, he smiles the smile of confidence and reassurance." The affair had been poorly timed in one way, for a week later Ingolf, Etta and I departed for our summer in Sweden, Ingolf consoled at least by Guy's farewell, "Hurry back."

When we reached Chicago Ingolf paused again in front of *Les Saltimbanques*, "overwhelmed with the tearful time three years ago. Douglas, where are you? How can I see Douglas again. The air is full of him." In Stockholm Ingolf waited in vain for a letter from Guy. At the

Sturebadet, Stockholm's equivalent to the "Y" pool, Ingolf noted some interesting possibilities, but did nothing about them.

Just how difficult it is to speak of Ingolf's creative life without touching at the same time on the emotional sources from which it sprang (the problem Bill Colvig warned me I would encounter if I tried to separate the two in a biography) can now be revealed in an account of the origins of a composition which Ingolf turned to after his return from Sweden. "In its very earliest and roughest stage," Ingolf played for Etta the beginning of the *Hymn* for piano solo on November 26, 1947. "It is wonderful with her, a complete whole," he wrote of this day, "So I am two complete wholes." However, it soon becomes evident that the inspiration for the piano work lay elsewhere. Ingolf was really thinking of Guy while writing this piece, the faithless lover whose letters had failed to appear in Mammi's mailbox. The friendship seems to have resumed in the fall, though clearly it was in its final stages of passion. On December 1, after deciding to rewrite a portion of the new piece, Ingolf notes a great tenderness growing in him for Guy: the *Hymn* "is all his piece. Gorgonio is there and the rock in the middle of the stream. That is a treasure that will never leave me, though he has already." On December 3 the work was finished. Practice was furious for the next few days and on December 7, on the eve of the first public performance, Ingolf brought Guy to the studio and ("the climax of so much in life"), played the work twice, – "and he is with me, the originator, for whom it was written, for whom it came!"

Ingolf and Guy continued to see each other for another year. They had drinks the week after a concert at Mike Lyman's restaurant downtown (Guy had eight martinis) and in January he and Guy made love in the studio – "Heaven opens itself again. How can one be so lucky?" The two went to the beach several times in 1948 and completed one trip to Mt. Whitney, but references to Guy (who married and moved out of state) disappear soon thereafter. Ingolf would wait quite some time for a sequel to this love affair, and even a visit from the once-loved Heini, the first personal contact in ten years with the last of his Zurich lovers, seems to have left him flat in 1948. He took his old friend to the "Y" and they had a rather "disappointing and boring" time on Hollywood Boulevard – this after a day in which Ingolf went to the beach with Etta and discovered once again, "She is so wonderful."

91. THE PUPPYCAT

The early Fifties did not provide for Ingolf the longed-for love affair that earlier episodes with Douglas or Guy had promised. The pattern of the Zurich years, casual sightings and quick assignations, was much more common. At the Hungarian Quartet concert in July, 1950, there appears "the little blonde crew cut whom I have seen for years." In March, 1951, Ingolf is driving on Wooster, in our Corning Street neighborhood, and he sees "the most beautiful sight" taking off his shoes and revealing well-formed feet and a consummate beauty that "knocks me for a loop." Something "very good and exciting" was sighted at the "Y" in November of 1951, but Ingolf had to rush back to campus for a *Consul* rehearsal.

His only success came at those parties thrown by his friend Fitz. Invitations here, or mountain outings with Fitz himself, did produce excitement and occasional catharsis. On January 12, 1950, on the eve of one of these all-gay parties, Ingolf (in mirror script) notes how he walked about all day pulsing in a sexual trance. One party invitation from the era reads, "Leave at home your wife and mother / We'd much rather have your brother." In 1954 Ingolf succeeded in sneaking Fitz into his cabin at the Huntington Hartford Foundation.

On March 20, 1952, Ingolf was testing one of his sore knees in Griffith Park. A black car began to follow him along the road. When he started up the trail the car's driver got out and followed as well. Together these strangers lay down in a secluded patch of underbrush, Ingolf completely passive. At last he extricated himself from his young ("too young") pursuer. "Will I see you again?" "Who knows?" It is not clear from the journal who spoke first. Ingolf found the experience rather shattering – "am ripe to get lost again," he added, "and inwardly probably yearn for that agony." He also noted a conflict concerning youthful lovers (for he was now on the eve of his fortieth birthday) – "it is both magnetically attractive and forbiddingly holy." (Ingolf was not attracted to the very young, to teenagers for instance, and he would have been the last person to take advantage of an immature partner.) A few days after the Griffith Park incident he returned to the scene of the unexpected tryst and walked by the abandoned "nest" in the underbrush. "The hillside swarms with peculiarities," he wrote, but "it is very dull." We didn't call the Hollywood Hills the Swish Alps for nothing.

In all these years only a few figures seem to have caused Ingolf's heart to beat again; one was a man named Walter, whom he met underwater at the "Y" pool on July 17, 1950 – "that loosens an avalanche of damned emotions." The two agreed to meet in two days. Ingolf ploughed through his summer school classes on the 19th, counting the minutes before he could go swimming again with this new unattainable male presence. On the 25th they met again, Ingolf just getting through his work on a music appreciation test before rushing to the pool. Walter asked him if he were free that evening. "Have to work," Ingolf answered, "So the choice is made. Just because it is so difficult to call E, 'not coming for dinner.'" The irony of this story is that when he did get home that night it was "to bed – very lovely with E. My lovely wife." "Through these confrontations with reality," he summed up the poolside experience, "some of the overheated excitement is wearing off."

This excitement, as we have seen, could not be conveyed on any sustained basis to his wife. I could not find a single 1949 reference in the journals that would give us any clue to the erotic relationship between my mother and my stepfather. A canasta party at the Kellers, drives to the beach, a little four-hand Schubert, reading aloud from Mark Twain, a walk in the Baldwin Hills – by such gestures the two kept alive their love for one another. Ingolf, in spite of "my particular kind of impotence" remained attracted to Etta – "Etta looks beautiful in black velvet and shells," he wrote the night of the Stravinskys' New Year's Eve Party, December 31, 1950. "I love her so much. I love Etta," he wrote in January, 1952, but physical expressions of "love, real love" were rare, and his comments on their twelfth wedding anniversary, in March, 1952, reveal his sense of always being in the wrong before this exceptional mate: "I am so grateful to Etta for being herself, for having stayed with me."

Etta has left us some evidence of her own feelings abut Ingolf and their relationship. These come in fragmentary literary jottings, never transcribed from pencil in many instances. I can see another intriguing character, perhaps a successor to Valentine Cactus, in the children's play, "A Tangled Yarn," which I performed with the Keller kids and others in the famous garage with its secret studio, whose open door we used for exits and entrances in this production:

> Hello, I'm the palace Puppycat.
> As you can see, I'm made like that;
> I can bark, but I also meow –
> Nobody knows why or how.
> All I know is that I cause
> Lots of mischief with my paws.
> Got a minute? Stay and see
> How they put a stop to me.

In the sketches for her detective novel of the mid-Fifties, Etta also has references to sexual ambiguity. Ma Grafton, her detective, chides herself for jumping to conclusions:

> Suppose you're a fellow and you are slender, and your hair is beautiful, and your nails are exquisitely groomed and there is somewhat too much distance between your dilated nostrils and your upper lip, and your glance was a practiced blank, and you walk as though one thigh were Romeo and the other Juliet, loath to part more than absolutely necessary, and I thought: *aha*, it would turn out that you could fight a man twice your size, that nature groomed your hair, to which you were indifferent, that your mother denied you desserts until you were habituated to caring for your nails, that you had just caught a whiff from the gas main, that by now the novocaine would have worn off your upper lip, that you learned to freeze your features while in the FBI, that you had two groin injuries in Korea and your three little ones were home fighting over your bronze star...That's how reliable my judgement is.

At the end of "A Tangled Yarn," the Puppycat becomes all dog after having his whiskers and tail pulled, but Ingolf could not be dealt with so easily. The rewarding and beautiful "break-through times," when he was totally and lovingly present, were, for Etta, in spite of her vows of celibacy, sufficient compensation for all those times of self-absorption and gay absence.

Ingolf's erotic impulse also seems to have been at low ebb during the first Schruns sabbatical. There are very few overt references to sexual activity ("Wonderful with E." I take to be one of these), and Ingolf does not seem to have engaged in any homoerotic activity while away from Los Angeles in 1952 and 1953. There is only the briefest catalogue of passing infatuations and none is mentioned more than once. On October 25, after a day of skiing, Ingolf was waiting in Bludenz for a connection back to Schruns – a train service whose engineer was frequently his own landlord, Mr. Netzer:

> In the station sits a face, princely, making all others look coarse and heavy. If it were only possible to remember it forever. Blue grey ski jacket and ski pants. Tall, noble, slender build. Gets into the Schruns train and sits opposite, how very fortunate. High cheekbones, narrow high forehead, full lips – occasionally he looks up from below with Douglas' expression, that hurts. His voice is deep, like Douglas... Gets off at Tschagguns – may I remember."

Ingolf never saw this lad again and life in Schruns does not seem to have altered the patterns of gay longing and husbandly frustration. "The personal problem, the brake, seems to get stronger," he wrote on April 14, 1953, "I have to think it out and get to the bottom of what turns the switch off always." As usual such erotic distance never lead to total estrangement, for there were always many other activities that my parents, soon installed in our Clarington apartment, lovingly shared – trips to the beach, walks on the pier, endless movies, concerts, ballets, an active social life with their wide circle of friends. "I wept like an idiot over your love letter," Etta wrote to Ingolf in Tanglewood in July, 1955, "in part because I love and miss you, in part because of your mentioning your 'inadequacies' and how I 'put up' with them. I don't know if I can ever make clear to you from what utterly different standpoints you and I view what you call inadequacy."

Ingolf's erotic life was still at a low ebb as he entered the mid-Fifties. A creative paralysis was paralleled by a sexual hiatus and when Ingolf refers to feeling "almost neurotically tense and frustrated" one cannot tell whether it is men or notes that are in short supply. He looked for the former incessantly, even in locations which, strictly speaking, belonged to the "other world," the dormitory at Eugene, the lake at Tanglewood.

On May 15, 1954, Ingolf reports a lack of courage after failing to follow up on a significant exchange of glances in a shower cubicle in the Hollywood "Y." "On the one hand frustration," he concluded, "on the other how marvelously alive and full of love and warm longing." The young man in question is described as at "the perfect stage of youth and strength and decency," and it should not come as a shock to attentive readers that Ingolf would never have seen anything indecent in his *own* behavior. He was a man who could commend his graduate students to potential employers for their "altogether wholesome personality" or turn down a subscription to the *Daily News* because the tabloid printed "filth" (crime and gossip) not fit for a child's eye, and then cruise the "Y" with a clear conscience. "How the queens and I flash and stare," he wrote after a shower room incident on Pearl Harbor Day, 1954, "somebody else is interested too – I touch him – on the way out it is all very, very wonderful – oh, if I could have had him!!"

On January 25, 1955, Ingolf received a proposition from a young man at the "Y" and the two arranged a meeting later that night in front of Woodbury College. "Bottomlessly excited and happy and glowing," Ingolf arrived at eight. At ten he gave up his vigil "in utter greyness. Now this is difficult to get over. I will never see him again." But four months later "the unbelievable happens. Woodbury College is there again." I shall call the young man Norman, in part because I am not certain if I have deciphered his real name correctly – Ingolf's tiny slashing script approaches illegibility when affairs of the heart are being discussed – and partly because Norman turns out to be another married man. He had two children, he sang in the church choir, and he made a date to meet Ingolf during his next visit to the "Y," four weeks hence, on June 17. The week preceding the rendezvous was one of intense excitement for Ingolf. "The continuous, continuous undercurrent of the most wonderful warmth and anticipation" pervaded a holiday he had undertaken to Baja with Etta. On the fateful day Ingolf decorated his studio with flowers before driving to the "Y." Norman was not waiting for him and Ingolf sat down to wait and smoke a cigarette – "What if he doesn't come?" "Then the face, walking up – salmon colored shirt, grey tie, Ingolf, if ever a face had to be remembered, it is this. Brown soft eyes, long straight nose, horizontal eyebrows – and that baritone voice like a cradle of down." "I think it is better if I don't see you today," Norman began, "I should never have made this date." "I waited for this so long," Ingolf protested, "you'll have to let me down easy." Numb with shock, Ingolf nevertheless succeeded in getting Norman into a coffee shop. "Have you ever tried to overcome a bad habit?" Norman asked. Ingolf suggested a correspondence, but the reply was, "I don't see what purpose writing would serve." Later Norman passed in front of Ingolf's locker at the "Y." "This is hard to write," the day's journal entry begins, "the blow hitting so deep that first a shock then a terrible scar are the effect." "It is all lost," Ingolf warned himself, "I must not give in, this will have to be overcome quickly (not like Peter), the disappointment must be conquered." As he drove back to campus he could only report, "I feel dead inside – the soul is not in me." Norman's image continued to haunt for several days – "the afterglow of a sun that never rose." "I will never get over the Norman defeat," Ingolf wrote a few weeks later at Tanglewood, "He was the best, the most beautiful, the most desirable, the most sensuous oh why did I ever have to miss him."

Who knows how long Ingolf would have moped over the lost Norman had it not been for a Sierra Club outing, soon after his return from Tanglewood, in late August, 1955. On the 28th, the second day of a backpacking trip in the Southern Sierras, he mentions for the first time the man who would be the most important male figure in his adult life, Bill Colvig.

92. PAN

"Had been wondering about him all along," Ingolf noted in his journal for August 28, 1955, "but his being so athletic and manly, had not dared to hope." "On this rock," the story continues, "an arm stretched out meets another arm and then it happens." On his recorder Bill played the melody later used by Ingolf in the *Couperin Variations* and that night they made their first joint campsite together. Bill lead the group to the top of Mt. Tyndall the next day: "There stands Bill, being photographed, red shirt, smiling face, all power and grace and manly strength, it just chokes me – what a dream come true."

The 30th was a rest day near Hourglass Lake. Animal exchanges of affection near a deserted tarn were followed by reading aloud. Bill read a portion of Rachel Carson's latest article in *The New Yorker*, Ingolf read *One* magazine. "In sleeping bag," Ingolf wrote, "I have to tell Bill how much I love him." On September 1, as the party climbed Mt. Russell, Bill saved some snow and made daiquiris. On September 2 he refused to follow the rest of the hikers to the next campsite over the regular "manure trail," and he and Ingolf climbed over the Hale-Young cirque alone. "Discuss political questions," Ingolf added, "and find that we feel much the same way...Do a Kwan-Yin Shadow Dance at the night's campfire near Timberline Lake." On September 3rd Bill climbed Whitney alone and on his return he and Ingolf made love, drank daiquiris, "Get quite high and silly, dance around, feel glorious." A fellow camper, tactfully calling out before arriving at their sleeping place, woke them on the final morning of the expedition. A last embrace behind a tree at Whitney Portal preceded the terrible moment of good-bye. When he reached L.A. that night Ingolf dashed off a note to his new friend, jumped on my bicycle, and, "in a state of utter transport," pedaled to the post office. "I must tell you," he wrote to Bill, "that this past week has been as close to pure happiness as I have ever had." Ingolf was again in love.

This letter, posted with so much urgency at three in the morning, was only the first in a long series of personal statements of love and affection which my stepfather sent to the San Francisco electrician. He wrote to Bill nineteen times in 1955, fifty-eight times in 1956, thirty-six times in 1957 – in all approximately three hundred times over the next fifteen years. These letters supplement his journals, make whole some of the fragmentary references there, and provide further testimony on his extremely complex private life in the Fifties and Sixties.

The day after his return Ingolf went to the beach with Etta, for once finding himself completely undisturbed by the beautiful shapes and creatures he spotted there because, as he wrote to Bill, "nothing that the eye saw could possibly penetrate into a place that was so completely happy in the thoughts of our days together." The next day we read of a "lovely time with E. who wakes me," and on September 7 of a phone call to Fitz, whom he visited on the 15th. The next day he met Norman by accident at the "Y," " more beautiful and lovely than ever – what frustration." On the 18th he paced up and down on the beach before getting up the courage to follow another customer into a gay house of recreation. In these short days we have all the strands of Ingolf's multifaceted sex life.

One of the newest elements in this tapestry was provided by the homosexual clubs and spas, the bathhouse ambience which would become familiar news to observers of the social scene in later years. Ingolf first mentions his awareness of such places and his hunger for what he might taste there on June 15, 1954 – "The problem to be solved: I will have to go, sooner or later, to Crystal." Cowardice held him back until July 3 when, driving out of the Hartford Foundation after lunch, he made his first "descent into hell...a world of strange, shadowy creatures floating about, waiting, whispering, an odd daylight underworld...But for me, as always, reality is the only cure. One good sight but then at last a very disappointing let-down release." At Janee's on September 18, 1955, there was someone who "excites me so much that we don't have much fun." On October 7 a very hot and sweet Latin body provided "the loveliest experience." From the outset Ingolf's use of the baths was fraught with hazard. One had to sign to get in, but there was no protection against the occasional police raid and both Janee's and the Rendezvous were evidently closed briefly in the next few months.

My mother-in-law was the first person to call my attention to the British music hall ditty, "No One Loves A Fairy When He's Forty." This sentiment was no laughing matter to my stepfather. Immersed in a culture that idolized youth, athleticism and beauty, Ingolf must have sensed that there were some things which weightlifting at the "Y" could not overcome. Though he possessed an excellent build and prided himself on being in shape, Ingolf also knew that as a bald, bespectacled middle-aged man he must now lack many erotic opportunities that his intended partners possessed so abundantly. "Why this cloud over me," he protested in August, 1955, age forty-three, "if I were dull, ugly, unpleasant – but I'm not, and yet I cannot get close to anything I like – oh hell." "Am I so unattractive," he asked the following December, "getting too old?" It was Ingolf's complaint that he often attracted only middle-aged partners because he himself appeared to be middle-aged. Furthermore in the "Dantesque cavern, with its floaty spirits in dark doorways," sex was often "too brief, hasty, anonymous." Ingolf, a man who craved fellowship as well as sex is reduced to referring to his anonymous partners as "things," – "There are nice things, one thing comes up but no reaction."

He embarked in earnest upon this form of erotic release only after the homosexual impulse flowed to the surface in his relationship with Bill. Another factor may have been that Fitz now seemed to have a permanent partner – "so the idyll is shattered," Ingolf wrote on September 7, 1955, "adjustment will be difficult – go out and fend for yourself – the road of the baths and streets and god knows what – yet I am happy for him." Fitz remained a close friend after all, and Ingolf continues to report parties, pornography exhibitions and mountain outings experienced in the company of his pal. Fitz was, after all, the only figure in whom he could confide the full story of his romance with Bill Colvig.

The journals indicate that Ingolf did mention Bill's *name* to Etta and his stepson in his account of his recent Sierra trip, but we can be quite certain that there were no details about the special relationship he now hoped to pursue. The latter is made clear in the many letters sent north in the next three weeks, requests for Bill's photograph, remembrances of their week in the mountains, anguished appeals for a rendezvous as soon a possible. "I want to write nice and objective and controlled words, and before I know it they turn into a love letter," so Ingolf begins on September 7, "As for myself, I feel physically wonderful, but my heart aches. It is both a sad and vitalizing feeling and so I can only hope that it will keep on aching." The two agreed to meet at the end of November.

The "longest, longest, most interminable day," November 23, 1955, arrived at last. "Ill with anticipation," Ingolf dropped Etta off at school and drove to the "Y," where, ironically, he shared a bench with the reluctant Norman. The afternoon lessons crawled by and at four he rushed to the airport and flew to Fresno. A few minutes late, Bill arrived in his car and the two drove up the Wawona Road to a Yosemite campsite, where a double sleeping bag presaged the resumption of their affair. On the 25th Ingolf wrote, "This day *all* happiness – it can't go higher – this is the all – how have I deserved it all, so late, now, at last." Later in San Francisco Ingolf was introduced to the gay society in which Bill was so at home; they played Mozart four-hand. On the drive to the airport on the 27th, "Can't take my eyes off his." "B. pursues me," he wrote the next day, "he is in my blood. I am just going to pieces and yet I am so happy that all this is given to me." "At home everything is fine," Ingolf wrote to Bill (he had, after all, skipped out on his family's Thanksgiving celebrations), "I give a convincing and fairly detailed account of the Sierra Club trip to Yosemite (also telling about you and what an ideal mountain companion you are and that you extended a standing invitation to me to visit you in San Francisco sometime). So everything is smooth and unruffled."

One may wonder how Ingolf's new relationship affected his existing family life. Etta was not slow to sense the threat which Bill's presence signalled. She tried very hard to behave as if nothing were going on, but Ingolf noted a change in her behavior. "Etta is far away, in her own little corner," he noted on November 10, "making a show of domesticity whenever I get a questioning glance on my face." "Etta is such a problem," he wrote on December 1, "just her silent presence is fraught with tension – she is so far away but I don't do anything to bring her closer. I resent her keeping away from my professional life, but what do I do for her?" One curious but bittersweet dividend in Ingolf's new romance is that the newly undammed erotic energies included Etta in their wash; thus he also mentions a number of moments of intimacy with his wife at the same time that he remains obsessed by Bill.

"This man drives me out of my mind," the entry for December 2 begins, "every fiber longs for Bill and cannot live without him...The way out would be to find a really satisfying boy down here in L.A. – that takes time and going out." Ingolf could not take his wife into his arms without first thinking of Bill, but he could not think of a life without her, nor could he share his real life with her. He could not, for instance, share with her his new happiness. He speaks of his own "scylla and charybdis: between home guilt feelings and sexual frustration."

On December 16 Ingolf received his next invitation to San Francisco. This time he would go there to "compose." "Well, he seems like a real friend," Etta said when Ingolf, red as a beet, broke the news to her on my eighteenth birthday, January 6, 1956. On January 22, amid "an ocean of emotion," Ingolf arrived in San Francisco. Bill was not in the mood ("I am in a bottomless pit again"), but things soon improved – "In one week make up for the years of frustration and suffering of a lifetime." There followed visits to the local "Y" and the local baths, though Ingolf could hardly have found a more satisfying partner than the one he now possessed. He and Bill went on walks, to restaurants, to museums, they played music together. In Golden Gate Park Ingolf chatted with a policeman who said, "Our biggest problem is degeneracy."

On January 31 my stepfather flew back to L.A. and resumed his bigamous existence, Etta's husband, Bill's wife. Bill delighted his lover by writing that the recent visit had convinced him he was "not meant to live alone – you spoiled me." "Oh Bill, Bill," Ingolf wrote in his daybook , "*how can we get together?*... What a mess have I made of my life – but who could have known that after all the waiting *this* would happen?" I have a feeling that Ingolf even considered applying now for a position at Berkeley.

He eased the frustration of separation with several visits to the "Y." "A wonderful thing happens," he wrote on February 24. Another bather, excited by Ingolf's presence, led his potential partner into the "Quiet Room," and locked the door as the two wet animal bodies sought each other. On March 1, after a rehearsal at the Congregational Church, Ingolf went to the "Y" steam bath where "two middle-aged men begin to do me." But three weeks later he and Bill joined a Sierra Club expedition to the Havasu country in Arizona: "Can we have enough time together if we are part of the group, and without raising too many raised eyebrows about such a buddy-buddy clique?"

Bill had a cold when the two met up for this expedition in Bakersfield. "I don't care," a happy Ingolf wrote, "just to be with him is enough." On the descent to Havasu Falls they made a cradle-love nest away from the other hikers, had rum drinks and got quite high. During the day they explored the beautiful sculptured canyons and at night "there was the most *wonderful* love." Bill brought out his recorder and piped Ingolf up the steep return trail at the end of the trip. Then they quarreled and Ingolf now had the cold. In front of a mirror in Barstow Bill said, "You know I'm an old whore. If somebody young should come along who likes mountains and music I'll take up with him and let you go." But the next morning the two were full of affection for one another. "We are necking like two adolescents," one of them said, "like two Hollywood fruits." "See you in June," Ingolf said as Bill got into his own car in Bakersfield. "Let's hope so," was the reply.

At a Clarington dinner that night thoughts of Bill were so strong that Ingolf started to cry. Etta looked up from her wine. "What's the matter dear?" she asked. However she had already provided the answer herself in another of her remarkable letters, which, in his absence, she had added to the pile of accumulated correspondence:

Dearest,

...In expressions of this kind, one has two risky choices; either to be vocal, and let the expression degenerate into an unthinking, highly emotional free-for all, or to write, and envision the reader inevitably interpreting irony where none exists, and looking for hidden left handed criticism...

Mixed in with your actually transfiguring joy of the last few weeks, you have, in parallel, given so many evidences of conscience, that I am moved to set down in black and white, the better to invite your thought, what you should long ago have been convinced of: I do not consider your erotic duality a problem; I am exceedingly happy with you as you are...Please do me the kindness not to translate me into a Monument of Patience, a Brave Little Woman, who deserved Better, the All-understanding All-mother, a Great Spirit putting A Good Face on a Bad Matter, or something equally mawkish. I have not always been this objective...Exactly how we achieved what we now have, I have neither the ability nor the wish to figure out. Suffice it to say that our "times of wine" are joyous to such a degree, that I do not give "our times of water" or even "times of drought" a second thought. Nor can I, in view of your unquestionable supremacy over me in intimacy, and my contentment therein, fret over your intimacies elsewhere...

I long ago became disabused of the notion that any one person can mean all things to any one other person...Quite apart from any erotic considerations, the very propinquity in which two bound people live tends at one and the same time both to deepen the bond and to blur it....Taking this into account, I think that on the whole, and on all planes, you and I are rather remarkably unblurred, or well-profiled to each other, and that our record for enjoying each other's company is especially felicitous.

...Formerly you were not above making semi-snide remarks about my popularity. Last week, by way of complete reversal, you suddenly came up with the idea that I should ask one of my "young friends" to take me out (to the Kabuki Dancers)! Such a totally untypical suggestion coming from you would have amazed me, if I had not known why you had the impulse to make it. Since one of the main purposes in writing this letter is to attempt to get you to abandon such ethical contortions as superfluous, you will see why your suggestion was not only revealing but saddening. Can you try, at least, to disburden your mind? To relax and untwist yourself? Why don't you just get down on your knees and thank God that your blood is singing?

Etta then offered the evidence needed to convince Ingolf that she was not being especially clever in divining the presence of a new gay relationship. She noted how Ingolf had once left two glossy photos of Guy lying about at Corning Street, a letter from Fitz on the living room table in Schruns – "Your relations with those of your own sex was no news, and scarcely a matter of concern." "For the facilitating of your maximum freedom," Etta noted, she had ceased asking Ingolf about appointments, had taken the number of male callers but not asked for their names, and had offered no indication of her marital status to callers – unless they were female callers. As for his current love, Etta could only assure Ingolf that it was indeed "marvelous to be so shaken," but "awful to live so far from one who inspires it." Then she revealed that Ingolf had left a photo of Bill in the stamp drawer – "one of the most fascinating and endearing faces I have seen in years, the kind that brings to mind the imp-god Pan." Etta concluded that she would never ask Ingolf to give her the names, dates, and facts relevant to his gay life: "There is not even the remotest reason to discuss it verbally. You will know, after reading and thinking about it, just how much of it you feel is correct, pertinent, or ash-can material."

At the mid-point in their married life Etta also summarized her continued willingness to participate in such an unlikely liaison:

> My adaptivity toward you...is in part, as I have tried to explain, a kind of generosity I can well-afford out of the fullness of what to me is a good life. I feel I must repeat this so you will not read any undue masochism, or even an altruism which isn't there, into everything I have said.
>
> But as to my vast resilience, per se, which must at times seem either superhuman or stupidly saintly to you, it is neither. It is merely the product of years of experience, extending far back to before I met you. By now it is almost like a muscular reflex. For one thing, we went to such different "nursery schools." In my case, it was adapt and develop self-reliance, or perish. I have not perished. It is quite true that during the first years of our life together this plasticity of mine was so sorely tried that it was very nearly stretched beyond repair (and what I did to you was no adventure in paradise, either). That I retrieved it, that it is as good as new, I cannot underscore enough, is due to the fact that you have changed so much within yourself and toward me. To put it quite bluntly, and not to include the myriad other things that make life with you as sweet as it is, when I have come fresh from your arms and have felt what I was made to feel, I

can handle any amount of effrontery made me about your other life by curious dimwits, and I am left indifferent by fresh evidences of your continuing to have it.

Etta did take time to warn Ingolf once again about the need for discretion:

> Discretion cannot be overestimated when one is, as you are, academically affiliated, as well as making your home with a highly perceptive and sensitive adolescent who, on the one hand, is already fully aware of what the phenomenon is, but on the other, should he ever have to connect it with you, could be nothing but shattered. For he does not yet have his mother's means of evaluating it or tossing it off.

Etta did advise Ingolf that his activities in the gay world *were* the subject of gossip. Ingolf might want to ignore this, but such naiveté was only a consequence of:

> your still incredible lack of sophistication, and your persistent belief that what you don't want known can automatically of course never be known, your belief that because something has gone well up until now, it will of course always go well, or your potentially always risky preference for trusting your luck rather than troubling yourself about taking precautions.

Etta elaborated: "That you have been seen in public places has been relayed to me, again not by clairvoyance. It has been by innuendo, by question, and by direct report." Etta cited the example of one of her fellow graduate students who "since he generally handed in excuses instead of assignments by reason of being allergic to any sustained mental effort, disliked me especially for being just the reverse. So he singles me out for his special target, and it was hard to evade him...all this with his hideously toothy leer." Etta also wanted to warn Ingolf about the notorious indiscretion of his secret friends, advice she felt well qualified to give after ten years as a ballet accompanist:

> One can say, however, without fear of contradiction, as I learned in my more than a decade of intimate association with them...that they are inordinately indiscreet, have a very marked propensity for gossip,

and are prodigious (tho amusing) liars. There are some exceptions, but not many...From my own experience: Nothing was sacred. They were always reading me and one another love letters sent them in all confidence, and to ask them to shut up is like asking Niagara Falls to do likewise.

Now, Etta feared, Ingolf might pay dearly for the blabbing of some garrulous gayboy. A Ph.D. candidate, she reported, had recently been shooed off campus after being found out, and perhaps Ingolf's bosses "could not afford to take anything but a morally negative stand" should *his* secret life be uncovered.

So my mother rescued her husband once again. Her complaints were directed only at the method and manner of his other life; that he could have *it* and her at the same time was made clear at last. Ingolf, the spoiled child at Mammi's knee, had succeeded, at perhaps some cost to his own character, in preserving that freedom without consequence that his strong-willed personality demanded. With a wife like Etta you could do anything, including the pursuit of a male lover in another city, and get away with it. Responsibility for your own behavior could always be deflected to the stronger shoulders of the loyal wife. As he embraced Etta in bed after reading his welcome home letter, Ingolf could only marvel at his good fortune – "It is too much, too much, how have I deserved such love and devotion?"

93. AN INTERESTING LIFE

On April 14, 1956, Ingolf took time out to re-read Etta's most recent letter, "which again moves me enormously – if I could only talk to her." On the 22nd he notes, "practice at home, then feel should be with Etta, go to bed, it starts all right, then fizzles, she cries." At about this time Ingolf discovered a bandana which Bill had left in his car during the Havasu trip. "I was tempted to keep it, " he wrote, "but then I told myself not to act like a damn fetishist...Life goes on in its two planes again (half of me is not here at all, and sometimes more than half – one plane the here and the now, the other the continuous presence of you in my thoughts and feelings." Yearning for Bill was constant over the next few months, though Ingolf did manage to get in one visit to San Francisco over the Memorial

Day holiday. "I don't really excite him any more," he agonized on the first day, but things improved and a few days later he reports sitting and waiting for Bill to return from work, "my husband." Etta had seen him off as he left for San Francisco, saying, "Have a good time." She greeted him on his return with the comment, "You do lead an interesting life."

"I must say," Ingolf wrote to Bill on July 4, that ever since I have known you I have become quite changed inside. Changed in so many ways, loosened up in so many ways." Ingolf was in Tanglewood when he wrote this and perhaps he was thinking of the wild period of experiment that he had recently completed in New York. He had picked up a young man in the shower at the Sloane House Y.M.C.A. in New York on June 13th – "quite unexpected, but very lovely." On June 22nd he had crossed over to New Jersey because someone had told him to check out the Howard Street baths. On the 26th, at the 125th Street Baths, Ingolf had settled for a "primitive colored boy" – "it's bad, the lowest gutter." The next morning he was joined by Etta – but he still found time to visit the "Y."

A month after his arrival on the east coast, however, he reports a serious illness. "Very worried, it is getting worse, what is it??" The next day he identifies the problem in his journal – "the pain in the rear, etc. gets worse, is quite bad. The big worry: is it what Bill said might happen?" "Can hardly wait to see doctor," he added on the 15th, "will I be able to tell him?" A young, pretty doctor examined Ingolf on the 16th and prescribed sulfa and baths for "an infection." "I don't have the nerve to ask him the *real* question," Ingolf moaned. Still worried about what he had picked up in the New York baths he faithfully followed the course of treatment, but there was little improvement. On the 24th he sought out another doctor – "I tell him everything (almost – the rest he'll have to put together himself.)" Penicillin was prescribed this time, but after swallowing a lot of pills Ingolf discovered that his body was unable to tolerate this medicine. He was ill with penicillin poisoning for several days, reading Boswell and Bevenuto Cellini in bed. I have it from Etta, who described only the last stages of this Tanglewood illness (and skipped over its origins), that Ingolf was afflicted by horrible swelling; he notes an inability to stand on his own two feet because of this. Weakness and dizziness plagued him for a week after he was able to rise, at last, on August 2. Thereafter, as anonymous sex became more and more important in his life, the risk of venereal infection lurked in the background continuously – and broke to the surface on more than one occasion. Two years later, on July 16, 1958, for instance, he sought out Dr. Edel – "have to tell him just that it *is* possible. The next day there was a positive diagnosis, then a brief delay while a substitute for penicillin was rooted out. An appointment on July 25 resulted in the entry, "I'm clean again as a newborn babe – so *that's* over with." Another doctor, while treating him for a throat infection in February, 1961, delicately informed him "en passant" that "the other tests were negative." "Of course," Ingolf bristled , "after all those antibiotics." By this time Ingolf had definitely rejected the notion that any amendment in his reckless life style was needed in order to avoid such problems. Indeed as the Dahls passed through New York on their way back to L.A. only a few days after getting the all-clear from the first Tanglewood episode, Ingolf was well enough to try his luck at the Everard Baths, an ill-fated establishment that years later burned to the ground with a terrible loss of life to the gay community.

Three days after returning from Tanglewood Ingolf left for San Francisco and a four week mountaineering expedition in the Cascades with Bill Colvig. On August 23rd he and Bill arrived in Portland, Ingolf excited by the prospects at the Portland "Y," but sulking because there was no letter from Etta waiting for him there. In Seattle it was Bill who wanted to go to the baths – "expensive and nothing," a disapproving Ingolf wrote, "just some old fat fags." A pain in Ingolf's right side on September 4 put an end to their mountaineering. Four days later he checked into a San Francisco hospital to have an x-ray and discovered he was suffering from a cracked rib which, Bill later told me, probably resulted from the overenthusiastic bear hug which one mountain buddy had visited upon the other. After the hospital visit the two went to a gay club, Ingolf in tears because, he feared, Bill no longer found him attractive. (But nothing is said about Bill's reaction when, during the course of this trip, he dropped Ingolf off for a night of romantic reunion, after many years, with Guy.) On September 9 Ingolf went to see Viveca Lindfors in *Miss Julie* and came home to Bill's arms once more – "so good, after promiscuity, to return to the arms of one whom one loves."

Ingolf liked to convince himself that he was not a promiscuous personality and that given the right opportunity and the right partner (such as Bill) he would have been happy to have had a permanent and monogamous relationship with one man only. I dispute this. One of the things he liked about his visits to 1403 Montgomery Street was that he and Bill could *both* go looking for new excitement in the steam rooms of San Francisco. His love for Bill did nothing to diminish his mania for casual sex in Los Angeles and, caught in the vice of this new urgency, he devoted himself to seeking ever wider opportunities for queer quickies. He trekked over the Swish Alps, he continued to have luck at the "Y" ("Ingolf," he warned himself on June 8, "one day you'll surely get caught."), he made his first visit to the Melrose Baths on April 28, 1956: "Oh what beauty and music," he wrote, after witnessing two young boys in embrace. But he found himself pushed aside by all the attractive denizens of the baths. "I see myself getting old, slipping," he had written after looking at the Havasu slides, "the discrepancy between the glowing inside and the sliding, falling outside." This was about the time that Ingolf gave up a habit that had always delighted the rest of his family; on mountain trips he would leave his shaving tools behind and surprise us on his return with a quickly grown beard. I realize now that he stopped this when he began to notice all the grey hairs in his whiskers, a sight that his vanity could no longer endure. Now at the Melrose Baths he watched the bodies in the snake pit, "exciting and sordid and so disturbing that it shakes me to my feet," and reflected on his own exclusion from this scene, the dangers of being spotted by someone he knew, the contrast between the "anonymity of this animal copulation" and his times with Bill – "with Bill everything is *bright*, and confident, and clean and good."

On September 11, 1956, as he went through the mail that had accumulated while he had been away on his recent mountaineering expedition, he opened something he described as a "bombshell." It was not another letter from Etta. Instead Ingolf Dahl, newly promoted full professor, recently inducted member of ASCAP, respected family man, mentor to the young, seeker after purity, defender of justice and friend of the nuns, learned that he had been kicked out of the Y.M.C.A.!

We were meant to laugh in 1979 when the Village People told us that it's fun to stay at the Y.M.C.A. – where you can do whatever you feel and hang out with all the boys. But we can perhaps also appreciate that the "Y" has not always been so amused by the purposes to which the gay community put its athletic facilities. In 1956 there was even less tolerance and understanding in this matter than might prevail today. The letter which Ingolf received was dated September 6 and was signed "Very truly yours" by the membership secretary of the Downtown Branch. It was brief, to the point, and not to the point at the same time – "Dear Mr. Dahl: The Membership Department has been instructed to cancel your membership as of this date. Within the prerogative of the YMCA no reason is assigned."

Complaining of a "*heavy* cloud over soul and heart," Ingolf spent the next few days in numb depression. At the root of his agony lay two conflicting realizations: his dismissal was against all standards of due process and fair play on the one hand and, on the other, he *was* guilty of behavior that might legitimately be deemed unacceptable by the "Y." He was unable to recall any specific incident which might have been observed, and his anger at the thought of an informer was considerable. "The most grotesque thing," he wrote Bill, "is that this calamity should have happened just to me – when you think of the many who are *really* wild (which I am not!) and who get away with everything over the years. But it is probably true that I have always been too naive, trusting, straightforward, guileless – and probably careless."

Bill urged him to pursue the matter with higher authorities in the Y.M.C.A. organization. Ingolf wrote the first draft of a letter on September 16, demanding a meeting. "I believe I am fairly courageous and manly myself and may be able to carry it through," he wrote to Bill on that date, but the wisdom of such a course soon came into question. "In spite of all the emotional bruises over the years my shell has remained fairly soft and I can be easily hurt," he added, "one other factor is that you are responsible to nobody but yourself and I am not." Though he probably made no comments on the incident to Etta – for fear of the inevitable I Told You So lecture – Ingolf did confer with his gay friends and he may even have spoken to an attorney. Some of his advisors encouraged him to fight, and one was quoted as saying, "This letter is written by an organization that has not the guts to speak openly and honestly." On September 23 he spoke to Fitz for the first time. "Without reasons to satisfy them," Ingolf paraphrased his friend's remarks, "they wouldn't have taken the step...I'll never find out who informed, will never be taken back." Fearing that a fuss might lead to a blacklisting in other cities, Ingolf decided not to demand a meeting but to save face instead by writing the following disingenuous letter to the membership secretary:

Dear Sir:

Returning to this city after an absence of several months I find your letter of September 6, which was not forwarded to me. I do now recall that on my last visit to the YMCA gymnasium, on August 13 or 14, I inadvertently forgot to pay in advance the charge for the steam room facilities. That day the man in charge, in checking up, asked if everyone there had paid the fee, and I immediately recalled that I had neglected to do so, after which I apologized, signed my name, and finally paid on my way out.

In 12 years this is the first time I ever neglected to pay the fee for these facilities. With that length of membership I think it extremely trivial to base your actions on this incident, particularly inasmuch as I was not aware of having been remiss at any other times. I wish hereby to protest your letter of September 6 and to state I consider it unfair.

I notice that my membership was paid up to September 30, so that there would be no refund coming to me, but you may consider this letter as a resignation from membership on my part.

There was no response to this letter. On October 7 Ingolf wrote to Bill that the chapter was finally closed, "I went down there last week to pick up the stuff in my basket, it was a strange feeling." Ingolf missed the "Y" very much, not merely because of the erotic possibilities which were now denied him, but because he had been a genuine user of the pool, the track, and the weight room. This I know not merely from the journals but because once, during my teens, he took me there for a run. Gradually he began to use campus facilities at U.S.C. for his athletic endeavors, but he tried not to indulge in any other activities there: you could never tell when one of your students might be in the next shower stall. And that student might number his own stepson among his friends.

It was Etta's task to devise a strategy for dealing with this "perceptive and sensitive adolescent." In the late spring of 1956 she gave Ingolf an undated letter which illustrates perfectly the fog of lies in which we were expected to take our breath in those days. Ingolf was considering a Sierra Club mountain climbing expedition in Alaska. "Dearest," Etta wrote:

...As you already know, I think you should go. My only real reservation was as to your physical ability to master the effort involved, but if you feel you have the stamina and the mountaineering know-how, that is enough for me...I understand and appreciate too...that being on a trip with your dear friend will be just about the crowning touch, since I assume he is going, too.

Etta then proposed that she and Ingolf "cook up" some financial hocus-pocus about the trip, which would be costly, in order to avoid any unnecessary accusations from relatives and friends who might possibly think of other ways in which the money might be better spent:

Anthony, like all adolescents, is inclined to judge his parents much more harshly than he will one day; his judgements are immature and not to be taken seriously. But, whether immature or not, his business or not, he has read the Sierra bulletin, knows the minimum cost involved, and to him, in the light of what is left of our check each month and our lament about lack of income, as well as the list of things we are always saying we can't afford – it will seem like sheer self-indulgence on your part.

Ingolf should tell all concerned that the fee in the *Sierra Club Bulletin* was for non-members only, that from New York to White Horse the League of Composers was paying the fee, and that someone else was providing free return transportation by truck. "This is a simple, straightforward story and all you have to do is tell it straight and consistently." As a further kindness to Etta, Ingolf was requested to:

Tell Anth that your friend Bill is going, if he is. He feels left out and put out if you don't share your friends with him a little bit. You did it so nicely after the Havasu trip. It needn't be much. And make a composer's conference or something plausible to him about your Ojai trip, whenever it is to be. Children do not digest parental mysteries well. They merely feel "left out."

Still perturbed by his expulsion from the "Y," Ingolf reported on October 31, 1956, that, "these bottoms of depression come too quickly together...The deep blackness. Bill – and Etta – and the gay life – and the composing career – and the outdoors – these just pull me apart." On December 21 he added, "am shut up, frustrated, lonesome, keyed up sexually and dammed up creatively." Writing to Bill on January 12, 1957, he noted that a recent performance of *Das Lied Von Der Erde* had left him in tears – "My whole adolescence and youthful emotions and sentiments are wrapped up in this piece." Then he concluded, "But it feels good to have a real emotional jag once in a while (particularly when brought on by beautiful music), and in a way I am rather happy that I'm still capable of strong feeling (some people would say: then why doesn't he show it in his music?) and feel sorry for those who aren't."

Was Etta capable of strong emotions? In spite of a number of successful sexual encounters with her husband, and her acceptance of his affair with Bill, it is obvious that she was not completely happy with his nocturnal rambles in Los Angeles. When, in February, 1957, he told her that he planned to have dinner with some of the boys, she got into such a state that he had to arrive home the next day with roses – "she smiles again, it's OK." This was the same day that the two later celebrated the completion of the *Piano Quartet*.

Because Etta didn't want to know the details of Ingolf's gay existence he gradually fell into the habit of hiding them altogether, going out after a few hours in the studio, where he had no telephone, and returning late at night. On March 23, 1957, he went to a party in the afternoon, got coaxed into seeing a production of Gide's *Immoralist* ("parts of it strike home") and had to come home with some improvised excuse in mid-evening – "fortunately," he noted after Etta had swallowed his explanation, "the deception works."

The Los Angeles bath scene continued to offer Ingolf both release and frustration. His need for gay contact was so intense now that he could fit in a stop at one of these establishments at the end of a day that would have put anyone else in his own bed. On October 14, 1956, to illustrate, Ingolf had private composition students at 9: 00 and 10:00; auditions and orchestra organization at 11:00; a meeting of the Executive Committee at 12:00; he conducted Haydn and Cimarosa with the Orchestra from 1:00 to 3:00; heard more auditions from 3:00 to 3:30; gave a conducting class from 3:30 to 5:15; ate dinner in the Orange Cafe; practiced at Clark House from 6:00 to 7:30; played through three Brahms quartets with the American Chamber Players at 7:30; had a drink with two quartet members after that; and *then* went in search of a new bath he had heard about in the Valley.

Frequently there were complaints about the pickings. On December 17, 1956, the only partners available were "a bunch of elderly psychopaths – and they don't even have each other (nobody has one, except myself!)...(Does this really make me an elderly psychopath?)" On January 1, 1957, he reported that in one bath house visit he was the only customer when he first arrived, "but a little later somebody else, rather nice, came in, and inasmuch as he found nobody there but a bald, middle-aged (albeit rather spunky and muscular) mad musician, he put up with him." In October, 1957 he found another bath with a gay emphasis, Brooks Beverly, but his experiences continued to be only partially satisfactory: "I just ain't got it," he wrote on February 1, 1958, "not at all or not anymore. There seems just nothing I like that I can get close to." "The dirty old neurotics" within his reach now made him feel like a dirty old neurotic himself, and there is no question that Ingolf *was* suffering from a form of sexual mania, by which I do not mean homosexuality. His inability to reach any form of permanent sexual fulfillment was the tragedy of his later years, even though the repetitive nature of his torment dulls our sympathy for his agony.

His affection for Bill Colvig *did* remain constant throughout this period. On April 7, 1957 Ingolf wrote to Bill that he had declined the opportunity to address an audience at an NAACC concert on *how* he came to write *Variations on an Air by Couperin* – "I would have been driven to tell where and by whom I first heard the Couperin, and with my wife in the audience, who would have understood quite well, it would not have been tactful (although she knows, and approves, that the piece is dedicated to you – but there is no point in rubbing things in.)" While conducting the *Alto Rhapsody* on October 6 Ingolf noted to Bill, "I kind of dedicated the performance to you," tracing for his friend the homosexual referents in the original Goethe text.

"You write I should stop making such a fuss about you," Ingolf had written to Bill on my 19th birthday, January 6, 1957, "Don't you think I am trying really hard to fight this preoccupation with you...I will even go so far as to try to bring to my mind all the instances of your faults, your childishness, your crudities, your excesses. As if it would make any difference whatsoever. You might as well try to stop the stream from running downhill."

Between November 1956 and May 1958 Ingolf saw Bill on eight occasions, all but one involving a visit to San Francisco. The longest of these, which included stops in the Sierras, the Wind River Range in Wyoming, and the Canadian Rockies, lasted for two months in the summer of 1957. A grateful Ingolf summed up the state of his emotional life when he concluded, "I really live for these few and short times we are together."

94. MR. WONDERFUL

During the Kaweah trip of 1958, undertaken in the company of a small Sierra Club group, Ingolf does mention that, at their own campsite, "B and I have a little jam session," but it is obvious that the intensity of the affair was beginning to wane. After our Sierra trip of 1959, during which I had my first chance to see the famous San Francisco mountain man on the trail, Bill and Ingolf remained behind for a few days in the Mt. Williamson area. Again there is a reference to "ripping one off" on August 30, but by now the two were facing issues of incompatibility "I feel adequate and walk well," my stepfather protested, but he could no longer maintain Bill's trail speed. The latter was clearly unhappy about being held back and referred to Ingolf as an "elderly man." "This hurts," Ingolf added – "should this be the end?" Bill stubbornly refused to attempt a summit *Ingolf* wanted to conquer – "Now the incompleteness again, just having everything in life *short* of the crucial final span (small and yet all-importantly big!) Everything is just short that much of reaching *the* point." That evening Bill made juice from elderberries. Ingolf threw his up. Bill suffered from a stiff neck, was "bitchy and unwell." The two remained best buddies thereafter, lovers on occasion, and fellow climbers many times, but Bill was now involved in extensive solo mountain climbing trips all over the world, and Ingolf must surely have realized by this time that the aspirations he had once held for their relationship would now fall well short of the mark.

I take it as a sign of this more casual attitude that Ingolf could now welcome his San Francisco friend into his own home, Bill making the first of several stops at Cheremoya on the way to mountain climbing destinations in late 1959. Predictably, Etta and Bill became good friends and correspondents and it was Etta who urged Bill to visit during their next trip to Europe. I remember his Los Angeles visits; Bill would be pressed into some household fix-it chore, where his skills as an electrician or carpenter could be captured by Etta.

When Ingolf left some of his clothes in San Francisco, something he managed to do quite often, it was Etta who would have to retrieve them now – "Would you mind very much sending down the white orlon shirt Ingolf left up there. The reason is that the frayed cuffs need turning before he can wear it again."

Etta's attitude toward this sharing of her spouse was, at least in the case of these long-term relationships, remarkably tolerant, if not insanely self-sacrificial. She is reported to have embraced Ingolf in the presence of another of his gay friends with the comment, "Isn't he wonderful. And isn't it wonderful that we can all have him!"

Bill surprised Ingolf by showing up in the audience of a Museum concert in which the *Variations on an Air by Couperin* was played. Spotting him in the audience, Etta was overheard explaining to her friends that Bill was Ingolf's mountain climbing buddy from San Francisco, that one of the pieces was dedicated to him, that he was very shy. After much gesturing, she succeeded in getting Bill to move his seat next to her own. The once volatile and threatening entanglement had been tamed, and Ingolf and Bill now used their time together almost exclusively for mountain adventures. "Memories of a warmer heart," flashed through Ingolf's mind as he and Bill drove for a second time over northwestern territory in the summer of 1960. There remained, of course, an immense residue of affection and respect. "After you flew south," Bill wrote at the end of this trip, "I realized all over again how fortunate I was to have met you. Each trip I learn to like you all over again and enjoy your company all the more. You're so goddam human."

Ingolf's other extracurricular activities in sex continued to follow the pattern we have by now become accustomed to. "A quick release" is a phrase which appears with some frequency in accounts of visits to the dozen or so bath houses which Ingolf visited on a regular basis – Melrose, Westside, Gower, Pico, Brooks Beverly and Ventura, Hyperion, Orlando, even one in El Monte – those "madhouses of instant sex," to use Bill Colvig's phrase. Ingolf was so successful in driving these erotic needs into a separate and protected compartment in his mind that he could visit Etta in her hospital bed in the afternoon and slip into the steam room of a gay health club that night. What might his occasionally dilatory students have thought had they known what opportunities their last-minute cancellations presented to their randy professor? (There is even one entry to indicate that Ingolf broke his own rule by engaging in a brief encounter in the Physical Education building after a meeting of the Executive Committee in 1960 and that, violating another, he enjoyed the sexual company of a former student during the same period.)

But Ingolf enjoyed no grand passion. The costume parties at Fitz's were no longer quite the occasion they had once been. And the bathhouse scene provided the usual mixture of marvelous sightings, lost opportunities, venereal scares, and anonymous adventure. Anonymity was only one curse. The partner might be "strictly passive" or "primitive," the other customers might be "strictly Square," you might have to settle for a "quick do with a fatso," or the clientele might be so wonderful that, by contrast, you found yourself "totally out of their class and age." Ingolf complained about the boredom of repetition, the same "stupid stuff." He often arrived too late at night ("the steam isn't even hot," he grumbled on December 22, 1964), and to make the disaster complete his glasses got broken. He worried that he might be spotted at the baths, and that his nocturnal prowling might disturb his wife upstairs.

There were triumphs. At the Pico baths on July 12, 1963, a slender young man with a lovely face and a polite manner ("not a hustler") accepted Ingolf's embrace in a brief moment of "lyric beauty." On June 4, 1965, he left the Honors Convocation on campus to enter the steam room at the Melrose Baths, finding it to be "the proverbial snake pit with the nicest things in it, just fantastic – the biggest melee I've been in." On February 18, 1966, he reports another hour of happiness at the Orlando. He had just given a lift to four 13-14 year-olds but far from exciting him, these teenagers had alarmed him – "their conversation frightening – the obscenity, the hidden violence – dim view of the future." At the baths the disapproving guardian of the commonweal reports a fabulous encounter – "The greatest beauty and strength – 'what an angel you are' – all is there but the wings. He wants nothing and gives it all." After wishing Ingolf a good night and sweet dreams the angel was gone. "How have I deserved this?" a grateful Ingolf asked. Then he knelt on the floor and offered a prayer of thanks.

Such experiences were rare. "Lots of dark and depressed thoughts about emotional situation," he wrote on July 26, 1965, "Should really become a bigamist, but how can that be managed – can't even find room for everything in my life right now – but these quick dos as last night are so very unsatisfactory and depressing." Only an insatiable need could have driven my stepfather to participate in encounters so full of disappointment and expense. Indeed, Ingolf's habit, like other addictions, was costly. When there was no action in one place he would often head for another – "Very expensive dud ," he reported after a disillusioning night in 1960.

How to take advantage of the bath scene when Ingolf traveled away from Los Angeles was a problem. He was stimulated by some sights in the Schruns sauna during the second sabbatical, but concluded, "It would be so nice, but in such a small place – what complications." He was too ill during his winter trip to Stockholm to engage in any sexual activities, and his only opportunity for "fun and release" came on occasional visits to Zurich. He visited the Everard Baths in late August, 1962, and again in January, 1963, when he travelled east for the American premiere of his *Trio*. Here he met a man named Russell and the two arranged what proved to be a disastrous rendezvous in Russell's Brooklyn apartment. It was during this visit, as we have noted earlier, that he met, at a publisher's party, that other journal-keeping composer, Ned Rorem. Reading through one of Rorem's books in 1967 Ingolf wrote, "What a camp, what exhibitionism, what gall...can't tear myself away." Ingolf found some of Rorem's diaries "tiresome," but above all he was jealous of the author – "if I had had a tenth of this 'life' in earlier years (when I too wasn't bad looking or bad in bed.)"

During his away games Ingolf rarely encountered anyone with whom he had anything more than casual contact – "a quick do" in the steam room of a bath in Seattle before his Bellingham lecture in 1963, a successful coupling at the Morgan Baths on the eve of an *Aria Sinfonica* performance in Buffalo in 1965, complaints that he could find no bath at all in puritanical Cincinnati. For that matter, someone put a Keep Out! sign at the entrance to one of his favorite Griffith Park hunting spots in more tolerant L.A. in November, 1965.

On New Year's Day, 1967, Ingolf went late at night to a club called Samson & Delilah. In a private room he was stimulated by a "marvelously endowed" young one, but the real excitement came when someone rapped on the door and whispered, "Cops!" Ingolf scampered wildly into a more public steam room and there fell into conversation with a chemistry professor I shall call Nigel. "Turns out to be a most worthwhile person," Ingolf wrote of his new friend. They talked science, before turning to sex. "He is the best in every way, how did I deserve it...I am completely aflame again." Unfortunately Ingolf had no idea how to reach the chemist and inquiries at all the local colleges proved unsuccessful. This was a desperate moment for Ingolf, "flooded with that feeling again, thought it would never happen...how great personal-sexual fulfillment helps the creative spark." (This remark serves to remind us that on January 31, 1965, as Ingolf was resting from a primitive "do" in the steam room of Ventura Brooks, ideas for the ending of the last movement of the *Aria Sinfonica* came flooding forth.) Now, "The whole agony of Peter is being repeated," he complained on January 9, 1967, "the search, the wondering what he does now, that if I see him he would be with someone else or just fluff me off – would he?"

Since there was so much disappointment in his current sex life it is not surprising that Ingolf frequently dwelt – as the name of Peter reminds us – on ancient relationships, successful and unsuccessful – for each had at least offered the promise of happiness at some time. Many times his thoughts returned to Hamburg and the tragedies of a teenager's broken heart. He mourned the loss of Edat, Barbara and Kurt – "oh Kurt – where are your bones smouldering and the flesh that I loved and love still." When Barbara Kruger-Sachse died, Ingolf was disturbed by bad dreams – "the overwhelming sadness that all that is lost...her nobility, grace, beauty, fire, inspiration, greatness of gifts and giving – gone, gone..." He did hear again from Guy and managed a second reunion with him in 1963. On February 3, 1961, he had been surprised by another voice from the past – "Douglas calls, of all things. Feel stiff and embarrassed in E.'s presence. He wants to visit me." In fact the two did meet, a number of years later, during a CMP conference with took Ingolf to New York on January 20th, 1967 (a date he has noted in his journal as the anniversary of the death of his father). Ingolf was sitting in his hotel room after a dinner party when the phone rang. "Deep and effeminate both," the voice of Douglas scolded him for not having called. Ingolf rushed to get dressed. In Douglas' apartment, "the flood, the revelations – all along it was not only one way. I did mean something, I mean something now – we talk and talk." Overwhelmed to be taken back after twenty-three years, Ingolf did not sleep a wink as he lay beside the boyish body, "the same sweet lips, so touching, so sad." Ingolf moved from the Americana into Douglas' apartment. "That this was in the stars," Ingolf wrote, "this utter vindication, the solution, resolution of the anguish and suffering of 1944." Only a few days later, after driving to the campus on the afternoon of January 23rd, Ingolf reports unhappiness at the fact that he has received no word from the elusive Nigel during his absence – "Will have to learn to live with the fact (oh, no!) of never seeing him again – Ingolf you are grabby really – But to have an East Coast and West Coast Douglas would have been so nice. Then he drove home to give "a *real* 'hello' kiss to Etta. I wish she would love me."

Ingolf returned to Douglas' side as he began his leave of absence on February 12, 1967. "From now on," Ingolf reported, "the problems gradually become apparent and open and real and crystallized in his drinking...Our interests are far apart." Disturbed by the barking of Douglas' dogs, Ingolf did not sleep a wink, and "Still no real sex, which I crave so much." "At last some fulfillment" was reported on the next day, and Ingolf visited Douglas a second time on the eve of his departure for Europe in April. This was a month for remembrance of things past, for on the 10th, just after leaving the MacDowell Colony, Ingolf had spent a night with the last of his Swiss lovers, Heini, in Rockport, Massachusetts. "The heart is silent across the centuries," Ingolf wrote of this disappointing encounter, "what was, was."

I have a feeling that, increasingly, Etta came to resent Ingolf's gay life style, especially his nocturnal wanderings, not so much because she disapproved of their homoerotic character but simply because her husband was not around at the odd moment when she craved his company or support. The separate quarters in which he now slept gave him the opportunity of slipping out discreetly late at night – "does she know that I went out last night?" he asks on July 28, 1960. I have no doubt that he was missed more than once, and this uncertainty about his whereabouts could not have helped the troubled relationship with a wife who had undergone her second mastectomy that February.

Of course she had welcomed Bill Colvig into her home, even encouraged him to bring his sleeping bag into Ingolf's room during the 1966 Ojai Festival. She accepted an invitation to a New Year's Eve party at Fitz's in 1965 (though Ingolf went alone the next year), and she gave many other signs of her acceptance of Ingolf's foothold in gay society. But it was a different matter when it came to her accommodating the less stable, anonymous and furtive liaisons which Ingolf pursued at all hours (from, not in) his apartment below. "She is still up – everything seems OK," he wrote after a late night on July 5, 1966. But when he asked her what she wanted for her 60th birthday, later that year, she answered, "More of you." She was speaking less poetically but perhaps more trenchantly when, in protest at Ingolf's driving too quickly over the country roads near Alt-Aussee in 1967, she asked, "Do you want to exchange me for two 30 year-olds?"

That her depression was deepening is evident from the nervous collapse she endured during the second sabbatical in the spring of 1962. As I have noted earlier, Ingolf never seemed to understand why Etta, who was seven years his senior and suffering, by 1965, from a third malign attack on her body, might have resented his ill-timed and inconsistent attentions, why she preferred the curtain of silence to the open air of an unpalatable truth. And that truth was that in Ingolf she possessed a sexual being whose love she could not encompass, whose life style made him a stranger on many occasions, and whose very whereabouts were often a mystery. These factors surely help explain her depression, her untypical introversion, the "wall," which he complains of so often in these years. He sensed that he was a part of this process and, at the same time, he did not know how to reverse it. Re-reading his journal for 1940, as they approached their 25th wedding anniversary, Ingolf noted – "Poor Etta – to have got stuck with *that* thing – and poor Ingolf too – the inadequacies, the frustrations, the delusions – How did we last?"

Etta prided herself on an ability to rise above judgment and blame, at least in the case of her beloved husband. In "Eric Forth and Back," the children's verse she worked on in 1965, another biologically ambivalent creature appears, but it cries out for our sympathy, not our antipathy:

But now Eric was drawing again. He made an octopus and then he
made an eel.

"These two combined," he said, "should give an interesting new
creature with arms a block long."

Just the thing," her majesty explained, "for our chathletes!"

You may have it week-ends and I'll have it Mondays," said the
Chempress. "In between it will rest."

When Chalec had brushed the creature into life it began to sing sadly:

I used to be an octopus,
I used to be an eel,
And now that I am both of them
I don't know how to feel!
I don't know *how* I feel!
I really don't,
I certainly don't know how I *feel*!

I used to to live in water,
And now I must live on land.
And all this weight upon my arms
Is more than I can stand!
It's really more,
It's certainly more,
It's more that I can *stand!*

And on which night of the week was Etta sure to have her husband at
her side? Was his behavior in any way responsible for her agony? Of course
she would have us believe otherwise, but I do not doubt for a moment
that this perpetual sublimation of her justifiable resentment contributed
significantly to her malaise.

95. SUGARDADDY

Midway into his 1967 sojourn in Europe, Ingolf concluded a period of
Alpine skiing on May 24 and, before returning to his wife in Alt-Aussee,
tried his luck at the Ottenweg Baths in Zurich:

Right on entrance, a dark-eyed beauty smiles at me (*why?*) and I
make a play, he flirts back. Tuck my courage in both hands, against
better knowledge, dress with him in cubicle. He's waiting outside.

Lovely, very young. He speaks first, "Wie stehts" or some such. Walk along to car, he shows me pictures. Take him to dinner (sugardaddy) elegant and nice. Tell without inhibition about I.D.

The two agreed to meet again, and Ingolf spent several desperate hours vainly trying to ring the number his young friend had given him. "Shit and double shit," he complained, before returning to the anonymous turmoil of the baths, "deserve it to run after such young golddiggers." The next morning Ingolf parked in front of the young man's Zurich flat, waiting "very pessimistically." "And then," the story continues, "miracle, that face – he's rushing out, is surprised – 'you didn't phone.'" Ingolf drove Hugo, as I shall call him, from Zurich to Lucerne, where this twenty-seven year-old hotel clerk was employed. "Conversation a little strained sometimes," Ingolf admitted, "because we have so little in common." The older man was not allowed to come up to Hugo's apartment but, "in dark hall downstairs he grabs my (excited) loins – so everything shall be OK."

Ingolf decided to spend the rest of his abbreviated mountain vacation in a Lucerne hotel room. He showered and shaved and waited for Hugo to come off-duty. They drank and went to Ingolf's room – "He is so direct, so simple. All is lovely and too short...when he comes back from bathroom he gets me with a whore's know-how, what a boy." Ingolf was soon besotted with his new companion – "the regularity of his eyebrows, long amber limbs, the beauty of the skin – how lucky, lucky I am, how could this still come to me?" "For your age," Hugo told him, "you have a good body."

Ingolf was in love again. As he began the long drive back to Alt-Aussee the next day he noted that, "The animal is purring. World is singing and *everything seems possible*." "Etta is home and is so happy that I came early," he continued, "the double life again." "I need a kiss and a drink in that order," he told her. He drank a scotch and ate the dinner Etta had fixed for him, "Lovely to see her relief and happiness." Almost immediately a yearning for Hugo overwhelmed him.

Ingolf was surely ready for another love affair. Douglas, it was obvious, could not fill the need for adventure, and the long missing chemist, Nigel, was a once-encountered dream. But it was perhaps inevitable that Ingolf, in the final flowering of his erotic energies, was now to embark not on one, but two affairs simultaneously.

His attempt to secure partners in Bad Ischl was not successful until almost the end of his stay in Alt-Aussee. On August 16 he was doing errands in the town where previous frustrating experiences at the sauna had once lead him to devour three pieces of cake at the Cafe Zauner in recompense. As he crossed the street on this day he was struck by a motor scooter. His glasses landed on the pavement, but he suffered only bruises. Continuing on his errands, he picked up Etta's coat at the cleaners, bought a ballpoint pen for himself, and had a look around Ischl station ('nothing"). At the sauna his luck improved. "*Now* it happens in shower room – a *young* blonde kid with *that* look at me, straight in the face, but I think hell he's too young and probably doesn't mean it." But he did, and was soon diving beneath Ingolf's legs in the pool. The two made a date to meet at Hallstatt at ten that night. Ingolf had half a mind not to go but at last he put his sneakers on and hid a blanket in the car. Dieter, as I shall call this young man, showed up at last and the two drove to a deserted road for fun and games beside the car. They made a date for the next day, Ingolf already worrying about "the problem of telling E. – just say vaguely at breakfast about errand in Bad Aussee." Too upset to compose ("Life vs. Art"), Ingolf waited nervously until rendezvous time. Dieter was not there. In a state, Ingolf returned to sit and stew at his desk, staring into space, full of the blackest thoughts. At night he returned to Hallstatt – "He's there..." Another night of love-making followed and after that, for Ingolf was soon to leave Austria, months of affectionate correspondence – though this relationship never seems to have generated the emotional electricity released by Hugo. The latter passion continued to smoulder for months.

The first letter to Hugo was dispatched on May 27, the day after Ingolf's return from Lucerne. Many followed, each begging for a reunion. A draft of a letter written on May 29 survives:

> You are one of the most attractive persons I have ever met and I still can't quite understand how it was possible that everything happened as it did. You have probably already half forgotten, but to me every minute, every word, every sight is as strongly present as it was then... a look at your face is enough to cure all the ills of this world.

On June 1 Ingolf sent Hugo some cufflinks from a store in Bad Aussee. The older man asked for a photo and waited to see if there was any response to his many communications. At last an answer came on June 5 – "it is as sweet and lovely as can be" – though Hugo now asked Ingolf to use a woman's name on the return address of future correspondence, perhaps "Prinzessin Inge Dahl." The princess proposed another Lucerne rendezvous at the end of the summer, clearly living much of the rest of his stay in Austria in a state of fevered anticipation. "I know," he wrote in his journal on June 11, "that this is no *real* relationship, that I am being an infatuated old fool, that worlds of age, intellect, compatibility, etc. separate us. To hell with it – what would I not give to see those eyes again." On June 16 Hugo accepted Ingolf's plan for an August meeting in Switzerland. Feeling vindicated before "all those who have killed me" – even those whose crimes were almost forty years old – Ingolf gloried in his victory – "I can't believe it is possible." There was to be a music festival in Lucerne at the time and this provided a plausible cover story for Etta. Ingolf wrote off for many concert tickets and then discovered that Hugo had an interest in only one or two. With visions of the naked Hugo dancing before him, Ingolf lay down in the Alpine sun – like some latter day Gustave von Aschenbach – claiming he "must make myself attractive for H." He sent candy to Lucerne on July 7.

We can speculate on Etta's reaction to this budding romance, our interest piqued by Ingolf's admission that the letter containing Hugo's snapshot was actually thrown down onto his desk by his wife. If her usual reaction is any clue, however, we must conclude that she *said* not a thing about this affair. She claimed, after all, a reluctance to spoil Ingolf's sense of adventure by making herself a part of that other world. In a letter of April 14 she had speculated if "my having become acceptable to these people – has as it must – changed your relationship with them, and I would feel terrible to think that I was an intruder, no matter how involuntarily and no matter how sympatico we have all become." Etta had broadened the scope of this letter to include one last swipe at her mother-in-law:

> I'm afraid your long, deep, early draught of "love" in the guise of uncritical approbation and 1000 percent cheerful companionship (which no really normal person can either give or accept) left a terrible mark on you. You will immediately reply that you *do* know when I am angry at the situation and not you, and that you *don't* mind criticism motivated by my love and my desire to see you more

truly characterful. In that case why do 3/4 of your responses take the form of apologies? Are you aware of your remarks as absolutely laden with guilt, and that you spend I don't know how much time in making rationalizations – which are not only transparent but *unnecessary?*

That Etta was thinking about Ingolf's sexual behaviour in these remarks becomes clearer in the next paragraph, "I only trust that I have never (the mere fact of our marriage) stood between you and anybody, though it is quite possible I unwittingly have." Are we to conclude that the letter-slamming wife who tossed one of Hugo's missives on her husband's desk was only being angry at the *situation* and not at her undoubtedly guilt-ridden spouse? This may have been *her* rationalization, but not even a scholastic theologian could split hairs that finely. Thus tension rippled beneath the surface of the Alt-Aussee calm in which the Dahls were now to play hosts to all those summer visitors. When Dorothy and I arrived, Ingolf drove us to Hallstatt, scene of his recent trysts with Dieter. He remained behind in Alt-Aussee for two days after we had left with Etta. On the 26th – "the day has finally come" – he undertook the twelve-hour car journey to Lucerne.

For the next few days he kept an extended journal on separate sheets in his "memory drawer." Hugo, a little embarrassed by Ingolf's early arrival at his pensione, gave his friend a little peck on the cheek – "those eyes, eyes, eyes again." "It is just as good as the first time," Ingolf wrote of their love-making. After a restaurant dinner Ingolf doped himself with two seconal and a darvon in an attempt to get *some* sleep next to the slumbering idol. Not as tired as he had expected ("the juices still flow") Ingolf began the 27th by giving his lover a massage – "to massage that body, to feel every inch of it – a paean – sharp hip bones, long legs, touching shoulder blades, enhanced by gold chain and cross." That afternoon the two checked into a Basle hotel, entered a local bath, and went to the movies and a gay bar before making love again. Ingolf checked into a Lucerne hotel after the two had visited Freiburg on the 29th ("These days are like weeks"). He took his friend on a hike – "Hugo is certainly no mountain man, but maybe I could train him (at Mammoth?)...On way down tell him all about myself, Anth, etc, and he is quite impressed." The two looked for a spot where Ingolf could take some provocative photographs; this process was continued late at night, after Hugo had finished a shift at his hotel. On the 30th the two spent the morning at the lake, then Ingolf shopped for presents for his friend and actually went to a concert while Hugo completed his work for the night. Ingolf was distraught because it was their last night together. Both cried. Ingolf dropped his friend off but was too overcome to continue his journey. Hugo came back to the car to urge his friend to "go away." "I love you," Ingolf sobbed.

The next morning my stepfather placed a pot of chrysanthemums before Hugo's door and drove to Zurich, uncertain if he would ever see his lover again. Nevertheless, in a year in which there had already been reunions with Douglas and Heini, one more was about to occur, for on this day he had a rendezvous with Edat, his very first lover, the Hamburg painter with whom he had maintained a lifelong correspondence. "He is white," Ingolf reported, "a little filled up, handsome as ever, 65...We make out as good as always, on floor of his room. Very tender afterwards."

That night Ingolf put the car on a train in Basle and took a berth in a sleeper. One night was spent in Hamburg itself as he made arrangements to have the Volkswagen shipped back to Edi Schaar. He dined in an elegant 19th century restaurant – "the first toast to Pappi," whose world this was, "But nothing in town has touched a string, a chord, nothing has directly spoken, it is all second hand, thought, visual and cerebral memory only. And thoughts of floating ghosts (Barbara –). At last tears again and a toast to the empty chair across: to you Hugo – to youth, beauty, affection, charm."

On September 2 Ingolf flew to Copenhagen, where he was enchanted to meet someone named Erik in the City baths. The two went to Ingolf's hotel room but the previous occupant had not checked out yet – "do it on floor anyway (risky!)" After an opera performance that night Ingolf went to the Tivoli and a series of gay bars. At the El Toro Negro one of his drinking buddies began rifling through his pockets. Unwisely he took two of these strangers back to his hotel room, where his wallet disappeared altogether. "Lesson," Ingolf wrote after calculating his losses (twenty dollars and credit cards), "never with two, never with Mediterraneans, so foolish, foolish, and I didn't at all like them." As I recall Etta used a minor taxi accident as a cover story to explain the loss of her husband's billfold. The next morning, with a great sigh of relief, he discovered that the thieves had not used the baggage claim check in his wallet to steal his suitcases at the Copenhagen airport. A short muzak-ridden flight to Stockholm followed.

"The relief," a chastened Ingolf reported as he stepped off his plane in Sweden, "to be in a solid milieu after the squalor of this morning. The many worlds." "Most eager to see Etta again," he added on September 10 in Reykjavik, where he was at last reunited with his wife. "When she doesn't come to wake me at first, afraid she might be hurt by escapades and imagining the consequences. But she comes right away and it is as warm and lovely as ever. Someday I must tell her and get permission to let H. stay at Cheremoya. But we are now very close again (if only –)." On September 12 they flew to New York where Ingolf even managed a few minutes in a bath on 58th Street ("not one to play with me") before they returned to the terminal for a flight to Los Angeles. At home a letter from Hugo was waiting.

Ingolf's first creative priority upon his return to America was completion of *A Cycle of Sonnets*, a work that he had started in Alt-Aussee. He used as his text three of Petrarch's sonnets, portions of which should now be included in the prose translation of Dr. Robert E. Blake:

> *Solo e pensoso* ("Now I believe that mountains and shores, / rivers and woods know what is the tenor / of my life, which is hidden from others."; *Benedetto sia 'l giorno* ("Blessed be the day, the month, the year, / the season, the time, the hour and the moment, / the lovely country and the place, where I was overcome / by two beautiful eyes which now have bound me;" and *Ne così bello il Sol giammi levarsi* ("I saw Love, and the bow He was drawing, / in such guise that since then my life has not been safe, / yet my soul still longs to see this vision again.

Surely the significance of these texts in Ingolf's recent history is obvious; we have once again to face the vanity of isolating the creative life from the emotional one. Added to the score by the composer, are the initials of Douglas in the first movement, and of Hugo in the second and third.

Ingolf did continue to have a number of contacts with Douglas. "What happened, where is he, my heart still wants him," Ingolf wrote on March 30, 1968. On February 1, 1969, following a Washington meeting, Ingolf flew to New Jersey to spend two nights with his old friend. "I feel so vital, boyish, strong, next to him," he added, but it was clear that the passion was gone and that Ingolf could only wonder over all those hours of anguish he had squandered in 1944. "Dear Douglas, what a shadow of yourself you are now," Ingolf mused on April 6, 1969, the twenty-fifth anniversary of their first Boston rendezvous. On May 28 Ingolf received some startling news, "Douglas is married – may they be happy." So ended this very long relationship.

At home Ingolf soon threw himself into his two worlds. "Just to hear a friendly gay voice," he would often ring one of his Hollywood pals. This world, it is curious to note, satisfied only one longing. "The squares," he wrote after a hike in October, 1968, "are infinitely more congenial and enjoyable as friends than the gays I know." Fitz was still a friend and so was Bill Colvig, who visited L.A. in 1967; this was an important year for Ingolf's old mountain buddy, who now began to share his life with someone else from Ingolf's world, the composer Lou Harrison – whom Ingolf had known since 1944. In March, 1968, Etta and Ingolf were invited to Aptos to celebrate Bill's birthday. Bill and Lou visited Cheremoya in January, 1969 and that September Ingolf spent some time with these old friends at Tassajara.

Correspondence with Dieter began almost immediately after Ingolf's return from Europe. On September 19, 1967, Ingolf had the Broadway dispatch a bottle of Canoe to Austria. "What is happening to me?" Ingolf asked on October 13 as Dieter's letters became more affectionate, "want a man and (D.) could be *just* that." Then Dieter began to write of a girlfriend – "How is *that* going to work out, that this queen is taking the het. route??" When news of an engagement came in June, Ingolf, with the voice of bitter experience, expressed consternation over this direction – "how to rescue that boy – feel like seeing a friend run in front of a truck." Ingolf sent a small check and in return got photos of the wedding – another dream dashed.

On October 5 Ingolf opened another letter from Hugo. A visit was possible! In "unbearable excitement" and tremendously agitated at the prospect, Ingolf went to a bath the next day and, without proper precautions, submitted himself to the attacks of a large black man. The next few days were spent worrying about the likelihood of yet another venereal infection and fretting over the possibility that Hugo might soon arrive (and worrying that the first possibility might spoil any joy in the second). A blood test ordered by a nice but naive physician proved negative, which was just as well because on October 10 Hugo confirmed his arrival plans. Ingolf spent a sleepless night before approaching his wife on the subject of guests. "E. is again an angel," he reported on the 11th, "'*Yes*, of course your friend can stay.' I am fantastically relieved." "E. is so affectionate," he wrote on October 26, the night before Hugo's arrival.

Hugo was introduced to Etta at U.S.C. on the 27th – "he begins to charm her which he finally does." Indeed my mother seems to have made some effort to include Hugo as *her* guest also. The three went on outings together, to Laguna Beach for instance, to the movies, to nightclubs. Etta and Hugo played cards. Ingolf turned over his bedroom to his friend and slept upstairs in my old room. But a pattern was soon established – "Sneak down at night," he wrote on that first night, "2 A.M. leave him asleep." During the next few days Hugo was introduced to one of Ingolf's worlds as they visited Fitz and the gay bars. "The body and warmth beside me," Ingolf wrote after another nocturnal visit to his friend's bed, "I love him so much, but what can be?" On November 4 Ingolf went hiking with Bill. Hugo was not to be found when he returned. "Early down to studio," Ingolf reported after several vain searches during the night, "and the door is *locked*. Stand in front of it, head against door and feel the lowest point. Am just dismally down. It takes all day to make up with H. but finally do." Within a few nights Ingolf was again in possession of the warmth and nearness he craved, leaving his lover as the dawn broke, climbing surreptitiously through an upstairs window so as to maintain a charade which his wife could not possibly believe.

On November 10 the two took off for a Palm Springs weekend. Hugo scored a big hit in a gay bar in Desert Hot Springs but grew weary of the desert hike Ingolf had been looking forward to. Trying to overcome a growing dependency, Ingolf took Hugo to the Samson & Delilah baths and had a "grand time in steam room with a very nice butch type" while Hugo observed morosely. "It is nonsense to say that I have a victory over him – I am his slave – the perspective of the past: for decades, my whole youth, the frustrated desire for just this...and now the miracle." On the 14th Ingolf offered to sponsor the immigration of his friend to the United States, but Hugo was more interested in making dates with some new L.A.

acquaintances. On the 18th another driver put an end to the life of Ingolf's Peugeot, parked down on Beachwood, and, in a vile mood, Ingolf made do with rent-a-cars while a rejecting Hugo ("Does it always have to be sex?") got ready for a solo trip to Mexico.

Days were spent in yearning. "It is all so hopeless and impossible," Ingolf wrote on November 24, "an older man being so totally infatuated with someone so incompatible in so many ways." On December 5 Lou Harrison called and Ingolf's attempt to describe his plight ended in hysterical tears. The heading for December 9 reads "the last two days on earth," for on this date Hugo returned for another brief visit before departing Los Angeles for good. "When I get upstairs at 8:30," Ingolf reported, "E. says 'Hugo called early this a.m.'" "Why didn't you connect me?" Ingolf snapped ("I am so cruel to E – all these things she has to put up with. – ") When Hugo appeared the two made love one last time and the next day went horseback riding. On the morning of the 11th Ingolf drove Hugo to the airport. "We are not well matched," the stricken lover had to conclude that night, "I have to give up too much for him, he is a drifter, etc, and yet I love him..."

96. INTO THE ABYSS

Only a few days passed after Hugo's departure, on December 11, 1967, before Ingolf began to yearn for his lost lover, who was still touring the eastern United States. Just when he had convinced himself that the affair was over, Hugo called collect on December 20 – "I *live* again!" On December 30 a letter also arrived – too wrought up to read it in Etta's presence, Ingolf took it downstairs: Hugo *was* considering emigration to the United States. This distant prospect did not diminish Ingolf's immediate yearning and on January 27, 1968, he added, "The continuous longing for Hugo (just the thought of his hands, lovelier than any I know, or his eyebrows –) and the knowledge that even if he were here it could not possibly work out." On February 4 Etta was awakened by another collect call at 5:30 A.M; this time she did not connect Ingolf. Hugo returned to Switzerland at the end of February but by the end of June he had returned to New York to study hotel management. He called Ingolf on July 18 – "hearing him is so *exciting* and fills the day with light."

On a number of occasions Ingolf permitted himself the fantasy of imagining what life might be like with Hugo or another gay mate. At a straight dinner party on December 27, 1967, he had tried to imagine, "How would I be there with H. instead of E.?" Two days later he complained, "All the time it is clear that I am just hungry, famished, for a mate – someone close in my bed. I have E. yet feel so dismally forsaken." "My whole purpose in life," he wrote on January 13, "is now to find another man like Hugo." Casual strangers were appraised by this standard – "this one I could live with." I hope I am not overstating the case when I propose that Ingolf was now closer to mental imbalance than in any period in his life since the days of Peter.

Never before had Ingolf been more active in the baths. A schedule of twice monthly visits gave way to one of twice weekly. With "thoughts of H. pulsating all the time," Ingolf had three unsatisfactory tricks on December 28, 1967 – a passive young one, a Jew, and a partner with one eye. As soon as he learned of Etta's recovery from her fourth cancer surgery in January, 1968, he rushed to Samson & Delilah for four tricks. The search for new contact spots did not stop at the baths. Ingolf reports encounters in the hills, in Ferndell, in the campus libraries, even – after all these years – in the Y.M.C.A. shower room (albeit the one in New York).

As he had once referred to his partners as "things," so now, more likely than not, he categorized them according to some social shorthand – a beer truck driver he met in Victory Park, "a nice youngish unpretty fattish Jewboy" at Melrose, a horsey set Republican who whipped out pictures of the wife and kids after a "do" in a 58th street bath in New York. Repulsed and attracted by the sights before him he paints a portrait of himself in a New York gay bar on June 11, 1969: "I am the way-off detached 'baldy-grampa' observing – but their gay banter is adorable – I feel at home here."

Even Ingolf recognized the existence of an emotional disturbance in this fevered mania. "Too restless for work," he wrote on October 6, 1967, "just can't do anything beyond the physical – the drive, yearning, preoccupation like a teenager, and at my age and with everything that should be done." "I'm wrought up beyond words, like the worst adolescent," he confessed on June 14. Bill Colvig suggested, "I think you need to move 100 miles away from the nearest bath in order to get inspired to do something else for a change. Such as composing!"

And Etta? Of course there were continuous expressions of love and affection for his wife on Ingolf's part – contemporaneous with his passion for Hugo or his dreams of a male mate or his nocturnal adventures. Listening to the Stravinsky *Violin Concerto* on October 12, 1967, Ingolf was impelled to embrace Etta, "She is, is, is – the music and her warmth – ." On New Year's Eve, "E comes early and lies down with me. I am so overjoyed, and half asleep, fling both my arms around her. We need physical contact so much!" A new sun deck and a storeroom were added to the upstairs portion of the house at this time. "A close, lovely peaceful moment" on the deck is recorded on May 19, 1968. Ingolf despaired of finding permanent gay happiness precisely because he was still in love with his wife. But given the nature of this relationship theirs was a love governed by recrimination and guilt.

Ingolf felt guilty at every step of his affair with Hugo. He felt guilty when he pined over some imaginary gay mate, when he had to flee from an ailing wife in order to satisfy a compulsion in the shower room of some gay club. He was hurt when she told him on January 31, 1968, "You should give up composing. You cannot make the continuous sustained work and effort." He blamed her for denying him the freedom to do anything he wanted, whenever he wanted to do it – "E., unspoken, holds me back from the frivolities, this is too impossible – when I need the outdoors so much." But it wasn't the outdoors she had in mind when, after dinner on the previous December 22, she had asked, "Will I see you still this evening?" only to hear Ingolf answer, "I don't think so." Nor was she reassured when a letter from Dieter arrived on January 25. "Whose European handwriting is this?" she asked. Her husband, cursing himself for not thinking to name his Alpine guide, answered lamely, "Oh, someone I know." Etta and Ingolf now discussed Hugo's character and Etta had a few unkind things to say. Ingolf didn't want to hear them. On February 18 he announced he was "going for a walk" before heading for S&D – and received "that look" from his wife.

On June 2 they began the first of two summer vacation trips together, spending ten days in Yosemite. Bobby Kennedy was shot while they were staying at the Glacier Point Hotel. On his fifty-sixth birthday Ingolf reports, "E. becomes quite loose talking about our days of poverty – her family relations…I can't talk about my emotional life." On August 2 they were again on the road, this time to Ensenada in Baja California. Etta almost passed out once, presumably from the heat, but Ingolf was pleased to note how well she did on a long walk and, on their return to Cheremoya on August 10, how "E. calls Lillian and bubbles over with happiness." I have a feeling that both of these observations may have been written in justification, after the fact, for the next night the evidence suggests that my mother may have tried to end her own life.

Her motivation on the night of August 12 is obscure. I can certainly think of reasons why a woman in the grip of cancer might have wished a speedy death. And perhaps she saw at last no hope of Ingolf recovering from *his* illness, love of Hugo and the world he represented. But I am not convinced that she deliberately set out, with forethought, to destroy herself on the night in question. When Ingolf got up on the morning of the 13th he found a note, "Aspirin and heat pad would not help had bad sacro-iliac? pain and took another seconal and benedril." In fact, since Etta had suffered from such pains before, he decided to let her sleep. In the early afternoon Larry Moss came by for a visit, the two old friends whispering so as not to wake her up. At 4:00 Ingolf became alarmed when he couldn't rouse his wife. He phoned Fred Kahn, who advised him to observe her pupils by flashlight. Fred then came himself and suggested that Etta would eventually wake by herself. Ingolf prepared to spend the night by her bedside and brought his sleeping bag upstairs. Throughout "the night when all the bats of horrible imagination flutter around me," he listened for the rattle of her breathing. At one point her comatose figure slipped out of bed and Ingolf had great difficulty in putting her back. He then moved her bed against the wall to prevent a recurrence of this incident. In the morning he called Fred again and then, in panic, an ambulance. The unconscious Etta was taken to hospital where early in the afternoon she opened her eyes for the first time. Assured of her survival, Ingolf rushed compulsively to the Corral Baths where he failed to gain admission. At the Regency later that afternoon, he got himself screwed by someone described as a "gee-gaw-goo moron." With flowers he rushed back to the hospital. Etta whispered an ambiguous, "How did you find me? The agony of that pain, it was ghastly, ghastly, poor Ingolf, I'm sorry, so sorry."

The next morning he returned to the hospital, "first time E. is really awake." Lillian was also there and Fred came for a conference. Lillian recalled that Fred asked, "Do you know any reason why Etta would have wanted to kill herself?" Ingolf said, "No, I don't know of any, do you Lillian?" My aunt, who knew nothing of Ingolf's private life, nevertheless answered without hesitation, "Yes, several." August 15 was the date set for Etta's next visit to East Lansing and it was now necessary for Ingolf to advise us that she would not be coming. Dorothy was at home when he called and she recalls that he was almost incoherent. "Just can't control myself," he wrote of the same conversation. He was calmer when he phoned Bill Colvig and when I called him later. His version of the events made room only for the accidental overdose theory and, indeed, I don't believe that it was ever determined just how many pills Etta had taken in her half-drugged state. Needless to say, following a lifelong pattern, neither party passed on to me any of the actual details of this incident. Back at the hospital husband and wife held hands while a nurse told Etta, "You must take B12 so God can help you."

Tests taken in the hospital showed Etta to be in satisfactory shape, but the hospital psychiatrist, who routinely interviewed drug overdose cases, had yet to give his report. Ingolf mentions walking with Etta down the corridors outside her room – "the abyss remains covered as it has been for so long now and all the talk remains on the surface. Both E. and I are suffering but we have none to talk to." On the 18th Fred Kahn called Ingolf at 8:30 in the morning, "The psychiatrist saw her and I talked to her." "Can you tell me?" Ingolf asked. He quotes my cousin as follows: "It has nothing to do with cancer or sacro-iliac – it was just a way of punishing you. She thinks you are a genius and probably wants you to write a symphony every week – you have probably passed the age of your greatest creativity – also, she has never fulfilled her own creative potential. She would not go into other aspects...on that night it just seemed so easy to do it." I tried without success to see this psychiatric report, though Fred confirmed to me in December, 1978, that he was under the impression that at some point on the fateful night Etta *had* willed her own death. Ingolf was crushed by the news – "What a burden – and yet about the other huge part of reality one can't talk. Of course she is right, but what to do? – to punish me – Blows, blows, blows, square on the head and in the heart." Then he remembered that on the night in question he had left an incriminating postcard in the outgoing mail pile.

Etta came home on the 19th, "Open the front door. Embrace and tears, wordless tears." In her absence the bed had been pulled away from the wall again – "and what now?" Ingolf asks. Four days later my mother flew to Lansing for her scheduled visit. She made no allusion to any of these dark matters. The story of her "suicide," like so many other aspects of this life hidden from others, would not come to me in any form until she was no longer among the living.

In September she and Ingolf made the first of three short trips to Borrego in the desert. The second of these visits, in late December, was followed by a bout of Hong Kong flu for Etta and a mild pneumonia, but on the whole she seemed to get along well in the year following her August hospitalization. She fussed over every plant at Cheremoya, busied herself in correspondence and gossip, and made plans for the next sabbatical. In August 1969 she visited Lansing once again. It was the last time for mother and son.

Ingolf continued to hunger for her affection and to discourage it by his behavior at the same time. "Etta comes and snuggles up and it feels so good – echoes," he wrote on December 20, 1968. When he spent several weeks in Hawaii the following summer he overwhelmed her with daily postcards and letters and complained when she didn't respond quickly enough. "If I lived alone," he mused on August 4, after a bath house affair, "I could have this when I pleased – Oh, these chains. And yet – on Thursday when I get Etta back – it feels right too and comfortable and relaxed. So to continue under the strain of the double life." Etta still angered him with her suggestions that he give up composing – "that is hard," he wrote on April 12, 1969, "and all evening I can't shake it. As if writing weren't hard enough. I need every ounce of encouragement I can get to go on, and she, closest, hits hardest – how she must hate me." But five days later, after a rehearsal of the *Aria Sinfonica,* Etta was backstage to embrace a weeping Ingolf – overcome with tears of joy at hearing his work finally performed to his liking.

On September 21, 1969, he provided Bill Colvig with a summary of the relationship in its final stages: "How I wish...to get some things talked out between Etta and me, but that has proved quite impossible.

For reasons that I can understand and respect, she is just too bitter about certain things, and in spite of her admirable rationality...it is impossible to talk, and so, for all these last years, we are sliding lightly along over the thin cover of the abyss."

On September 28, 1968, Ingolf used the occasion of a New York business trip to spend another night with Hugo. "How I love that guy," he added the next day, "but now am not so frantic." Hugo moved about a great deal in the next few months but he and Ingolf kept in contact by post and phone. Summarizing this affair for his sister at the end of the year, Ingolf wrote, "With all the pain and complications and desperate situations it was still wonderful because being in love is wonderful..."

In his last autumn in Los Angeles my stepfather lived out, therefore, a life whose pattern he could not relinquish. A Texan in a VW camper, a medical technician from Santa Ana, a boyish Mexican, a hairdresser from Monrovia, an affectionate middle-aged Chinese, the list of Griffith Park and bathhouse contacts marched on. Ingolf died a decade or so before the first deaths from the AIDS virus were recorded. Can anyone doubt that he would have been among the prime targets for this plague had he survived?

In spite of his chronic complaints about his "fettered existence" as Etta's husband and the longing for a permanent male mate there does come, late in the game, an admission that the present pattern is at least convenient – for it provides "an outlet without any frustrating long entanglement in which I have to stoop to someone's level, spend lots of time while feeling guilty about spending it and bored by the many extraneous paraphernalia attendant upon the one thing." "How could I ask a man to share my life in which there is so little room for any other person?" he asked on December 30. The brief satisfactions available to a closet queen (for so he now described himself) in the "joyless paradise-hell of fornication" were perhaps the most efficient way of managing his passions while still acting as Etta's husband. Promiscuity, precisely because it called for no commitment or entangling relationships, helped preserve the love affair of Ingolf and Etta.

Thus, on February 4, 1970 my parents took themselves, their luggage, their grievances, their love, his lung complaints and her inoperable tumor to Switzerland, where this story had begun. They were about to celebrate their thirtieth wedding anniversary. In Paris on the 6th Ingolf spent a night with

Wolf, his companion of the early Thirties – it was "just as if we hadn't seen each other for a third of a day, and not a third of a century." On the 13th Ingolf had a rendezvous with the beloved Hugo; in fact the two of them accompanied Etta on her first visit to Dr. Brunner, who supervised her chemotherapy at the Zieglerspital in Bern. Ingolf listened intently while Hugo listed the broken hearts he had left in his wake; Hugo's eyebrows, his hands, his sweet face still delighted this elderly sick man, who said goodbye to his last great love that afternoon. The two were to have gone on a skiing trip, but Ingolf's health would not permit this. They never saw each other again.

Correspondence with Dieter continued for some months. Ingolf had joined American Express so that Dieter could send him letters in care of the Bern office. Then he discovered that there was no Bern office, and letters were sent to his Frutigen address. "Did E. see it lie on desk??" Ingolf asks on March 24th. "So she got over her mad because of yesterday's envelope," he adds on April 7. On April 13 Ingolf records, "Letter from Dieter – his wife expecting – wants to see me for a week – has got fat – and I'm so dead." Nostalgia alone survived. "Have coffee and kirsch with a toast to Douglas, 26 years ago today," he reported on April 6. On the 30th he had occasion to walk through the corridors of the University of Zurich, his thoughts full of his purgatory as Peter's worshipper all those many years ago – "And where is today's Peter?" Over thirty-five years had passed since those turbulent episodes during his Swiss apprenticeship and Ingolf was still looking at faces.

He had arrived in Europe with a list of clubs and baths, but he hadn't the time or energy to do much about them now. "The anonymous passionate fleshpots at home are so much better," he reported after a visit to a Bern sauna on April 14. Eight days later he had a brief fling with a local town planner who complained that after eight years of marriage he and his wife could no longer live happily together because of the *language* barrier, he being German, she French.

As his illness gained strength his desire, which had somehow flourished in spite of his many recent ailments, at last ebbed. Looking through a gay magazine (perhaps one of those discovered by Holger a few months later) he reported that nothing "gives the slightest reaction – it looks like an anthropological newspaper." There was even some talk about adding hormones to his list of medicaments – "this neuter existence is awful." By the end of April his bathhouse days had come to an end.

On June 2, after the trip to Greece had been curtailed because of his breathing problems, Ingolf lay in bed in a Zurich hotel room and noted that Etta was his remaining consolation. "E. is an angel," he added, "does everything...she is so gentle and loving in direct proportions to my helplessness, sickness, feeling old and slow." "If I were like last year," he added with some astuteness, "and bouncing and tricking with all kinds of guys the times would be different – so it is to her, as it was to Mammi's *advantage*, to have a 'sick child' – it is *hers*."

Etta died eight days later. For the first time in thirty years Ingolf was a free man; no reproachful eye would gaze balefully in his direction when he went out for a late night walk, no impediment existed any longer in his quest to find a male mate. But none of this was to be. As we have seen in earlier chapters, the only emotion he could summon, in the short time remaining to him, was grief. Guiltily, he returned to earlier entries in which he had prayed for independence and crossed these out in his daybook. He lived the last few weeks of his life in the shadow of his wife's memory. That other world is not mentioned. When his wife was no more, ironically, his sexual obsessions were gone as well.

97. DEFINING DAHL

On August 30, 1970, carrying Ingolf's briefcase filled with 40 pounds of manuscripts, I flew alone to Los Angeles. I delivered the case to Lawrence Morton, who prepared a catalogue of its contents. I spent one week in California, visiting Cheremoya briefly, conferring with the attorney for the Dahl estate, Tobias Klinger, and stopping at U.S.C. for talks with Grant Beglarian, Dean of the School of Music. He told me that it would take at least two highly qualified persons to fill the void left by Ingolf's death. By the end of the week, overwhelmed by the tasks that remained for me to do, I was ready to retreat to my home in Michigan, limping aboard the plane with the first symptoms of one of Ingolf's own maladies, gout.

In spite of his history of bad health Ingolf had maintained a robust physique and a youthful manner to the end, and the tragedy of his early death deepened the wound of his passing. Many of his older associates outlived him – even "the old man," Igor Stravinsky, survived his protégé by several months and other figures, from a senior generation, did as well: Nadia Boulanger and Dame Gracie Fields outlived Ingolf by nine years. Indeed his own mother perished only in 1976, aged eighty-eight, too deep in her senility to understand that her firstborn son was gone. Even Lawrence Morton, whose ill-health had been a constant source of anxiety in our household, outlived Ingolf by almost seventeen years. Ingolf's siblings have each outlived him by almost four decades; indeed, as I write this in 2008, each of them is still alive!

Lawrence was one of the many figures from Ingolf's musical world who devoted himself to commemorating the fallen composer. Written tributes included an obituary article written by Lawrence for the September 1970 *Overture*, Michael Tilson Thomas' eulogy in the September 20th issue of the *Los Angeles Times*, and Halsey Stevens' "In Memoriam" in the Fall-Winter 1970 edition of *Perspectives of New Music*. One could add that MTT offered a significant musical memorial the following January when he led the Boston Symphony Orchestra in several highly successful performances of the Dahl *Saxophone Concerto*, with Harvey Pittel as soloist. In May 1973 Gail Kubik lead a testimonial round table discussion on Ingolf's life and career on station KSPC. Concert stage commemorations began only a week after Ingolf's death, when it was decided to add a lone excerpt from Copland's *Twelve Dickinson Songs*, "Why Do They Shut Me Out Of Heaven?" to a program honoring Copland on *his* seventieth birthday. "It was too late to put it on the printed program, so Aaron merely announced it from the stage – very simply, without emotion or tears," Lawrence wrote, "though many of us had our own deep feelings about the occasion."

At U.S.C. a Dahl Memorial Fund, in honor of Ingolf and Etta, was established to aid scholars and preserve Dahl manuscripts. Copland served as chairman of the honorary committee of this fund, whose other members included Robert Craft, Lawrence Foster, Ernst Krenek, Zubin Mehta, Gregor Piatigorsky, Vera Stravinsky and Michael Tilson Thomas. Monday Evening Concerts and the University were joint sponsors of "A Musical Tribute to the Memory of Ingolf Dahl," held on September 21, 1970. "Bovard Auditorium was filled to capacity with many people who had come for this special tribute," Grant Beglarian wrote, "No words were spoken, just the music performed extremely well by so many of Ingolf's admirers."

Many of the musicians endorsed their checks to the Dahl Memorial Fund at the end of the concert. Ten years later, when the School of Music moved to new quarters, a courtyard was named in Ingolf's honor.

Don Michalsky, who organized a memorial concert on October 13, 1970 at the Orange Country Chamber Concerts, dedicated his 1971 *Cantata Memoriam* to the Dahls. At the 25th Ojai Festival, in May 1971, Gerhard Samuel added the following dedicatory note to the program:

> The Ojai festival wishes to pay its respects to the memory of two great musicians whose work has been so much a part of the history of the festivals, Ingolf Dahl and Igor Stravinsky. Where the older Stravinsky changed the course of music, Dahl changed the course of many a young life fortunate to be under his guidance. We are grateful for the precious personal memories and contacts left to us by Ingolf Dahl and Igor Stravinsky.

On that year's program there was another dedication, albeit private and unannounced. Inspired by Lou Harrison, Bill Colvig had begun a new career as a performer and maker of Asian instruments. At Ojai, he had an unaccompanied solo on the Chinese hsün during the Sunday morning performance. The music depicted two Chinese gentlemen, lifelong friends, drinking wine at a mountain pass where one of them is to cross over, never to return. Two years later Michael Tilson Thomas included *A Noiseless Patient Spider* in a concert called "Homage to Five Ojai Composer/Conductors," which also included work by Stravinsky, Foss, Boulez, and Copland.

Perhaps the most significant of these early testimonial concerts was that presented at the Bing Theater of the County Museum of Art on November 21, 1971 – for this was an all-Dahl program featuring some of the Ingolf's most recent music, including the Frutigen compositions. It was again a joint project of U.S.C. and the Monday Evening Concerts. In 1977 a section of the Dahl *Trio* was performed at festivities marking the 50th anniversary of the Lichtwarkschule in Hamburg; both Gert and Anna-Britta were in attendance. On October 5, 1981 the U.S.C. School of Music inaugurated the Ingolf Dahl lectures in the History and Theory of Music. On May 7 and 8, 1983 A Tribute to Ingolf Dahl concert was held at U.S.C. – ironically and mistakenly as part of the Scandinavia Today series. In the 20th year after the composer's death the School of Music also presented

An Evening of the Music of Ingolf Dahl in Hancock Auditorium on April 29, 1990.

I wrote an afterward for the program notes of the latter event, and I have been called on to write notes about my stepfather on a number of occasions since then. I wrote the program notes that accompanied Michael Tilson Thomas' presentation of the *Tower of Saint Barbara* at the Ojai Festival of 1994 and the liner notes for the all-Dahl CD, "Defining Dahl," which Decca issued on its Argo label in 1995; MTT, utilizing his Miami-based New World Symphony, again conducted *Barbara*, with the *Saxophone Concerto*, the *Hymn* and the *Music For Brass Instruments* as the other works on the disc.

In addition to overseeing the Dahl publication list, I have also inherited the task of assisting other scholars in their work. This process began when James Berdahl visited East Lansing while working on his doctoral dissertation. I was visited in London by Peter Heyworth when he was doing research on the second volume of his *Otto Klemperer: His Life And Times*. And I spent a good deal of time offering materials to Dorothy Lamb Crawford, whose 1995 *Evenings On And Off The Roof* followed the careers of Peter Yates and Lawrence Morton (as well as that of Ingolf) in her well-documented history of the famous concert series. More recently, I have shared with her other materials as she completes a work on L.A.'s émigré composers for a volume to be published by Yale University Press. Mark A. Nicolay also produced a useful article on my stepfather's career ("Emigré Composers in Los Angeles: Ingolf Dahl (1912-1970") for the U.S.C. publication *Coranto* in 1992. There have been a number of doctoral dissertations on aspects of Ingolf's compositions.

It came as some surprise to me that my stepfather, in many ways so unsystematic a manager of his own affairs, had actually thought to leave a will, a handwritten document that he left with my uncle, Morris Keller, shortly before his departure for Europe in 1970. There were five beneficiaries: to U.S.C. he left his books and manuscripts; to Michael Tilson Thomas he left a collection of the autographed sketches of other composers; he left some money (through his insurance policies and the TIAA death benefit) to his sister. He left cash to a beneficiary I had never heard of, someone described in the will simply as a "friend," and this was one of those early mysteries I had to wrestle with – until I discovered who Hugo actually was.

I was the fifth beneficiary; to me he left his musical estate and the house in Hollywood. Accordingly, Dorothy and I drove to California in the summer of 1971 to dispose of this property and its contents.

While Rick Lesemann worked downstairs in the studio, cataloguing Ingolf's library and manuscripts, Dorothy and I wrestled with the ghosts of my parents in the rest of the house. Many people expressed a desire to have some memento of the Dahls and I was eager to make appropriate bestowals. Don Michalsky claimed the topographic maps that he and Ingolf had used on many a Southern California hike. Bill Colvig and Lou Harrison visited us at Cheremoya and I loaded them down with much of Ingolf's camping equipment. The Steinway was made ready for a sea voyage to Stockholm and I prepared for shipment to Michigan many items of furniture and decoration, the family photo albums, the journals, the professional and personal correspondence. Many artifacts that had once been a part of my parents' lives have remained a part of mine, first in East Lansing and then in London. I wore Ingolf's wristwatch for many years and I still use the Swiss Army knife that Bill Colvig gave him in 1959; I used the knife to repair the window of a volunteer's cabin on an Israeli kibbutz in 1980. A few miles away there is a young pine tree in the Balfour Forest which I planted in my mother's name in 1977.

We had to throw out a great deal of just plain junk, making endless trips to the bottom of the stairs. We often discovered that the frugal and forward thinking Etta had three of everything: one item still in use, one ready for use, and the discarded version waiting for recall in case of an emergency. I trimmed all the foliage which, in the absence of its loving owners, had grown to embrace the beloved yellow house. At the end the place became an emptiness, with little to remind us of the passionate spirits who had once inhabited its rooms. Our relatives shared out the last unclaimed possessions, often choosing items for sentimental rather than practical reasons. I gave the clothes of my parents to a Jewish old folks home.

I would have liked to keep the house myself, but I lived too far away to manage this. Donald Aird suggested turning Cheremoya into a place of accommodation for impoverished music students and Hugo, with his new legacy, evidently considered buying the place, but nothing came of these ideas. Banks were reluctant to make loans on a house with no access for automobiles and it was with some difficulty that I at last made arrangements for the sale of 2486 Cheremoya. This act did make it possible for Dorothy and me to become homeowners ourselves in East Lansing, just as Anna-Britta, emboldened by her inheritance, was able to extricate herself from life in Iceland and to begin again in Stockholm.

Joseph Szigeti was only one of a number of figures who wrote to me to emphasize the nature and scope of my duties as conservator of the Dahl musical estate. His letter of August 18, 1970 (with its final evidence of the success of one of Ingolf's many myths) contained the stricture: "I am sure you are aware of the responsibilities of those who remain after the passing of a composer like Ingolf...There is a great deal to be done both in Sweden and America to give his compositions a place in the sun...A great deal of attention and vigilance on your part will be necessary."

The world of music publishing into which I was suddenly plunged was unknown territory for me. I was surprised at the amount of effort required for this task and there were some unhappy chapters. The firm of Alexander Broude, for instance, ceased to exist in about 1975, and the Dahl titles which it had handled passed for a number of years into a kind of musical limbo. I had better success with Joseph Boonin (whose editor was Ingolf's Hamburg friend Kurt Stone), who took an interest in publishing a number of Dahl works, even accepting the responsibility for handling the blueprint reproduction of all unpublished pieces (and there were still many of these). Boonin also published a catalogue, compiled by James Berdahl, describing the availability of all of Ingolf's titles. In 1977 European American Music assumed responsibility for all of the contracts I had signed with Boonin and, as Ingolf's chief publisher, this firm has continued to administer the materials in their care. The number of Dahl titles in publication is now twice what it had been in Ingolf's own lifetime.

Naturally I had to rely on the advice of a number of Ingolf's friends in my work for the musical estate, Lawrence Morton (who would himself orchestrate the *Hymn*), Kurt Stone, and Donal Michalsky among them. I had three paramount goals in the years following Ingolf's death – to bring to first performance the *Elegy Concerto* for violin and orchestra and the *Symphony Concertante* for two clarinets and orchestra, and to help in the production of the recording of the Dahl solo piano music, which was performed by Charles Fierro and released on the Orion label in 1975.

For the revision of the two unfinished concerti I was able to rely on the good offices of Donal Michalsky, who went to work on the violin piece first. On May 1, 1971, he wrote, "I'm glad to say it is less of a problem than I suspected for Ingolf's sketch is *very* complete." In program notes he explained:

> Most of the short-score clearly indicated the instruments assigned to each note. The problem in general was to decipher the manuscript... some parts were overwritten several times in layers of colored ball-point (red, blue, green). Which color level is the last or intended version I decided by studying the many verbal scratchings and notes in the margin...

As examples of the latter, Don cited such comments as "don't 'wail' so much!" and "*courage* – sing it *straight*" and when "they say, as they will, how *can* somebody be so naive, let 'em!" The first performance of this fourteen-minute work came at the Memorial Concert of November 21, 1971, with Daniel Lewis conducting the U.S.C. Chamber Orchestra and Eudice Shapiro as soloist. Donal reported that while working on the composition he was visited by Ingolf in a dream. As the two ascended the last peak, Don put questions to his mentor – "There are two versions of the cadenza, do you want the first, the second, or both – one after the other as a paraphrase." At this point Ingolf threw out his arms, shrugged his shoulders and offered a definitive "Huh?"

In January, 1973, Don also agreed to see what could be done with the *Symphony Concertante*. The problems here were more complex. Ingolf, by Don's reckoning, had attempted revision on eight occasions, each signaled by a new writing implement, and he had taken the score to Frutigen, presumably to begin a ninth attack on the manuscript. Most of Ingolf's suggestions, Don determined, involved *cuts* in the original, so that it would be possible to produce a version close to the composer's final wishes – without having to write any new sections. Realization of the project owed much to the persistence of the clarinetist Richard Waller, and after Don had completed his revision in June of 1975 and the long and expensive task of preparing parts had been finished, Dorothy and I drove from Lansing to Cincinnati on March 5, 1976 to hear the world premiere, with Waller and Carmine Campione as soloists and the Cincinnati Symphony conducted by Thomas Schippers. The thrill of hearing the work performed at last was mixed for us with undercurrents of grief. Ingolf was not the only figure whose presence was missed at the premiere. In the early hours of January 1, 1976 a fire had swept through the Balboa home of Donal Michalsky, killing our friend, his new wife, his two infant sons and two overnight guests.

Sometime in the following year I reached the decision to write the story of Ingolf and Etta. I think in some ways I had always harbored such an intention, but it was to take me many years to determine the scope of the project and my approach to it. I do remember mentioning the idea to Michael Tilson Thomas in June of 1977, when I met my ghost-brother for the first time back stage at Meadowbrook, where he had just conducted the Detroit Symphony in a performance of Mahler's *Eighth*. In the winter of 1978-1979 I spent several weeks in California, interviewing friends of my parents, going through papers at U.S.C. and talking with Bill Colvig (who died in 2000) and Lou Harrison (who died in 2003) in Aptos. Michael and I had a long talk in a booth of Musso & Frank's grill on Hollywood Boulevard, one of Ingolf's old hangouts. In June of 1979 Dorothy and I made our third visit to Sweden, where I was assisted in my inquiries by Holger and Anna-Britta. Then I settled down for a year of intensive labor in London, and even finished one complete draft in 1980. The version you now read is my third attempt.

The passing of Ingolf Dahl elicited a long series of comments on his personality and the role he had played in the artistic circles of his city. Indeed, not a few people have expressed their belief that the musical life of Los Angeles never recovered from the premature death of my stepfather in 1970. In 1979 Halsey Stevens wrote, "Ingolf remains for me the exemplar of the Compleat Musician – the composer of great persuasion, the pianist of surpassing ability, the astute pedagogue. Very few wear so becomingly so many hats." Pushed to define the most significant accomplishments of his mentor in the *Los Angeles Times* memorial of September 20, 1970, Michael Tilson Thomas had argued that:

> Ingolf was above all a real composer. His output of more than 30 compositions includes masterworks...He never took the easy or fashionable way out in his works and would revise them until, like the works of Bach and Ockegham he much admired, they had a

sense of oneness, of tension and balance and hidden craft like a work of architecture.

Writing about his friend's work in 1968, Peter Yates had warned that, "Since 'originality' became a popular fetish a few years ago, it has been increasingly difficult to distinguish, among the serried uniforms of the avant-garde, the plain coats of the few genuine originals." "Whatever its other merits (and there were many)," Halsey Stevens wrote in *Perspectives of New Music*, "Dahl's music convinces by its absolute honesty, its freedom from faddism, its unshakeable logic, its concern for enduring values; at the same time, it is invested with a wit that often borders on irony. In a way, it is like Dahl himself, never content with approximations, seeking always the one right word." Elliott Carter wrote in 1979, "As a composer, his work continues to impress me. Each work that I know is outstandingly well written for the combination, very imaginative, compelling and fascinating as music and each is an important contribution to contemporary music."

In establishing the Dahl Memorial Fund, Grant Beglarian argued that:

> It is fitting that Professor Dahl's memory should be kept alive at the University as a norm by which we judge our daily work in music. A consummate craftsman, impatient with the shoddy and expedient, Professor Dahl, throughout the years he taught at USC instilled in his many students a deep respect for the traditions of musical excellence...

A "total integrity" in artistic matters was certainly one of the features of Ingolf's personality most valued by friends like Gail Kubik. And the belief that there are standards by which each artist might measure himself has often been cited by those who have continued to work under Ingolf's influence. "For the rest of my life, whenever I ponder an artistic decision or think of what would be the most exciting, important and courageous thing to do," Michael Tilson Thomas wrote, "his voice will be there giving with humor, conviction and love his always sage advice."

98. WELL...I DON'T KNOW

If Etta's escapades during her first honeymoon gave Leroy a lifelong preference for monogamy and travel by land, I would add that my research into the story of Ingolf and Etta gave me a lifelong preference for candor and the comforts of family life. The mismatched couple who were my parents nurtured in their son a craving for security, a sense of order that seemed to be so absent in my childhood home where, when they were not hiding things from me by speaking German to one another, they were clearly out of step with one another on too many occasions or following mysterious agendas I could not penetrate.

But while it is fair to speculate on the effects of such discord on the five-year old Anthony, I am less inclined today to give Nurture the nod over Nature than I used to be. Etta believed that all of Ingolf's deficiencies could be traced to bad upbringing; I am more inclined to believe that his "deficiencies," and my own, were as much part of the genetic code as over-fastidious toilet training or smotherly love. Nevertheless I would not recommend bringing up a child in the kind of atmosphere that poisoned our world on N. Westmorland Avenue. My puzzlement over the simplest exchange of affection between a man and a woman, my loneliness when I returned to an empty house or lay awake in the darkness waiting for *someone* to come home – much of this I can now see as the inevitable consequences *not* of the exigencies of "work," as such incidents were usually explained to me, but of the demands of unsatisfied Eros in the hearts of my parents. One happy parent would have been enough for me, perhaps, but two miserable ones was surely not the best environment for someone with Baby Tony's intelligence and sensitivity.

The lies that were perpetuated to protect Ingolf during my teens also poisoned much of my home life at a later period as well. I have written in an earlier section about the difficult times my mother and I endured in my late adolescence. Immature judgment or no, I can now see that my sense of injury had a basis in a reality which was steadfastly withheld from me by my mother, withheld as a duty of love for her husband – whose every indulgence (sheer or not) she seemed willing to grant, even at the cost of *our* domestic tranquility. How much easier this would have been for me had I gone away to university, instead of living at home while attending college. But, as her comments on family finance prove, such a choice did not seem to be possible in our world, where every bit of surplus income, I can now see, was committed elsewhere.

In laboring on the history of my family, surely the greatest conflicts for me came with work on my stepfather's journals. I do not speak of the technical difficulties, the problems of translation or deciphering his tiny script. The diaries were problematic primarily because they carried with them the full weight of Ingolf's self-absorption and self-indulgence. Of course he treasured his debilitating neuroses and neither he nor Etta ever sought any relief from the agonies of their married life in the profession of psychiatry. His behavior, ever more compulsive, constituted a kind of sexual madness. I am, in fact, comforted by this assertion, for by positing a psychological source for much of his behavior I am in an easier position, as Etta's son, to forgive that which would otherwise be unforgivable.

Through these daybooks I have been able to let Ingolf speak for himself on as many occasions as possible, for he approached each entry with a persistent frankness. It is precisely because he was so candid, so sensitive to his own fate at every moment, that I have some doubts about the journals as a true reflection of my stepfather's character. Those who knew Ingolf well will have difficulty matching the image of the friend they loved with the picture of the spoiled egomaniac who raves incessantly through these diaries. Self-preoccupation is a habit of humanity, but it is rare to have as detailed a record of it as that which Ingolf Dahl left behind. What the rest of us may think, Ingolf committed to paper. What the journals do not tell us is that Ingolf mastered his egotism in the great majority of his life encounters and, far from purposefully inflicting his suffering on others, he considered it a life duty to dispel unhappiness whenever he could. To students, colleagues and friends he will always be remembered as a kindly and generous personality and the fossilized self-love which the diaries preserve will never outweigh the altruistic gestures through which he was so loved and respected.

"I think one of the outstanding characteristics of Ingolf," Donald Aird wrote, "was his kindness." "I think of him as a person having great sensitivity, kindness, humor, humility," Grace-Lynne Martin added. "I must tell you," Harvey Pittel remembered, "That he spent 45 minutes on the phone with me once telling me why I should take swimming rather than play base clarinet in the orchestra. He felt I would be a better rounded person and that the idea of the renaissance man helped make better musicians." The hours that Ingolf spent in trying to find jobs and performance opportunities for students and friends are not reflected in the diaries, though one gets a better glimpse into this element of his character in the dozens of thank you letters that crowd his correspondence files. "Dear Ingolf," Lillian Steuber had written some ten years before his death, "Your curious impulse to tell me the other evening that I was a 'great artist' came at a time when I needed particularly to hear it. Surely it could not have come from a more treasured source. Thank you."

There was about Ingolf an indefinable sweetness, an innocence even, a naiveté that made him an endearing figure to many, not excluding his wife. Etta – who had so much to resent in the opposite qualities, his self-centeredness, his single-minded pursuit of sexual release, his penchant for money-saving travel ordeals, his self-inflicted artistic traumas – never saw these negative aspects as any reason for abandoning her love for the wonderful man whom so many others admired. Other family members, my mother-in-law for instance, were prepared to remind Etta that she was too often the victim of this crushing self-absorption. And no doubt, in her acceptance of the role of suffering servant, she paid dearly for the abandonment of her own creative potential and the rewards of a career of her own. But in spite of such difficulties Etta always had a defense for the great man. As difficult as it may be to weigh the costs of her own self-sacrifice on some abstract scale of justice, it has to be agreed that at the end the "dear self-sacrificing girl," as Trude Rittman called her, chose all the agonies of life with Ingolf as more rewarding that that colorless desert that would have been life without him.

Etta also made this choice on my behalf and I would certainly not want to argue, at any point, that I would have wished this choice undone. Sharing Ingolf's life was full of the greatest opportunities for me. Of course I suffered from the usual disappointments and resentments, the normal ones and those endemic to life in the shadow of a star. If anything, however, I craved more of his company, not less, but, as I could not have it, it became all the more important to me to carve out my own identity, to succeed in areas where no comparison could be made, that is to leave his Los Angeles at the first time a reasonable professional opportunity beckoned.

Ten years earlier, to follow some of the characters who peopled the early pages of this book, Dora Linick, my step-grandmother, if there is such a designation, died. Adolph Linick, my grandfather, died in 1967 at the age of 97. On my rare visits to Laurel Avenue during his old age he would always slip me a dollar bill. Once I heard him complain, in the wake of the Holocaust, "God must hate the Jews!" His son, my father Leroy, died in 1986. *His* son, my half-brother Timothy, took his own life at age 42 in 1989. For years I dutifully phoned my stepmother Del, the least loved but longest-lived member of this generation of giants, to sympathize with her on her many tragedies. She died in 1993. Lillian Keller, Etta's sister, died in 1994 and her husband Morry the following year. Sid Weisman died in 1981 but my Aunt Elsie, who long presided over the Laurel scene, died only in 2000, aged 101. My wife and I visited her, my cousin Virginia, and other members of the dwindling Linick family on annual visits to California, where we stayed in the little apartment in the garage that was once used by my grandfather's chauffeur.

On the morning of January 16, 1980 I rose in drowsiness from my bed and recorded the following dream. Ingolf and Etta had come lovingly to wake me from my sleep. Ingolf had read a chapter of this biography and had complained to Etta about the use of the word "stepfather." "Don't you think," he asked, "that a word like that diminishes our relationship?" "Don't worry," I responded, "When you read more of the book you'll see that I've written in such detail about our relationship that no one will doubt our closeness. In fact the book is really about you, not me, and I'm calling it "Ingolf" or "Ingolf and Etta." At this moment, perhaps detecting a potential assault on his privacy, he began to splutter, getting red in the face – 'Well...I don't know."

Naturally the decision to write about Ingolf's private life was not an easy one for me and I have not been immune to feelings of guilt and betrayal, which, indeed, some may wish to hurl at me now that the story is fully told. I would not want to leave the impression that this volume is merely an act of vengeance, a last chapter in a rather ordinary father-son conflict. On November 21, 1979, when I was well into the present project, I had recorded another dream. I dreamed that Ingolf and I had agreed to fight. I chose to escape his wrath by running through a forest, but he was soon upon me. We cracked at each other with rolled newspapers and I landed all the blows, even snatching his weapon from his hand. At the end of the pummeling he was lying on the ground in his nightshirt and saying, "I think we've had enough of this now." "So do I," I replied. The dream invites a number of interpretations but at the time I saw it only as a reflection of the struggle between Ingolf's sense of privacy and my desire to tell the truth at last.

What plans did my parents have for their memories? I have never come across any instructions in this matter. If Ingolf gave the matter any thought at all he must have known that all these secrets, in the absence of any other directive, would some day be mine, and that I would be left to do with them what I wished. How could he, for instance, have named Hugo in his will, and imagine that no questions would be asked?

Ingolf was extremely successful in keeping his homoerotic life hidden from others, but after his death it was a surprise to me to discover that the secret was already out in many places, alive and well in the rumor mill. My mother-in-law, citing a career in hairdressing, said she had *always* suspected. But to have *any* opinion on the subject was to have enjoyed an advantage over me in this matter. Mine was the biggest ignorance of all and I have tried many times to understand how the evidence could have escaped my notice.

I will never be able to answer definitively two pressing questions: how could I have gone through life to age 32 without knowing anything of my stepfather's sexual identity and, if I had known, would this have been the devastating blow to my mental well-being that Etta imagined?

As for the first question, I can only say that the "perceptive teenager" was simply taken in. I don't believe I ever expected my stepfather to have *any* interest in sex (that was left for us troubled adolescents); it would not have occurred to me that he had such passions or that they could be centered on his own gender. I was asked directly by Paul Glass if Ingolf was gay and I participated in no cover up in vehemently denying the suggestion. Repression was at work, no doubt, too. When, during the 1961 sabbatical, Ingolf continued to receive his subscription to *The Mattachine Review*, which he had carelessly failed to cancel, I could see that it was a gay publication but could assume that it represented just another one of those unpopular causes that my stepfather, in his defense of civil liberties, had proposed to add to his catalogue of good works. And when I ran into him once in the lobby of a classic film house, which I was visiting with some of my pals, and he was accompanied by a dark-haired young man not much older than myself, and he smiled somewhat embarrassedly and said, "Mother didn't want to see this film," I gave myself no reason to delve any further.

As for my reactions, had the full truth been known to me, well there is no doubt that, as a teenager, I would have had great difficulty with the news. Even in my early twenties I was not immune from the gay bashing prejudices of my peers. I laughed with a snicker when friends would go through their litany of gay jokes – "What do you call an Irish queer? A gay lick. What do you call a Spanish queer? A señor eater." When asked by a fellow little magazine editor what I thought about homosexuals, I responded hatefully – perhaps sensing a come-on – "I think they all need help!" I do note from the reading of my own college era journals that I defended the rights of "faggots" in arguments with my former Hamilton classmates, Mike Taxer and the aspiring actress Luana Anders, but basically I knew very little about gays and their culture in those closeted days. Ironically it was my mother who would, with her practiced antennae, identify the gays among my college pals and warn me against them – not so much because she feared a seduction but because she classified such people as "notoriously undependable."

But a few years later the situation was very different. I had many valued and dependable gay friends and colleagues, and Etta knew this. Still, the curtain remained lowered on the family gay. As in the case of Ingolf's Jewish forebears, I would have to wait until both parents were gone to experience the full weight of this revelation and this deception.

Many people, not excluding his siblings, warned me away from a complete investigation into so private a personality. They were challenged by Bill Colvig, speaking for another constituency, who wrote in 1974, "I can't think for a minute that Ingolf would have wanted 'that' side of his life kept quiet." Sometime in 1967 Ingolf himself added a paragraph to a "Think Sheet" at the end of his journal. He had been on his way to Indiana on July 30, 1966, and, with time to kill in Chicago, he had observed "two goodlooking Swiss boys talking: "All my life," he added, "I tried to be something I wasn't – talk Schwyzerdüütsch – be a Swede – be a married man – be a composer – be a twelve-tone composer – is it too late to try to start being who I *am*...is it too late for 'honesty'?" I discovered that it was not even possible, let alone honest, to talk about Ingolf the artist or the composer without including the personal element that many may find difficult to encompass in their view of the friend they still mourn.

About Ingolf's role as a "great humanist figure," which was how MTT summarized the life of his mentor in our chat at Musso & Frank's, I cannot see how such a characterization is diminished by a demonstration that the humanist was also human. I agree with Michael that Ingolf and Etta had decided that there was much in life that is absurd and painful, but that existence can be redeemed in art. Their life together was a work of art. That Ingolf should have waged so successful a battle against the deficiencies of his own character is a testimony to his courage and his contribution as an artist.

There has been much discussion in the present volume devoted to Ingolf's failure to forge the dazzling personal career he so often craved. His social life and his compositions never seemed to acquire that ease of communication that sustain many gifted creators, those titans whose ability to tap into the well-springs of their being allow them to produce a copious and enviable body of artistic endeavor. Ingolf labored under levels of repression that were antithetical to such a process. He did not choose to be who he was, nor did he choose to make his true self available to the wider world. He lived and died without the luxury of candor, and that he may have disfigured his own reality because he had to worry about a perceptive and sensitive adolescent in his own home has caused me more guilt over the years than any qualms I may now have about revealing his private life over a third of a century after his death.

I still mourn the passing of those wonderful people who were my parents. I still want their advice and still long for their approval. Every one of my own accomplishments in life has failed to satisfy, in part because *they* have not been here to share my happiness. I miss Etta's search for spelling errors in my manuscript. I miss the sound of Ingolf clearing his throat, his questioning glance, the fingers scratching at his scalp in abstracted concentration, his, "Well...I don't know."

AFTERWORD

I had no way of knowing, when I first started my work on a biography of Ingolf Dahl, that I would still be laboring over this project almost thirty years later. When I began to sift through the materials left behind by my stepfather and by my mother, Etta, this couple had been dead only eight years or so. I was therefore able to ask for the assistance of a number of their contemporaries, who supplied me with written commentaries and shared with me in person many of the memories that were still fresh in their minds. Had this project reached a speedy conclusion – one draft was completed during a sabbatical leave from Michigan State University in 1980 – each of these generous benefactors would have received a specific words of thanks from me at this point. Sadly, many will not have lived long enough to read their names now, and this is one of the great tragedies of the enterprise for me: many of those most interested in the lives of the Dahls will never have unravelled for them the many mysteries that this pair crafted so artfully. I do thank all of those kind souls who provided information, most of which I gathered in 1978 and 1979; their names are an integral part of the text now.

I have not included footnotes in this volume. Such notes would be of limited use to scholars for, at the present moment, I would say that over ninety percent of the references are to documents that only I possess. Most of these are citations from my stepfather's journals, the writings of my mother, and from correspondence – letters written to them or to me, almost all of which I still retain. I believe that in most instances it will be clear from my text who said what and to whom. Under any circumstances, this, the first definitive biography of Ingolf Dahl, is a personal testimony and not a work which requires a bibliography or footnotes. It is up to others to carry on the research and the debate. Dahl scholarship begins anew here.

In the construction of the index that follows I have tried to include categories that would be of specific use to those undertaking additional research. I have included the names of academic and cultural institutions and organizations, of all titles, and the names of individuals – when such names have been presented in full and authentic detail in the text.

I would also like to thank a number of individuals who, over the years, have read drafts of this biography and who have helped me with their comments. With one exception, all can see what their suggestions have helped produce: my wife of forty-three years, Dorothy, died on July 12, 2007.

I left academia twenty-five years ago but I still remember my academic etiquette sufficiently to report that my original project was supported by an All-University Research Grant from Michigan State University.

The cover photo is credited to the photo department of the University of Southern California. Finally I would also like to thank Rob Taggart, of the London office of the Associated Press, for his assistance in the preparation of the photographs used in this book.

Anthony Linick
London
February 21, 2008

INDEX

In the very long index that follows I have tried to include references useful to those interested in the lives of my parents, and I have eliminated those that refer only to my own. Should anyone require the latter as well, I can supply these as an attachment if you would write to me at the email address mentioned in the section entitled "About The Author."

ABOUT THE AUTHOR

Anthony Linick was born in Los Angeles in 1938 and educated in the city's schools, including Alexander Hamilton High School. In 1955 he entered the University of California at Los Angeles where, majoring in history, he completed his BA in 1959 and his Ph.D. five years later. While still an undergraduate he began work on the little magazine, *Nomad* (1959-1962), which he co-edited with Donald Factor. This background also contributed to his choice of dissertation topic, *A History of the American Literary Avant-Garde Since World War II*.

In 1964 he and Dorothy Goldstone were married in Los Angeles and the following year they moved to East Lansing, Michigan, where Anthony took up a post as Professor of Humanities at Michigan State University. He taught a variety of courses in Western Civilization, literature and contemporary culture here and published a number of articles on popular culture topics, American and British. Indeed, the Linicks began to spend more and more time in England, including a sabbatical year begun in 1979; in 1981 they moved to London.

Here Anthony began a twenty-year teaching career at the American School in London, in St. John's Wood, offering many courses, first in the high school social studies department and then the English department, where he served as department head from 1994 to 2002, the year he retired. Dorothy also worked at the American School as a special projects coordinator; earlier she had held the post of director of student services at the American College in London.

After retirement the Linicks worked on a number of writing projects; while Dorothy concentrated on fiction Anthony completed an introduction to long-distance footpath walking in Britain, *A Walkers Alphabet* (a volume that will be published shortly), this biography of his stepfather, and *Strictly Come Barking or Life Among The Dog People of Paddington Rec*, which was published by AuthorHouse in 2008. He can be contacted at AnthonyLinick@compuserve.com.